Few economic events have had a more profound or enduring impact than the German hyperinflation of 1923, still remembered popularly as a root cause of Hitler's rise to power. Yet in recent years many historians have argued that inflationary policies were, on balance, advantageous to post-1918 Germany, both boosting growth and helping to reduce reparations. The scholarly consensus is that there was no viable alternative to inflation.

In *Paper and iron* Niall Ferguson takes a different view. Focusing on the influential Hamburg business community, he exposes the flaws in the contemporary justifications for inflationary policies. The inflation, he argues, did severe damage to the German economy, eroded the foundations of bourgeois society and discredited Weimar's welfare state. Above all, it did nothing whatever to reduce reparations.

Alternative policies might in fact have stabilised the German currency in 1920. To explain why such policies were not adopted, the author points to long-term defects in the political economy of the Reich. He suggests that there was a thirty-year 'era of inflation' after 1897 in which the inadequacy of the Reich's fiscal and monetary institutions allowed economic interest groups to wield excessive power. This internal imbalance of power was reversed only in the 1930s. Thus *Paper and iron* reveals not only the Wilhelmine origins of Weimar's failure. It also casts new light upon the origins of the Third Reich.

Paper and iron

for my parents

Paper and iron

Hamburg business and German politics in the era of inflation, 1897–1927

NIALL FERGUSON

Jesus College, Oxford

CAMBRIDGE
UNIVERSITY PRESS

Published by the Press Syndicate of the University of Cambridge
The Pitt Building, Trumpington Street, Cambridge CB2 1RP
40 West 20th Street, New York, NY 10011-4211, USA
10 Stamford Road, Oakleigh, Melbourne 3166, Australia

© Cambridge University Press 1995

First published 1995

Printed in Great Britain at the University Press, Cambridge

A catalogue record for this book is available from the British Library

Library of Congress cataloguing in publication data
Ferguson, Niall.
Paper and iron: Hamburg business and German politics in the era of inflation,
1897–1927 / Niall Ferguson.
p.   cm.
Includes bibliographical references (p.   ) and index.
ISBN 0-521-47016-1 (hc).
1. Hamburg (Germany)–Economic conditions. 2. Inflation
(Finance)–Germany–Hamburg–History–20th century. I. Title.
HC289/H2F47 1995.
338.943'515–dc20   94-13455   CIP

ISBN 0 521 47016

Contents

Figures

Preface

In recent years, the historiography of the German inflation has itself developed inflationary tendencies. The academic printing presses have been kept almost as busy as the Reichsbank's in the early 1920s, such has been the volume of literature published on the subject. Nevertheless, I make no apologies for adding these pages to the paper flood. Most studies of the inflation concentrate on the years 1914–24. I have sought to describe a rather longer 'era of inflation' running from 1897 to 1927, and to show the links from the hyperinflation of 1922/3 to the second great inflation of the 1940s. Most authors emphasise to some degree the role of economic interest groups in causing the inflation and undermining the Republic; I have tried to suggest that corporate power was as much a product as a cause of the German Reich's weakness as a modern state. Finally, most recent work has tended to conclude that there was no alternative to inflationary policies in the circumstances of 1919–23; indeed, some historians have seen positive advantages in these policies. I argue not only that these advantages have been exaggerated, but also that alternative, less inflationary policies could conceivably have been pursued, with less disastrous consequences.

In the inflation, it was possible to pay off debts with worthless money. I hope the following expressions of gratitude will offer slightly better recompense to my many intellectual creditors. Professor Norman Stone and Dr Hartmut Pogge von Strandmann acted as my successive doctoral supervisors in Oxford: I am grateful to them both. Others who at various stages have read and commented on the manuscript as a whole include Dr Jonathan Steinberg, Dr Anthony Nicholls, Professor Harold James and Dr Theo Balderston. Numerous others have read individual chapters, or have commented on extracts when I have presented them at seminars. In particular, I would like to thank Professor Knut Borchardt, Professor Richard Evans, Professor Barry Supple, Professor Tim Blanning, Dr Michael John, Dr Chris Clark, Dr Brendan Simms and Dr Avner Offer. I would also like to express my gratitude to Dr Angus Macintyre, Sir John Plumb and Mr Maurice Cowling for their support and counsel over the years.

I have been greatly assisted by the staff at the following archives: the Staatsarchiv Hamburg, where Dr Gabrielsson was unfailingly polite and helpful in the early stages of my research; the archive of M.M. Warburg & Co., Hamburg; the archive of Hapag–Lloyd AG, Hamburg; the Bundesarchiv, Potsdam (or Zentrales Staatsarchiv, as it then was); the Bundesarchiv, Koblenz; the Politische Archiv des Auswärtigen Amts, Bonn; the Prussian State Archive (Stiftung Preußischer Kulturbesitz), Berlin–Dahlem; the Haniel Archiv, Franz Haniel & Cie. GmbH, Duisberg; the Hamburg Weltwirtschaftsarchiv; the National Archives, Washington, DC; the archive of the Federal Reserve Bank of New York; the John Fitzgerald Kennedy Library in Boston; the Seeley G. Mudd Manuscript Library at Princeton; the Sterling Library at Yale; the Baker Library at Harvard; the Public Record Office at Kew; and the Foreign Office Library at Cornwall House. I should like to express my gratitude to the late Eric Warburg and his son Max A. Warburg for permission to use the Max Warburg Papers; as well as to Alick Goldsmith, HM Consul General in Hamburg, who introduced me to Eric Warburg, but could not, alas, persuade the Hamburg Handelskammer to open its archive to me.

The Scottish Education Department, the German Academic Exchange Service, the Stiftung FVS, the British Academy and the Master and Fellows of Christ's College provided generous financial support for my archival work. The secretarial staff at Peterhouse and at Jesus, Oxford, also provided much practical assistance in the preparation of the manuscript. Georgina Capel, my agent, William Davies, my publisher, and Anne Rix, my copy-editor, have been models of efficiency. I would also like to thank Edward Lipman and Andrew Vereker for their help with the proofs and index.

Finally, I would like to thank my wife, Susan, for giving me something worth working for; and my parents – for everything. This book is dedicated to them.

Abbreviations

AA	Auswärtiges Amt
AEG	Allgemeine Elektrizitätsgesellschaft
AfS	*Archiv fur Sozialgeschichte*
AHR	*American History Review*
Allg.	Allgemeines
AOM	Arnold Otto Meyer
AVHA	Arbeitgeberverband Hamburg-Altona
BAK	Bundesarchiv Koblenz
BAP	Bundesarchiv Potsdam
B&V	Blohm und Voß
BB	Bürgerbund
CEH	*Central European History*
CVDBB	Centralverein des Deutschen Bank- und Bankiergewerbes
DDP	Deutsche Demokratische Partei
DHSG	Deputation für Handel, Schiffahrt und Gewerbe
DKH	Detaillistenkammer Hamburg
DMA	Demobilmachungsamt
DNVP	Deutschnationale Volkspartei
DVP	Deutsche Volkspartei
EcHR	*Economic History Review*
FA	Firmenarchiv
GFM	German Foreign Ministry
G&G	*Geschichte und Gesellschaft*
GHH	Gutehoffnungshütte
GKH	Gewerbekammer Hamburg
GStA	Geheimes Staatsarchiv
HA	Hapag Archive
Hapag	Hamburg-Amerikanische Packetfahrt-Aktien-Gesellschaft
HB	Holtzendorff Berichte
HG	Hamburgische/Hanseatische Gesandter, Berlin.
HJ	*Historical Journal*
HKH	Handelskammer zu Hamburg
HKHP	Handelskammer Plenarsitzung
HV	Holtzendorff to Vorstand
HZ	*Historische Zeitschrift*
JCH	*Journal of Contemporary History*

JEcH	*Journal of Economic History*
JMH	*Journal of Modern History*
KDR	Kriegsausschuß der deutschen Reederei
KDW	Kriegsausschuß der deutschen Werften
KPD	Kommunistische Partei Deutschlands
NAW	National Archives, Washington
NDG	Norddeutsche Gruppe des Gesamtverbandes deutscher Metallindustrieller
PA/AA	Politisches Archiv des Auswärtigen Amts
P&P	*Past and Present*
PG	Preußische Gesandter
Pol. Corr.	Politische Correspondenz
Prot.	Protokoll
RAM	Reichsarbeitsminister(ium)
RdI	Reichsverband der deutschen Industrie
RFM	Reichsfinanzminister(ium)
RGB	*Reichsgesetzblatt*
RK	Reichskanzler/kanzlei
RKEAB	Reichskommissar für die Ein- und Ausfuhrbewilligung
RKfdÜöO	Reichskommissar für die Überwachung öffentlicher Ordnung
RMfW	Reichsminister(ium) für Wiederaufbau
RMfwD	Reichsminister(ium) für die wirtschaftliche Demobilmachung
RMI	Reichsminister(ium) des Innern
RSA	Reichsschatzamt
RWM	Reichswirtshaftsminister(ium)
RWR	Reichswirtschaftsrat
Sen.	Senat
SJfDR	*Statistisches Jahrbuch für das Deutsche Reich*
SK	Senatskommission für die Reichs- und Auswärtigen Angelegenheiten
SPD	Sozialdemokratische Partei Deutschlands
StAH	Staatsarchiv Hamburg
Sten. Ber.	Stenographische Berichte
SVS	Schriften des Vereins für Sozialpolitik
USPD	Unabhängige Sozialdemokratische Partei Deutschlands
VfZ	*Vierteljahrshefte für Zeitgeschichte*
VHEx	Verein Hamburger Exporteure
VHR	Verein Hamburger Reeder
VSWG	*Vierteljahrsschrift für Sozial- und Wirtschaftsgeschichte*
WA	Warburg Archive
ZAG	Zentralarbeitsgemeinschaft
ZEG	Zentral-Einkaufsgesellschaft
ZfG	*Zeitschrift für Geschichtswissenschaft*
ZVDG	Central Association of German Wholesalers
ZVHG	*Zeitschrift des Vereins für hamburgische Geschichte*

Introduction

I

Blood and iron, gold and iron, coal and iron, rye and iron – these are among the most vivid images in the history of the German Reich. We think of Bismarck's speech to the Prussian Diet's budgetary committee in September 1862,[1] of Bleichröder's financing of the iron Chancellor's wars,[2] of Keynes's comment on the economic roots of German power,[3] of Kehr's stress on the role of agrarian and industrial interest groups in Wilhelmine politics.[4] This book, however, turns away from these more familiar themes of German historiography, to consider the relationship between paper and iron – in particular, between the paper instruments which financed the economic life of Germany's largest port, and the iron ships built there to transport and protect its commerce; more generally, between the paper notes and bonds produced by the Reich printing press in Berlin's Oranienstraße, and the industrial and military power of the Reich itself. The principal question it seeks to address is: what were the causes and consequences of the German Reich's chronic susceptibility to inflation?

It is fair to say that, until relatively recently, historians tended to be more interested in deflation than inflation as a factor in the historical development of the German Reich. The two economic events which were seen as having had the most decisive influence on modern German history were, firstly, the *Gründerkrach* of 1873–4 and the subsequent period of stagnation, linked by Rosenberg and others to the crisis of liberalism in the late 1870s;[5] and, secondly, the Slump of 1929–32,

---

[1] L. Gall, *Bismarck. The White Revolutionary*, vol. I: *1815–1871* (London, 1986), p. 204.
[2] F. Stern, *Gold and Iron. Bismarck, Bleichröder and the Building of the German Empire* (London, 1977).
[3] J.M. Keynes, *The Economic Consequences of the Peace* (London, 1919), p. 75.
[4] E. Kehr, 'Englandhaß und Weltpolitik', in H.-U. Wehler (ed.), *Der Primat der Innenpolitik. Gesammelte Aufsätze zur preußisch-deutschen Sozialgeschichte im 19. und 20. Jahrhundert* (Berlin, 1970), pp. 149–77.
[5] H. Rosenberg, *Große Depression und Bismarckzeit* (Berlin, 1967); *idem*, 'The Political and Social Consequences of the Great Depression of 1873–1896 in Central Europe',

usually seen as the main cause of the collapse of the Weimar Republic.[6]
In the popular mind, however, equal if not greater importance has
long been attached to the 1923 hyperinflation, the 'memory' of which
is frequently cited to explain the relative stringency of recent (West)
German monetary policy.[7] Of course, few Germans now living have
first-hand recollections of events which took place seventy years ago.
Leaving aside oral tradition, this 'memory' therefore owes at least some
of its longevity to post-war textbooks on modern German history,
which have tended to advance one or more of three negative theses
about the inflation – that it was caused by irresponsible fiscal and
monetary policies; that it benefited 'greedy industrialists' while 'stripping the middle classes of their savings'; and that it contributed
significantly to the rise of Hitler. According to Golo Mann, for instance,
'whole sections of the population were expropriated and an age-old
confidence was destroyed and replaced by fear and cynicism'; a view
echoed by Hajo Holborn and Erich Eyck.[8] Influential Anglo-Saxon
writers of the same generation advanced similar interpretations. According to A.J.P. Taylor:

The former rentiers became resentful of the republic [. . .] and ready to follow
the first demagogic saviour not blatantly from the industrial working class.
The inflation, more than any other single factor, doomed the republic.[9]

Gordon Craig explicitly blamed the inflation on the 'self-interest and
irresponsibility of German business, which was known for its anti-
republican stance', attributing subsequent support for Nazism to the
'wounds' it left 'in the collective psyche' of the *Mittelstand*:[10]

That the bulk of the lower middle class looked to Adolf Hitler as a saviour
was due less to the Great Depression of the Thirties [than] to the memory of
the great inflation of 1923. [. . .] For millions of Germans, that unprecedented
and bewildering event hopelessly compromised faith in representative government.[11]

in J.J. Sheehan (ed.), *Imperial Germany* (New York, 1970), pp. 39–60. See also A.
Gerschenkron, *Bread and Democracy in Germany* (Ithaca, 1989), pp. 42–7; H.-U.
Wehler, *The German Empire* (Leamington Spa, 1985), pp. 32–9.
[6] For contrasting interpretations: D. Abraham, *The Collapse of the Weimar Republic.
Political Economy and Crisis* (Princeton, 1981); H. James, *The German Slump. Politics
and Economics 1924–1936* (Oxford, 1986).
[7] D. Marsh, *The Bundesbank. The Bank that Rules Europe* (London, 1992), esp. pp.
18, 29, 99ff.
[8] G. Mann, *The History of Germany since 1789* (London, 1987), pp. 588–95; H.
Holborn, *A History of Modern Germany*, vol. III: *1840–1945* (London, 1969), pp.
595–601; E. Eyck, *A History of the Weimar Republic*, vol. I (Oxford, 1962), p. 171.
Cf. F. Meinecke, *Die deutsche Katastrophe* (Wiesbaden, 1965), pp. 54f.
[9] A.J.P. Taylor, *The Course of German History* (London, 1961), pp. 227f.
[10] G.A. Craig, *Germany, 1866–1945* (Oxford, 1981), pp. 450–6.
[11] *Idem*, *The Germans* (Harmondsworth, 1984), pp. 120f.

Similar verdicts can be found in many more recent textbooks;[12] and although they have been substantially qualified as a result of the recent enormous concentration of scholarly resources on the inflation,[13] they have certainly not been overturned.

Such critical views owe a considerable debt to a book, *Le Vicende del Marco Tedesco*, published by the Italian economist Costantino Bresciani-Turroni in 1931.[14] According to Bresciani, 'the fundamental cause[s] of the paper inflation and consequently of the depreciation of the mark' were 'the budget deficit' and errors in 'banking policy', both of which he traced back to the outbreak of the war.[15] The

[12] See, e.g., A.J. Nicholls, *Weimar and the Rise of Hitler* (London, 1979), pp. 74ff.; H. Schulze, *Weimar: Deutschland 1917–1933* (Berlin, 1982), pp. 34–9; V. Berghahn, *Modern Germany. Society, Economy and Politics in the Twentieth Century* (Cambridge, 1987), pp. 67–72; M. Fulbrook, *Germany 1918–1990. The Divided Nation* (London, 1991), p. 34. See also F.K. Ringer, *The German Inflation of 1923* (New York, 1969); A. Ferguson, *When Money Dies. The Nightmare of the Weimar Collapse* (London, 1975); W. Guttmann and P. Meehan, *The Great Inflation: Germany, 1919–1923* (London, 1975).

[13] Under the informal leadership of Gerald Feldman and others, a series of important volumes of essays on the inflation has been produced since 1978: O. Büsch and G.D. Feldman (eds.), *Historische Prozesse der Deutschen Inflation 1914 bis 1924. Ein Tagungsbericht* [*Einzelveröffentlichungen der historischen Kommission zu Berlin*, Bd. 21] (Berlin, 1978); G.D. Feldman, C.-L. Holtfrerich, G.A. Ritter and P.-C. Witt (eds.), *Die deutsche Inflation. Eine Zwischenbilanz* [*Beiträge zu Inflation und Wiederaufbau in Deutschland und Europa 1914–1924*, Bd. 1] (Berlin/New York, 1982); idem, *Die Erfahrung der Inflation* [*Beiträge zu Inflation und Wiederaufbau in Deutschland und Europa 1914–1924*, Bd. 2] (Berlin/New York, 1984); idem, *Die Anpassung an die Inflation* [*Beiträge zu Inflation und Wiederaufbau in Deutschland und Europa 1914–1924*, Bd. 8] (Berlin/New York, 1986); idem, *Die Konsequenzen der Inflation* [*Einzelveröffentlichungen der Historischen Kommission zu Berlin*, Bd. 67. *Beiträge zu Inflation und Wiederaufbau in Deutschland und Europa 1914–1924*] (Berlin, 1989); G.D. Feldman and E. Müller-Luckner (eds.), *Die Nachwirkungen der Inflation auf die deutsche Geschichte, 1924–1933* (Munich, 1985). For a survey of some of this literature see M. Schneider, 'Deutsche Gesellschaft in Krieg und Währungskrise 1914–1924', *AfS*, 16 (1986), pp. 301–20.

[14] C. Bresciani-Turroni, *Le Vicende del Marco Tedesco* (Bocconi, 1931), translated as *The Economics of Inflation. A Study of Currency Depreciation in Post-War Germany* (London, 1937). Bresciani was in Germany for most of the 1920s, representing Italy on the Reparations Commission and its successor. Cf. the less well-known German accounts by E. Schultze, *Not und Verschwendung. Untersuchungen über das deutsche Wirtschaftsschicksal* (Leipzig, 1923); A. Jessen, *Finanzen, Defizit und Notenpresse, 1914–1922* (Berlin, 1923); K. Elster, *Von der Mark zur Reichsmark. Die Geschichte der deutschen Währung in den Jahren 1914 bis 1924* (Jena, 1928); P. Beusch, *Währungszerfall und Währungsstabilisierung* (Berlin, 1928); F. Hesse, *Die deutsche Wirtschaftslage von 1914 bis 1923. Krieg, Geldblähe und Wechsellagen* (Jena, 1938).

[15] Bresciani, *Inflation*, pp. 42–51, 47–74, 75–82, 155–82. Those historians who use the phrase 'the inflation' to refer only to the year 1923 overlook the protracted nature of the crisis. Most accounts identify between three and six phases: in Bresciani's case, 1914–18; 1918–19; July 1919 to February 1920; February 1920 to May 1921; May 1921 to July 1922; July 1922 to June 1923; June 1923 to December 1923: ibid., pp. 25–38. Cf. F.D. Graham, *Exchange, Prices and Production in Hyperinflation Germany 1920–1923* (Princeton, 1930), p. 153; K. Laursen and J. Pedersen, *The German Inflation, 1918–1923* (Amsterdam, 1964), pp. 17–21.

consequences of the collapse of the currency, he argued, were almost entirely negative: falling productivity, a misallocation of resources, 'profound disequilibrium in the economic organism', 'the vastest expropriation of some classes of society that has ever been effected in time of peace', and declines in public health and morality:

> It annihilated thrift [. . .] It destroyed [. . .] moral and intellectual values [. . .] It poisoned the German people by spreading among all classes the spirit of speculation and by diverting them from proper and regular work, and it was the cause of incessant political and moral disturbance. [. . .Moreover,] by reinforcing the economic position of those classes who formed the backbone of the 'Right' parties, i.e. the great industrialists and financiers, (it) encouraged the political reaction against democracy.[16]

When Lionel Robbins wrote his Foreword to the English version of Bresciani's book in 1937 he merely added what appeared with hindsight to be an obvious conclusion: 'Hitler is the foster-child of the inflation.'[17]

Bresciani's emphasis on fiscal and monetary policy as the cause of inflation was echoed by numerous contemporaries. Particularly in 1921 and 1922, many foreign observers – and a few German commentators[18] – were loud in their criticisms of excessive government borrowing. Indeed even some of those who were inclined to defend the government's policy – Keynes, Frank Graham and the Reichsbank itself – acknowledged that fiscal and monetary laxity played at least some role in the collapse of the currency.[19] There have, of course, been significant refinements of this view under the influence of more recent monetarist theory, particularly with respect to the final phase of hyperinflation.[20] Moreover, with more sophisticated definitions of

---

[16] *Ibid.*, pp. 183, 215, 261f., 275, 286, 314f., 330ff., 404.

[17] *Ibid.*, p. 5.

[18] W. Eucken, *Kritische Betrachtungen zur deutschen Geldproblem* (Jena, 1923); A. Hahn, *Geld und Kredit* (Tübingen, 1924). On contemporary theories of inflation in Germany, see Bresciani, *Inflation*, pp. 42–7; H.S. Ellis, *German Monetary Theory, 1865–1933* (Cambridge, Mass., 1934), pp. 203–95; K. Hardach, 'Zur zeitgenössischen Debatte der Nationalökonomen über die Ursachen der deutschen Nachkriegsinflation', in H. Mommsen, D. Petzina, B. Weisbrod (eds.), *Industrielles System und Politische Entwicklung in der Weimarer Republik*, vol. I (Düsseldorf, 1977), pp. 368–75; C.-D. Krohn, 'Helfferich contra Hilferding. Konservative Geldpolitik und die sozialen Folgen der deutschen Inflation, 1918–1923', *VSWG*, 62 (1975), pp. 62–92; *idem*, *Wirtschaftstheorien als politische Interessen. Die akademische Nationalökonomie in Deutschland, 1918–1933* (Frankfurt am Main, 1981).

[19] J.M. Keynes, *A Tract on Monetary Reform* (London, 1923); Graham, *Hyperinflation*, pp. 5ff., 35–48. For the Reichsbank's expressions of fiscal orthodoxy in July 1919 see C.-L. Holtfrerich, 'Reichsbankpolitik 1918–1923 zwischen Zahlungsbilanz- und Quantitätstheorie', *Zeitschrift für Wirtschafts- und Sozialwissenschaft*, 13 (1977), pp. 193–214.

[20] See esp. P. Cagan, 'The Monetary Dynamics of Hyperinflation', in M. Friedman, *Studies in the Quantity Theory of Money* (Chicago, 1956), pp. 25ff., T.J. Sargent and

money than Bresciani's, historians have been able to identify subtle variations in the course and dynamics of the inflation.[21] Webb, in particular, has applied recent theoretical work on the role of expectations and the demand for money in the inflationary process to provide a more sophisticated model of the relationship between fiscal policy, monetary expansion and price movements.[22] Nevertheless, the kernel of Bresciani's explanation of the inflation remains more or less intact, even in studies which identify more profound 'structural' factors as the causes of fiscal and monetary expansion.[23]

Bresciani's negative view of the economic, social and political consequences of the inflation was also shared by numerous contemporaries, and remains influential. Willi Prion had been among the first economists to suggest that inflation investments might be based on 'illusory profits', concealing 'substance loss'; and the more recent work of Lindenlaub has done much to reinforce Bresciani's scepticism on this point, suggesting that engineering firms rarely took 'flight into real values' in response to increased inflation.[24] Likewise, Feldman, James

N. Wallace, 'Rational Expectations and the Dynamics of Hyperinflations', *International Economic Review*, 14 (1973), pp. 328ff.; idem, 'Rational Expectations and the Theory of Economic Policy', *Journal of Monetary Economics* (1976), pp. 169ff.; M. Khan, 'The Variability of Expectations in Hyperinflations', *Journal of Political Economy*, 85 (1977), pp. 817–27; R.L. Jacobs, 'Hyperinflation and the Supply of Money', *Journal of Money, Credit and Banking*, 9 (1977), pp. 287ff.; J.A. Frenkel, 'The Forward Exchange Rate, Expectations and the Demand for Money: the German Hyperinflation', *American Economic Review*, 67 (1977), pp. 653ff.; idem, 'Further Evidence on Expectations and the Demand for Money during the German Hyperinflation', *Journal of Monetary Economics*, 5 (1979), pp. 81–96; M.K. Salemi, 'Adaptive Expectations, Rational Expectations and Money Demand in Hyperinflation Germany', *Journal of Monetary Economics*, 5 (1979), pp. 593–604; M.K. Salemi and T.J. Sargent, 'The Demand for Money during Hyperinflation under Rational Expectations: II', *International Economic Review*, 20 (1979), pp. 741–58; A. Abel, R. Dornbüsch, J. Huizinga and A. Marcus, 'Money Demand during Hyperinflation', *Journal of Monetary Economics*, 5 (1979), pp. 97–104.

21 Cf. G. Merkin, 'Towards a Theory of the German Inflation: Some Preliminary Observations', in Feldman *et al.* (eds.), *Zwischenbilanz*, pp. 25–47.

22 S.B. Webb, 'Money Demand and Expectations in the German Hyperinflation: A Survey of the Models', in N. Schmukler and E. Marcus (eds.), *Inflation through the Ages. Economic, Social, Psychological and Historical Aspects* (New York, 1983), pp. 435ff.; idem, 'Government Debt and Inflationary Expectations as Determinants of the Money Supply in Germany, 1919 to 1923', *Journal of Money, Credit and Banking* (1985), pp. 479ff.; idem, 'Fiscal News and Inflationary Expectations in Germany after World War I', *Journal of Economic History*, 46, 3 (1986), pp. 769–94; idem, *Hyperinflation and Stabilisation in Weimar Germany* (New York/Oxford, 1989), pp. 9, 21–3, 30, 44–8, 51.

23 C.-L. Holtfrerich, *The German Inflation, 1914–1923* (Berlin/New York, 1986); G.D. Feldman, *The Great Disorder. Politics, Economics and Society in the German Inflation* (New York/Oxford, 1993).

24 W. Prion, *Zwei Vorträge über Scheingewinne* (Jena, 1922); D. Lindenlaub, 'Machinebauunternehmen in der Inflation 1919 bis 1923: Unternehmenshistorische

and others have stressed the damage done to the banking system by the inflation;[25] while Balderston has identified important links between the inflation and the subsequent weakness of the German capital market.[26] Pessimistic views of the impact of the inflation on workers' living standards have, of course, been popular among Marxist historians,[27] and have recently been underlined by Robert Scholz.[28] Similarly, the idea of the inflation as a material crisis of the bourgeoisie – which Bresciani had derived from the seminal work of Fritz Eulenberg[29] – continues to feature in the scholarly literature. Whether as *rentiers*, shopkeepers, professionals or salaried employees, middle-class groups continue to be seen by many historians as the inflation's principal material losers.[30] The idea of the inflation as a time of moral or cultural upheaval has also recently been reinforced by historians who have noted the coincidence of the inflation with increased criminality,

Überlegungen zu einigen Inflationstheorien', in Feldman *et al.* (eds.), *Zwischenbilanz*, pp. 49–106; *idem, Machinebauunternehmen in der Inflation 1919 bis 1923: Unternehmenshistorische Untersuchungen zu einigen Inflationstheorien* (Berlin/New York, 1985). For other sceptical views on this point see James, *German Slump*, pp. 125–30; Webb, *Hyperinflation*, pp. 84f., 100f.

[25] G.D. Feldman, 'Banks and Banking in Germany after the First World War', in Y. Cassis (ed.), *Finance and Financiers in European History, 1880–1960* (Cambridge, 1993), pp. 243–62; H. James, 'Banks and Bankers in the German Interwar Depression', in *ibid.*, pp. 263–73; James, *German Slump*, pp. 128ff., 140ff. Cf. M. Pohl, 'Die Situation der Banken in der Inflationszeit', in Büsch and Feldman (eds.), *Historische Prozesse*, pp. 83ff.; C.-L. Holtfrerich, 'Auswirkungen der Inflation auf die Struktur des deutschen Kreditgewerbes', in Feldman and Müller-Luckner (eds.), *Nachwirkungen*, pp. 187–208.

[26] T. Balderston, 'Links between Inflation and Depression: German Capital and Labour Markets, 1924–31', in Feldman and Müller-Luckner (eds.), *Nachwirkungen*, pp. 157–84; *idem, The German Economic Crisis, 1923–1932*, (Berlin, 1993), esp. pp. 184ff.

[27] See, e.g., H. Mottek, W. Becker and A. Schröter, *Wirtschaftsgeschichte Deutschlands. Ein Grundriß*. Bd. III: *Von der Zeit der Bismarckschen Reichsgründung 1871 bis zur Niederlage des faschistischen deutschen Imperialismus 1945* (Berlin, 1974), p. 246; K. Gossweiler, *Großbanken, Industriemonopol, Staat* (Berlin, 1971), pp. 143–55; J. Kuczynski, *Die Geschichte der Lage der Arbeiter unter dem Kapitalismus*. Bd. V: *Darstellung der Lage der Arbeiter in Deutschland von 1917/18 bis 1932/33* (Berlin, 1966), p. 150; C.-D. Krohn, *Die große Inflation in Deutschland, 1918–1923* (Cologne, 1977), p. 35; H. Burg, *Inflation und Klassenkampf. Ursachen, Widersprüche und Konsequenzen der Inflation in Imperialismus* (Berlin, 1977).

[28] R. Scholz, 'Lohn und Beschäftigung als Indikatoren für die soziale Lage der Arbeiterschaft in der Inflation', in Feldman *et al.* (eds.), *Anpassung*, pp. 278–322. See also M. Niehuss, *Arbeiterschaft in Krieg und Inflation. Soziale Lage und Schichtung der Arbeiter in Augsburg und Linz, 1910–1925* (Berlin/New York, 1984).

[29] F. Eulenberg, 'Die sozialen Wirkungen der Währungsverhältnisse', in *Jahrbücher für Nationalökonomie und Statistik*, 122, 6 (1924), pp. 748–94.

[30] See for example Graham, *Hyperinflation*, pp. 14, 241f.; James, *German Slump*, p. 48; P.J. Lyth, *Inflation and the Merchant Economy, The Hamburg Mittelstand, 1914–1924* (New York/Oxford/Munich, 1990); A. Kunz, 'Variants of Social Protest in the German Inflation: The Mobilisation of Civil Servants in City and Countryside, 1920–1924', in Feldman *et al.* (eds.), *Anpassung*, pp. 323–56.

changing sexual mores – even the art of Expressionism.[31] Finally, the argument that inflation undermined the political stability of the Republic by alienating middle-class groups has been persuasively developed by Childers, Jones and others.[32] Borchardt has stressed the way the fear of inflation reduced the options open to policy makers in the Slump.[33]

There is a further, international dimension to the case against the inflation. From 1919 onwards, there were many foreign observers who believed that the Germans were deliberately stimulating inflation to avoid paying reparations – a view recently revived by historians like Marks, Schuker and, most recently, Kent.[34] Their argument is that Germany could have paid more if the German government had been willing to depress domestic demand sufficiently to generate an export

[31] G.D. Feldman, 'Weimar from Inflation to Depression: Experiment or Gamble?', in *idem* and Müller-Luckner (eds.), *Nachwirkungen*, pp. 385–402; *idem*, *Great Disorder*, pp. 527–55; J. von Kruedener, 'Die Entstehung des Inflationstraumas. Zur Sozialpsychologie der deutschen Hyperinflation, 1922/23', in Feldman *et al.* (eds.), *Konsequenzen*, pp. 213–86; D. Peukert, 'The Lost Generation: Youth Unemployment at the End of the Weimar Republic', in R.J. Evans and D. Geary (eds.), *The German Unemployed* (London/Sydney, 1987), pp. 188f.; *idem*, *The Weimar Republic. The Crisis of Classical Modernity* (London, 1991), pp. 71–6. See also J. Willett, *The New Sobriety, 1917–1933: Art and Politics in the Weimar Period* (London, 1978), pp. 82f.; *idem*, *The Theatre of the Weimar Republic* (New York/London, 1988), pp. 85, 190; C. Usborne, *The Politics of the Body in Weimar Germany. Reproductive Rights and Duties* (London, 1991), pp. 69ff.

[32] L.E. Jones, '"The Dying Middle": Weimar Germany and the Fragmentation of Bourgeois Politics', *CEH*, 5 (1972), pp. 23–54; *idem*, 'Inflation, Revaluation and the Crisis of Middle Class Politics: A Study of the Dissolution of the German Party System, 1923–1928', *CEH*, 12 (1979), pp. 143–68; *idem*, 'Die Rückwirkungen der Inflation auf die Entwicklung des deutschen Parteiensystems in der Weimarer Republik', in Büsch and Feldman (eds.), *Historische Prozesse*, pp. 288–94; *idem*, 'In the Shadow of Stabilisation: German Liberalism and the Legitimacy Crisis of the Weimar Party System', in Feldman and Müller-Luckner (eds.), *Nachwirkungen*, pp. 21–41; T. Childers, 'Interest and Ideology: Anti-System Politics in the Era of Stabilisation, 1924–28', in *ibid.*, pp. 1–20. See also G.D. Feldman; 'The Historian and the German Inflation', in Schmukler and Marcus (eds.), *Inflation through the Ages*, pp. 386–99.

[33] K. Borchardt, 'Inflationsgefahren in der Weltwirtschaftskrise? Zu den Spielräumen der Brüningschen Wirtschaftspolitik, 1930–1932', in W. Engels *et al.* (eds.), *International Capital Movements, Debt and Monetary System. Essays in Honour of Wilfried Guth* (Mainz, 1984), pp. 21–42; *idem*, 'Das Gewicht der Inflationsangst in den wirtschaftspolitischen Entscheidungsprozessen während der Weltwirtschaftskrise', in Feldman and Müller-Luckner (eds.), *Nachwirkungen*, pp. 233–60.

[34] S. Marks, 'Reparations Reconsidered: A Reminder', *CEH*, 2, 4 (1969), pp. 356–65; 'The Myths of Reparations', *CEH*, 11 (1978), pp. 231–55; S. Schuker, 'Finance and Foreign Policy in the Era of the German Inflation: British, French and German Strategies for Economic Reconstruction after the First World War', in Büsch and Feldman (eds.), *Historische Prozesse*, pp. 343–61; *idem*, 'American "Reparations" to Germany, 1919–1933', in Feldman and Müller-Luckner (eds.), *Nachwirkungen*, pp. 335–83; B. Kent, *The Spoils of War. The Politics, Economics and Diplomacy of Reparations, 1918–1932* (Oxford, 1989).

surplus. Matters were made easy by the large amounts of foreign lending made available during and after the inflation; yet the Germans deliberately elected to continue inflationary monetary and fiscal policies, in the belief that allowing the mark to fall against the dollar would make the collection of reparations impossible. The implication of these arguments is that it was Germany which destabilised the post-war international order, in a vain attempt to wreck the reparations system. Whereas the French had approached the peace process with the best of intentions, hoping to establish some kind of economic partnership in Europe, and the Americans were willing to finance, albeit privately, European reconstruction, the Germans adopted a policy of sabotage. The result was an international crisis which culminated in the occupation of the Ruhr and did permament damage to Franco-German relations.[35]

Yet there have always been those who took a less severe view of the inflation. At a meeting with the American ambassador in Berlin in June 1922, the German Foreign Minister Walther Rathenau and the industrialist Hugo Stinnes offered two differing justifications for German policy:

[Rathenau] held [. . .] that inflation was no worse economically than controlling rents and maintained it only took from those who had and gave to those who had not, which in a country as poor as Germany was entirely proper. Stinnes [. . .] declared the choice had been between inflation and revolution and as between the two he favoured inflation.[36]

For Stinnes, inflation was 'the only way of giving the population a regular employment, which was necessary to secure the life of the nation'.[37] 'It was,' he told Houghton some months later, 'politically necessary to put at work three million men coming back from the war. It was [. . .] a question of your money or your life.'[38] The Hamburg banker Carl Melchior made a similar point:

It was politically and socially necessary at the time and [. . .] could it have been controlled, no permanent harm would have occurred. It was not planned. It came about from the tremendous budget deficiency at the close of the war, when they had no funds. It became involved in the creation of new capital

---

[35] W.A. McDougall, *France's Rhineland Diplomacy 1914–1924. The Last Bid for a Balance of Power in Europe* (Princeton, 1978); M. Trachtenberg, *Reparation in World Politics: France and European Economic Diplomacy 1916–1923* (New York, 1980); S.A. Schuker, *The End of French Predominance in Europe. The Financial Crisis of 1924 and the Adoption of the Dawes Plan* (Chapel Hill, 1976).

[36] NAW, RG 59, 862.00/1128, Houghton to State Dept., 25.6.22. Cf. Feldman, *Great Disorder*, pp. 447ff.

[37] James, *German Slump*, p. 42.

[38] NAW, RG 59, 862.00/1199, Houghton to Secretary of State, 27.12.22.

to enable industry to hire the returning soldiers. It grew out of control owing to the demands on German resources from abroad.[39]

Elsewhere he argued that the huge deficit on the state railways was necessary 'to avoid putting [. . .] 100,000 disposable employees [. . .] onto unemployment benefit and thus handing them over to political radicalism'.[40] Writing in November 1923, his senior partner Max Warburg underlined the point: 'It was always a question of whether one wished to stop the inflation and trigger the revolution.'[41]

For many years historians tended to be sceptical of such views, precisely because they were expressed by businessmen: they amounted, it was assumed, to cynical justifications for policies in which they and their firms had an economic interest.[42] The Communist Georg Grosz's cartoons of bloated inflation profiteers in books like *Abrechnung folgt!* were simply the most vivid expression of the widely held view that 'big business' derived substantial material benefits from inflation at the expense of other social groups.[43] This view, albeit with substantial scholarly refinement, has proved remarkably persistent. Historians since Bresciani have suggested at least six distinct ways in which 'the inflation' was advantageous to business interests. It has been suggested that inflation reduced wage costs in real terms, because payments to workers lagged behind price increases,[44] and that it reduced the real value of business debts, interest payments and dividends.[45] Moreover, the tax burdens on business were eroded by inflation to levels far below what they would have been under conditions of stability, principally because protracted payment periods eroded the real value of profits and income taxes.[46] Indeed, business benefited doubly from

[39] *Ibid.* Cf. H.J. Rupieper, *The Cuno Government and Reparations 1922–1923. Politics and Economics* (The Hague/London/Boston, 1976), p. 198.

[40] WA, Politische Correspondenz 1921, Melchior to S. Japhet, 15.1.21.

[41] WA, 'Jahresbericht 1923', p. 43.

[42] Gossweiler, *Großbanken*, pp. 135f., 143ff. For a recent such view, see A. von Specht, *Politische und wirtschaftliche Hintergründe der deutschen Inflation, 1918–1923* (Frankfurt am Main, 1982).

[43] G. Grosz, *Abrechnung Folgt* (Berlin, 1923), pp. 14, 18f., 41.

[44] Bresciani, *Inflation*, pp. 104f., 233; Graham, *Hyperinflation*, pp. 197, 313.

[45] Bresciani, *Inflation*, pp. 104f.; Laursen and Pedersen, *German Inflation*, p. 118; C.S. Maier, *Recasting Bourgeois Europe. Stabilisation in France, Germany and Italy in the Decade after World War I* (Princeton, 1975), p. 82; Holtfrerich, *Inflation*, pp. 200f; Specht, *Politische Hintergründe*, pp. 35, 102, 148; J. Flemming, C.-D. Krohn and P.-C. Witt, 'Sozialverhalten und politische Reaktionen von Gruppen und Institutionen im Inflationsprozeß. Anmerkungen zum Forschungsstand', in Büsch and Feldman (eds.), *Historische Prozesse*, pp. 258f.

[46] Bresciani, *Inflation*, pp. 66, 71f, 105; Maier, *Recasting Bourgeois Europe*, p. 82; P.-C. Witt, 'Finanzpolitik und sozialer Wandel in Krieg und Inflation 1918–1924', in Mommsen *et al.* (eds.), *Industrielles System*, I, pp. 414–24; Holtfrerich, *Inflation*, pp. 134–7.

fiscal policy because of the many subsidies paid by the wartime and post-war governments to industry.[47] All of this inflated profits, allowing high levels of investment in plant and buildings – investments which in themselves made sense as a hedge against currency depreciation.[48] Thus while ordinary Germans went hungry,[49] German industry went on an investment spree, aided and abetted by Reichsbank credits at low or negative real interest rates.[50] Finally, the depreciation of the mark boosted business in an additional way, by giving German products a substantial competitive advantage on the world market, allowing 'business to recapture many foreign markets'.[51] In addition to these purely 'economic' benefits which business allegedly derived from inflation, two more political advantages have also been suggested: namely that inflation helped to contain the revolutionary threat posed to German capitalism in 1918–23;[52] and, furthermore, that it helped business evade the heavy tax burdens which would have been imposed on it had the German government succeeded in 'fulfilling' the London schedule of reparations.[53]

From the evidence of such economic benefits, it has been but a short step to the conclusion that businessmen were *responsible* for the inflation. The liberal journalist Georg Bernhard expressed this view clearly when he denounced Stinnes in October 1923: 'He has woven intrigues against every Government which he was afraid would put in order the internal conditions of Germany. [. . .] His system of politics [. . .has] aimed at the maintenance of inflation and disorder.'[54] Historians have frequently echoed this accusation, levelling it more generally at 'the great economic groups' and 'a conspiracy of the industrial classes [. . .] to impede the reform of the public finances and to sabotage all proposals for the reform of the exchange'.[55] For example:

---

[47] Bresciani, *Inflation*, p. 196; James, *German Slump*, pp. 170f.
[48] Bresciani, *Inflation*, pp. 196–201; Graham, *Hyperinflation*, pp. 88ff., 93f., 242, 323f.; Laursen and Pedersen, *Inflation*, pp. 95–8, 124ff.; Maier, *Recasting Bourgeois Europe*, p. 82; Specht, *Politische Hintergründe*, pp. 35, 102, 148; Peukert, *Weimar Republic*, p. 65.
[49] Depressed consumption is seen as having been a corollary of high investment; see Bresciani, *Inflation*, pp. 329f, 332f.; Graham, *Hyperinflation*, pp. 302–5.
[50] Bresciani, *Inflation*, p. 75–82.
[51] *Ibid.*, pp. 101, 105, 293; Graham, *Hyperinflation*, pp. 187, 193, 260; Maier, *Recasting Bourgeois Europe*, pp. 67f., 71, 82; von Specht, *Politische Hintergründe*, p. 43.
[52] Maier, *Recasting Bourgeois Europe*, passim. Cf. idem, 'Inflation and Stabilisation in the Wake of Two World Wars: Comparative Strategies and Sacrifices', in Feldman et al. (eds.), *Erfahrung*, p. 114.
[53] Specht, *Politische Hintergründe*, pp. 33, 38; Kent, *Spoils of War*, pp. 64f., 169.
[54] Bresciani, *Inflation*, p. 105. For similar, earlier allegations by Bernhard see StAH, SK II, II A4 Fasc. 29 Inv. 1, HG to SK, 30.1.23; 9.2.23.
[55] Bresciani, *Inflation*, pp. 57f., 74, 102–4, 330ff.: 'The power of the great industrialists and [. . .] profiteers increased [. . .] There was established [. . .] the dictatorship of heavy industry – an industrial feudalism pitted against the nation.' Cf. Graham,

'The government came increasingly under the influence of business interests who initially were the chief beneficiaries of the inflation. [. . .] The head of the government which carried on the inflationary financing of the Ruhr industrialists in 1923 was [himself] a man of big business.'[56] Such an interpretation clearly fits into a broader theme of German historiography. Most obviously, for Marxist–Leninist historians, the inflation was simply one episode in the story of German 'monopoly capitalism'. But there is also a degree of continuity in Western writing, leading from the work of Stegmann, Saul and others on the increasingly 'organised' capitalism of the Wilhelmine period,[57] via Feldman and Kocka's work on the war,[58] to the work of Weisbrod and others on the role of business interests in the collapse of Weimar and the establishment of the Third Reich.[59] The common factors in this admittedly far from homogeneous literature are an emphasis, firstly, on the role of heavy industry as the most powerful of business interests, secondly, on its increasing organisational concentration at the level of the concern, the cartel and the pressure group, and, finally, on its fundamentally malignant political role. Thus, from Saul's *Kaiserreich* to Weisbrod's Weimar, there is a theme of industrial sympathy for authoritarianism, combined with antagonism towards both parliamentary democracy and organised labour. The inflation years thus appear as the transitional phase, with Feldman's industrialists coming to

Hyperinflation, pp. 11, 281; Maier, *Recasting Bourgeois Europe*, pp. 69, 224, 414; P.-C. Witt, 'Staatliche Wirtschaftspolitik in Deutschland 1918–1923: Entwicklung und Zerstörung einer modernen wirtschaftspolitischen Strategie', in Feldman *et al.* (eds.), *Zwischenbilanz*, pp. 151–79.

[56] D.H. Aldcroft, *The Twenties. From Versailles to Wall Street, 1919–1929* (Harmondsworth, 1987), pp. 136f.

[57] D. Stegmann, *Die Erben Bismarcks. Parteien und Verbände in der Spätphase des Wilhelminischen Deutschlands. Sammlungspolitik 1897–1918* (Cologne, 1970); K. Saul, *Staat, Industrie und Arbeiterbewegung. Zur Innen- und Sozialpolitik des Wilhelminischen Deutschlands 1903–1914* (Düsseldorf, 1974). For the recent revival of Hilferding's idea of 'organised capitalism', see the essays in H.-A. Winkler (ed.), *Organisierter Kapitalismus* (Göttingen, 1974), esp. J. Kocka, 'Organisierter Kapitalismus oder Staatsmonopolistischer Kapitalismus? Begriffliche Vorbemerkungen', in *ibid.*, pp. 19–35; and the comments in G. Eley, 'Capitalism and the Wilhelmine State: Industrial Growth and Political Backwardness, 1890–1918', *HJ*, 21 (1978), pp. 737–50.

[58] G.D. Feldman, *Army, Industry and Labor in Germany, 1914–1918* (Princeton, 1966); idem, 'German Big Business between War and Revolution: The Origins of the Stinnes-Legien Agreement', in G.A. Ritter (ed.), *Entstehung und Wandel der modernen Gesellschaft. Festschrift für Hans Rosenberg zum 65. Geburtstag* (Berlin, 1970), pp. 312–41; idem, 'Der deutsche Organisierte Kapitalismus während der Kriegs- und Inflationsjahre, 1914–1923', in Winkler (ed.), *Organisierter Kapitalismus*, pp. 150–71; J. Kocka, *Klassengesellschaft im Krieg. Deutsche Sozialgeschichte 1914–1918* (Göttingen, 1973).

[59] B. Weisbrod, *Schwerindustrie in der Weimarer Republik. Interessenpolitik zwischen Stabilisierung und Krise* (Wuppertal, 1978); idem, 'Economic Power and Political Stability Reconsidered: Heavy Industry in the Weimar Republic', *Social History*, 4 (1979), pp. 241–63.

resemble their pre-war allies, the *Junker*, in their desire to stave off long-term economic decline by political means;[60] and Maier's 'business spokesmen' exercising a 'veto power' against stabilisation after 1921 in a rehearsal of their later role during the Slump.[61] The central theme of Feldman's *magnum opus* is the growth of industrial power – personified by Stinnes – at the expense of public authority.[62]

However, it has proved difficult for historians to maintain that the inflation offered so many advantages to German business without raising the possibility that, as Graham suggested, 'the balance of material gains and losses' for the economy as a whole was 'on the side of gains'.[63] This was the argument developed in the 1960s by two Scandinavian Keynesians, Laursen and Pedersen,[64] and, certainly, there is some evidence to support it. Wagenführ's figures suggest increases in industrial output in 1920, 1921 and 1922,[65] as do the statistics for agricultural production;[66] while estimates for real national income or net national product – for what they are worth – also point to a three-year period of rapid growth.[67] Moreover, it has been argued that, because the inflation led to high rates of investment, it created a potential for growth which only the depressed conditions of the post-1924 period prevented from being put to use;[68] a point borne out by other case

[60] G.D. Feldman, *Iron and Steel in the German Inflation, 1916–1923* (Princeton, 1977), p. 466.

[61] Maier, 'Inflation and Stabilisation', pp. 114f.

[62] Feldman, *Great Disorder, passim*.

[63] Graham, *Hyperinflation*, pp. 321, 324.

[64] Laursen and Pedersen, *Inflation*, p. 123.

[65] R. Wagenführ, 'Die Industriewirtschaft. Entwicklungstendenzen der deutschen und internationalen Industrieproduktion, 1860–1932', in *Vierteljahreshefte zur Konjunkturforschung*, Sonderheft 31 (Berlin, 1933), pp. 22, 28, 56.

[66] Cf. Holtfrerich, *Inflation*, p. 182; James, *German Slump*, pp. 250f.

[67] Graham, *Hyperinflation*, pp. 245ff.; Laursen and Pedersen, *Inflation*, pp. 84–8, 120; F.-W. Henning, *Das industrialisierte Deutschland 1914 bis 1972* (Paderborn, 1974), pp. 42, 47, 49; Witt, 'Finanzpolitik und sozialer Wandel', p. 424; Holtfrerich, *Inflation*, p. 224. These figures are to a large extent the products of guesswork, because of the unreliability and patchiness of contemporary data. They are used in this study to allow aggregate macroeconomic comparisons, however rough, with the preceding and succeeding periods.

[68] Graham, *Hyperinflation*, pp. 88ff., 93f., 242, 278f., 306–13, 323f.; Laursen and Pedersen, *Inflation*, pp. 95–8, 124ff.; M. Nussbaum, 'Unternehmenskonzentration und Investitionsstrategie nach dem Ersten Weltkrieg', *Jahrbuch für Wirtschaftsgeschichte* (1974), pp. 51–67; D. Petzina, *Die deutsche Wirtschaft in der Zwischenkriegszeit* (Wiesbaden, 1977), p. 83; P. Czada, 'Große Inflation und Wirtschaftswachstum', in Mommsen *et al.* (eds.), *Industrielles System*, I, pp. 386–94; W. Abelshauser, 'Inflation und Stabilisierung. Zum Problem ihrer makroökonomischen Auswirkungen auf die Rekonstruktion der deutschen Wirtschaft nach dem Ersten Weltkrieg', in Büsch und Feldman (eds.), *Historische Prozesse*, pp. 161–74; W. Abelshauser and D. Petzina, 'Krise und Rekonstruktion. Zur Interpretation der gesamtwirtschaftlichen Entwicklung Deutschlands im 20. Jahrhundert', in W.H. Schröder and R. Spree (eds.), *Historische Konjunkturforschung* (Stuttgart, 1981), pp. 75ff.; D. Petzina, 'Was there a Crisis before the Crisis?', in J. Baron von Kruedener (ed.), *Economic Crisis and*

studies suggesting a more positive picture of inflation investment than Lindenlaub's.[69] Finally, there is no doubting the fact that in 1920, 1921 and 1922, German employment levels were unusually high by international standards. Unemployment had all but vanished in Germany in mid 1922, averaging around 1.5 per cent of trade union members, compared with roughly comparable figures of 14 per cent and 11 per cent in the UK and US respectively.[70] From this comparative perspective, there seems much to recommend Graham's conclusion that 'Germany accomplished the actual process of transition from the war to a stable post-war monetary structure at a lower real cost' than Britain and the US.[71] Even if their conclusions are less positive than Graham's, most recent economic history textbooks have been at pains to stress these advantages of inflation, at least for the pre-hyperinflation period.[72]

From this more positive view of the economic impact of inflation has followed a parallel reassessment of its social consequences. Not only was unemployment low; evidence has been produced to suggest that in real terms wages and consumption were eroded less by inflation than had previously been thought.[73] It was not just an elite of profiteers who gained from the inflation; workers (especially the unskilled)

Political Collapse. The Weimar Republic 1924–1933 (New York/Oxford/Munich, 1990), pp. 9–12.

[69] P. Czada, *Die Berliner Elektro-industrie in der Weimarer Zeit. Eine regionalstatistische-wirtschaftshistorische Untersuchung* (Berlin, 1969); J. Reulecke, 'Phasen und Auswirkungen der Inflation 1914–1923 am Beispiel der Barmer Wirtschaft', in Büsch and Feldman (eds.), *Historische Prozesse*, pp. 175–87; A. Gladen, 'Der Ruhrbergbau in der Inflationszeit', pp. 188–96.

[70] Graham, *Hyperinflation*, pp. 278f., 317f.; Laursen and Pedersen, *Inflation*, pp. 77, 123; Petzina, *Deutsche Wirtschaft*, p. 16. Cf. D. Petzina, 'Arbeitslosigkeit in der Weimarer Republik', in W. Abelshauser (ed.), *Die Weimarer Republik als Wohlfahrtsstaat. Zum Verhältnis von Wirtschafts- und Sozialpolitik in der Industriegesellschaft*, *VSWG*, Beiheft 81 (1987), pp. 239–59.

[71] Graham, *Hyperinflation*, pp. 289, 318–21. Cf. Laursen and Pedersen, *Inflation*, p. 123.

[72] G. Stolper with K. Häuser and K. Borchardt, *The German Economy 1870 to the Present* (London, 1967), pp. 72–93; K. Borchardt, 'Wachstum und Wechsellagen, 1914–1970', in H. Aubin and W. Zorn (eds.), *Handbuch der deutschen Wirtschafts- und Sozialgeschichte*, Bd. II (Stuttgart, 1976), pp. 696–703; Henning, *Das industrialisierte Deutschland*, pp. 63–83; F. Blaich, *Der schwarze Freitag. Inflation und Wirtschaftskrise* (Munich, 1985), pp. 9–58; H.-J. Braun, *The German Economy in the Twentieth Century. The German Reich and the Federal Republic* (London/New York, 1990), pp. 33–41.

[73] W. Abelshauser, 'Verelendung der Handarbeiter? Zur sozialen Lage der deutschen Arbeiter in der großen Inflation der frühen zwanziger Jahre', in H. Mommsen and W. Schulze (eds.), *Vom Elend der Handarbeit* (Stuttgart, 1982), pp. 445–76; A. Kunz, 'Verteilungskampf oder Interessenkonsensus? Einkommensentwicklung und Sozialverhalten von Arbeitnehmergruppe in der Inflationszeit 1914 bis 1924', in Feldman *et al.* (eds.), *Zwischenbilanz*, pp. 347–84. Cf. Holtfrerich, *Inflation*, pp. 227–62; Webb, *Hyperinflation*, pp. 78, 84.

enjoyed relatively high real wages; while big and small rural landowners benefited from mortgage debts being liquidated.[74] Even the undoubted levelling effect of the inflation on both incomes and wealth has been portrayed in a positive light by Holtfrerich;[75] while Hughes has suggested that the losses suffered by savers and investors were less severe than was once thought.[76]

In turn, such positive views of the social consequences of inflation have led to new perspectives on its political causes and effects. Where earlier accounts portrayed big business as the essentially selfish manipulators of the process, the idea of more generalised benefits has led to a more 'structural' view of the inflation as the product of an 'inflationary consensus' between industry and labour.[77] Pre-war antagonism between German employers and the trade unions was dissolved in the *Burgfrieden* of the war, and turned to active partnership with the outbreak of the Revolution in November 1918 and the formation of the 'Central Working Community'. Workers also had an interest in inflation because expansionary monetary and fiscal policies would maintain employment levels, and, given the ease with which nominal wages could be adjusted through collective bargaining, would reduce real income differentials in society as a whole. In this light, the inflation brought halcyon days for German organised labour: a time of restricted working hours, widespread and frequent collective bargaining, binding arbitration in the event of a dispute and statutory representation on works' councils.[78] It was only after the inflation had burnt itself out in 1923 that the 'corporatist' honeymoon came to an end, with the divorce taking place

---

[74] On this second point, see Gerschenkron, *Bread and Democracy*, pp. 108ff.; J. Osmond, 'Peasant Farming in South and West Germany during War and Inflation 1914 to 1924: Stability and Stagnation', in Feldman *et al.* (eds.), *Zwischenbilanz*, pp. 189–307; R.G. Moeller, 'Winners as Losers in the German Inflation: Peasant Protest over the Controlled Economy', in *ibid.*, pp. 263–75.

[75] Holtfrerich, *Inflation*, pp. 265–78; Laursen and Pedersen, *Inflation*, pp. 72–82, 108–22, 123.

[76] M. L. Hughes, *Paying for the German Inflation* (Chapel Hill, North Carolina, 1988); idem, 'Economic Interest, Social Attitudes and Creditor Ideology: Popular Responses to Inflation', in Feldman *et al.* (eds.), *Zwischenbilanz*, pp. 385–408.

[77] C.S. Maier, 'Die deutsche Inflation als Verteilungskonflikt: soziale Ursachen und Auswirkungen im internationalen Vergleich', in Büsch and Feldman (eds.), *Historische Prozesse*, pp. 329–42; idem, 'Inflation and Stabilisation', p. 114; idem, *Recasting Bourgeois Europe*, pp. 114, 228–31; C. Kindleberger, 'A Structural View of the German Inflation', in Feldman *et al.* (eds.), *Erfahrung*, pp. 10–33; Flemming *et al.*, 'Sozialverhalten und politische Reaktionen'; A. Kunz, 'Inflation als Verteilungskampf. Eine Bilanz der neueren Forschung', in Abelshauser (ed.), *Weimarer Republik*, pp. 171–84. Cf. L.N. Lindberg and C.S. Maier, *The Politics of Inflation and Economic Stagnation* (Washington, 1985).

[78] On the role of organised labour see H. Potthoff, *Gewerkschaften und Politik zwischen Revolution und Inflation* (Düsseldorf, 1979); H.-A. Winkler, *Von der Revolution zur Stabilisierung. Arbeiter und Arbeiterbewegung in der Weimarer Republik, 1918–1924* (Berlin/Bonn, 1984).

somewhere between the Ruhr iron industry lockout and the fall of the Great Coalition.[79]

This 'structural' interpretation of inflation can be applied to fiscal policy as well as to labour relations. It was frequently argued by contemporaries (notably Keynes) that no government could survive the social strains of trying to eliminate the budget deficit. Inflation was the only tax which was politically acceptable.[80] Thus Haller estimated that tax levels would have needed to have exceeded 35 per cent of national income to pay for reparations, war pensions and debt service without further government borrowing; a level of taxation which, he suggested, would have been politically intolerable, given the far lower tax rates to which Germans were accustomed.[81] Inflation is thus said to have 'secured the parliamentary form of government for the period of the Weimar Republic', in that any attempt to have stabilised fiscal and monetary policy would have led to social upheaval and the fall of the government.[82] In short, there was no alternative.[83] Finally, it should be noted that doubt has been cast on the link between inflation and middle-class support for National Socialism. Support for parties explicitly aiming at the revaluation of savings was relatively limited after 1924;[84] while Falter's work on the elections of 1930 and 1932 has in any case undermined the idea that the Nazi vote had an exclusively middle-class character.[85]

Perhaps the most influential element in the 'structural' case for the defence is, however, the role of international constraints, in particular reparations. In part, this is simply an extension of the view summarised

---

[79] On the idea of 'corporatism' as a model of cooperation betwen capital and labour, see C.S. Maier, 'The Politics of Inflation in the Twentieth Century', in F. Hirsch and J.H. Goldthorpe (eds.), *The Political Economy of Inflation* (Harvard, 1978), pp. 37–92; U. Nocken, 'Corporatism and Pluralism in Modern German History', in D. Stegmann, B.-J. Wendt and P.-C. Witt (eds.), *Industrielle Gesellschaft und politisches System. Beiträge zur politischen Sozialgeschichte. Festschrift für Fritz Fischer zum 70. Geburtstag* (Bonn, 1978), pp. 37–56; W. Abelshauser, 'Freiheitlicher Korporatismus im Kaiserreich und in der Weimarer Republik', in *idem* (ed.), *Weimarer Republik*, pp. 147–70.

[80] J.M. Keynes, *A Revision of the Treaty* (London, 1922); *idem*, *A Tract on Monetary Reform* (London, 1923), p. 36. Cf. Laursen and Pedersen, *Inflation*, pp. 10, 70, 121ff.; Borchardt, 'Wachstum und Wechsellagen', pp. 698ff.

[81] H. Haller, 'Die Rolle der Staatsfinanzen für den Inflationsprozeß', in Deutsche Bundesbank (ed.), *Währung und Wirtschaft in Deutschland, 1876–1975* (Frankfurt am Main, 1976), pp. 137–41. Cf. K. Borchardt, 'Germany's Experience of Inflation', in *idem*, *Perspectives on Modern German Economic History and Policy* (Cambridge, 1991), p. 135; Holtfrerich, *Inflation*, pp. 124–37.

[82] Haller, 'Rolle der Staatsfinanzen', p. 151.

[83] A similar argument can be advanced that a stricter monetary policy (i.e., increases in the discount rate) by the Reichsbank would have been counterproductive, given the high level of public sector debt: see H. Schacht, *The Stabilisation of the Mark* (London, 1927), pp. 50f.; Webb, 'Government Revenue', p. 56.

[84] Hughes, *Paying for the German Inflation, passim*.

[85] See most recently, J.W. Falter, *Hitlers Wähler* (Munich, 1991).

above that fiscal balance was impossible. The German budget was
already badly out of kilter after the war, it is argued; but the Allies'
demand for cash reparations of around 3 bn. gold marks *per annum*
(issued in May 1921) made fiscal collapse inevitable.[86] A further argument was more frequently advanced by contemporaries, however:
namely that, even if the money could have been raised in taxation, a
structural deficit on the German balance of payments would have made
it impossible to obtain the equivalent gold or foreign currency required
by the Allies. According to Keynes's tract *The Economic Consequences
of the Peace*, the loss of Germany's colonies, most of her overseas
investments, almost her entire merchant fleet and over a third of her
coal and iron-producing capacity condemned the German economy to
an acute balance of payments crisis, which attempts to collect cash
reparations could only compound.[87] Keynes himself did not initially
make the link to inflation explicit; but, as the depreciation of the mark
progressed, and, as the level of cash reparations was laboriously set,
the view gained ground inside Germany that there was a causal link
from reparations to inflation. The essence of the balance of payments
theory was that Germany could not achieve a current account surplus
out of which to pay cash reparations, and was therefore obliged to
buy hard currency by selling paper marks, thus driving down the
exchange rate, pushing up import prices and hence the domestic price
level.[88] Two factors made the achievement of such a surplus unlikely.
Firstly, the argument that the 'transfer problem' could be solved
by solving the budgetary problem, although theoretically satisfactory,
implied a sharp contraction in German consumption – intolerable for
reasons already discussed. Secondly, as Keynes and others argued from
an early stage, such an export surplus was not in the interests of the
collectors of reparations themselves.[89] A conclusion frequently drawn
is that German governments were therefore right to seek to undermine

[86] Haller, 'Rolle der Staatsfinanzen', pp. 137f.; D. Felix, 'Reparation Reconsidered with
a Vengeance', *CEH*, 4, 2 (1971), pp. 171–9; P. Krüger, 'Das Reparationsproblem der
Weimarer Republik in fragwürdiger Sicht', *VfZ*, 29 (1981), pp. 21–47; Holtfrerich,
Inflation, pp. 137–55; Webb, *Hyperinflation*, pp. 54, 104, 107. See also B. Eichengreen, *Golden Fetters. The Gold Standard and the Great Depression, 1919–1939* (New
York/Oxford, 1992), pp. 125–51.
[87] Keynes, *Economic Consequences*, pp. 103–210.
[88] See, e.g., M.J. Bonn, *Die Stabilisierung der Mark* (Berlin, 1922). Cf. Bresciani,
Inflation, p. 45; Graham, *Hyperinflation*, pp. 134, 117–49, 153–73; Merkin, 'Towards
a Theory of the German Inflation'.
[89] J.M. Keynes, 'The Economic Consequences of the Paris Settlement', 31.1.21/1.2.21,
in E. Johnson (ed.), *The Collected Writings of John Maynard Keynes*, vol. XVII
(Cambridge, 1977), pp. 207–13; idem, 'The New Reparations Proposals', 6.5.21, in
ibid., p. 234; 'The New Reparations Settlement: Effect on World Trade', 28.8.21,
in *ibid.*, pp. 249–56.

the system of reparations by allowing currency depreciation to accelerate. As Graham stressed, the depreciation of the currency boosted German exports.[90] This should have put pressure on the Allied economies, forcing them to accept that reparations could only be paid at the expense of Allied industry. The Germans were therefore not only justified, but tactically wise to place the blame for the depreciation of the currency on the impact of reparations on the balance of payments. In Graham's words, the view was 'by no means without justification that improvement in the public finances would lead to still more severe exactions. [. . .] Reparations [. . .were] probably considerably diminished by reason of the collapse of the currency'.[91] Depreciation (and hence inflation) was therefore, according to Holtfrerich, 'in the national interest' – the most effective way of 'persuading the rest of the world of the need for a reduction of the reparations burden'.[92] Indeed, the strategy had a double advantage: because so much of the money lent to Germany in the period was never repaid, one historian has gone so far as to speak of 'American "Reparations" to Germany'.[93]

2

This book's first objective is to challenge these arguments in defence of the inflation. It questions the idea that inflation boosted growth, suggesting that the benefits enjoyed in the years 1920–2 were outweighed by the costs of disastrous economic performance in the hyperinflation phase, and by the longer-term damage done to the German economy. It also questions the argument that inflation stimulated investment in 'real values', suggesting that, if anything, rising inflation deterred investment and concealed 'substance-losses' caused by inadequate allowance for depreciation. Where investment did take place, it frequently proved to be 'misinvestment' in the post-stabilisation period. Finally, the devastating impact of inflation on the capital market and banking system is adduced as evidence that, far from postponing economic crisis, the inflation ensured that the Slump was uniquely severe in Germany.

Secondly, it questions the idea that inflation was socially stabilising. Although the inflation brought exceptionally high employment levels

---

[90] Graham, *Hyperinflation*, pp. 174–97, 209, 214–38, 248.

[91] *Ibid.*, pp. 4, 7–9, 11, 30–5, 248, 321. Keynes made a similar point in 1929: see Keynes, *Collected Writings*, XI, p. 365.

[92] C.-L. Holtfrerich, 'Die deutsche Inflation 1918 bis 1923 in internationaler Perspektive. Entscheidungsrahmen und Verteilungsfolgen', in Büsch and Feldman (eds.), *Historische Prozesse*, p. 327. Cf. Borchardt, 'Wachstum und Wechsellagen', p. 700.

[93] Schuker, 'American "Reparations" to Germany, 1919–1933', in Feldman and Müller-Luckner (eds.), *Nachwirkungen*, pp. 335–83.

in 1921 and 1922 and led to a more equal distribution of income, it is by no means clear that this greater equality led to greater social harmony. For example, the inflation years witnessed unprecedented industrial strife, sporadic food riots, recurrent political violence and increased criminality. Moreover, the purely material effects of the inflation's radical redistribution on German society may have been less damaging than its cultural and even psychological effects. The 'silent bourgeois revolution' of the nineteenth century[94] had inculcated an intricate set of values – the virtue of industry and thrift, the sanctity of property and contract, the importance of *Bildung* and *Kultur*. In wiping out the assets of savings banks, private schools and all kinds of voluntary associations, the inflation effectively undermined the institutions on which those values were based, and thus the values themselves.

This in turn casts doubt on the idea that inflation was politically stabilising. For one thing, the role played by businessmen and their organisations in promoting inflationary policies did much to discredit capitalism in the eyes of those bourgeois groups – small businessmen, professionals, civil servants, rentiers – who lost out. By undermining the authority of the courts, the crisis also tended to discredit the rule of law in the eyes of expropriated creditors. Indeed, by effectively using private savings to liquidate the debts of the state, it may be said to have discredited the political authority of the Republic itself. Hyperinflation thus in many ways ruled out the emergence in Germany of the kind of parliamentary conservatism which emerged in inter-war Britain, where all the propertied classes, from big business to small shopkeeper, could be united on a platform of sound money against the interests of organised labour.[95] This is not to say that the inflation made Hitler inevitable. But, because of the inflation, the Weimar system reestablished in 1924 was built on foundations of sand; and, when it began to collapse in 1930, it was far harder to argue against Hitler's alternative.

Finally, and perhaps most importantly, this study challenges the notion that inflationary policies were in Germany's national interest, because they were the most effective way to demonstrate the impossibility of reparations. In fact this strategy failed, because its architects overestimated the extent to which currency depreciation would stimu-

[94] D. Blackbourn, 'The Discreet Charm of the Bourgeoisie: Reappraising German History in the Nineteenth Century', in *idem* and G. Eley, *The Peculiarities of German History. Bourgeois Society and Politics in Nineteenth Century Germany* (Oxford, 1984), pp. 159–205.
[95] Cf. R. McKibbin, 'Class and Conventional Wisdom. The Conservative Party and the "Public" in Inter-war Britain', in *idem*, *The Ideologies of Class: Social Relations in Britain, 1880–1950* (Oxford, 1990), pp. 259–93.

late German exports, and overlooked the fact that inflationary policies, in the context of a world recession, were more likely to stimulate imports. Although it was rational to want to reduce the level of reparations, the German strategy of revision by economic means wholly backfired, as it relieved rather than increased the pressure on the British and American economies.

In short, this book argues that the various economic, social, political and diplomatic arguments advanced, at the time and since, in defence of inflationary policies are, on balance, mistaken. In a sense, it therefore represents a return to Bresciani. However, the book has a second object, and that is to demonstrate that an alternative was possible, since the strongest objection to Bresciani's view has always been that there was none. Here the historian treads on treacherous ground; 'counter-factual' history is, after all, abhorrent to those for whom the historian's main purpose is to 'understand' the contemporary con-straints on decision makers, not to recommend 'better' courses of action with the advantage of hindsight. Yet as the historian elucidates the contemporary arguments against stabilisation, he cannot help but be struck by the poor quality of the economic information – and the crudeness of the calculations – on which those arguments were based. Clearly, many influential contemporaries were persuaded by the argu-ment that reducing government deficits and stabilising the growth of the money supply, particularly in the context of heavy reparations demands, would lead to an economic crisis so severe that it would destabilise the Republic. Clearly too, many believed that allowing the mark constantly to depreciate against other currencies would give German exporters an advantage over their competitors which would, in turn, give Germany political leverage. But the historian can legit-imately ask if these views exaggerated the probable costs of an earlier stabilisation, or the benefits of sustained currency depreciation. The argument advanced here is, firstly, that a stabilisation of monetary and fiscal policy *could* in theory have been achieved in 1920 without a British-style recession; indeed, without a recession as severe as that which did occur in Germany 1923/4. The reason this did not happen had as much to do with the desire to avoid reparations as with the fear of domestic disorder; yet subsequent events disproved the thesis that currency depreciation would bring about a decisive revision of the peace terms. A policy of stabilisation, by contrast, would have exerted real pressure on the Allies. True, the cuts in public expenditure and reductions in credit which such a policy would have entailed would probably have necessitated some political shift to the Right. However, Weimar governments were eventually forced to use authori-tarian methods in 1923 and 1924 to contain the social and economic

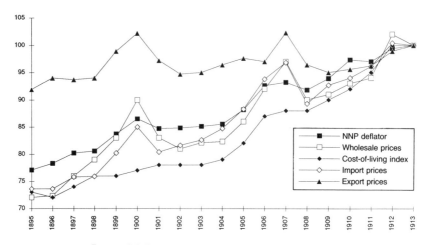

Figure 0.1 Pre-war inflation, 1895–1913 (1913=100)
Sources: Hoffmann *et al.*, *Wachstum*, pp. 99ff., 607f., 615; Jacobs and Richter,
'Grosshandelspreise', pp. 82f.; Bry, *Wages*, pp. 325f.

consequences of hyperinflation. Had they employed these powers to
end inflation in 1920, a conservative regime might have emerged which,
even if somewhat less democratic than Weimar, would have been
infinitely less dangerous than the regime which emerged thirteen years
later.

3

As that hypothesis implies, economic alternatives, however 'feasible',
could not have been implemented without some measure of change to
the mechanisms which determined fiscal, monetary and general economic policy. The third and final object of this book, however, is to
show how very difficult such change was for the German Reich. This
is best done by setting the inflation in a longer-term perspective, seeing
it less as the product of war and revolution, and more as the product
of fundamental institutional weaknesses dating back to the Reich's
origins and persisting even after the currency reform of 1923/4. For
the years 1914–23 were not the only inflationary years between 1871
and 1945. The Reich was established in an inflationary boom between
1867 and 1872. After 1897, the Wilhelmine Germany experienced
gentle – though to contemporaries striking – inflation until 1913 (see
figure 0.1). There was similar though less sustained inflation (of retail
prices) between 1924 and 1929; while the history of the Third Reich

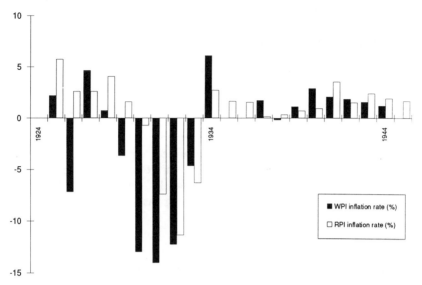

Figure 0.2 Inflation and deflation, 1924–1945
Source: Bundesbank (ed.), Währung und Wirtschaft, p. 416

was one of suppressed inflation after 1933 (see figure 0.2), and a second collapse of the currency in the 1940s, lasting until the (Western) currency reform of 1948 and the division of Germany.

Of course, the peculiarity of this experience should not be exaggerated. A 200 year survey of wholesale prices in Germany shows that there were major inflationary episodes both before (1799–1809) and after (1971–81) the existence of the Reich, both associated – like the decades 1914–24 and 1938–48 – with war-related shocks.[96] Moreover, it could be argued that the inflations of the period 1867–1947 were not peculiar to Germany, and therefore cannot help us to explain the 'special path' down which Germany went in the 1930s, if not before. Comparative indices suggest that, apart from the extreme episodes at the end of the world wars, nineteenth- and early twentieth-century price movements were roughly synchronised in the major European economies (Germany, Britain and France), with the United States converging after the Civil War.[97] Indeed, this argument can plausibly be applied to the 'great' inflation of 1918–23 too, since a number of

[96] Indeed, one could expand a discussion of German inflation to include experiences in the 17th and 18th centuries: the *Kipper- und Wipperzeit* and Frederick the Great's war finance, to say nothing of medieval problems of dearth.

[97] A. Jacobs and H. Richter, 'Die Grosshandelspreise in Deutschland von 1792 bis 1934', *Sonderhefte des Instituts für Konjunkturforschung*, 37 (1935), pp. 34, 41.

the new post-war Republics in Central Europe (notably Austria, Hungary and Poland), as well as revolutionary Russia, had hyperinflationary or near-hyperinflationary experiences comparable with that of Germany.[98] Most countries in continental Europe in fact had inflationary problems in the wake of the First World War, and even Britain and the United States were not unaffected.[99] The inter-war period as a whole is notorious as a time when the international monetary system malfunctioned, whether because the United States failed to don the mantle of international monetary hegemon, or because the world's central banks failed to cooperate as they had done before 1914.[100] On the other hand, much the same could be said of Germany's experience of the Slump, which clearly cannot wholly be separated from its international context. The question, in both cases, is whether anything stands out about the German experience.

In fact, German consumer prices rose faster than French, British and American between 1875 and 1913.[101] The 1923 hyperinflation was significantly more protracted and extreme than those in Hungary, Poland or Russia, or in Austria the year before; indeed, only one episode in European history (Hungary after the Second World War)

[98] Bresciani, *Inflation*, pp. 22f., 161–5; Cagan, 'Hyperinflation', pp. 25–117; T.J. Sargent, 'The Ends of Four Big Inflations', in R.E. Hall (ed.), *Inflation: Causes and Effects* (Chicago, 1982), pp. 41–97. On Austria: W. de Bordes, *The Austrian Crown: Its Depreciation and Stabilisation* (London, 1924); E. März, *Austrian Banking and Financial Policy: Creditanstalt at a Turning Point, 1913–1923* (London, 1984); G. Ostruba, 'Inflation in Österreich während und nach dem Ersten bzw. Zweiten Weltkrieg. Ein Vergleich', in Büsch and Feldman (eds.), *Historische Prozesse*, pp. 418–31; H. Kernbauer and F. Weber, 'Die Wiener Grossbanken in der Zeit der Kriegs- und Nachkriegsinflation', in Feldman *et al.* (eds.), *Erfahrung*, pp. 142–87. On Hungary: E.A. Boross, 'The Role of the State Issuing Bank in the Course of Inflation in Hungary between 1918 and 1924', in Feldman *et al.* (eds.), *Erfahrung*, pp. 188–227. On Poland: Z. Landau and J. Tomaszweski, 'Poland Between Inflation and Stabilisation 1924–1927', in Feldman *et al.* (eds.), *Erfahrung*, pp. 270–94. On Russia: S.S. Katzenellbaum, *Russian Currency and Banking, 1914–1924* (London, 1925); E.H. Carr, *The Bolshevik Revolution, 1917–1923*, vol. II (Harmondsworth, 1983), pp. 136–50, 247–59, 343–57.

[99] Aldcroft, *Versailles to Wall Street*, pp. 127f.; Petzina, *Deutsche Wirtschaft*, p. 82. Cf. R. Nurske, *The Course and Control of Inflation. A Review of Monetary Experience after World War I* (Geneva, 1946); J.H. Rogers, *The Process of Inflation in France, 1917–1927* (New York, 1929); D.E. Moggridge, *British Monetary Policy 1924–1931. The Norman Conquest of $4.86* (Cambridge, 1972); M. Friedman and A.J. Schwartz, *A Monetary History of the United States, 1867–1960* (Princeton, 1963).

[100] C.P. Kindleberger, *The World in Depression, 1929–1939* (London, 1973); F. Hirsch and P. Oppenheimer, 'The Trial of Managed Money', in C. Cipolla, *The Fontana Economic History of Europe*, vol. V (London, 1976), pp. 603ff.; C. S. Maier, 'The Two Post-war Eras and the Conditions for Stability in Twentieth Century Western Europe', in idem, *In Search of Stability. Explorations in Historical Political Economy* (Cambridge, 1987), pp. 153–84; Eichengreen, *Golden Fetters, passim*.

[101] A. Sommariva and G. Tullio, *German Macroeconomic History, 1880–1979. A Study of the Effects of Economic Policy on Inflation, Currency Depreciation and Growth* (London, 1987), pp. 89ff.

has seen such drastic currency depreciation.[102] Similarly, the German experience of suppressed inflation in the 1930s was unusual in an international context of deflation and depreciation. Moreover, it bears saying that, of all the twentieth-century economies to be afflicted by acute inflationary episodes, Germany's was the most advanced; its bourgeois social structure more dependent than those of more rural economies on the stability of paper assets. How, then, are we to account for the comparative instability of prices throughout the Reich's history?

It is, of course, possible to seek the answer to this question in the unusual power of economic interest groups in German history – as we have seen, an approach long favoured by historians. Certainly, an important theme of this study is the powerful dynamic which propelled German business forward from the mid 1890s towards ever-greater levels of output, investment and concentration. The growing appetite of German firms for credit and capital before 1914 undoubtedly contributed to the gentle inflation of the pre-war years. Moreover, the momentum of the upswing after 1897 encouraged some businessmen to begin disbelieving in the trade cycle, with its inevitable troughs. Thus, when confronted with the need for contraction during and after the war, many preferred to seek refuge in the phoney boom provided by inflation. As the American ambassador shrewdly noted in December 1922:

The German bankers and industrialists [. . .] have had plenty of experience in a constantly growing and expanding volume of industry and trade; they have had no experience whatever, until the present, in a decreasing volume of trade, such as [. . .] the US and England have experienced several times. [103]

A similar reluctance to see gross profits reduced lay behind the hostility of business towards taxation, particularly after 1924. Of equal importance, on the other hand, was the growing power of trade unions in Germany to push up wages. Although this became (and has remained) a controversial issue in the mid to late 1920s, in fact it was a feature of the German economy from the mid 1890s.

However, while the power of economic organisations certainly played a part in Wilhelmine and Weimar inflations, the problem was magnified by the peculiar institutional structure of the Reich. Inflation, as Knut Borchardt has said, is primarily a political phenomenon,[104] reflecting a failure of monetary and fiscal institutions. If German economic

---

[102] Cagan, 'Hyperinflation'; Maier 'Inflation and Stabilisation', pp. 115ff.; Aldcroft, *Versailles to Wall Street*, pp. 145–50.
[103] NAW, RG 59, 862.00/1199, Houghton to Secretary of State, 27.12.22.
[104] Borchardt, 'Germany's Experience with Inflation', p. 135.

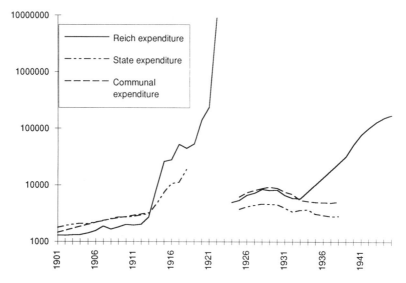

Figure 0.3 Public spending by tier of authority, 1901–1945 (m. marks)
Sources: Andic and Veverka, 'Government Expenditure' pp. 244f.; Witt,
Finanzpolitik, pp. 377, 380; Roesler, *Finanzpolitik*, pp. 196ff., 201; Witt, 'Tax
Policies', pp. 154–9; James, *German Slump*, p.52; Balderston, *Economic Crisis*,
p. 226.

interest groups were able to push up prices and wages, it was because
monetary and fiscal policy created an inflationary environment in which
this was possible. It is important to appreciate the broader significance
of this point in the German case. The creation of a national currency
by liberals in the 1870s had been more than a device for uniting
Germany economically – like the Customs Union, the railways and
the unified system of weights and measures. The mark coin was an
important symbol of German nationhood, which antedated more emotive symbols such as a national anthem and flag, to say nothing of a
unified tax system or time zone. The perennial weakness of the currency
must therefore be understood as a symptom of the weakness of the
Reich as a political entity.

This was threefold. Firstly, it reflected the Reich's fundamental
fiscal weakness. There were two phases of unsustainably rapid growth
in public spending: from 1891 to 1917, after which military and
political collapse rapidly eroded the state's role; and from 1925 to
1943, after which, once again, came collapse (figures 0.3 and 0.4).
The central problem was the persistent failure of taxation to keep pace
with these increases: there were recurrent public sector deficits from
the mid 1890s until the 1940s, reaching peaks in the war years. Even

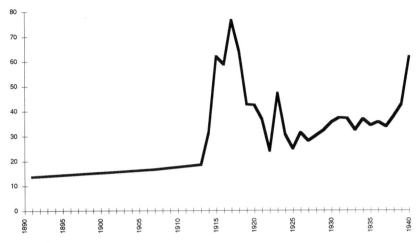

Figure 0.4 Public spending as a percentage of NNP, 1890–1940
Sources: Witt, 'Finanzpolitik', pp. 424f.; Witt, 'Tax Policies', pp. 154–9; Andic and Veverka, 'Government Expenditure' pp. 243f.; Balderston, *Economic Crisis*, p. 217; James, *German Slump*, pp. 52, 375f.; Milward, *War*, p. 78.

in the year of the utmost fiscal stringency, 1931, there was still a public sector deficit of 2.7 per cent of NNP.[105] This led in turn to unsustainable increases in public debt: from 49 per cent of NNP to around 240% in 1918, from 33 per cent in 1930 to around 390 per cent in 1944. Clearly, there were fundamental defects in the fiscal system. Firstly, the three-tiered system of public finance dispersed responsibility for revenue raising and expenditure too widely between Reich, federal states and local communes. Only in the 1930s did the central government establish control over the lower tiers' spending and borrowing policies. Secondly, there was a persistent discrepancy between the political demand for public expenditure, particularly on social welfare and defence, and the political tolerance of taxation.

Moreover, inflation reflected fundamental flaws in the German monetary system, particularly with regard to the power of the Reichsbank, which never established effective instruments to regulate public and private credit. Long-run monetary growth in nominal terms traced two roughly exponential paths between 1890 and 1923, and between 1933 and 1947, punctuated by the deflationary episode of 1929–32. In real terms, monetary growth was steadily upward until the onset of rapid

[105] Balderston, *Economic Crisis*, p. 417.

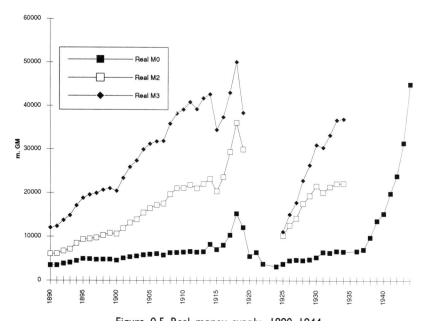

Figure 0.5 Real money supply, 1890–1944
Sources: Hoffmann *et al.*, *Wachstum*, pp. 814f.; Holtfrerich, *Inflation*, pp. 17,
50f.; Bundesbank (ed.), *Währung und Wirtschaft*, p. 416; James, *Reichsbank*,
pp. 365–8; Bry, *Wages*, pp. 442–9, 440–5.

inflation (see figure 0.5). The determinants of this growth were, firstly,
the demands of the private sector for credit, which were especially
important before the war and in 1922; secondly, the demands of the
public sector for short-term borrowing, especially between 1914 and
1923 and from 1931 to 1945; and, thirdly, international flows of capital
during German membership of the gold standard (1890–1914, 1924–
31). The Reichsbank's persistent failure to balance these factors partly
reflected the lack of theoretical sophistication of those in charge of
monetary policy. However, of greater significance was the fundamental
inadequacy of the powers at their disposal. The Reichsbank failed to
impose minimum reserve requirements on the credit banks; it had no
system of open market operations to regulate the effect of government
borrowing on the money supply; and it proved incapable of regulating
capital flows without imposing severe restrictions on capital movement.

Finally, inflation reflected the recurrent conflict between, on the one
hand, fiscal and monetary policy and, on the other, trade policy. The
German trade deficit in the years 1919 to 1923, though large, was not
unique; for most of its pre-1914 history the Reich had run a trade
deficit, although earnings from German capital exports and 'invisible'

exports of services sufficed to finance this; and, after 1924, the trade deficit persisted, save in the recession years of 1926 and 1932 (see figure 0.6). German policy makers repeatedly tried to reduce these deficits: by erecting tariff barriers between 1878 and 1914 and again after 1925, and by pursuing various policies designed to stimulate exports after the war, notably the depreciation of the mark between 1919 and 1923 and the deflationary policies of 1930–2. Yet the export surplus which was so often seen as desirable – particularly when Germany had a large external debt – proved elusive. Why? The answer suggested here is that, quite apart from structural inelasticities relating to German industry's demand for raw materials, other elements of economic policy ran counter to the desire for a positive trade balance. Firstly, apart from the period 1919–23, the exchange rate was either tied to gold or, as in the periods 1914–18 and 1933–45, pegged by exchange controls, thus eliminating the easiest device for eliminating a persistent payments deficit. Secondly, the policies of fiscal and monetary laxity, outlined above, tended to widen rather than narrow the trade gap.

The overarching themes of this study are therefore: the defects of the Reich's fiscal and monetary institutions, and the tension between the domestic and international objectives of economic policy. These institutional defects of the Reich's political economy are seen as the critical determinants of its perennial monetary instability.

It only remains to explain the choice of Hamburg as the focus for this study. The first and most obvious reason is that it was, of all the major economic centres of Germany, among the most commercial and financial, rather than industrial, in its structure. Hamburg was economically a 'special case': more international in its orientation, with even its major industries – notably ship-building – dependent on buoyant trade for their business. Analysing its experience therefore provides a valuable counterweight to the traditional historical emphasis on the role of heavy industry. Secondly, there are a priori grounds for thinking that Hamburg might have had a special interest in certain aspects of the inflationary process. One is that, as a major centre of German trade, Hamburg must have been strongly affected by and interested in the fluctuations in the German exchange rate which occurred in the inflation period. Another is that, as a major shipping centre, the city must have been involved in what was perhaps the most striking case of intensified investment during the inflation: the reconstruction of the German merchant fleet.[106] Analysis of the effects of inflation in these areas provides valuable answers to the question

---

[106] For a positive view of the inflation in Hamburg, see U. Büttner, *Politische Gerechtigkeit und sozialer Geist. Hamburg zur Zeit der Weimarer Republik* (Hamburg, 1985), pp. 140–5.

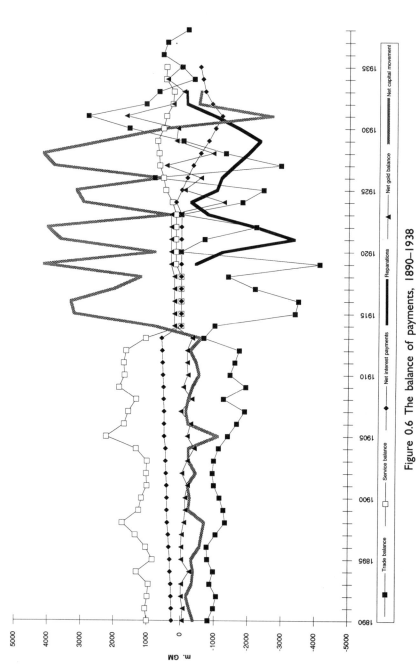

Figure 0.6 The balance of payments, 1890–1938

Sources: Hoffmann et al., *Wachstum*, pp. 262, 817f.; Bresciani, *Inflation*, pp. 85, 234; Graham, *Hyperinflation*, p. 265; Laursen and Pedersen, *Inflation*, pp. 69, 101; Kent, *Spoils of War*, p. 392, Holtfrerich, *Inflation*, pp. 147, 212, 288; Hardach, *First World War*, p.33; Schuker, 'American "Reparations"', pp. 378f.; Webb, *Hyperinflation*, pp. 33, 37, 108.

how far inflation benefited business by stimulating German exports and investment. Politically too, it merits attention. It was one of the Revolution's centres, the last major city to be occupied by the Reichswehr in 1919, and the scene of two abortive Communist risings in 1921 and 1923. If the inflation was in part intended to contain working-class radicalism by forging a consensus between business and labour, we would expect to find evidence of it here. The experience of Hamburg also offers important insights into the relationship between inflation, social trauma and the rise of National Socialism, given the city's much-vaunted cosmopolitanism and liberalism in the pre-war years. Did inflation undermine Hamburg's character as a 'special case', so that it too went down Germany's 'special path' to catastrophe?[107]

The principal reason for concentrating on Hamburg, however, is the unusually high political profile of Hamburg businessmen at the national level during the early Weimar period. Was it merely fortuitous that the 'man of big business' who was Chancellor at the time of the hyperinflationary crisis of 1923 was Wilhelm Cuno, head of the Hamburg–Amerika shipping line? Why was such an important role played in the international financial diplomacy of the period by the banker Max Warburg and his partner Carl Melchior? The national and international importance of Hamburg business has until now been more or less neglected by historians, with a few exceptions – not least because, on the whole, they sought to exercise their influence 'behind the scenes'. This study uses private papers and firm archives, in conjunction with official papers, to reconstruct their story, tracing their rise to influence (and subsequent fall) from the Wilhelmine period to the 1930s. The importance of their political role means that this is not intended only as a 'regional' study, but rather as a contribution to the economic and political history of the German Reich as a whole, as well as to the history of international economics and politics between the wars.

Chapter 1 sets the scene, describing the pre-war development and structure of Hamburg's dynamic commercial economy, its materially stratified but culturally integrated society, its evolving corporative (and corporatist) polity, and the benefits it derived from its membership of the federal Reich. In contrast, chapter 2 describes the devastating impact of the war on Hamburg. It crippled the city's economy, intensified social division, polarised politics and created an appetite for post-war recovery at any price. The consequences of this crisis are traced in chapter 3, which describes the impact of the November Revolution.

---

[107] See P.E. Schramm, *Hamburg – Ein Sonderfall in der Geschichte Deutschlands. Vorträge und Aufsätze* (Hamburg, 1964).

Politically, this was as much a bourgeois as a proletarian revolution, but its outcome was determined by economic factors: the dearth imposed by the Allied blockade and the inflationary explosion generated by continuing government deficits and labour radicalism. Chapter 4 concentrates on external forces – the power of the Allies over Germany after the armistice – and traces the central role of Hamburg business in the economic diplomacy of the peace process. It was their argument that the peace would lead to economic crisis and political revolution; the chapter seeks to explain why these predictions were not fulfilled. Chapter 5 outlines the opportunity for lasting stabilisation which arose in 1920 and explains how this was squandered by misconceived fiscal, monetary, trade and labour policies. Above all, as chapter 6 argues, it was the argument that continued currency depreciation could undermine the system of reparations by boosting exports which encouraged governments to continue with inflationary policies. Yet the strategy, strongly supported by Hamburg business, did not work. Instead of forcing revision, depreciation weakened Germany's position, forcing its advocates to adopt an increasingly confrontational stance. This came to a head with the appointment of Cuno as Reich Chancellor and the French occupation of the Ruhr, described in chapter 7, which seeks to explain why the experiment of government by business ended with the collapse of the currency and, very nearly, of the Reich itself. Finally, chapter 8 explores the legacy of the inflation, and suggests that the stabilisation achieved in 1924 was bound to be short lived. The economic, social and political damage done by hyperinflation was too profound; and the reforms of 1924 did not go far enough to end the instability of monetary policy, the fiscal system and the balance of payments. By a final irony, it was fear of inflation which drove the Brüning government into its suicidal policy of deflation. Only after 1933 was the Reich's political economy altered sufficiently to achieve recovery without inflation; and even this was to prove unsustainable.

This, then, is the view from Hamburg of an era of inflation which began in the Wilhelmine boom of the late 1890s and continued for three decades until the Weimar deflation of 1928–32. At one level, it is an economic history; but my object has been to set the economic analysis in its social, political and diplomatic context. Unfashionably, the story has a hero: the banker Max Warburg. Inevitably, because of what followed, it is a tragedy.

I

Golden years

On 11 June 1913, a leviathan was launched in Hamburg. Weighing over 52,000 gross tons, the *Imperator* not only established the Hamburg–Amerika shipping line as the largest in the world; with its two later sister ships, the *Vaterland* and the *Bismarck*, it confirmed Hamburg's shipyards as equal to any in Britain. The 'Hapag''s publicity department described the *Imperator* as 'a work of gigantic forms', of 'gigantic realities and still more gigantic portents', and illustrated the point with scale drawings showing the upended ship alongside the Hamburg *Rathaus*, Ulm cathedral and the Wartburg.[1] In a similar vein, the ship-builders Blohm and Voß trumpeted that the still bigger *Vaterland* had been 'built on the biggest slip, had received her equipment under the biggest crane, and [. . .] would be launched in the biggest floating dock in the world'.[2]

This economic giganticism is open to a variety of interpretations. Clearly, to many contemporaries, these leviathans embodied the great advances made by German industry and engineering since the mid nineteenth century. Yet from a purely economic standpoint, they were of dubious value. As expensive as they were immense, the three ships catered almost exclusively for luxury transatlantic passenger traffic and were not expected to break even; indeed, it was assumed by the Hapag that they would be subsidised by the line's freight business. Their social significance seems more obvious. With their marble sinks and electric heating, they were built for the delectation of a wealthy, cosmopolitan elite by an army of semi-skilled manual workers housed in the poorly plumbed, under-heated 'rent-barracks' of Hamburg's proletarian quarters. That the *Imperator* was launched in a year of unparalleled labour conflict on the Hamburg waterfront would seem to confirm the ship's role as a symbol of early twentieth-century class inequality. Yet the ships also symbolised the ambivalence of the social

---

[1] V. Plagemann (ed.), *Industriekultur in Hamburg. Des Deutschen Reiches Tor zur Welt* (Munich, 1984), p. 65.
[2] B. Huldermann, *Albert Ballin* (London/New York/Toronto/Melbourne, 1922), pp. 113f.

elite for which they were designed. The man who conceived them, Albert Ballin, was a self-made Jewish businessman, sneered at by the populist writer Gorch Fock as 'a petty village grocer'.[3] The man whose helmeted bust stood in the *Imperator*'s ballroom, and who assisted the Iron Chancellor's granddaughter at the launching of the *Bismarck*, was the Hohenzollern German Emperor, a confirmed anti-Semite. The ships were decorated in a pot-pourri of historicist styles, ranging from the pseudo-Roman to the mock Tudor, as if to disguise their technological modernity.

Their political significance was no less complex. To name them 'Emperor', 'Fatherland' and 'Bismarck' might seem at first sight an expression of simple patriotism; but to Ballin the launching of the *Bismarck* by the Kaiser represented a posthumous reconciliation between the two men; while the idea that the *Vaterland* should be built by men once dubbed *vaterlandlose Gesellen* by the Kaiser himself had obvious piquance. Moreover, in outdoing Britain at what Britain did best, the ships gave a vivid expression to the German challenge to British economic power. The significance of this at a time of mounting international tension was – despite pointed assurances that the *Imperator* was a 'ship of peace' – obvious, at least to the leader-writers of the British popular press. The launch of the *Imperator* therefore symbolised not only the triumphalism of German economic success, but also the social 'shadow side' of that success, and its ambiguous political implications both at home and abroad. Just five weeks before, the *Titanic* – the ship which the *Imperator* was to have rivalled – had struck an iceberg and sunk. The *Hamburger Fremdenblatt's* suggestion that German hubris might invite a comparable nemesis was to prove prescient.[4] This chapter is accordingly concerned with hubris: with that inflation of economic aspirations, symbolised by the *Imperator* and its sisters, which was the harbinger of the inflation itself.

Business in Hamburg

Along with London, Liverpool, Rotterdam, Antwerp and New York, the city of Hamburg was one of the elite of great Atlantic entrepots which flourished in the century between the battle of Waterloo and the battle of the Marne – the British age of free trade, industrialisation, imperialism and the gold standard. Never before had goods, people, information and capital moved so freely across oceans as they did

---

[3] 'Ein kleiner Dorfkrämer': quoted in Plagemann, *Industriekultur*, p. 64.
[4] *Hamburger Fremdenblatt*, Illustrierte Rundschau, 4. Beilage, 24 May 1912, no. 120, p.20.

before 1914; and it was from these movements that the great entrepots profited. Hamburg had, of course, been a centre of commerce since the Middle Ages; but as the case of Lübeck showed, mercantile tradition alone was no guarantee of continuing prosperity. Hamburg had adapted to changing circumstances: drawing on Dutch examples and emigrants in the sixteenth century, detaching itself from the war-torn German hinterland in the seventeenth, and gravitating towards France in the eighteenth.[5] Similarly, as Britain came to dominate the Atlantic economy after 1815, Hamburg evolved into an 'outpost' of English commerce; as trade with the Americas burgeoned, Hamburg founded its own outposts between Boston and Brazil; and as the industrialisation of Western and Central Germany gathered pace, so Hamburg's free port became 'the German Reich's gateway to the world'.[6] Between 1816/20 and 1856/60, the tonnage of ships coming into Hamburg's harbour increased by a factor of five; by 1860, almost a million tons of goods worth over 330 m. marks were entering the port annually.[7] Hamburg's foreign imports grew at a rate of 5.5 per cent per annum between 1885 and 1913; the corresponding figure for exports (after 1890) was 5.3 per cent. By 1913, as much as 42 per cent of German imports and 38 per cent of German exports passed through Hamburg.[8] The city's share of total world trade was in the region of 4.5 per cent by the eve of the First World War. Of the other continental ports, only Rotterdam had a comparable volume of trade.[9]

[5] M. Lindemann, *Patriots and Paupers. Hamburg 1712–1830* (New York/Oxford, 1990), pp. 33ff.; W.O. Henderson, *The Rise of German Industrial Power 1834–1914* (London, 1975), pp. 26, 64, 113.

[6] E. Baasch, *Geschichte Hamburgs, 1814–1918*, Bd. II (Hamburg, 1925), pp. 159–87; R. Hauschild-Thiessen, *Bürgerstolz und Kaisertreu. Hamburg und das deutsche Reich von 1871* (Hamburg, 1979), pp. 79–97; E. Böhm, *Überseehandel und Flottenbau. Hanseatische Kaufmannschaft und deutsche Seerüstung* (Hamburg, 1972), pp. 66f. Cf. C.T. Freytag, *Die Entwicklung des Hamburger Warenhandels 1871–1900* (Berlin, 1906); L. Wendemuth and W. Böttcher, *Der Hafen von Hamburg* (Hamburg, 1927).

[7] W. Jochmann and H.-D. Loose (eds.), *Hamburg. Geschichte der Stadt Hamburg und ihre Bewohner*, Bd. I (Hamburg, 1982), pp. 443–7.

[8] Calculated from *Statistisches Handbuch für den hamburgischen Staat* [henceforth *Statistisches Handbuch*] *1920* (Hamburg, 1921), pp. 153f., 162, 165; W.G. Hoffmann, F. Grumbach and H. Hesse, *Das Wachstum der deutschen Wirtschaft seit der Mitte des 19. Jahrhunderts* (Berlin, 1965), pp. 520, 524. The growth rates are geometric; the figures for Hamburg's shares of total German trade (in current prices) have been arrived at by deducting imports from and exports to the rest of Germany from the officially published Hamburg trade statistics. Cf. the lower figures of 20 per cent or 36 per cent sometimes cited: e.g., R.J. Evans, *Death in Hamburg. Society and Politics in the Cholera Years 1830–1910* (Oxford, 1987), p. 29; M. Grüttner, *Arbeitswelt an der Wasserkante* (Göttingen, 1984), p. 29.

[9] H. Flügel, *Die deutschen Welthäfen Hamburg und Bremen* (Jena, 1914), pp. 308f., 351; H. Meyer, *Hamburg als Güterumschlagsplatz vor und nach dem Kriege* (Hamburg, 1930), p. 107.

Hamburg's economy can be analysed in a number of ways: firstly, in terms of flows of goods. Of the total volume flowing into Hamburg in 1913, two-thirds arrived by sea, a fifth by rail and a little less by river. The corresponding figures for the goods leaving Hamburg were 48 per cent by sea, 14 per cent by rail, and 30 per cent by river.[10] Around 31 per cent of the goods arriving in Hamburg by all means of transport originated in the rest of Germany before 1913, 22 per cent came from the rest of continental Europe, slightly less (19 per cent) from the British Isles, and around 10 per cent apiece from North America and Latin America. The share of African, Asian and Australasian markets was therefore small (together around 9.5 per cent), though these were the city's fastest-growing markets. Hamburg's exports were more concentrated in Europe: around 36 per cent of the goods leaving Hamburg went to other parts of the Reich; while those bound for the rest of continental Europe accounted for only slightly less. Of the remainder, most went to the Americas (13 per cent) or the British Isles (around 8 per cent).[11] Clearly, therefore, Hamburg's biggest single 'trading partner' was the rest of the Reich, with substantial rail consignments arriving in Hamburg from the industrial West (the Ruhr, Rhineland and Westphalia), and shipments of imported goods going down the Elbe to Central Germany.[12] Hamburg's biggest single *foreign* trading partner was Britain and her Empire, which altogether accounted for a quarter of the city's import volume, though a considerably smaller amount (7 per cent) of her exports.[13] Finally, foodstuffs accounted for around a quarter of the value of sea-borne imports and 17 per cent of the value of exports; raw materials and semi-finished goods for around two-thirds of imports and a third of

[10] In money terms, 60 per cent arrived by sea; 29 per cent arrived by rail and 11 per cent by river; 57 per cent left by sea; 24 per cent by rail and 19 per cent by river – indicating that river traffic mainly carried low-value, bulky goods: *Statistisches Handbuch 1920*, pp. 153f., 162; Meyer, *Güterumschlagsplatz*, pp. 37–40.

[11] Calculated from: *Statistisches Handbuch 1920*, pp. 164–7; *Statistisches Handbuch 1925*, pp. 134f., 144f.; *Statistisches Jahrbuch für die Freie und Hansestadt Hamburg* [henceforth *Statistisches Jahrbuch*] *1928/29*, pp. 130–2, 145–7. Expressed in money terms, the relative shares are significantly different: for sea-borne trade only, Western Europe (including Great Britain) accounted for 20/25 per cent (imports/exports); Latin America and the Caribbean for 23/18 per cent; North America for 17/11 per cent; Asia for 15/9 per cent; Africa and the Middle East for 12/15 per cent and Scandinavia, the Baltic and Northern Russia for 6/15 per cent.

[12] Meyer, *Güterumschlagsplatz*, pp. 101–6. In money terms, and including rail and river traffic, around 36 per cent of all goods entering Hamburg came from the rest of the Reich; 27 per cent of all goods leaving Hamburg went to German destinations.

[13] *Ibid.*, p. 95; *Statistisches Handbuch 1925*, pp. 134f., 144f. In money terms, the respective figures are significantly higher: 31.5 per cent and 24 per cent, indicating the high level of trade in manufactured products between the two Empires.

exports; while finished goods accounted for only a tenth of imports, but over half the value of exports.[14] The core of Hamburg's business was therefore the import to Germany of primary and intermediate goods and the export of finished German manufactures, though there was also a substantial transit trade.[15]

An alternative way of analysing Hamburg's economy is to consider the structure of economic organisation and employment. The city's role as an entrepot meant that its economic structure differed significantly from that of other large German cities. Whereas in Berlin, Düsseldorf or Leipzig over 50 per cent of the working population was employed in the category 'industry and manufacturing' in 1907, the corresponding figure for Hamburg was just 36 per cent, compared with 39.9 per cent employed in commerce ('trade and transport').[16] Such broad headings, of course, embraced a multitude of quite different forms of enterprise. 'Trade' (*Handel*), for example, included not only the mercantile world of the counting house, the bourse and the bank, but also a plethora of agents, auctioneers and brokers, to say nothing of the tens of thousands of retailers (and over 2,000 street hawkers) who supplied the population's daily needs. Similarly, the transport sector included not only a handful of huge shipping lines, but also the various coastal and river companies, the railway and tram system, and the numerous small enterprises which conveyed goods over shorter distances by road. Manufacturing too was heterogeneous; while the banks of the Elbe were dominated by huge shipyards, thousands of artisans laboured in small workshops in the city centre, and the traditional manual skills involved in furniture-making or cobbling continued to thrive alongside the newer technologies of the electrical and chemical sectors.

Certain elements of Hamburg's commercial sector are difficult to subject to close scrutiny: the 16,000 retailers and 4,000 or so brokers

[14] The principal imports in money terms were coffee, hides, wool, copper, saltpetre and rubber; the main exports were iron manufactures, refined sugar, machines, cotton goods and coffee. Cf. Meyer, *Güterumschlagsplatz*, p. 108; *Statistisches Handbuch 1925*, pp. 136–141, 146–52; *Statistisches Jahrbuch 1928/1929*, pp. 132–43, 145–59.

[15] I.e., goods entering and leaving Hamburg's free port without entering the German customs area. Because of the nature of the available statistics, it is impossible to quantify this exactly.

[16] *Statistische Mitteilungen über den hamburgischen Staat*, No. 4, 'Die Gewerbebetriebe im hamburgischen Staat 1907' (Hamburg, 1915), pp. 41–92; *Statistik des Deutschen Reiches*, Bd. 217 (1907), i, 365–73; Bd. 408 (1925), pp. 24–31; Bd. 416 (1925), pp. 6, 54–78. Cf. V. Ullrich, 'Die Hamburger Arbeiterbewegung vom Vorabend des Ersten Weltkrieges bis zur Revolution 1918/19' (Diss., Hamburg, 1976), pp. 5f.; P.J. Lyth, 'The Experience of Urban *Mittelstand* in the German Inflation of 1914 to 1923: the Case of Hamburg' (Ph.D. thesis, East Anglia, 1984), p. 75.

of 'mobile' and 'immobile' property have left behind little trace of their activity.[17] The mercantile world which centred around the bourse, by contrast, set out to impress posterity with grand architecture and self-congratulatory publications – and not without success. The apparent cultural and political hegemony of Hamburg's merchants in the nineteenth and early twentieth centuries has sometimes given rise to exaggerated impressions of their economic significance.[18] In fact, the bourse was home to perhaps a thousand relatively small family firms engaged in importing and exporting commodities and manufactures,[19] the majority of them late eighteenth- and nineteenth-century firms which had established themselves in America, Asia and Africa as these began to develop into trading partners for industrialising Europe.[20] One or two firms in each major regional market tended to stand out from the multitude – whether because of relative size, antiquity, or the personalities of those who ran them: in the Far East, A.O. Meyer and J.C. Godeffroy; in West Africa, C. Woermann and G.L. Gaiser; in East Africa, Wm. O'Swald; in the Americas, Johs. Schuback & Söhne, which rose to preeminence under the leadership of the Amsinck family.[21] Such firms generally employed at the most a hundred people (some in the Hamburg office, some overseas), had a narrow capital base (usually composed of family wealth), and made their money at the margin out of the commissions and percentages they charged suppliers and buyers. Because of the hazards of international transport, risks were high and income erratic: of the thousand firms of the 1900s only a handful have left traces of their existence, and often those, like

[17] Cf. Lyth, '*Mittelstand*', p. 45; and *idem, Inflation and the Merchant Economy*, pp. 38–44.

[18] Cf. P.E. Schramm, *Hamburg, Deutschland und die Welt. Leistung und Grenzen hanseatischen Bürgertums in der Zeit zwischen Napoleon I und Bismarck. Ein Kapital deutscher Geschichte* (Munich, 1943); *idem, Deutschland und Übersee. Der deutsche Handel mit den anderen Kontinenten insbes. Afrika, von Karl V. bis zum Bismarck: Geschichte der Rivalität im Wirtschaftsleben* (Brunswick/Berlin/Hamburg/Kiel, 1950); as well as the numerous publications on individual firms by M. Möring and the *Wirtschaftsgeschichtliche Forschungsstelle*.

[19] G. Jantzen, *Hamburgs Ausfuhrhandel im 20. Jahrhundert* (Hamburg, 1953), p. 28; E. Böhm, *Überseehandel und Flottenbau. Hanseatische Kaufmannschaft und deutsche Seerüstung, 1879–1902* (Hamburg, 1972), p. 12. Nearly 6,000 firms were registered on the bourse, but only around 860 were fully fledged *Überseehäuser*.

[20] See H. Washausen, *Hamburg und die Kolonialpolitik des Deutschen Reiches, 1880–1890* (Hamburg, 1968), pp. 67–75, 80–96.

[21] E. Helfferich, *Zur Geschichte der Firmen Behn, Meyer & Co. und Arnold Otto Meyer*, 2 vols. (Hamburg, 1967); K. Schmack, *J.C. Godeffroy & Sohn. Kaufleute zu Hamburg* (Hamburg, 1938); T. Bohner, *Die Woermanns. Vom Werden deutscher Größe* (Berlin, 1935); E. Hieke and A. Dreyer, *Zur Geschichte des deutschen Handels mit Westafrika. Das hamburgische Handelshaus G.L. Gaiser (1859–1939)* (Hamburg, 1941); E. Hieke, *Zur Geschichte des deutschen Handelshaus Wm. O'Swald & Co.* (Hamburg, 1939); M. Möring, *1757–1957. 200 Jahre Johannes Schuback & Söhne. Familie und Firma in Hamburg* (Hamburg, 1957).

Woermann's, which diversified into the related fields of shipping or banking. They and their like in entrepots throughout the world were the foot-soldiers of free trade and informal imperialism, the rank-and-file of the 'cosmopolitan bourgeoisie' of the nineteenth century.[22] By the turn of the century, however, the first intimations of obsolescence were detectable. True, family firms like the Amsincks, the Schramms and the O'Swalds were less decadent than their Lübeck counterparts, portrayed by Thomas Mann in *Buddenbrooks*.[23] But the imperative of family control and the tendency for individuals to remove their share for a comfortable retirement imposed limits on the size of the firm's capital, and this could mean acute vulnerability in times of crisis. To speak of 'Buddenbrooks in reverse' is too sanguine.[24] The future lay with more complex forms of economic organisation.

The growth of trade fostered the development of all the other branches of the Hamburg economy, in particular transport. It was shipping which dominated the transport sector,[25] from the huge liners of the Hapag to the tugs of the port and the barges of the Elbe. As striking as the four-fold growth in the volume of traffic in the three decades before 1914 was the shift in ownership.[26] In the 1870s, over half of the shipping entering Hamburg had been British; however, by 1913, the British share in Hamburg's sea traffic had fallen to just 29 per cent, while ships flying the German flag accounted for 60 per cent of the total.[27] The German merchant fleet had grown to become the world's second largest (after the British), accounting for around 13 per cent of total world tonnage.[28] With 1,372 sea ships amounting to

---

[22] Cf. C.A. Jones, *International Business in the Nineteenth Century. The Rise and Fall of the Cosmopolitan Bourgeoisie* (Brighton, 1987).

[23] See O. Hintze, *Die Niederländische und Hamburgische Familie Amsinck*, 3 vols. (Hamburg, 1932); P.E. Schramm, *Neun Generationen. 300 Jahre deutscher 'Kulturgeschichte' im Lichte der Schicksale einer Hamburger Bürgerfamilie*, 2 vols. (Göttingen, 1963, 1965). Cf. R.J. Evans, 'Family and Class in the Hamburg Grand Bourgeoisie, 1815–1914', in D. Blackbourn and R.J. Evans (eds.), *The German Bourgeoisie* (London/New York, 1991), pp. 115–39.

[24] Schramm, *Neun Generationen*, p, 401.

[25] Though mention should also be made of the internal communications provided by tens of thousands of horses, and extensive tram, underground and elevated rail systems: R. Postel, 'Hamburg', in *idem*, *Grundriß zur deutschen Verwaltungsgeschichte, 1815–1945*. Bd. 17: *Hansestädte und Oldenburg* (Marburg/Lahn, 1978), pp. 70, 203. Cf. E. Kipnase, *Die Hamburger Hochbahn AG in verkehrspolitischer und sozialpolitischer Beziehung* (Berlin, 1925).

[26] Grüttner, *Arbeitswelt*, p. 28.

[27] Evans, *Death in Hamburg*, pp. 29f.; *Statistisches Handbuch 1924*, p. 238 (figures for registered tonnage of ships arriving in the Hamburg port).

[28] BAP RFM 46583 N.Reg. 324/49, Handelskammer Bremen, 'Denkschrift betr. eine größere deutsche Trampdampferflotte', 30 June 1915; R. Krohne, 'Der Zusammenbruch und der Wiederaufbau der deutschen Seeschiffahrt', in B. Harms (ed.), *Strukturwandlungen der Volkswirtschaft*, Bd. II (Berlin, 1928), pp. 218–49.

around 1.9 m. registered tons (and employing over 25,000 sailors),
Hamburg accounted for over a third of German merchant tonnage in
1914.[29]

For this armada of commerce, the transport of people was as important as the transport of commodities. By 1913, there were over 160
separate regular services linking Hamburg to the rest of the world,
and around 620 departures per month.[30] Many of these covered short
distances with small vessels; indeed, some of the older shipping lines
continued to rely on sail to traverse the North Sea.[31] It was transatlantic
emigration, however, which provided the shipping companies' biggest
business. Throughout the nineteenth century, and particularly in the
1840s, 1850s and 1880s, there were high levels of German emigration,
mainly to the United States: altogether, just under 2.9 million Germans
left the Reich between 1871 and 1914.[32] In addition, around 5.8 million
non-Germans (mostly from Eastern Europe) emigrated through the
principal German gateways, Bremen and Hamburg.[33] The most celebrated beneficiary of this exodus was Albert Ballin. The second son
of a minor Jewish entrepreneur who had arrived in Hamburg from
Denmark in the 1830s, Ballin was always something of an outsider in
Hamburg. Like the giant ships which were his most spectacular monument, his adopted motto – 'My field is the world' – expressed an
economic ambition quite different in quality and extent from that of
a Schramm or an Amsinck (though the older shipping families were
quick to recognise and employ his talents). He was a bold business
innovator, first undercutting the established steerage rates as the agent
of the English Carr Line; then, as director and later managing director
of the Hapag in the 1890s, negotiating international agreements on
transatlantic rates, while at the same time expanding and diversifying

---

[29] Postel, 'Hamburg', pp. 68f. Cf. V.P. Rood, 'The Hamburg Merchant Marine 1866–
1914' (Ph.D. thesis, University of Wisconsin, 1985); O. Mathies, *Hamburgs Reederei,
1814–1914* (Hamburg, 1924).

[30] Meyer, *Güterumschlagsplatz*, pp. 92f. Cf. A. Kludas, *Die Geschichte der deutscher
Passagier-Schiffahrt I: 1850–1914* (Hamburg, 1986).

[31] For histories of some of the older lines see, e.g., H.G. Prager, *F. Laeisz* (Herford,
1980); E. Hieke, *Rob. M. Sloman Jr.* (Hamburg, 1968); M. Möring, *75 Jahre
Carsten Rheder* (Hamburg, 1979); E. Verg, *Unter der blauen Flagge. 150 Jahre H.M.
Gehrekens* (Hamburg, 1980).

[32] G. Hohorst, J. Kocka and G.A. Ritter, (eds.) *Sozialgeschichtliches Arbeitsbuch*, Bd.
II, *Materialien zur Statistik des Kaiserreichs 1870–1914* (Munich, 1978), p. 38. Cf.
M. Walker, *Germany and the Emigration, 1816–1885* (Cambridge, Mass., 1964); P.
Marschalck, *Deutsche Überseewanderung im 19. Jahrhundert. Ein Beitrag zur soziolog-
ischen Theorie der Bevölkerung* (Stuttgart, 1973).

[33] J. Wertheimer, *Unwelcome Strangers: East European Jews in Imperial Germany*
(Oxford/New York, 1987); Evans, *Death in Hamburg*, p. 281; M. Just, 'Hamburg
als Transithafen für osteuropäische Auswanderer' in Museum für Hanseatische Geschichte (ed.), '*Nach Amerika!*' (Hamburg, 1970), pp. 49–54.

into freight and luxury travel.[34] With a fleet of 175 ocean-going ships
(and nineteen more under construction) and a payroll of 29,000 people,
the Hapag was, as we have seen, the world's biggest by 1913,[35]
dwarfing the other Hamburg lines, and rivalled in Germany only by
the Bremen-based North German Lloyd.[36] Of particular interest is the
financial scale of Ballin's achievement. In the sixteeen years before the
war, he increased the firm's gross income by a factor of seven, financing
the huge expansion of the company's fleet by a proportional increase
in its share capital, and the issue of 70 m. marks of fixed interest
debentures ('priority loans'). With fixed assets valued at 289 m. marks,
liquid assets worth 54 m. marks and net profits equal to 17 per cent
of share capital, the Hapag's balance sheet epitomised the expansion
made possible by combining the essential economic elements of paper
and iron.[37]

Despite attempts to promote it with fairs (and even specially composed waltzes), industry in Hamburg was, to a large extent, the
dependant of commerce.[38] Hamburg had no mines, no large foundries,
and few textile mills – the classic enterprises of industrialisation.
Instead, its manufacturers either served the needs of the city's population, processed imported raw materials for markets outside Hamburg,
or provided the commercial sector with its essential plant. Regulated
until 1865 by the city's guilds, the manufacturing sector retained a
substantial number of very small artisanal enterprises.[39] By contrast,

[34] L. Cecil, *Albert Ballin. Business and Politics in Imperial Germany* (Princeton, 1967),
pp. 15–61; Henderson, *German Industrial Power*, pp. 204ff.; E. Rosenbaum, 'Albert
Ballin. A Note on the Style of his Economic and Political Activities', *Leo Baeck
Institute Yearbook*, 3 (1958), pp. 257ff. Cf. P.F. Stubmann, *Mein Feld is die Welt,
Albert Ballin – sein Leben* (Hamburg, 1920); and the astute comments of the American
Consul Stewart: NAW, RG 59, 862.00/911, Report of 5 April 1920.

[35] H.J. Witthöft, *Hapag. Hamburg-Amerika Linie* (Herford, 1973). The Hapag had been
set up originally by the established firms of Laiesz and Godeffroy: see G. Ahrens
and R. Hauschild-Thiessen, *Die Reeder: Laiesz/Ballin* [*Hamburgische Lebensbilder 2*]
(Hamburg, 1989). Cf. K. Heimer, *Geschichte der Hamburg-Amerika Linie*, 2 vols.
(Hamburg, 1927); K. Roggendorf, 'Die Entwicklung und Bedeutung der H.A.L.
unter Berücksichtigung der Vor- und Nachkriegszeit' (Diss., Erlangen, 1922); T.
Guttmann, *Die Hamburg-Amerika Linie* (Berlin, 1947).

[36] Cf. K. Brackmann, *50 Jahre deutsche Afrika-Schiffahrt. Die Geschichte der Woermann-
Linie und der Deutschen Ost-Afrika-Linie* (Berlin, 1935); O. Harms, *Deutsch-Australische
Dampfschiffahrtsgesellschaft, Hamburg* (Hamburg 1933).

[37] Figures from Hapag, *Jahresbericht 1913*.

[38] Plagemann, *Industriekultur*, p. 85. See in general G. Stenzel, 'Die Industrie', in
Deutsche Auslands-Gemeinschaft (ed.), *Hamburg in seiner politischen, wirtschaftlichen
und kulturellen Bedeutung* (Hamburg, 1921); H. Reymann and K. Johannsen, *Hamburg
als Industrieplatz* (Hamburg, 1930); E. von Lehe and R. Wiemar, 'Industrie und
Gewerbe in Hamburg', in *Heimatchronik der Freien und Hansestadt Hamburg* (Cologne,
1967).

[39] Thirty-seven per cent of those working in manufacturing in 1907 were in firms with
fewer than ten employees: *Statistische Mitteilungen*, 'Die Gewerbebetriebe', pp. 41–

the city's biggest industrial employer before the war was the construction industry (see figure 1.1), which benefited from the expansion of the city's port facilities after 1880[40] and the transformation of Hamburg's housing following the social crises of the 1890s.[41] Also providing for the city's own requirements, and employing almost as many people, were the city's cleaning, clothing, furniture, food and power-generating sectors.[42] Because Hamburg had remained outside the Customs Union during the early phases of North German industrialisation, those manufacturers who aimed at the markets of other German states (particularly that of Prussia) tended to be located outside the city-state's formal border – in towns like Altona and Pinneberg to the west, or Wandsbek and Barmbek to the east.[43] Factories like the New York–Hamburg Rubber Goods Co. or the Norddeutsche Affinerie were therefore not, strictly speaking, Hamburg firms; though the expansion of Hamburg's residential suburbs meant that by 1913 the distinction was scarcely visible to the eye.[44] The same was true of much of Hamburg's engineering industry – not quite the city's largest sector, but certainly the sector with the largest individual firms.[45] This branch of the economy was dominated by a few firms so immense that one contemporary

92; *Statistik des Deutschen Reiches*, Bd. 217, i, 365–73. Cf. E. Lüth, *Hamburg und sein Handwerk, 1873–1973* (Hamburg, 1973).

[40] A. Kludas, D. Maass and S. Sabisch, *Hafen Hamburg* (Hamburg, 1988), p. 35; Postel, 'Hamburg', p. 70; H.-J. Teuteberg, 'Die Entstehung des modernen Hamburger Hafens (1886–1896)', *Tradition*, 17 (1972), pp. 257–91; H. Kutz-Bauer, *Arbeiterschaft, Arbeiterbewegung und bürgerlicher Staat in der Zeit der Grossen Depression, 1873–1890* (Bonn, 1988), pp. 108f., 419f.; Plagemann, *Industriekultur*, pp. 28–31, 57f.

[41] *Statistisches Handbuch 1920*, p. 125; Lyth, 'Mittelstand', pp. 419, 421f. Cf. C. Wischermann, *Wohnen in Hamburg vor dem Ersten Weltkrieg* (Münster, 1983); H.-J. Nörnberg and D. Schubert, *Massenwohnungsbau in Hamburg. Materialien zur Entstehung und Veränderung Hamburger Arbeiterwohnungen und –siedlungen 1800–1967* (Berlin, 1975).

[42] V. Ullrich, 'Arbeiterbewegung', p. 14; E. Klessmann, *Geschichte der Stadt Hamburg* (Hamburg, 1981), p. 477; R. Schubach, *Die Entwicklung der öffentlichen Elektrizitätsversorgung in Hamburg* (Hamburg, 1982).

[43] Besides the great staples of modern consumption, tobacco and coffee, firms in these areas produced rubber, glass, mineral oil and agricultural fertilisers: cf. E. Samhaber and O.A. Friedrich, *100 Jahre Weltwirtschaft im Spiegel eines Unternehmens (Phoenix Gummiwerke AG)* (Hamburg, 1956); W. Ehricht, 'Hamburgs Mineralöl-Handel und -Industrie' (Diss. Hamburg, 1926); M. Möring, *Das Lebenswerk Carl Wilhelm Ohlmanns* (Hamburg, 1953). There was also a small chemicals sector, which included a major Nobel explosives factory, and a metal-processing sector specialising in zinc and copper: M. Möring, *100 Jahre Zipperling, Kessler & Co.* (Hamburg, 1958); G. Hans, *Die Entwicklung der Firma P. Beiersdorf & Co.* (Hamburg, 1915); G. Buxell, *100 Jahre Dynamit Nobel* (Troisdorf, 1965); K. Prior, *100 Jahre Norddeutsche Affinerie* (Hamburg, 1966).

[44] Plagemann, *Industriekultur*, pp. 77–83.

[45] The principal branches of the engineering sector were land vehicle manufacture (2,026 employees), machine-building (7,201), and ship-building (6,427): *Statistische Mitteilungen*, 'Die Gewerbebetriebe', pp. 45ff.

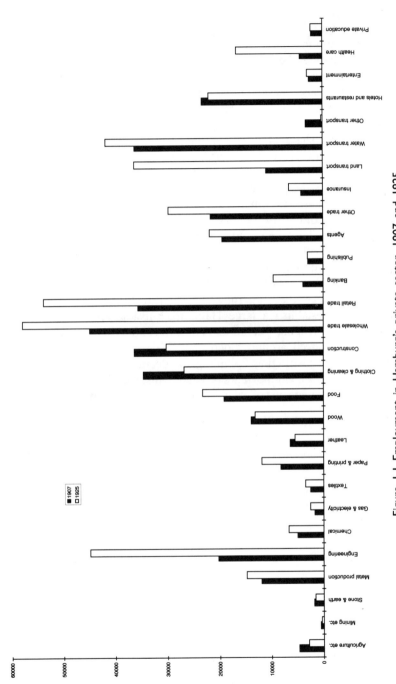

Figure 1.1 Employment in Hamburg's private sector, 1907 and 1925

Sources: *Statistische Mitteilungen, Nr.* 4 'Die Gewerbebetriebe im hamburgischen Staat 1907' (Hamburg, 1915), pp. 41–92; *Statistik des Deutschen Reiches*, Bd 416 (1925), pp. 6, 54–78.

observer was moved to describe them as 'capitalist works of art'.[46] These were the shipyards.

Like the shipping lines, the German shipyards grew at a remarkable rate in the decades before the First World War. By swiftly adopting British techniques and securing a rising share of domestic contracts (including the large naval orders placed by Tirpitz after 1895), the industry achieved average annual output growth rates of around 9 per cent in the three decades after 1885.[47] Indeed, between 1892 and 1913, it increased its share of world output from 7.3 per cent to 14 per cent.[48] Although there were important firms in Rostock (AG Neptun), Stettin (Vulkan) and Danzig (F. Schichau and J.W. Klawitter), the Wasserkante was the principal location of German ship-building. Hamburg alone accounted for (on average) 15 per cent of German production between 1910 and 1913, and about the same percentage of total employment.[49] There remained a number of small firms, relics from the days of wood and sail;[50] but they were dwarfed by the great shipyards – Blohm & Voß, which had 10,853 employees by July 1914, and the older Reiherstieg, with 3,560.[51] It was a further sign of the Elbe's importance that, in 1909, the Stettin Vulkan considered it worthwhile to establish a large Hamburg subsidiary, with the clear purpose of challenging Blohm & Voß's position there in 1909; by 1913, this employed around 7,000 men.[52] These were the two firms entrusted with constructing Ballin's giant floating palaces.

Money – and economic news – made this world go round. The extraordinary expansion of Hamburg's commerce and its industry

---

[46] M. Cattaruzza, *Arbeiter und Unternehmer auf den Werften des Kaiserreichs* (Wiesbaden, 1988), p. 48 n.

[47] Calculated from G. Leckebusch, *Die Beziehung der deutschen Seeschiffswerften zur Eisenindustrie an der Ruhr in der Zeit 1850–1930* (Cologne, 1963), p. 123. Cf. Cattarruza, *Arbeiter und Unternehmer*, pp. 7ff., 54–61; E. Strobusch, *Deutscher Seeschiffbau im 19. und 20. Jahrhundert* (Bremerhaven, 1975); W. Treue, 'Innovation, Know-How, Rationalisation in the German Ship-building Industry 1860–1930', in H. Pohl (ed.), *Innovation, Know-How, Rationalisation and Investment in the German and Japanese Economies* (Wiesbaden, 1982), pp. 103–23.

[48] BAP RFM 46583 N. Reg. 324/49, Handelskammer Bremen, 'Denkschrift'; Henderson, *German Industrial Power*, pp. 198–201; F.M. Walker and A. Slaven (eds.), *European Ship-building. 100 Years of Change* (London, 1983), p. 78. Cf. P. Stubmann, *Gegenwart und Zukunft der Seeschiffahrt* (Berlin, 1916); W. Huth, *Der deutsche Schiffbau und seine Zukunft* (Nieder-Ramstadt bei Darmstadt, 1921).

[49] Calculated from A. Goetz, *Schiffbau und Schiffahrt. Ein Kapitel von Gestern und Morgen* [*Mitteilungen des Archivs für Schiffbau und Schiffahrt*] (Hamburg, 1916).

[50] Stülcken & Sohn employed 800, Heinrich Brandenburg 600 and the Schiffswerft und Maschinenfabrik 300: Ullrich, 'Arbeiterbewegung', pp. 8f. Cf. E. Hieke, *H.C. Stülcken Sohn* (Hamburg, 1955).

[51] H.G. Prager, *Blohm & Voß* (Herford, 1977), pp. 56–103; *Blohm & Voß Hamburg 1877–1927* (Hamburg, 1927); W. Kresse, *Aus der Vergangenheit des Reiherstiegwerft in Hamburg* (Hamburg, 1927).

[52] Cattaruzza, *Arbeiter und Unternehmer*, pp. 29, 58; Leckebusch, *Beziehung*, pp. 23f.

before 1914 would not have been possible without corresponding developments in the city's financial markets[53] and the commercial press and telegraph wires which served them.[54] The bourse was the centre of most financial activity, for it was here that the city's commodity markets, shipping exchange, insurance exchange[55] and stock exchange were all located.[56] Established merchant banks – such as L. Behrens & Sons, Berenberg, Goßler & Co. and Conrad Hinrich Donner – were principally concerned with discounting commercial bills, promissory notes issued to finance protracted transactions.[57] However, the late nineteenth century saw a widening of financial opportunities, and no private bank did more to exploit these than the house of M.M. Warburg.[58] The Warburgs had established themselves in Altona in the late seventeenth century, but for four generations remained little more than minor money changers. In the wake of the Napoleonic Wars, however, the firm succeeded in establishing itself as one of the Rothschilds' agents in Hamburg, finally supplanting its rival Salomon Heine in 1865, and almost trebling its capital between 1848 and 1870.[59] In the succeeding years, its interests expanded to embrace straightforward commercial bill transactions, arbitrage, securities dealing and state loan issues; but it remained a relatively minor concern, reliant on its connections with more eminent houses such as Bleichröder's.[60] It was only after 1900, under the inspired direction of Max Warburg, the

[53] In 1909, there were 258 banks in Hamburg, compared with 515 in Berlin and 135 in Frankfurt: M. Pohl, *Hamburger Bankengeschichte* (Mainz, 1986), p. 97. Cf. E. Achterberg, *Kleine Hamburger Bankengeschichte* (Hamburg, 1964); H. Fahning, *Bankplatz Hamburg* (Hamburg, 1956).

[54] The main business newspapers were the *Hamburgische Börsenhalle* and its stable-mate the long-established *Hamburgische Correspondent*: Böhm, *Flottenbau*, pp. 15ff. Cf. E. Baasch, *Geschichte des Hamburgischen Zeitungswesens* (Hamburg, 1930), pp. 121–51.

[55] See W. Heyn, *Das schaffende Hamburg. Hamburg als Versicherungsstadt* (Hamburg, 1939); *300 Jahre Hamburger Feuerkasse* (Hamburg, 1976).

[56] G. Klein, *400 Jahre Hamburger Börse. Eine geschichtliche Darstellung* (Hamburg, 1958).

[57] W.E. Mosse, *Jews in the German Economy. The German-Jewish Economic Elite* (Oxford, 1987), p. 200; *175 Jahre L. Behrens & Söhne* (Hamburg, 1955); M. Möring, *Johann Berenberg, Goßler & Co.* (Hamburg, 1962): idem, *175 Jahre Conrad Hinrich Donner* (Hamburg, 1973). Cf. H. Tummescheit, 'Die Entwicklung der Hamburger Merchant Bankers unter besonderer Berücksichtigung der heute noch bestehenden Firmen' (Diss. Hamburg, 1962); C.P. Kindleberger, *A Financial History of Western Europe* (London, 1984), pp. 121f.

[58] E. Rosenbaum and A.J. Sherman, *M.M. Warburg & Co. 1798–1938. Merchant Bankers of Hamburg* (London, 1979); A. Vagts, 'M.M. Warburg & Co. Ein Bankhaus in der deutschen Weltpolitik, 1905–1933', *VSWG*, 45 (1958), pp. 289–398. See also R. Chernow, *The Warburgs. The Twentieth Century Odyssey of a Remarkable Jewish Family* (London, 1993). D. Farrer, *The Warburgs. The Story of a Family* (New York, 1975) is journalistic and unreliable.

[59] Rosenbaum and Sherman, *M.M. Warburg & Co.*, pp. 1–64.

[60] *Ibid.*, pp. 84–90.

second of Moritz Warburg's five sons, that the bank entered the elite
of international finance houses.[61] Connected by the marriages of two
younger sons, Paul and Felix, to the powerful New York house of
Kuhn, Loeb & Co., Warburg's became a leading firm in the growing
international market for state bonds, including those of the Reich and
the Prussian state.[62] Between 1895 and 1913, the firm's balance sheet
grew from 30 m. marks to 118 m. marks.[63] Yet Max Warburg's refusal
to convert the family bank into a joint-stock company placed limits
on the bank's expansion. By comparison, the three major joint-stock
banks, the Norddeutsche Bank, founded in 1856, the Commerz- und
Diskontobank, founded in 1870, and the Vereinsbank, were able to
grow larger.[64] It was these firms which led the way in Hamburg's
delayed *Gründerzeit* after 1880, helping to finance the construction of
the free port, the expansion of the merchant fleet and the other large
investments necessitated by the city's commercial expansion.[65]

By 1914, then, Hamburg had developed quite sophisticated capital
and money markets. The annual number of share issues on the Hamburg stock market had risen to between thirty and forty, bringing the
total of quoted shares to over 900 m. marks.[66] There was a still larger
market in mortgages,[67] as well as five savings banks with deposits
totalling 417 m. marks.[68] Finally, as an indicator of monetary growth,

[61] M. Warburg, *Aus meinen Aufzeichnungen* (Hamburg, 1952), pp. 15ff. There are three
different versions of Warburg's memoirs in existence: the heavily edited 1952 version,
published privately; a three volume typescript dating from the 1930s, which repro-
duces large extracts from the firm's internal annual reports, and an English version
which differs in minor respects from the original (both in WA). In the notes these
will be referred to as *Aufzeichnungen*; Aufzeichnungen MSS; and Diaries.
[62] Vagts, 'M.M. Warburg & Co.', pp. 300f., 336f.; K.E. Born, *International Banking
in the 19th and 20th Centuries* (Leamington Spa, 1983), pp. 127f.; G. Stolper, K.
Häuser and K. Borchardt, *The German Economy, 1870 to the Present* (London, 1967),
p. 31.
[63] Rosenbaum and Sherman, *M.M. Warburg & Co.*, p. 107.
[64] Pohl, *Bankengeschichte*, pp. 96–101; Born, *International Banking*, pp. 87–92, 169;
Kindleberger, *Financial History*, p. 127.
[65] See *90 Jahre Commerzbank in Hamburg* (Hamburg, 1961); *Hundertjahre Vereinsbank
in Hamburg* (Hamburg, 1956); and the bank's published annual reports, in the
Hamburg Weltwirtschaftsarchiv.
[66] Pohl, *Bankengeschichte*, p. 97; *Vierteljahreshefte zur Statistik des Deutschen Reiches*
(1914), I, pp. 181–3; *Ergänzungsheft* II, p. 11; *Vierteljahreshefte zur Statistik des
Deutschen Reiches* (1915), I, pp. 112–14.
[67] The city's real estate was mortgaged to nearly 70 per cent of its market value of
around 4 bn. marks: Lyth, '*Mittelstand*', pp. 451, 460 n. R. Deumer, *Das Hamburger
Hypotheken-Kreditwesen* (Hamburg, 1917).
[68] The two main savings banks were the Hamburger Sparcasse von 1827 and the Neue
Sparcasse von 1864. Significantly, nearly 80 per cent of their assets were held as
mortgages: *Statistisches Handbuch 1920*, pp. 364–8; G. Offermann, *Die Geschichte
der Neuen Sparcasse von 1864* (Hamburg, 1959); G. Albrecht, *Vom Sparen in Hamburg.
Hundert Jahre Neue Sparcasse von 1864* (Hamburg, 1964); A. Paquet, *Die Alte*

the turnover of the Hamburg branch of the Reichsbank grew annually by 3.9 per cent between 1890 and 1913; while the volume of direct debit ('Giro') transactions grew two and a half times.[69] These various forms of money provided the liquidity without which the iron wheels of commerce and industry could not have turned. Yet it would be misleading to suggest that those wheels always turned at a smooth and even speed. Although Hamburg's growth in the nineteenth century was unprecedented, it was subject to sometimes quite severe fluctuations. In the two decades after 1790, war generated first a boom and then, after 1799, a bust.[70] A financial crisis in the United States in August 1857 revealed the fragility of the entire Hamburg credit system: 145 firms with obligations of 340 m. marks banco[71] failed, and the city's venerable clearing bank, the Hamburger Bank, had to be bailed out by a loan from the Austrian Creditanstalt.[72] Hamburg was less affected than Berlin by the *Gründerkrach* of 1873 and the subsequent period of relative economic stagnation once known as the 'Great Depression', thanks in part to the economic expansion associated with the construction of the free port.[73] But the vagaries of the trade cycle ensured that there were leaden years even among the golden ones after 1895: 1908/9 saw a severe trade recession, and growth was sluggish in 1913.[74] Fluctuations were even more marked in industry: there was a pronounced recession in ship-building between 1907 and 1910 (see figure 1.2). Indeed, when one compares the aggregate real income figures available for Hamburg with those available for Prussia after 1885, it

Sparcasse (Hamburg, 1927); O. Karen, *Die Hamburger Sparkasse von 1827 in den Jahren 1892 bis 1925* (Hamburg, 1927).

[69] *Statistisches Handbuch 1920*, pp. 260f.

[70] Lindemann, *Patriots*, pp. 35f.; A. Herzig, 'Einleitung', in idem, D. Langewiesche and A. Sywottek (eds.), *Arbeiter in Hamburg. Unterschichten, Arbeiter und Arbeiterbewegung seit dem ausgehenden 18. Jahrhundert* (Hamburg, 1982), p. 10.

[71] The mark banco was a unit of account used by the Hamburger Bank, equivalent to 8.3 g. silver or 1.50 of the German marks established in 1875: H. Sieveking, 'Die Hamburger Bank, 1619–1875', in *Festschrift der Hamburgischen Universität ihrem Ehrenrektor Herrn Bürgermeister Werner von Melle zum 80. Geburtstag am 18.October 1933 dargebracht* (Hamburg, 1933), pp. 20–110.

[72] H. Böhme, 'Wirtschaftskrise, Merchant Bankers und Verfassungsreform. Zur Bedeutung der Weltwirtschaftskrise von 1857 in Hamburg', ZVHG, 54 (1968), pp. 77–128; E. Baasch, 'Zur Geschichte der Handelskrise von 1857', ZVHG, 30 (1929), pp. 81–105; G. Ahrens, 'Die Überwindung der hamburgischen Wirtschaftskrise von 1857 im Spannungsfeld von Privatinitiative und Staatsintervention', ZVHG, 64 (1978), pp. 1–29. See also Rosenbaum and Sherman, *M.M. Warburg & Co.*, p. 37.

[73] Kutz-Bauer, *Arbeiterschaft*, pp. 28f., 106.

[74] Cf. R. Spree, *Wachstumstrends und Konjunkturzyklen in der deutschen Wirtschaft von 1820–1913* (Göttingen, 1978); E.W. Axe and H.M. Flinn, 'An Index of General Business Conditions for Germany, 1898–1914', in *Review of Economic Statistics*, 7 (1925), pp. 263–87.

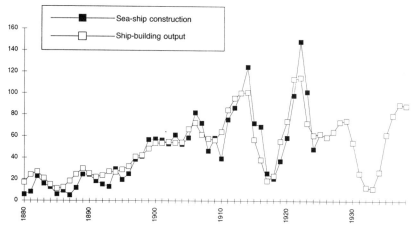

Figure 1.2 German ship-building, 1880–1938 (1913 = 100)
Sources: Leckebusch, *Beziehung*, p. 124; *Statistisches Jahrbuch für das Deutsche Reich, 1921/2, 1924/5;* Bresciani, *Inflation,* p. 194n.; Graham, *Hyperinflation,* p. 306.

is clear that Hamburg's growth was lagging behind its much larger neighbour.[75] In this climate, bankruptcy was an ever-present threat, particularly for the city's many small firms. There were 843 bankruptcies in 1877/8, and even in 1913, 311 firms went to the wall.[76]

To be able to resist the laws of the market – or at least temper the punishments it meted out – called for greater resources and organisational sophistication than could be mustered by the average firm. An important aspect of Hamburg's economic structure in this regard was the clear distinction which existed between big and small business. Hamburg's was a relatively polarised economy; unusually high proportions of the workforce were employed either in very small (under ten employees) or in very large firms (over 1,000) – a mere four companies (the Hapag and the three big shipyards) employed around

---

[75] Average annual growth rates of real income for Hamburg: 1885–1900, 2.10 per cent; 1900–1913, 1.75 per cent; for Prussia: 2.49 per cent and 3.20 per cent: calculated from figures in V. Hentschel, *Wirtschaft und Wirtschaftspolitik im wilhelminischen Deutschland. Organisierter Kapitalismus und Interventionsstaat?* (Stuttgart, 1978), pp. 80f., 97; Ullrich, 'Arbeiterbewegung', p. 28; Hohorst *et al.,* (eds.), *Sozialgeschichtliches Arbeitsbuch,* II, pp. 101f.; D. Petzina, W. Abelhauser and A. Foust (eds.), *Sozialgeschichtliches Arbeitsbuch,* Bd. III, *Materialien zur Statistik des Deutschen Reiches 1914–1945* (Munich 1978), p. 102. Clearly, this reflected the 'catching up' of rural areas as well as the industrial expansion of areas like the Ruhr and Berlin.

[76] Kutz-Bauer, *Arbeiterschaft,* p. 110; Lyth, *Inflation,* p. 165.

a tenth of the city's working population.[77] In terms of capital, twelve joint-stock companies had a total share capital equivalent to around half the total shares quoted on the Hamburg bourse,[78] with the top twelve family firms not far behind.[79] 'Big business' in Hamburg thus meant an elite group of firms: merchant houses like Schuback & Söhne; the shipping lines R.M. Sloman, the Hapag and the Woermanns; the shipyards Blohm & Voß, Vulkan and Reiherstieg; the Commerzbank, the Vereinsbank, the Norddeutsche Bank and Warburg's. There were close ties between these firms: the Hapag was the shipyards' biggest single private customer, and the banks were well represented on the supervisory boards of the shipping firms.[80] In addition, these firms shared other distinguishing features: in particular the rising level of bureaucratic organisation which was characteristic of larger firms at the turn of the century.[81]

Big business in Hamburg had more in common than mere size and organisational sophistication, however. Firstly, all these firms clearly had a considerable interest in maximising the movement of goods, people and capital through Hamburg. Not only the banks and shipping lines but also the shipyards had a vested interest in a liberal trade policy; for it was on this that Hamburg's prosperity largely rested. Secondly, as a result of decades of extremely rapid economic growth, Hamburg's big firms had acquired what might be called the habit of expansion. Max Warburg, Albert Ballin, the Woermanns and the Blohms personified a highly dynamic entrepreneurial culture, which regarded increasing turnover, high profits and (particularly in the

---

[77] 43 per cent of private sector employees worked in firms with fewer than eleven persons in 1907 (Reich as a whole: 38 per cent); 10 per cent in just nine companies with more than 1,000 employees (Reich as a whole: 5 per cent): *Statistik des Deutschen Reiches*, Bd. 217 (1907), p. 365; Hoffmann *et al.*, *Wachstum*, p. 212; Hohorst *et al.* (eds.), *Sozialgeschichtliches Arbeitsbuch*, II, p. 75. Cf. Ullrich, 'Arbeiterbewegung', p. 5; Lyth, '*Mittelstand*', p. 282. Concentration was, however, higher in the industrial Ruhr: Hentschel, *Wirtschaft und Wirtschaftspolitik*, pp. 30, 54, 95.

[78] StAH, FA Blohm & Voß 264, Schiffbau-Treuhand Bank report 19 July 1921; BAP, RFM 46582 N.Reg. 322/275–85, 'Gutachten: Aufstellung von Grundsätzen für die Festsetzung der Zuschläge'; *Vierteljahreshefte zur Statistik des Deutschen Reiches* (1914), *Ergänzungsheft* II, p. 11.

[79] In 1917, their total capital amounted to 328.2 m. marks: H.-K. Stein, 'Interessenkonflikte zwischen Großkaufleuten, Handelskammer und Senat in der Frage des Zollanschlusses Hamburgs an das Reich 1866–1881', in *ZVHG*, 64 (1978), pp. 81–9.

[80] Max Warburg and Max Schinckel of the Norddeutsche Bank were members of the Hapag's supervisory board: Hapag *Jahresbericht 1913*; and Ballin persuaded the Blohms to take financial advice from Warburg. Adolph Woermann was a board member of Blohm & Voß, a supervisory board member of the Hapag, the Levant Line, the Hamburg–South American Line and Dynamit AG, and a director of the Norddeutsche Bank: Washausen, *Kolonialpolitik*, p. 69.

[81] J. Kocka, 'Industrielles Management: Konzeption und Modelle in Deutschland vor 1914', *VSWG*, 56, 3 (1969), pp. 332–72; *idem*, 'Capitalism and Bureaucracy in German Industrialisation before 1914', *EcHR*, 34 (1981), pp. 453–68.

shipping industry) high investment as the norm. It was this addiction
to expansion which the *Imperator* so perfectly symbolised. These two
characteristics played a major role in determining the way Hamburg
business responded when its golden age abruptly ended.

Bourgeois society and its values

The social history of late nineteenth-century Hamburg has, like the
social history of the German Reich as a whole, tended to be presented
as the history of material inequality and class conflict.[82] That there
was great inequality can scarcely be denied: one need only compare
photographs of a slum in the city's Altstadt with the Warburgs' idyllic
summer house in Blankenese to appreciate the material gulf between
a docker and a banker.[83] Yet the historical significance of the 'emancipatory and democratic strivings' by the organised 'workers' movement'
to reduce these material disparities should not be exaggerated at the
expense of other social forces. Of equal, if not greater importance were
the internal dynamics of bourgeois society. It was the emancipation of
economic energies by capital which did most to transform traditional
urban society; and the key to its stability lay less in the attitudes of
other classes than in the relation between the material and cultural
values of the bourgeoisie itself.[84]

One danger of relying on the concept of class is that one loses sight
of the extraordinary fluidity of late nineteenth-century urban society.
In 1811, 132,000 people had lived in the state of Hamburg; in 1913,
eight times as many did, making it one of the twenty largest cities in
the world, and the second city of the Reich – the German Glasgow.[85]
Hamburg was no procreative paradise, however: indeed, the birth-rate

[82] Cf. the essays in J. Berlin (ed.), *Das andere Hamburg. Freiheitliche und demokratische
Bestrebungen in der Hansestadt seit dem Spätmittelalter* (Hamburg, 1981); Herzig *et
al.* (eds.), *Arbeiter in Hamburg.*

[83] See the photographs reproduced in Plagemann, *Industriekultur*, pp. 241, 259; I.
Warburg-Spinelli, *Erinnerungen 1910–1989. 'Die Dringlichkeit des Mitleids und die
Einsamkeit, nein zu sagen'* (Hamburg, 1990), pp. 15–38.

[84] Cf. Blackbourn and Eley, *Peculiarities*, esp. pp. 159–205; J. Kocka, *Bürger und
Bürgerlichkeit im 19. Jahrhundert* (Göttingen, 1987); *idem* (ed.), *Bürgertum im 19.
Jahrhundert. Deutschland im europäischen Vergleich*, 3 vols. (Munich, 1988);
Blackbourn and Evans (eds.), *German Bourgeoisie*. For current work on the history
of the bourgeoisie in Hamburg see J. Breuilly *et al.*, 'Zustände und Prozesse – Ein
Projekt zur Sozialgeschichte Hamburgs im 19. Jahrhundert', in Verein Hamburg-
Jahrbuch, *Hamburger Zustände. Jahrbuch zur Geschichte der Region Hamburg*, I (1988)
pp. 1ff.

[85] *Statistisches Handbuch 1929/30*, pp. 12f. Its growth was most rapid from around
1870, the average annual rate of increase rising from 1.54 per cent (1821–70) to
2.85 per cent (1871–1913); Hohorst *et al.* (eds.), *Sozialgeschichtliches Arbeitsbuch*, II,
p. 51.

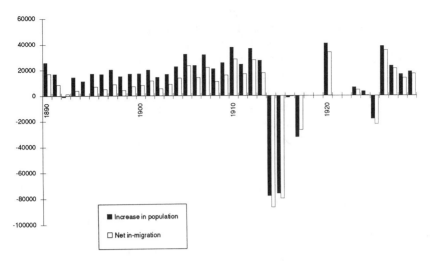

(i) Migration and population: Hamburg, 1890–1928

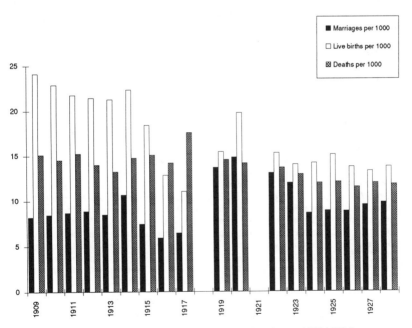

(ii) Marriage, birth and death rates in Hamburg, 1890–1928
Source: Statistisches Handbuch, 1929/30, pp. 12f., 32, 51, 61.
Figure 1.3

fell sharply from its secular peak in the 1870s (39.4 births per 1,000 inhabitants) to 22.2 per 1,000 in 1913; while mortality rates remained above 20 per 1,000 until the turn of the century (see figure 1.3).[86] With its overcrowded slums, polluted air, and archaic sanitation system, the city was a death trap, prey to epidemics of smallpox (in 1871), typhus (in the 1880s), and cholera (in 1892).[87] Yet it exerted an irresistible economic attraction. Around 58 per cent of the total increase between 1871 and 1910 was due to net in-migration, and the proportion of the population actually born in Hamburg steadily declined to less than half.[88] In 1907, only 35.6 per cent of workers in manufacturing were Hamburg born, compared with a third again from the rest of North Germany, a quarter from elsewhere in Germany and 5 per cent from abroad.[89] *Wanderlust* persisted in the form of high labour mobility – only a third of workers had been in the same job for more than five years.[90]

People came to Hamburg to work. Around 46 per cent of the population were in employment in 1907, including 73 per cent of all those aged between 16 and 60, 38 per cent of men over seventy and over a third of all unmarried women;[91] and for most, work meant manual labour. In 1907, just over half the working population (52.8 per cent) were categorised as 'workers'; however, such a broad category obscures the enormous diversity of work done. The biggest single

---

[86] *Statistisches Handbuch 1929/30*, pp. 51, 61; Hohorst *et al.* (eds.), *Sozialgeschichtliches Arbeitsbuch*, II, p. 56.

[87] Evans, *Death in Hamburg*, esp. pp. 180–226, 252–60, 533. For improvements in health provision after the cholera epidemic, see also the figures in Hohorst *et al.* (eds.), *Sozialgeschichtliches Arbeitsbuch*, II, pp. 152f.; Büttner, *Politische Gerechtigkeit*, p. 205.

[88] *Aus Hamburgs Verwaltung und Wirtschaft*, 4. Jg. (April 1927), p. 104. The 1907 census revealed that over 100,000 born Hamburgers lived in another state; compared with 420,000 in-migrants: Hentschel, *Wirtschaft und Wirtschaftspolitik*, pp. 30, 82–8. The peaks of net in-migration were in 1885–90 and 1905–10, with adult men in search of work accounting for the majority of the new arrivals.

[89] Grüttner, *Arbeitswelt*, p. 85; Ullrich, 'Arbeiterbewegung', p. 18; cf. Kutz-Bauer, *Arbeiterschaft*, p. 112. In general, K. Bade, 'Massenwanderung und Arbeitsmarkt im deutschen Nordosten von 1880 bis zum Ersten Weltkrieg. Überseeische Auswanderung, interne Abwanderung und kontinentale Zuwanderung', *AfS*, 20 (1980), pp. 265–323; D. Langewiesche, 'Wanderungsbewegungen in der Hochindustrialisierungsperiode. Regionale interstädtische und innerstädtische Mobilität in Deutschland 1880–1914', *VSWG*, 64 (1977), pp. 1–40.

[90] Ullrich, 'Arbeiterbewegung', p. 23. In 1907, 8,586 workers left the employ of Blohm & Voß; 9,074 were taken on: Cattaruzza, *Arbeiter und Unternehmer*, p. 77.

[91] *Aus Hamburgs Verwaltung und Wirtschaft*, 4. Jg. (1927), pp. 106f. Only *rentiers*, lunatics, prisoners and (apart from around 5 per cent to 10 per cent of them) children and wives were exempt: *Statistik des Deutschen Reiches*, Bd. 408 (1925), p. 100. This was in line with the national participation ratio: G. Bry, *Wages in Germany 1871–1945* (Princeton, 1960), p. 25; J. Reulecke, 'Veränderungen des Arbeitskräftepotentials im Deutschen Reich 1900–1933', in Mommsen *et al.* (eds.), *Industrielles System*, I, p. 88.

occupational group – 11.4 per cent of the working population – were employed as domestic servants, most of them young unmarried women: hardly the rank-and-file of the proletariat.[92] The most numerous male manual workers were fitters, builders, seamen and dockers; but there were comparable numbers of women who spent their days toiling over sewing machines and wash tubs.[93] Moreover, a growing proportion of the working population – nearly 15 per cent in 1907 – did work which depended more on literacy than physical strength or manual skill: generating and regulating the increasing volume of paperwork required by the modern economy and state. These were the clerical workers, like the artisans' sons from Eppendorf who, as one contemporary described them, 'set off every morning for the city with their stiff hats and white shirts, and were thus lost to [. . .] the self-reliant *Kleinbürgertum* [. . .] – the first representatives of an ambitious but still uncertain petty-bourgeoisie, full of their semi-education and drawing their knowledge from the daily newspaper'.[94] Finally, there were those classified as 'self-supporting': the owners of property (around a fifth of the working population), including the self-employed proprietors of firms and professionals, but also (somewhat illogically, but reflecting their comparable status) senior managers and civil servants. By far the greatest number of these (just under half) were either shopkeepers or artisans – groups which contemporaries saw as the core of a traditional 'old' *Mittelstand*, similar in their means to the 'new' *Mittelstand* of clerical employees.[95] 'Big' businessmen – the owners, directors and senior managers of Hamburg's largest firms – were, by comparison, a tiny occupational elite, even more exclusive than the professional elite.[96]

[92] *Hamburger Statistische Monatsberichte*, June 1926, 'Die berufliche und soziale Gliederung der Bevölkerung Hamburgs nach den Zählungen von 1925 und 1907'; Lyth, '*Mittelstand*', pp. 73–5, 106, 109, 186, 280, 340. Hamburg's female employment rate (c. 25 per cent) was below the national average (c. 34 per cent): Hohorst *et al.* (eds.), *Sozialgeschichtliches Arbeitsbuch*, II, p. 66; Reulecke, 'Veränderungen des Arbeitskräftepotentials', p. 88; Hentschel, *Wirtschaft und Wirtschaftspolitik*, p. 91. Cf. K. Schleger, 'Mistress and Servant in Nineteenth Century Hamburg', *History Workshop Journal*, 15 (1983), pp. 60–77.

[93] Ullrich, 'Arbeiterbewegung', pp. 24f.; *Statistik des Deutschen Reichs*, Bd. 217, pp. 365–71.

[94] Karl Scheffler in his autobiographical novel *Der junge Tobias*, quoted in Schramm, *Neun Generationen*, II, pp. 397f. The ratio of white-collar to manual workers was above average in Hamburg: cf. Lyth, '*Mittelstand*', pp. 73, 109; Hohorst *et al.* (eds.), *Sozialgeschichtliches Arbeitsbuch*, II, pp. 55, 67.

[95] Lyth, '*Mittelstand*', pp. 266f., 280, 340. See in general D. Blackbourn, 'The *Mittelstand* in German Society and Politics, 1871–1914', *Social History*, 4 (1977), pp. 409–33.

[96] See in general J. Kocka, *Unternehmer in der deutschen Industrialisierung* (Göttingen, 1975); Y. Cassis, 'Wirtschaftselite und Bürgertum. England, Frankreich und Deutschland um 1900', in Kocka (ed.), *Bürgertum im 19. Jahrhundert*, II, pp. 9–34. On the

More than anything else, work – its availability, its degree of difficulty and discomfort, its duration and its recompense – determined the quality of an individual's life. From an employer's standpoint, the labour market was doubly flexible: not only did migration levels respond to economic conditions, but there was a high level of casual employment in sectors subject to seasonal fluctuation. This was of especial importance on the waterfront, where a substantial proportion of dockers and ship-building workers were subject to periodic unemployment.[97] By contrast, clerical workers (particularly the 13,000 in the public sector) expected a high degree of job security.[98] Conditions ranged from the hellish (boiler-cleaning), to the hazardous (riveting), to the merely humdrum (book-keeping),[99] while the average working week varied from fifty-three up to eighty-two hours.[100] Of paramount importance was pay. Hamburg had the highest per capita income of all the German states, 72 per cent above the Reich average in 1913.[101] However, relatively sluggish aggregate growth and the high level of in-migration meant that Hamburg's real per capita income was in fact falling.[102] Moreover, the distribution of income was – as in Berlin – highly inequitable, with little sign of the disparity between rich and

professions, see H. Siegrist (ed.), *Bürgerliche Berufe* (Göttingen, 1988); G. Cocks and K.H. Jarausch (eds.), *German Professions 1800–1950* (Oxford, 1990); K.H. Jarausch, *The Unfree Professions. German Lawyers, Teachers and Engineers, 1900–1950* (Oxford, 1990).

[97] Dockers were usually hired on a daily basis; and average monthly employment fluctuated by as much as +/−12.5 per cent: H.J. Bieber, 'Der Hamburger Hafenarbeiterstreik 1896–1987', in Herzig *et al.* (eds.), *Arbeiter in Hamburg*, pp. 229–45; Grüttner, *Arbeitswelt*, pp. 31, 34. Cf. Hermann Blohm's praise for Hamburg's reserve army of unemployed, quoted in Cattaruzza, *Arbeiter und Unternehmer*, p. 82.

[98] Lyth, *'Mittelstand'*, p. 186; L. Lippmann, *Mein Leben und meine amtliche Tätigkeit. Erinnerungen und ein Beitrag zur Finanzgeschichte Hamburgs* (Hamburg, 1964), p. 442.

[99] Bieber, 'Hafenarbeiterstreik', pp. 100–4; Ullrich, 'Arbeiterbewegung', pp. 25–44; Cattaruzza, *Arbeiter und Unternehmer*, p. 51.

[100] Ullrich, 'Arbeiterbewegung', pp. 34f. In German industry as a whole, the average working week fell in length from sixty-six hours in the 1880s to fifty-seven hours in 1914, leaving more time for leisure. Hoffmann *et al.*, *Wachstum*, pp. 213f.; cf. W. Nahrstedt, *Die Entstehung der Freizeit. Dargestellt am Beispiel Hamburgs. Ein Beitrag zur Strukturgeschichte und zur strukturgeschichtlichen Grundlegung der Freizeitpädagogik* (Göttingen, 1972).

[101] Hohorst *et al.* (eds.), *Sozialgeschichtliches Arbeitsbuch*, II p. 79; D. Petzina, *Die deutsche Wirtschaft in der Zwischenkriegszeit* (Wiesbaden, 1977), p. 172. Cf. T.J. Orsagh, 'The Probable Geographical Distribution of German Income 1882–1962', *Zeitschrift für die gesamte Staatswissenschaft*, 124 (1968); H. Hesse, 'Die Entwicklung der regionalen Einkommensdifferenzen im Wachstumsprozeß der deutschen Wirtschaft vor 1913', in W. Fischer (ed.), *Beiträge zu Wirtschaftswachstum und Wirtschaftsstruktur im 16. und 19. Jahrhundert* (Berlin, 1971), pp. 261–79.

[102] At an average annual rate of −0.54 per cent between 1885 and 1900; and −0.85 per cent between 1900 and 1913; compared with figures for Prussia of 1.17 per cent and 1.1 per cent: see note 75.

poor diminishing.[103] Income tax statistics show that, in 1871, the bottom 83 per cent of taxpayers accounted for 32 per cent of total taxable income, while the top 1.5 per cent accounted for 29 per cent. In 1916, the bottom 83 per cent had increased its share to just 35 per cent; but the percentage of taxpayers who earned 29 per cent of the total had fallen to just 1 per cent. Indeed, in absolute terms the gap had widened. Allowing for changes in purchasing power, the percentage of taxpayers in the lowest of five composite income bands had risen from 49 per cent to 83 per cent; the figure for the top tax band had fallen from 0.1 per cent to 0.02 per cent, representing a mere forty-four individuals – the proprietors of firms like Sloman and Behrens, or an exceptional company director like Ballin – who paid tax on incomes over 500,000 marks.[104] By contrast, the average self-employed shopkeeper or artisan's income was perhaps around 5,000 marks: 1 per cent of top business earnings.[105] Differentials in the public sector were less enormous: a senior (grade one) civil servant earned 9,768 marks annually, a second grade civil servant or an average white-collar worker 40 per cent as much, a grade three civil servant 25 per cent as much, and an ordinary state clerical employee 20 per cent as much.[106] Private sector clerical salaries were lower, ranging from as little as 721 marks to 2,700 marks.[107] Workers' incomes are more difficult to calculate. In 1895, dockers' daily wages ranged from 2.00 marks to 4.20 marks; but, because of seasonal unemployment, over two-thirds earned below 500 marks annually, and only 5 per cent over 1,500.[108] Journeymen in crafts like baking, carpentry or plumbing

---

[103] Of nineteen provinces, states and cities for which income tax evidence is available in 1913, Hamburg had the sixth largest proportion of earners (51.3 per cent) below the 900 marks annual income threshold; but the largest proportion earning above 6,000 marks (4.4 per cent): Hentschel, *Wirtschaft und Wirtschaftspolitik*, pp. 80f., 98. See also the Pareto coefficients in Hoffmann *et al.*, *Wachstum*, pp. 512–15; and the figures for other states in H. Kaelble, *Industrialisation and Social Inequality in Nineteenth Century Europe* (Leamington Spa, 1986), pp. 14–48. Cf. A. Jeck, *Wachstum und Verteilung des Volkseinkommens. Untersuchungen und Materialien zur Entwicklung des Volkseinkommensverteilung in Deutschland 1870–1913* (Tübingen, 1970).

[104] Calculated from figures in Hohorst *et al.* (eds.), *Sozialgeschichtliches Arbeitsbuch*, II, p. 129; *Statistisches Handbuch 1920*, pp. 244f.; Lippmann, *Leben*, pp. 384f. Cf. Stein, 'Interessenkonflikte', pp. 89f.; Mosse, *Jews in the German Economy*, p. 213; Evans, *Death in Hamburg*, pp. 50, 73–8, 408, 533; Ullrich, 'Arbeiterbewegung', pp. 33f.; Schramm, *Neun Generationen*, II, p. 389.

[105] Ullrich, 'Arbeiterbewegung', p. 33.

[106] *Hamburger Statistische Monatsberichte*, Sonderbeitrag (Hamburg, 1924), 'Die Wirkungen der Geldentwertung auf die Gehälter der Beamten und Staatsangestellten in den Jahren 1919 bis 1923', p. 78.

[107] Lyth, '*Mittelstand*', pp. 129f.

[108] Grüttner, *Arbeitswelt*, pp. 49, 51; Bieber, 'Hafenarbeiterstreik', pp. 104f.

were paid rather more, on a daily or weekly basis.[109] The hourly wage rates quoted for ship-builders (which ranged from 17 pfennigs to 65 pfennigs) had limited significance in practice, since the majority of shipyard workers were paid according to the system of piecework (*Akkord*), whereby gangs of workers were paid for specific tasks. There was an elaborate system of wage differentials; and translating these into annual figures is complicated further by the high levels of overtime which were usual in the shipyards.[110] Average annual earnings for manual workers in the pre-war period have been estimated at around 1,800 marks; but a top skilled worker could earn closer to 2,500 marks; while the average unskilled worker's income could rise to as much as 2,170 marks with overtime bonuses.[111] Compared with the differentials at the upper reaches of the income scale – within the bourgeoisie – the gap between the average shopkeeper, clerk or small businessman and the average blue-collar worker was therefore relatively narrow.

Such statistics require amplification and qualification, however. For one thing, despite the notoriety of the inflationary decade after 1914, prices also fluctuated in the pre-war years. Between 1874 and 1887, the estimated cost of living fell at an average annual rate of between 1.5 per cent and 1.7 per cent; but in the succeeding years to 1913 it rose by between 0.9 per cent and 1.5 per cent per annum,[112] and Hamburg prices were higher than the average, having fallen less in the Great Depression.[113] For most people, the cost of living principally meant the cost of food. The average worker spent around half his wages on a high-fat, low-protein diet of rye bread, potatoes, fish and pork, washed down with sugared coffee and beer.[114] Then came rent,

[109] In 1913, their daily pay ranged from 5.00 marks (baking) to 7.38 marks (building): Lyth, *Inflation*, p. 86. On building workers, see Bry, *Wages*, pp. 104, 371, 437.
[110] Cattaruzza, 'Hamburger Modelle', pp. 47f., 165–71; Ullrich, 'Arbeiterbewegung', pp. 25, 36–9; BAP, RFM 46585 N. Reg. 329/114.
[111] Ullrich, 'Arbeiterbewegung', pp. 30–3. There were also wide income differentials according to sex and age: female workers earned around half to two thirds of this, junior clerks earned only 720 marks; young manual workers 572 marks.
[112] See the indexes of Kuczynski and Desai in Bry, *Wages*, pp. 354f. and A. Desai, *Real Wages in Germany 1871–1913* (Oxford, 1968).
[113] Kutz–Bauer, *Arbeiterschaft*, pp. 97f.; Evans, *Death in Hamburg*, p. 71. The cost of living for an average working-class family is estimated to have risen at 1.29 per cent annually between 1895 and 1913: Grüttner, *Arbeitswelt*, p. 54. Ullrich's figures suggest an inflation rate of 2.3 per cent: Ullrich, 'Arbeiterbewegung', p. 29. However, inflation did not significantly erode real incomes: for reasons to be discussed, wages generally kept pace with prices: Grüttner, *Arbeitswelt*, p. 55; Ullrich, 'Arbeiterbewegung', p. 30. Cf. R. May, *Kosten der Lebenshaltung in Hamburg seit 1890* (Munich/Leipzig, 1915) [*Schriften des Vereins für Sozialpolitik*, Bd. 145, 4. Teil, 1].
[114] Ullrich, 'Arbeiterbewegung'; Evans, *Death in Hamburg*, pp. 161–76. On the pre-war working-class diet, see A. Offer, *The First World War: an Agrarian Interpretation* (Oxford, 1989), pp. 39–53.

which accounted for as much as a fifth of the income of those earning less than 1,200 marks.[115] There was little left over to save: workers accounted for only around 7 per cent of savings accounts at the Neue Sparcasse, and generally owned only the most rudimentary property.[116] To save and to own was to be bourgeois; and, in this sense, it was true that social differences rested more on 'inherited and acquired wealth' than on the more complex distinctions of occupation and income.[117] Yet even within this propertied elite there were subdivisions. Around 600,000 people had savings accounts worth a total of 390 m. marks; but the average account contained just over 600 marks.[118] By contrast, just 40,000 people owned property worth more than 10,000 marks;[119] and half that number again – 2 per cent of the population – owned the city's real estate, valued at 4.76 bn. marks.[120] Once again, there was a tiny elite at the top: in 1880, there were seventy-two millionaires, of whom just sixteen had private fortunes worth more than 5 m. marks.[121] The richest man in Hamburg before the war, the shipowner Henry Sloman, was reputedly worth 60 m. marks.[122]

Probably the most visible expression of wealth and income differentials was the distribution of housing. Although the city's geographical extent increased with the settlement of peripheral areas like Bergedorf and Ritzebüttel, the density of population continued to rise, reaching nearly 1,500 inhabitants per kilometre before the war;[123] and Hamburg had an exceptionally high percentage of families living in cellar apartments, sharing flats with other families or sub-letting rooms to lodgers.[124] The problems of overcrowding were not evenly spread, however.

[115] The pressure for cheap accommodation was such that rents of smaller properties (with only one heated room) rose ahead of average inflation: Grüttner, *Arbeitswelt*, pp. 53, 104; Desai, *Real Wages*, p. 124; Ullrich, 'Arbeiterbewegung', p. 29. Only 4.4 per cent of residences were owner-occupied in 1910.

[116] *Statistisches Handbuch 1920*, p. 367.

[117] Evans, *Death in Hamburg*, p. 34.

[118] *Statistisches Handbuch 1920*, pp. 364f.

[119] Lippmann, *Leben*, p. 384. Its total value was 5.753 bn. marks. Around 70 m. marks was passed on every year through inheritance: *Statistisches Handbuch 1920*, p. 249.

[120] Lyth, 'Mittelstand', pp. 403f., 460; *Statistisches Handbuch 1920*, p. 125; *Statistik des Hamburgischen Staates*, 25 (1910), p. 1; 29 (1919), p. 1. Real estate in turn acted as the security for mortgage loans, among the most popular forms of investment before the war.

[121] See the lists in Stein, 'Interessenkonflikte', pp. 81–9. Cf. Schramm, *Neun Generationen*, II, p. 389; Kindleberger, *Financial History*, p. 189; Mosse, *Jews in the German Economy*, pp. 6–9, 201f., 213, 391f.; R. Martin, *Jahrbuch der Millionäre in den Hansestädten* (Berlin, 1912).

[122] Evans, *Death in Hamburg*, p. 15.

[123] *Aus Hamburgs Verwaltung und Wirtschaft*, 4. Jg. (April, 1927), p. 104; Hentschel, *Wirtschaft und Wirtschaftspolitik*, p. 88.

[124] Kutz-Bauer, *Arbeiterschaft*, pp. 107f.

The Alley Quarters of the central Altstadt and Neustadt which, in the
midst of the 1892 cholera epidemic, inspired the damning comment,
'I forget I am in Europe',[125] might have been partially cleared by
1913; but slum conditions persisted in nearby St Georg and St Pauli;
while the newer working class 'rent barracks' on the eastern edge of
the city were a world apart from the elegant villas of Harvestehude
and Rotherbaum on the West side of the Alster lake where the
Amsincks, Ballins, Blohms, Berenberg-Goßlers and Warburgs all
lived.[126] Over a fifth of taxable income and a third of income tax
receipts came from those two areas, where a mere 5 per cent of the
population lived.[127] The vital importance of this residential 'segre-
gation'[128] becomes clear when one compares mortality rates in the
'West End' with those in the 'inner city'. Because of the insanitary
conditions of the slums and the lack of resources to combat disease,
the poor were more likely to die of tuberculosis, typhoid or cholera
than the rich.[129] Throughout his life, the banker's son Aby Warburg
had an acute terror of epidemics; yet the fact that he had survived
typhoid as a child is in itself revealing. It was by no means irrational
of his brother Max, who continued to work seventeen hours a day in
the city centre during the cholera epidemic of 1892, to 'have the
certain feeling that I was immune'.[130] The mortality rate among those
earning more than 50,000 marks was 4.8 per thousand; for those on
less than 1,000 marks, the figure was 61.9, nearly thirteen times
higher.[131]

Such was Hamburg's bourgeois society at the turn of the century –
a society of frenetic economic activity and persistent material inequality.
It might be thought that such a society was doomed ultimately to be
overthrown by a revolution of the poor and propertyless, and this is
often the implication of accounts which centre on the revolution of
1918/19.[132] Yet this is by no means certain. For bourgeois society had
other values – moral and cultural values – which tended to mitigate,
if not to legitimise, its unequal material complexion.

The most fundamental social cement was provided by family life.
The majority of men and women married between the ages of twenty

---

[125] Quoted in Evans, *Death In Hamburg*, p. 305. Cf. M. Grüttner, 'Soziale Hygiene
und soziale Kontrolle. Die Sanierung der Hamburger Gängeviertel, 1892–1936', in
Herzig *et al.* (eds.), *Arbeiter in Hamburg*, pp. 359–72.
[126] Cf. Plagemann, *Industriekultur*, pp. 228–54.
[127] *Statistisches Handbuch 1920*, pp. 246f.
[128] Evans, *Death in Hamburg*, pp. 53f.
[129] *Ibid.*, pp. 182–202, 433–69.
[130] Warburg, *Aufzeichnungen*, p. 14; E.H. Gombrich, *Aby Warburg. An Intellectual
Biography* (Oxford, 1970), pp. 19f., 88.
[131] Evans, *Death in Hamburg*, p. 408.
[132] See below, chapter 3.

and thirty (women tending to marry at a slightly earlier age), and
although the divorce rate had begun its rise (from 4.7 per cent of
marriages in 1890/4 to 10.9 per cent in 1913), divorcees remained a
tiny minority (0.6 per cent of the population in 1910).[133] Similarly,
although the birth rate had also begun to decline, improvements in
health (particularly, as we have seen, among wealthier groups) meant
that families remained large. In 1910, 42.5 per cent of German families
had five or more members; 10.1 per cent had eight or more.[134] A not
untypical case was that of Moritz and Charlotte Warburg, who had
seven children between 1866 and 1879, all but one of whom lived to
be over sixty. Albrecht O'Swald and his wife had six children at
around the same time; while in the previous generation Johannes and
Emilie Schuback had produced twelve children, only one of whom
died in infancy.[135] At one level, the nineteenth-century family was a
simple economic unit, with a clear division of labour between the
husband, who worked, the wife, who maintained the home, and the
children, who prepared for work and marriage.[136] Within the propertied
bourgeoisie, this economic role became more complex; here the family
often formed the foundation for the firm, and the transfer of capital
between generations, as well as the maintenance of a family's social
position, called for careful choices about the education and marriage
of children.[137] As Percy Schramm recalled of his own elite milieu
around 1900: 'How one was inter-related, what the name of the father's
firm was, how well-born the mother was – naturally, these were the
things one had to know.'[138] The Schramms were linked by marriage
to the O'Swalds, the Rupertis, the Mercks and the Amsincks, who in
turn were related to the Berenberg-Goßlers, the Willinks and the

---

[133] *Aus Hamburgs Verwaltung und Wirtschaft*, 4. Jg. (April 1927), p. 105; *Statistisches Handbuch 1929/30* (1930), p. 42; *Statistische Mitteilungen*, Nr. 18, 'Die Bevölkerung der Stadt Hamburg vor und nach dem Krieg nach Geschlecht, Alter und Familienstand', table 1.

[134] W. Jaide, *Generationen eines Jahrhunderts. Wechsel der Jugendgeneration im Jahrhundertrend. Zur Sozialgeschichte der Jugend in Deutschland, 1871–1985* (Opladen, 1988), p. 44; Hentschel, *Wirtschaft und Wirtschaftspolitik*, p. 64 n. The average household in Hamburg had 4.09 members: *Aus Hamburgs Verwaltung und Wirtschaft*, 4. Jg. (April, 1927), p. 104.

[135] Warburg, *Aufzeichnungen*, pp. 1–13; Schramm, *Neun Generationen*, II, pp. 404–8; Evans, 'Family and Class', p. 120.

[136] Only 5.5 per cent of women in employment were married: calculated from *Statistik des Deutschen Reiches*, Bd. 217 (1907), pp. 365–71. Cf. R. Dasey, 'Women's Work and the Family: Women Garment Workers in Berlin and Hamburg before the First World War', in R.J. Evans and W.R. Lee (eds.), *The German Family* (London, 1981), pp. 221–56; Plagemann, *Industriekultur*, pp. 255–66.

[137] Cf. J. Kocka, 'Familie, Unternehmer und Kapitalismus', *Zeitschrift für Unternehmensgeschichte*, 24. Jg. (1979), pp. 91–135.

[138] Schramm, *Neun Generationen*, II, p. 425.

Westphals.[139] Of equal if not greater importance as a foundation for
the success of a bourgeois family was the effective division of fraternal
responsibility. The Amsinck family, for example, pursued a strategy
of bifurcation, with one son in each generation becoming a lawyer,
while the others went into business. Comparable patterns of diversifi-
cation emerge in the case of the Schramms, the O'Swalds; while the
Blohm brothers concentrated their efforts on business.[140]

However, the case of the Warburgs illustrates the way in which
family life changed in the course of the nineteenth century. The
children of Sara and Aby Warburg all married into other business families;[141] but in the next generation only three of Moritz and
Charlotte's seven children married conventionally.[142] Marriage based
on individual affection began to challenge marriage as a socio-economic
strategy for the family as a whole.[143] Similarly, there was a clear
diminution in the control which parents were able to wield over their
sons' vocational choices.[144] Max had to be dissuaded from pursuing a
military career; Paul from studying science; and the parents failed to
prevent both Aby from relinquishing his birthright in preference for
the study of art history, and Felix from abandoning business for a life
of leisure and philanthropy.[145] It therefore seems fair to say that the
large and closely knit bourgeois family had passed its zenith by the
turn of the nineteenth century. A note of self doubt is detectable in
Aby Warburg's disparagement of the banking dynasties of the Italian
Renaissance, or in the tendency of Percy Schramm's aged great-aunt

---

[139] *Ibid.*, pp. 401–8; Evans, 'Family and Class', pp. 122f.

[140] On the Amsincks, see Evans, 'Family and Class', pp. 118–26. On the Schramms
and O'Swalds, see Schramm, *Neun Generationen*, II, esp. pp. 404–8 on the brothers
Albrecht and William O'Swald, who were both in business, both married Rupertis,
and lived as neighbours in the Klopstockstrasse. On Hermann and Rudolph Blohm,
see Prager, *Blohm und Voß*, pp. 56–103.

[141] Rosenbaum and Sherman, *M.M. Warburg & Co.*, p. 46.

[142] Warburg-Spinelli, *Erinnerungen*, pp. 445, 456, 458; J. Attali, *A Man of Influence. Sir Siegmund Warburg, 1902–1982* (London, 1986), p. 124; James P. Warburg Diary MSS, pp.
1–32, James P. Warburg papers, John Fitzgerald Kennedy Library, Boston; Gombrich,
Aby Warburg, pp. 93–109; Chernow, *Warburgs*, pp. 57–68, 103–27.

[143] H. Rosenbaum, *Formen der Familie. Untersuchungen zum Zusmannenhang von Familien-
verhältnissen, Sozialstruktur und sozialem Wandel in der deutschen Gesellschaft des 19.
Jahrhunderts* (Frankfurt, 1982), pp. 251–379; R. Sieder, *Sozialgeschichte der Familie*
(Frankfurt am Main, 1987), pp. 125–45.

[144] On the brothers' characters, Rosenbaum and Sherman, *M.M. Warburg & Co.*,
p. 94; Warburg-Spinelli, *Erinnerungen*, pp. 48–51, 126, 444f., 447–51, 453f., 458–
60; James P. Warburg, 'A Book for Jimmy, Jennifer and Philip', MSS, pp. 32f.,
Paul Warburg Papers, Ser. II, Box 10, Folder 128, Sterling Library, Yale. Cf. C.
Adler, *Felix M. Warburg, A Biographical Sketch* (New York, 1938).

[145] Warburg, *Aufzeichnungen*, pp. 8–13; Chernow, *Warburgs*, p. 38; Warburg-Spinelli,
Erinnerungen, pp. 447, 449–51; Gombrich, *Aby Warburg*, p. 22.

to confuse her own family with the Borgias.[146] This was a mood perfectly captured, of course, in Thomas Mann's first novel, *Buddenbrooks. Verfall einer Familie*, first published in 1901. Although based largely on Mann's own Lübeck family, the Buddenbrooks are the archetypal Hanseatic merchant dynasty, grown prosperous in the eighteenth century, but condemned to decline by unhappy marriages, fraternal strife and the decline of the family's entrepreneurial spirit, exacerbated by exposure to Schopenhauer and Wagner.[147] The book was widely read in Hamburg, finding its way into the well-documented library of Max Schramm, and clearly struck dissonant chords. Percy Schramm felt compelled to contrast his mother's family with the Buddenbrooks; while the Warburgs can hardly have been oblivious to the book's general significance, having had more than their fair share of troubled marriages, to say nothing of a son who succumbed to the arts, having only narrowly survived typhus.[148] Even before the storm that lay ahead, the great families were conscious of their own vulnerability.

After the familial, the most traditional social bonds were those provided by religion. Around 90 per cent of the population throughout the nineteenth century was formally Lutheran, and the city was in many ways imbued with Protestantism's peculiar ethic. The secular values of work, however, tended to take precedence over the spiritual values of religious observance, a priority symbolised by the demolition of the city's Gothic cathedral and five other churches to make way for new sea walls and sewers in the early nineteenth century.[149] For those at the top of the social hierarchy, like the banker Max von Schinckel, orthodox Lutheran piety clearly retained its appeal; but by the turn of the century there was increasing pressure from within the clergy for 'liberal' reforms to counter the low level of church attendance among 'the great mass of people'.[150] By contrast, comparable divisions within the city's Jewish community

---

[146] Gombrich, *Aby Warburg*, pp. 128, 151f., 155; Schramm, *Neun Generationen*, II, pp. 415f.

[147] On the links between the book and Mann's own family, see E. Heller, *Thomas Mann, The Ironic German* (Cambridge, 1981), pp. 27–67; M. Vogtmeier, *Die Familien Mann und Buddenbrook im Lichte der Mehregenerationen-Familientherapie. Untersuchungen zu Thomas Manns 'Buddenbrooks. Verfall einer Familie'* (Frankfurt, 1987).

[148] Schramm, *Neun Generationen*, II, p. 401; Gombrich, *Aby Warburg*, pp. 19f.

[149] Evans, *Death in Hamburg*, p. 36. On the religious composition, see *Aus Hamburgs Verwaltung und Wirtschaft*, Jg. 4 (1927), p. 105; Hohorst *et al.* (eds.), *Sozialgeschichtliches Arbeitsbuch*, II, p. 53. Cf. G. Daur, *Von Predigern und Bürgern. Eine Hamburgische Kirchengeschichte von der Reformation bis zur Gegenwart* (Hamburg, 1970).

[150] E. Rohrmann, *Max von Schinckel* (Hamburg, 1971); Evans, *Death in Hamburg*, pp. 102, 356.

at the beginning of the nineteenth century had been contained, allowing
the orthodox *Synagogenverband* and the liberal *Tempelverband* to worship
separately under the umbrella of the *Gemeinde*.[151] One reason for this
relative harmony was the limited degree of social polarisation within the
Jewish community compared with the Lutheran. The mid nineteenth
century was a time of collective prosperity for the Jews of Hamburg, as
legal restrictions upon them were gradually lifted, and their preferred
forms of economic activity (above all, self-employment in commerce)
flourished.[152] In 1871, 75 per cent of the Jewish population had lived in
the 'inner city' areas of the Altstadt, Neustadt, St Pauli and St Georg;
by 1914, the majority lived in the 'West End', predominantly in the
Rotherbaum area, as well as in Harvestehude.[153] In 1897, 27 per cent of
Jews paid tax in the top two tax brackets, compared with 11 per cent of
the population as a whole.[154] Yet in other respects, the Jewish community
was in decline. In 1811, 4.87 per cent of the population had been Jewish;
by 1910 that figure had fallen to 1.87 per cent, reflecting the relatively
low Jewish birth rate and the paucity of new Jewish settlement in Hamburg.[155] Moreover, there were signs that religious observance and participation in the community were beginning to fall. The grandparents and
parents of the five Warburg brothers were strict in their observance of
the Sabbath;[156] but the next generation, with the exception of the young-

[151] I. Lorenz, *Die Juden in Hamburg zur Zeit der Weimarer Republik. Eine Dokumentation*,
Bd. I (Hamburg, 1987), p. xv. The Jewish community had its roots in the late
seventeenth-century Ashkenazi settlement in Altona; by the nineteenth century, there
was little trace of the Portuguese Sephardic Jews who had settled in Hamburg after
1550: *ibid.*, p. xlv; J. Whaley, *Religious Toleration and Social Change in Hamburg,
1529–1819* (Cambridge, 1985), pp. 9ff., 206; Rosenbaum and Sherman, *M.M.
Warburg & Co.*, pp. 16f.

[152] P. Freimark, *Die Hamburger Juden in der Emanzipationsphase, 1780–1870* (Hamburg,
1989); M. Zimmermann, *Hamburgischer Patriotismus und deutscher Nationalismus. Die
Emanzipation der Juden in Hamburg* (Hamburg, 1979); H. Krohn, *Die Juden in
Hamburg. Die politische, soziale, kulturelle und politische Entwicklung einer judischen
Großstadtgemeinde nach der Emanzipation, 1848–1918* (Hamburg, 1974); G. Marwedel,
Geschichte der Juden in Hamburg, Altona und Wandsbek (Hamburg, 1982).

[153] The triangular area between Bundesstraße and Rotherbaumchaussee was known as
'Little Jerusalem' such was the concentration of Jewish residence: Lorenz, *Die Juden
in Hamburg*, p. lxv. Cf. Evans, *Death in Hamburg*, p. 392f.; I. Lorenz, '"Ahasver
geht nach Eppendorf": Zur Stadtteilkonzentration der Hamburger Juden im 19. und
20. Jahrhundert', *Informationen zur modernen Stadtgeschichte* (1987), pp. 23–9. On
Jewish employment, Lorenz, *Die Juden in Hamburg*, pp. lxx–lxxi.

[154] *Ibid.*, p. lxxiv.

[155] *Ibid.*, pp. xlii, xlv, li; *Statistisches Handbuch 1920*, p. 466. By comparison, the
proportion of Catholics in the population rose from 2 per cent to 5 per cent: C.
Linckmeyer, *Das katholische Hamburg in Vergangenheit und Gegenwart* (Hamburg,
1931).

[156] Sarah conducted the regular Friday evening family service (even after the death of
her daughter Marianne), and her sons Moritz and Siegmund, a cantor, had a
synagogue installed in the family house: Warburg, *Aufzeichnungen*, pp. 2f.; Warburg-
Spinelli, *Erinnerungen*, p. 43; Rosenbaum and Sherman, *M.M. Warburg & Co.*, p. 46.

est son Fritz, was less pious. Max's attendance at the synagogue was formal rather than faithful; while Aby first abandoned the kosher diet at university, and then married a Gentile.[157] Albert Ballin did likewise.[158] We know with hindsight that the increasing number of such matches did not herald the assimilation of the Jewish community into an elite defined in material rather than religious terms; yet there was much additional evidence which seemed to point in that direction. Along with formal emancipation came the acceptance of Jews not only as commercial and professional partners, but also as officials in associational life and public administration, and friends in social life.[159] Only a persistent undercurrent of anti-Semitism – overt at times of popular unrest, latent within the social elite – provided a reminder that the achievements of the nineteenth century might one day be revoked.[160] Bürgermeister Johann Georg Mönckeberg had no objection to his daughter Mathilde living with Aby Waburg and his wife while studying in Florence, and the Warburgs were also on friendly terms with Senator Max Schramm; but Schramm's mother included Jews in the four groups unacceptable as husbands, and Max Warburg had no doubt that there was 'much latent anti-Semitic feeling' in Hamburg.[161]

More than anything else, it has been argued, a common bourgeois culture acted to transcend the occupational, material and religious divisions of nineteenth-century society. Central to this was the idea of

---

[157] Warburg-Spinelli, *Erinnerungen*, pp. 52f., 444; Gombrich, *Aby Warburg*, pp. 25, 81f., 93, 137; Chernow, *Warburgs*, pp. 73f.

[158] Cecil, *Ballin*, pp. 27f.

[159] For example: Isaac Wolffson was elected President of the Hanseatic Lawyers' Chamber; Leo Lippmann and Max Warburg played leading roles in the Hamburg state's financial affairs; Paul Wallich was elected a member of the exclusive Hamburg Rowing Club; and Cäsar Wolf was a leading mason: Lorenz, *Die Juden in Hamburg*, p. cxxxvi; Lippmann, *Leben*; Warburg, *Aufzeichnungen*; W.E. Mosse, *The German-Jewish Economic Elite 1920–1935. A Socio-Cultural Profile* (Oxford, 1989), p. 152; *1737–1987. Ein Vierteljahrtausend Freimaurer in Hamburg. Aus dem Leben und Wirken der ältesten deutschen Loge. 'Absalom zu den drei Nesseln' Nr. 1, Hamburg* (Hamburg, 1987), pp. 83–8.

[160] On anti-Semitic riots in the 1830s, Evans, *Death in Hamburg*, pp. 392f.; on hostility to Jewish immigrants in transit from Eastern Europe, Wertheimer, *Unwelcome Strangers*, p. 14.

[161] Warburg-Spinelli, *Erinnerungen*, p. 446; Schramm, *Neun Generationen*, II, pp. 414, 451; Cecil, *Ballin*, p. 36. Cf. Schramm, *Hamburg, Deutschland und die Welt*, pp. 411–24; Baasch, *Geschichte Hamburgs*, II, pp. 106ff. From a large literature, see also J. Toury, *Soziale und politische Geschichte der Juden in Deutschland 1847–1871. Zwischen Revolution, Reaktion und Emanzipation* (Düsseldorf, 1977); D. Sorkin, *The Transformation of German Jewry, 1780–1840* (Oxford, 1987); W.E. Mosse (ed.), *Juden im wilhelminischen Deutschland 1890–1914* (Tübingen, 1976); S. Volkov, 'Jüdische Assimilation und jüdische Eigenart im Deutschen Kaiserreich. Ein Versuch', *G&G*, Jg. 9 (1983), pp. 331–48; idem, 'Die Verbürgerlichung der Juden in Deutschland. Eigenart und Paradigma', in Kocka (ed.), *Bürgertum im 19. Jahrhundert*, II, pp. 343–71.

Bildung – of formal education and private cultivation.[162] However, historians have tended to discount Hamburg as a stronghold of the *Bildungsbürgertum*; indeed, the city's cultural reputation in the nineteenth-century is for philistinism and materialism. Typically, one visitor commented in the 1840s, 'The relationship between art and business life in Hamburg is rather like the relationship between Roman law and Hamburg's own law: the former only applies where the latter does not exist, or is not contradicted by it' – a view echoed by an Intendant of the early nineteenth century theatre at the Gänsemarkt, who thought the Hamburg public the 'least cultured (*ungebildeteste*) I have ever encountered'.[163] The poet Heine, nephew of the Hamburg banker Salomon, fled the 'disgusting merchant's nest' in 1831, as did Brahms when he was passed over for the job of director of the city's concert hall; while the director of the Hamburg *Kunsthalle*, Alfred Lichtwark, despaired at the lack of patronage for the fine arts.[164] Such verdicts are perhaps slightly misleading. The late nineteenth century saw a rapid expansion of the system of formal education in the city. With the diminution of church control over education, the near monopoly of secondary education enjoyed by the sixteenth-century Johanneum grammar school[165] was ended, so that, by 1913, an additional two *Gymnasien* existed, as well as the *Realgymnasium* of the Johanneum (founded in 1837), five *Oberrealschulen* and seven *Realschulen*.[166] Altogether, there were twenty publicly constituted secondary schools before the war, with over 630 teachers and 11,200 pupils; while at the primary level, there were nearly 200 *Volksschulen* with around 3,500 teachers and 112,000 pupils.[167] There were also two lycées for girls, and around twenty private schools for Catholics, Jews and other minority groups.[168] In addition, although Senator Werner von Melle's proposal for a university was defeated in 1913, important steps had been taken at the level of higher education, with the revival of the traditional system of public lectures in 1895, the building of the first

---

[162] See J. Kocka (ed.), *Bildungsbürgertum im 19. Jahrhundert*, Bd. I: *Bildungsbürgertum und Professionalisierung in internationalen Vergleich* (Stuttgart, 1985); Bd. IV: *Politischer Einfluß und gesellschaftliche Formation* (Stuttgart, 1989); U. Engelhardt, '*Bildungsbürgertum'. Begriffs- und Dogmengeschichte eines Etiketts* (Stuttgart, 1986).

[163] Plagemann, *Industriekultur*, pp. 295f., 304.

[164] *Ibid.*, pp. 305, 312ff., 331.

[165] E. Kelter, *Hamburg und sein Johanneum im Wandel der Jahrhunderte 1529–1929. Ein Beitrag zur Geschichte unserer Vaterstadt* (Hamburg, 1928); D. Klemenz, *Die Religionsunterricht in Hamburg von der Kirchenordnung von 1529 bis zum staatlichen Unterrichtsgesetz von 1870* (Hamburg, 1970).

[166] P.-R. Schulz (ed.), *Wilhelm-Gymnasium Hamburg 1881–1981. Eine Dokumentation über 100 Jahre Wilhelm-Gymnasium* (Hamburg, 1981); Postel, 'Hamburg', p. 65.

[167] *Ibid.* Cf. H. Milberg, *Schulpolitik in der pluralistischen Gesellschaft. Die politischen und sozialen Aspekte der Schulreform in Hamburg, 1890–1935* (Hamburg, 1970).

[168] Postel, 'Hamburg', p. 65; Büttner, *Politische Gerechtigkeit*, p. 213.

lecture hall on Moorweide, and the establishment of the *Kolonialinstitut* in 1908.[169] The absence of a local university was, in any case, no obstacle to higher learning: Hamburg students, like most German students, wandered between the great universities.[170]

On the other hand, there is no mistaking the fundamental subordination of aesthetic values to material values which lay at the heart of Hamburg's bourgeois culture. Typically, most businessmen preferred to support vocational institutes, of which there were around thirty-seven, rather than a university – a not unreasonable preference given their own tradition of a 'practical' *Lehrzeit* working abroad.[171] Social status, in other words, rested on economic and occupational *Selbständigkeit*, rather than on classical education. Similarly, the rule of law – that most fundamental of bourgeois values – was defended with reference not to legal theory but to economic interest: 'The protection of the law cannot be withdrawn from [. . .] creditors,' declared the Senate in 1857, 'or we shall destroy [not only] confidence in [. . .] the law as the foundation of our state and our independence, [but also] our very existence as a commercial city'.[172] The maintenance of *Treu und Glauben* – equity and good faith – was imperative for a society which depended on the honouring of contracts and promissory notes.[173] These – along with work, parsimony and profit – were the fundamental values of bourgeois Hamburg; and they were not confined to the world of work. Historians have identified the voluntary association as a distinctively bourgeois institution in the nascent 'public sphere' of the late eighteenth and nineteenth century.[174] Characteristically, among the most numerous clubs in Hamburg were savings clubs.[175]

Of course, there were self-conscious efforts to create spheres of activity distinct from the economic. Businessmen ceased to live above their offices and affirmed the values of family life – dining in the

---

[169] Schramm, *Neun Generationen*, II, p. 442; J. Bolland, 'Die Gründung der "Hamburgsichen Universität" ', in *Universität Hamburg, 1919–1969* (Hamburg, 1969), pp. 21ff.

[170] Evans, *Death in Hamburg*, p. 7; Gombrich, *Aby Warburg*, pp. 25, 47.

[171] For some typical examples of business education, see Handelskammer Hamburg (ed.), *Repräsentanten der Hamburger Wirtschaft, 1850–1950* (Hamburg, 1984), pp. 110–12, 119f.; Warburg, *Aufzeichnungen*, pp. 8–13.

[172] Böhm, 'Wirtschaftskrise', p. 99.

[173] Cf. R. Tilly, 'Unternehmermoral und -verhalten im 19. Jahrhundert. Indizien deutscher Bürgerlichkeit', in Kocka, *Bürgertum im 19. Jahrhundert*, II, pp. 35–64.

[174] T. Nipperdey, 'Verein als soziale Struktur in Deutschland im späten 18. und frühen 19. Jahrhundert', in idem, *Gesellschaft, Kultur, Theorie* (Göttingen, 1976), pp. 174ff.; O. Dann (ed.), *Das Vereinswesen und bürgerliche Gesellschaft in Deutschland* (Munich, 1984); Blackbourn and Eley, *Peculiarities*, pp. 195f; J.R. Eidison, 'German Club Life as a Local Cultural System', *Comparative Studies in Society and History*, 32 (1990), pp. 357ff.

[175] H. Freudenthal, *Vereine in Hamburg, Ein Beitrag zur Geschichte und Volkskunde der Geselligkeit* (Hamburg, 1968), p. 519.

company of deferential wives, cowed children and a clutter of Biedermeier furniture.[176] This was *Sittlichkeit*; to be distinguished from the regulated brothels and the 'free markets [for the] product love' in the Altstadt, Neustadt and St Pauli areas.[177] The values of private friendship could also be distinguished from the values of business.[178] One could, like Max Schramm, pursue literature in the privacy of one's own library – a remarkable collection of 5,000 volumes, the annotated catalogue of which provides an invaluable insight into the *großbürgerlich* intellect.[179] More commonly, cultural interests were pursued in the institutionalised, sociable milieu of an association. The *Vereine* of the late eighteenth century tended to be concerned with questions of public welfare (notably the problem of poverty);[180] however, in the nineteenth century, associations proliferated which were principally concerned with leisure, including not only cultural pursuits but also sporting activities: the Philharmonic Society, the various choral societies, the Art Association, the Literary Society, as well as the Hamburg Racing Club, and a host of gymnastic, shooting and rowing clubs.[181] Certain sectors of the public sphere had attained sufficient popularity to rely on the market for their financial existence: this was true of the city's newspapers and its eight theatres.[182] But others, like the various chari-

[176] See the description of Max Schramm's domestic life in Schramm, *Neun Generationen*, II, pp. 436–9.

[177] Plagemann, *Industriekultur*, pp. 255–60, 267ff.; A. Urban, *Staat und Prostitution in Hamburg, 1807–1922* (Hamburg, 1927); M. Deutelmoser and B. Ebert, '"Leichte Mädchen", hohe Herren und energische Frauen', in Berlin (ed.), *Das andere Hamburg*, pp. 140ff.; R.J. Evans, 'Prostitution, State and Society in Imperial Germany', *P&P*, 70 (1976), pp. 106ff.

[178] See for example Ballin's friendship with Carl Fürstenberg, in which 'personal and business matters' were kept 'separate': Mosse, *German Jewish Elite*, p. 133.

[179] Schramm, *Neun Generationen*, pp. 445–53. In addition to revering Goethe, Schramm was an avid reader of Ranke, Treitschke and Meinecke. He admitted to finding Nietzsche's philosophy incomprehensible, thought Bebel's memoirs the work of a 'philistine', and was suspicious of Houston Stewart Chamberlain and Julius Langbehn.

[180] F. Kopitzsch, 'Aufklärung, freie Assoziation und Reform: Das Vereinswesen in Hamburg im 18. und frühen 19. Jahrhundert', in A. Herzig (ed.), *Das alte Hamburg (1500–1848/49). Vergleiche, Beziehungen* (Hamburg, 1989), pp. 209–34; idem, 'Die Hamburgische Gesellschaft zur Beförderung der Künste und nützlichen Gewerbe (Patriotische Gesellschaft von 1765) im Zeitalter der Aufklärung', in R. Vierhaus (ed.), *Deutsche patriotische und gemeinnützige Gesellschaften* (Munich, 1980), pp. 71ff.; O. Brenner, 'Die Patriotische Gesellschaft in Hamburg im Wandel von Staat und Gesellschaft', in *idem, Neue Wege der Verfassungs- und Sozialgeschichte* (Göttingen, 1968), pp. 335–44. Cf. F. Kopitzsch, *Grundzüge einer Sozialgeschichte der Aufklärung in Hamburg und Altona*, 2 vols. (Hamburg, 1982); Lindemann, *Patriots and Paupers*.

[181] Freudenthal, *Vereine*, pp. 71–287; Plagemann, *Industriekultur*, pp. 301–7, 312–14; A. Freytag, *Geschichte des Hamburger Rennclubs und seiner Rennen, 1927–1951* (Hamburg, 1952).

[182] Baasch, *Geschichte des Hamburgischen Zeitungswesens*; Plagemann, *Industriekultur*, pp. 296–300; Postel, 'Hamburg', p. 66.

table foundations in the city, relied on the rich to finance them. Between 1908 and 1913, over 15 m. marks were bequeathed in wills to secular charitable foundations – around 9 per cent of all the money left by the deceased.[183] The world of *Kultur*, in short, depended on the material world. Percy Schramm's eccentric great aunt Anna Jencquel could only indulge her fondness for Heine's poetry, billiards and Russian cigarettes with the aid of 300,000 marks inherited from her father.[184] And even Aby Warburg could only immerse himself in the minutiae of classical and Renaissance symbolism (and lay the foundations for his immense *kulturwissenschaftlich* library) with money from those 'fearful *Zinsmenschen*', his brothers.[185] To describe the city which produced Warburg or Lichtwark as philistine is too crude – though Warburg himself did so.[186] Liszt, Joachim and Clara Schumann performed there; Richard Strauss and Hans von Bülow conducted there. But the new concert hall on the Holstenplatz was paid for by the shipowner Carl Laiesz; and the Impressionist paintings that found their way to Hamburg were mainly collected by the banking family Behrens. Ultimately all values in Hamburg rested on money values.

The urban polity

The election of a Hamburg Senator was a picturesque affair. Having emerged as the successful candidate after three rounds of deliberation between Senate and Bürgerschaft, the new Senator was formally congratulated by the existing Senators, resplendent in their ruffs and gowns, followed by representatives of the city's principal associations, 'professors with Prussian stiffness, judges and councillors with ten-syllable titles, aunts and cousins, members of the citizens' associations, lawyers in droves, police chiefs and civil servants', and finally representatives of the clergy. Swearing-in came only after several days spent receiving these visitors, and was followed by a traditional breakfast of egg and chocolate in the *Rathaus*.[187] Such was the public aspect of the Free and Hanseatic State. The question which historians have posed is whether this combination of anachronistic dress and ritual accurately reflected the persistence of an 'old regime' in Hamburg, or whether it masked an altogether more 'modern' system of class rule. Was

---

[183] *Statistisches Handbuch 1920*, p. 251.
[184] Schramm, *Neun Generationen*, II, pp. 415f.
[185] Gombrich, *Aby Warburg*, pp. 40, 130f., 325f.
[186] In a satirical sketch entitled 'Hamburger Kunstgespräche', which mocked the conventional artistic tastes of his parents-in-law: Gombrich, *Aby Warburg*, p. 93.
[187] Schramm, *Neun Generationen*, II, pp. 433–6. Cf. Evans, *Death in Hamburg*, pp. 25, 99.

Hamburg's patrician oligarchy merely a facade behind which 'the power of mercantile, banking and industrial interests' exercised hegemony?[188]

Hamburg's system of urban government was the product of successive conflicts traceable back to the challenges posed in the fifteenth century by a rebellious citizenry (the *erbgesessene Bürger*) to the authority of the governing council (*Rat* or *Senat*), a body composed mainly of wealthy merchants.[189] From the 1520s, this conflict became entangled with the question of religion as the Senate sought to impose Lutheranism – and hence its own power – on a reluctant clergy.[190] It succeeded, and the Orthodox settlement of 1580 endured for almost a century before friction between Senate and citizenry precipitated a fresh political crisis, not resolved until the introduction of an imperially sponsored constitution of 1712. It was at this point that sovereignty was formally divided between an executive Senate, composed of equal proportions of lawyers and merchants, and a legislative Bürgerschaft, restricted to the owners of real estate and the holders of deaconal and other offices.[191] The subsequent history of urban government in Hamburg is in many ways the history of the redefinition of this second entity – of the qualifications, rights and responsibilities of a *Bürger*. In the 1720s and 1760s, Patriotic Societies asserted the need for a more active policy to alleviate the lot of the growing population of labouring poor, as well as for greater toleration of non-Lutherans.[192] However, in the wake of occupation by revolutionary France and post-Napoleonic restoration, bourgeois voluntary associations became more concerned with their own interests than with those of the poor, as Enlightenment paternalism gave way to *Vormärz* liberalism.[193] The Great Fire of 1842, the revolutionary events of 1848 and the economic crisis of 1857 enabled organisations representing various interests – the lawyers, the property owners, the Jews – as well as *Bürgervereine* representing particular localities gradually to expand their political influence, so that in 1860 the constitution was once again revised, formally separating the church

---

[188] Compare H. Holborn, *A History of Modern Germany 1840–1945*, vol. III (London, 1969), p. 19; E.K. Bramsted, *Aristocracy and the Middle Classes in Germany* (Chicago, 1964), p. 152; Blackbourn and Eley, *Peculiarities*, p. 235; Evans, *Death in Hamburg*, pp. 105, 528f., 546–9; R.A. Comfort, *Revolutionary Hamburg. Labor Politics in the Early Weimar Republic* (Stanford, 1966), p. 15.

[189] Postel, 'Hamburg', p. 72.

[190] Whaley, *Religious Toleration*, pp. 13, 23–8.

[191] *Ibid.*, pp. 12–20, 28–37. Cf. F. Kopitzsch, 'Hamburg zwischen Hauptrezess und Franzosenzeit', in W. Rausch (ed.), *Die Städte Mitteleuropas im 17. und 18. Jahrhundert* (Linz, 1981), pp. 181–210.

[192] *Ibid.*, pp. 38–43; Lindemann, *Patriots and Paupers*, passim.

[193] M. Lindemann, 'Unterschichten und Sozialpolitik in Hamburg, 1799–1814', in Herzig et al. (eds.), *Arbeiter in Hamburg*, pp. 61–70; B. Mehnke, *Armut und Elend in Hamburg. Eine Untersuchung über das öffentliche Armenwesen in der ersten Hälfte des 19. Jahrhunderts* (Hamburg, 1982).

and the state and giving office-holding notables and property owners fixed quotas of Bürgerschaft seats.[194]

The most striking feature of Hamburg's polity as it evolved was its corporative character: Hamburg was, in all but name, a *Ständesstaat* – despite the claim of one contemporary that there was 'only a single *Stand*, that of the *Bürger*'.[195] The most venerable collectivities, the religious communities, continued to play an important and distinct role in the organisation of education and welfare; but the majority of the city's political institutions more or less corresponded to identifiable socio-economic interests. Thus the Senate was dominated by an elite of interrelated patrician families like the Amsincks, the Sievekings, the Westphals and the Burchards.[196] The redefinition of the citizenship qualification after 1860 as a voluntary 30 mark tax had the effect of reducing the percentage of the population entitled to elect the Bürgerschaft from 18 per cent to 4 per cent in 1890,[197] so that the majority of deputies were businessmen, and the loose groupings within the assembly (the 'Rights', the 'Lefts' and the 'Left Centre') corresponded to social and occupational sub-groups of the bourgeoisie.[198] Most striking of all, the business community – the *Kaufmannschaft* – enjoyed its own privileged representation in the Chamber of Commerce, which had a substantial influence over economic and financial policy.[199]

If the period between 1840 and 1860 saw a successful bid for representation within the urban polity by such bourgeois groups, the next major challenge came with the rise of various organisations representing the city's manual workers. The traditional organisation of

[194] Evans, *Death in Hamburg*, pp. 41–7. On 1848 in Hamburg, see W. Schmidt, *Die Revolution von 1848–9 in Hamburg* (Hamburg, 1983); D. Langewiesche, '1848/49: Die Revolution in Hamburg – eine vergleichende Skizze', in Herzig (ed.), *Das alte Hamburg*, pp. 177–90. On political associations, A. Obst, *Geschichte der Hamburger Bürgervereine* (Hamburg, 1911); R. Hauschild-Thiessen, *150 Jahre Grundeigentümer Verein in Hamburg von 1832 e.V. Ein Beitrag zur Geschichte der Freien und Hansestadt Hamburg* (Hamburg, 1952). On the changes to the constitution, J. Bolland, *Die hamburgische Bürgerschaft in alter und neuer Zeit* (Hamburg, 1959); M. Asendorf, F. Kopitzsch, W. Steffani and W. Termin (eds.), *Geschichte der hamburger Bürgerschaft. 125 Jahre gewählter Parlament* (Berlin, 1984); F.-M. Wiegand, *Die Notabeln. Untersuchungen zur Geschichte des Wahlrechts und der gewählten Bürgerschaft in Hamburg 1859–1919* [*Beiträge zur Geschichte Hamburgs*, Bd. 30] (Hamburg, 1987).

[195] Quoted in Herzig, 'Einleitung', in *idem et al.* (eds.), *Arbeiter in Hamburg*, p. 11.

[196] Evans, *Death in Hamburg*, pp. 14–27.

[197] *Ibid.*, pp. 40f., 47f. A. Cord, 'Die soziale Schichtung der Hamburger Bürgerschaft von 1859 bis zum Jahre 1921. Ein Beitrag zur parlamentarischen Geschichte des Kaiserreichs' (Diss. Hamburg, 1961).

[198] Kutz-Bauer, *Arbeiterschaft*, pp. 17, 425; Evans, *Death in Hamburg*, pp. 44f.

[199] See E. Böhm, *Anwalt der Handels – und Gewerbefreiheit: Staat und Wirtschaft* [*Beiträge zur Geschichte der Handelskammer Hamburg*, Bd. 2] (Hamburg, 1981); E. Baasch, *Die Handelskammer zu Hamburg 1665–1915*, 3 vols. (Hamburg, 1915); Handelskammer Hamburg, *Dokumente zur Geschichte der Handelskammer Hamburg* (Hamburg, 1965).

labour had distinguished between guild members, apprentices and the underclass – the *Pöbel* – outside the guilds;[200] and roughly analogous divisions between the skilled and the unskilled persisted even after the guilds began to lose their dominant position. For instance, the organisations which emerged after 1840, notably the Hamburg Workers' Education Association, the Lassallean General German Workers' Association and the first labour unions (in the tobacco and textile industries) had their roots in the guild tradition and drew much of their political inspiration from 'bourgeois' liberal ideas.[201] However, there is no doubt that from around 1880, with the rapid expansion of employment in the harbour and of the city's industries, Hamburg entered a new era of industrial relations. The shallow organisational roots put down by union *Fachvereine* in the 1860s and 1870s flourished, with the combination of high labour demand, long and intense working hours, rising prices and housing shortages providing ideal conditions for labour organisation. In 1880, there were eight 'free' (i.e., socialist) trade unions in Hamburg, with 1,544 members; ten years later there were over eighty, with 40,000 members.[202]

Recent historians of late nineteenth-century Hamburg have tended to suggest that this challenge met with concerted resistance from a near-monolithic bourgeoisie, entrenched in the Senate, Bürgerschaft and Chamber of Commerce. The Senate has been portrayed in some accounts as little more than the executive arm of the Hamburg commercial community, dominated by 'the patriarchs of the business community'; the Bürgerschaft as a forum for 'the reconciliation (of) the interests of the different fractions of capital'; and the Chamber of Commerce as the representative of 'the most tightly knit and highly organised concentration of capital in Germany'.[203] Yet the idea of a

---

[200] S. Petersen, '"Hest ock dahl legt?" August 1791: Generalstreik in Hamburg', in Berlin (ed.), *Das andere Hamburg*, pp. 36–47; H. Herzig, 'Organisationsreform und Bewußtseinsprozesse Hamburger Handwerker und Arbeiter in der Zeit 1790–1848', in *idem et al.* (eds.), *Arbeiter in Hamburg*, pp. 95–108. Cf. H. Laufenberg, *Hamburg und sein Proletariat im achtzehnten Jahrhundert: Eine wirtschaftshistorische Vorstudie zur Geschichte der modernen Arbeiterbewegung im niederelbischen Städtegebiet* (Hamburg, 1910).

[201] J. Breuilly, 'Kontinuität in der hamburgischen Arbeiterbewegung von 1844 bis 1863?', in Herzig *et al.* (eds.), *Arbeiter in Hamburg*, pp. 139ff.; T. Offermann, 'Arbeiterbewegung, Bürgertum und Staat in Hamburg, 1850–1862/3', in *ibid.*, pp. 121ff. Cf. J. Breuilly and W. Sachse, *Joachim Friedrich Martens und die deutsche Arbeiterbewegung* (Göttingen, 1984).

[202] Kutz-Bauer, *Arbeiterschaft*, pp. 109, 131; K. Saul, 'Machtsicherung und Gegenoffensive. Zur Entstehung des Arbeitgeberverbandes Hamburg-Altona, 1888–1890', *ZVHG*, 72 (1986), pp. 107, 136f.; Cattaruzza, *Arbeiter und Unternehmer*, pp. 98–121. Cf. H. Laufenberg, *Geschichte der Arbeiterbewegung in Hamburg Altona und Umgegend*, 2 vols. (Hamburg 1911, 1931).

[203] See Comfort, *Revolutionary Hamburg*, p. 21; Evans, *Death in Hamburg*, pp. viii, 101f., 104f., 528f., 549; Lyth, '*Mittelstand*', pp. 60f., 66f.; Ullrich, 'Arbeiterbewegung', pp. 45f. There are, significantly, close parallels between this account and contempor-

united bourgeois front against socialism is misleading. In fact, the rise of working-class organisations had the contrary effect of exposing divisions of economic interest and ideology within the *Bürgertum*, and gave rise to new 'corporatist' or 'collectivist' institutions which lay outside the framework of the traditional 'corporative' polity.

In this process, a decisive role was played by the ship-builder Hermann Blohm. Convinced that 'Social Democracy' (shorthand for the labour movement as a whole) could only be 'countered effectively by keeping the Social Democrats on short rations and firing anyone who is an active Social Democrat',[204] Blohm set out to organise Hamburg's employers into combative, anti-labour associations. The Association of the Iron Industry, established by Blohm in 1888 to counter strike action by the various metal-workers' organisations, set the organisational pace, using lockouts, strike-breaking tactics, blacklists and a politicised labour exchange to undermine the position of the labour organisations.[205] The results were impressive, and Blohm capitalised on his successes by establishing, in March 1890, the United Association of German Metal Industrialists and the Hamburg-Altona Employers' Association (AVHA), the first action of which was to match the Social Democrats' May Day strike with a general lockout.[206] The employers' victory was crushing: within months, the major unions had lost over half their members; by 1895, further depleted by the cholera epidemic, total membership had plummeted to just over 11,000.[207] In the aftermath, the employers were able to expand their activities to include the organisation of 'yellow unions' and the imposition of more rigid work discipline, as well as to expand their membership. In 1890, around 50,000 employees were within the ambit of the AVHA; by 1913, over 8,300 companies and 129,000 employees.[208]

The 'Hamburg model' of industrial relations was unusual in that firms sought to combat unionisation by concerted and often confrontational action. As one employers' spokesman put it, relations between

---

ary Social Democrat rhetoric: the SPD press also tended to lump together 'the patrician clique that rules Hamburg', 'the shop-keeper interest', 'the ship-owners, the coffee kings, the traders, the brokers (and) the speculators': Evans, *Death in Hamburg*, p. 389.

[204] K. Saul, ' "Verteidigung der bürgerlichen Ordnung" oder Ausgleich der Interessen? Arbeitgeberpolitik in Hamburg-Altona 1896 bis 1914', in Herzig *et al.* (eds.), *Arbeiter in Hamburg*, p. 264.

[205] Cattaruzza, *Arbeiter und Unternehmer*, p. 128; Saul, 'Arbeitgeberverbandes', pp. 108f.

[206] *Ibid.*, pp. 105f., 126f.; Saul, 'Verteidigung', p. 264; Cattaruzza, *Arbeiter und Unternehmer*, pp. 142f.; W.D. Hund, 'Der 1. Mai 1890', in Berlin, *Das andere Hamburg*, p. 119.

[207] Hund, '1. Mai', pp. 119–25; Saul, 'Arbeitgeberverbandes', pp. 107, 136f.

[208] *Ibid.*, p. 129; Saul, 'Verteidigung', pp. 261, 264–8; Cattaruzza, *Arbeiter und Unternehmer*, pp. 164, 172ff.; M. Cattaruzza, 'Das "Hamburgische Modelle" der Beziehung zwischen Arbeit und Kapital. Organisationsprozesse unf Konfliktverhalten auf den Werften 1890–1914', in Herzig *et al.* (eds.), *Arbeiter in Hamburg*, p. 249.

capital and labour in Hamburg were like relations 'between the governments of two warring nations', and the object of Blohm and his
associates was to involve as many employers as possible, large and
small, in the struggle.[209] However, attempts to export the Hamburg
model to other parts of Germany had only limited success. In part,
this was because confrontational tactics seemed less appropriate in the
more concentrated heavy industrial sector, where firms were able to
impose effective in-house bans on unionisation, and where paternalistic
company welfare schemes could be introduced.[210] In addition, the
Hamburg model revealed its own limitations in practice. If the objective
had been to roll back unionisation, it failed. In 1891, there were
around 21,500 trade union members in Hamburg; in 1900, 37,500;
and in 1913, 142,800 – 42 per cent of the city's working population,
with the proportion rising above 70 per cent in Blohm's own industry
and in the docks.[211] Moreover, the creation of a national General
Commission in Hamburg itself and the emergence of large, sectoral
unions like the Metal Workers' Union and the Transport Workers'
Union marked significant advances in union organisation.[212] Employers
in sectors other than the iron industry found themselves unable to
resist trade union pressure to run the labour exchanges on a joint
(paritätisch) basis; while the 'yellow unions' were neither large enough
nor reliable enough to be counted as a success.[213]

Above all, the Hamburg model had the disadvantage that it antagonised the state authorities. The Senate had been willing to provide the
AVHA with police support for its first May Day lockout; but it grew
increasingly concerned about the potential consequences for public
order of the employers' confrontational approach, turning down
requests by the employers for official bans on the May Day holiday
and on picketing.[214] An important turning point came with the dockers'
strike of November 1896. Initially, the Senate had been willing to
support the shipping lines against the strikers; but as the dispute

---

[209] Saul, 'Verteidigung', pp. 271, 277.

[210] G. Eley, 'Capitalism and the Wilhelmine State: Industrial Growth and Political
Backwardness, 1890–1918', *HJ*, 21 (1978), pp. 737–50.

[211] J. Schult, *Geschichte der Hamburger Arbeiter, 1890–1919* (Hamburg, 1967), pp. 106–
7, 135; Hund, '1. Mai', p. 131; Cattaruzza, *Arbeiter und Unternehmer*, p. 157; idem,
'Hamburgische Modelle', p. 248.

[212] K. Tenfelde, 'Der Durchbruch der Freien Gewerkschaften Deutschlands zur Massenbewegung im letzten Viertel des 19. Jahrhunderts', in G.A. Ritter (ed.), *Arbeiterbewegung, Parteien und Parlamentarismus* (Göttingen, 1976), pp. 55–101; K. Schönhoven,
*Expansion und Konzentration. Studien zur Entwicklung der Freien Gewerkschaften im
wilhelminischen Deutschland, 1890–1914* (Stuttgart, 1980); H.J. Varain, *Freie Gewerkschaften, Sozialdemokratie und Staat. Die Politik der Generalkommission unter der
Führung Carl Legiens, 1890–1920* (Düsseldorf, 1956).

[213] Saul, 'Verteidigung', pp. 268ff., 278f; Cattaruzza, *Arbeiter und Unternehmer*, p. 220.

[214] Ibid., pp. 274, 280.

escalated into a full-scale general strike involving 16,500 workers, paralysing the city's commerce and culminating in two days of rioting in the inner city, a rift opened between the AVHA, which hoped to deliver 'an annihilating blow to Social Democracy', and the authorities, who sought to mediate between the two sides.[215] These attempts at mediation prefigured a phase of less confrontational industrial relations in Hamburg. Although the strike ended after nearly three months with a victory for the employers and prosecutions of some 500 strikers, a Senatorial Enquiry into conditions in the docks led to a number of concessions to the workforce, and opened the way to regulated collective bargaining on the waterfront.[216] Further indications of a shift from confrontation to collectivism came in the wake of the inconclusive shipyard strike of 1900 and the dock lockout of 1906. In 1907, collective negotiations took place for the first time between the Metal Workers' Union and the United Association of Metal Industrialists, leading to a reduction in the working week from sixty to fifty-six hours; and a major strike in 1910 ended in compromise, despite an attempt by Blohm to revive the lockout weapon.[217] Nevertheless, it would be wrong to interpret these as an irreversible shift towards the 'corporatism' associated with the early Weimar Republic and with more recent German labour history. There were limits to the discipline which the increasingly centralised trade union organisation could impose on such a mobile and volatile workforce; and grassroots disenchantment with the General Commission's consensual policy came to a head in July 1913, when 14,000 shipyard workers went on strike in defiance of the Metal Workers' Union leadership.[218] Of 799 wage disputes recorded between 1910 and 1913, no fewer than 212 led to strikes, involving over 50,000 employees.[219] It was confrontation, not corporatism, which secured the reductions in working hours and increases in nominal

---

[215] H.-J. Bieber, 'Die Hamburger Hafenarbeiterstreik 1896/1897', in Herzig et al. (eds.), *Arbeiter in Hamburg*, pp. 229–45; *idem*, 'Der Streik der Hamburger Hafenarbeiter 1896/1897 und die Haltung des Senats', *ZVHG*, 64 (1978), pp. 91–148; M. Grüttner, 'Mobilität und Konfliktverhalten. Der Hamburger Hafenarbeiterstreik 1896/7', in K. Tenfelde and H. Volkmann (eds.), *Streik* (Munich, 1984), pp. 143–61. Cf. C. Legien, *Der Streik der Hafenarbeiter und Seeleute in Hamburg Altona* (Hamburg, 1897).

[216] Rieber, 'Streik der Hamburger Hafenarbeiter', pp. 146ff.

[217] Cattaruzza, *Arbeiter und Unternehmer*, pp. 183–207; Cattaruzza, 'Hamburgische Modelle', pp. 250ff.; Saul 'Verteidigung', pp. 270–7.

[218] R. Neuhaus, 'Zum Arbeitskampferfolg der Gewerkschaften vor dem Ersten Weltkrieg. Streik und Aussperrung auf den Werften 1910', *Internationale wissenschaftliche Korrespondenz zur Geschichte der deutschen Arbeiterbewegung*, 20 (1984), pp. 498–508; Cattaruzza, *Arbeiter und Unternehmer*, pp. 219f.; Cattaruzza, 'Hamburgische Modelle', pp. 254ff.; Saul, 'Verteidigung', p. 278.

[219] Ullrich, 'Arbeiterbewegung', p. 43.

wages which were the labour movement's main achievements in pre-war Hamburg.[220]

The Senate's attempts to adopt a neutral stance in industrial disputes in part reflected the conflicts of interest within the Hamburg bourgeoisie which the labour question exposed. Even within the business community, the enthusiasm of the big industrial employers like Blohm for confrontation was not universally shared, and differences were magnified by the structure of the Chamber of Commerce, which gave greater influence to merchant houses than to industrial firms. In 1914, eighteen of its twenty-four members were in commerce; 4 were bankers; while there was only a single shipowner and a single industrialist.[221] Blohm managed to secure the creation of an Industrial Committee within the Chamber of Commerce in 1900; but he and Ballin clearly preferred to act through the newer sectoral and employers' associations established in the 1880s.[222] Nor was this shift away from the established organs of representation confined to the shipping industry. Around 200 merchant firms established a separate Hamburg Exporters' Association in 1903; and the pre-war decade witnessed a proliferation of similar associations, such as the East Asian Association, concerned less with labour relations than with trade policy.[223] Similarly, although Blohm sought to include the thirty-three guilds in his employers' organisation, the policy towards labour advocated by the artisans' Crafts Chamber (*Gewerbekammer*) differed in a number of respects from that favoured by the ship-builders, not least because the bakers and brewers had to contend with consumer boycotts as well as strikes.[224] Nor was the association representing the city's property owners always in accord with the representatives of 'mobile capital': typically, the residents of Eimsbüttlerstrasse objected when the employers' labour exchange was moved there, because of the detrimental effect of queues

---

[220] *Ibid.*, pp. 34–7, 40–4.
[221] *Handelskammer Jahresbericht 1914*, pp. 6f.; Saul, 'Verteidigung', pp. 264ff.
[222] Cecil, *Ballin*, pp. 38f.
[223] Cf. G. Jantzen, *Hamburgs Ausfuhrhandel im XX. Jahrhundert. Ein Beitrag zur Geschichte eines deutschen Kaufmannstandes und des Vereins Hamburger Exporteure, 1903–1953* (Hamburg, 1953); E. Schwenck, *25 Jahre Verein Hamburger Exporteure* (Hamburg, 1928); E. Maack, *Reeder, Schiffe und ein Verband. Zentralverein Deutscher Rheder* (Hamburg, 1957); *Ostasiatischer Verein Hamburg-Bremen zum 60-jährigen Bestehen 1900–60* (Hamburg, 1960).
[224] Lyth, *'Mittelstand'*, pp. 266f., 273, 278, 288f., 317f.; Saul, 'Arbeitgeberverbandes', p. 118; idem, 'Verteidigung', p. 273. Cf. *Denkschrift zum 60jährigen Stiftungsfest des Hamburger Gewerbe-Vereins von 1867* (Hamburg, 1927); S. Volkov, *The Rise of Popular Anti-Modernism in Germany. The Urban Master Artisans, 1873–1896* (Princeton, 1978); H.-G. Haupt, *Die radikale Mitte. Lebensweise und Politik von Handwerkern und Kleinhändlern in Deutschland seit 1848* (Munich, 1985).

of unemployed workers on property values.[225] While industrialists were mainly preoccupied with the growth of the trade unions, other bourgeois groups had different concerns – for example, the emergence of the cooperative or consumers' movement, the second of organised labour's three 'pillars' in Hamburg. Its flagship, the Consumption, Building and Saving Society 'Produktion' was established in 1899 to provide cheap housing and food on a cooperative basis, and, having accumulated around 70,000 members, seventy-three shops and an annual turnover of 21 m. marks by 1913, was viewed with considerable hostility by Hamburg's shopkeepers.[226] On the other hand, the Chamber set up to represent the shopkeepers' interests in 1904 was equally hostile to capitalist department stores.[227] Like the white-collar employees who formed themselves into union-like (but anti-socialist) associations – notably the Association of Commercial Clerks and the German National Commercial Employees' Association – the shopkeepers saw themselves as part of a *Mittelstand* which was aligned with neither capital nor labour.[228]

The fissiparity of the bourgeoisie is underlined by the differing responses elicited by the rise of the third and most political of the labour organisations, the Social Democratic Party. Bebel's birthplace was, in his words, 'the capital city of German socialism': a centre of the early workers' education movement and of Lassalle's socialism, it became the SPD's main base in the period of the Anti-Socialist Law, and returned Social Democrats to represent one after another of its three Reichstag

[225] Cattaruzza, *Arbeiter und Unternehmer*, p. 141. Cf. Hauschild-Thiessen, *150 Jahre Grundeigentümer*.

[226] W. Ahrens, 'Die sozialistische Genossenschaftswesen in Hamburg 1890–1914. Ein Beitrag zur Sozialgeschichte der Arbeiterbewegung' (Diss. Hamburg, 1970); J. Rieger, M. Mendel and W. Postelt, *Die Hamburger Konsumgenossenschaft 'Produktion'* (Hamburg, 1949); *60 Jahre Grosseinkaufs-Gesellschaft Deutscher Konsumgenossenschaft mit beschränkter Haftung Hamburg* (Hamburg, 1954). Cf. E. Hasselmann, *Geschichte der deutschen Konsumgenossenschaften* (Frankfurt am Main, 1971); A. Weuster, *Theorie der Konsumgenossenschaftsentwicklung. Die deutschen Konsumgenossenschaften bis zum Ende der Weimarer Zeit* (Berlin, 1980).

[227] H.T. Götz, *Die Detaillistenkammer Hamburg, 1904–1929* (Hamburg, 1929). Cf. Lyth, '*Mittelstand*', pp. 319f., 337. Cf. R. Gellately, *The Politics of Economic Despair: Shopkeepers and German Politics 1890–1914* (London/Beverly Hills, 1974).

[228] I. Hamel, *Völkischer Verband und nationale Gewerkschaft. Der Deutschnationale-Handlungsgehilfen Verband 1893–1933* (Frankfurt am Main, 1967). Cf. J. Kocka, 'White Collar Employees and Industrial Society in Imperial Germany', in G. Iggers (ed.), *The Social History of Politics* (Leamington Spa, 1985), pp. 113ff. See in general D. Blackbourn, 'The *Mittelstand* in German Society and Politics 1871–1914', *Social History*, 4 (1977), pp. 409–33; *idem*, 'Between Resignation and Volatility: the Petite Bourgeoisie in Nineteenth Century Germany', in G. Crossick and H.-G. Haupt (eds.), *Shopkeepers and Master Artisans in Nineteenth Century Europe* (London, 1984), pp. 35ff.

seats.[229] Not surpisingly, given these electoral successes, one of the Hamburg SPD's principal objectives was to reform the restricted franchise used in Bürgerschaft elections.[230] In 1896, this had been amended so that an annual minimum income qualification replaced the voluntary *Bürgerrecht* as the basis for elections to half the seats in the Assembly. However, the steady upward trend of nominal wages from the mid-1890s gradually undermined the exclusivity of the threshold, which had been set at just 1,200 marks. In 1894, 21 per cent of those qualified to vote in Reichstag elections could vote in Bürgerschaft polls; by 1904, however, the proportion had risen to 29 per cent, and in 1905 twelve SPD deputies were elected with 38 per cent of this 'general' vote.[231] Again, this creeping democratisation – an early indication that inflation could be the worker's friend – might have been expected to call forth a united response from the Hamburg *Bürgertum*; but, in practice, attempts still further to restrict the general franchise merely exposed new divisions.[232] To begin with, although the majority of the Hamburg SPD's 68,000 members were male workers, a significant number were drawn from the *Mittelstand* – clerical employees and artisans – as well as the bourgeois intelligentsia.[233] In addition, the Senate was divided over the franchise issue, with some Senators wishing to erode the privileged position of the property owners, who were guaranteed forty of the 152 seats,[234] and opposing the decision taken in 1906 to sub-divide the general franchise into two or three bands (along the lines of the Prussian three-class franchise).[235] As it happened, the 1906 'franchise robbery' – which entitled those earning more than 2,500 marks (around 28,000 voters) to elect twice as many deputies as those earning between 1,200 and 2,500 marks (around 49,000) – could not halt the Social Democratic advance. By 1913 there were 20 SPD deputies, and there had been a marked reduction in the number of deputies who were self-employed businessmen.[236]

Bourgeois divisions over the franchise issue were closely linked to the second challenge which the rise of Social Democracy posed to the traditional Hamburg polity. The SPD not only stood for more demo-

[229] Kutz-Bauer, *Arbeiterschaft*, p. 20.
[230] Comfort, *Revolutionary Hamburg*, p. 26.
[231] Evans, *Death in Hamburg*, pp. 542–6.
[232] See H.W. Eckardt, *Priviligien und Parlament. Auseinandersetzungen um das allgemeine und gleiche Wahlrecht in Hamburg* (Hamburg, 1980); R.J. Evans, ' "Red Wednesday" in Hamburg. Social Democrats, Police and Lumpenproletariat in the Suffrage Disturbances of January 17, 1906', *Social History*, 4 (1979), pp. 1–31.
[233] Schult, *Hamburger Arbeiter*, pp. 238–89; Comfort, *Revolutionary Hamburg*, p. 27; Bieber, 'Hafenarbeiterstreik', p. 96; Cattaruzza, *Arbeiter und Unternehmer*, p. 235.
[234] U. Büttner, 'Vereinigte Liberalen und Deutsche Demokraten in Hamburg, 1906–1930', *ZVHG*, 63 (1977), p. 6.
[235] Bolland, *Bürgerschaft*, pp. 67ff.
[236] Evans, *Death in Hamburg*, p. 549.

cratic political representation; it also envisaged an expanded role for the state, particularly in fields such as public health, education and welfare provision. This 'reformist' tendency was particularly strong in Hamburg. As Otto Stolten assured the Bürgerschaft, his party had no wish to 'turn the small state of Hamburg into a socialist state' (adding disarmingly: 'We Sozis aren't crackpots'); but it did wish to do away with the night-watchman state which bore the blame for the cholera epidemic.[237] To demonstrate its bona fides, the party put its extensive organisation at the service of the authorities during the epidemic, distributing leaflets and suspending public meetings. At a time when bourgeois interest groups, notably the property owners and the shipping lines, were being less than cooperative, this did not fail to impress the authorities. As Wilhelm Liebknecht noted: 'The Senate no longer regards the socialists as a gang of conspirators and revolutionaries with whom no dealings are possible, but rather as people who can be drawn into cooperation with it.'[238] Such cooperation was not put on a regular footing, it is true – not least because bourgeois observers rightly discerned a gap between the assurances of the 'respectable' SPD leadership and the conduct of the 'rougher' elements it attracted. Moreover, the policies adopted by the Senate to modernise the Hamburg state after the crises of the 1890s did not always accord with Social Democrat aspirations. The programme of slum clearance which 'decanted' 20,000 people from the inner city Alley Quarters to new working-class suburbs was a measure of 'social control' which enjoyed more support from waterfront employers, for example,[239] as was the 'Prussianisation' of the police force.[240] On the other hand, such measures were aimed at elements of the working class from which the SPD was anxious to distance itself; and other Senate policies – the expansion of educational and health provision, the efforts at impartial arbitration in the labour market, and the improvements in the city's public

[237] Bolland, *Bürgerschaft*, pp. 69f.
[238] Evans, *Death in Hamburg*, pp. 314–46, 368–76, 478–86. Cf. *idem*, 'Die Cholera und die Sozialdemokratie: Arbeiterbewegung, Bürgertum und Staat in Hamburg während der Krise von 1892', in Herzig *et al.* (eds.), *Arbeiter in Hamburg*, pp. 203–14.
[239] M. Grüttner, 'Soziale Hygiene und soziale Kontrolle. Die Sanierung der Hamburger Gängeviertel 1892–1936', in *ibid.*, pp. 359–72; Plagemann, *Industriekultur*, pp. 18f.
[240] A. Lessat, 'Vom "Corps der Nachtwache" zur modernen Schutzpolizei. Aus der 150jährigen Geschichte der Polizeibehörde', in *Hundertfünfzig Jahre Hamburger Polizei 1814–1964* (Hamburg, 1964); G. Stolz, 'Die Schutzpolizei in Altona und Wandsbek, 1869–1937', *ZVHG*, 63 (1977), pp. 35–68. Cf. R.J. Evans, *Kneipengespräche im Kaiserreich, Stimmungsberichte der Hamburger Politischen Polizei 1892–1914* (Hamburg, 1989); M. Grüttner, 'Unterklassenkriminalität in Hamburg. Güterberaubungen in Hamburger Hafen, 1888–1923', in H. Reif (ed.), *Volk und Obrigkeit* (Frankfurt am Main, 1984), pp. 153–84.

transport – could only be viewed as advances by the party.[241] It is also striking that the new expenditures necessitated by such policies were financed in a relatively progressive way. As the state's budget rose to around 230 m. marks in 1913 (of which around 22 per cent was spent on 'social' provision), the bulk of increased expenditure was financed by new direct taxation or by borrowing: nearly 60 per cent of total state revenue came from direct taxes in 1913, while the state debt rose from 481 m. marks in 1903 to 842 m. marks on the eve of the war.[242] These tendencies implied a degree of convergence between Social Democrat and bourgeois reformism as conceived within the expanding state bureaucracy, which by 1914 numbered close to 14,000.[243]

As in the economic sphere, bourgeois political responses to the growth of Social Democracy were far from unified. In the wake of the franchise 'robbery', left-liberal opponents of the measure established the United Liberals,[244] whose programme of state impartiality on labour issues, educational reform and increased welfare provision reflected the belief of Friedrich Naumann that workers could be wooed away from Social Democracy through 'positive' integration. The United Liberals were far from being radicals; it was conspicuous that the party held out against supporting female suffrage, for example, and favoured only a gradual shift to universal male suffrage.[245] However, to many businessmen, its conciliatory stance on Social Democracy was unpalatable, and the founding of the Hamburg League Against Social Democracy in 1907 confirmed the existence of an overtly confrontational bourgeois camp.[246] Above all, the rise of organisations like the Anti-Semitic Electoral Association and the German Social Reform Party in the 1890s underlined the absence of an anti-proletarian bourgeois front. The anti-Semites blamed 'the alien Jewish people' for the 'disintegration of the *Mittelstand*'; but located Jewish influence at the top of bourgeois

---

[241] Evans, *Death in Hamburg*, pp. 529ff.; Saul, 'Arbeitgeberverbandes', pp. 122, 133; J. Flemming, 'Wege zum sozialen Frieden? Anfänge staatlicher Arbeitsmarktpolitik in Hamburg', in Herzig *et al.* (eds.), *Arbeiter in Hamburg*, pp. 283–98.

[242] *Statistisches Handbuch 1920*, pp. 242f., 248ff.; *Statistisches Jahrbuch für das Deutsche Reich 1914*, pp. 356–60; Lippmann, *Leben*, pp. 169–77; J. Brandt, *Hamburgs Finanzen von 1914 bis 1924* (Hamburg, 1924), p. 15. Hamburg's finances differed from those of other German states, since in Hamburg state and communal functions were merged.

[243] Lyth, *Inflation*, p. 155. On the expansion and reform of the civil service see Evans, *Death in Hamburg*, p. 543.

[244] Büttner, 'Vereinigte Liberalen', pp. 1–34. Cf. E. Lüth and H.-D. Loose (eds.), *Bürgermeister Carl Petersen 1868–1933* (Hamburg, 1971).

[245] Büttner, 'Vereinigte Liberalen', p. 10; R.J. Evans, *The Feminist Movement in Germany, 1894–1933* (London, 1976), pp. 225f.

[246] Cf. G. Eley, *Reshaping the German Right. Radical Nationalism and Political Change After Bismarck* (New Haven/London, 1980), esp. pp. 229–35.

society – in the Senate, the Bürgerschaft and even at the Kaiser's court.[247] Leading figures in the movement included officials of the Hamburg-Altona Employers' Association and the German National Commercial Employees' Association; but some Social Democrats evidently saw it as a rival for working-class as well as petty-bourgeois votes.[248] To say the least, the temporary political success of the anti-Semites at the turn of the century exemplifies the limitations of a class-based analysis of Hamburg's urban politics.

From 1890 onwards, then, the traditional, corporative Hamburg polity came under increasing strain, primarily due to the development of working-class organisations in the city's new workplaces and residential areas. Far from putting up a united opposition to these organisations, the various different elements of the Hamburg bourgeoisie responded in often contradictory and conflicting ways. The emergence of employers' associations, petty bourgeois 'defensive' organisations, a progressive left-liberal party, an anti-socialist conservatism and an anti-Semitic movement testified to the political fissiparity of the Hamburg bourgeoisie, and intimated the obsolescence of the traditional institutions of urban government. Clearly, Martin Haller's huge *Rathaus* building, erected next door to the Chamber of Commerce and bourse between 1886 and 1897 to house the Senate and Bürgerschaft, was intended to impress upon the world the vitality and integrity of the old system; but, like so much self-consciously historicist public architecture of the period, it was at least in part the product of a sense of insecurity.[249] By 1914, other 'stones of Hamburg' had come to acquire at least comparable significance. The buildings erected (on the Viennese model) to house the financial, postal and judicial administrations on the 'Ring' between the Dammtor and Holstentor symbolised the growing importance of the state bureaucracy.[250] The huge neo-classical Hapag building on the banks of the inner Alster and the Florentine M.M. Warburg office behind it in the Ferdinandstraße were powerful representations of commercial and financial power; just as the mighty cranes of the Blohm and Voß yard at Steinwerder or the smokestacks of Menck and Hambrock in Ottensen

---

[247] K.-G. Riquarts, 'Der Anti-Semitismus als politische Partei in Schleswig-Holstein und Hamburg 1871–1914' (Diss. Kiel, 1975), pp. 357–75; Evans, *Death in Hamburg*, p. 390; Cecil, *Ballin*, pp. 131f.; Büttner, *Politische Gerechtigkeit*, pp. 124f. Cf. P.W. Massing, *Rehearsal for Destruction* (New York, 1949); P.G.J. Pulzer, *The Rise of Political Anti-Semitism in Germany and Austria* (London, 1988); R.S. Levy, *The Downfall of the Anti-Semitic Parties in Imperial Germany* (New Haven, 1975).

[248] Saul, 'Arbeitgeberverbandes', p. 129; D. Blackbourn, 'The Politics of Demagogy', *P&P*, 113 (1986), pp. 152–84; Evans, *Death in Hamburg*, pp. 554f.

[249] Plagemann, 'Industriekultur', pp. 32ff.

[250] *Ibid.*, pp. 174f.; C.E. Schorske, *Fin-de-siècle Vienna. Politics and Culture* (Cambridge, 1981), pp. 24–115.

embodied that of Hamburg's industry. Finally, the imposing *Gewerk-schaftshaus* in Besenbinderhof and the offices of the Consumers' Associ-ation next door to it testified to the pretensions of organised labour to be accorded comparable status. These edifices were evidence less of class division than of the emergence of a new class of bureaucrats – civil servants, managers and labour functionaries – claiming to act on behalf of government, capital-owners and labour, but increasingly pursuing their own administrative objectives.

Cosmopolitan bourgeoisie and nation state

The process of bureaucratisation described above has been seen by one recent historian as symptomatic of a more general 'Prussianisation' of Hanseatic political life after the turn of the century.[251] Underlying this interpretation is the idea that prior to 1867, when the 'free city' reluctantly joined the North German Confederation, Hamburg had been more English than German: cosmopolitan in culture, liberal in economics and politics and amateurish in its administration.[252] These traditions persisted in the first decade of Hamburg's membership of the Reich, taking the form of a particularism which gave the city-state authorities the reputation of being 'the worst Germans we have'.[253] However, the rise of Social Democracy in the 1880s led, it is argued, to a 'mental transformation' within the Hamburg ruling class; and by the turn of the century 'the success of the protective tariff and the colonial policies and the enthusiasm sparked by the fleet' had 'cast a pall of social opprobrium on the old [. . .] bourgeois [. . .] traditions, which had been associated with the free trade opposition'.[254] The concept of 'Prussianisation' thus brings Hamburg, in spite of its historic peculiarities, under the umbrella of that influential historical school which identifies, as the root of Germany's failure to 'establish [. . .] a democratic order', the political 'capitulation' of the German bourgeoisie before the absolutist, militarist Prussian state, with its dominant agrar-

[251] Evans, *Death in Hamburg*, pp. viii, 88f., 106, 562f.
[252] See, e.g., Craig, *The Germans*, p. 23.
[253] Quoted in Stern, *Gold and Iron*, p. 399. Cf. H. Böhme, *Frankfurt und Hamburg. Des Deutschen Reiches Silber- und Goldloch und die allerenglischste Stadt des Kontinents* (Frankfurt, 1968).
[254] Kutz-Bauer, *Arbeiterschaft*, pp. 423, 428f.; E. Kehr, 'The Genesis of the Prussian Reserve Officer', in *idem*, *Economic Interest, Militarism and Foreign Policy in German History* (Berkeley, 1977), p. 106. Cf. *idem*, *Schlachtflottenbau und Parteipolitik 1894–1901* (Berlin, 1930), pp. 236–45; *idem*, 'Soziale und finanzielle Grundlagen der Tirpitzschen Flottenpropaganda', in H.-U. Wehler (ed.), *Der Primat der Innenpolitik* (Berlin, 1965), pp. 134–9.

ian ruling elite.[255] It was hostility to socialism and susceptibility to the benefits of imperialism which lured the once-liberal Hamburg bourgeoisie down the 'special path' leading ultimately to the 'catastrophe' of National Socialism.[256] This general interpretative framework has been widely criticised in recent years, as historians have looked more closely at the social history and culture of the German bourgeoisie, and at the political history of the pre-1914 Reich.[257] The specific case of Hamburg too requires reappraisal. There is no doubt that the attitude of Hamburg's bourgeoisie towards the idea of German unity and the practice of Prussian political leadership in Germany altered significantly between 1840 and 1900. In the 1840s, nationalists like Wilhelm Hocker and Heinrich Schacht were a politically radical minority; in the 1860s, the Prussian envoy was forced to protest about an anti-Prussian play at the Carl-Schultze Theatre which satirised 'Wilhelm König and Fritz Fischmarkt'; while in 1870 Julius von Eckardt was struck by the universal particularism of the older generation 'who had glimpsed the light of the world between the Alster and the Elbe'.[258] On the other hand, the enormous success of the 1859 Schiller Festival (despite the restrictions imposed by the Senate and Church) testified to the growth of national feeling in Hamburg; while the celebrations which followed the Prussian military victory of 1870/1 marked the shift to a specifically *kleindeutsch* enthusiasm.[259] It would be wrong, however, to portray German nationalism and particularism as mutually exclusive: as elsewhere in Germany, there was a studied effort to marry the political culture of state and empire, whether by singing 'Hamburgs Wohlergehen' after 'Deutschland über alles', or by placing the allegorical figure of 'Hammonia' ahead of 'Germania' in the elaborate parades

---

[255] R. Dahrendorf, *Society and Democracy in Germany* (New York, 1967), pp. 14f. For the classic formulation of this view see H.-U. Wehler, *The German Empire 1871–1918* (Leamington Spa, 1985), *passim*.

[256] Cf. B. Faulenbach, ' "Deutscher Sonderweg." Zur Geschichte und Problematik einer zentralen Kategorie des deutschen geschichtlichen Bewußtseins', *Aus Politik und Zeitgeschichte*, 33 (1981), pp. 3ff.; H. Grebing, *Der 'deutsche Sonderweg' in Europa 1806–1945. Eine Kritik* (Stuttgart, 1986); J. Kocka, 'German History before Hitler. The Debate about the German "Sonderweg" ', *JCH*, 23 (1988), pp. 3–16.

[257] T. Nipperdey, 'Wehlers *Kaiserreich*. Eine kritische Auseinandersetzung', *G&G*, 1 (1975), pp. 539ff.; R.G. Moeller, 'The Kaiserreich Recast? Continuity and Change in Modern German Historiography', *Journal of Social History*, 17 (1984), pp. 655–83; V. Berghahn, 'Der Bericht der Preußischen Oberrechnungskammer. Wehlers *Kaisserreich* und seine Kritiker', *G&G*, 2 (1976), pp. 125ff.

[258] Plagemann, *Industriekultur*, pp. 296, 298f., 305, 315; Schramm, *Neun Generationen*, II, pp. 308, 314. Cf. Evans, *Death in Hamburg*, pp. 4ff.

[259] Plagemann, *Industriekultur*, pp. 287ff.; Schramm, *Neun Generationen*, II, pp. 305ff. On subsequent celebrations of Sedan Day at the Johanneum school, see *ibid.*, p. 480.

organised by Veterans', Gymnasts' and other associations in the 1880s
and 1890s.[260] It is true that Kaiser Wilhelm II's maritime enthusiasms
brought him into contact with many leading Hamburg figures, above
all Albert Ballin; that a number of Hamburg families were ennobled
or married into the aristocracy; and that the 'cult' of Bismarck which
sprang up after his dismissal was especially strong in Hamburg.[261] But
to regard this as evidence of 'feudalisation' or 'Prussianisation' is
misleading:[262] a sense of loyalty to Kaiser and Reich was in no way
incompatible with the traditional cosmopolitanism of the Hamburg
bourgeoisie. Max Warburg's banking apprenticeship in Paris and
London; his brothers' emigration to New York; and the family's marital
links to families in the United States, England, Sweden and Russia –
none of this struck the second son as incompatible with a strong sense
of German patriotism.[263] As a child, Percy Schramm wore English
clothes and read 'Humpty Dumpty', but was hardly unmoved by the
uniformed parades with which his school marked Sedan Day and the
Kaiser's birthday.[264] His uncle Ernst lived in Brazil for thirty years,
but made a point of visiting the battlefields of Alsace-Lorraine in 1871,
and was exhilarated by the sight of a German naval vessel in San
Francisco (and a performance of *Tannhäuser* in New York) the following
year.[265]

It is not difficult to see why this reconciliation of particularism,
nationalism and cosmopolitanism was so easily achieved before 1914
when one examines the institutional structures of the Kaiserreich.
From a political standpoint, Hamburg gained much and lost little by
acceding to the North German Confederation in 1867 and the Reich
in 1871. Repeated occupations during the Napoleonic Wars, followed

---

[260] G. Jaacks, *Festzüge in Hamburg 1696–1913. Bürgerliche Selbtsdarstellung und Geschichtsbewußtsein* (Hamburg, 1972); and *idem*, 'Hermann, Barbarossa, Germania und Hammonia. Nationalsymbole in Hamburger Festzügen des Kaiserreichs', in *Beiträge zur
deutschen Volks- und Altertumskunde*, 18 (1979), pp. 57–66. Cf. C. Applegate, 'Localism and the German Bourgeoisie: the "Heimat" Movement in the Rhenish Palatinate
before 1914', in Blackbourn and Evans (eds.), *The German Bourgeoisie*, pp. 224–54.

[261] Cecil, *Ballin*, pp. 50, 98; Mosse, *German-Jewish Economic Elite*, p. 197; Vagts,
'M.M. Warburg & Co.', pp. 330f.; H. Tramer, 'Die Hamburger Kaiserjuden', in
Bulletin des Leo Baeck Instituts, 3 (1960), pp. 177–89; Schramm, *Neun Generationen*,
II, pp. 383, 385, 393, 478; Böhm, *Flottenbau*, pp. 18, 99f.; Stein, 'Interessenkon-
flikte', pp. 69f.; Evans, *Death in Hamburg*, p. 561.

[262] Simply because John Berenberg-Goßler was ennobled and fought a duel with Graf
Königsmarck in 1912 does not mean that he had ceased to be bourgeois: cf. M.S.
Coetzee, *The German Army League. Popular Nationalism in Wilhelmine Germany*
(Oxford, 1991), p. 94; U. Frevert, 'Bourgeois Honour: Middle-Class Duellists in
Germany from the Late Eighteenth to the Early Twentieth Century', in Evans and
Blackbourn (eds.), *German Bourgeoisie*, pp. 255–92.

[263] Warburg, *Aufzeichnungen*, esp. pp. 8–15.

[264] Schramm, *Neun Generationen*, II, pp. 463, 480.

[265] *Ibid.*, p. 308.

by Prussian occupation in 1849 and Austrian occupation two years later – to say nothing of the fate of Frankfurt in 1866 – clearly demonstrated the vulnerability of a free city in a continent increasingly dominated by nation states. Accounting for just 0.8 per cent of the Reich's total territory, and around 1.2 per cent of its population, Hamburg clearly gained greatly in security, without having to make an especially onerous contribution to the Reich's military forces.[266] Although the representatives of the Senate in the constitutional negotiations between 1867 and 1871 were extremely hostile to Prussia's 'imperialism', the twenty-five member states of the Reich were initially pooling only a limited amount of their non-military powers, principally in the realm of foreign policy.[267] Of course, with just one representative in the Federal Council (*Bundesrat*), Hamburg had little chance of resisting further steps towards political centralisation; but the hostility of successive Prussian Ministries and of the large South German states to such steps meant that the threat to state prerogatives remained relatively limited before 1914. The Reich's bureaucracy remained small; the legal unification of Germany proved a protracted process; and the states retained control of policing, communications, education and other such 'social' functions, the importance of which was, as the case of Hamburg illustrates, to increase rapidly after around 1890. Certainly, there were occasions when the centre sought to impose its authority on the (still) 'Free and Hanseatic City', as over the 1878 Anti-Socialist Legislation, or when the Hamburg system of legalised brothels came under attack from the Left in the Reichstag after 1900.[268] But in other respects, it might be said, the Reich and the state tended to grow apart rather than together. The main reason for this was the difference between the Reichstag franchise and the restricted franchises operated in the various states, which had the effect (as Bismarck had intended) of reducing significantly the representation of the 'bourgeois' parties, particularly in urban electoral districts. National Liberalism triumphed in the 1870s as the party of professional and business elites;[269] but the

---

[266] Postel, *Hamburg*, pp. 61, 78; Hohorst *et al.* (eds.), *Sozialgeschichtliches Arbeitsbuch*, II, pp. 47, 167. The Prussian War Ministry consciously restricted the number of conscripts taken from urban areas: see most recently, S. Förster, *Der doppelte Militarismus: die deutsche Heeresrüstungspolitik zwischen Status-quo-Sicherung und Aggression, 1890–1913* (Stuttgart, 1985), pp. 91–143.

[267] H.G. Schönhoff, *Hamburg im Bundesrat. Die Mitwirkung Hamburgs an der Bildung des Reichswillens 1867–1890* (Hamburg, 1967), pp. 11ff., 29.

[268] J. Jensen, *Presse und politische Polizei. Hamburgs Zeitungen unter den Sozialistengesetz 1878–1890* (Hanover, 1966); I. Blatt, 'Die Stellung bürgerlicher Hamburger Zeitungen zur Einführung des Sozialistengesetzes', *ZVHG*, 73 (1987), pp. 61–96; Evans, *Feminist Movement*, pp. 17, 52.

[269] Böhm, *Flottenbau*, pp. 13ff. Of the twenty-one liberal Reichstag deputies from Hamburg before 1890, eleven were businessmen; see M. Schwarz, *MdR. Biographisches Handbuch des Reichstags* (Hanover, 1965).

combination of universal suffrage and increased electoral participation in the 1880s and 1890s 'dished' the notables, who failed or were unable to adapt to the conditions of mass politics. Not only were they gradually driven from the Reichstag by the SPD; Hamburg's businessmen found themselves under attack from anti-Semites, who branded Hamburg 'a modern Sodom and Gomorrah', from agrarians, who lambasted Hamburg's opposition to tariffs from the 'national' standpoint, and even from feminists, who condemned the power of 'economic interests' in politics.[270] The renunciations of party-political activity by Hamburg businessmen after 1900 can therefore be seen as typical expressions of a bourgeois 'apoliticism' which sought to rationalise electoral defeat by questioning the legitimacy of democratic institutions. Max von Schinckel's argument that 'party politics' required an unacceptable 'sacrifice of conviction' was a familiar Wilhelmine refrain; but the Lübeck-born civil servant Arnold Brecht was more candid:

Families from the upper strata who lived in North Germany [. . .] generally had little contact with politics, if we disregard occasional outbursts of patriotic feeling, hero-worship (Frederick the Great, Bismarck) and negative reactions to the opinions of other groups, considered 'political', in contrast to one's own 'objective' views [. . .] National Liberal[s] [. . .] enthused about free trade, a flourishing industry, a strong navy and colonies. Social Democrats were 'public enemies' and heads were wagged over 'ultramontane' Catholics. This way of thinking was natural. Whoever tended towards the Left or the Right – they were the politicians.[271]

When Albert Ballin insisted that he was 'too preoccupied with [his] business [. . .] for the conscientious exercise of a Reichstag mandate', he was not abandoning political activity altogether – merely indicating a redirection of his political energies into less hostile political environments: the diplomatic and journalistic circles which brought him into contact 'behind the scenes' with Chancellor Bülow and the Kaiser himself.[272]

As Brecht's and Ballin's comments suggest, it was above all economic issues – 'free trade, a flourishing industry, a strong navy and colonies' – which the Hanseatic bourgeoisie liked to think of as transcending

---

[270] Evans, *Death in Hamburg*, p. 390; idem, *Feminist Movement*, p. 76; Böhm, *Anwalt der Handelsfreiheit*, pp. 130–6.

[271] M. von Schinckel, *Lebenserinnerungen* (Hamburg, 1929); A. Brecht, *The Political Education of Arnold Brecht. An Autobiography 1884–1970* (Princeton, 1970), p. 3.

[272] Cecil, *Ballin*, pp. 114–18, 136, 141f. On the comparable retreat of bourgeois notables into local politics see J.J. Sheehan, 'Liberalism and the City in Nineteenth Century Germany', *P&P*, 51 (1971), pp. 116–37. Cf. Blackbourn and Eley, *Peculiarities*, pp. 241–51.

politics. If the political sacrifices involved in joining the Reich were minimal, then the economic benefits were substantial; and perhaps this more than anything explains the conversion of the Hamburg bourgeoisie to the national cause. The *tableaux* of 'The Elbe's Course' staged at the 1907 festival of the Association of German Engineers illustrate the contemporary view: from the turnips at the Elbe's source to the pottery of Meissen to the shipping lines and industry of Hamburg – all the Reich's economic forces were united in 'Germany's upward struggle'.[273] In fact, the initial phases of Hamburg's economic integration into the Reich – or, to be precise, into the Customs Union – were anything but harmonious. Following Bismarck's return to protectionism in 1878/9, the Prussian government set out to end the anomaly whereby Hamburg remained outside the *Zollverein* by threatening to incorporate Altona and St Pauli into the tariff area. However, tenacious negotiation by Johannes Versmann at the Bundesrat and an effective campaign by the elite group of businessmen who favoured creating a free port area resulted in a compromise which was highly favourable to Hamburg – not least because the Reich agreed to subsidise the construction of the free port area.[274] Hamburg business remained strongly opposed to the protectionist policies of the 1880s and early 1900s, where these impeded the import of grain and other goods through Hamburg; but the free port ensured that German tariffs did not disrupt Hamburg's transit trade.[275] Moreover, Bismarck's reluctant acceptance of German colonial expansion in the 1880s did much to reconcile the Hanseatic commercial community to Reich economic policy. Adolf Woermann, who had expressed profound mistrust of Bismarck during the Customs Union negotiations, was transformed into the 'royal merchant' when his and the Chancellor's views on colonisation in West Africa coincided; and Hamburg businessmen (notably William O'Swald and Justus Strandes) came to play an important role in the Colonial Society in the 1890s, a time when Hamburg's trade links with Africa and the Far East were expanding rapidly.[276]

[273] Freudenthal, *Vereine in Hamburg*, p. 542.

[274] E. Böhm, 'Wirtschaft und Politik in Hamburg zur Zeit der Reichsgründung', *ZVHG*, 64 (1978), pp. 31–54; Stein, 'Interessenkonflikte', pp. 55–90; O. Becker, 'Bismarcks Kampf um die Eingliederung der Hansestädte in die Zolleinheit', in A. v. Brandt and W. Koppe (eds.), *Städtwesen und Bürgertum als geschichtliche Kräfte* (Lübeck, 1953); C.M. Mueller, 'Die Auseinandersetzung über Hamburgs Zollanschluß an das Deutsche Reich 1833–1888. Hamburgs Entwicklung von einer Freihafenstadt zu einer Stadt mit Freihafen' (Diss., Freiburg, Switz., 1988); Baasch, *Geschichte Hamburgs*, II, pp. 188–219; A. Kludas, D. Maass and S. Sabisch, *Hafen Hamburg*, pp. 34f.

[275] E. Wiskemann, *Hamburg und die Welthandelspolitik von den Anfängen bis zur Gegenwart* (Hamburg, 1929), pp. 203–328; Böhm, *Anwalt der Handelsfreiheit*, pp. 109–35.

[276] G. Jantzen, 'Adolf Woermann. Ein politischer Kaufmann in den Wandlungen und Spannungen der imperialistischen Epoche des Reiches', in O. Brunner and D. Gerhard (eds.), *Europa und Übersee. Festschrift für Egmont Zechlin* (Hamburg, 1961),

It is, above all, the construction of a large German battleship fleet which is seen as having cemented Hamburg's economic and political links to Berlin. Historians have traditionally devoted more attention to the domestic-political functions which Tirpitz's naval programme was supposed to perform than to the economic benefits it brought to the ship-building industry. Kehr saw the 'conversion' of men like Ballin and Woermann to the naval cause as an important indication of their political reorientation to the Right; though it has been argued persuasively that, by emphasising the navy's importance for German commerce, Ballin and his associates were principally concerned to counter the influence of agrarian interest groups over trade policy.[277] What is certain is that the 1898–1913 naval programme marked the beginning of a singularly close relationship between the Reich government and the major German shipyards. Altogether eighty-six naval vessels were constructed in that period, of which sixty-three were built by a small group of private shipyards: Schichau, Vulkan, Germania, Howaldt (after 1908) and Blohm & Voß, the last of which all but monopolised the construction of large cruisers.[278] The significance of the navy for the German economy as a whole should certainly not be exaggerated: it absorbed little more than 1–2 per cent of total iron and steel production. But for the ship-building industry, naval orders could account for as much as 25 per cent of total output in a year of depressed private orders such as 1907; and between 1892 and 1914, over 20 per cent of Blohm & Voß's total output was for Tirpitz.[279] Inevitably, this led to increasingly intimate relations between the shipyards and the state. Although the yards were never able to achieve a level of cartelisation comparable with that in the iron and steel industry, the five big yards were still able to exert considerable leverage in negotiations with the Navy Office, individually or through the Association of German Seaship Yards.[280] The 1884 Post Service Subsidy Law, the discussions in 1901 about placing counter-cyclical naval orders, and the first interventions by the authorities in labour disputes

---

pp. 171–91; Washausen, *Kolonialpolitik*, pp. 55–179. Cf. A. Coppius, *Hamburgs Bedeutung auf dem Gebiete der deutschen Kolonialpolitik* (Berlin, 1905), pp. 127–76.

[277] Kehr, 'Social and Political Foundations', pp. 80–3; Böhm, *Flottenbau*, pp. 77–131.

[278] Leckebusch, *Beziehung*, pp. 61–72; Böhm, *Flottenbau*, pp. 146ff.; Cattaruzza, *Arbeiter und Unternehmer*, p. 22.

[279] Hentschel, *Wirtschaft und Wirtschaftspolitik*, pp. 153ff.; Cattaruzza, *Arbeiter und Unternehmer*, p. 26; GHH, 4001012012/0, Scholz Report (1924); Böhm, *Flottenbau*, p. 147.

[280] Leckebusch, *Beziehung*, pp. 53–83. Cf. Hentschel, *Wirtschaft und Wirtschaftspolitik*, pp. 99–118; G.D. Feldman, *Iron and Steel in the German Inflation, 1916–1923* (Princeton, 1977), pp. 27–50.

on the waterfront in 1910 were indications that relations between the Reich and the shipping industry could become closer still.[281]

A similar tendency can be seen in the relations between the Reich and those Hamburg banks which became involved in capital export before 1914. Contemporaries were aware of the international diplomatic leverage which could be gained through capital export. As Albert Ballin put it in April 1914, Britain and France 'subdue foreign states with their money, [and thus] they extend their political spheres of power'; sentiments expressed similarly by Chancellor Bülow in 1908.[282] But it was Max Warburg who was probably the most ardent proponent of *Weltpolitik* through capital export. From 1904, when he became involved in a major loan floated by the Japanese government to finance its war with Russia, Warburg became increasingly preoccupied with the politics of international finance: 'I did what any sound banker must do in such cases: I went straight to the Foreign Office in Berlin.'[283] Warburg's involvement in official attempts to assert German influence in China, Morocco and Portuguese Angola certainly entitled him to claim that 'no banking house in Germany has interested itself so determinedly for Germany's activity in the colonies than ours';[284] even if his efforts brought, in his own words, 'little return'.[285] Indeed, the events of 1911, when he became entangled in Kiderlen's ill-conceived attempt to challenge French predominance in Morocco, merely served to confirm the relative weakness of the German capital market compared with those of Britain and France: the withdrawal of French short-term deposits from Berlin caused a sharp fall on the stock market.[286]

The vulnerability of the German financial markets to such capital outflows exposed one of the major paradoxes of Germany's economic unification. Monetary unification was among the most enduring liberal achievements of the 1870s, and Hamburg had played an important

---

[281] Leckebusch, *Beziehung*, pp. 23, 52; Henderson, *German Industrial Power*, pp. 201f.; Cattaruzza, *Arbeiter und Unternehmer*, pp. 16, 45, 180–92, 204–7; V. Berghahn, *Der Tirpitz Plan* (Düsseldorf, 1970), pp. 139ff.; *idem*, *Germany and the Approach of War in 1914* (London, 1973), pp. 27f., 92f.

[282] F. Fischer, *War of Illusions. German Policies from 1911 to 1914* (London/New York, 1975), pp. 449f., 457; D.E. Kaiser, 'Germany and the Origins of the First World War', *JMH*, 55 (1983), p. 455.

[283] Warburg, *Aufzeichnungen*, p. 19.

[284] *Ibid.*, p. 24.

[285] For details, see Vagts, 'M.M. Warburg & Co.', pp. 318–29, 342–6, 378; Chernow, *Warburgs*, pp. 144–7.

[286] WA, 'Jahresbericht 1911'; R. Kroboth, *Die Finanzpolitik des Deutschen Reiches während der Reichskanzlerschaft Bethmann Hollwegs und die Geld- und Kapitalmarktverhältnisse (1909–1913/14)* (Frankfurt am Main, 1986), pp. 56f.

role in it. The mark-banco of the Hamburg Bank (founded in 1619
as a clearing centre for international transactions) was one of the mark's
direct antecedents.[287] As the legislation establishing a unitary system
of coinage and a central bank for the Reich was laboriously formulated
between 1870 and 1875, Hamburg experts like the Chamber of Commerce *Syndikus* Alfred Soetbeer and Max von Schinckel played an
influential role; and it was a sign of Hamburg's importance in the
monetary system that it was one of only five states to be represented
directly on the *Direktorium* of the Reichsbank.[288] The German monetary
system as it emerged in the 1870s represented a compromise between
centralisers and particularists, free traders and agrarians, bullionists
and bimetallists, banking school and currency school. Thus the Reichsbank Law of March 1875 defined the central bank's role as being 'to
regulate the money supply in the entire Reich area, to facilitate the
balancing of payments and to ensure the utilisation of the available
capital'.[289] In practice, however, the bank was denied the instruments
necessary to fulfil such a dirigiste role. In its international role, the
Reichsbank was essentially a passive channel through which the gold/
sterling standard functioned. Given the growth of the German trade
deficit, the dependence of the German economy on short-term foreign
credits and the predominance of London and Paris as financial centres,
the bank had only limited control over capital flows, as became evident
in crises such as that of 1907 or late 1911.[290] At the same time,
despite a double restriction on the circulation of paper money (a fixed
contingent of 250 m. marks, breaches of which were taxable, and a
one-third gold or gold-equivalent reserve ratio), the Reichsbank wielded
only minimal control over the domestic money supply, for two reasons.
Firstly, the growth of the 'great' joint stock banks – Deutsche Bank,
Disconto-Gesellschaft, Dresdner Bank, Darmstädter and Berliner Handelsgesellschaft – created immense reservoirs of credit which the
Reichsbank, in the absence of minimum reserve requirements or a

---

[287] Sieveking, 'Die Hamburger Bank 1619–1875', pp. 100–10.
[288] Böhm, 'Wirtschaft und Politik', p. 36; Rosenbaum and Sherman, *M.M. Warburg &
Co.*, pp. 72ff.; R. Zilch, *Die Reichsbank und die finanzielle Kriegsvorbereitungen von
1907 bis 1914* (Berlin, 1987), pp. 145–8.
[289] K. Borchardt, 'Währung und Wirtschaft', in Deutsche Bundesbank (ed.), *Währung
und Wirtschaft in Deutschland 1876–1975* (Frankfurt am Main, 1976), p. 17.
[290] A. Sommariva and G. Tullio, *German Macroeconomic History, 1880–1979. A Study
of the Effects of Economic Policy on Inflation, Currency Depreciation and Growth*
(London, 1987), pp. 83–120; K. Werling, 'Der Preis- und Einkommensmechanismus
der Goldwährung. Untersuchung am Beispiel Englands und Deutschlands zwischen
1880 und 1914' (Diss. Hamburg, 1962); M. Seeger, *Die Politik der Reichsbank von
1876–1914 im Lichte der Spielregeln der Goldwährung* (Berlin, 1968); W. Mosbacher,
'Reichsbank und Bank von England im Goldstandard vor 1914', *Bankhistorisches
Archiv*, 1 (1975).

significant level of short-term government borrowing at the Reichsbank, could not regulate. Secondly, the development of the direct debit or 'Giro' system of payments in Germany allowed *de facto* monetary growth which was not constrained by the note-issue restrictions.[291] This meant that, although currency in circulation in Germany grew at around 3.2 per cent annually between 1890 and 1914, total monetary growth as a result of increased bank mediation was much more rapid.[292] For Hamburg, these peculiar features of the German monetary system had three significant consequences. Firstly, because Hamburg was itself a net creditor on the short-term international capital account, crises of the sort which disrupted the Berlin money market in 1907 and 1911 were less acutely felt.[293] On the other hand, Berlin increasingly came to dominate the German money and capital markets: the proportion of business conducted at the Reichsbank branch in Hamburg compared with the central office in Berlin sank steadily; and increasingly the Hamburg joint stock banks moved the centre of their operations to Berlin.[294] Finally, monetary expansion (along with the rising level of tariffs on food imports) contributed to the inflation already mentioned above, albeit at the gentle annual rate of around 1 per cent after 1890. This did not go unnoticed. Contemporaries were in no doubt that there was a link between the rising cost-of-living and the increase of the SPD vote in the 1912 elections: as one commentator had noted in September 1911, 'Some people talk about Morocco; everyone talks about the rise in the cost of living.'[295] Although it was only after 1907 that the first steps were made to make low denomination notes available for ordinary transactions, it is clear that the era of monetary stability – of 'the hard [. . .] half-thaler [. . .] coated in the sweat of one and a half working days'[296] – was drawing to a close just twenty years after the Reichsbank's birth.

Similar ambiguities emerge when one turns to the Reich's financial system. To a state with a strong particularist streak such as Hamburg, Bismarck's decision 'to stick more to the confederation of states [model] while in practice giving [the North German Confederation] the character of a federal state' had much to recommend it.[297] A division of fiscal

---

[291] Hentschel, *Wirtschaft und Wirtschaftspolitik*, pp. 136–43; Zilch, *Die Reichsbank*, pp. 17–57; Borchardt, 'Währung und Wirtschaft', pp. 46f.

[292] Zilch, *Die Reichsbank*, p. 184.

[293] Cf. Kroboth, *Finanzpolitik*, pp. 62f. for Warburg's sanguine view of the situation in 1912.

[294] *Statistisches Handbuch 1920*, pp. 260f.; Kindleberger, *Financial History*, p. 127; Pohl, *Bankengeschichte*, pp. 96–101. The Norddeutsche Bank was in fact taken over by the Disconto-Gesellschaft in 1895.

[295] Fischer, *War of Illusions*, pp. 96f., 102.

[296] Cattaruzza, *Arbeiter und Unternehmer*, p. 167.

[297] Gall, *Bismarck. The White Revolutionary*, p. 317.

responsibility which confined the Reich to the revenues from taxes on salt, beer, tobacco, coffee and spirits left the budgets of the twenty-five states relatively intact; and the provisions of Article 70 of the Reich constitution specified that, if the Reich required more money, it would have to request 'matricular contributions' (i.e., assessed in proportion to population) from the states, or obtain new taxes from the Reichstag.[298] Not surprisingly, the Hamburg government opposed all Bismarck's subsequent attempts to free the Reich from 'begging for contributions at the doors of the individual states'. However, from around 1897, the shortcomings of the federal financial system began to make themselves felt, as a consequence of rapid increases in public expenditure at all levels of government. Between 1890 and 1913, total public spending in Germany grew at around 5.4 per cent annually, increasing the share of public spending in NNP from 14 per cent to nearly 19 per cent.[299] Although the rise in defence spending caused by the navy was partly responsible, in fact it was increased social and infrastructural spending at the state and local levels which accounted for the bulk of the increase, as well as the Reich government's policy of *Sammlungspolitik*, which relied on fiscal stimuli to rally the political parties behind the government – tariffs and rebates for farmers, naval contracts and colonies for business, social insurance for workers.[300] All three tiers of government initially tried to finance these new expenditures by borrowing: in 1905, over a fifth of total Reich revenue was raised from the sale of government bonds, and between 1901 and 1913, over 45 per cent of total capital market issues were public sector loans. Total public debt rose from 11.6 bn. marks to 26.7 bn. marks between 1890 and 1913, with the states accounting for over half the total (see figure 1.4). The result was an increasing debt-service burden (11 per cent of total spending in 1913), and an overstretching of the capital market reflected in rising interest rates and falling bond prices. Yet reforms of the financial system were

---

[298] W. Gerloff, *Die Finanz- und Zollpolitik des Deutschen Reiches 1867–1913* (Jena, 1913); F. Terhalle, 'Geschichte des deutschen Finanzwirtschaft vom Beginn des 19. Jahrhunderts bis zum Schluss des zweiten Weltkrieges', in W. Gerloff and F. Neumark, *Handbuch der Finanzwissenschaft* (Tübingen, 1952), pp. 274–89; P.-C. Witt, *Die Finanzpolitik des Deutschen Reiches, 1903–1913* (Lübeck, 1970).

[299] See figure 0.4. S. Andic and J. Veverka, 'The Growth of Government Expenditure in Germany Since the Unification', *Finanzarchiv*, 23 (1964), pp. 169–278; D.E. Schremmer, 'Taxation and Public Finance: Britain, France and Germany', in P. Mathias and S. Pollard (eds.), *The Cambridge Economic History of Europe*, vol. VIII. *The Industrial Economies: the Development of Economic and Social Policies* (Cambridge, 1989), pp. 315–494.

[300] Hentschel, *Wirtschaft und Wirtschaftspolitik*, pp. 146–63. Cf. D. Stegmann, *Die Erben Bismarcks. Parteien und Verbände in der Spätphase des wilhelminischen Deutschlands. Sammlungspolitik, 1897–1918* (Cologne, 1970); G. Eley, '*Sammlungspolitik*, Social Imperialism and the German Navy Law of 1898', *Militärgeschichtliche Mitteilungen*, 15 (1974), pp. 29–63.

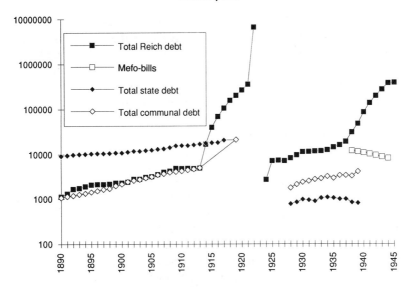

Figure 1.4 Public debt, 1890–1945 (m. marks)
Sources: Hoffmann et al., Wachstum, p. 791; Kroboth, Finanzpolitik, p. 489;
Roesler, Finanzpolitik, p. 201; Witt, Finanzpolitik, p. 386; Sommariva and
Tullio, Macroeconomic History pp. 237ff.; James, German Slump, p. 375,
Bundesbank (ed.), Währung und Wirtschaft, p. 401.

impeded by two political obstacles: the reluctance of the states and communes to relinquish their effective monopoly on direct taxation, and the political concessions required to secure the Reichstag's support for tax reforms. Even after protracted political battles between 1908 and 1913 had led to the introduction of a Reich inheritance tax, a small capital gains tax and a one-off property and income tax, the fiscal balance remained tilted against the Reich, which received only 35 per cent of total revenues, the bulk of it (around 60 per cent) still from indirect taxes.[301]

The financial impasse was in many ways the most important political issue of the Wilhelmine period; and the Hamburg government and business community were as much to blame for the problem as the larger states and interest groups. The Senate opposed the 1913 Defence Contribution on particularist grounds; the Chamber of Commerce, while happy to support increased military spending, vehemently opposed taxes which fell on financial transactions or business income.[302] There were those, notably Max Warburg, who sought to play a more constructive role; but

[301] Kroboth, Finanzpolitik; P.-C. Witt, 'Reichsfinanzen und Rüstungspolitik', in H. Schottelius and W. Deist (eds.), Marine und Marinepolitik im kaiserlichen Deutschland, 1871–1914 (Düsseldorf, 1981), pp. 146–77.
[302] Böhm, Flottenbau, pp. 235–44; idem, Anwalt der Handelsfreiheit, pp. 130f.

when Warburg attempted to broach the subject of financial reform with
the Kaiser, he merely provoked the shrill response that it was Russia not
Germany which was 'going bust'.[303] Warburg persuaded the Chamber of
Commerce to lend its support to the Hansabund, and at the time of the
financial debates which helped topple Chancellor Bülow from office,
drafted a memorandum in which he denounced the fiscal stalemate in
prophetic terms: 'If we carry on our financial policy in the same way,
we will be guilty of financial asset-stripping; and, one fine day, we will
find that we can only make good the damage with the greatest possible
sacrifice – if we can make it good at all.'[304] Yet Warburg remained a
defender of the states' privileged position with respect to direct taxation;
and his constitutional argument (that the power of the Reichstag must
necessarily be increased) alienated more conservative figures like Max
von Schinckel. Whatever the economic arguments for financial reform,
few businessmen were willing to accept the constitutional implications
of increased centralisation and increased parliamentarisation.[305]

It has been argued that the leaders of Wilhelmine Germany sought to
divert attention from such domestic-political dilemmas by pursuing an
aggressive foreign policy.[306] Certainly, the Hamburg *Bürgertum* was not
slow to involve itself in those organisations like the Pan German League,
the Navy League and the Army League which, at least initially, seemed
to offer a revival of the 'national' spirit of the 1860s and 1870s through
Weltpolitik. The Navy League in Hamburg was set up by leading businessmen such as Adolf Woermann, Albert Ballin and William
O'Swald, and included representatives of the Senate, the Bürgerschaft,
the various Chambers and the principal bourgeois *Vereine*, as well as the
veteran liberal and Bürgermeister Johannes Versmann as its President.[307]
There was a similar 'establishment' complexion to the Pan German
League when it was first established in Hamburg in 1892, and to the
Army League, founded in 1913.[308] 'Anti-national' organisations like the

---

[303] Warburg, *Aufzeichnungen*, pp. 29–33.
[304] Max Warburg, 'Die geplante Reichsfinanzreform. Wie vermeiden wir, daß aus
der Beseitigung der Reichsfinanznot eine Bundesstaatsfinanznot entsteht?', Sterling
Library, Yale University, Paul M. Warburg Papers, Ser. II, Box 8, Folder 118;
Böhm, *Anwalt der Handelsfreiheit*, pp. 138–45. See also his later paper presented at
the German Banker's Conference in 1912, 'Geeignete und ungeeignete Mittel zur
Hebung des Kurses des Staatspapiere', WA, Folder XIX, Gesammelte Vorträge.
[305] For conflicting views on how far there was *de facto* parliamentarisation before 1914:
Wehler, *German Empire*, pp. 52–65, 72–83; M. Rauh, *Föderalismus und Parlamentarismus im wilhelminischen Reich* (Düsseldorf, 1972).
[306] D. Groh, '"Je eher, desto besser!" Innenpolitische Faktoren für die Präventivkriegsbereitschaft des Deutschen Reiches 1913–14', *Politische Vierteljahresschrift*, 13 (1972),
pp. 501–21; Wehler, *German Empire*, pp. 192–201.
[307] Böhm, *Flottenbau*, pp. 173–223.
[308] *Ibid.*, pp. 67f.; Coetzee, *Army League*, pp. 27, 46, 93.

pacifist movement or the Zionist movement were viewed with hostility.[309]
Yet Hamburg's economic prosperity was too dependent on good relations
with England for the city's elite to be comfortable with the increasingly
radical tone of the radical nationalist 'opposition' in the years before
1914; and after 1911, the Senate publicly distanced itself from both the
Navy League and the Pan Germans. As early as 1909, Ballin expressed
his disquiet at the effect of the naval programme on both domestic and
foreign politics:

In two years what will we have for this accelerated naval construction – a
new financial catastrophe or a war? [. . .] If we do not come to an understanding [with England] we must very quickly proceed to financial reform, and
with this reform [domestic] developments can take a very serious turn.[310]

At around the same time, the British Admiralty was working out a
strategy which it claimed would be 'a certain and simple means of
strangling Germany at sea': 'The mills of our sea power (though they
would grind the German population slowly perhaps) would grind them
"exceedingly small" – grass would grow in the streets of Hamburg
and widespread dearth and ruin would be inflicted.'[311] Hamburg had
much to fear not merely from the Reich's financial crisis, but more
particularly from the mounting international crisis which the Reich's
armaments policy appeared to be causing.

The economic benefits of Reich membership for Hamburg seemed
unquestionable in 1914. An economy which, since 1890, had grown
at an average annual rate of 2.8 per cent, with its exports growing
still faster at 4.9 per cent, appeared to be the ideal hinterland for a
major entrepot.[312] In that sense, the 'Prussianisation' of the Hamburg
bourgeoisie requires little explanation; though it would be better
described as 'Germanisation'. The political culture of Hamburg
acquired new characteristics, associated with the institutionalisation of
nationalism through education and the political process; but retained
much of its traditional particularism and cosmopolitanism. However,
the harmony of Hammonia and Germania so often represented in
public concealed underlying structural problems of the Reich's political
system: in particular of its monetary and fiscal systems. The German
mark was a symbol of national sovereignty; but as a currency, it was
prey to fluctuations of international capital flows and domestic credit
generation. The Reich's fiscal structure was a bottom-heavy edifice

[309] R. Chickering, *Imperial Germany and a World Without War* (Princeton, 1975),
     pp. 54f., 401; Mosse, *German-Jewish Economic Elite*, p. 97.
[310] Cecil, *Ballin*, pp. 159f.
[311] Offer, *Agrarian Interpretation*, p. 232.
[312] Figures calculated from Hoffmann *et al.*, *Wachstum*, pp. 26f., 520f.

which allowed undemocratic states and communes to horde the swelling receipts of direct taxation and 'crowd out' the capital market, leaving the Reich vulnerable to allegations from its democratic assembly that it financed militarism by means of dear bread. One of the principal attractions of Reich membership had been the increased security it promised. Yet because of the Reich's fiscal system, Germany was in fact spending less on defence as a proportion of GNP than either France or Russia.[313] In chapter 2, the consequences of these structural defects are examined.

[313] N. Ferguson, 'Germany and the Origins of the First World War: New Perspectives', *HJ*, 35, 3 (1992), pp. 725–52.

2

The sinews of war

On 21 June, 1914, following a banquet held in his honour in Hamburg, the German Emperor Wilhelm II gave Max Warburg a notorious analysis of Germany's 'general situation':

He was worried about the Russian armaments [programme and] about the planned railway construction; and detected [in these] the preparations for a war against us in 1916. He complained about the inadequacy of the railway-links that we had at the Western Front against France; and hinted [. . .at] whether it would not be better to strike now, rather than wait.

Warburg 'advised decidedly against' this:

[I] sketched the domestic political situation in England for him (Home Rule), the difficulties for France of maintaining the three year service period, the financial crisis in which France already found itself, and the probable unreliability of the Russian army. I strongly advised [him] to wait patiently, keeping our heads down for a few more years. 'We are growing stronger every year; our enemies are getting weaker internally.'[1]

The exchange is open to a variety of interpretations. That the Kaiser was willing to confide in a banker in this way would seem to confirm the importance of business interests in Wilhelmine high politics. That the Kaiser was contemplating the idea of a 'preventive' or preemptive war against Russia even before the Sarajevo assassination would appear to confirm that the German government premeditated war in 1914. That Warburg immediately assumed that to 'strike now' meant to strike against England, France and Russia would seem to contradict the idea that the German government intended to 'localize' any confron-

---

[1] WA, 'Jahresbericht 1914', pp. 1f. This passage was crossed out in pen at a later date, probably when Warburg was compiling his *Aufzeichnungen* in the 1940s. Cf. 'Jahresbericht 1920' (for Warburg's account of the meeting before the Weimar *Untersuchungsausschuß*); Warburg, Aufzeichnungen MSS (1914); Warburg, *Aufzeichnungen*, p. 29. The published account is cited in E. Zechlin, 'Bethmann Hollweg, Kreigsrisiko und SPD 1914', *Der Monat* (January 1966), p. 21; A. Hillgruber, *Germany and the Two World Wars* (Cambridge, Mass., 1981), p. 38; Fischer, *War of Illusions*, p. 471.

tation between Austria and Russia over the Balkans. Finally, that
Warburg saw Germany's rivals as suffering more from domestic weakness than Germany would seem to run counter to the thesis that the
war was precipitated by the German government to counter a domestic
political crisis within Germany. What is beyond dispute is that Warburg
was aware of the argument for a preventive war, and rejected it. Yet,
despite being kept relatively well informed of developments during the
July Crisis, he and Ballin were powerless to influence the process of
decision making in Berlin. The war which broke out in August 1914
did more damage to the economy of Hamburg than to that of any
other major German city, exposing as illusory the idea that Hamburg's
particular and cosmopolitan interests were compatible with the national
interest of the Reich as defined in Berlin. It is therefore tempting to
regard it as nemesis, after the hubris embodied by the *Imperator* –
whose sister-ship the *Vaterland* was launched in the same week as the
Kaiser's conversation with Warburg.

In the years after 1908, the growing conviction that Germany could
not 'afford a race in dreadnoughts against the much wealthier British',
coupled with anxieties about the economic consequences of a clash
with England had led Ballin and Warburg to distance themselves from
Tirpitz and to favour a policy of Anglo-German detente.[2] Along with
Sir Ernst Cassel, Ballin was one of the principal architects of the visit
of the British War Minister Lord Haldane to Berlin in February
1912, which he hoped would pave the way for an Anglo-German
rapprochement. The decision of Tirpitz and the Kaiser to press on with
a new navy bill on the eve of Haldane's arrival in Germany has
sometimes been seen as having torpedoed an agreement; but in reality
the German proposal, whereby Germany would agree to limit her
naval programme in return for a British commitment to remain neutral
in any continental war, was based on a misunderstanding of British
policy.[3] Ballin and Warburg continued to hope that Britain could be
persuaded to remain neutral if it were made obvious that Germany's
only objective in defeating France was to secure territory in Africa.
Indeed, Warburg's three visits to London in February, April and June
1914 to discuss German investment in Morocco, Nyasaland and Brazil

---

[2] Berghahn, *Germany and the Approach of War*, pp. 68, 78. For Warburg's anxieties, WA, 'Jahresbericht 1908', 'Jahresbericht 1912' It is significant that Warburg saw in 1912 the possibility of an Austrian clash with Russia over the Balkans leading to 'further complications (Germany *contra* France and England)'.

[3] Warburg, *Aufzeichnungen*, pp. 27ff.; Cecil, *Ballin*, pp. 161–5, 180–200. Cf. J. Steinberg, 'Diplomatie als Wille und Vorstellung. Die Berliner Mission Lord Haldanes im Februar 1912', in Schottelius and Deist (eds.), *Marine und Marinepolitik*, pp. 263–82.

led him to hope that 'an extraordinary amity between the Germans
and England' might have 'broken out'.[4] However, none of this – nor
agreements reached over Portuguese Angola and the Berlin–Baghdad
railway – affected Britain's continental policy. As was made clear in
December 1912 and again in July 1914, Britain would not stand aside
if 'the position of France as a power' was threatened.[5]

It seems clear that Bethmann also hoped for British neutrality, as
part of a complex (and not very well calculated) gamble that swift
military action by Austria-Hungary against Serbia would cement the
Triple Alliance and divide the Triple Entente.[6] During the July Crisis,
Ballin was sent to London by Jagow to exert pressure on Haldane
and Churchill over the Anglo-Russian naval talks, news of which had
only just reached Berlin.[7] In effect, he rehearsed for Churchill on 25
July the argument that Bethmann was later to put to Goschen on the
night of 29 July: in the event of a German victory over France,
Germany would take 'nothing from her in Europe, not an inch of her
territory, only some colonies to indemnify us'.[8] Yet this argument, as
Bethmann realised too late, cut no ice in London. What was not fully
appreciated in Hamburg was that, if this diplomatic calculation mis-
fired, the military calculation outlined by the Kaiser to Warburg in
June could be advanced to justify German mobilisation. It was the
German General Staff which ultimately secured the mobilisation orders,
the ultimata and declarations of war which unleashed the conflict; and
this was more than just a reaction to the Russian general mobilisation,
finally approved by the Tsar on July 30. The Chief of the General

---

[4] Pohl, *Bankengeschichte*, p. 110.
[5] Z.S. Steiner, *Britain and the Origins of the First World War* (London, 1983), pp.
94–109.
[6] G. Schmidt, 'Contradictory Postures and Conflicting Objectives: the July Crisis', in
G. Schöllgen (ed.), *Escape into War? The Foreign Policy of Imperial Germany* (Oxford/
New York/Munich, 1990), pp. 143ff.; Berghahn, *Germany and the Approach of War*,
pp. 139f., 145, 191f., 200; I. Geiss, *July 1914. The Outbreak of the First World War:
Selected Documents* (London, 1967), pp. 122ff., doc. 30. See also K.D. Erdmann,
'Zur Beurteilung Bethmann Hollwegs', *Geschichte in Wissenschaft und Unterricht*, 15
(1964), pp. 525–40; E. Zechlin, 'Deutschland zwischen Kabinettskrieg und Wirtsch-
aftskrieg: Politik und Kriegsführung in den ersten Monaten des Weltkrieges 1914',
HZ, 199 (1964), pp. 347–458; K.H. Jarausch, 'The Illusion of Limited War. Chancel-
lor Bethmann Hollweg's Calculated Risk, July 1914', *CEH*, 2 (1969), pp. 48–76;
E. Zechlin, *Krieg und Kriegsrisiko: Zur deutschen Politik im Ersten Weltkrieg*
(Düsseldorf, 1979). For the view that German objectives were more extensive, F.
Fischer, *Griff nach der Weltmacht. Die Kriegszielpolitik des kaiserlichen Deutschlands,
1914–1918* (Düsseldorf, 1961); and for the argument that there was a systematic
German plan for war from late 1912, *idem*, *War of Illusions*.
[7] Cecil, *Ballin*, pp. 200–7.
[8] Cf. Geiss, *July 1914*, docs. 139, 167. For the view that this was Bethmann's true
objective, see Kaiser, 'Germany and the Origins of the First World War', pp. 442–74.

Staff, Moltke, had in fact been arguing for a preventive strike against Russia since March 1914, on the grounds that, because of new armaments programmes in France and Russia, Germany would within a few years have lost the capability to win a war against them.[9] Warburg had been dismissive of the Kaiser's argument for a preventive war; and historians have often suggested that it was disingenuous.[10] Certainly, the banker's argument that time was on Germany's side had some economic foundation. It is true that Russia's population, GNP and iron and steel production were all growing faster than those of Germany, and that British rates of capital export gave it an advantage in overseas influence. On the other hand, Germany's exports were growing faster than its European rivals': its gross domestic capital formation was the highest in Europe, and, in terms of population, GNP and steel production, it was growing substantially faster than its Western rivals. Yet the military position did not fully reflect Germany's economic advantage. Although, according to the German General Staff, the German army totalled around 2.15 million men at its full wartime strength, simple addition suggested that, in the event of a war, Russia, Serbia, France, Britain and Belgium would be able to field 64 per cent more soldiers than Germany and Austria-Hungary.[11] This reflected a widening gap in rates of peacetime conscription.[12] According to the German General Staff, 83 per cent of those eligible for military service in France performed it, compared with 53 per cent in Germany.[13] The comparable figure for Austria-Hungary was 29 per cent.[14] Another way of illustrating the point is to consider the proportion of gross national product spent

[9] Berghahn, *Germany and the Approach of War*, pp. 164–7; Geiss, *July 1914*, pp. 65–8, docs. 3, 4. Cf. N. Stone, *The Eastern Front 1914–1917* (London, 1975), pp. 37–43.

[10] Fischer, *War of Illusions*, pp. 461–70; H. Pogge von Strandmann, 'Germany and the Coming of War', in *idem* and R.J.W. Evans (eds.), *The Coming of the First World War* (Oxford, 1988), pp. 118f.

[11] Reichsarchiv, *Der Weltkrieg 1914–1918. Erste Reihe: Die militärischen Operationen zu Lande* (Berlin, 1925), pp. 38f.

[12] On the eve of the war, the Russian and French armies had increased their total peacetime strength to 2,272,000, compared with a combined German and Austrian strength of 1,239,000; whereas, in 1904, the combined German–Austrian strength had exceeded the Franco-Russian by 371,180. The growing disadvantage was equally clear in terms of total numbers called up in 1913/14: 585,000 to 383,000: Förster, *Der doppelte Militarismus*, pp. 28, 37, 96f., 129, 190, 248; A. Bucholz, *Moltke, Schlieffen and Prussian War Planning* (New York/Oxford, 1991), pp. 62, 67, 159; Berghahn, *Germany and the Approach of War*, p. xii; *Statistisches Jahrbuch für das Deutsche Reich* (1914), p. 343.

[13] Reichsarchiv, *Der Weltkrieg*, pp. 11–21; Förster, *Der doppelte Militarismus*, p. 205.

[14] G.E. Rotheberg, *The Army of Francis Joseph* (West Lafayette, 1976); P.M. Kennedy, *The Rise and Fall of the Great Powers. Economic Change and Military Conflict from 1500 to 2000* (London, 1988), p. 307; Stone, *The Eastern Front*, pp. 17–36; W. Rutherford, *The Russian Army in World War I* (London, 1975).

on defence in the pre-war decades. In absolute terms (and setting aside the impact of the Boer War and the Russo-Japanese war), the German, French, Russian and British military budgets were not separated by much, with Germany outstripping France after 1905, and Russia outstripping Germany by 1913. But in terms of percentages of GNP, Germany consistently lagged behind. In 1913, the Reich was spending just 3.5 per cent of GNP on defence;[15] more than Britain (3.1 per cent) and her own ally Austria-Hungary (2.8 per cent), but less than France (3.9 per cent) and Russia (4.6 per cent).[16] The reason for this discrepancy was evidently not the absence of 'militarist' sentiment in Germany,[17] but the domestic political obstacles to higher defence spending arising, on the one hand, from conservatism within the Prussian military establishment, and, on the other, from the Reich's federal and parliamentary fiscal system, as outlined in the previous chapter. Whereas Russia, France and Britain all had more or less centralised fiscal systems, only Germany's ally Austria-Hungary had a comparable (and indeed worse) fiscal constraint. It is in this limited sense only that the war can be said to have had domestic political origins: domestic politics convinced Moltke that Germany was doomed to lose the arms race, and should therefore strike sooner rather than later.

The limits of the older argument that the German 'ruling elites' (including business interest groups) precipitated war to avert a domestic political crisis[18] become clear if one considers the ambivalent public

[15] Estimates of German defence spending in 1913/14 vary from Roesler's 1,664 m. marks (3.0 per cent of GNP) to Witt's 2,406 m. marks (4.4 per cent of NNP) depending on the method of computation. The figures worthy of consideration are: Andic and Veverka, 'Government Expenditure', pp. 189, 205, 263; Witt, *Finanzpolitik*, pp. 380f.; Schremmer, 'Taxation and Public Finance: Britain, France and Germany', in Mathias and Pollard (eds.), *Cambridge Economic History of Europe*, vol. VIII, p. 474; Hentschel, *Wirtschaft und Wirtschaftspolitik im wilhelminischen Deutschland*, p. 149; K. Roesler, *Die Finanzpolitik des Deutschen Reiches im Ersten Weltkrieg* (Berlin, 1967), p. 195; *Statistisches Jahrbuch für das Deutsche Reich* (1914), pp. 348–55.

[16] For details, see Ferguson, 'Germany and the Origins of the First World War: New Perspectives', pp. 725–52; *idem*, 'Public Finance and National Security: the Domestic Origins of the First World War Revisited', *P&P*, 142 (1994), pp. 141–68.

[17] J. Dülffer and K. Holl, *Bereit zum Krieg. Kriegsmentalität im wilhelminischen Deutschland 1890–1914* (Göttingen, 1986).

[18] See A.J. Mayer, 'Domestic Causes of the First World War', in L. Krieger and F. Stern (eds.), *The Responsibility of Power* (London/Melbourne, 1968), pp. 286–300; Groh, ' "Je eher, desto besser!" ' pp. 501–21; M.R. Gordon, 'Domestic Conflict and the Origins of the First World War: the British and German Cases', *JMH*, 46 (1974), pp. 191–226; P.-C. Witt, 'Innenpolitik und Imperialismus in der Vorgeschichte des Ersten Weltkrieges', in K. Holl and G. List (eds.), *Liberalismus und imperialistischer Staat* (Göttingen, 1975), pp. 24ff.; Wehler, *German Empire*, pp. 192–201. Cf. W. Mommsen, 'Domestic Factors in German Foreign Policy before 1914', *CEH*, 6, 1 (1973), pp. 3–43; J. Joll, *The Origins of the First World War* (London, 1984), pp. 108–18.

reaction to the outbreak of war in Hamburg. There is no question
that, as in most major European cities, the outbreak of war did coincide
with an upsurge of patriotic feeling in certain circles: the excited crowds
which gathered from 25 July at the Alster Pavilion on Jungfernstieg had
their counterparts not only in Munich and Berlin, but also in Paris
and London.[19] The language used by the shipowner Richard Krogmann
(a man involved in the policy of *rapprochement* with England) in a
speech to mark the Kaiser's birthday in January 1914 serves to illustrate
the bellicose mood of the *Bildungsbürgertum* on the eve of war:

> And I am sure that if our honour is challenged, the Kaiser will draw his
> sword; and when the Kaiser calls and the trumpets sound, a murmur will go
> through the German oak forest [. . .] From another world, Kaiser Wilhelm I
> will stretch out his arm in blessing over Germany.[20]

While young men like the fifteen-year old Percy Schramm or the poet
Richard Dehmel rushed to the colours, their female relatives were
seized by religious fervour: Schramm's sister Ruth exulted that 'our
people have come to God', and his aunt Emmy's reaction was overtly
millenarian:

> It all must come to pass; for it is foretold in the Bible, and we can only
> thank God if Satan's rule is soon to be destroyed. Then will come at last the
> true Empire of Peace, with our Lord Jesus Christ as ruler![21]

This was a mood which persisted throughout the first months of the
war, with trains leaving for the Front decorated with flowers, and
crowds gathering to celebrate the victory at Tannenberg outside the
stock exchange.[22] Yet behind this euphoria there lay a profound and
justified anxiety. One recent account has tried to suggest that while
the bourgeoisie exulted, the proletariat fretted;[23] but it is clear that
anxiety was not class specific. As at the time of the second Moroccan
Crisis and the Balkan War, the threat of war triggered a flight into
liquid assets on the financial markets. Warburg's began to 'realise what
could be sold, and reduce our engagements' immediately after the
Sarajevo assassination; and by 20 July the main Hamburg banks had

[19] V. Ullrich, *Kriegsalltag. Hamburg im ersten Weltkrieg* (Cologne, 1982), pp. 10–14.
Cf. Joll, *Origins of the First World War*, pp. 171–200; J.-J. Becker, *1914: Comment
les français sont entrés dans la guerre* (Paris, 1977).

[20] H. Pohlmann, *Richard C. Krogmann 1859–1932. Leben und Leistung eines hamburgischen Kaufmanns und Reeders* (Hamburg, 1986), pp. 203–14. Cf. Schramm, *Neun
Generationen*, II, p. 480; Plagemann, *Industriekultur*, p. 307.

[21] Schramm, *Neun Generationen*, II, pp. 467–9. Cf. K. Vondung, 'Deutsche Apokalypse
1914', in *idem, Das wilhelminische Bildungsbürgertum* (Göttingen, 1976), pp. 153–
51; M. Greschat, 'Krieg und Kriegsbereitschaft im deutschen Protestantismus', in
Dülffer and Holl (eds.), *Bereit zum Krieg*, pp. 33–55.

[22] Schramm, *Neun Generationen*, II, p. 480.

[23] Ullrich, *Kriegsalltag*, pp. 10–21.

to take measures to counter a panic on the stock exchange.[24] The earliness of the crisis in Hamburg was probably due to a series of official indications that war was imminent. On 18 July, the Kaiser requested that Ballin be informed of possible mobilisation; three days later, the Reich Chancellery wrote to the Senate about the need for regional labour exchanges to allocate labour in the event of a war; and on 23 July (i.e., on the day it was sent), the Foreign Office sent Langwerth von Simmern to Hamburg with a copy of the Austrian Ultimatum to Serbia.[25] When news reached Hamburg on the evening of 28 July that the German government had rejected Grey's proposal for a conference of foreign ministers in London, there was such acute panic on the Hamburg bourse that Warburg felt compelled to contact the Wilhelmstraße. Zimmermann authorised him to announce that although the German government did not regard the proposed conference as 'feasible', nevertheless 'the negotiations from Cabinet to Cabinet, which had already been initiated with the utmost success, would be continued'. Although this – wholly disingenuous – statement was greeted with applause, the bourse was not reopened that evening.[26] The subsequent entry of England into the war plunged Albert Ballin into a despair which startled even Warburg.[27] Nor was it just in business circles that the prospect of war inspired anxiety. The art historian Aby Warburg was thrown into mental turmoil by the war: too old to serve and fearful of the consequences of defeat, he obsessively collected evidence from newspapers to rebut Entente allegations of atrocities by German troops.[28] Whereas for many, like the young Percy Schramm, the war presented an opportunity to act out nationalist fantasies,[29] a few recognised the fulfilment of Bebel's prophecy – war meant 'the twilight of the gods of the bourgeois world'.[30]

War economics

The magnitude of the risk being taken by the German General Staff only became apparent with the failure of the Schlieffen Plan at the

---

[24] WA, 'Jahresbericht 1914', pp. 2ff.

[25] Geiss, *July 1914*, p. 134; StAH, DHSG II, Spez. XXXIV 23a, Reich Chancellor to Senate, 21.7.14; WA, 'Jahresbericht 1914', p. 3.

[26] *Ibid.*; *Hamburger Börsenhalle*, 28.7.14.

[27] Cecil, *Ballin*, pp. 210–14; Warburg, *Aufzeichnungen*, p. 34. By contrast, Warburg and the shipowner Krogmann remained hopeful of a swift victory until September and November respectively.

[28] Gombrich, *Aby Warburg*, p. 206; Chernow, *Warburgs*, pp. 175–8, 193–6, 203f.

[29] See in general M. Eksteins, *Rites of Spring. The Great War and the Modern Age* (London, 1989), pp. 55–93, 193–7.

[30] W.J. Mommsen, 'The Topos of Inevitable War in Germany in the Decade before 1914', in V.R. Berghahn and M. Kitchen (eds.), *Germany in the Age of Total War* (Totowa, 1981) pp. 23–45.

Marne and the Austrian setbacks against Russia: for, once the continental hammer-blow had failed, Germany was confronted by the full economic and military might of the British Empire. Even if one takes only the British Isles into account, the Triple Entente had a combined GNP around 60 per cent larger than that of the Central Powers.[31] The resources of the Empire in terms of manpower and food supplies, as well as the huge reservoir of overseas capital which Britain could liquidate to finance the fighting, greatly increased the economic differential.[32] Much therefore depended on the efficiency with which Germany was able to mobilise her inferior resources. German businessmen and politicians were perhaps more ideologically predisposed to accept large-scale state intervention in economic life than their British counterparts: it is tempting to contrast the semi-official slogan of 'business as usual' favoured by the Asquith government with the visions of an irreversible abandonment of the capitalist system in favour of 'war socialism' conjured up by Walther Rathenau and Wichard von Moellendorff.[33] Yet, despite the extensive theorising about economic planning which went on in Germany during the war, it is a striking fact that the German war economy performed less well in practice than the more pragmatically run British.[34] In part, this was because British economic warfare against Germany was more effective than Germany's against Britain. In the case of Hamburg, there were several distinct respects in which enemy action caused damage, the first and most important being the disruption caused by British naval action to German sea-borne trade. The Hamburg shipping journal *Hansa* noted on 1 August that if Britain entered the war 'economic life [would] suffer a collapse unprecedented in history'.[35] As noted above, trade between Hamburg and the British Empire accounted for nearly a third of the value of the city's sea-borne imports and a quarter of the value of its exports in 1913, substantially higher figures than for Germany as a whole.[36] But British naval supremacy and the effectiveness of British pressure on neutrals meant that the disruption of Hamburg's trade was far greater than even the most pessimistic contemporaries had anticipated. The inability of the German navy to challenge British

[31] P. Bairoch, 'Europe's GNP: 1800–1975', *Journal of European Economic History* (1976), pp. 281, 303.

[32] See Offer, *Agrarian Interpretation*; K. Burk, *Britain, America and the Sinews of War, 1914–1918* (Boston and London, 1985).

[33] H. Pogge von Strandmann (ed.), *Walther Rathenau. Industrialist, Banker, Intellectual and Politician. Notes and Diaries 1907–1922* (Oxford, 1985), p. 189.

[34] See G.D. Feldman, *Army, Industry and Labour in Germany 1914–1918*, *passim*; W. Fischer, 'Die deutsche Wirtschaft im Ersten Weltkrieg', in N. Walter (ed.), *Deutschland. Porträt einer Nation*, Bd. III: *Wirtschaft* (Gütersloh, 1985).

[35] *Hansa*, 1.8.14.

[36] *Statistisches Handbuch 1925*, pp. 134f., 144f.

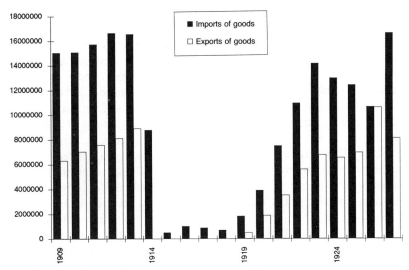

Figure 2.1 Hamburg's foreign trade by volume, 1909–1927 (tons)
Sources: *Statistisches Handbuch 1920*, p. 153; Büttner, *Staats- und Wirtschafts-krise*, p. 687; Brandt, *Finanzen*, p. 92; Meyer, *Hamburg*, p. 107.

control of the North Sea meant that German merchant shipping in port at the outbreak of war was effectively cut off from all foreign markets save the Scandinavian.[37] The result was that, while German imports by 1915 had fallen to around 55 per cent of their pre-war level, Hamburg's collapsed to just 2.4 per cent, rising only slightly (to 4.3 per cent) in 1918 (see figure 2.1).[38] There was inactivity at the Hamburg docks; and the majority of the city's overseas commercial houses found themselves redundant. Johannes Amsinck compared the situation with the time of the Napoleonic Wars: 'Our business is stone dead'; while Ballin railed against the 'sickening' and 'wretched shopkeepers' methods' adopted by the British 'with the sole purpose of excluding us from the world market'.[39] Nor, as gradually became apparent, was this to be a temporary exclusion confined to the period of hostilities, since the protraction and scale of the conflict caused

[37] Offer, *Agrarian Interpretation*, pp. 300–9; G. Hardach, *The First World War 1914–1918* (Harmondsworth, 1987), pp. 11–19; C.P. Vincent, *The Politics of Hunger. The Allied Blockade of Germany 1915–1919* (Athens, Ohio, 1985).

[38] Wartime statistics from Ullrich, 'Arbeiterbewegung', pp. 221f.; Lyth, '*Mittelstand*', p. 77. The evidence also suggests a 96 per cent fall in Hamburg's exports, compared with a fall of 75 per cent for Germany as a whole.

[39] Möring, *Johannes Schuback & Söhne*; A. von Tirpitz, *Deutsche Ohnmachtspolitik im Weltkriege* (Hamburg/Berlin, 1926), p. 68.

permanent structural changes to the world economy. The subtraction of European industrial output from the world market as a result of its diversion into war production opened the way for a significant increase in industrial production outside Europe, particularly in the United States, but also, on a smaller scale, in Japan, India and South America.[40] This was a blow to Hamburg's exporters; but it had its most serious consequences for other sectors of the economy, in particular for ship-building. Here it is necessary to qualify the distinction between enemy action and government action; for it was above all the German strategy of unrestricted submarine warfare which precipitated the dramatic wartime expansion of American ship-building output from 8 per cent to 56 per cent of new construction. From the point of view of German ship-builders, this new American capacity became a most unwelcome source of competition in the depressed post-war years.[41]

British economic warfare was not confined to blockading the enemy; of equal importance was the policy of sequestration of German overseas assets initiated with the first Alien Enemies (Winding Up) Ordinances in October 1914. In 1914, Germans held overseas investments worth between 20 and 28 bn. marks. As a result of British, French, Russian and later American legislation, as much as 16.1 bn. marks of this was confiscated, much of it in the British Empire.[42] Short-term investments and credits could in many cases be liquidated: between the outbreak of war and March 1915, Warburg's were able to repatriate around 241 m. marks, so that only around 70.7 m. marks was still owed by foreigners to Hamburg lenders in 1917.[43] However, many of Hamburg's overseas assets were less easily liquidated. Merchant houses with branches in British territory found themselves summarily expropriated: Behn, Meyer & Co. lost 'millions' as a result of the sequestration of

---

[40] Hardach, *First World War*, p. 245; Petzina, *Deutsche Wirtschaft*, pp. 6f; H. Levy, *Die Weltmarkt 1913 und heute* (Leipzig/Berlin, 1926), pp. 9–15, 45–59, 78f., 85f.; Wiskemann, *Hamburg und die Welthandelspolitik von den Anfängen bis zur Gegenwart*, pp. 282–7, 336f.

[41] Hardach, *First World War*, p. 45.

[42] See the various estimates in J.M. Keynes, *The Economic Consequences of the Peace* (London, 1919), pp. 161, 165 (pre-war German estimates); *The Economist*, 'Reparations Supplement', 31.5.24, p. 6 (the McKenna Committee's estimate); H.G. Moulton and C.E. McGuire, *Germany's Capacity to Pay. A Study of the Reparation Problem* (New York, 1923); Hoffmann *et al.*, *Wachstum*, p. 262; Henderson, *German Industrial Power*, p. 240; Kindleberger, *Financial History*, p. 225; Hardach, *First World War*, pp. 4, 289. German representatives tended to claim larger losses: see, e.g., HA, NL Cuno, Melchior and Cuno, Deposition for Brussels Conference, 18.12.20. It should be noted that up to 12 bn. marks was invested in Germany by foreigners in 1914; Henning, *Industrialisierung*, p. 135.

[43] WA, 'Jahresbericht 1914', p. 5; StAH, DHSG II, III C 53 (1919), DHSG 16. Sitzung, 4.11.19. Warburg's also shifted German assets to neutral havens like Amsterdam and Stockholm; NAW, RG 59, 763 72112/3531; /10531a; /7840.

its assets in Singapore and Penang, Wm. O'Swald & Co. lost around
40 m. marks in East Africa, while G.L. Gaiser lost 10 m. marks in
West Africa.[44] Particularly hard hit were the shipping lines. As a result
of sinking or confiscation, the German shippers lost up to 639 ships
with a total tonnage of 2.3 m. gross tons – 44 per cent of the total
pre-war merchant fleet.[45] Recorded wartime losses for Hamburg were
less severe, amounting to 28 per cent of total pre-war tonnage. Not
only did the Hapag lose twelve ships which were in Entente harbours
at the start of the war, and a further fifteen, sunk in action in the
first nine months of hostilities, but the eighty-three ships in neutral
ports, and many of the eighty in German, were rendered useless; the
former because they could not risk sailing home, the latter because,
as ocean-going vessels, they were unsuitable for the Baltic and coastal
trade.[46] However, the impact of enemy action on the shipping lines
provides a further instance of damage made worse by German government policy. The losses suffered by the shipping lines would not have
been so severe had it been possible to charter or sell at least some of
the tonnage to neutral lines, particularly the 109 ships in US harbours;
but government anxieties that the ships, if sold or even chartered to
neutrals, might be used to provision the Allies, meant that only around
fifty-five small vessels with a tonnage of 170,000 were disposed of.[47]
Ballin was only able to sell nine of the Hapag ships trapped in foreign
harbours, and ultimately had assets worth around $100 m. seized in
the United States alone, including thirty-seven ships.[48] It is not surprising that many of those businessmen whose companies were expropriated by the British turned away from their pre-war Anglophilia and
supported the idea of colonial transfers from Britain to Germany in
the event of a German victory. But as the war progressed, Hanseatic

[44] StAH, FA AOM 1, Bd. 6, F. Witthoefft to J. Lütjens, 29.9.14; Witthoefft to
Ostermeyer, 1.12.14; Witthoefft to Ostermeyer, 9.1.15; Bd. 9, Witthoefft to von
Rechenberg, 18.3.18; Schramm, *Neun Generationen*, II, pp. 489f.; D. Kersten, 'Die
Kriegsziele der Hamburger Kaufmannschaft im Ersten Weltkrieg' (Diss. Hamburg,
1962), pp. 42ff. For compensation claims from commercial interest-groups, StAH,
DHSG II, Spez. XXXIV, No. 77.

[45] BAP, RWM 764/268–301, 'Verluste der deutschen Handelsflotte'; Krohne, 'Der
Zusammenbruch und Wiederaufbau der deutschen Seeschiffahrt', in Harms (ed.),
Strukturwandlungen der deutschen Volkswirtschaft, Bd. II, pp. 218–49; GHH, 408213/
0, 'Beteiligung der GHH an einer Schiffswerft', 17.3.18. These figures exclude
sailing boats and unconfirmed losses reported by the shipping lines.

[46] Hapag, *Jahresbericht, 1914–20*; Cecil, *Ballin*, pp. 215–31. Cf. Roggendorf, 'Die
Entwicklung und Bedeutung der H.A.L. unter Berücksichtigung der Vor- und
Nachkriegszeit'.

[47] BAP, RFM 46583 N. Reg. 324/3, RSA Notiz, 2.10.15; NAW, RG 39, G 756, Navy
Department to Treasury, 9.2.27.

[48] H.-H. Kohlhaus, 'Die Hapag, Cuno und das deutsche Reich, 1920–1933' (Diss.
Hamburg, 1952), pp. 77ff.; Cecil, *Ballin*, pp. 218–44.

dissatisfaction increasingly came to be focused on Berlin rather than London. As Ballin put it in an angry letter to the Ministry of the Interior: 'Our company [. . .] has [. . .] lost practically all its ships except a very few. The losses are not so much due to capture on the part of the enemy as to the measures taken by our own government.'[49]

This was only one of numerous aspects of the government's organisation of the war effort which alienated Hamburg business. In part, this reflected the disappointment of high expectations. Most businessmen had shared the contemporary assumption that the German military authorities were a model of efficiency. In August 1914, Ballin was able to 'derive some pleasure from the magnificent discipline and accomplishment of the General Staff', one of only two organisations he still considered 'beyond reproach' (the other, now that the Hapag was ruined, being the Catholic Church).[50] In reality, the military and civilian authorities proved ill-prepared for the strains of a protracted war. In Berlin, the Ministry of the Interior had been unresponsive to pre-war pressure from industrialists for the creation of an 'Economic General Staff' to coordinate resource allocation.[51] In Hamburg, Ballin had been asked by the military authorities to draw up plans for wartime food supply in 1912; but little had been done to implement these.[52] Instead, the outbreak of war was followed by near-farcical improvisation. On 6 August, Ballin and Warburg were driven to Berlin to discuss the question of food imports with officials of the Ministry of the Interior, the Treasury Office, the Foreign Office and the Reichsbank. The chaos of the journey (during which they were repeatedly stopped by armed civilians searching for spies) was matched by the confusion of the meeting, which foundered on the erroneous assumption of the Foreign Office representative that Germany would be able to make use of the American merchant marine.[53]

Contemporaries and some later historians sought to portray the German war economy as a new kind of economy: 'the planned economy', 'state socialism', the 'common economy', 'state-monopoly-capitalism', 'organised capitalism'.[54] All of these exaggerate the degree of conceptual coher-

---

[49] Huldermann, *Ballin*, p. 230.
[50] Cecil, *Ballin*, pp. 212f.
[51] L. Burchardt, *Friedenswirtschaft und Kreigsvorsorge. Deutschlands wirtschaftliche Rüstungsbestrebungen vor 1914* (Boppard am Rhein, 1968).
[52] Cecil, *Ballin*, p. 216 n.
[53] WA, 'Jahresbericht 1914', p. 6; Warburg, *Aufzeichnungen*, pp. 34f.
[54] Among the more influential of contemporary analyses were W. von Moellendorff, *Deutsche Gemeinwirtschaft* (Berlin, 1916) and R. Goldscheid, *Staatssozialismus oder Staatskapitalismus* (Jena, 1917). For the Marxist perspective, A. Schröter, *Krieg-Staat-Monopole 1914–1918* (Berlin, 1965). Cf. F. Zunkel, *Industrie und Staatssozialismus. Der Kampf um die Wirtschaftsordnung in Deutschland 1914–1918* (Düsseldorf, 1974); H.G. Ehlert, *Die wirtschaftliche Zentralbehörde des Deutschen Reiches, 1914–1919. Das*

ence and practical cohesion involved. The fundamental principle that the vastly increased needs of the armed forces should be met by placing contracts with private companies, working with a view to profit (as opposed to expanding the state armaments sector), remained intact throughout the war. The most fundamental effects of the war economy on Hamburg therefore related to the volume of military contracts the state's industrial firms received.[55] Typically, textile- and food-processing firms were able to shift to producing uniforms and rations for the Front: by December 1915, Hamburg had supplied 6 m. marks – around a third – of the army's textile needs, and a further 11 m. marks was provided in the ensuing three months. But munitions contracts were much less plentiful. In late 1916, there were thirty-four firms producing fuses, and 58 producing grenades; but only fifteen of these firms employed more than 100 people, and a further fifty-eight firms suitable for munitions work had none.[56] By 1918, munitions contracts in Hamburg averaged 4.6 m. marks per month; and there were persistent complaints that Hamburg was being discriminated against by the 'centralising' Berlin authorities.[57] It was characteristic of the problems which beset the federal Reich during the war that such complaints had a strong particularistic overtone; indeed, in its attempts to balance the competing interests of the separate states, the War Ministry resorted to allocating contracts on a matricular basis (i.e., in proportion to state populations) – a patently absurd system.[58]

Such complaints tended to overlook the disproportionate role played by Hamburg ship-building and engineering firms in naval and particularly submarine production. At first sight, as figure 2.2 shows, increased orders for naval vessels clearly did not compensate in volume terms for the fall in demand for merchant vessels: ship-building output fell by 44 per cent in the first year and a half of the war, and by 1917 had fallen to around a fifth of its pre-war level.[59] Yet the war appears to have been surprisingly good for the shipyards in financial terms. Net profits at Blohm & Voß, which received orders for ninety-seven submarines during the war, rose steadily

Problem der Gemeinwirtschaft in Krieg und Frieden (Wiesbaden, 1982); and G.D. Feldman, 'Der deutsche organisierte Kapitalismus während der Kriegs- und Inflationsjahre 1914–1923', in Winkler (ed.), *Organisierter Kapitalismus*, pp. 150–71.

[55] Ullrich, 'Arbeiterbewegung', pp. 221–6; StAH, DHSG III, Pr. VI 3, Gewerbekammer to DHSG, 23.4.17.

[56] StAH, DHSG III, Pr. VI 3, Detaillistenkammer to DHSG, 16.12.15, 13.3.16; Pr. VI 7, DHSG to HKH, 19.10.16; BAP, RMfW 1565, 'Industrielle Abrüstung', 1919/20.

[57] StAH, DHSG III, Pr. VI 2, Adolf Bernstein to DHSG, 17.2.17; Pr. VI 5, Ausgleichstelle der Bundesstaaten für Heereslieferungen (1918); Pr. VI 4, HKH Munitionsbeschaffungsstelle to Heeresauftragsamt für das Hamburgische Staatsgebiet, 4.6.18.

[58] StAH, DHSG III, Pr. VI, 3, Kriegsministerium Abschrift, 20.1.17. For specific companies which benefited from war contracts: Möring, *100 Jahre Zipperling, Kessler & Co.*; Prior, *100 Jahre Norddeutsche Affinerie*.

[59] See figure 1.2. Cf. Wagenführ, 'Die Industriewirtschaft', p. 23.

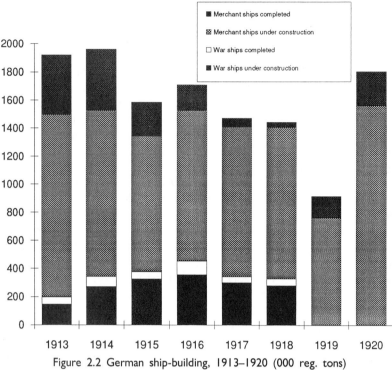

Figure 2.2 German ship-building, 1913–1920 (000 reg. tons)
Source: NAW, RG 59, 862.00, Stewart Report, 1.

throughout the war from 1.37 m. marks in 1914/15 (11.4 per cent) to
2.7 m. marks (13.5 per cent) in 1917/18 – above average even for the iron
and steel industry. The firm was able to expand its capacity to around
600,000 gross tons per annum – acquiring a new dock and machine factory
from a smaller yard – to expand its share capital from 12 m. marks to 20 m.
marks, and to increase its workforce from 10,250 to 12,555.[60] This was by
no means exceptional: between 1914 and 1920, the thirteen main German
shipyards increased their capital by 120 per cent. While employment in
engineering overall only rose by 6.6 per cent during the war, in the shipyards it rose 52 per cent.[61] The government was in no doubt that 'the ship-

[60] BAP, RFM 46124, 'Besprechung über die Schiffsraumbeschaffung nach dem Krieg',
     7.7.16; Wiskemann, *Welthandelspolitik*, p. 329; Ullrich, 'Arbeiterbewegung', pp. 224,
     363. Once again, the firm benefited from its links to the Navy Office; see Hermann
     Blohm's letter to Tirpitz of 1926, recalling the latter's encouragement to the firm to
     go over to submarine production: Tirpitz, *Ohnmachtspolitik*, p. 660.
[61] BAP, RFM 46582 N.Reg. 322/312, Gutachten. The corresponding employment
     figures for Vulkan are 4,300 and 10,863; and for Stülcken, 855 and 1,005; Ullrich,
     'Arbeiterbewegung', pp. 224f.

building industry has [. . .] done much better during the war than in the preceding peacetime years', and indeed accused the shipyards of concealing the true extent of their profits 'whether through depreciation allowances or transfers of all kinds'.[62] This may have exaggerated the benefits of wartime contracts: the principal reason for expanding the workforce was the much lower quality of the workers available as a consequence of indiscriminate conscription.[63] Blohm & Voß's profits, if deflated to allow for inflation, can be shown to have risen only slightly from the trough of 1914; and the yard's expansion was in many ways a gamble on the anticipated post-war boom in demand for shipping.[64] On the other hand, there is little doubt that the government was over-generous in its payments for war contracts: turnover per man rose by 69 per cent at Vulkan between 1913 and 1916, while material used per unit of wages fell by 20 per cent – a fact which may partly explain the yards' hostility to supervision by the Naval Office.[65]

The main innovations of the war economy on the supply side were the delegation of monopolistic controls over the distribution of raw materials to trusts made up of the industrial consumers of raw materials – the so-called 'war companies' – over which a new official body, the War Raw Materials Office, exercised supervision, and the delegation of certain industrial production targets to industrial cartels.[66] The War Raw Materials Office and the War Corporations were heavily criticised by Hamburg businessmen from the outset: Max Warburg opposed the creation of the Metal Corporation, arguing for a less 'bureaucratic' system in 1914; while the Chamber of Commerce denounced the system as 'an exclusion of business individuality'.[67] This partly reflected the ideological commitment of Hamburg business to *laissez faire*;[68] but the target of Hanseatic antagonism was less the centralisation of distribution *per se* than its control by industry. It was feared that the war companies would exacerbate the already existing tendency towards vertical integration within the German economy, increasing industrial control over imports and exports at the expense of independent commercial interests. There was some justification for such fears. It proved impossible to prevent the Imperial (later Central) Purchasing Corporation (*Einkaufsgesellschaft*) –

---

[62] BAP, RFM 41624 Alt. Reg. 2954, 'Gutachten: die Verwaltungskosten der Werften'.
[63] See StAH, FA B&V 13, Bd. II, Firmenleitung, 10.1.17, 20.12.17.
[64] StAH, FA B&V 13, Bd. 1, Firmenleitung, 17.9.14.
[65] BAP, RFM 46582 N.Reg. 322/306; StAH, FA B&V, Firmenleitung 26.11.14.
[66] O. Groebel, *Deutsche Rohstoffwirtschaft im Weltkrieg* (Stuttgart, 1930); K. Wiedenfeld, *Die Organisation der Kriegsrohstoff-bewirtschaftung 1914–1918 im Dienste des deutschen Monopolkapitals* (Berlin, 1955); Hardach, *First World War*, pp. 58–61; Feldman, *Iron and Steel*, pp. 67f.; idem, *Great Disorder*, pp. 52ff.
[67] Warburg, *Aufzeichnungen*, pp. 92, 100; Böhm, *Anwalt der Handelsfreiheit*, p. 151.
[68] *Ibid.*, pp. 148–52, 272–82.

set up by Ballin and Warburg in August 1914 to coordinate imports –
from being moved from Hamburg to Berlin.[69] Although the Hamburg
banks, in particular Warburg's, were able to play an important role in
the financing of imports from Sweden, Romania and Holland,[70] difficulties arose in the export trade, largely as a consequence of the government's desire to restrict iron and steel exports by producers chafing at
the price restrictions imposed by the steel cartel.[71] The export licensing
system introduced in January 1917 effectively gave the industrial associations direct control over all export transactions – a development which
appeared to pose a serious threat to the future autonomy of Hamburg's
export houses.[72] The spectacle of economic power being concentrated in
Berlin around the War Committee of German Industry and its satellites
filled Hamburg business circles with alarm: Berlin, as Ballin commented
in December 1917, was 'the big sponge which soaks everything up'.[73]

It has been claimed that 'the industry [. . .] which suffered most from
the war and the peace' was the iron and steel industry.[74] Hamburg's
economy – with the exception of the shipyards – fared worse.[75] In the
case of the big shipping lines and the small merchant houses, there is
no question that they suffered more immediate capital losses during the
war than any other sector: the Hapag's post-war accounts recorded a 25
per cent fall in the real value of its total assets, rising to 53 per cent if
only its physical assets are considered. Moreover, their incomes were
dramatically reduced: calculations based on the Hapag's post-war
accounts suggest that they were able to earn only 43.9 m. gold marks
during the war years – an 84 per cent fall in annual earnings.[76] Among
the banks, Warburg's was able to establish a satisfactory share of wartime
import finance, and its balance sheet (adjusted for inflation) at the end
of the war showed a 50 per cent increase on 1913 (118 m. marks to
176 m. marks).[77] But the picture was blacker for the smaller merchant
banks: only Berenberg-Goßler's succeeded in maintaining a satisfactory
level of business.[78] Because of legal restrictions imposed on the stock

---

[69] See the material in BAP, Zentraleinkaufsgesellschaft; Cecil, *Ballin*, p. 216; Warburg,
Aufzeichnungen, pp. 34–6.
[70] WA, 'Jahresbericht 1915', pp. 3f.; 'Jahresbericht 1916', p. 5; 'Jahresbericht 1918',
Anlage 35. Cf. Feldman, *Iron and Steel*, p. 55.
[71] *Ibid.*, pp. 60–7.
[72] *Ibid.*, pp. 72–7.
[73] Kersten, 'Kriegsziele'. Cf. the comments of Franz Witthoefft in StAH, FA AOM,
Witthoefft to Ostermayer, 19.5.16: 'Business here is more or less crippled; more or
less everything is monopolised by the state'.
[74] Feldman, *Iron and Steel*, pp. 11f.
[75] Bresciani, *Inflation*, p. 288.
[76] Calculated from Hapag, *Jahresbericht*, 1914–20.
[77] Calculated from figures in Rosenbaum and Sherman, *M.M. Warburg & Co.*, pp.
107, 116.
[78] Pohl, *Bankengeschichte*, p. 113.

market, banks specialising in industrial finance also faced difficulties:[79] both the Vereinsbank and the Norddeutsche Bank contracted in real terms during the war, while the Commerzbank only prospered by continuing its pre-war expansion into other German regions.[80] A good indication of the relatively poor wartime performance of Hamburg's economy was the contraction of the city's aggregate joint stock capital. While the Reich's total share capital fell only 14 per cent in real terms during the war, Hamburg's fell by over a third.[81]

Perhaps the most obvious symptom of Hamburg's decline was the increasing penetration of the city's economy by 'outsider' capital; and perhaps the best proof that Hamburg fared worse than the Ruhr and Berlin is the identity of the outsiders concerned. Hugo Stinnes built up substantial shareholdings in a number of the major Hamburg shipping lines, including the Hapag and the merged Woermann Lines, with the obvious intention of buying up the weakened lines after the war and merging them into his Hamburg-based concern, the AG Hugo Stinnes für Seeschiffahrt und Überseehandel.[82] Similarly, Alfred Hugenberg sought to gain control of the Transocean-Gesellschaft, a Hamburg-based transatlantic cable company.[83] Of more lasting significance were the incursions by the AEG and the Gutehoffnungshütte into Hamburg. Among Rathenau's pet projects for the AEG during the war was to invest in air transport and ship-building, and he identified in Ballin a suitably enterprising partner in the transport sector. Between them, Rathenau and Ballin planted the seeds of the future Lufthansa; but this was a long-term investment, and it was the new ship-building project which they both recognised as offering opportunities for immediate profits in the post-war years.[84] Two separate ideas converged: for light, diesel-motor powered ships, and for American-style mass-production based on standardised components and assembly-line shipyards.[85] However, it was Paul Reusch's desire to secure a peacetime outlet for the Gutehoffnungs-

[79] Share issues on the Hamburg bourse fell from 43 (1913) to 28 (1914); and did not resume again until 1917 (5) and 1918 (18): *Vierteljahreshefte zur Statistik des Deutschen Reiches* (1914), I, pp. 181–3; (1915), I, pp. 112–14; (1917), II, pp. 75–6; (1918), II, pp. 73–4.

[80] Pohl, *Bankengeschichte*, p. 120.

[81] Calculated from: *Vierteljahreshefte zur Statistik des Deutschen Reiches, Ergänzungsheft* II (1914), p. 11; (1915), p. 9; (1916), p. 9; (1917), p. 11; (1918), p. 11; (1920), p. 106.

[82] Ballin was unable to keep Stinnes out and was forced to grant him a seat on the Hapag supervisory board; see HA, 'Stinnes Akten'; P. Wulf, 'Schwerindustrie und Seeschiffahrt nach dem Ersten Weltkrieg: Hugo Stinnes und die HAPAG', *VSWG*, 67 (1980), pp. 1–21.

[83] WA, 'Jahresbericht 1915', p. 6; Mosse, *German-Jewish Economic Elite*, p. 266.

[84] Leckebusch, *Beziehung*, p. 101.

[85] W. Claviez, *50 Jahre Deutsche Werft, 1918–1968*, (Hamburg, 1968), pp. 10–20; *Gutehoffnungshütte Denkschrift Nr. 30*, Bd. III (Oberhausen, 1930), pp. 29–43.

hütte's steel production which provided the decisive impetus for the establishment of Deutsche Werft on the undeveloped Finkenwerder peninsula. Reusch established a controlling interest in the new company; and by June 1918 construction was sufficiently far advanced for the company to accept contracts for twenty-five submarines.[86] Thus, by 1918, one of the leading companies in the sector alleged to have suffered most as a result of the war had established itself in what had been the heart of Hamburg's industry; an apt symbol for the relative decline of Hamburg business under the conditions of the war economy.

The supply side of the German war economy was thus increasingly dominated by the industrial concerns and their umbrella organisations: not only did they control the production of essential materials, but also, to a striking extent, they were able to control their prices, allocation and export. The efficiency of this system is, to say the least, open to question. Clearly, the disruption to trade and the diversion of factors of production into the work of destruction led to declines in output in most combatant countries; just as the poor harvests of the war years led to a world-wide fall in agricultural output. However, the problem of falling output was particularly severe in Germany. The available index suggests that Net National Product contracted at an annual rate of around 4 per cent during the war (see figure 2.3).[87] In agriculture, there were below-average yields in 1915 and 1916, and harvests of around 60 per cent of the 1910–14 average in 1917/18.[88] The available statistics reveal a fall of the same order in industrial production: output fell at an annual rate of around 11 per cent (see figure 2.4).[89] This cannot wholly be blamed on the shortages of imported materials caused by the blockade; for Germany was able to run a substantial trade deficit with her Scandinavian and continental neighbours of between 11 and 15 bn. gold marks, and there were significant achievements in the field of import substitution.[90] Nor can it wholly be blamed on the inevitable diversion of men and material to the Front. Rather, it is a plausible hypothesis that the German war

---

[86] GHH, 408213/0, Reusch to Karl Haniel, 11.5.18; GHH, 300193012/2, Konsortialvertrag.

[87] P.-C. Witt, 'Finanzpolitik und sozialer Wandel in Krieg und Inflation 1918–1924', in Mommsen *et al.* (eds.), *Industrielles System*, I, p. 425.

[88] Holtfrerich, *Inflation*, p. 180; Hardach, *First World War*, pp. 108f.; R. Berthold, 'Die Entwicklung der deutschen Agrarproduktion und der Ernährungswirtschaft zwischen 1907 und 1925', *Jahrbuch für Wirtschaftsgeschichte*, IV (1974), pp. 83ff. Cf. J. Lee, 'Administrators and Agriculture: Aspects of German Agricultural Policy in the First World War', in J.M. Winter (ed.), *War and Economic Development* (Cambridge, 1975), pp. 229ff.

[89] Wagenführ, 'Die Industriewirtschaft', p. 23.

[90] Bresciani, *Inflation*, pp. 83–3; Hardach, *First World War*, p. 33. Cf. the figures given by Wagenführ for the volumes of imported raw materials transported by rail: Wagenführ, 'Industriewirtschaft', p. 21.

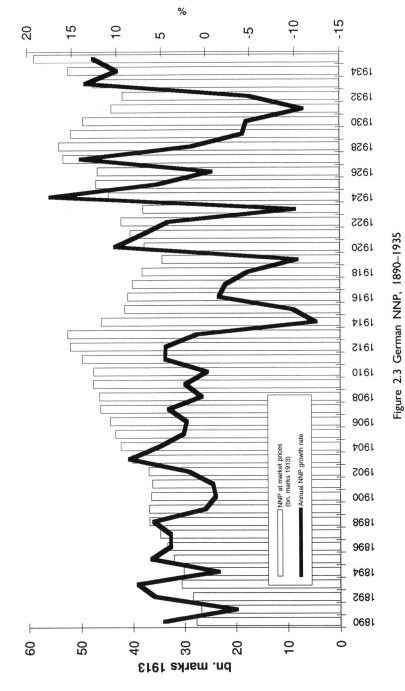

Figure 2.3 German NNP, 1890–1935
Sources: Hoffmann *et al.*, *Wachstum*, pp. 827f.; Witt, 'Finanzpolitik', p. 424f.

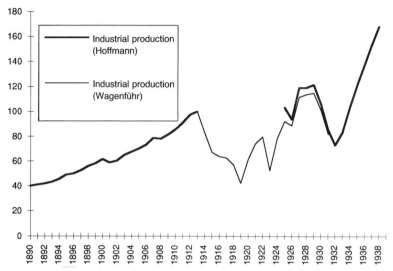

Figure 2.4 German industrial output, 1890–1939 (1913 = 100)
Sources: Hoffmann et al., *Wachstum*, p. 358; Wagenführ, 'Industriewirtschaft',
p. 219.

economy was characterised by serious misallocation of raw materials and
factors of production. Electrical ouput during the war years was on average a third higher than in 1913; but with the exception of non-ferrous
metals, all major industrial indicators fell – steel by 13.5 per cent, coal
by 16.5 per cent, metal products by 20.1 per cent, pig iron by 33.6 per
cent and textiles by 56.4 per cent. At the same time, indicators of consumer production do not indicate significantly greater contraction;
indeed, tobacco production rose during the war, while the output of
sugar fell less than the output of pig iron (see figures 2.5, 2.6 and 2.7).[91]
Although the railway authorities exceeded pre-war levels of investment
in locomotives by 23 per cent, the volume of goods transported by rail
had fallen to 59 per cent of pre-war levels by 1917.[92]

One reason why the German war economy's performance was less
than optimal lies on the demand side. Clearly, in all combatant countries, governments were obliged by the unanticipated scale of the war
to appropriate a far greater share of output than ever before. In the
early stages of the war, the sudden competition for resources between
government procurement agencies and consumers precipitated liquidity

---

[91] Calculated from Hoffmann et al., *Wachstum*, pp. 358f., 383ff., 390–3; Feldman, *Iron
and Steel*, pp. 474f.; Wagenführ, 'Industriewirtschaft', pp. 23ff.
[92] Graham, *Hyperinflation*, pp. 307f.; Hohorst et al. (eds.), *Sozialgeschichtliches Arbeitsbuch*, II, p. 82.

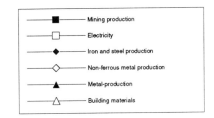

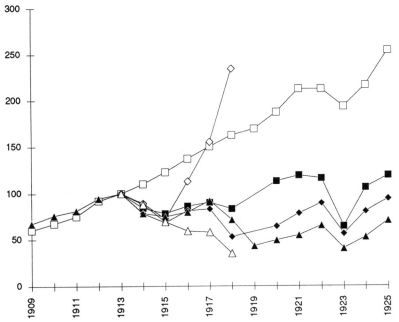

Figure 2.5 Heavy industrial production, 1909–1925 (1913 = 100)
Sources: Statistisches Jahrbuch für das Deutsche Reich, 1921/2, 1924/5;
Hoffmann *et al., Wachstum,* pp. 358, 383–5, 388, 390–5; Wagenführ,
'Industriewirtschaft', p. 219; Bresciani, *Inflation,* pp. 193f., 198; Graham,
Hyperinflation, pp. 387, 293, 306; Roesler, *Finanzpolitik,* p. 221.

crises as people sought to withdraw savings and buy up stocks in
anticipation of future shortages. To avert bank crashes and bankruptcies, debt moratoriums were resorted to (as in France), or the laws
governing the convertibility of paper money into gold were formally
or informally suspended.[93] In the longer term, governments sought to
finance the war by a combination of increased taxation and borrowing,
with the emphasis on the latter. Insofar as borrowing took the form

[93] J. Lawrence, M. Dean and J.-L. Robert, 'The Outbreak of War and the Urban
Economy: Paris, Berlin and London in 1914', *EcHR,* xlv, 3 (1992).

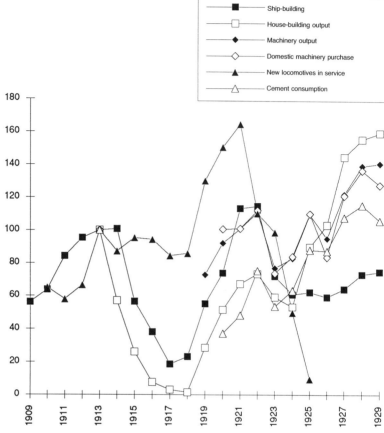

Figure 2.6 Investment indicators, 1909–1929 (1913 = 100)
Sources: Hoffmann et al., Wachstum, pp. 358, 383–5, 388, 390–5; Wagenführ,
'Industriewirtschaft', p. 219; Bresciani, Inflation, pp. 193ff, 198; Graham,
Hyperinflation, pp. 287, 293, 306; Holtfrerich, Inflation, pp. 182f., 201; Balder-
ston, Economic Crisis, p. 74.

of the sale of war bonds to the public, its impact was simply to
substitute saving for consumption. However, to compensate for lags
in the sale of war bonds, all governments borrowed from their central
banks, or introduced new forms of government promissory notes to
pay for government purchases – both of which devices led to monetary
expansion. It was the degree of expansion, coupled with the degree
of physical shortage which determined the level of wartime inflation
in the combatant countries. In this regard, it is striking that German

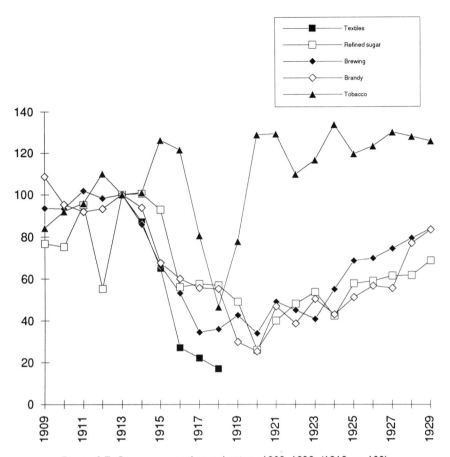

Figure 2.7 Consumer goods production, 1909–1929 (1913 = 100)
Sources: Hoffmann *et al., Wachstum*, pp. 358, 383–5, 388, 390–5; Wagenführ,
p. 219; Bresciani, *Inflation*, pp. 193f., 198; Graham, *Hyperinflation*, pp. 287,
293, 306; Petzina *et al.* (eds.), *Sozialgeschichtliches Arbeitsbuch*, III, p. 61;
Bry, *Wages*, p. 26; Roesler, *Finanzpolitik*, p. 221.

financial and monetary performance was worse than that in Britain,
France or Italy – though it was not as disastrous as that in Russia.[94]
   As with the allocation of goods, this failure stemmed partly from
inadequate preparedness. In 1907, Max Warburg had presented a
paper to the Association of German Banks and Bankers on the subject

[94] T. Balderston, 'War Finance and Inflation in Britain and Germany', *EcHR*, 42
(1989), pp. 222–44, Hardach, *First World War*, p. 81; Kindleberger, *Financial
History*, pp. 295f.; Feldman, *Great Disorder*, pp. 25–51.

of 'Financial Readiness for War' in which he estimated the annual cost of the war at 22 bn. marks.[95] This was a higher figure than most other commentators anticipated;[96] but still an underestimate. In fact, annual Reich expenditure on the war averaged 30 bn. marks, or roughly 84 m. marks per day. Between 1914 and 1918, total Reich spending rose by a factor of five; the spending of the states by a factor of four. Including the communes and social insurance system, total public spending rose from around 18.5 per cent of NNP before the war to 76 per cent at its peak in 1917.[97] As elsewhere, only a limited proportion of this expenditure was met out of taxation. Ordinary Reich revenues (from tax) covered just 13.7 per cent of total expenditures, despite the introduction from 1916 of new consumption taxes (on coal and beverages, for example), of a turnover tax and of 'war levies' on capital gains and a tax on excess profits. The states covered only a third (35 per cent) of their expenditure with taxation.[98] Instead, in accordance with the prevailing theory of war finance and as in all combatant countries, the bulk of spending was financed by borrowing; though unlike Britain, France and Russia, Germany was only able to borrow a limited amount abroad. Total foreign lending (largely credits from suppliers of imports) probably amounted to around 8 bn. gold marks, compared with around 17 bn. gold marks which Britain was able to borrow in the US.[99] The greater part of the burden of borrowing therefore fell on the German capital market. Beginning in September 1914, the Reich issued tranches of war loans every six months, so that by the end of the war the Reich funded debt had reached 99.3 bn. marks, a twenty-fold increase. However, as the public sector deficit spiralled (reaching a peak of 71 per cent of NNP for the Reich and states combined in 1917), the level of borrowing exceeded the public's

[95] WA, XIX, Gesammelte Vorträge, M.M. Warburg, 'Finanzielle Kriegsbereitschaft und Börsengesetz', 5.9.07. For a similar figure, cf. J. von Renauld, Die finanzielle Mobilmachung der deutschen Wehrkraft (Leipzig, 1901).
[96] See, e.g., J. Riesser, Finanzielle Kriegsbereitschaft und Kriegsführung (Jena, 1913); O. Schwartz, Die finanzielle Stellung der europäischen Großmächte, zugleich im Hinblick auf ihre finanzielle Kriegsbereitschaft (Stuttgart, 1913). Cf. Haller, 'Finanzpolitik', pp. 115f.
[97] W. Lotz, Die deutsche Staatsfinanzwirtschaft im Kriege (Stuttgart, 1927), p. 104; Witt, 'Finanzpolitik', pp. 424f.; Hardach, First World War, pp. 150–4; Roesler, Finanzpolitik, pp. 197ff. See also Bresciani, Inflation, p. 47; Graham, Hyperinflation, p. 7. Cf. figure 0.4.
[98] Roesler, Finanzpolitik, pp. 196–201; Haller, 'Finanzpolitik', pp. 131–4; Hardach, First World War, pp. 157f.; Kindleberger, Financial History, pp. 292f.
[99] Bresciani, Inflation, pp. 83ff.; Hardach, First World War, pp. 140–50. For details on the role of Warburg's in arranging supplier credits to the Reich in Scandinavia in WA, 'Jahresbericht 1916'; 'Jahresbericht 1917', II. Teil; 'Jahresbericht 1918', Anlage 35. Altogether, credits totalling 824.6 m. kronen were negotiated. The bank was also apparently able to place some German war loans in New York in the early months of the war.

willingness to lend long to the government. From September 1916, the amount of war bonds sold was consistently less than the amount of floating debt in circulation.[100] By November 1918, the Reich's floating debt had reached 51.2 bn. marks, 34 per cent of the total Reich debt. The state of Hamburg's debt had risen from 842 m. marks to 1.75 bn. marks, of which around 57 per cent was floating debt.[101]

What was distinctive about German war finance was not so much the level of public borrowing, but the extent to which it gave rise to monetary expansion. In the years before 1914, the German monetary authorities had devoted considerable attention to the question of how best to counter a war-induced liquidity crisis (such as there had been in 1870/1). In the light of the financial crises of 1907 and 1911, the Reichsbank President Havenstein had pursued a policy of increasing the Reichsbank's gold reserve, by encouraging the use of other forms of money, such as banknotes (formally declared legal tender only in 1909), cheques and giral payments. By 23 July, the gold reserve had reached 1.36 bn. marks; in addition to which there remained the war treasure in the Julius Tower, which was increased in 1913 to around 200 m. marks.[102] At the same time, preparations had been made for the establishment, in the event of war, of state loan banks (*Darlehnskassen*), empowered to issue special notes (*Scheine*) against securities; as early as 1912, 550 m. marks of these notes had been printed in anticipation of a conflict.[103] Havenstein was well aware, in other words, that the public flight into liquidity would be unprecedented in the event of a war. However, largely because he was unsuccessful in his efforts to persuade the joint stock banks to pursue similarly prudent reserve policies, these preparations did not suffice. On 31 July 1914, having lost 103 m. marks in gold within a week, the Reichsbank illegally suspended gold convertibility, an action which was retrospectively legalised four days later.[104]

The legislation of 4 August created the potential for unlimited monetary growth through four simple modifications to the Reichsbank's reserve rule. The threshhold beyond which the Reichsbank had to pay tax on note issues was suspended; state loan bank notes were given

---

[100] Roesler, *Finanzpolitik*, pp. 206f.; Holtfrerich, *Inflation*, p. 117; Hardach, *First World War*, p. 159. Comparative figures for France and Britain in Schremmer, 'Public Finance', p. 470. Schremmer's point that the level of borrowing rose by a higher factor in Germany is misleading, since the increase is less than in Britain and France when one includes the German state and local debts. See figure 1.4.

[101] Roesler, *Finanzpolitik*, pp. 204f.; Lippmann, *Leben*, pp. 262–5; Brandt, *Hamburgs Finanzen*, pp. 15–25.

[102] Zilch, *Die Reichsbank und die finanzielle Kriegsvorbereitungen*, pp. 92–114.

[103] *Ibid.*, p. 122.

[104] *Ibid.*, pp. 138ff.

equal status to gold in the Reichsbank's primary (one-third) reserve; and Reich Treasury bills were given equal status to trade bills in the secondary (two-thirds) reserve. Finally, it was allowed that state loan bank notes could be issued against war bonds.[105] This meant that not only short-term borrowing led to money creation; in theory, long-term Reich bonds, sold to the public for cash, could be used as security for loans from the state loan banks, whose notes, when taken to the Reichsbank, could be used as security for a loan of Reichsbank notes: a potentially unstoppable monetary merry-go-round. In practice, financial institutions and the public did not take full advantage of these monetary opportunities. The major banks and industrial concerns were increasingly willing to hold non-interest-bearing treasury bills because of their liquidity, so that from mid 1917 on, more than half of the Reich's floating debt was held outside the Reichsbank.[106] Typically, large banks held around half of their assets in the form of Treasury bills by 1918; and found their reserve ratios rising.[107] Moreover, after 1915 relatively few holders of war bonds used them as security for state loans.[108] Nevertheless, the annual rate of monetary growth was still significantly above that in Britain (around 14 per cent for cash in circulation);[109] and it is clear that the state loan bank notes were the key to the process. By the end of the war, 15.6 bn. marks of these had been issued (mostly to local authorities), of which around two thirds circulated as cash, while the rest had ended up in the Reichsbank's reserve, where they accounted for 15 per cent of total assets, and two thirds of the primary reserve. They thus were doubly responsible for the 38 per cent annual growth rate of cash in circulation – a rate substantially ahead of that for M2 or M3 (including time and savings deposits) (see figure 2.8).[110]

In the light of German monetary laxity, one might expect German price inflation to have been more severe than that elsewhere. Yet this was not so. After an initial surge in the first eleven months of the war, largely a consequence of panic-buying and supply bottlenecks, official wholesale prices were relatively stable until mid 1917 (see figure 2.9). The average wartime inflation rate of around 20 per cent (again for wholesale prices) was less than in France (36 per cent) and Britain

[105] Holtfrerich, *Inflation*, pp. 114ff. Cf. Feldman, *Great Disorder*, pp. 26–51.
[106] *Ibid.*, pp. 67f.; Haller, 'Finanzpolitik', pp. 121–30.
[107] Roesler, *Finanzpolitik*, p. 220; Pohl, *Bankensgeschichte*, p. 119.
[108] Roesler, *Finanzpolitik*, pp. 212–15. By December 1918, just 5.5 per cent of state loan bank notes had been issued against war bonds.
[109] Kindleberger, *Financial History*, p. 295.
[110] Roesler, *Finanzpolitik*, pp. 208ff., 216; Graham, *Hyperinflation*, p. 216; Haller, 'Finanzpolitik', pp. 121–30; Holtfrerich, *Inflation*, pp. 50–4. Joint-stock bank deposits grew at 25 per cent annually; savings bank deposits at 10 per cent.

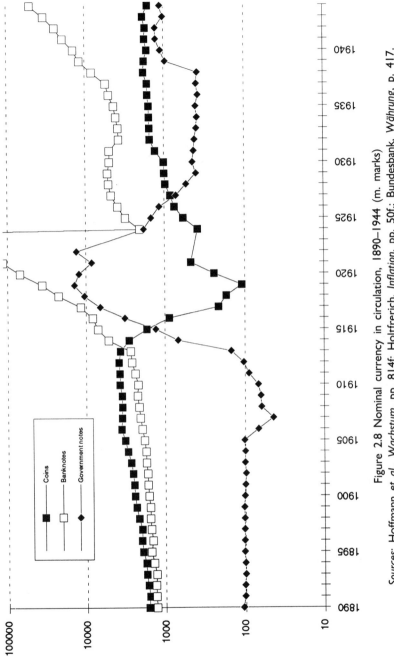

Figure 2.8 Nominal currency in circulation, 1890–1944 (m. marks)

Sources: Hoffmann *et al.*, *Wachstum*, pp. 814f; Holtfrerich, *Inflation*, pp. 50f.; Bundesbank, *Währung*, p. 417.

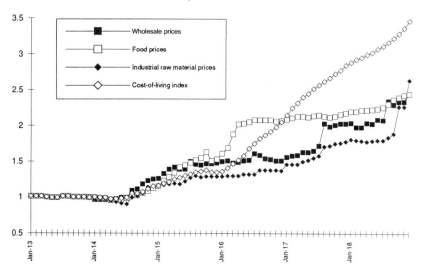

Figure 2.9 Wartime inflation, 1914–1918 (1913 = 1)
Sources: Bry, *Wages*, pp. 422–9, 440–5; *Zahlen zur Geldentwertung*, p. 5;
Roesler, *Finanzpolitik*, p. 227.

(23 per cent); although it is clear that the cost of living rose twice as fast in Germany (32 per cent) as in Britain (16 per cent).[111] Why did German prices not rise further? The answer lies principally in the controls on industrial prices imposed by the system of syndication and allocation; and the series of ordinances which were passed against profiteering (*Wucher*), forestalling and regrating (*Kettenhandel*), which principally affected the retail trade. These measures identified the problem of inflation in archaic terms as one of 'dearth' (*Teuerung*), and attempted to prohibit price increases by wholesalers and retailers.[112] Initial measures introduced in August and October 1914, which empowered state governments to act against excessive prices proved ineffectual; and it was not until 1915/16, with the introduction of rationing for essential foods, maximum prices for food and raw materials, the creation of local Price Supervisory Boards, the law against *Kettenhandel*, and the legal ruling condemning 'abnormal profits' that price control was effective.[113] In addition, new measures were also introduced to insulate the currency from the detrimental effects of the suspension of gold convertibility and the growing trade deficit on the

[111] Figures calculated from Holtfrerich, *Inflation*, p. 17; Petzina, *Deutsche Wirtschaft*, p. 82; Hardach, *First World War*, p. 172.
[112] Feldman, *Army, Industry and Labour*, pp. 97–117, 471f.
[113] Hardach, *First World War*, pp. 115–17, 199.

exchange rate, thus limiting the inflationary impact of imports. These included an official compulsion for importers to negotiate credits only in foreign currency and for exporters (who were encouraged to export by subsidised domestic prices) to secure payment in foreign currency, and, later, blanket exchange and import controls.[114] The effects of these measures, however, were not merely to check the upward trend in the official price index. Price controls distorted the market when they created artificial differentials,[115] led to the development of black markets for goods in demand, hence exacerbating shortages on the official market, and encouraged producers to reduce the quality of goods sold at official prices.[116] Inflation, in other words, was merely suppressed. It seems probable that this growing 'overhang' of frustrated purchasing power carried with it a high price in terms of economic efficiency.

Dearth in Hamburg

The 'exaltation' of the days of August 1914 appeared to many observers to have transcended all social divisions.[117] For the first time, Social Democrats in the Reichstag voted for military expenditure, publicly accepting the argument that the war was one of defence against Tsarism.[118] At an interdenominational service in front of the Reichstag, a congregation sang Protestant and Catholic hymns together; nor did Jews, feminists or homosexuals feel themselves excluded.[119] In Hamburg, the Bürgerschaft passed a resolution affirming that 'Merchant and worker have joined hands; with united strength each sets about his work'; and throughout the war, the Hamburg Senate repeatedly praised the 'splendid' and 'patriotic' conduct of the local Social Democrat leadership.[120] Yet few observers could deny that by 1916, if not before, the *Burgfrieden* had begun to crumble. Recent historians have seen this as an inevitable consequence of material polarisation: the war economy led to a heightening of class division, paving the way for

---

[114] F. Kleine-Natrop, *Devisenpolitik in Deutschland vor dem Kriege und in der Kriegs- und Nachkriegszeit* (Berlin, 1922); *Hamburger Fremdenblatt*, 130, 12.5.23 (a useful summary of the exchange controls introduced since 1916).

[115] For price differentials, see Roesler, *Finanzpolitik*, pp. 225–7; Bresciani, *Inflation*, p. 442.

[116] Holtfrerich, *Inflation*, pp. 79–94.

[117] F. Meinecke, *Die deutsche Erhebung von 1914* (Stuttgart, 1914); and his retrospective comments in *Die deutsche Katastrophe* (Wiesbaden, 1946), pp. 43ff.

[118] See in general S. Miller, *Burgfrieden und Klassenkampf. Die deutsche Sozialdemokratie im Ersten Weltkrieg* (Düsseldorf, 1974).

[119] Eksteins, *Rites of Spring*, p. 61.

[120] Ullrich, *Kriegsalltag*, p. 17; Lüth and Loose, *Bürgermeister Carl Petersen*, pp. 41f.; Schramm, *Neun Generationen*, I, p. 453; Comfort, *Revolutionary Hamburg*, p. 66.

revolution in 1918/19.[121] However, a more useful insight may be
Meinecke's, that the war economy created a conflict between individual
freedom and the power of 'a state whose very essence is organisation',
and whose pursuit of 'technicalism, rationalism and the socialism of
the ration-card' led inevitably to compulsion.[122] British historians have
become increasingly preoccupied with the progressive social effects of
the increased state intervention necessitated by the war. Put simply,
war reduced social inequality in Britain.[123] By contrast, the German
state in the First World War appeared to increase inequality by its
interventions, favouring some social groups and penalising others.
Relations between classes became less important during the war compared with relations between special interest groups and the state.
Material outcomes reflected as much the priorities of the increasingly
large and powerful state bureaucracies[124] as the relative political power
of economic groups.

The allocation of manpower provides one obvious illustration of the
arbitrary workings of the German state. Clearly, an inevitable inequality
of the war was the greater sacrifice of those men required to risk their
lives in the miserable conditions of the Fronts, compared with those
who remained at home. The state's objective was to match enemy
military manpower while at the same time optimising domestic production of food and materiel. In the German case, the number of men
under arms rose from 2.9 million in the first month of war to 4.4
million by the beginning of 1915, and over 7 million at its peak in
early 1918. Of the 13 million who at one time or another 'served',
some 2.4 million lost their lives (18 per cent); 4.3 million were wounded
(of whom as many as 2.7 million were permanently disabled); and 1
million were taken prisoner.[125] Their removal from the labour force
could only partially be compensated for by the increased employment
of women (an additional 5.2 million), the use of prisoners-of-war
(900,000) and imported foreign labour (360,000).[126] It is not necessary
to attach a cash value to each dead soldier to appreciate that this was

[121] J. Kocka, *Facing Total War* (Leamington Spa, 1984). For Hamburg, see Ullrich,
'Arbeiterbewegung', e.g., pp. 282f.
[122] Meinecke, *Deutsche Katastrophe*, p. 44.
[123] A.S. Milward, *The Economic Effects of Two World Wars in Britain* (London/Basing-
stoke, 1984); J.M. Winter (ed.), *The Great War and the British People* (Basingstoke,
1985).
[124] It is important in this regard to stress the multiplicity of public authorities. Not
only did the military, Reich, state and local officials frequently find themselves in
conflict; as public powers were delegated to private organisations (e.g., the industrial
associations), these too joined the bureaucratic fray.
[125] R. Bessel, *Germany after the First World War* (Oxford, 1993), pp. 5, 73, 79.
[126] Petzina *et al.* (eds.), *Sozialgeschichtliches Arbeitsbuch*, III, p. 27; Henning, *Industrialisierte Deutschland*, p. 34.

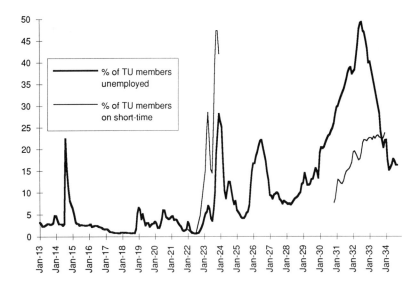

Figure 2.10 Unemployment and short-time work in Germany, 1913–1934
Source: Bry, Wages, pp. 398–402, 432.

economically detrimental.[127] A comparison of the age and sex structure of Hamburg's population in 1910 with that in 1919 reveals an unprecedented loss of human capital: war, unlike cholera, claimed men in their prime.[128] Some degree of loss was inevitable, of course; but the reduction in manpower in Hamburg was above average: of 120,000 men called to arms from Hamburg, 34,519 (28 per cent) were killed and 13,482 were registered as war-wounded seven years after the war's end.[129] Despite a 13 per cent increase in the number of women in employment, total employment in Hamburg fell by 28 per cent during the war.[130] Moreover, because of the relative lack of discrimination with which troops were mobilised in the early part of the war, the dead and maimed included many skilled workers.[131]

In the immediate aftermath of the outbreak of war, labour shortages were not the problem, but rather temporary unemployment caused by the closure of firms (see figure 2.10).[132] As the number of unemployed

[127] Cf. E.L. Bogart, *Direct and Indirect Costs of the Great World War* (Oxford, 1920).
[128] *Statistische Mitteilungen über den hamburgischen Staat*, Nr. 18 (1920), pp. 9f.
[129] Büttner, *Politische Gerechtigkeit*, p. 22.
[130] Ullrich, 'Arbeiterbewegung', pp. 229–31. Cf. *Statistisches Jahrbuch 1925*, p. 246.
[131] Schult, *Hamburger Arbeiter*, p. 135.
[132] Kocka, *Facing Total War*, p. 22; Petzina, *Deutsche Wirtschaft*, p. 10. For statistics see Petzina *et al.* (eds.), *Sozialgeschichtliches Arbeitsbuch*, III, p. 119; Holtfrerich, *Inflation*, p. 199; Bry, *Wages in Germany*, p. 432.

reached 28,000 in August (of whom around 9 per cent were from
'business circles'), there were anxious discussions of the problem in
the Senate – probably prompted by the creation of a Central Labour
Exchange at the Reich level, rather than anonymous threats of
'upheaval, riot, revolution and burglary upon burglary'.[133] However,
compared with the extent of the disruption in Berlin (to say nothing
of Paris), as well as with subsequent unemployment peaks, the crisis
of August 1914 was a minor one. Worst affected were the docks,
where employment fell by 73 per cent in the course of August; but
in the course of September, the process of conscription rapidly solved
the unemployment problem.[134] Around half of the Hapag's employees
were called up and 40 per cent of contracted dockers.[135] By January
1915, firms like Blohm and Voß which had substantial war contracts
were requesting the return of skilled workers called up since August;
and by December 1915 the firm was for the first time forced to employ
women and prisoners-of-war.[136]

The immediate consequence of conscription was to weaken the
Hamburg trade unions, as total membership dropped from 142,799 to
67,151 in 1915 and 44,342 in 1918 – a 70 per cent fall.[137] By October
1916, only 22 per cent of shipyard workers were still unionised.[138]
This contraction of the unions' constituency – a process which had in
fact already begun with the unofficial strike of 1913 – greatly diminished
the effectiveness in Hamburg of the tripartite system of industrial
relations which emerged at the national level and culminated in the
Auxiliary Service Law of December 1916.[139] The military authorities
in Altona and the Senate both appear to have hoped that state mediation
and union representation could reduce friction between workers and
employers on the waterfront, and they were encouraged by the conciliatory stance of the Metal Workers' Union representative Koch.[140]

---

[133] StAH, DHSG II, Spez. XXXIV 23a, Auszug aus dem Protokolle des Senats, 14.8.14;
27a, HKH to DHSG, 24.8.14; Ullrich, *Kriegsalltag*, pp. 17–21.

[134] StAH, DHSG II, Spez. XXXIV 27a, Hafenbetriebsverein to DHSG, 25.8.14, 28.8.14.

[135] *Ibid.*; Cecil, *Ballin*, pp. 215–31.

[136] StAH, FA B&V 13, Firmenleitung, 14.1.15, 19.11.15. By February 1916, 500
women and 450 POWs were employed: *ibid.*, Firmenleitung, 3.2.16. In fact women
lacked the physical strength required for work in the yards, and only ever accounted
for 3 per cent of the workforce at Blohm & Voß, while the share of youths employed
only rose from 7 per cent to 9 per cent: B&V, 249, Bd. 1, 268; 264; B&V, 13,
Bd. 2, Firmenleitung, 23.8.18, 13.9.18.

[137] Schult, *Geschichte der Hamburger Arbeiter*, pp. 106f., 135.

[138] Ullrich, 'Arbeiterbewegung', pp. 248f.

[139] See Feldman, *Army, Industry and Labour, passim*; Hardach, *First World War*, pp.
63–9, 179f.; G. Mai, *Kriegswirtschaft und Arbeiterbewegung in Württemberg 1914–1918*
(Stuttgart, 1983); H.-G. Husuung, 'Arbeiterschaft und Arbeiterbewegung im Ersten
Weltkrieg: Neue Forschungen über Deutschland und England', *HZ*, Sonderheft 15
(1986), pp. 611–64.

[140] Ullrich, 'Arbeiterbewegung', pp. 258f., 265ff., 365; *idem*, *Kriegsalltag*, pp. 105–8.
On the implementation of the Auxiliary Service Law in Hamburg, see StAH, DHSG

However, confrontational tactics persisted on the waterfront. On the employers' side, Blohm & Voß sought to compensate for labour shortages by lengthening working hours and increasing work intensity, taking advantage of trade union weakness to do so. Junior managers and foremen sometimes took these tactics to extremes: in March 1916, instructions had to be issued discouraging 'forms of words towards insubordinate workers such as: 'You're headed for the trenches'; and a year later, shifts lasting over twenty-four hours were ruled excessive.[141] Workers responded in a variety of ways; more often resorting to individual and spontaneous acts than to collective strike action.[142] There was a recurrent problem of indiscipline at Blohm & Voß: lunch breaks were extended, work was half-hearted, absenteeism was rife and there was routine theft of tools and wood suitable for burning.[143] Above all, workers took advantage of the high demand for their services to change jobs regularly: traditionally high labour mobility reached unprecedented levels, so that 10,000 workers had to be replaced at Blohm and Voß in the year after October 1916 – a problem which the Auxiliary Service Law exacerbated by recognising the worker's right to change job for a higher wage.[144] Finally, as in other industrial areas, the no-strike agreement concluded in August 1914 gradually crumbled. In October 1916, the rejection by Blohm & Voß of a wage claim led to the first major strike of the war; there were major strikes at Vulkan four months later and again in May 1917; and there was a Hanseatic echo of the national strike wave of January 1918.[145]

In one sense, the impact of the war on the labour market did tend

III, Pr. II 3 Bd. I, DHSG Sitzung, 14.12.16; HKH to DHSG, 15.12.16; DKH to DHSG, 15.1.17; HKH to DHSG, 16.1.17. Altogether, 105 companies were affected by the regulation concerning the creation of works committees.

[141] StAH, FA B&V 13 Bd. I, Firmenleitung, 31.1.16; Bd. II, Firmenleitung, 5.4.17. Cf. H.-J. Bieber, 'Die Entwicklung der Arbeitsbeziehungen auf den Hamburger Großwerften (Blohm & Voß, Vulkanswerft) zwischen Hilfsdienstgesetz und Betriebsrätegesetz', in G. Mai (ed.), Arbeiterschaft in Deutschland 1914–1918. Studien zu Arbeitskampf und Arbeitsmarkt im Ersten Weltkrieg (Düsseldorf, 1985), pp. 77–153.

[142] In 1909, 1910 and 1913, Hamburg workers had been a significant percentage (between 4 and 11 per cent) of those involved in strike action in Germany as a whole; but the effect of the war on the Hamburg economy greatly weakened the capacity of the labour force for collective action. Cf. V. Ullrich, 'Massenbewegung in der Hamburger Arbeiterschaft im Ersten Weltkrieg', in Herzig et al. (eds.), Arbeiter in Hamburg, pp. 407–18.

[143] See, e.g., StAH, FA B&V 13 Bd. I, Firmenleitung, 5.11.14; 15.4.15; 29.4.15; 18.2.16; Bd. II, Firmenleitung, 13.9.17; 15.11.17; 20.12.17; 25.4.18.

[144] Ullrich, 'Arbeiterbewegung', p. 232; StAH, FA B&V 13, Bd. II, Firmenleitung, 4.1.17; 18.1.17; GStA, Rep. 90j, Kriegsakten Nr. 5, 'Zusammenstellung der Monats-Berichte der Stellv. Generalkommandos', p. 7.

[145] Ullrich, 'Arbeiterbewegung', pp. 258f., 265ff., 367, 579f.; idem, 'Der Januarstreik 1918 in Hamburg, Kiel und Bremen. Eine vergleichende Studie zur Geschichte der Streikbewegung im Ersten Weltkrieg', ZVHG, 71 (1985), pp. 45–74.

to make society more equal. Labour shortages in strategic sectors gave bargaining power to groups – for example, unskilled shipyard workers – who were traditionally at the lower end of the income scale. Whether through strike action or changing jobs, metal workers were able to secure significant nominal increases in wages; certainly more than were achieved by many salaried employees, a fact overlooked by historians concerned to portray the war in terms of the immiseration of the working class. Between July 1914 and October 1918, the hourly wage of an average male worker at Blohm & Voβ rose by 113 per cent (from 64 pfennigs to 136 pfennigs); while a youth employed at the same yard earned 85 per cent more than in peacetime and a textile worker earned 74 per cent more. By comparison, a junior clerical worker earned only 62 per cent more, a bookkeeper only 37 per cent more and a chief cashier a meagre 30 per cent more. All groups therefore experienced losses in real terms; but manual workers did better than white-collar employees (see figures 2.11 and 2.12).[146] This success was a testament to the effectiveness of spontaneous or 'unofficially' organised action in circumstances of high demand for labour and political anxiety about working-class disaffection.

However, such evidence of social 'levelling' requires qualification. It was a hallmark of the war economy that nominal income levels were subject to considerable distortion, depending on the attitude of the state towards particular groups. The success of metal-workers' wage demands owed much to the military authorities' desire to avoid stoppages in submarine construction, for example.[147] Similarly, the willingness of the state to compensate some groups for material losses occasioned by the war led to obvious cases of favouritism. For example, those who had lost assets overseas were quick to seek compensation from the public purse; but success depended on the ability to lobby effectively in Berlin. This was beyond the organisational resources of the merchant houses.[148] By contrast, Albert Ballin's tactics in his campaign to secure compensation for the shipowners provide an important illustration of the development of corporate lobbying in wartime. Ballin transformed the Berlin bureau of the Hapag into a lobbying department under the direction of Arndt von Holtzendorff, the brother

---

[146] Workers' wages from B&V 249 Bd. 1; 268; Ullrich, 'Arbeiterbewegung', pp. 241f; Hardach, *First World War*, pp. 197f. White-collar wages from Lyth, '*Mittelstand*', pp. 154f. See in general on real wages during the war: Kocka, *Facing Total War*, pp. 17–22.

[147] See, e.g., Ullrich, 'Arbeiterbewegung', pp. 265ff.

[148] StAH, DHSG II, Spez. XXXIV, No. 77, Verein Westafrikanischer Kaufleute to Reichskolonialminister Solf, 22.1.15. The Reich Treasury Office consistently opposed any compensation measure which might lead to a generalised indemnification of overseas companies.

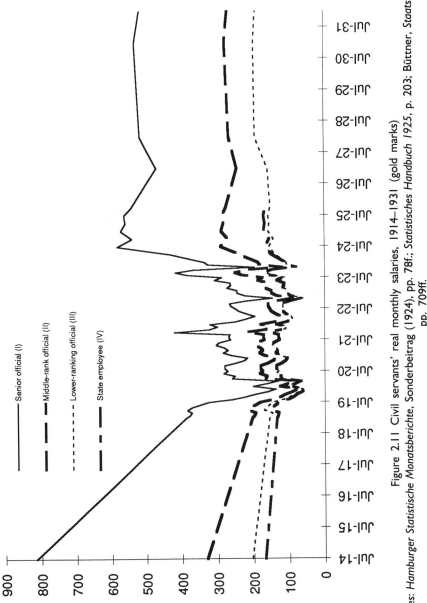

Figure 2.11 Civil servants' real monthly salaries, 1914–1931 (gold marks)

Sources: Hamburger Statistische Monatsberichte, Sonderbeitrag (1924), pp. 78f.; Statistisches Handbuch 1925, p. 203; Büttner, Staatskrise, pp. 709ff.

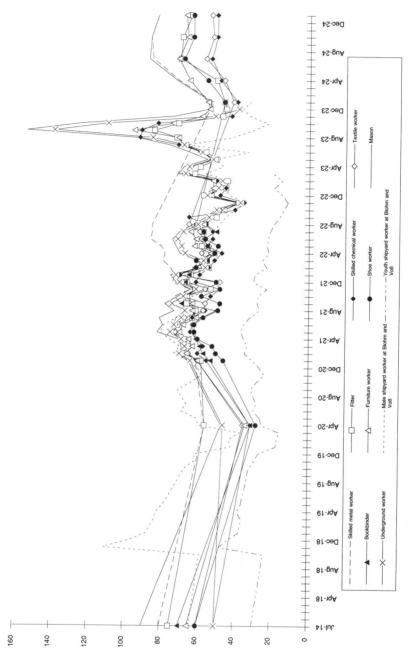

Figure 2.12 Workers' real hourly wage rates, 1914, 1918–1924 (gold pfennigs)

Sources: *Statistische Mitteilungen über den hamburgischen Staat,* 13 (1922); *Hamburger Statistische Monatsberichte* 1. Jg. (May 1924), p. 98; StAH, FA B&V 249, Bd. 1; 268; 139; 1286 Bd. 2.

of Admiral von Holtzendorff. The Prussian's social cachet made him ideally suited to the task of wining and dining officials and politicians; and the regular 'gentlemen's evenings' in the Viktoriastraße (next door to the Rathenaus) became a familiar part of Berlin's wartime salon society, which ministers (including Helfferich, Delbrück, Zimmermann and Roedern) and politicians (such as Stresemann, Erzberger and Westarp) did not scruple to attend.[149] At the same time, Ballin entrusted the Association of German Shippers secretary and Reichstag deputy Peter Stubmann with the task of mobilising parliamentary backing for a bill compensating the shippers, and forged close links with Reich officials, notably the Reich Treasury official Wilhelm Cuno, which ultimately led to Cuno's leaving the civil service to work for the Hapag.[150] Ballin's arguments for compensation – that the shipping lines played an indispensable role in the German economy, that they had suffered exceptional losses because of the war, that the government was partly to blame for these, and that insurance funds would not suffice because of the rising costs of ship-building – were grudgingly accepted in Berlin.[151] After a prolonged wrangle during which the shippers' demands rose from 50 m. marks to 1.5 bn. marks, the government finally agreed to pay compensation equal to the pre-war value of all freight ships lost or damaged, the cost of repairing the ships which had languished in dock since 1914, as well as 50–70 per cent of any price increase for reconstruction completed within four years of the end of the war, and 20–55 per cent for work finished in the subsequent five years – a revealing indication of official inflationary expectations.[152] These monies began to be advanced to the shipping

---

[149] Ballin commented revealingly that 'it would be a shame for your evenings if the false impression arose that they did not serve national issues but private interests'; Cecil, *Ballin*, p. 253.

[150] *Ibid.*, pp. 236–41, 320; BAP, RFM 46124, Reichschatzamt Vermerk, 7.7.16.

[151] BAP, RFM 46579 N.Reg. 315/113–19, Ballin to Graf Roedern, 8.6.17; 41624/150 Reichsamt des Innern Sitzung, 12.4.17: 'He [State Secretary Richter] admitted that the general situation of the shippers was still more difficult than in the other branches of commerce and industry and that the general interest in the revitalisation of the German shipping lines was very much greater.'

[152] Details of negotiations between the shippers, the Interior Ministry and the Treasury Office in BAP, RFM 46124/101–67. On the drafting of the Compensation Law, 41624/182–254; *Sten. Ber. Reichstag*, 114. Sitzung, 11.7.17, pp. 3554f.; 117. Plenarsitzung, 20.7.17, p. 36116; 119. Sitzung, 3.10.17, pp. 3638–49; 120. Sitzung, 4.10.17, pp. 3651–75; 126. Sitzung, 11.10.17, pp. 3874–79; *RGB*, Nr. 201, 1917, pp. 1025–9, Nr. 6132, Gesetz über die Widerherstellung der deutschen Handelsflotte, 7.11.17. Cf. Hapag, *Jahresbericht, 1914–20*; Kohlhaus, 'Die Hapag', p. 16; Cecil, *Ballin*, pp. 242–7. The measure was viewed with suspicion by the Hamburg banks because it challenged their traditional control over the financing of Hamburg ship-building. Immediately after the bill was passed the Commerzbank, the Vereinsbank and Warburg's set up the German Ship Mortgage Bank with a paid-up capital of 2.5 m. marks, which in its first year of activity lent 3.5 m. marks to shipping lines using

lines (formally as loans disbursed by a new Reich Committee) in the course of 1918.[153]

Such generous handouts by the Reich were unusual. However, it is clear that, at the state level, similar loans and subsidies were made available to smaller firms. In the early months of the war, the Hamburg state, in conjunction with the major Hamburg banks, set up a number of institutions designed to avert small-business bankruptcies by providing easy loans.[154] In August 1914, a Loan Bank for Mortgages was set up with 200 m. marks of state funds to make loans against mortgage bonds (an asset popular with small investors in the city); though it only lent out 30 m. marks in the war years.[155] The Hamburg Bank of 1914 was set up with a capital of 15.85 m. marks (of which the Hamburg state provided 5 m. marks) to rescue commercial firms in difficulties, and lent around 13.75 m. marks during the war.[156] Finally, the Assistance Bank for Artisans was set up with 3 m. marks of state funds to assist those small manufacturers whose businesses had 'suffered because of the war'; between 1914 and 1918, it lent 2.59 m. marks, of which 42 per cent was still owing at the end of the war.[157]

Such loans and subsidies were just one of the forms of preferential treatment which developed during the war. In a similar way, the failure of the government to impose higher direct taxation attested to the powerful political position of business; for it was business, and especially industry, which made the biggest gains in income and wealth during the war. Even in Hamburg, where business did relatively poorly during the war, interest groups succeeded in fending off higher tax burdens. The wartime tax measure which was most energetically opposed by Hamburg business interests was the turnover tax (*Umsatzsteuer*), a flat levy on all business activity introduced in June 1916. This posed a serious threat to commercial interests because of the lack of vertical integration in commerce and the tendency for imported goods in particular to change hands numerous times on the bourse. In a typical example of wartime buck-passing, Max Warburg therefore proposed as an alternative a sales tax on finished goods which

seventeen existing ships as security: WA, 'Jahresbericht 1917', p. 16, Anlage 29; *50 Jahre Deutsche Schiffsbeleihungsbank* (Hamburg, 1968).

[153] By June 1918, the Hapag had received 79.9 m. marks (with a further 20.2 m. following in June and 19.9 m. marks in August); the German Australian Line 20.3 m. marks; the Woermann Line 4.97 m. marks; Sloman's 2.58 m. marks; and the German East African Line 7.23 m. marks: BAP, RFM 41624 Alt. Reg. 2954.

[154] This was the preferred alternative to a moratorium: WA, 'Jahresbericht 1914', p. 7; Warburg, *Aufzeichnungen*, pp. 36ff.

[155] Pohl, *Bankengeschichte*, p. 107; Lyth, 'Mittelstand', p. 412; Lippmann, *Leben*, pp. 266ff.

[156] Pohl, *Bankengeschichte*, pp. 108f.

[157] Lyth, 'Mittelstand', pp. 293f.; Brandt, *Finanzen*, pp. 15–19.

would have fallen upon retailers and consumers; and the Hanseatic Chambers of Commerce, supported by the Hamburg Senate, finally secured important concessions for 'intermediary trade', including an exemption for exporters. In its final form, the turnover tax thus weighed most heavily on the small business groups such as retailers, artisans and manufacturers not represented in the Chamber of Commerce.[158]

It was, however, the state's response to the problem of 'dearth' which most clearly illustrated the relative weakness of such smaller and less-organised economic interests. Shortages, particularly of food, clearly posed the greatest threat to social stability during the war; and the authorities were swift to respond to signs of popular dissatisfaction on this issue.[159] The Hammerbrook food riot of March 1915 led to the introduction of ration cards in Hamburg; the Barmbek riot of August 1916 prompted the setting up of the War Provisions Office (KVA); and the biggest outbreak of unrest, at the nadir of the 'turnip winter' in February 1917, forced an increase in the potato ration.[160] In July 1918, 'in spite of apparently sufficient wages', there was a strike at the Vulkan yard because of 'the almost complete lack of potatoes [and] the absence of fruit and vegetables'. The arrival of additional supplies sufficed to end the strike.[161] Increased supply was clearly the best way of averting 'an elemental eruption of the neglected and disenfranchised parts of the population' – a significant choice of words, in view of the events of 1905/6.[162] However, when no additional supplies were to be had, the authorities had two further options. As Social Democrats and consumers' associations requested, food prices could be subsidised through state purchasing and distribution: around 80 m. marks out of a total wartime expenditure of 348 m. marks was spent by the KVA and its predecessor in this and other related efforts.[163] Alternatively, the prices charged by wholesalers and retailers could be controlled. This was first done by the military authorities in

---

[158] Böhm, *Anwalt der Handelsfreiheit*, pp. 165–71. Nevertheless, those who had opposed the tax most vehemently were dissatisfied even with the compromise achieved; and set up a Hamburg branch of the Central Association of German Wholesalers (ZVDG) with a view to lobbying directly in Berlin rather than through the Chamber of Commerce.

[159] Ullrich, *Kriegsalltag*, pp. 39–47, 51–62. Cf. A. Roerkohl, 'Die Lebensmittelversorgung während des Ersten Weltkrieges im Spannungsfeld kommunaler und staatlicher Maßnahmen', in H.-J. Teuteberg (ed.), *Durchbruch zum modernen Massenkonsum. Lebensmittelmärkte und Lebensmittelqualität im Städtewachstum des Industriezeitalters* (Münster, 1987), pp. 309–70.

[160] Ullrich, 'Arbeiterbewegung', pp. 268–74, 277–82, 352–62.

[161] *Ibid.*; Comfort, *Revolutionary Hamburg*, p. 32.

[162] The phrase is Johannes Amsinck's; quoted in Möring, *200 Jahre Johannes Schuback*.

[163] Lippmann, *Leben*, pp. 206–39, 262–5; Lyth, 'Mittelstand', pp. 349ff.

August 1914, when maximum prices were introduced for certain goods. However, it was not until the September 1915 Bundesrat ordinance for the creation of Price Supervisory Boards that a coherent policy of price control emerged. The Price Supervisory Board set up in October 1916 was carefully designed by the Hamburg Senate to be sympathetic to the interests of business.[164] However, there was considerable pressure from Berlin on the Board to implement the price regulations strictly;[165] and, despite a barrage of criticism,[166] it is clear that it did not neglect its duties: in 1917 alone there were 1,538 successful prosecutions, leading to the closure of 5,551 firms, custodial sentences totalling 12,208 days and fines totalling 92,300 m. marks.[167] Protests in the Bürgerschaft reveal the extent of disaffection among small businessmen; and an attempt by Senate spokesmen to lay the blame on inexperienced lawyers for 'the witch-hunt against business' deceived no one.[168] The problem was insoluble: the Chamber of Commerce was accused by the Berlin authorities of exercising a moderating influence on the Price Board; but in reality, the Board was acting under pressure from Berlin, while the Chamber's protests were 'read by a Saxon *Regierungsrat* and then thrown in the bin'.[169]

In order to appease the mass of consumers, price controls thus made shopkeepers the scapegoats for problems of shortage and monetary expansion which were in no sense their responsibility. Similar sacrifices were exacted from what had been, before the war, one of the most powerful political forces within Hamburg: the property owners. Despite the exodus of men to the Front, there remained some pressure on the housing stock because of the sharp fall in house-building caused by the war: between 1915 and 1918, just 1,923 new homes were added to the Hamburg housing stock, compared with 17,780 in the two

---

[164] The city board's thirty non-official members were predominantly businessmen, including Georg Simon, chairman of the Exporters' League, and the merchants Carl Bunzel and Rudolf Crasemann: StAH, DHSG III, Pr. IV 11 Bd. I, Sen. Prot., 16.10.15. In the same way, there were representatives of the various branches of the food trade on an advisory council to the KVA: DHSG III, Pr. 2 1b. Cf. Lyth, '*Mittelstand*', pp. 343ff.

[165] StAH, DHSG III, Pr. IV 10 Bd. 1, DHSG to Senate, 10.2.17; Price Supervisory Board to Kriegswuchersamt, 11.5.18.

[166] See, e.g., StAH, DHSG III, Pr. IV 24 Bd. 1, HKH to DHSG, 24.9.15; DHSG, Pr. IV 11 Bd. 1, Price Supervisory Board to Kriegswuchersamt, 5.3.17; ZVDG Eingabe, May 1917. Cf. Lyth, '*Mittelstand*', pp. 343f.; Böhm, *Anwalt der Gewerbefreiheit*, pp. 153–61; Götz, *Detaillistenkammer Hamburg*, pp. 58–70.

[167] Figures from StAH, DHSG III, Pr. IV 70.

[168] *Sten. Ber. der Bürgerschaft*, 20. Sitzung, 28.11.17, pp. 407f.; *Neue Hamburger Zeitung*, No. 610, 29.11.17; StAH, DHSG II, Pr. IV 70, DHSG Prot., 20.12.17; 29.1.18; DHSG Eingabe January 1918; DHSG II, III C 52, DHSG Prot., 3. Sitzung, 5.3.18.

[169] StAH, DHSG III, Pr. IV 11 Bd. 1, Bürgerschaft interpolation by Eddelbüttel, 9.1.18.

pre-war years.[170] However, a succession of regulations controlling rents meant that the war was the property owners' nemesis. The Property Owners' Association estimated the cost of the war to its members at 80 m. marks, largely as a result of compulsory rent reductions which were imposed on over half the existing tenancies in Hamburg during the war.[171]

In aggregate terms, the burdens of war were shouldered by all Germans. The 240 per cent rise in the cost of living affected everyone to some extent, as did the 24 per cent fall in real per capita incomes, or the 52 per cent fall in average per capita consumption of meat (see figure 2.13).[172] The increased incidence of lung disease and the overall rise in mortality rates during the war also suggest a picture of general immiseration.[173] But the narrowing of differentials in nominal pay meant that a shipyard worker lost far less in real terms (9 per cent) than a senior civil servant (52 per cent). Put another way, in 1914, the civil servant's monthly income had been roughly five times that of the worker; by 1918, it was less than three times as great.[174] Evidence from tax returns would seem to confirm this picture of levelling: the share of total income going to the top 0.5 per cent of taxpayers appears to have fallen between 1913 and 1916.[175] Moreover, those on lower incomes benefited disproportionately from restrictions on the price of basic foodstuffs and rent; while price control was not strict enough to prevent the development of a large black market to which city-dwellers with spare cash and contacts in the countryside readily turned.[176] Above all, wartime controls had highly differentiated effects on wealth. Between 1913 and 1918, the number of savings accounts in Hamburg rose by 34 per cent, while the real value of the average deposit fell by 69 per cent.[177] The large issues of war bonds also had the effect of spreading asset ownership more widely.[178] Certain

---

[170] Petzina et al. (eds.), Sozialgeschichtliches Arbeitsbuch, III, p. 124.

[171] Lyth, 'Mittelstand', pp. 408, 414f., 461 n. 16, 430.

[172] Witt, 'Finanzpolitik', pp. 424f.; Bry, Wages, pp. 233, 422–9, 440–5; Holtfrerich, Inflation, p. 255; Petzina et al. (eds.), Sozialgeschichtliches Arbeitsbuch, III, p. 109.

[173] Ibid., pp. 32f., 155; Statistik des Hamburgischen Staates, 31 (1921).

[174] Cf. the complaint in the civil servants' journal Der Bureaubeamte that '18-year-olds in industry today can earn more than a Bureauassistent and electrical fitters more than a Hamburg Oberassistent': Lyth, 'Mittelstand', p. 195.

[175] Lippman, Leben, pp. 384f.; Statistisches Handbuch 1920, pp. 244f. But cf. the Pareto coefficient calculations for Prussia, which suggest a significant widening of income distribution: Petzina et al. (eds.), Sozialgeschichtliches Arbeitsbuch, III, p. 106. See in general, W. Zimmermann, A. Günther and R. Meerwarth, Die Einwirkung des Krieges auf Bevölkerungsbewegung, Einkommen und Lebenshaltung in Deutschland (Stuttgart/Berlin/Leipzig, 1932).

[176] See Offer, Agrarian Interpretation, pp. 56f.; Ullrich, 'Arbeiterbewegung', pp. 234f.

[177] Calculated from Statistisches Handbuch 1920, pp. 364f.

[178] See StAH, FA B&V 13, Bd. 1, Firmenleitung, 2.9.15 for attempts to sell war bonds to shipyard workers.

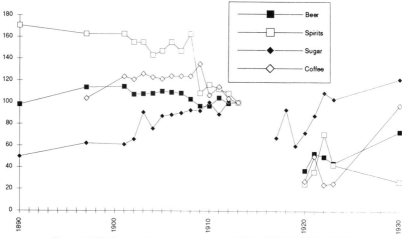

Figure 2.13 Per capita consumption, 1890–1930 (1913 = 100)
Sources: Petzina *et al.* (eds.), *Sozialgeschichtliches Arbeitsbuch*, III, p. 121; Bry,
Wages, p. 233.

kinds of existing wealth, meanwhile, were penalised by government regulation. Share values stagnated, as did the real estate market. It was only those bourgeois groups who made a direct entrepreneurial contribution to the war effort who appeared to accumulate wealth: certainly, the Warburgs, with private capital in the bank worth 22.8 m. marks in 1917, showed little sign of impoverishment.[179]

All this makes it tempting to conclude that the war had shifted the balance of socio-economic power away from the *Mittelstand*, towards, on the one hand, the working class and, on the other, big business.[180] The possibility, already hinted at before 1914, that the interests of the Hamburg elites and the workers' organisations might converge was realised as price and rent controls were used to subsidise working-class living standards at the expense of retailers and landlords; or as civil servants' salaries were held down, while the nominal wages of workers in strategic sectors were allowed to rise. This was certainly how it appeared to the military authorities:

Fruit and fresh vegetables [. . .] are purchased by the upper ten thousand and the now universally well-paid workers, who have no need to shirk the high

---

[179] WA, 'Jahresbericht 1917', II. Teil.
[180] See J. Kocka, 'The First World War and the *Mittelstand*. German Artisans and White Collar Workers', *JCH*, 8 (1973), pp. 101–23; Lyth, '*Mittelstand*', esp. pp. 40, 474. Cf. A. Günther, *Die Folgen des Krieges für Einkommen und Lebenshaltung der mittleren Volksschichten Deutschlands* (Stuttgart/Berlin/Leipizig, 1932).

prices. But the situation is becoming increasingly difficult for the *Mittelstand* or the civil service (*Beamtentum*), upon whom the burdens of the war weigh most heavily.[181]

Yet it would be misleading to portray the social impact of the war simply as a material squeezing of the petty-bourgeoisie between labour and capital. The real significance of the war economy lay in its differential impact on the sub-groups within classes. For example, the experience of the Schramm family – a Senatorial family at the pinnacle of the Hamburg *Großbürgertum* – illustrates that the trauma of deprivation was not confined to the *Mittelstand*. For Ruth Schramm, dearth was more than just a matter of physical deprivation; it was a moral and cultural humiliation. The 'lugubrious and unfriendly public', the war profiteers, the corruption and violence of 1917 – all this represented a grotesque mockery of the ideals of the *Burgfrieden* three years before. To have to eat meat-paste made from the Alster swans was symbolic of Hamburg's degradation; to have to buy food on the black market represented a stark break with 'the principles which held firm for me before 1914'.[182] When her brother returned to the family home from the Front in December 1918, he found that his parents had taken in a lodger on the second floor and closed up the ground floor to save on heating. Although they still ate with silver spoons, he at once recognised 'the end of the grand-bourgeois lifestyle'.[183]

The politics of war and peace

Physical deprivation and material shortages may help to explain why Germany ultimately could not win the war on the Western Front.[184] However, nations have continued to fight wars under far worse conditions than those experienced by Germans in 1918: the Soviet Union suffered catastrophic military defeat and economic collapse in 1941/2, yet fought on. Nor, on the other hand, do material factors explain why the German Reich continued to fight the war to the point of complete military and political collapse. States in stronger positions than that of Germany in 1917 have sought to negotiate peace rather than risk ultimate defeat. The German state, it appears, lacked at once the internal cohesion to wage a total war, and the diplomatic sophistication to negotiate from a position of relative strength. Its collapse

---

[181] GStA, Rep. 90j, Nr. 5, 'Zusammenstellung der Monatsberichte der Stellv. General-kommandos', p. 6 (3.7.17).
[182] Schramm, *Neun Generationen*, II, p. 495.
[183] *Ibid.*, 501.
[184] Bessel, *Germany*, pp. 39ff.

therefore had as much to do with political as with material factors. It reflected a crisis of legitimacy, not supply.[185]

The war had been justified by the German General Staff as necessary to preempt a deterioration in Germany's strategic position: it was to be a swift strike aimed principally at preventing the completion of the Russian armaments programme. However, English intervention, failure at the Marne and Austrian weakness on the Eastern Front led to a military stalemate, with its nadir at Verdun and the Somme in 1916. Given the substantial economic superiority of the Triple Entente, it would have been logical for the German government to have sought either a negotiated peace, or at least some kind of diplomatic shift in the balance of forces which would have increased the chances of military victory. However, the longer the war went on and the greater the sacrifices it entailed, the greater became expectations of its ultimate rewards. The formulation of war aims, which began as a preliminary to negotiation, rapidly escalated into a public debate involving economic interests, ideology and domestic politics, as well as grand strategy. Not only did Germans disagree about what they were fighting for; they disagreed about their chances of winning, and even about how political choices as important as that between war and peace should be arrived at.

From the moment that Bethmann Hollweg's September programme raised the possibility of annexations of ore-rich territory from France and Belgium and the formation of a Central European Customs Union, economic interests were brought into play in the war aims debate. In May 1915, the six principal economic associations submitted their petition on war aims; but already the Hansabund's withdrawal from this united front had exposed the absence of consensus.[186] Indeed, it might be said that the *Burgfrieden* among business interest groups broke down more quickly than that between business and labour. The idea of annexations of all or part of Belgium had some support in Hamburg among men like Rudolf Crasemann and Richard Krogmann; but on the whole most Hamburg businessmen shared Ballin's view that there should be 'no annexation' since 'English policy cannot sacrifice Belgium to us'. The most that could be achieved was 'economic and military dependence [. . .] especially for the ports', by which was meant principally Antwerp, the civil government of which was entrusted to a succession of Hamburg Senators.[187]

[185] Cf. Offer, *Agrarian Interpretation, passim*; N. Ferguson, 'Food and the First World War', *Twentieth Century British History*, 2, 2 (1991), pp. 188–95.
[186] Fischer, *Griff nach der Weltmacht*, pp. 184ff.; Hardach, *First World War*, pp. 226–9.
[187] Pohlmann, *Richard Krogmann*, pp. 214f.; Cecil, *Ballin*, pp. 261–6; Schramm, *Neun Generationen*, II, p. 491.

Similarly, the Chamber of Commerce, led by Ballin and Warburg, spoke out against the idea of *Mitteleuropa*, stressing the limited importance of trade with Central Europe for Germany.[188] For Hamburg, colonial acquisitions were a more attractive prospect, and much effort was expended within the Chamber of Commerce on drawing up a shopping-list of territory which might be acquired from France or England in the event of victory. However, even here there was dissension, as the main mercantile firms disputed the relative merits of German colonies in Africa and Asia.[189]

To some extent, the bitter disagreements within the business community on the subject of war aims reflected the conflicting economic interests of those concerned. Ballin and Warburg, who were generally lukewarm about annexations and inclined to favour a negotiated peace, were clearly influenced by the vulnerability of their businesses to a sustained disruption of transatlantic commerce. By contrast, Hermann Blohm, who by 1917 had emerged as a firm supporter of Hindenburg and Ludendorff's Supreme Command and war *à outrance*, may have been influenced by the generals' commitment to the construction of a large German submarine fleet. On the whole, however, ideological and political factors probably played a more important part than economic self interest in determining positions in the debate. When the Pan German League attacked the Chamber of Commerce for opposing the annexation of Belgium, it accused Hamburg of repeating its particularist error in resisting the *Zollverein*: 'Not for the first time has Hamburg taken a negative stance at the moment of a great German advance.'[190] Yet even Max Warburg argued in the course of 1916 for the creation of German 'colonies' in the Baltic territories of Latvia and Courland:

The Latvians would be easily evacuated. In Russia, resettlement is not regarded as cruel in itself. The people are used to it [. . .] Those alien [i.e. non-Russian] peoples who are of German descent and are currently so ill-treated can be allowed to move into this area and found colonies. [These] do not need to be integrated into Germany, but must merely be affiliated, albeit with cement, so that their slipping back to the Russian side is ruled out.[191]

---

[188] Cecil, *Ballin*, pp. 275, 316; WA, 'Jahresbericht 1918', Anlage 20, 'Rede gehalten auf der Versammlung der Deutschen Gesellschaft für Völkerrecht, Kiel' (September, 1918).

[189] Kersten, 'Kriegsziele', *passim*.

[190] *Ibid.*

[191] WA, 'Jahresbericht 1916', pp. 13; Warburg to Ballin, 10.3.16; Anlage 7, Warburg to Wahnschaffe (Under State Secretary at the Reich Chancellery), 19.5.16. This proposal almost certainly relates to informal meetings in Stockholm between Warburg's brother Fritz and the Vice-President of the Russian Duma, Protopopov: Chernow, *Warburgs*, pp. 177ff.

The views of Richard Krogmann were little different.[192] Had such a reshaping of the Russo-German border area been achieved on a sustainable basis, it would have enjoyed broad, if not universal, support from Hamburg business.

Yet by the time Warburg's vision of 1916 was realised at Brest Litovsk, a deep rift had opened up between him and Krogmann. While the latter welcomed Ludendorff's creation of puppet states in the Baltic, Poland and the Ukraine and 'rejoice[d] that these men are at the top',[193] Warburg denounced the treaties of 1918 as 'thinly veiled annexation, with an all too transparent facade provided by the right of national self-determination'.[194] Their disagreement reflected above all their different assessments of Germany's bargaining position. Warburg, like Ballin, took a relatively pessimistic view of Germany's chances in a war against the Triple Entente – and regarded a war against the United States as hopeless. For that reason, they took the view that some diplomatic adjustment was needed to improve the military odds: hence their involvement in 1915 in attempts to win new allies for Germany (Italy, Romania, Bulgaria, Sweden), and their advocacy of separate peaces either with Russia (Ballin's favoured strategy) or England (Warburg's).[195] Above all – and uniquely in Hamburg – Warburg opposed the lifting of restrictions on submarine warfare, on the grounds that, however great the impact on British food supplies, the risk of alienating the United States was too grave: 'If America is cut off from Germany,' he argued in February 1916, 'that means a 50 per cent reduction in Germany's financial strength for the war, and an increase of 100 per cent for England's and France's [. . .] Everything should [. . .] be done to avoid a breach with America.'[196] 'The war is lost if [unrestricted submarine war] goes ahead: financially, because our loans will no longer be bought; economically, because the masses of raw materials which we continue to get from abroad and which we cannot do without will be cut off.'[197] For Warburg,

---

[192] Pohlmann, *Richard Krogmann*, pp. 240f.

[193] *Ibid.*, pp. 220–33.

[194] WA, 'Jahresbericht 1918', Anlage 13, 'Bemerkungen über die östlichen Freidensverträge und die deutschen Kriegsziele', 1.5.18.

[195] WA, 'Jahresbericht 1915', pp. 2–5; 'Jahresbericht 1916', Warburg to Ballin, 2.2.16; Warburg, *Aufzeichnungen*, pp. 39–48; Cecil, *Ballin*, pp. 272, 276–84, 295f., 307; E. Jaeckh, *Der Goldene Pflug* (Stuttgart, 1955), pp. 189f.; L. Haupts, *Deutsche Friedenspolitik. Eine Alternative zur deutschen Machtpolitik des ersten Weltkrieges* (Düsseldorf, 1976), pp. 113f.

[196] WA, 'Jahresbericht 1916', Warburg to Ballin, 2.2.16. See also: 'Jahresbericht 1915', p. 5, Anlage 8; 'Jahresbericht 1916', p. 22; 'Jahresbericht 1917', pp. 3f., Warburg to Langwerth von Simmern, 26.1.17; 'Jahresbericht 1918', Anlage 31, Warburg to Admiral von Holtzendorff, 8.8.18; Vagts, 'M.M. Warburg & Co.', p. 361; Warburg, *Aufzeichnungen*, pp. 53f. For Ballin's nervous support of the submarine war, Cecil, *Ballin*, pp. 272f., 285–7, 299.

[197] Haupts, *Friedenspolitik*, p. 119.

the German response to Wilson's 'peace without victory' note of 22 January 1917 was not conciliatory enough:

We cannot pay any heed to the dangerous views prevalent in our 'piazza'. The *Basser- and Stresemänner* are really less important than our relations with America. If we end up at war with America, we will face an enemy with such moral, financial and economic strength that we will have nothing more to hope for from the future; that is my firm conviction.[198]

Warburg went unheard: the restrictions on submarine warfare were again lifted, and in just over two months, the United States declared war on Germany. Yet far from being vindicated by the events of 1917, Warburg – who by now had made contact with a number of pacifist writers including Martin Hobohm and Walther Schücking[199] – appeared discredited. The collapse of Russia and the military victory on the Eastern Front gave fresh impetus to those who opposed negotiation. Indeed, it was the publication of the Treaty of Brest Litovsk in March 1918 which helped torpedo an attempt by Warburg (acting on Chancellor Hertling's instructions) to hold unofficial talks about Belgium with the American ambassador in Holland.[200]

It was inevitable that the war aims debate would become inextricably bound up with the debate on Germany's constitutional arrangements. Even before the war, Bethmann had acknowledged that a war would strengthen the hand of the Social Democrats and might 'topple many a throne'; and the concessions necessary to maintain the economic *Burgfrieden* – official recognition of trade union power and formal provision for workers' councils – had obvious political implications. The debate on war aims lent an additional urgency to the question of the location and distribution of political power. Those who felt that diplomatic opportunities were being squandered questioned not only the calibre of the Foreign Office but also the extent of the Reich Chancellor's subordination to the military. Those for whom Bethmann was a 'traitor' and a 'criminal against the Fatherland'[201] wished con-

---

[198] WA, 'Jahresbericht 1917', Warburg to Langwerth von Simmern, 26.1.17.

[199] For the Organisation Hobohm, Haupts, *Friedenspolitik*, pp. 103, 119f., 123, 132f. For Warburg's involvement with Walther Schücking and the German Association for International Law: WA, 'Jahresbericht 1916', 'Kriegsziele'; 'Jahresbericht 1917', p. 12; 'Jahresbericht 1918', p. 9.

[200] WA, 'Jahresbericht 1918', p. 3; Warburg, *Aufzeichnungen*, p. 58; Prinz Max von Baden, *Erinnerungen und Dokumente* (Stuttgart/Berlin/Leipzig, 1927), pp. 248, 252, 66of. Warburg cannot have been unduly optimistic, since the German government was still insisting on 'minor cessions' of Belgian territory 'in order to have assurances [. . .] that Belgium would not be used as a *pied à terre* by the English and the French'. He must also have been well aware of the terms to be imposed on Russia, since Melchior was acting as a financial expert at Brest Litovsk: 'Jahresbericht 1917', untitled document on Melchior's activity.

[201] Pohlmann, *Richard Krogmann*, pp. 220f.

versely to see the power of the generals increased. War aims – whether annexations, *Mitteleuropa*, the status quo ante or a revolutionary peace based on self determination or working-class solidarity – came to be identified with domestic aims: dictatorship, some degree of parliamentarisation, or revolution. Events between February and September 1917 made the alternatives clear. In the wake of the February Revolution in Russia, the founding of the Independent Socialist Party at Gotha gave organisational substance to the idea of 'peace through democratisation' and pushed the Majority Social Democrats in the same direction. In the Reichstag, the SPD allied with the Centre Party and the Progressives to pass a resolution calling for peace without 'forced cessions'. But Bethmann, having persuaded the Kaiser to accept democratisation of the Prussian franchise, was ousted by Hindenburg and Ludendorff and replaced by the nonentity Michaelis; a move endorsed by Wolfgang Kapp's new Fatherland Party.[202]

In Hamburg, demonstrations featuring pacifist as well as political and economic slogans dated from August 1916, but reached a peak in late 1917.[203] The authorities responded initially by arresting radical activists; but at the same time liberals in the Senate and Bürgerschaft, taking their cue from national events, felt obliged to consider reforming the Hamburg franchise, as 'a way of calming the less well-off members of the population and supporting the influence of their moderate leaders'.[204] Significantly, outright democratisation was rejected by both the United Liberals and the Fraction of the Rights (in effect, the National Liberals in the Bürgerschaft), on the grounds that some kind of corporatist overrepresentation of *Bildung* and *Besitz* was necessary in a state as heavily urbanised as Hamburg: both wished to retain the special representation of the notables, if necessary by sacrificing the property owners' privileges.[205] Yet even this went too far for some. Krogmann and Max von Schinckel had been hesitant to support Kapp when he had approached them with the idea of the Fatherland Party in the summer of 1917; but the opening of the franchise issue forced the Hamburg conservatives to act. The founding of the Hamburg Conservative Association in July was followed in October by the

---

[202] Wehler, *German Empire*, pp. 215ff.; Stegmann, *Erben Bismarcks*, pp. 497–519.
[203] Ullrich, 'Arbeiterbewegung', p. 275; Ullrich, *Kriegsalltag*, pp. 31–8, 114–22, 134–45. Cf. GStA, Rep. 90j, Nr. 5, 'Zusammenstellung der Monatsberichte der Stellv. Generalkommandos', 3.12.17.
[204] Ullrich, 'Arbeiterbewegung', p. 371.
[205] Büttner, 'Vereinigte Liberalen', p. 9. In July 1917, it was agreed to repeal the 1905 restriction of the franchise, and, in October 1918, to transfer sixteen of the property owners' seats to those elected by the general franchise.

establishment of a Hamburg branch of the Fatherland Party, which by 1918 had attracted 10,000 members.[206]

It was perhaps inevitable that Max Warburg's support for a negotiated peace and some degree of constitutional reform would make him a target for the Right, and that the hostility would take an anti-Semitic form.[207] In December 1917 Warburg was proposed by the Senate as its preferred candidate in a Senatorial election; but to his surprise and disappointment, he was rejected by the Bürgerschaft, a rebuff which the press interpreted as anti-Semitic.[208] It was a humiliation which made a mockery of Warburg's deeply felt patriotism. For his contribution to the economic war effort, he had been awarded the Iron Cross in August 1916.[209] His son Eric and partner Carl Melchior were among the 2,900 Hamburg Jews who served in the army.[210] After April 1917, he had been forced to sever all ties with his brothers in the United States.[211] Yet the idea persisted that Warburg put his international ties – economic, familial and racial – before his national loyalty.[212] The experience of the Warburgs illustrates well the strains which the war placed on those cosmopolitan elites who, before 1914, had found it relatively easy to reconcile their national and international interests. Paul Warburg encountered very similar antagonism in the United States on account of his 'foreign connections'. Despite having become an American citizen in 1910, making a major contribution to monetary reform in the US and helping to organise the wartime 'Liberty Loan', Warburg felt obliged to resign his position as Vice-Governor of the Federal Reserve Board in August 1918, following 'agitation to the effect that a naturalised citizen of German birth, having near relations prominent in German public life, should not be permitted to hold a

---

[206] Ullrich, 'Arbeiterbewegung', pp. 378, 517–48; *Kriegsalltag*, pp. 123ff.; Pohlmann, *Richard Krogmann*, pp. 233, 241f. For the Blohm brothers' support of the Fatherland Party, see StAH, B&V 13 Bd. 2, Firmenleitung, 18.10.18.

[207] W. Jochmann, 'Die Ausbreitung des Antisemitismus', in W.E. Mosse (ed.), *Deutsches Judentum in Krieg und Revolution 1916–1923* (Tübingen, 1971), pp. 409ff.

[208] WA, 'Jahresbericht 1917', p. 9; *Hamburger Echo*, 8.12.17.

[209] WA, 'Jahresbericht 1916', p. 13.

[210] Chernow, *Warburgs*, pp. 155–74, 196ff.; Attali, *Siegmund Warburg*, p. 92; Lorenz, *Die Juden in Hamburg*, I. p. cxxx.

[211] 'For years [Paul and I] wrote to one another almost every day. When the world war made that impossible, it was as if I had been cut off from my second "I"'; Warburg, *Aufzeichnungen*, pp. 3–7.

[212] In 1915, Admiral von Holtzendorff alleged that Warburg opposed unrestricted submarine warfare because of his economic interests in the US: WA, 'Jahresbericht 1915', p. 5. It was also alleged that his American relatives at Kuhn, Loeb & Co. were unwilling to lend to Germany, but were lending to the Entente: 'Jahresbericht 1915', pp. 4a, 4b, 4c; Max Warburg to Paul Warburg, 9.10.15; Otto Kahn to Max Warburg, 20.10.15, 3.11.15.

position of great trust in the service of the United States'.[213] Warburg felt betrayed by President Wilson; yet his loyalties were undeniably divided. He had opposed American entry into the war, defended German submarine warfare, insisted in August 1917 that Germany had been 'defeudalised' and 'democratised', and tried to prevent his son joining the Naval Flying Corps.[214] Similarly, the war forced the Warburgs to reassess their attitudes to Judaism. The large exodus of Jews from Eastern Europe into Germany during the war prompted Max and Felix Warburg to investigate and seek to ameliorate conditions in Poland; just as the Balfour Declaration on Palestine caused Max Warburg to qualify his opposition to Zionism.[215]

Although Warburg came to see 'heavy industry and the Pan Germans' as the 'chief agitators' for continuing the war, he appreciated that theirs were not 'immediately realisable material motives'; rather, they had 'talked themselves into a craving for conquest (*Eroberungssucht*)'.[216] His colleague in the Chamber of Commerce, the merchant Franz Witthoefft, extended this criticism to the National Liberals in the Reichstag – 'People who get drunk with their own rhetoric in parliament [and] rush off in nationalist ecstasy, rather than practising *Realpolitik*.'[217] However, it was by no means easy to stake out a defensible position in the political middle ground, as the draft programme drawn up by Warburg and others for the Bürgerschaft Rights in September 1916 illustrates. Compared with earlier versions, the new programme dropped the phrase 'struggle against Social Democracy' as 'impossible under the present circumstances'; and abandoned the Fraction's traditional condemnation of 'the advancement of one-sided *Stand* or class interests'. It now referred to 'the furtherance of Hamburg's trade and shipping' as 'a special objective':

It was emphasised that it was precisely our Fraction which had to stand on the basis of a healthy *Hamburg* conservatism. However, the draft avoided using the

[213] Sterling Library, Yale University, Paul Warburg Papers, 535, Series 1, Box 2, Folders 21, 22 (material on Warburg's initial appointment to the Federal Reserve Board in July 1914); Box 4, Folders 43, 44, 47, 48, 49 (material on US war finance); Folder 53, Paul Warburg to President Wilson, 27.5.18; Folder 56, Benjamin Strong to Paul Warburg, 9.8.18, 10.8.18; Federal Reserve Bank, New York, Benjamin Strong Papers, 120.0 2) Paul Warburg to Benjamin Strong, 13.8.18.

[214] Paul Warburg Papers, Series 1, Box 3, Folder 42 (memoranda of February 1917); Series 2, Box 9, Folder 10 (undated memorandum); Series 1, Box 4, Folder 47, Warburg to Colonel House, 4.8.17; John F. Kennedy Memorial Library, Boston, James P. Warburg Papers, James Warburg Diary, pp. 1–32.

[215] Lorenz, *Die Juden in Hamburg*, p. cxxxvii; WA, 'Jahresbericht 1914', p. 11; 'Jahresbericht 1915', p. 5; 'Jahresbericht 1916', p. 16, Anlage 16, Max Warburg, 'Die Judenfrage im Rahmen der deutschen Gesamtpolitik', November 1916; 'Jahresbericht 1916', p. 21; Attali, *Siegmund Warburg*, p. 62; Chernow, *Warburgs*, pp. 173f. Cf. E. Zechlin, *Die deutsche Politik und die Juden im Ersten Weltkrieg* (Göttingen, 1969).

[216] WA, 'Jahresbericht 1917', p. 1.

[217] StAH, FA AOM 1, Bd. 7, Witthoefft to Rudolf Sieverts, 31.5.16.

term 'conservative' in order not to allow the mistaken impression that the Fraction shared the standpoint of the two Reich conservative parties. After very exhaustive discussions, the committee decided to omit the terms 'liberal' and 'conservative' from the programme entirely. Nevertheless, the proposed draft can leave no one in any doubt that the Fraction will continue to stand for the sound kernels of both the said tendencies.[218]

As noted above, such unpolitical rhetoric had been a feature of pre-war bourgeois politics; but the fissures which the war had opened within the Hamburg *Bürgertum* demanded a new level of obfuscation. The reality was that Warburg wanted an end to the war by negotiation, and he had to acknowledge that this would only be achieved by some degree of domestic reform, if only to increase the power of the Reich Chancellor over the military and to reduce the power of the heavy industrial lobby.[219] Such views drew him from July 1917 into the circle which wished to see Prince Max of Baden as Chancellor; but they also meant that he had little difficulty in finding common ground with the leader of the Majority Social Democrats, Friedrich Ebert, when the latter visited Hamburg in June 1918.[220] Inevitably, the centre ground tilted to the Left.

Inflationary expectations

If arguing over war aims and political reform had divided the business community, the question of post-war economics offered an opportunity to rally Hamburg business interests. The centralising and bureaucratising tendencies of the war economy had begun to cause disquiet in Hamburg at a relatively early stage in the war. However, it was only when it became clear that the government intended preserving the system of compulsory cartels, war companies and trade controls into peacetime that concern developed into concerted action. Inquiries by the Chamber of Commerce in 1916 revealed that the government was contemplating preserving the Central Purchasing Company's near monopoly over food imports after the war.[221] Despite efforts by the Chamber of Commerce to argue the case for returning to liberalised

[218] WA, 'Jahresbericht 1916', Anlage 13, September 1916.
[219] WA, 'Jahresbericht 1918', Anlage 21, Max Warburg, 'Gedanken zur Fortbildung unserer auswärtige und innere Politik als Grundlage einer Verständigung der Völker' (undated), esp. points 15, 16 and 18.
[220] WA, 'Jahresbericht 1917'; 'Jahresbericht 1918', pp. 11, 11a; Warburg, *Aufzeichnungen*, pp. 61ff.; Brecht, *Political Education*, p. 63. Even Ballin acquiesced in the invitation of leading Social Democrats to Holtzendorff's 'evenings' in Berlin: see correspondence in HA, HB, 1917–18.
[221] StAH, Krieg B II L 2 vol. I, HKH to HK Düsseldorf, 31.1.16.; DHSG III, Pr. 1 2 Bd. 1, Bericht über die Besprechung im RMI, 13.4.16.

trade, these plans became concrete under the Hindenburg–Ludendorff Supreme Command. It was announced that not only would the ZEG persist, but controls would be imposed on the allocation of shipping and foreign currency under a new body, the Commissariat for the Transitional Economy.[222] Details emerged following Bethmann's replacement as Chancellor by Michaelis, when the new Commissioner (who was in fact the Hamburg Senator Sthamer) announced his intention to allocate quotas of freight tonnage and foreign exchange directly to the industrial war corporations.[223] This caused uproar in Hamburg, as it implied not only the exclusion from post-war importing of the established commercial houses and the continuance of exchange controls, but also the subordination of the shipping lines to the Commissariat: in short, the subjugation of commerce to the war companies.

It quickly became apparent that Hamburg's commercial interests were ill-equipped to defend themselves against this threat: the demands tabled at a protest meeting of the Chamber of Commerce were simply ignored in Berlin, as were objections from bankers and shipowners.[224] The crisis revealed the extent to which the war had sown discord among Hamburg's commercial interests. Under the pressures of Allied sequestration and government regulation, special interest groups had increasingly sought to by-pass the traditional system of interest representation (*via* the Chamber of Commerce and the Senate), taking their case directly to the relevant authorities in Berlin. It was characteristic of this atmosphere of *sauve qui peut* that, as we have seen, the shipowners had been able to secure government compensation mainly through the lobbying efforts of Ballin and their own war committee in Berlin; and that, confronted with the Chamber of Commerce's compromise over the turnover tax, the wholesalers had joined the ZVDG. By 1917, independent lobbying in Berlin by sectoral associations was rife, with Alfred O'Swald acting independently on behalf of the Hamburg Import Trade League and the Hamburg Exporters' Association establishing a permanent Berlin war bureau. As Senator Sthamer complained, the various interest groups were making applications to Berlin 'unbeknown to the authorities':

Throughout the war, the associations had conducted their affairs directly through the Reich authorities, by-passing the Chamber of Commerce, which,

---

[222] *RGB*, p. 885, Bekanntmachung des Bundesrats, 3.8.16. On the background to this decision, Feldman, *Great Disorder*, pp. 87ff.; Bessel, *Germany*, pp. 49ff.

[223] StAH, DHSG III, Pr. 1 2 Bd. 1, HKH to Reichskommissar f. d. Übergangswirtschaft, 14.11.16; *ibid.*, Bd. 2, Sen. Prot., 15.12.16.

[224] StAH, SK, II, III A 1 a 8, HKH, 'Der Handel und die Übergangswirtschaft' (published resolution of the meeting of An Honourable Merchant, 25.7.17); Sen.

considering the need to balance the various interests of the associations, was most regrettable. The Hamburg Shipowners' Association (for example) had made itself wholly independent of the Chamber.[225]

Yet, as the commercial associations pointed out, such action had been necessary because 'industry is everywhere in more prominent positions and hears better and rather sooner than we in commerce what is afoot in the official departments'.[226] There was much debate as to what should be done to remedy this state of affairs, including a suggestion by Max Warburg that a Hanseatic version of *The Economist* be launched as a means of countering industrial influence over the press.[227] However, the device for increasing Hamburg's political effectiveness which won the broadest support was that of inviting delegations from the Reichstag to visit Hamburg. This was done on two occasions, under the direction of a new organisation, the Hamburg Committee for the Reconstruction of the Peacetime Economy, a body which reflected the success of the pro-peace wing of the business community in seizing the initiative in the battle against control.[228] In February, the Chamber of Commerce President, Heye, lambasted the government's economic policies before the entire Reichstag National Liberal fraction, decrying 'the concentration of all business transactions [. . .] in the hands of the war companies; [. . .] the almost exclusive distribution of army contracts to Berlin industry; [. . . and] the countless, commerce-inhibiting Bundesrat decrees'.[229] Then, as part of what Ballin called 'an assault on public opinion', the Chamber invited the entire Reichstag to Hamburg, for a further brow beating. It was Franz Witthoefft who best expressed the new mood:

We Hanseatic businessmen are extremely reluctant to gather in public protest meetings. But this reluctance reaches its limit if the possibility arises [. . .] that Hamburg's trade is to be disrupted by legal measures which are, in the circumstances, unnecessary [. . .] [The businessman is] fed up with having

Prot. 1.8.17; SK to Reich Chancellor, 2.8.17; Sen. Prot. 31.8.17; DHSG Abschrift, 1.9.17; Sen. Prot. 5.9.17.

[225] StAH, DHSG II, III C 52 (1918), 19. Sitzung, 23.10.18. See also *ibid.*, 11. Sitzung, 14.5.18.

[226] StAH, SK II, III A 1 a 8, 'Der Handel und die Übergangswirtschaft'.

[227] Böhm, *Anwalt der Handelsfreiheit*, p. 271. This was the origin of the journal *Wirtschaftsdienst*.

[228] The members of the committee included Ballin, Heye, O'Swald, Amsinck and Krogmann; see *Wirtschaftsdienst*, 37, 13.9.18, p. 869.

[229] F. Heye, 'Kriegswirkungen und Kriegswünsche Hamburgs', in Nationalliberaler Landesverband (ed.), *Hamburgs wirtschaftliche Zukunft. Verhandlungen der Hamburger Kaufmannschaft im Gegenwart der Nationalliberalen Reichstagsfraktion vom 22–24.2.18* (Hamburg, 1918). For the government's cool response, StAH, SK II, III A 1 a 8, Reichswirtschaftsamt to SK, 12.2.18.

his business fouled up by ill-considered government measures and [. . .] by government officials who believe that they can regulate the world economy, [equipped] with the formalistic schooling of the jurist.[230]

In a similar vein, Ballin spoke of 'the dangerous notion of running the national economy and international trade from the parade ground', and demanded 'freedom from the Berlin planned economy'. His Hapag lieutenant Bernhard Huldermann went still further, declaring that, because of Hamburg's doubts about the commitment of the government to liberal economic policy, 'we have joined the Opposition'.[231]

With its explicit attacks on the *Obrigkeitsstaat* and appeals to *laissez faire* liberalism, this rhetoric recalled the anti-Prussian sentiments of the particularists in the *Zollverein* debates of the 1860s and 1870s, and it did much to heal the divisions within the business community which the controversies over war aims and political reform had opened up. It was also typical of a general reaction by European businessmen against wartime economic regulation. Even in the heavy industrial camp, there were some voices calling for decontrol by the summer of 1918;[232] though in Germany, unlike Britain, the campaign for liberalisation was unsuccessful.[233] Yet the argument in favour of a rapid dismantling of the wartime 'command economy' had implications which extended beyond the ideological conflict between economic liberalism and state control. The opposition to centralised control of post-war imports in Hamburg rested on the optimistic view that, as soon as the war ended, it would be possible for Germany to resume her pre-war trading links overseas: lifting German government controls, it was argued, would allow a rapid influx of essentials. However, this argument appeared to overlook the likely inflationary consequences of deregulation. As we have seen, the German balance of payments was chronically in deficit, with a substantial import surplus and a collapse in revenue from 'invisibles'; while within Germany, war finance had generated an immense overhang of purchasing power. Only exchange controls (which had prevented the mark from falling below 58 per

[230] F. Witthoefft, 'Handel und Friedenswirtschaft', in Wirtschaftsdienst (ed.), *Wiederaufbau der Friedenswirtschaft. Vorträge und Reden anläßlich des Besuches des Deutschen Reichstages in Hamburg am 25. und 26. Juli 1918* (Hamburg, 1918).

[231] B. Huldermann, 'Schiffahrt und Friedenswirtschaft', *ibid*. Cf. Haupts, *Friedenspolitik*, pp. 93f., 110f., 147. With the armistice just a month away, Bürgermeister von Melle was still repeating these arguments: PA/AA, R3008, PG to AA, 11.10.18.

[232] Feldman, *Iron and Steel*, p. 80.

[233] In September 1918, two all-embracing statutes were passed which provided for the continuation of the war economy's restrictions into peacetime; see HKH, *Jahresbericht*, *1918*. For the British experience, see R.H. Tawney, 'The Abolition of Economic Controls, 1918–1921', *EcHR* (1943), pp. 1–30.

cent of its pre-war rate against the dollar) and price controls stood
between Germany and a price explosion. It is sometimes argued that
an important factor in the post-war inflation was the deficiency of
German monetary theory, owing in large part to the influence of the
'state theory of money' formulated by G.F. Knapp, who rejected
English bullionism and asserted that the value of money was a matter
for state fiat.[234] Was Hamburg business unconscious of the inflationary
dangers of deregulation?

In July 1918, Max Warburg appeared to confirm the idea of German
theoretical backwardness when he joked: 'Nowadays there are people
talking about monetary problems who still thought, until recently, that
"Valuta" was a girl's name.'[235] On the surface, however, the debate
in business circles in Hamburg in 1918 rehearsed the conventional
arguments for and against bullionism which had been heard in Britain
during and after the Napoleonic Wars.[236] Thus, while Max von
Schinckel described himself as 'an old [. . .] decided [. . .] gold currency man' and urged (with Franz Witthoefft) a swift return to gold
convertibility and the pre-war gold reserve ratio, Warburg maintained
that note issue should be governed by the requirements of 'productive'
economic activity, as reflected in the volume of 'sound' commercial
bills.[237] Yet the parallel with the Currency and Banking Schools is not
exact. The Hamburg opponents of bullionism were also among the
firmest supporters of Knapp, and Knapp's disciples Friedrich
Bendixen, Alfred Schmidt-Essen and Kurt Singer were all leading
lights in Warburg's creation, the periodical *Wirtschaftsdienst*;[238] while
Schinckel's bullionism was closer to that of Helfferich than that of
Peel. This is by no means the way one would expect the theoretical
lines to be drawn. In view of Knapp's reputation as the economic
theorist of the Prussian *Obrigkeitsstaat* and the association of metallism
with British liberalism, it seems paradoxical that the liberal Warburg

---

[234] See C.-D. Krohn, 'Geldtheorien in Deutschland während der Inflation, 1914–1924',
in Feldman *et al.* (eds.), *Anpassung*, esp. pp. 7–19; *idem*, *Wirtschaftstheorien als
politische Interessen. Die akademische Nationalökonomie in Deutschland, 1918–33*
(Frankfurt am Main, 1981); K. Hardach, 'Zur zeitgenössischen Debatte der Nationalökonomen über die Ursachen der deutschen Inflation', in Mommsen *et al.* (eds.),
Industrielles System, I, pp. 368–74.

[235] WA, 'Jahresbericht 1918', Anlage 22, M. Warburg, 'Währung und Wirtschaftsführung nach dem Kriege', 15.6.18; Warburg, *Aufzeichnungen*, p. 61.

[236] Kindleberger, *Financial History*, pp. 61ff.

[237] Rohrmann, *Max von Schinckel*, p. 237; StAH, FA AOM 1, Bd. 7, Witthoefft to
Jakob Riesser, 6.6.16; WA, 'Jahresbericht 1915', p. 4, Anlage 7, M. Warburg,
'Finanzielle Kriegslehren', 1.8.15; 'Jahresbericht 1918', Anlage 22, Warburg, 'Wäh-
rung und Wirtschaftsführung'.

[238] See, e.g., K. Singer, 'Wirtschaftspolitische Lehren des Krieges', in *Wirtschaftsdienst*,
33, 16.8.18; and A. Schmidt-Essen, 'Goldteuerung', in *ibid.*, 27, 13.9.18. Cf. Krohn,
'Geldtheorien', pp. 15–19.

appeared to sympathise with the Knappist position, while the conservative Schinckel was a metallist. Only when the practical preoccupations
of those concerned are made clear can their sometimes contradictory
theoretical positions – and the ultimate consensus in favour of inflationary policies – be understood.

Few influential voices in Hamburg disputed during the war that the
inflationary pressures in the German economy stemmed from government finance. In 1916, Warburg explicitly linked government borrowing with monetary expansion; and in June 1918, he urged a
reduction of government debt through 'the utmost parsimony and
tough taxes' as the only means of 'protecting us from the continuing
inflation with all its consequences'.[239] He never denied the need for
some kind of check on monetary growth, merely arguing that commercial activity (whether defined by the volume of real bills, or the trade
deficit) should determine the money supply, rather than a fixed gold
ratio.[240] Nor did Warburg have a material interest in a fiscal breakdown.
On the contrary, as he commented during the war with typical black
humour: 'If Germany should lose the war, and the Reichsbank finds
itself unable to honour its obligations to us, we will have no alternative
but to put an announcement in the papers saying: "Payments suspended on the field of honour. M.M. Warburg & Co.".'[241] On the
other hand, there was little fiscal room for manoeuvre by 1917/18.
Even Warburg had accepted Helfferich's argument that the war debt
would ultimately be liquidated by reparations from the vanquished
Entente: in November 1914, he had proposed 50 bn. marks as an
appropriate level of reparations for Germany to impose, assuming a
war lasting just four months. Although from the outset he acknowledged that 'the longer the war progresses [. . .], the greater will be
the discrepancy between the demands that we will be justified in
making and the ability of our enemies [. . .] to meet these', he
continued to envisage reparations as high as 100 bn. marks as late as
May 1918.[242] Without reparations, the only way of halting government
borrowing was by cutting spending and increasing taxes. Yet the
keystone of Hamburg's economy – the shipping and ship-building
industry – had become dependent on the continuation of high levels

---

[239] WA, 'Jahresbericht 1915', p. 4, Anlage 7, Warburg, 'Finanzielle Kriegslehren',
1.8.15; 'Jahresbericht 1918', Anlage 22, Warburg, 'Währung und Wirtschaftsführung'. Cf. the analysis in Lippmann, *Leben*, p. 262.

[240] WA, 'Jahresbericht 1915', Warburg to Glasenapp (Reichsbank Vice-President),
20.10.15.

[241] Warburg, *Aufzeichnungen*, pp. 44f.

[242] WA, 'Jahresbericht 1914', Anlage IV, 'Gutachten über eine mögliche Kriegsentschädi-
gung', 26.11.14; 'Jahresbericht 1918', Anlage 13, 'Bemerkungen über die östlichen
Friedensverträge und die deutschen Kriegsziele', 1.5.18.

of government subsidy, and had secured an agreement from the government which assumed continuing inflation for at least nine years after
the end of the war. Moreover, the levels of taxation needed to eliminate
the fiscal deficit filled businessmen with trepidation: there would be
'great taxes [. . .] which not only we, but also our children, will have
to endure'.[243] Finally, a deflationary strategy would inevitably mean a
surge in unemployment at the very time when large numbers of
troops were being demobilised. As Ballin observed ten days before
the armistice, even as things stood 'the housing, lighting, employment
and particularly the food problem' made social unrest likely. 'A
retreating army for which no housing is available, to which one cannot
guarantee food [. . .] which must cope without artificial light, [and]
which is forced to go out into the streets at four on a winter's
afternoon, naturally represents an extraordinary danger.'[244] The same
preoccupation dominated thinking in the new Reich Economics Office
as it prepared for demobilisation in 1918.[245] In other words, there
were strong economic, social and political arguments against ending
inflationary finance.

Similar arguments applied to the question of the exchange rate.
During the war, Warburg and others had supported the use of exchange
controls – as well as import restrictions – to prevent the mark from
depreciating.[246] In January 1916, Franz Witthoefft had warned that
even if Germany won the war, foreign loans would be necessary to
avoid a balance of payments crisis; 'but if speculation and the free
play of forces are allowed in the import of raw materials, even such
loans will scarcely suffice to restore our currency to its old level and
keep it there'.[247] This desire to defend the exchange rate almost certainly
related to the large foreign currency debts owed by business as a result
of outstanding pre-war transactions and wartime import credits like
those negotiated by Warburg's in Sweden: devaluation would irrevo-
cably increase the cost in mark terms of repaying these.[248] However,
Warburg was insistent that exchange controls could not be continued

[243] StAH, FA AOM 1, Bd. 7, Franz Witthoefft to Richard Witthoefft, 24.11.16.
[244] Ballin to Holtzendorff, 1.11.18, cit. Cecil, *Ballin*, pp. 342f.
[245] Bessel, *Germany*, p. 64.
[246] WA, 'Jahresbericht 1915', pp. 4, 4b, Anlage 6, M. Warburg, 'Wie können wir
und sollen wir die Auslandswechselkurse beeinflußen?', 1.1.16 (memorandum for
Reichsbank); Warburg to Havenstein, 10.3.16; 'Jahresbericht 1916', Anlage 19
(memorandum on exchange controls), 7.12.16; 'Jahresbericht 1917', pp. 11f., Anlage
18, Warburg to Havenstein, 25.6.17.
[247] StAH, FA AOM 1, Bd. 7, Witthoefft to HKH, 17.1.16; Witthoefft to Harms,
8.3.16.
[248] WA, 'Jahresbericht 1917', Anlage 36, M. Warburg, 'Behandlung der ante-bellum-
Schulden in den Friedensverträgen', 19.11.17; StAH, FA AOM 1, Bd. 9, Witthoefft
to Reich Justice Office, 17.11.17.

after the end of the war: 'The damage that would be done to our currency's reputation abroad by such measures [i.e., peacetime exchange controls] would necessarily be much more harmful than a short period of a large disagio and even temporarily very high prices on the food and raw material markets.'[249] The markets, he argued, should be left to set the currency at the appropriate level: 'The exchange rate must follow the lead of the economy; and after the war we must, whether we like it or not, pass through the purgatory of free prices to arrive at a new stability.'[250]

Why was Warburg prepared to let the mark float freely, despite the dangers that its depreciation might double or treble the burden of German foreign currency debts? The answer lies in the anticipated effect of a floating currency on exports. The immediate fall in the value of the currency would, he argued, stimulate German exports by making them cheaper for foreign purchasers, while at the same time making imports prohibitively expensive for German firms: after a period of depreciation and inflation, the balance of payments would accordingly adjust itself. In an important memorandum of September 1917, Ballin outlined the crucial argument:

[I regard] our gravely ailing currency as an admirable means of dispelling the hatred felt abroad towards Germany, and of overcoming the reluctance to trade with us [likely to be felt] by our enemies. The American who no longer gets for his dollar 4.21 marks worth of goods from us, but 6.20 marks worth, will rediscover his fondness for Germany.[251]

Thus it seemed in 1918. Germany, by exploiting the fall of the mark, could export her way back to currency stability, and reintegrate herself into the world economy; for not only would a floating mark allow an export boom which would ultimately restore the mark to pre-war parity (solving the foreign currency debt problem), it could also act as a diplomatic counter, exerting pressure on the Allies to accept Germany back into the international fold. It was this calculation which inclined Hamburg liberals like Warburg to collude with Knappist economists against those who argued for the maintenance of exchange controls and an immediate return to pre-war parity.

Thus, by 1918, an influential group of Hamburg businessmen – notably Warburg, Ballin and Witthoefft – had formulated a threefold strategy, based on ending the war by negotiation, shifting the consti-

---

[249] WA, 'Jahresbericht 1915', M. Warburg (untitled memorandum for Reichsbank), 24.11.16. Cf. 'Jahresbericht 1917', Anlage 23, Warburg, 'Übergangswirtschaft und Devisenregulierung', 6.7.17.
[250] WA, 'Jahresbericht 1918', Anlage 2, Warburg, 'Währung und Wirtschaftsführung'.
[251] Ballin to Huldermann, 6.9.17, quoted in Huldermann, *Ballin*, pp. 273f.

tution in the direction of parliamentarism and cooperation with the Majority Social Democrats, and reviving German commerce by means of deregulation and depreciation, even at the risk of further inflation. Of course, such ideas were not the sole property of Hamburg business: by the end of the war some industrialists (notably Hugo Stinnes) were also gravitating towards accommodation with the MSPD, chafing at the *Planwirtschaft* and looking forward to deregulation and a depreciation-led export drive.[252] But the strategy had a distinctive significance for Hamburg, because of the exceptional damage caused to the city's economy by the war, because of the pre-war reformism of its labour movement, and because of the aversion of its commercial interests to wartime economic controls. An 'inflationary consensus' therefore already existed in Hamburg business circles before the war's end, even if those concerned – unconsciously repeating their earlier delusions about the duration of the war – envisaged only a short period of post-war inflation.[253] It was not yet fully realised how overstretched the sinews of war had been.

[252] Feldman, *Iron and Steel*, pp. 55, 80. On Stinnes's contacts with Ballin at this time, see Cecil, *Ballin*, p. 334.
[253] James, *German Slump*, p. 126.

3

The political economy of revolution

A bourgeois revolution?

In 1914, Bethmann Hollweg had predicted that war might 'topple many a throne'. Beginning in February 1917 in Petrograd, his prophecy was fulfilled. Military failure and economic exhaustion precipitated a crisis of urban order, sweeping eastwards from the Russian capital to Vienna, Budapest and Berlin. The upheavals sufficed to despatch the defeated Eastern Empires – Tsarist Russia, Habsburg Austria-Hungary, Hohenzollern Germany and Ottoman Turkey; indeed, even the victorious Western states underwent substantial political alterations, including democratisation and Southern Irish secession in Britain. In this sense, there was a generalised European Revolution between 1917 and 1919, in which economic, pacifist, democratic, socialist and nationalist aspirations all played a part. However, the point which has traditionally preoccupied historians is that only in one country – Russia – was a radically socialist dictatorship established. Whereas in Russia, a high degree of 'social polarisation' could be exploited by a small but adaptable party claiming to represent the proletariat, elsewhere 'bourgeois Europe' was 'recast', whether by corporatist compromise (Germany, Austria and Poland), conservative containment (Britain and France), 'white' reaction (Hungary) or fascist counter-revolution (Italy).[1] In view of this contrast with events in Russia, German historians have long debated whether the Social Democrats were right to compromise with the military, industrial and administrative elites in order (as they argued) to avert 'Bolshevik chaos'; or whether an opportunity was missed in 1918/19 to transform German society and politics by using the democratic potential of the 'councils movement' to dilute the power of those 'anti-democratic' elites whose continued existence – arguably –

---

[1] F. Carsten, *Revolution in Central Europe 1918–19* (London, 1972); C.L. Bertrand, *Revolutionary Situations in Europe 1917–1922. Germany, Italy and Austria-Hungary* (Montreal, 1977); C.S. Maier, *Recasting Bourgeois Europe*. On Russia, R.G. Suny, 'Toward a Social History of the October Revolution', *AHR*, 88 (1983), pp. 31–52 provides useful points of comparison.

proved fatal to the Republic.[2] If a consensus has emerged in recent
years it is that, paradoxically, Germany was too advanced economically
for a Bolshevik-style coup to be possible; in any case, relatively few
contemporaries saw the councils of 1918/19 as an alternative to the
parliamentary system of Weimar, or doubted the need for some degree
of compromise with army, industry and bureaucracy, given the economic difficulties of demobilisation.[3]

Certainly, there was little room for manoeuvre once the military
leadership had admitted defeat, and once the Allies had resolved to
maintain economic sanctions until a peace treaty had been signed by
a German government of which they approved.[4] Under these circumstances, ambitious ideas for socialisation or government by councils
were not really practicable. However, it would be misleading to conclude, as the Hamburg civil servant Leo Lippmann did, that 'this
was no revolution of [. . .] new ideas'.[5] There were other important
possibilities besides socialism raised by the collapse of the old order,
particularly in liberal circles.[6] Disillusionment with the monarchy and
the military – once sacrosanct in the eyes of bourgeois Germany – as
well as the hopes raised by Wilson's Fourteen Points, opened the way
for a far more radical reappraisal of the institutions of the Reich than

---

[2] A. Rosenberg, *Imperial Germany and the Birth of the German Republic* (Boston, 1964);
W. Elben, *Das Problem der Kontinuität in der deutschen Revolution. Die Politik der
Staatssekretäre und der militärischen Führung von November 1918 bis Februar 1919*
(Düsseldorf, 1965); A.J. Ryder, *The German Revolution of 1918. A Study of German
Socialism in War and Revolt* (Cambridge, 1967). On the *Rätebewegung*: E. Kolb, *Die
Arbeiterräte in der deutschen Innenpolitik 1918–19* (Düsseldorf, 1962); G. Hillmann
(ed.), *Die Rätebewegung* (Reinbeck bei Hamburg, 1967); E. Kolb, 'Rätewirklichkeit
und Räteideologie in der deutschen Revolution von 1918–19', in *idem*, *Vom Kaiserreich
zur Weimarer Republik* (Cologne, 1972); V. Arnold, *Rätebewegung in der Novemberrevolution. Die Räte als Organisationsformen des Kampfes und der Selbstbestimmung*
(Hanover, 1978).

[3] G.D. Feldman, 'Wirtschafts- und sozialpolitische Probleme der deutschen Demobilmachung 1918/19', in Mommsen *et al.* (eds.), *Industrielles System*, II, pp. 618–36;
W.J. Mommsen, 'Die deutsche Revolution 1918–1920. Politische Revolution und
soziale Protestbewegung', *G&G*, 4 (1978), pp. 362–91; R. Rürup, 'Demokratische
Revolution und "dritter Weg". Die deutsche Revolution 1918/19 in der neueren
wissenschaftlichen Diskussion', *G&G*, 9 (1983), pp. 278–301; U. Kluge, *Die deutsche
Revolution 1918/19* (Frankfurt am Main, 1985); H.A. Winkler, 'Die Revolution von
1918/19 und das Problem der Kontinuität in der deutschen Geschichte', *HZ*, 250
(1990), pp. 303–19. See most recently Feldman, *Great Disorder*, pp. 99–125; Bessel,
Germany, *passim*.

[4] E. Kolb, 'Internationale Rahmenbedingungen einer demokratischen Neuordnung in
Deutschland 1918/19', in L. Albertin and W. Link (ed.), *Politische Parteien auf dem
Weg zur parlamentarischen Demokratie in Deutschland* (Düsseldorf, 1981), pp. 147–76.

[5] Lippmann, *Leben*, p. 271.

[6] See L. Albertin, *Liberalismus und Demokratie am Anfang der Weimarer Republik: Eine
vergleichende Analyse der DDP und der DVP* (Düsseldorf, 1972); L.E. Jones, *German
Liberalism and the Dissolution of the Weimar Party System* (Chapel Hill/London, 1988).

had been possible under the constraints of the Wilhelmine era.[7] Not
since 1848 had there been such far-reaching debates about the extent
of parliamentary as against executive power, about the level of democratic as opposed to corporate representation, about the degree of
political centralisation as against federal devolution, about the level of
economic regulation over liberal market forces. Arthur Rosenberg
called the November Revolution 'a middle class revolution won by
labour'; but that is to understate the contribution made by a part of
the bourgeoisie in its own right – often with the intention of countering,
or at least containing, the 'workers' movement'. At the same time,
the collapse of the Hohenzollern regime forced those repelled by both
socialism and liberalism to redefine their conservatism.[8] The fact that
this ideological ferment coincided with a time of national crisis, in
which German political sovereignty itself was clearly in jeopardy, makes
the historian's task doubly difficult. Ideological positions on domestic
politics were often rooted in analyses of Germany's international position. Some avowed liberals were, from an early stage, more concerned
with conciliating the Western powers than they were convinced of the
benefits of a parliamentary, democratic republic. Some socialists saw
alignment with Russia principally in terms of nationalist resistance
against the West.

This point is well illustrated by the case of Max Warburg. It was
the misconduct of German policy during the war which had convinced
Warburg of the necessity of political 'evolution' by October 1917 at the
latest; though it was not until the failure of Ludendorff's summer offensive the following year that he and the other liberals around Prince Max
of Baden had their opportunity. Ballin still hoped to awaken the Kaiser
to the need for negotiation and reform; but by 23 September, Warburg
had become convinced that it would be necessary for Prince Max to
'persuade the Kaiser to abdicate'.[9] His political objectives beyond this
were straightforward – parliamentarisation for the Reich, the preservation of the federal system and democratisation in Prussia. These

---

[7] See esp. W.J. Mommsen, *Max Weber and German Politics 1890–1920* (Chicago/
London, 1984), pp. 283–389.
[8] A. Mohler, *Die konservative Revolution in Deutschland 1918–1932. Grundriß ihrer
Weltanschauung* (Stuttgart, 1950); K. Fritzsche, *Politische Romantik und Gegenrevolu-
tion. Fluchtwege in der Krise der bürgerlichen Gesellschaft. Das Beispiel des 'Tat'
Kreises* (Frankfurt, 1976); J. Petzold, *Konservative Theoretiker des deutschen Faschismus.
Jungkonservative Ideologen in der Weimarer Republik als geistige Wegbereiter des faschistischen Diktatur* (Berlin, 1982).
[9] Cecil, *Ballin*, pp. 334ff.; WA, 'Jahresbericht 1918', pp. 4ff.; Anlage 1, Warburg
Angabe, 22.9.18; Anlage 8 (Warburg's account of Max of Baden's government);
Warburg, *Aufzeichnungen*, pp. 65f. Warburg still hoped to be able to 'retain the
dynasty'. For Ballin's subsequent conclusion that 'the Emperor [. . .] cannot do
anything but abdicate', see Fischer, *War of Illusions*, p. 462.

domestic reforms were in fact achieved by the government of Prince Max in the course of October 1918: the new government included two Social Democrats, and by the end of the month it had reformed the Prussian franchise and altered the Reich constitution to make the government responsible to the Reichstag. But Warburg's pessimistic view that Prince Max was coming to power 'too late' had already been confirmed four days before his appointment as Chancellor, when Ludendorff made his dramatic demand for 'immediate armistice to avoid catastrophe'. Warburg's argument against this 'panic' was a strong one: 'begging President Wilson for an armistice' would mean 'the capitulation of Europe to America' if it was done before 'the idea has taken root abroad that there had been a change in Germany'.[10] Without the leverage of a defensible Front, there was no sense in attempting to make a qualified acceptance of the Fourteen Points, as Warburg, Kurt Hahn and Konrad Haussmann had intended, and nothing to prevent Wilson from demanding further political reforms within Germany – including the end of the monarchy – as a precondition for negotiation.[11] When the navy then attempted to launch a last-ditch raid on Britain, the effect was to precipitate the Kiel mutiny, and unleash the spontaneous revolution from below.[12]

To Ballin and Warburg, it had been clear since early 1918 that some kind of popular revolution was likely.[13] This was a reasonable conclusion to draw from the events of January 1918, when strikes at the Vulkan and Blohm & Voß shipyards had spread throughout the city's engineering sector and culminated in anti-war demonstrations and the formation of a Workers' Council.[14] Only the imposition of military control had brought the situation under control; and by October 1918, this could clearly no longer be depended upon. Indeed, it was sailors on their way back to Kiel who brought the revolution to Hamburg on the night of 5/6 November. Local leadership was hesitant: as in January, the Hamburg Majority Social Democrats had responded to the strike call from Kiel by calling meetings in consultation with the military authorities, while the Independent Social Democrats had simply called for a socialist republic, then gone home. It

[10] WA, 'Jahresbericht 1918', Anlage 8; Warburg, *Aufzeichnungen*, p. 65; Vagts, 'M.M. Warburg', p. 367; Max von Baden, *Erinnerungen*, pp. 329f., 476; Haupts, *Deutsche Friedenspolitik*, pp. 144ff., 186–91, 196–9.

[11] WA, 'Jahresbericht 1918', Anlage 8; Brecht, *Political Education*, pp. 96ff.; Max von Baden, *Erinnerungen*, pp. 329f.

[12] See E. Kolb, *The Weimar Republic* (London, 1988), pp. 3–5; Holborn, *History of Modern Germany*, III, pp. 502ff.

[13] Cecil, *Ballin*, pp. 329, 342f.

[14] Ullrich, 'Arbeiterbewegung', pp. 517–48; StAH, FA B&V 13, Bd. 2, Firmenleitung, 31.1.18, 21.2.18.

was only when sailors roused the USPD leader Kalweit on the morning
of 6 November, informed him that the Altona military commander
had fled, and marched him down to the *Gewerkschaftshaus*, that the
Hamburg Workers' and Soldiers' Council came into being. The events
which had been halted by military intervention in January were now
repeated unchecked: the Blohm & Voß workers struck, and mass
meetings were held on the Heiligengeistfeld.[15]

The bourgeois reaction to these events was mixed. It was clearly one
of profound shock for those who, to the last, had refused to contemplate
either defeat or revolution. Only two weeks before, Max von Schinckel
and Richard Krogmann had secured the support of a majority on the
Chamber of Commerce for a resolution condemning the constitutional
reforms of Prince Max's government.[16] Now the full extent of the collapse was abruptly revealed as revolution manifested itself in a multiplicity of affronts to the bourgeois sense of order. On the night of 6
November, there was shooting in the streets. Soldiers and sailors, their
badges of rank symbolically stripped off, patrolled the city in cars flying
the red flag. Others searched the houses of the wealthy in Harvestehude
for food and weapons – an experience so alarming for one Senator and
his wife that they fled their house through the back door. Representatives
of the Workers' and Soldiers' Council even burst into the state opera
house, interrupting a performance of *Tannhäuser* during Elisabeth's
prayer to the Virgin in Act Three.[17] For some, the trauma was too much.
Albert Ballin, having been ousted from his office by the new Council
and abused by a crowd outside, took a fatal overdose of sleeping tablets.[18]

[15] See Ullrich, 'Arbeiterbewegung', pp. 615–46; Comfort, *Revolutionary Hamburg*, pp.
30–40; J. Stehling, 'Der Hamburger Arbeiter- und Soldatenrat in der Revolution
1918/19', in Herzig *et al.* (eds.), *Arbeiter in Hamburg*, pp. 419–28; W. Lamp'l, *Die
Revolution in Hamburg/Das groß-hamburgische Revolutionsrecht* (Hamburg, 1921), pp.
12ff.; P. Neumann, *Hamburg unter der Regierung des Arbeiter- und Soldatenrats.
Tätigkeitsbericht erstattet im Auftrage der Executive des Arbeiterrats Groß Hamburgs*
(Hamburg, 1919), pp. 3–12; Cattaruzza, *Arbeiter und Unternehmer*, p. 173. See also
H. Laufenberg, *Die Hamburger Revolution* (Hamburg, 1919); and in general R.
Rürup, E. Kolb and G.D. Feldman, 'Die Massenbewegung der Arbeiterschaft in
Deutschland am Ende des Ersten Weltkrieges, 1917–1920', *Politische Vierteljahresschrift*, 13 (1972), pp. 84–105.
[16] Warburg and Witthoefft blocked the motion by insisting it be carried unanimously:
WA, 'Jahresbericht 1918', Anlage 9 (Warburg Diary), 24.10.18; StAH, FA AOM
1, Bd. 10, 91, Witthoefft to Warburg, 4.11.18; Pohlmann, *Richard Krogmann*, pp.
24iff.; Rohrmann, *Max von Schinckel*, p. 227.
[17] See the Prussian envoy Köster's report: PA/AA, R3008, PG to AA, 6.11.18, 7.11.18;
and Arndt von Holtzendorff's account: HA, HV, Bd. I, Notiz 19.11.18; Schramm,
Neun Generationen, II, p. 498; Plagemann, *Industriekultur*, p. 300; Pohlmann, *Richard
Krogmann*, p. 245; Schröder, *Aus Hamburgs Blütezeit*, pp. 335ff.
[18] Cecil, *Ballin*, pp. 342f.; Kohlhaus, 'Die Hapag', p. 170; Chernow, *Warburgs*, p.
201; HA, HV, Bd. I, Notiz 19.11.18. Cf. T. Krause, 'Revolution in Altona. Die
"Novemberrevolution" – Entstehung eines bürgerlichen Traumas', in A. Sywottek
(ed.), *Das andere Altona. Beiträge zur Alltagsgeschichte* (Hamburg, 1984).

Others evidently hurried to remove their movable wealth to safety by smuggling it abroad.[19] Yet there were those who remained surprisingly calm in the face of the upheaval. The left-liberal Carl Petersen, recently elected a Senator, was confident that he 'would be able to come to an understanding with his old friends, the Majority Social Democrats'.[20] In the Chamber of Commerce, Franz Witthoefft was sure that, provided the Kaiser and Crown Prince stepped down, 'calm and order' would be restored 'in a relatively short time'.[21] At first sight this seems surprising, in view of the fact that the MSPD failed to gain control of the Workers' Council when it was elected, allowing the 'radical Leftist' Heinrich Laufenberg to proclaim the abolition of the Senate and Bürgerschaft on 12 November.[22] However, from an early stage there were indications that the threat posed to the status quo by the Council was less serious than it appeared. Bourgeois Hamburg was quick to regain the political initiative.

Historians of the November Revolution in Hamburg have tended to concentrate on the political compromise ultimately struck between the Majority Social Democrats and the city's traditional rulers in the Senate after the Bürgerschaft elections of March 1919. This compromise has been portrayed critically as a regional equivalent of the course adopted by Ebert and Scheidemann in Berlin, inevitably culminating in the occupation of Hamburg by the Reichswehr in July 1919 and the stifling of radical aspirations.[23] More recently, the political compromise has been put in a more positive light: the alliance of moderate socialists and progressive liberals which emerged in Hamburg and endured until 1933 illustrated what might have been achieved at the national level.[24] Both accounts suggest that bourgeois groups played an essentially passive role. In reality, however, the political 'turning points' of the traditional historiography were of limited significance compared with the economic compromises achieved in 1918/19; and, as at the national level, the initiatives for these more often than not came from the side of business.

It was Max Warburg who took the first steps in this direction. The day after the red flag had been hoisted over the Rathaus, on 13 November, Warburg led a delegation from the Chamber of Commerce

---

[19] StAH, DHSG III, Pr. V Bd. I, HKH to DHSG [date illegible], protesting at the ban on capital flight introduced in the course of November.
[20] F.-S. Baumann, *Um den Staat: Ein Beitrag zur Geschichte der Revolution in Hamburg* (Hamburg, 1924), p. 39.
[21] StAH, FA AOM I, Bd. 10, 97, Witthoefft to Clara Strandes 9.11.18.
[22] Ullrich, 'Arbeiterbewegung', pp. 644–52.; Comfort, *Revolutionary Hamburg*, pp. 39–41.
[23] Ullrich, 'Arbeiterbewegung', pp. 659–729.
[24] Büttner, *Politische Gerechtigkeit*, pp. 13–46; idem, *Hamburg in der Staats- und Wirtschaftskrise, 1928–1931* (Hamburg, 1982), p. 27.

to discuss the city's finances with Laufenberg. It was a tense confrontation:

He asked me what I thought about renewing the [state] treasury bills which we and our friends held. I replied we would proceed with renewing them, provided the Finance Deputation continued in the future, as it had done in the past, to determine the state's expenditure. Dr Laufenberg replied extremely coldly: 'You do not seem quite to appreciate who is in charge here.'[25]

But Warburg had the advantage over him. Already the state was having to print illegal 'emergency money' to cover its liabilities; and all the schemes envisaged by Laufenberg – job creation, payments for returning soldiers, unemployment benefits, higher salaries for public employees, and subsidised food – implied an increase in the state's dependence on the banks.[26] Laufenberg yielded, and after a further meeting with Warburg and five representatives of the Senate (over a somewhat uneasy lunch in the Rathaus), the Council agreed to repeal the proclamation of 12 November. Fritz Warburg and the bank's legal expert Ernst Spiegelberg then assisted with the drafting of new proclamations which, while distinguishing between the political power of the Workers' and Soldiers' Council and the administrative power of the Senate and Bürgerschaft, confirmed the Finance Deputation's sovereignty on matters of public finance.[27] Just ten days after abolishing the Senate and Bürgerschaft, Laufenberg had to acknowledge: 'The economy cannot be set in motion without the cooperation of the bourgeoisie [. . .] The proletariat [. . .] cannot by itself provide the resources [. . .] to run the state machine [. . .] in its own sense.'[28] Speaking in Berlin at the national Congress of Councils, he was still more explicit:

Germany has no more credit abroad [. . .] The only factor which one can bring into play is the personal credit which individual bourgeois capitalists enjoy abroad. In order to survive, the economic system which has hitherto existed cannot for the moment be dispensed with (quite right!) and hence, even if the bourgeoisie is excluded from the exercise of political power, there is no way of denying it influence over political power in another form.[29]

[25] Warburg, *Aufzeichnungen*, pp. 67f.; Pohlmann, *Richard Krogmann*, pp. 242f.; Rosenbaum and Sherman, *M.M. Warburg & Co.*, p. 152.
[26] Brandt, *Finanzen*, pp. 16–19; Lippmann, *Leben*, pp. 318f.
[27] WA, 'Jahresbericht 1918', pp. 12, 13, 13a; Anlage 36, Fritz Warburg, Tagebuchnotizen (4–23.11.18). For other accounts, see Comfort, *Revolutionary Hamburg*, pp. 46f.; Lamp'l, *Die Revolution*, pp. 95–109; Ullrich, 'Arbeiterbewegung', p. 652.
[28] Quoted in Ullrich, 'Arbeiterbewegung', p. 670.
[29] S. Miller and H. Potthoff (eds.), *Die Regierung der Volksbeauftragten 1918/19*. [*Quellen zur Geschichte des Parlamentarismus und der politischen Parteien*, I. Reihe Bd. 6] vol. I (Düsseldorf, 1969), pp. 185f.

These events had their parallel at the national level in the decision not to replace Havenstein as President of the Reichsbank, and in the hasty improvisation of Eugen Schiffer in the absence of formal authorisation for the issue of new Reich treasury bills.[30]

Financial leverage had its limits, of course. Warburg and his colleagues could do nothing but rail against the surge of wage demands unleashed by the revolution. But here too, even where its bargaining power had collapsed, business was quick to reconstruct its position. Concessions to the existing workforce had to be made in the short term; but just as in the Ruhr, where the industrial employers sought to contain their workforces by centralising bargaining in the form of a 'Central Working Community' (Zentralarbeitsgemeinschaft) with the workers' least radical representative, the unions,[31] so in Hamburg, a parallel effort was made to institutionalise, and hence to stabilise, the new economic balance of power. The idea of an Economic Council (Wirtschaftsrat) – a device intended to counteract the power of democratic assemblies which dated back to Bismarck – was hastily adapted to fit the revolutionary fashion for councils, and presented to Laufenberg, at the same time as the financial 'deal', as a progressive way of 'maintaining economic life'.[32] Laufenberg was so impressed by the idea that, as we have seen, he argued for its adoption at the national level. In fact, its sole function was, like the Zentralarbeitsgemeinschaft, to secure the position of the pre-revolutionary economic organisations – in the case of Hamburg, by placing the various corporate chambers on an equal footing with the Workers' Council, and thus, as Witthoefft noted, keeping 'the whole economy at least tolerably above water'.[33] Warburg insisted upon 'the fundamental distancing' of the Hamburg

[30] H. Habedank, Die Reichsbank in der Weimarer Republik. Zur Rolle der Zentralbank in der Politik des deutschen Imperialismus, 1919–1933 (Berlin, 1981), p. 34; Webb, Hyperinflation, p. 122; Feldman, Great Disorder, pp. 130–6.

[31] G.D. Feldman, 'German Big Business between War and Revolution. The Origins of the Stinnes-Legien Agreement', in G. Ritter (ed.), Enstehung und Wandel der modernen Gesellschaft (Berlin, 1970), pp. 312–41; idem, Iron and Steel, pp. 82–109; idem, 'The Origins of the Stinnes-Legien Agreement: A Documentation', Internationale wissenschaftliche Korrespondenz zur Geschichte der Deutschen Arbeiterbewegung, 19/20 (1972), pp. 45–102; idem, 'Die Freien Gewerkschaften und die Zentralarbeitsgemeinschaft 1918–1924', in H.O. Vetter (ed.), Vom Sozialistengesetz zur Mitbestimmung (Cologne, 1975), pp. 229–52.

[32] The idea of a Volkswirtschaftrat had been revived in Hamburg during the war; see Wirtschaftsdienst, 30, 26.7.18, pp. 718f.; but it was Warburg and Witthoefft who adapted the idea to the revolutionary situation: WA, 'Jahresbericht 1918', p. 13; Anlage 27, 'Entwurf für eine erste Resolution des Wirtschaftsrats'; StAH, FA AOM I, Bd. 10, 119, Witthoefft correspondence with Leuckfeldt. Cf. Ullrich, 'Arbeiterbewegung', p. 654. Other bourgeois groups did likewise, setting up Civil Servants' Councils and Teachers' Councils: Lyth, 'Mittelstand', pp. 208f.; Büttner, Politische Gerechtigkeit, p. 214.

[33] StAH, FA AOM I, Bd. 10, 119, Witthoefft to Oberlandsgericht Präsident, 29.11.18.

Economic Council from 'political questions'; but he clearly hoped that it would be possible to use the ZAG and the Economic Council as the foundations for a national economic 'parliament', with the obvious function of absorbing the workers' councils and reducing the power over economic affairs of any democratic assembly.[34]

That is not to suggest that the business community was opposed to democratisation. Certainly, those businessmen who had emerged as avowedly conservative during the war – such as Hermann Blohm, Richard Krogmann and Max von Schinckel – identified themselves early on with political organisations like the Nationalklub of 1919, which were more or less openly hostile to both democracy and republicanism.[35] However, the attitude of men like Warburg and Witthoefft towards democracy had clearly changed under the circumstances of 1918. True, their support for some kind of corporatist assembly based on the Economic Council – a central plank of Witthoefft's campaign as a DVP candidate for the National Assembly – implied a qualified form of democratisation. True, their attitude was also to some extent instrumental: the election of democratic assemblies at the state and national level was seen as the most effective way of isolating the radicals like Laufenberg, given the overwhelming support of the MSPD for the election of a National Assembly.[36] Laufenberg might insist on the political supremacy of the Workers' and Soldiers' Council, as he did at a stormy session of the Bürgerschaft on 27 November; but once the Council of People's Delegates in Berlin had approved a date for national elections, and once this had been not merely ratified but brought forward to 19 January by the Congress of Councils, the path to a democratised Bürgerschaft was clear.[37] Yet it is impossible to mistake the new and distinctive tone of political confidence which characterised Witthoefft's campaign. Witthoefft saw himself as the

---

[34] WA, 'Jahresbericht 1918', Anlage 27, 'Entwurf'; 'Jahresbericht 1919', Warburg to Walter Dauch, 2.3.19; 'Jahresbericht 1920', p. 31; HA, HV No. 983, Holtzendorff to Vorstand, 27.1.19; PA/AA, R3008, PG to AA, 10.2.19; Wirtschaftsrat Hamburg to Reich government, 21.3.19.

[35] On the Nationalklub, see B&V 241, Bd. 1, Carl Gottfried Gok, Schriftwechsel; on the General Secretariat for the Study and Combating of Bolshevism, another strongly conservative organisation, see Rohrmann, *Max von Schinckel*, p. 217.

[36] See, e.g., HA, HV, Bd. I, Holtzendorff to Vorstand, 1.12.18.

[37] Ullrich, 'Arbeiterbewegung', p. 680; Comfort, *Revolutionary Hamburg*, p. 55; StAH, NL Lamp'l, No. 2, pp. 205f. After Laufenberg's resignation as President of the Workers' and Soldiers' Council on 20 January, following an overwhelming MSPD success in the elections for the National Assembly, the Council passed a resolution setting the date for Bürgerschaft elections on 16 March. On the role of the Campaign Committee for the Hamburg Legislative Assembly, which pressed for swift Hamburg elections and represented around 300 'parties, professions and interest groups': BAP, RMI 16526, Nr. 8, Werbeausschuß to Ebert and Scheidemann, 28.1.19; StAH, FA AOM I, Bd. 10, p. 226, Witthoefft to H. Baehne, 24.1.19.

representative of the '*Erwerbsstände*', attempting to unite big and small business, *Bürgertum* and *Mittelstand*, in a single, united 'democratic party'.[38] Developing themes which had first been heard in the campaign against economic controls earlier in the year, he portrayed himself as an archetypal 'unpolitical German', whom the hard lessons of the war had galvanised into activism:

The war was initiated like a great duel, and the military conception of duelling honour overshadowed the businessman's readiness to seek compromise [. . .] We are responsible for the collapse, because we [. . .] only [. . .] thought about the expansion of our business, leaving politics to the politicians, diplomacy to the diplomats and military matters to the militarists [. . .] Until the outbreak of the revolution, I had never belonged to a political party, because I gave very little thought to politics. [. . .] Like a great many of my fellow *Bürger*, I found the principle: 'Politics corrupts the character' extraordinarily seductive. Everything was going just splendidly [. . .] The professional [. . .] politicians could talk themselves into a lather; the most one did was make fun of them. Political *laissez aller* was just fine – a passivity in outlook rooted in the German character, [which was] to be followed by a rude awakening [. . .] I regard [that] as a great mistake on my part [. . .] But my experience was little different from that of the majority of my fellow *Bürger*. Now we have all been shaken out of our political lethargy, and have the duty to be politically active [. . .] The dream of *Kaisertum* is now over.[39]

This was the authentic tone of a reactivated liberalism, explicitly distancing itself from the institutions and culture of the imperial era.

The events which followed the Bürgerschaft elections in March 1919 were therefore more than an act of grace by the Majority Social Democrats. In part, the political compromise accurately reflected the lack of social and political polarisation in Hamburg: at least a quarter of SPD voters were not manual workers, while around a fifth of employees earning less than 10,000 marks per annum voted for liberal candidates in the elections to the Great Workers' Council which replaced the revolutionary Workers' Council on 23 March.[40] The nine men selected by the Hamburg MSPD to become Senators were typical, quasi-bourgeois functionaries of the labour movement.[41] At the same time, the compromise

[38] StAH, FA AOM 1, Bd. 10, 100–8, esp. Witthoefft to Vogelstein, 19.11.18; 123, Witthoefft to Zentralausschuß hamburgischer Bürger-Vereine, 29.11.18; 164, Witthoefft to Fritz Brahm, 8[?].1.19; Witthoefft to W.O. Rose, 9.1.19; AOM 24, Fritz Brahm to Witthoefft, 28.12.18; Fritz Brahm to Witthoefft, 2.1.19; PA/AA, R3008, PG to AA, 10.1.19. On the difficulties in uniting DVP and DDP, cf. Büttner, 'Vereinigte Liberalen', pp. 14, 26; *idem*, *Staats- und Wirtschaftskrise*, pp. 30–4, 52–9.

[39] StAH, FA AOM 24 (four election addresses by Witthoefft dating from December 1918).

[40] *Statistisches Jahrbuch 1920*, p. 484; Comfort, *Revolutionary Hamburg*, pp. 62, 158–61.

[41] They were three senior journalists on the *Hamburger Echo*, three senior managers of the cooperative societies, one SPD secretary, one trade union secretary, and the head of a *Krankenkasse*: PA/AA, 3009, PG to AA, 1.4.19. See O. Stolten, H. Stubbe,

reflected the simple inertia of metropolitan administration, which had grown so complex by 1918/19 that only the most utopian revolutionaries contemplated a complete restructuring. Laufenberg complained in February that the MSPD was surreptitiously restoring the bourgeoisie to power by using pre-revolutionary civil servants to help run the Workers' and Soldiers' Council; but even he had been forced to recognise the indispensability of the Finance Deputation and the War Provisions Office in the first stormy weeks of revolution.[42] In agreeing to form a coalition Senate, half composed of existing Senators, despite winning an overall majority in the poll, the Majority Social Democrats openly acknowledged this dependence on 'bourgeois intelligence' in government as well as economic life.[43] Indeed, they even insisted that 'a man who is close to the old Hamburg families' be first Bürgermeister.[44] Of course, some bourgeois groups inevitably lost out as a result of democratisation – notably the 9,500 property owners, whose representation in the Bürgerschaft dwindled to just four seats under the democratic franchise, and small business, whose Economic League won just nine seats.[45] The business community, however, had never been as dependent as the *Mittelstand* on representation in the Bürgerschaft. Having convinced Laufenberg of his financial dependence on business in the first weeks of revolution, the decisive institutional victory from the point of view of business was the defeat of attempts to 'democratise' the Chamber of Commerce, and the confirmation of its role as the official mouthpiece of the business community.[46] Laufenberg had accepted only grudgingly the need for business representation on the Finance Deputation; but the SPD Senator Paul Hoffmann positively welcomed the 'expertise' of three Chamber of Commerce members on the Deputation for Commerce, Shipping and Manufactures.[47] It was a sign of the success with which the business community had defended its institutional position in the revolution that little was subsequently heard of the idea, aired before the March elections, to create a new economic assembly as a counterweight to the democratic Bürgerschaft.[48]

E. Krause and M. Leuteritz, *Der Kampf der Sozialdemokratie um das Rathaus in Hamburg* (Hamburg, 1927).

[42] PA/AA, R3008, PG to AA, 16.2.19. Cf. Büttner, *Staats- und Wirtschaftskrise*, p. 515 n. 81.

[43] PA/AA, R3008, PG to AA, 10.2.19, 22.3.19, 25.3.19; Comfort, *Revolutionary Hamburg*, pp. 58–65, 162.

[44] Bolland, *Bürgerschaft*, pp. 97ff.; Büttner, *Staats- und Wirtschaftskrise*, p. 27.

[45] Lyth, '*Mittelstand*', pp. 414f.

[46] Pohlmann, *Richard Krogmann*, pp. 243ff.; Büttner, *Staats- und Wirtschaftskrise*, p. 517 n. 116. An analysis of membership and office-holding in the Chamber during the 1920s reveals a high degree of continuity with the pre-war years: see the *Handelskammer Jahresberichte* for the years 1919 to 1930.

[47] Büttner, *Staats- und Wirtschaftskrise*, pp. 47f.

[48] PA/AA, R3008, PG to AA, 10.2.19.

Bourgeois political attention was not confined to the future structure of political power within the Hamburg state. The election of a National Assembly was merely the preliminary step towards a fundamental restructuring and reshaping of the Reich. Once again, the revolutionary debate on the constitution was conducted in the shadow of the Allied powers. No doubt in the months before Versailles some liberals tailored their constitutional prescriptions with one eye on the presumed tastes of the American President and public. But, as in the debate over political representation, the debate on the Reich's constitution and structure illustrates how the revolution liberated the bourgeois political imagination. Franz Witthoefft was not untypical in assuming that self determination would lead to the loss of non-German peripheral areas in exchange for German Austria and Luxemburg, in arguing for an indirectly elected President, and in sharing Hugo Preuß's vision of the break-up of Prussia, to allow the creation of more congruent federal states.[49] Although he wished to see 'a stronger Reich consciousness' and a 'unitary constitution', Max Warburg also argued for preserving the 'federal state', partly 'in the interests of the economy' and partly because a federal system would make it 'easier [. . .] for the other lands which wish to join Germany, such as German-Austria, to do so'. He too envisaged breaking up Prussia 'into its component parts'.[50] There was an element of Hanseatic opportunism here. Both men saw a redrawing of the Reich's internal boundaries as an opportunity to increase the extent of the Hamburg state, whether (as Witthoefft suggested) through union with the other Hanseatic ports, or, as was more commonly argued, by absorbing Prussian areas such as Altona and Wandsbek which were now economically inseparable from Hamburg. This vision of a 'Greater-Hamburg' or a 'Republic of Lower Saxony' had indeed been raised before the Revolution; but the conditions of flux after November 1918 appeared to offer a real prospect of success, particularly since Hugo Preuß was sympathetic.[51] Nevertheless, the readiness to rethink the most fundamental aspects of the Reich's structure is striking.

[49] StAH, FA AOM 24, Witthoefft, 'Das neue Deutschland' (undated manuscript, probably for his National Assembly election campaign in late 1918).

[50] HA, HV, Holtzendorff Notiz, 30.1.19; WA, 'Jahresbericht 1919', Max Warburg to Alice Warburg, 7.6.19; 'Jahresbericht 1920', Blatt 31.

[51] WA, 'Jahresbericht 1918', Anlage 18, 'Notiz für die Akte: Kommission für den Wideraufbau Hamburgs'; HA, HV, Holtzendorff to Vorstand, 15.12.18; BAP, 16526 RMI, Gen. Nr. 8, Max Warburg to Hugo Preuß (telegram), 29.12.18, Senator Predöhl to Hugo Preuß, 3.2.19; Herz (Workers' and Soldiers' Council) to Hugo Preuß, 6.2.19; SS Hirsch to RMI, 25.2.19. For hostile Prussian reactions: *ibid.*, AA to RMI, 11.12.18, Prussian government to RMI, 12.2.19. Cf. H.-D. Loose, 'Hansestaat oder Republik Niedersachsen? Territoriale Neuordnungspläne für Nordwestdeutschland in der Revolution 1918/19', *ZVHG* (1980), pp. 95–116.

There was, in other words, a kind of bourgeois revolution in Hamburg in the period from September 1918 to around March 1919. Liberal aspirations which had in many ways been suppressed in the Wilhelmine golden years revived amid the crisis of the Wilhelmine state. By no means all of the Hamburg *Bürgertum* reacted in this way; and to some extent, the responses of active liberals like Max Warburg and Franz Witthoefft were defensive strategies aimed, with a certain degree of cynicism, at containing the unpredictable forces of popular unrest. But there was a core of genuine liberal conviction behind the arguments for a restructured federal system and corporate representation alongside parliamentary democracy. Witthoefft's call for the unpolitical *Bürger* to end his quiescence and participate in the refounding of the Reich represented a conversion as profound as it was similar to those experienced by those more eminent spokesmen of the *Bürgertum*, Max Weber and Thomas Mann.

Dearth and disorder

There was, however, an illusory quality to the political debates of the 'bourgeois revolution' described above. The radical Left might only have a narrow organisational base; its ideas might appeal only to a minority; it might be prone to fragment.[52] But that did not guarantee the popular legitimacy of the political changes effected after November 1918. Popular aspirations in Germany, as in Russia in 1917, were intimately bound up with economic discontents. It was from the roots of shortage, unemployment and inflation that politicisation stemmed: beginning with demands for peace and democracy, but becoming increasingly radical if peace and democracy failed to provide bread, jobs and adequate wages. That had been the pattern in Petrograd after February 1917;[53] and in some ways it was repeated in Hamburg two years later.

There was no lack of awareness in Hamburg of the importance of improving food supplies. Not only was there a clear correlation between dearth and social unrest; the food question offered a further opportunity for Hamburg business to assert its indispensability to the new regime.

---

[52] On the complicated relations between the 'Left Radicals', the USPD, the Spartacists/KPD, the revolutionary shop stewards and the various short-lived syndicalist unions, see Ullrich, 'Arbeiterbewegung', esp. pp. 716f.; Comfort, *Revolutionary Hamburg*, pp. 84–108. There are revealing, if highly subjective, analyses of the Left in the reports of the Prussian envoy: PA/AA, R3008, PG Abschrift, 14.2.19; PG to AA, 7.4.19, 10.4.19, 24.5.19 and 18.6.19.

[53] On the experience in urban Russia, see S.A. Smith, *Red Petrograd. Revolution in the Factories 1917–1918* (Cambridge, 1983); D. Mandel, *The Petrograd Workers and the Soviet Seizure of Power* (London, 1984).

Just as Max Warburg had moved swiftly to assert the dependence of the Workers' and Soldiers' Council on the goodwill of the Hamburg banks, so the city's commercial interests were quick to offer their services to the Council of People's Deputies. On 11 November 1918, the Hapag's Berlin representative Arndt von Holtzendorff and Max Warburg contacted Friedrich Ebert, now head of the Council of People's Deputies, to discuss 'how we can use our ships to bring in food and raw materials as soon as possible after the conclusion of peace'.[54] The government promptly instructed the Hamburg and Bremen Workers' and Soldiers' Councils to cooperate with the shipping lines in preparing available vessels for any such imports.[55] It was a promising start. Indeed, so successful was Holtzendorff in convincing Ebert of his case that in February Ebert invited him to become his press secretary.[56] However, as Warburg implied, there was no guarantee that Ebert would have the final say in the matter: 'I hope,' he commented acidly, 'that we do not keep getting in with the wrong people in the new government, as we kept doing with the old.'[57] His fears were quickly realised when Senator Sthamer, on behalf of the Hamburg Council, approached the Central Purchasing Company, which referred him to the Reich Food Office, which initially agreed to allow imports to be organised 'on the basis of free trade', and then changed its mind.[58] Sthamer's reference to free trade reveals how Hamburg was seeking to exploit the revolutionary upheaval to undermine the earlier decision to maintain import-controls during the 'transitional' period. The failure of his initiative reveals the continued opposition of the Economics Office to policies of trade liberalisation. Although steps were taken – for example by the Hapag – to reestablish trading links with American meat exporters, 1918 ended without any significant increase in activity in the docks.[59] Witthoefft pessimistically anticipated 'yet more centralisation' from the new government.[60]

---

[54] HA, HV, Bd. I, Holtzendorff to Ebert, 11.11.18.

[55] Ibid., Holtzendorff to Vorstand, 16.11.18.

[56] Ibid., Cuno to Holtzendorff, 25.12.18; Holtzendorff to Cuno, 28.2.19. Holtzendorff declined, but his relations with Ebert continued to be of great value to the Hapag. Holtzendorff's evenings in Berlin continued to provide an important point of contact between Hamburg business and government ministers, notably Ebert and Noske. By June 1919, it had been nicknamed the 'Secret Club': ibid., Holtzendorff to Cuno, 30.5.19.

[57] Ibid., Warburg to Holtzendorff, 19.11.18.

[58] StAH, DHSG III, Pr. III 37, Sthamer to Zentraleinkaufsgesellschaft, 19.11.18; ZEG to Senate, 23.11.18; Strandes to Sthamer, 30.11.18.

[59] HA, XVI, Huldermann to Holtzendorff, 7.12.18; Wirtschaftsdienst, Nr. 49, 6.12.18, p. 1094; StAH, FA AOM 1, Bd. 10, 163, Witthoefft to Kraewel, 28.12.18.

[60] Ibid., 134, Witthoefft to Nolze, 12.12.18. Cf. the justification for continued regulation by the Economics Minister Müller: StAH, SK II, III A 1 a 1, Bd. I, Müller to SK, 13.1.19.

With the appointment of Rudolf Wissell as Economics Minister in place of August Müller after the January 1919 elections, his prediction was fulfilled. Wissell was impressed by the wartime State Secretary Wichard von Moellendorff's vision of a *Gemeinwirtschaft*, which involved replacing market forces throughout the economy with planning by tiers of 'self-regulating' corporations.[61] Industry was sceptical of von Moellendorff; on the other hand, as Jakob Reichert of the Association of German Iron and Steel Industrialists (VdESI) persuasively argued, there was a danger that the policy favoured by Stinnes, of a total lifting of wartime controls, might precipitate a backlash against the big iron and steel concerns because of its effect on prices.[62] The lifting of exchange controls in November and the subsequent fall of the mark from 7.43 to 15.08 marks/$ by July 1919 precipitated what was to become a considerable outflow of industrial goods, particularly of iron and steel, and hence an acute domestic shortage.[63] When it became clear that Moellendorff was not proposing his full-scale plan (which would have meant stricter cartelisation for industry at a time when the iron cartel was falling apart) but simply the application of self-regulation to foreign trade, industry was inclined to moderate its criticism.[64] Yet Wissell and Moellendorff's plan was mainly concerned with something which had not yet begun to happen, least of all in Hamburg: large-scale imports. Their argument was that without regulation there would be a flood of 'unnecessary' goods which would be detrimental to 'the protection of national labour' and would feed inflation by worsening the balance of payments.[65] It was therefore proposed to expand the wartime system of central boards (*Zentralstellen*), which had controlled wartime trade through a system of export licensing. The number of these boards would be multiplied

[61] See D.E. Barclay, 'A Prussian Socialism? Wichard von Moellendorff and the Dilemma of Economic Planning in Germany 1918–1918', *CEH*, 11 (1978), pp. 50–82; *idem*, 'Rudolf Wissell, *Planwirtschaft*, and the Free Trade Unions 1919 to 1923. Some Tentative Observations', in Büsch and Feldman (eds.), *Historische Prozesse*, pp. 295–308. Cf. Ehlert, *Die wirtschaftliche Zentralbehörde des Deutschen Reiches 1914 bis 1919;* H. Schieck, 'Der Kampf um die deutsche Wirtschaftspolitik nach dem Novembersturz 1918' (Diss., Heidelberg, 1958). See most recently, Feldman, *Great Disorder*, pp. 126–9, 138ff.

[62] Feldman, *Iron and Steel*, pp. 100–7.

[63] *Ibid.*, pp. 85, 118–22.

[64] *Ibid.*, pp. 108f.

[65] Wissell addressed the Hamburg Chamber of Commerce on 5 April, in the vain hope of heading off Hanseatic opposition: HA, HB, Holtzendorff Notizen, 4.4.19; StAH, Krg. B II b 121 c, Rede des Reichsministers Wissell in Hamburg 5.4.19; HKH *Jahresbericht, 1919*, p. 23. For the definitive memorandum to the Länder, see StAH, SK II, III A 1 a 1, Bd. I, RWM to Länder, 6.5.19.

to meet the more diversified requirements of peacetime commerce; they would become autonomous 'self regulatory bodies', and the trade unions would be given equal representation alongside the various industrial associations which had controlled the boards during the war.[66] This underestimated the complexity of normal trade, overestimated the altruism of the industrial associations, and gave the unions wholly inappropriate powers. With good reason, the plan was attacked not only by the Hamburg Chamber of Commerce (in a memorandum drafted by Warburg), but by the DDP ministers Dernburg and Gothein, the SPD Food Minister Schmidt, the Düsseldorf metal industries, the South German states, and finally, though in muffled tones, the new Imperial Association of German Industry (RdI).[67] By the end of June, with a new Chancellor in office, the Economics Ministry was in retreat, admitting feebly that the plan was 'a leap in the dark'; and on 12 July Wissell and Moellendorff resigned.[68]

This appeared to be a major victory for the advocates of trade liberalisation. Yet the practical impact of the Wissell plan had been negligible. In reality, the principal obstacle to free imports through Hamburg after October 1918 was not the Economics Ministry in Berlin, but the Allied decision to prolong the wartime blockade of Germany until a peace treaty had been signed.[69] English, French and American naval vessels lay at anchor in Hamburg's harbour;[70] but it was not until February 1919 that the first British Commission arrived to investigate the city's food supply, and a further month elapsed before the food promised in the armistice terms began to arrive.[71] Hamburg's weakness was open to exploitation. It emerged in March 1919 that the British secret service had been offering consignments of food and coal worth 400 m. marks to Hamburg firms (including

[66] *Ibid.*, Wissell to Senate, 15.5.19.

[67] HA, HB, Holtzendorff to Cuno, 26.5.19; StAH, SK II, III A 1a 1, Bd. I, Strandes (Hanseatic delegate to Reichsrat) to SK, 17.6.19; FA AOM 1, Bd. 10, 363, Witthoefft to Warburg, 6.6.19. Cf. Böhm, *Anwalt der Handelsfreiheit*, pp. 218–28; Maier, *Recasting Bourgeois Europe*, pp. 66, 142f., 144–59; Feldman, *Great Disorder*, pp. 140–4.

[68] StAH, DHSG III, Pr. III 37, Strandes to Sthamer 4.7.19; Feldman, *Great Disorder*, pp. 152–5.

[69] S.L. Bane and R.H. Lutz, *The Blockade of Germany after the Armistice 1918–1919* (Stanford, 1942); C.P. Vincent, 'The Post-World War I Blockade of Germany: An Aspect of the Tragedy of a Nation' (Ph.D. thesis, Colorado, 1980); *idem*, *The Politics of Hunger: the Allied Blockade of Germany, passim.*

[70] H. Schulze (ed.), *Das Kabinett Scheidemann* (Boppard am Rhein, 1971), p. 412.

[71] Lippmann, *Leben*, p. 246; HA, HV, Holtzendorff to Vorstand, Nr. 985, 3.2.19, 5.2.19, 2.4.19; Kohlhaus, 'Die Hapag', p. 11; Offer, *Agrarian Interpretation*, pp. 388f., 393ff.; NAW, RG 59, 862.00/492, American Mission to State Department, 28.3.19; StAH, SK I, C 2 a 5 Fasc. 13, Bd. 1; Haupts, *Friedenspolitik*, pp. 300–20.

Warburg's) in the hope of detaching any emergent Greater Hamburg
or Lower Saxon republic from Prussia.[72] Although representatives of
the Workers' and Soldiers' Council and the Senate showed interest in
the offer of food, not even the most ardent proponent of 'Greater
Hamburg' was willing to pay such a high political price.[73]

The consequence of all of this was that supplies of food in revolutionary Hamburg were extremely scant, and continued to be so until
around August 1919.[74] Indeed, disruptions to the transport system and
the return of troops from the Front meant that the situation rapidly
became worse than it had been during the war.[75] Of course, the impact
of food shortages on the German population during and after the war
is open to debate, and the extent of malnutrition has sometimes been
exaggerated. On the other hand, to portray the war as some kind of
extended *Kur* for the urban population, involving a salutary shift from
meat to fish and vegetables, would be to understate the miserable
quality of war rations. British and American as well as German
observers were struck by the psychological impact of undernourish-
ment, noting 'a high degree of nervous excitability' and a 'desire for
distraction at any cost'.[76] The possibility that this might express itself
in a second, more violent wave of revolutionary unrest was not to be
discounted. In late December, the radical leader Laufenberg attempted
to mobilise popular opposition to the Ebert-Scheidemann government
in the wake of the bloodshed in Berlin; and he did so again at the
time of the Spartakist coup in Berlin in January.[77] Although these
moves came to nothing, they revealed the precariousness of the situation, and the lack of any adequate force for preserving order in the
city. In a heated moment, Laufenberg had declared: 'Legal norms are
no longer valid, [. . .] the ordinary courts will no longer be recognised

[72] PA/AA, R3008, Grenzüberwachungsstelle Bentheim to Polizeipräsident Berlin,
10.3.19; PG to AA, 12.13.19; Rosen (ambassador in the Hague) to AA, 14.3.19;
PG to AA, 3.4.19; Schmidt to von Maltzan, 4.4.19; PG to Prittwitz, 28.5.19; PG
Abschrift, 5.6.19. Cf. O. Hovi, 'England und der Gedanke einer Hanserepublik im
Herbst 1918', *Publikationen des Instituts für allgemeine Geschichte, Universität Turko,
Finland*, 3 (1971), pp. 39–48. The British agents also offered financial support for
a separate Hamburg currency and separate representation at the peace conference.
[73] PA/AA, R3009, PG Abschrift, 5.6.19; PA/AA, R3010, Heise statement, 17.6.19;
Carl Petersen to Pantel, 29.7.19; StAH, FA AOM I, Bd. 10, Witthoefft to Warburg,
24.6.19.
[74] Lippmann, *Leben*, pp. 222–52; StAH, DHSG III, Pr. 2 1b (Note of meeting of
Kriegs-versorgumsamt), 12.8.19.
[75] Büttner, *Politische Gerechtigkeit*, pp. 24f. Demobilisation also exacerbated the housing
shortage: Lyth, '*Mittelstand*', p. 419 (table 1); *Statistische Mitteilungen über den
hamburgischen Staat*, no. 6, p. 15.
[76] Offer, *Agrarian Interpretation*, pp. 388ff.
[77] Neumann, *Hamburg unter der Regierung*, pp. 51, 59–61; Ullrich, 'Arbeiterbewegung',
p. 693; Comfort, *Revolutionary Hamburg*, pp. 53f.

and [. . .] violence alone will decide matters. The workers are ready to use the force at their disposal.'[78] The MSPD was able to organise large demonstrations against such 'anarchist terror'. But it was not clear that the bourgeoisie had any comparable force to mobilise in defence of the rule of law.

Responsibility for maintaining order in the wake of the revolution was initially supposed to rest with the Soldiers' Council. In the first days of the revolution, this had appeared a relatively conservative body, with officers seeking to maintain discipline and prevent looting.[79] However, an abortive putsch attempt against the Workers' Council aroused widespread suspicion of 'militarism' because of the role played by ex-officers, including three of the original members of the Soldiers' Council.[80] It was in an attempt to avoid a wholesale purge of officers and the formation of a 'Red Guard' (as Laufenberg demanded) that Walther Lamp'l, a Social Democrat officer on the Soldiers' Council, drafted the famous 'Hamburg Points' on military organisation, which were adopted at the December Congress of Councils in Berlin. Lamp'l's main intention in drafting the 'Points' was to confirm the supremacy of the Soldiers' Council on questions of order, and to establish the right of ex-officers to remain in charge of their troops (points 3 and 6). The more radical proposals (2, 5 and 7), calling for the election of officers, the abolition of badges of rank and the creation of a People's Army were, to some extent, sops to the Left.[81] The result was a political victory for Lamp'l, who ousted Heise as chairman of the Soldiers' Council and replaced the head of the Security Police.[82] From the point of view of security, however, the new system inspired only limited confidence; and increasingly, the business community looked to the Defence Minister Noske for support, impressed by his

---

[78] GHH, 300193012/4, Deutsche Werft report, 13.1.19.

[79] StAH, NL Lamp'l, 8b, 'Maßnahmen zur Bildung einer Volkswehr'. For early confidence that discipline would be maintained see Schramm, *Neun Generationen*, II, p. 499; Lippmann, *Leben*, p. 278.

[80] StAH, NL Lamp'l 2, 'Historische Bericht', pp. 171–6; Lippmann, *Leben*, pp. 680–3; Comfort, *Revolutionary Hamburg*, pp. 52f.; Neumann, *Hamburg unter der Regierung*, pp. 39–42. It was alleged that 'capitalists', including Max Warburg had made 500,000 marks available to the putschists, who were led by the editor of the *Hamburgische Correspondent*, Abter; but Warburg insisted that he had dismissed the plan as 'nonsensical': WA, 'Jahresbericht 1918' (Warburg statement), 11.12.18. Cf. Arndt von Holtzendorff's regret at the damage done by the 'doubtless well-intentioned putsch' in Berlin: HA, HV, Holtzendorff to Vorstand, 8.12.18.

[81] StAH, NL Lamp'l, 2, 'Historische Bericht', pp. 191–204; Miller and Pothoff (eds.), *Regierung der Volksbeauftragten*, I, p. 393. See also U. Kluge, *Soldatenräte und Revolution. Studien zur Militärpolitik in Deutschland 1918/19* (Göttingen, 1975); H. Oeckel, *Die revolutionäre Volkswehr 1918/19* (Berlin, 1968); E.-H. Schmidt, *Heimatheer und Revolution 1918* (Stuttgart, 1981).

[82] StAH, NL Lamp'l, 2, 'Historische Bericht', p. 213.

assurances that Lamp'l's 'Points' were only to be regarded as 'provisional', as well as by his ruthless suppression of the Spartacist putsch in Berlin.[83] When Noske sent 4,000 troops of the Gerstenberg Division to oust the *Räterepublik* in the neighbouring Hanseatic port of Bremen, Wilhelm Cuno (Ballin's successor at the Hapag) urged him to send additional troops to Hamburg.[84]

The reaction in Hamburg to Noske's move against Bremen gave a clear indication of the fragility of public order in the city and the volatility of the political atmosphere. Incensed at what they saw as Noske's desertion 'of proletarian ideas under the clever influence of the militarists', the Majority Socialists on the Workers' and Soldiers' Council joined the Independents and Radicals in condemning the 'utilisation of the old military system' against Bremen.[85] The reemergence of militarism as a political issue – a traditional rallying point for the Left – gave Laufenberg a golden opportunity. At a protest demonstration of the three left-wing parties, he urged 'support for Bremen with all military means'; and when the motion was rejected by the Soldiers' Council, his supporters overran a number of military posts, seizing a large quantity of rifles. This action in turn precipitated a strike by railway and postal workers in support of the Berlin government, paralysing the city's communications.[86] It was in this atmosphere of near chaos that the MSPD pushed through the decisive motion on the Workers' and Soldiers' Council for elections to a constituent Bürgerschaft.[87] The timing and swift execution of this decision suggests that the MSPD's main objective was to avoid a Bremen-style occupation by replacing the Council as quickly as possible with a government that would be acceptable in Berlin. At the same time, Lamp'l's supporters on the Soldiers' Council 'Committee of Seven' assured Noske

---

[83] HA, HV, No. 973, 5.1.19, reporting Noske's comments at one of Holtzendorff's 'evenings'.

[84] *Ibid.*, Holtzendorff Notizen, 29/30.1.19. Cuno was a civil servant whose wartime work for the War Food Office had led Ballin to offer him a job with the Hapag in November 1917. He was appointed his successor on 20 December 1918, on the assumption that the company's survival would depend initially on the quality of its relations with government, rather than entrepreneurial flair: Kohlhaus, 'Die Hapag', pp. 149, 167–86. As a Thuringian-born Catholic, Cuno appears at first sight an unlikely recruit to the Hamburg commercial elite – until one appreciates that he had married into the merchant family Wirtz in 1906.

[85] Comfort, *Revolutionary Hamburg*, pp. 69f.; Neumann, *Hamburg unter der Regierung*, pp. 73, 89–102; PA/AA, R3008, PG to AA, 4.2.19.

[86] PA/AA, R3008, PG to AA, 6.2.19; 7.2.19; 12.2.19; 14.2.19; 16.2.19; 20.2.19; Comfort, *Revolutionary Hamburg*, pp. 72f.; Neumann, *Hamburg unter der Regierung*, pp. 98–102; Baumann, *Um den Staat*, pp. 88–90.

[87] PA/AA, R3008, PG to AA, 10.2.19.

that it could 'maintain peace and order with our own men' and imposed a state of siege.[88]

Yet even before the celebrated political compromise between old and new could take place, there was a second challenge to public order. During negotiations at Trier in early 1919, the Allies pressed for the handing over of Germany's remaining merchant ships, ostensibly for the purpose of transporting food supplies to Germany. This had already caused difficulties in Hamburg when a new organisation, the German Seamen's League, had demanded a substantial wage increase as a condition for cooperating in the transfer.[89] The shipping companies warned that this would prompt the Allies to provide their own crews for the ships, leading to 'Bolshevik conditions in Hamburg', and appealed to Noske for support; but the Hamburg Workers' Council took the side of the *Seemansbund*.[90] Although the government's 'energetic intervention in Bremen' temporarily subdued the sailors' protest,[91] the first sailings of ships for England after the Brussels agreement of 15 March prompted renewed protests. By 19 March, the sailors were openly refusing to cooperate in the surrender of the ships, arousing fears of a general strike and a further bid by Laufenberg to launch a Bolshevik coup.[92] On the eve of the Bürgerschaft poll, the Prussian envoy in Hamburg was seeking contact with outside troops in the belief that Laufenberg was planning a 'putsch on the Berlin model'.[93]

The increasing popular unrest of March/April 1919 clearly had economic roots. When the railway workers struck, they demanded improved food supplies, as well as opposing Laufenberg's call to arms against Noske. The seamen sought improved wages. The discovery in early April that a consignment of food intended for the army was being allowed to rot in the free port nearly led to riots; and on 23 April there were outbreaks of looting in the city centre, St Pauli and Hammerbrook by crowds of youths and women, forcing Lamp'l to reimpose a state of siege.[94] Witthoefft's repeated warnings that, unless

---

[88] *Ibid.*, R3008, PG to AA (telephone transcript), 6.2.19; PG to AA, 12.2.19.
[89] HA, HV, Holtzendorff Notizen, 28.1.19; 30.1.19.
[90] *Ibid.*, Holtzendorff Notizen, 31.1.19; 1.2.19; 7.2.19.
[91] HA, HV, Holtzendorff Notizen, 9.2.19.
[92] PA/AA, R3009, PG to AA, 10.3.19; 13.3.19; 19.3.19; HA, HV, Hapag to Noske, 18.3.19; Holtzendorff Notizen, 18.3.19; 19.3.19; NAW, RG 59 862/5045/18, US ambassador in the Hague to State Department, 22.3.19. Cf. Büttner, *Politische Gerechtigkeit*, p. 24.
[93] PA/AA, R3009, PG to AA, 13.3.19.
[94] *Ibid.*, PG to AA, 4.4.19; 8.4.19; Noske to AA, 8.4.19; Pantel [PG Kanzleivorstand] to AA, 23.4.19; PG to AA, 26.4.19; StAH, Lamp'l NL, No. 8c, 'Maßnahmen betr. Sicherstellung der Verpflegung insbes. im Freihafen lagernde Lebensmittelvorräte der Intendanten des IX. Armeekorps'; Comfort, *Revolutionary Hamburg*, pp. 72f.

restrictions on commerce were lifted, Hamburg faced 'complete ruin [. . .] because there are 75,000 people too many living in our *Vaterstadt*'[95] were in no sense hyperbole: dearth meant that Hamburg in mid 1919 was indeed 'reaching boiling point':

It is looking very black for Hamburg [. . .] and I would not be surprised if suddenly an insurrection were to break out which put all earlier events in the shade. Our authorities are too slack, and are letting the reins slip.[96]

However, the form which popular resentment took as it reached its climax in the summer of 1919 cannot be characterised simply as hunger rioting. Nor did it much resemble the Russian-style Bolshevism feared by the Prussian envoy. Rather, popular discontent was tinged by distinctly nationalist, populist and even 'proto-fascistic' forms. For example, the hostility of the seamen was clearly directed as much against the Entente powers as against the shipowners: it was discerned that the confiscation of the German merchant fleet was more likely to lead to unemployment for German sailors than to increased supplies of food. Heinrich Laufenberg himself had from an early stage espoused 'national Bolshevik' arguments, calling in November 1918 for 'the immediate organising of national defence by revolutionary means and in alliance with Russia to protect the revolution against the imperialist Entente'.[97] Above all, popular hostility increasingly focused on the protracted peace conference at Versailles. The difficulty was that, apart from a few deputations of English and American officers, the victorious powers were scarcely visible in Hamburg.[98] It was for this reason that resentment came to focus on the social group which – whether by cooperating in handing over the merchant fleet, engaging in mysterious talks with English agents, or actually representing Germany at the peace conference – appeared to be their accessories: the business community. Businessmen were not only held to blame for shortages and high prices; with Warburg, Melchior, Cuno and Witthoefft all involved in the diplomacy of the peace treaty,[99] business was also blamed for Germany's national humiliation. Moreover, in the case of Warburg and Melchior, whose diplomatic activities were well known, this national feeling could be expressed in anti-Semitic terms.

In the light of his wartime experiences, Warburg was well aware of

---

[95] StAH, FA AOM 1, Bd. 10, 363, Witthoefft to Warburg, 6.6.19.

[96] *Ibid.*, Witthoefft to Eduard Rosenbaum, 6.6.19.

[97] O.-E. Schüddekopf, *Linke Leute von Rechts. Nationalbolschewismus in Deutschland 1918–1933* (Frankfurt, 1972), pp. 100ff.

[98] Significantly, the Prussian envoy took the view that it would reduce social unrest if American troops could be stationed in Hamburg to control the distribution of food: PA/AA, R3009, PG to AA, 8.4.19.

[99] See chapter 4.

the dangers facing a Jewish businessman who entered politics in a revolutionary situation. He had refused Max of Baden's offer of the post of Finance Minister in September 1919 on the grounds that he 'knew the Germans, and knew that they would never accept a Jewish Finance Minister. On the other hand, the Social Democrats would see me as a representative of capitalism.'[100] He was equally careful to avoid being given too prominent a role in the peace negotiations. As he put it: 'We simply [can]not be too careful [. . .] It is important that the current democratic/social democratic combination prevails without acquiring a capitalist-Jewish hue.'[101] For the same reason, he declined to stand as a candidate in the Bürgerschaft elections.[102] Yet his self effacement was to no avail. Recently established anti-Semitic or '*völkisch*' organisations like the *Deutschvölkische Partei*, the *Hammerbund* or the *Schutz- und Trutzbund* were sufficiently influential in Hamburg by early 1919 to shift the existing Pan German League and the new conservative *Sammlungspartei*, the DNVP, in an anti-Semitic direction.[103] At the end of May, there was a scuffle at the bourse when a member of the *Schutz- und Trutzbund* began handing out anti-Semitic leaflets directed against Warburg's role at Versailles.[104] However, it was not just Jewish businessmen who came under attack. At the same time there was an aggressive press campaign against Franz Witthoefft in the Social Democrat *Hamburger Echo*, alleging that his political and diplomatic activities had mercenary motives.[105] When the German peace delegation's finance experts were deliberating whether to publish their report criticising the Allied terms, Warburg wrote to Witthoefft from Versailles, asking that his name be omitted from the published version. Witthoefft replied:

You say you want me to keep your name secret, in case they try to murder you [. . .] You can console yourself with my situation, because being murdered is a far more likely prospect for me here in Hamburg than for you in Versailles. Scarcely a day goes by without me being attacked in the most virulent fashion

---

[100] Warburg, *Aufzeichnungen*, p. 64.
[101] WA, 'Jahresbericht 1918', Anlage 5, Max Warburg to Fritz Warburg, 7.10.18.
[102] Warburg, *Aufzeichnungen*, p. 68.
[103] PA/AA, R1010, Rechenberg to AA, 29.8.19; W. Jochmann (ed.), *Nationalsozialismus und Revolution. Ursprung und Geschichte der NSDAP in Hamburg 1922–1933. Dokumente* (Frankfurt am Main, 1963), pp. 5–10, 25f.; U. Lohalm, *Völkischer Radikalismus. Die Geschichte des Deutschvölkischen Schutz- und Trutzbundes, 1919–1923* (Hamburg, 1970); A. Roth, *Aus der Kampfzeit des Deutschvölkischen Schutz- und Trutzbundes – Eine Erinnerungsschrift vom ehem. Hauptgeschäftsführer Alfred Roth* (Hamburg, 1939). On the influence of anti-Semitism in the Hamburg DNVP, see Lorenz, *Die Juden in Hamburg*, II, p. 1005.
[104] Warburg, *Aufzeichnungen* MSS, 23.6.19; HKHP, 31.5.19.
[105] StAH, FA AOM 1, Bd. 10, 335, Abschrift 24.4.19; 375–9, Witthoefft to *Hamburger Echo*, 7.6.19.

in the Social Democratic press [. . .] When I tell you that they have already shot at me through the window in Carlstraße, you may get some idea of how I feel.[106]

When Warburg returned to Hamburg from Versailles he found it once again under a 'state of siege', and, on being informed that he was on a Spartacist assassination list, departed for Switzerland.[107] Hostility to the Allies, hostility to the new MSPD-dominated government, hostility to businessmen and hostility to Jews: all of these were articulated in the hungry months from March to June 1919.

When Witthoefft expressed the fear that the authorities in Hamburg were 'letting the reins slip', he was alluding to the failure of Walther Lamp'l to forge a credible police force out of the revolutionary 'Security Force'. With around 13,000 men organised on the basis of Lamp'l's 'Points', the *Sicherheitswehr* was as much a job creation scheme for unemployed soldiers as a police force; and there were occasions when it appeared more a threat to public order than its bulwark.[108] There were repeated requests to send Reichswehr troops to Hamburg; but Noske, preoccupied with events in Munich and Bremen, could only spare a single officer, Major Lothar Danner, to oversee the creation of a local Home Guard (*Einwohnerwehr*).[109] The Ministry of the Interior had envisaged the Home Guard being drawn from 'reliable members of all sections of the population'; but in practice the volunteer force which took shape in the spring of 1919 was a bourgeois affair, composed of young ex-officers and students. Mobilised in the middle-class suburb of Bahrenfeld, the 400 young men descended on St Pauli on 24/5 March to quell the looting which had broken out there. With their volumes of Baudelaire in their pockets, they too were moved by the spirit of the bourgeois revolution:

Almost none [of the volunteers] had ever had an opportunity to see at such close quarters the poverty and depravity of a big city [. . .] This experience awakened and sharpened our social consciousness and intensified the feeling – which from the outset had been strongly present among the volunteers – of obligation, transcending all party allegiances towards the people whose will it was [our] sad task to execute.[110]

---

[106] *Ibid.*, 386, Witthoefft to Warburg, 10.6.19.
[107] WA, Warburg *Aufzeichnungen* MSS [n.p], 'June 1919'.
[108] StAH, Lamp'l NL, 'Historische Bericht', pp. 191–4; PA/AA, R3009, PG to AA, 8.4.19; Schramm, *Neun Generationen*, II, 502.
[109] L. Danner, *Ordnungspolizei Hamburg. Betrachtungen zu ihrer Geschichte 1918–1933* (Hamburg, 1958), pp. 11–15; Comfort, *Revolutionary Hamburg*, pp. 68–71; StAH, SK II, II VI B 1 Fasc. 2, RMI to Länder, 18.3.19.
[110] Schramm, *Neun Generationen*, II, pp. 502–5; H. Dähnhardt, *Die Bahrenfelder. Geschichte der Zeitfreiwilligenkorps Groß-Hamburg in den Jahren 1919/20* (Hamburg, 1925).

However, the citizens of St Pauli were more inclined to view the Bahrenfelder as a 'class troop'; and older bourgeois observers feared their action would merely be 'provocative'.[111] A more cautious voluntarist response to the threat of disorder was the Burghers' League (*Bürgerbund*) set up in late April by a group of around 250 civil servants and businessmen (including Franz Witthoefft) and incorporating a number of the anti-radical organisations like the Anti-Bolshevik League, the League for the Protection of German Culture and the Private Information Bureau, set up in the wake of the November events.[112] Like the Bahrenfelder, the *Bürgerbund* also employed unpolitical rhetoric:

> The *Bürgerbund* does not wish to conflict with the Workers' Council. [. . .]
> 1. The *Bürgerbund* does not engage in party politics. 2. It stands for law, morality and order. 3. The concept of *Bürger* means the equal rights of all citizens, irrespective of occupation [and is] infused with the democratic outlook.
> 4. [It also stands for] resistance to dictatorial and terroristic minorities.[113]

However, the *Bürgerbund* rejected armed action, envisaging as its ultimate weapon a 'defensive strike' by the bourgeoisie in the event of a general workers' strike aimed at the 'overthrow [of] the existing political order'.[114]

Supposedly 'unpolitical' voluntary associations like the Bahrenfelder and the *Bürgerbund* had deep roots in the bourgeois political tradition; but it is clear that neither represented an effective security force. Nevertheless, when Noske himself visited Hamburg on 27 May to review the city's police arrangements, it was the 'discipline, [. . .] good tone [and] true comradeship' of the Bahrenfelder which he commended; the *Sicherheitswehr*, which failed to keep a USPD-organised demonstration of the war-wounded at bay, he decided to dissolve.[115] At the moment of the most acute economic crisis, therefore, Lamp'l was instructed to sack 7,000 men from the *Sicherheitswehr*, and reduce the pay of the remainder in preparation for their absorption by the Reichswehr.[116] Predictably, the men used Lamp'l's own 'Points' to contest these changes, and open mutiny seemed imminent. The result was that, despite repeated requests for Reichswehr troops by the Prussian envoy's deputy, the Hamburg authorities were left all but defenceless.[117]

---

[111] *Ibid.*; PA/AA, R3009, PG to AA, 1.4.19.
[112] *Ibid.*, R3009, PG to AA, 28.4.19; StAH, FA B&V 1204, Vorstand des Bürgerbundes für Hamburg-Altona und Wandsbek, 1. Sitzung, 13.5.19.
[113] *Ibid.*
[114] *Ibid.*, Vorstand des Bürgerbundes Sitzung, 24.6.19.
[115] PA/AA, R3009, PG to AA, 27.5.19.
[116] *Ibid.*, PG to AA, 5.6.19.
[117] *Ibid.*, Rechenberg to Prittwitz, 7.6.19; Rechenberg to Prittwitz, 20.6.19.

With good reason, neither Max Warburg nor Franz Witthoefft felt
safe in Hamburg by June 1919. In the event it was another businessman, Jakob Heil, who fell victim to popular discontent, when rumours
began to circulate in late June that his pickled meat factory was using
the carcases of cats, dogs and rats in its brawn (*Sülze*). Heil was
subjected to a ritualised punishment which would seem familiar to
students of the eighteenth-century urban 'moral economy'. He was
paraded into the town centre in a wheelbarrow by a crowd and then
deposited in the Alster.[118] The following morning, a crowd congregated
in the Rathausmarkt, demanding that the responsible officials of the
War Provisions Office be brought to account; and there were scattered
attacks on food stores.[119] The fact that dog carcases were hung from
lamp-posts and the 'guilty men' subjected to ritual humiliations
(stripping, mock trials) suggests that the demonstration was at first
relatively 'unpolitical'. However, on the afternoon of 24 June, the
USPD leader Bergmann egged on the crowd to occupy the Rathaus;
and at this point the situation became more earnest. Lamp'l decided
to relieve the Rathaus by leading the Bahrenfelder into action in a
motorised assault; but the shortcomings of the volunteer force were
soon revealed. When the surrounded Bahrenfelder opened fire, the
crowd retaliated, killing ten of them and taking the rest prisoner. By
the evening, the bourse had been set alight, the city jail opened, the
Rathaus occupied, and the railway station sealed off.[120]

At an early stage, Holtzendorff and Warburg had endorsed the
Prussian representative's plea for Reichswehr troops to be sent from
Stettin.[121] However, once again, there was a hasty effort by the left-wing
parties to avert military intervention. A 'Committee of 12', composed
of equal numbers of MSPD, USPD and KPD works' council members,
sought to patch together a compromise to 'protect Hamburg from
bloodshed at all costs'.[122] The Committee called for the preservation
of order by a people's militia (the old *Sicherheitswehr*) and urged the
rioters to release the hostage Bahrenfelders.[123] For a moment, the

---

[118] For details on the Sülze riots see the material in: StAH, Sen. Cl. VII Lit. Mo. Nr. 12
vol. 24 Fasc. 1–18, 'Unruhen in Hamburg 1919–20'; Sig. A 320, 'Zeitungsausschnitt
Sammlung Heilsche Sülze, 1919'; Lamp'l NL, Nr. 9, 'Bürgerschaft Untersuchungs-
kommission betr. sog. Sülzeunruhen, 1919–20'. Cf. H. Ebeling, *Schwarze Chronik
einer Weltstadt. Hamburger Kriminalgeschichte 1919–1945* (Hamburg, 1980), pp. 16–
26; Comfort, *Revolutionary Hamburg*, pp. 74f.; Danner, *Ordnungspolizei*, pp. 17–21.
[119] Lippmann, *Leben*, pp. 253f.
[120] PA/AA, R3009, Pantel (telephone) to AA, 24.6.19; Pantel to AA, 25.6.19; Rechenberg (telephone) to Prittwitz 25.6.19; Rechenberg to Prittwitz (AA), 26.6.19;
Schramm, *Neun Generationen*, II, pp. 483, 508.
[121] PA/AA, R3009, PG to AA, 26.6.19; HA, HB, Cuno to Holtzendorff, 24.6.19.
[122] Comfort, *Revolutionary Hamburg*, pp. 76f.; Danner, *Ordnungspolizei*, p. 17.
[123] *Hamburger Echo*, 26.6.19; Comfort, *Revolutionary Hamburg*, p. 77; PA/AA, R3009,
Rechenberg to Prittwitz (AA), 26.6.19.

compromise appeared to stay the Reichswehr forces. This time, however, Noske chose to act. At his instruction, General Paul von Lettow-Vorbeck – veteran of the South West African Herero war – occupied Hamburg with a huge force of some 10,000 men, backed up by artillery and torpedo boats. Despite rumours of thousands of rifles being in the hands of the insurgents, there was no resistance to speak of.[124]

Historians of the socialist movement have tended to see the arrival of the Lettow troops as a watershed, marking a decisive setback for the Left and ushering in a period of right-wing *revanche*.[125] Yet this ignores the ambiguous nature of the popular protest itself. It is true that the radical Left had opportunistically sought to exploit an initially 'unpolitical' riot, issuing radical communist manifestos calling for 'the end of the money economy and the annulment of all material obligations' and directing the crowd against the new Hamburg government.[126] But the anti-Semitic *Schutz- und Trutzbund* had been equally active, issuing pamphlets which claimed that Heil was Jewish and portrayed the incident as symptomatic of 'Jewish rule'.[127] Moreover, the arrival of the Reichswehr did not solve the fundamental problem which had sparked off the trouble in the first place. As one observer pointed out within days of the occupation, stability would only be guaranteed once proper supplies of food were available: 'When the people who are currently fomenting discontent are properly fed, their enthusiasm for unrest will subside.'[128] Moreover, it was significant that when representatives of 'the influential men of Hamburg [. . .] in particular [those representing] the industrial works' met officers from Lettow's staff, the main topic of discussion was whether the shipyards would be prepared to supplement the soldiers' pay.[129] The end of

---

[124] PA/AA, R3009, Rechenberg to Prittwitz, 27.6.19, 28.6.19; Pantel to AA, 29.6.19; Senate (telephone) to AA, 28.6.19; Rechenberg to Prittwitz, 1.7.19. For Noske's assurances that he would intervene, see HA, HB, Holtzendorff to Cuno, 27.6.19; A. Golecki (ed.), *Das Kabinett Bauer* (Boppard am Rhein, 1980), p. 20; P. Wulf (ed.), *Das Kabinett Fehrenbach* (Boppard am Rhein, 1972), p. 45.

[125] See, e.g., Comfort, *Revolutionary Hamburg*, pp. 77f.

[126] PA/AA, R3009, Rechenberg to Prittwitz (AA), enclosed fly-sheet *Freie Sozialisten*, 26.6.19. As its attack on *Geldwirtschaft* suggests, high prices were at the root of the riots, as they were in similar disturbances in Harburg; *ibid.*, Oberbürgermeister Harburg to AA, 28.6.19.

[127] Jochmann, *Nationalsozialismus*, pp. 25–8, 33f.; Lorenz, *Die Juden in Hamburg*, II, pp. 1001–14. See also PA/AA, R3010, Rechenberg to AA, 29.8.19, and Comfort, *Revolutionary Hamburg*, p. 149.

[128] PA/AA, R3010, Rechenberg to Prittwitz, 5.7.19. This was the cue for a reiteration of the now-familiar Hanseatic litany of complaint about goverment restrictions on trade.

[129] GHH, 300193012/4, Deutsche Werft to Reusch, 11.7.19. The yards offered 110,000 marks. Cf. StAH, Lamp'l NL, Korps Lettow-Vorbeck to Senat, [?].7.19.

unrest also witnessed a resumption of wage demands from the railway workers.[130] In any case, Lettow's army did not tarry; by mid July, all but three battalions had left; and yet another attempt had to be made to create an effective locally recruited security force – this time to be called the 'Security Police'.[131]

The wage–price spiral

The military suppression of disorder in July 1919 was thus only a temporary solution to Hamburg's problems; only a significant improvement in the economic situation could guarantee that unrest would not recur. In one respect at least this began to happen in the wake of the Sülze riots, as the ending of the blockade allowed the city's commercial heart to begin beating again, albeit softly. Trade figures for the immediate post-war period are few and unreliable; however, the two available series indicate that imports into the free port returned to about 11 per cent of their pre-war level in 1919, exports to 5 per cent.[132] True to its assurances, the commercial community began to deliver increased supplies of food in the second half of the year. Yet food shortages were only one aspect of post-war economic instability, and bread riots were only one of a number of popular responses to economic pressure which characterised the revolutionary period. Indeed, looting shops and lynching businessmen were relatively extreme responses to the problem of dearth; a more common reaction was to seek compensation from employers by demanding higher wages (to allow for higher prices) or shorter working hours (which, in the straitened circumstances of 1918/19, allowed more time for queueing and foraging for food).

The November Revolution manifested itself in the workplace as an unprecedented explosion of labour demands to which employers, suddenly deprived of military support, had no option but to accede. In the shipyards, the principal demands were for substantial increases in wages, the narrowing of wage differentials, the introduction of the eight-hour day, the abolition of piecework, strike pay and the extension

[130] PA/AA, R3010, Rechenberg to AA, 7.7.19.
[131] The new *Sicherheitspolizei* was set up under one of Lettow-Vorbeck's officers, Colonel Völckers; StAH, FA B&V 1204, *Bürgerbund* Vorstand, 15.7.19. For the recriminations against Lamp'l in the bourgeois press see esp. StAH, Lamp'l NL, W. Lamp'l Nr. 9, 'Die Unruhen und die öffentliche Unsicherheit in Hamburg (Eine Entgegnung)'. Cf. N. Steinborn, 'Militärs auf Abruf – zur Rolle und Entwicklung der Hamburger Polizei', in Verein Hamburg-Jahrbuch (ed.), *Hamburger Zustände. Jahrbuch zur Geschichte der Region Hamburg*, I, pp. 13–18.
[132] See figure 2.1 The notorious export 'orgy' of 1919, when heavy industry took advantage of the difference between German domestic prices and 'world market' prices to 'dump' iron and steel on the booming European market was largely a Ruhr/Rhineland affair: Maier, *Recasting Bourgeois Europe*, p. 70.

of the powers of the wartime works' councils. Significantly, it was these councils – transformed into revolutionary workers' councils – which articulated the demands, rather than official union spokesmen. At Blohm and Voß, the eight-hour day, the abolition of piecework and 'wholly extraordinary minimum wages' of between 160 and 240 pfennigs per hour had to be conceded 'under the current duress'.[133] Nominal hourly wages for an average male worker nearly doubled as a result of the Revolution, rising from 213 pfennigs to 405 pfennigs, though they were lowered in January 1919 to 361 pfennigs. The nominal weekly pay of a Hamburg shipyard carpenter rose by 57 per cent.[134] Deutsche Werft attempted to resist these wage rates, on the grounds that the company was in too embryonic a state to be able to afford them, but it was overruled by the Workers' Council.[135] Warnings by Senator von Melle to the Council not to 'push matters too far' fell on deaf ears; on the same day as his warning, a number of harbour employers were arrested for their opposition to the new wages.[136] Workers' representatives were insistent that 'for the transitional period the question of wages is to be determined not according to productivity, but according to what the worker needs. The stomach question has the same significance for unskilled, trainee and skilled workers.'[137]

Like their counterparts in the Ruhr, employers in Hamburg initially sought to contain this upsurge of labour radicalism by embracing the traditional representatives of labour, the trade unions, as equal negotiating partners. The Economic Council had been set up to create a formal relationship between the revolutionary Workers' Council and the existing Hamburg Chambers of Commerce, Crafts and Retailing, thereby implicitly diminishing the authority of the Workers' Council. In the same way, national negotiations between business organisations and the trade unions, institutionalised in the *Zentralarbeitsgemeinschaft* or conducted in conjunction with the new Demobilisation Office, were intended to diminish the importance of the works' councils which had spearheaded the revolutionary upsurge. As early as 7 December 1918,

---

[133] StAH, FA B&V 13, Bd. 2, Firmenleitung, 16.11.18, 18.11.18; Firmenleitung to Betriebsleiter, 23.11.18.

[134] Figures from StAH, FA B&V 249, Bd. 1; 268; 139; 1286, Bd. 2; BAP, RFM 46585/329/113.

[135] GHH, 300193012/4, Arbeiterrat declaration, 11.11.18; Sozialpolitische Abteilung des Arbeiter- und Soldatenrats to Deutsche Werft, 22.11.18; Deutsche Werft directors meeting with Workers' Council, 29.11.18; Deutsche Werft to Reusch, 30.11.18; Deutsche Werft (monthly report), 1/2.1.19; BAP, RMfwD, 25/055, Deutsche Werft to DMA, 23.12.18; /050, Deutsche Werft to DMA, 30.12.18.

[136] Ullrich, 'Arbeiterbewegung', p. 654; Büttner, *Politische Gerechtigkeit*, p. 30.

[137] BAP, RMfwD, 65/190–1, DMA Sitzung, 10.12.18; 164–8, DMA Sitzung, 29.12.18; 161–3, Erklärung der Werften, 29.12.18; 153–60, DMA Sitzung (Hamburg), 29.12.18, 30.12.18.

there were appeals by the German shipyards to the Demobilisation
Office to reexamine the question of the abolition of piecework and the
new revolutionary wage rates.[138] Some headway was made on the
question of regional differentials, so that the wage rates imposed in
Hamburg were not applied uniformly along the Baltic coast, where
labour was traditionally cheaper.[139] But attempts by the trade union
representatives to make concessions on the question of piecework over
the heads of the works' councils precipitated a rash of wildcat strikes
and shopfloor violence on the waterfront.[140] When the Hamburg unions
called a meeting in early January to discuss the question of wage
reduction, 25,000 workers demonstrated on the Heiligengeistfeld to
express 'the greatest mistrust of the trade union leaders'.[141] Cries of
'Down with the *Gewerkschaftsbonzen*' gave a clear indication of the
extent to which the trade unions' wartime collaboration with government and business had alienated rank-and-file workers. As one union
leader admitted: 'The workers' and sailors' councils have annulled the
agreements made by the trade unions [. . .] The conditions in the
coastal cities are so radical and irrational because, thanks to Russian
examples and agitation, [. . .] workers who were already moving away
from the trade union[s] have wholly broken away from them.'[142] By
March, it was generally acknowledged that the revolutionary wage
increases were irreversible.[143]

However, there was one vital factor working in the employers'
favour: as soldiers returned from the Front and the demand for
armaments dried up, so unemployment began to rise. By January
1919, there were 6.6 million workers registered as unemployed at the

---

[138] BAP, RMfwD, 23/2, Staatskommissar für Demobilmachung to Demobilmachungs-
kommissare in Aurich, Königsberg, Hamburg etc., 7.12.18; 65/190–1, 'Notiz über
die Sitzung [. . .] im DMA mit Vertretern der Arbeitgeber und -nehmer der Werften
über Regelung der Lohnfrage', 10.12.18; 23/18, State Commissioner for Demobilisation to Prussian Minister for Trade and Industry, 4.1.19.

[139] BAP, RMfwD, 25/080, Reg. Präs. Danzig to DMA, 8.12.18; Reg. Präs. Stettin to
DMA, 8.12.18; Handelskammer zu Elbing to DMA, 11.12.18; Schichau-Elbing to
DMA, 13.12.18; 65/178–87, 'Sitzung im DMA', 10.12.18; 65/192, DMA telegram,
13.12.18; BAP, RFM 46584 N. Reg. 328/380, Abschrift (telegram from DMA to
Demobilisation Commissars), 13.12.18; BAP, RMfwD, 23/5, Abschrift (agreement
on three-class regional pay scale), 30.12.18.

[140] StAH, FA B&V 13, Bd. 2, Firmenleitung, 13.12.18; 20.12.18; 27.12.18; BAP,
RMfwD, 24/53, Nitzsche to DMA, 18.12.18; 73, B&V to DMA, 19.12.18; RMfwD,
65/18–19, DMA Sitzung, 20.12.18; 23/19–25, Schichau to DMA, 23.12.18; 65/169–
77, DMA Sitzung (Hamburg), 28.12.18.

[141] *Hamburger Echo*, Nr. 8, 6.1.19; BAP, RMfwD, 65/140–51, Vermerk über DMA
Sitzung (Hamburg), 6.1.19. Cf. Comfort, *Revolutionary Hamburg*, pp. 88ff., 94.

[142] BAP, RMfwD, 65/206–10, DMA Sitzung, 26.11.18.

[143] BAP, RMfwD, 67/14, Deutsche Metallarbeiter-Verein to DMA, 8.3.19; WA, 'Jahresbericht 1919', Wirtschaftsrat to Warburg, 25.2.19; Rudolf Sieverts to Max Warburg,
26.2.19; Warburg to Sieverts, 27.2.19,

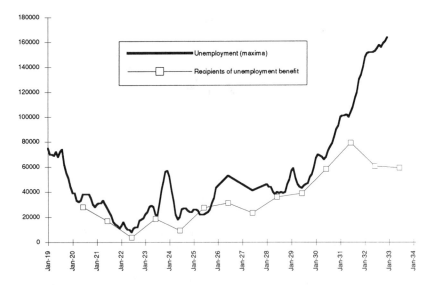

Figure 3.1 Unemployment in Hamburg, 1919–1933
Sources: Lippmann, *Leben,* p. 314; Büttner, *Staats- und Wirtschaftskrise,* pp.
241, 397, 679; *idem, Politische Gerechtigkeit,* p. 145.

national level; the number in Hamburg rose from a negligible number
in September 1918 to 38,710 in early December and 75,000 at the
beginning of February 1919 (see Figures 2.10 and 3.1).[144] As early as
22 November, the Chamber of Commerce was warning of 60,000
redundancies in firms dependent on military contracts.[145] Typically,
around 1,500 dock workers had returned from the war by March
1919, of whom only 700 could be found work.[146] Employment at
Blohm & Voß fell from 12,555 in July 1918 to just 5,713 in March
1919 (see figure 3.2).[147] Under less volatile political circumstances, it
might have been possible for employers to use this slump in the labour
market to reverse the wage increases of November. However, anxieties
about the political consequences of high unemployment were such that
this option was ruled out. Indeed, the dominant MSPD members of
the Reich government saw the creation of 'job opportunities [. . .] for
our workers and returning [. . .] soldiers' as their primary objective.[148]

[144] Büttner, *Politische Gerechtigkeit,* p. 27; Comfort, *Revolutionary Hamburg,* p. 68.
[145] StAH, DHSG III, Pr. VI 12, HKH to DHSG, 22.11.18.
[146] StAH, DHSG II, Spez. XXXIV 57 b, Kaiverwaltung to DHSG, 7.12.18; 3.3.19.
[147] For similar conditions at Deutsche Werft, GHH, 300193012/4 (DW monthly report),
14.1.19. Total employment in German ship-building in January 1919 was 76,934:
BAP, RFM 46524 N. Reg. 328/145–6.
[148] Specht, *Wirtschaftliche Hintergründe,* pp. 12f.; Maier, *Recasting Bourgeois Europe,*
p. 63.

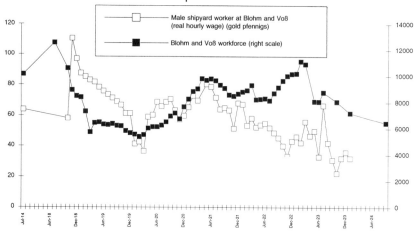

Figure 3.2 Wages and employment at Blohm & Voß, 1918–1924
Source: StAH, FA B&V.

It was with this in mind that the Demobilisation Office had been set up; and it was this which gave the Hamburg employers their leverage.

The argument has often been advanced that the heavy industry of the Ruhr wielded exceptional political power in the early years of the Weimar Republic.[149] But the argument that war contracts should be continued to avoid unemployment applied in Hamburg too, where the shipyards were paid to keep building submarines throughout November.[150] 'Over-hasty lay-offs of workers could lead to [a] serious situation': this was something on which the Workers' Council and Hamburg business could agree.[151] On the other hand, there was no question that sooner or later the war contracts had to end. In the wake of the armistice, the big iron and steel producers fell into disarray at this prospect, hurriedly seeking to dispose of their suddenly superfluous output (and clear their foreign currency debts) by exporting, irrespective of cartel agreements and domestic customers.[152] Munitions factories in Hamburg likewise pleaded with the Berlin purchasing agencies to increase their prices in line with the increased

[149] Feldman, *Iron and Steel*, p. 83.
[150] HA, HV, Bd. I, Holtzendorff to Direktion, 19.11.18; StAH, FA B&V 13, Bd. II, Firmenleitung, 27.12.18.
[151] StAH, DHSG III, Pr. VI 11, DHSG Registratur, 13.11.18; Arbeiter- und Soldatenrat 10. Kommission to Reichsmarineamt, 21.11.18. For the Council's attempts to maintain employment levels by securing locomotive contracts for the shipyards, see StAH, Lamp'l NL, 2, 'Historische Bericht', p. 163; DHSG III, Pr. VI 13, Niederschrift über die Sitzung betr. Umstellung der Werften auf Herstellung von Eisenbahnmaterial am Sonnabend, 15.2.19.
[152] Feldman, *Iron and Steel*, pp. 85–90. On the termination of approximately half of the outstanding war contracts, see *idem, Great Disorder*, p. 128.

wage costs of the revolution; but in vain.[153] By comparison, the Hamburg shipping industry had a stronger case for continuing government subsidies, because of the Reich's wartime commitment to finance the reconstruction of the German merchant fleet. It was this, combined with projections of a post-war global shortage of merchant vessels, which convinced industrialists like Stinnes and Reusch that shipbuilding would be a buoyant sector in the post-war years.[154] Indeed, Stinnes himself was soon pressurising the Demobilisation Office to stop 'throwing away money on building more war-ships purely in order to keep workers employed [. . .] It would be far more sensible to treat the money as [. . .] further advances for [the reconstruction of] the merchant fleet.'[155]

The argument that was advanced in Hamburg was simple. As the management of Blohm and Voß put it:

The socialist government has promised the people bread. Only agriculture and industry can provide it. This task is made extremely difficult for industry, because at present no contracts are [. . .] to be had due to the irresponsibly high wages [. . .] The closure of the yard lies in the realm of possibility.[156]

Cuno went still further on behalf of the shipping lines: 'If the Reich does not intervene, then Germany's entire economic life can lie down and go to sleep, [. . .] for all time ruined.'[157] The Reich had committed itself to rebuilding the merchant fleet, and was now also committed to creating employment; but revolutionary wages in the shipyards meant that the funds available to the shipping lines no longer sufficed. If the government could not induce the workers to accept lower wages, then it would have to pay for the additional costs or face a wave of redundancies, 'financial collapse' and 'unrest'.[158] These warnings were heard sympathetically at the Demobilisation Office:

It was imperative that the shipyards immediately begin work on the merchant fleet. On the other hand, the shipping lines naturally did not want to order ships with the enormously high wages. There was no option but to increase

---

[153] StAH, DHSG III, Pr. VI 12, HKH to DHSG, 22.11.18; DHSG Registratur, 23.11.18; HKH to DHSG, 26.11.18; DHSG III, Pr. VI 11, Kriegsmaterial-Beschaffungsstelle der Gewerbekammer to Heeresauftragsamt, 7.12.18; 10.12.18; Heeresauftragsamt to DMA, 9.12.18; HKH to DHSG, 10.12.18. The Chamber of Commerce estimated that the revolution had effectively increased labour costs by 15 per cent.

[154] Feldman, *Iron and Steel*, p. 70. For Gutehoffnungshütte projections of demand for shipping, GHH, 300193012/4, Deutsche Werft to Reusch, 3.12.18; 23.1.19; Claviez, *Deutsche Werft*, p. 32.

[155] HA, HV, Holtzendorff to Vorstand, 15.11.18.

[156] StAH, FA B&V 13, Bd. II, Firmenleitung, 29.11.18.

[157] BAP, RMfwD, 65/201–5, DMA Sitzung, 27.11.18.

[158] BAP, RMfwD, 24/67, HKH to DMA, 20.12.18.

the Reich advance correspondingly, since the workers had to be provided for, and in the present critical time, what did 100 million matter?[159]

Indeed, Koeth's officials were soon arguing for a programme of subsidies aimed at maintaining full employment in the ship-building industry for 'one and a half to two years'.[160] The Defence Ministry too had no doubt that 'the creation of jobs irrespective of financial or other considerations [is], along with adequate food provision, the best means of restoring peace and order in the country'.[161] However, it took weeks of wrangling before agreement could be reached between the shipping lines, the shipyards and the Reich Treasury on the extent and nature of the additional payments to be made.[162] It was not until April 1919 that agreement had been reached on the financing of around 350 ships under construction, leaving a further sixty-six contracts under dispute – notably the *Bismarck*, the last of the Hapag's three leviathan liners, still lying unfinished at the Blohm & Voß yard. By the end of April, the forty-two German yards had orders for 391 ships altogether (with a total tonnage of 45.5 m. tons), around 45 per cent of which were already under construction. Hamburg lines accounted for eighty-four of the orders; Hamburg yards for 110 of the ships ordered.[163]

---

[159] HA, HV, Holtzendorff to Direktion, 19.11.18.

[160] BAP, RMfwD, 65/19–55, DMA Sitzung, 8.2.19.

[161] BAP, RFM 46584 N.Reg. 328/249, Noske to RFM, 1.4.19. See for similar views Bessel, *Germany*, pp. 67, 95, 105, 143.

[162] BAP, RMfwD, 65/206–10, DMA Sitzung, 26.11.18; /201–5, DMA Sitzung, 27.11.18; RFM 46584 328/9, Vermerk, 27/28.11.18; 328/4, RFM Sitzung, 28.11.18; 328/1, DMA Notiz, 5.12.18; 328/5, KDR to DMA, 6.12.18; 328/15–17, RSA Staatssekretär Schiffer to KDR, 27.12.18; RFM 46580 N. Reg. 318/147, Blohm & Voß to DMA, 30.12.18; RMfwD, 25/111–21, Blohm & Voß to DMA, 31.12.18; RFM 46584 N. Reg. 328/223, KDR to DMA, 3.1.19; 328/27, RSA to KDR, 5.1.19; RFM, 46580 N. Reg. 318/165, RFM to Reichsausschuß für Wiederaufbau der Handelsflotte, 17.1.19; RMfwD, 65/92–6, DMA Sitzung, 17.1.19; /97–134, DMA Sitzung, 23.1.19; / 56–80, DMA Sitzung, 24.1.19; RFM 46584 328/88, RSA Sitzung, 24.1.19; 328/81, RSA Sitzung, 25.1.19; 328/36, RSA to Cuno, 8.2.19; RMfwD, 65/16–18, DMA Sitzung, 8.2.19; RFM 46584 328/220, Cuno to RFM, 1.3.19. The main difficulty was whether to regard the payments for the revolutionary wage increases as distinct from the provisions made for inflation under the wartime compensation legislation of November 1917. It was decided to pay the additional costs caused by the revolution directly to the shipyards using the wartime cost–plus *Regie* system, on condition that the shipping lines would ultimately repay any sums advanced which exceeded the inflationary mark-up agreed in 1917 by 50 per cent. A further sticking-point was whether the new agreement (the *Überteuerungsabkommen*) would apply for the first four years of the Compensation Act, or merely for a notional revolutionary period of three months. It was finally agreed that the agreement would apply to all ships under construction by 28 November or ordered within a year of 1 November 1918. 30 per cent of any sums still outstanding after four years would have to be paid by the shippers within ten years. For the final agreement, see BAP, RFM 46584 328/164, 'Formulierung des Überteuerungsabkommen', 13.2.19; 46580 N. Reg. 317/44, Niederschrift 5.12.19. Cf. Kohlhaus, 'Die Hapag', pp. 17, 34.

[163] BAP, RFM 4654 N.Reg. 328/284, 394. On the *Bismarck* dispute, RFM 46584 328/231–306.

The negotiations between government and business over revolutionary wages give a number of important insights into the relationship between the state and industry in the first months of the Weimar Republic. 'We are businessmen,' declared a spokesman for the shipping lines during one particularly acrimonious meeting: 'It is our duty, as the managers of other people's capital, to accept no obligations which could lead to the ruin of our company [. . .] You cannot expect us to give the shipyards full employment.' This awoke 'a certain alarm' on the part of Koeth, the head of the Demobilisation Office, who questioned the 'loyalty' of the shippers. Another official present was more explicit:

The government certainly has an interest in the regularisation of labour relations; but the shipyards and shipping lines have a greater interest still. It is they who will be hit first if anarchy breaks out in the coastal cities. I admit that the government is principally responsible for ensuring order. But it is impossible for it to keep economic life under such a tight rein that every strike can be stopped at once. That cannot even be done by force of arms [. . .] The shipping lines are adopting an attitude which is too mercenary and insufficiently national and social.[164]

However, this rhetoric concealed a simple reality: the Reich had given the German shipping industry what amounted to a hand-out in the form of a blank cheque. The provisions for repayment on which the Treasury Office so doggedly insisted in both the compensation and 'top-up' agreements made virtually no allowance for continued inflation; and as the Hapag director Huldermann put it: 'The inflation will not be overcome this year.'[165]

The subsidies paid to the shipping industry were symptomatic of the way in which the revolution negated any fiscal savings brought by peace. 'What did 100 million matter?' was, as noted above, the initial response of the Demobilisation Office to requests from the shipping industry for additional assistance.[166] Nor, for all Moellendorff's grand schemes, was the Economics Ministry view much different: 'The Reich will have to hold its purse wide open', noted one official during the *Überteuerung* negotiations.[167] Even Schiffer, who, as Finance Minister, struggled to restrain Koeth, conceded that 'millions [would] have to be spent, even if we cannot be sure that we will get them back'.[168] The consequences were predictable. In November, the Treasury Office

[164] BAP, RMfwD, 65/97–134, DMA Sitzung, 23.1.19; RFM 46584 328/84–7, Vermerk über die Sitzung [. . .] über Handelsschiffbau, 23.1.19.
[165] BAP, RMfwD, 65/97–134, DMA Sitzung, 23.1.19.
[166] HA, HV, Holtzendorff to Direktion, 19.11.18.
[167] BAP, RMfwD, 65/206–10, DMA Sitzung, 26.11.18.
[168] Specht, *Wirtschaftliche Hintergründe*, p. 15; Feldman, *Great Disorder*, pp. 130–6.

had earmarked 300 m. marks for the merchant fleet, of which 60.8 m. marks had been spent by March 1920.[169] Of 10.3 bn. marks worth of outstanding war contracts, only 2.4 bn. marks were cancelled without some financial compensation.[170] Moreover, the policy adopted by the Bauer government in mid 1919 of subsidising food prices led to further expenditures totalling at least 5 bn. marks in the second half of that year.[171] Such open-handedness ensured that total Reich spending in 1919 was, in nominal terms, 20 per cent higher than in 1918.[172] It is true that in real terms, total public spending fell by around 40 per cent, reducing the state's share of net national product from 64 per cent to 43 per cent.[173] However, that has its principal explanation in the inflationary consequences of fiscal policy. Among the many side effects of the revolution was a substantial fall in government revenue, due to the breakdown of the budgetary process and the system of assessment and collection. Reich revenue in 1919 was 50 per cent below the level of the previous year; so that the government deficit rose by some 24 bn. marks (an increase of 173 per cent) (see figure 3.3).[174] As during the war, the consequent 44 per cent increase in the floating debt was reflected in a monetary expansion of a similar order: currency in circulation rose by around 50 per cent.[175] As Schiffer confessed: 'Since the revolutionary events of November, all we have done is keep printing.'[176] His successor Dernburg spoke openly of an 'Assignat economy': 'The National Assembly passes a resolution. On the basis of this resolution, notes are printed. That is our money [. . .] We have a purely paper currency.'[177] Even Havenstein admitted 'that the growth of the money supply has its origin for the most part in the growth of the floating debt'; and called for 'immediate far-reaching reductions of the Reich's spending and [. . .] immediate obtainment of new revenues'.[178]

Nor was it only at the Reich level that the transition from monarchy to republic was smoothed with open-handed spending; at the municipal level too, public spending leapt up in 1918/19, largely because of the

---

[169] BAP, RFM 46124 Alt. Reg. 2954, Geschäftsbesprechung des Reichsausschusses für den Wiederaufbau der Handelsflotte, 18.11.18; 46583 324/297–300, Übersicht betr. Anträge von Reedereien auf Erstattung von Überteuerungskosten.
[170] Feldman, *Great Disorder*, p. 128; Bessel, *Germany*, p. 98.
[171] Feldman, *Great Disorder*, p. 155.
[172] Roesler, *Finanzpolitik*, pp. 196–200.
[173] Witt, 'Finanzpolitik', pp. 424f.; S.B. Webb, 'Fiscal News and Inflationary Expectation in Germany after World War I', *JEcH*, 46, 3 (1986), p. 779. See figure 0.4.
[174] Roesler, *Finanzpolitik*, pp. 196–200.
[175] Figures from Holtfrerich, pp. 50, 53.
[176] Specht, *Wirtschaftliche Hintergründe*, pp. 10f.
[177] *Ibid.*, pp. 18f.
[178] Webb, *Hyperinflation*, p. 25.

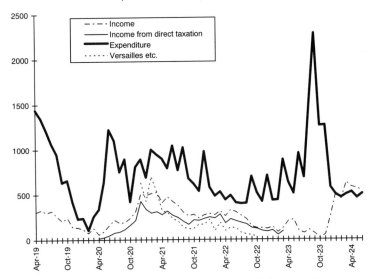

Figure 3.3 Real monthly Reich finances, 1919–1924 (m. gold marks)
Sources: Bresciani, *Inflation*, pp. 437ff.; Graham, *Hyperinflation*, pp. 44f.; Witt, 'Tax Policies', pp. 156f.; Eichengreen, *Golden Fetters*, p. 146.

decision to delegate the provision of unemployment relief to local authorities. This was especially true in Hamburg, where liberal bureaucrats and reformist Social Democrats readily agreed on the need to combat social and political instability with welfare measures rather than coercion. Even as the Revolution was unfolding in November, a Labour Office was hastily set up with a monthly budget of 8 m. marks for the relief of unemployment.[179] It established labour exchanges, public works programmes and paid generous doles of up to 93 marks per week (for an average family).[180] Indeed, even the realisation of Bürgermeister von Melle's long-postponed plan for a Hamburg University was justified as a way of reducing youth unemployment.[181] Nor were these merely temporary expedients. The watchword of the new Social Democrat Senators after March 1919 was 'social policy', as suggested by their initial choice of portfolios: welfare, health, youth

[179] StAH, Lamp'l NL, No. 2, pp. 211–12, 'Erwerbslosenfürsorge', 23.12.18; BAP, RAM 33333/ Nr. 1199, Reich Labour Ministry to National Assembly, 29.10.19; Schramm, *Neun Generationen*, II, p. 500; Brandt, *Finanzen*, pp. 16–19. See in general Feldman, *Great Disorder*, pp. 118ff.

[180] Büttner, *Politische Gerechtigkeit*, p. 149; Comfort, *Revolutionary Hamburg*, pp. 61f.

[181] GStA, Rep. 842, Justizministerium 936, 102–6, von Melle to Prussian Justice Minister, 6.1.19; Ausschuß der Studierenden der juristischen Fakultät Hamburg to Prussian Justice Minister, 4.2.19. By July 1920, there were 2,893 students at the University: NAW, RG 59 852.00/990, Stewart to State Department, 10.7.20.

policy and vocational training.[182] In practice, this meant a permanent increase in the state budget to finance the building of new housing, schools and hospitals, and to pay the salaries of hundreds of new state employees.[183] Admittedly, not all of this was financed by short-term borrowing, as at the Reich level. In January 1919 the city-state issued an unlimited series of 4.5 per cent Hamburg bonds; and in the extraordinary international speculation in mark assets that was to gather momentum throughout 1919/20, they sold strongly: the first series in 1919 raised 48.65 m. marks.[184] Nevertheless, the state, like the Reich, found its expenditures increasingly outstripping its income: the deficit was 370 m. marks for 1919, taking the state debt to 2.3 bn. marks.[185]

Such fiscal policies would have had inflationary consequences under almost any circumstances; but the fact that public sector deficits soared at the same time as wartime controls on prices were weakened meant that the Revolution unleashed a price explosion. The average annual inflation rate for wholesale prices during the war had been 20 per cent. In the year after November 1918, the figure leapt to 190 per cent (see figure 3.4). Moreover, the ending of import restrictions and exchange controls magnified inflation still further as wartime liquidity was unleashed on the world market. When the Bauer government lifted exchange controls in September 1919, the mark plummeted to 99.11 marks/$ in February 1920.[186] Consequently, the prices of imported goods rose by over 300 per cent in 1919.[187] To some extent, these pressures were mitigated by continuing controls on food prices and rents, so that the cost-of-living index rose only by around 50 per cent in the year after the Revolution (see figure 3.5).[188] Nevertheless, the effect of this inflation on real incomes was severe. The gains in wages won by manual workers in the first weeks of the Revolution were simply wiped out. Because nominal wage rates at Blohm & Voß remained unchanged between January and November 1919, real wages in fact fell steadily, reaching a nadir of around half pre-war levels in March 1920.[189] Public employees fared equally badly. Salaries were

[182] Büttner, Staats- und Wirtschaftskrise, p. 664; Bolland, Bürgerschaft, pp. 102ff..

[183] Büttner, Politische Gerechtigkeit, pp. 150, 205; idem, Staats- und Wirtschaftskrise, pp. 42f., 514 n., 515 n.; Lyth, 'Mittelstand', pp. 418f., 423f.; Lippmann, Leben, pp. 323–54, 442. Between 1918 and 1923, 9,665 new homes were built, while the number of public sector employees rose from 37,523 (1914) to 46,446.

[184] Lippmann, Leben, pp. 320f.; Büttner, Politische Gerechtigkeit, p. 151.

[185] Brandt, Hamburgs Finanzen, p. 19.

[186] Feldman, Iron and Steel, p. 472.

[187] See figure 3.4.

[188] Between January and December 1919, the real value of the average rent in Hamburg fell from 53 per cent of the pre-war level to 10 per cent; Hamburger Statistische Monatsberichte, June 1924, Sonderbeitrag 3, pp. 118f. Cf. Lyth, 'Mittelstand', pp. 426–8, 432, 457; Büttner, Politische Gerechtigkeit, pp. 149f.

[189] See figure 2.12.

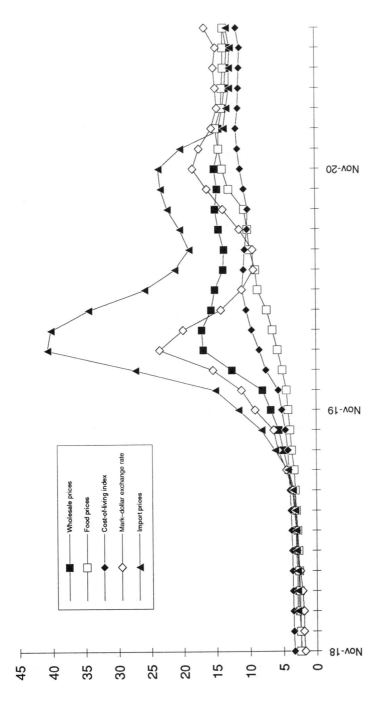

Figure 3.4 Inflation from revolution to relative stabilisation, 1918–1921 (1913 = 1)

Sources: Bry, *Wages*, pp. 422–9, 440–5; *Zahlen zur Geldentwertung*, pp. 16f.; Holtfrerich, *Inflation*, p. 17; Laursen and Pedersen, *Inflation*, pp. 133–5.

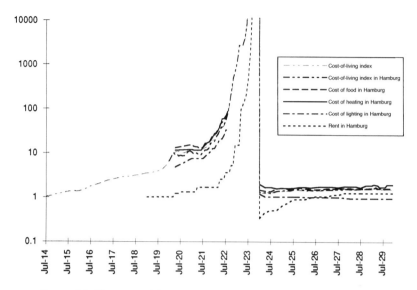

Figure 3.5 The cost of living in Hamburg, 1914–1929 (1914 = 1)
Sources: *Statistiche Mitteilungen*, 13 (1922), pp. 36f.; *Hamburger Statistische Monatsberichte* (May 1924), p. 100; *HSM*, 1 (June 1924), pp. 118f.; *Statistiches Handbuch 1929/30* (1930), p. 259.

only increased once in the course of 1919, with the result that their real value by March 1920 had fallen to between 15 and 40 per cent of pre-war levels.[190]

The implications of this for industrial relations in Hamburg can be gleaned from a speech made by Rudolf Blohm in December 1919, at the moment when his workers' real wages were nearing their all-time low.[191] Posing the question 'How can we win our workers back?', Blohm began with a blunt attack on the idea of corporatist consensus between capital and labour:

> The [idea of] eternal economic peace, in the sense that there should never be conflicts between workers and employers, is as much of a utopia as the eternal peace between nations of which the pacifists dream. The relationship between employee and worker is inherently one of opposition.[192]

In November 1918, the bourgeoisie had suffered 'a nervous breakdown'; it had pursued a 'policy of concessions', forgetting that its real duty was

[190] See figure 2.11.
[191] StAH, B&V 1203, R. Blohm, 'Wie gewinnen wir unsere Arbeiter zurück?'; 11.12.19; reported in *Bremer Nachrichten*, 12.12.19. Blohm was toying with the idea of standing as a DNVP candidate in the 1920 Reichstag elections.
[192] *Ibid.*

to strive to provide the workers with what they had before the war: a secure, remunerative opportunity for work [. . .and to banish] the spectre of unemployment. It has been emphasised in vain on the side of the employers that high wages in themselves do not bring happiness, and indeed only lead to inflation (*Geldwentwertung*).

As in the days of Bismarck's social insurance legislation, he added, it was for the government to mitigate the vagaries of the labour market, for example, by introducing a 'comprehensive housing policy'.[193] These remarks were a gloss on the policy adopted by Blohm's firm throughout 1919. This was to use unemployment and inflation to roll back the gains made by the workforce in November 1918, and to leave the state to alleviate the resulting misery. Even as real wages were slashed, the Blohm & Voß workforce continued to contract, falling by half between October 1918 and February 1920.[194] This was partly because of serious shortages of coal, but mainly because the firm's management believed there was no point in trying to compete for work until wages had been reduced and the bargaining position of labour weakened. Production took second place to waging a counter-revolution in industrial relations.[195] Diametrically opposed to the strategy advocated in the Ruhr by Hugo Stinnes (who saw the inflationary wage–price spiral as a means of expanding his concern), Blohm's view exemplified the combative stance taken by the Hamburg shipping industry in 1919.[196] The attempt to 'roll back' the gains of the revolution culminated in the successful reintroduction of the system of piecework, the abolition of which had been, alongside the introduction of the eight-hour day, the principal gain won by shipyard workers in November.[197] After the failure (by a narrow margin) of an attempt to achieve this by means of a collective vote on the issue in all the North German shipyards, the major Hamburg yards proceeded individually.[198] Within around a year of the 'nervous breakdown' of November 1918, the revolution in the workplace thus appeared to have been substantially undone.

---

[193] *Ibid.*
[194] See figure 3.2.
[195] For the management's increasingly aggressive attitude, StAH, FA B&V 13, Bd. II, Firmenleitung, 17.4.19, 30.5.19, 17.7.19, 28.8.19, 30.10.19.
[196] See, e.g., StAH, FA B&V 139, Schlichtungsausschuß (H.C. Stülcken), 7.8.19. On Stinnes, see Feldman, *Iron and Steel*, pp. 118–22; Maier, *Recasting Bourgeois Europe*, p. 68.
[197] StAH, FA B&V 13, Bd. 2, Firmenleitung, 27.6.19; Sen. Cl. 1 Lit. T No. 9b, vol. 89, HKH to DHSG, 6.9.19; FA B&V 1405, Bd. I, Hermann Blohm to Chamber of Commerce, 26.8.19. Cf. HA, HB, Holtzendorff to Cuno 1.6.19.
[198] On the reintroduction of piecework, StAH, Sen. Cl. 1 Lit. T No. 9b, vol. 89, HKH to DHSG 6.9.19; FA B&V 13, Bd. II, Firmenleitung 27.6.19, 11.12.19; GHH, 300193012/5, Deutsche Werft to Reusch, 1.11.19; 5.12.19. Cf. Specht, *Politische Hintergründe*, p. 39 n.

Yet in two respects, the employers' victory was less secure than it seemed. The first related to the idea of 'socialisation' – a nebulous term used in the period after November 1918 to denote policies as diverse as nationalisation, co-determination and employee share-ownership.[199] In the first chaotic months of revolution, threats to 'socialise everything' by radicals like Laufenberg aroused little anxiety in business circles. It was characteristic of the ambiguity of those days that, while Franz Witthoefft privately scoffed at 'the great theorist' Laufenberg,[200] Fritz Warburg could enthuse:

We can only hope that things carry on along these lines, [for] then, instead of a Bolshevik state, Germany will become the freest democracy in the world, with far-reaching socialisation, though without any suppression of the freedom of the individual.[201]

This was easily said, since, in practice, socialisation appeared to be a threat to heavy industry, not to commerce or finance. Although coal was nationalised, threats that the new government might nationalise the shipping industry – using the high subsidies it was being asked to pay as a pretext – were never translated into action.[202] However, when 'socialisation' was effectively redefined to signify giving works' councils some kind of role in managerial decision making, attitudes in Hamburg perceptibly hardened. The limited works' council legislation mooted in April 1919 was seen by employers as a device to make the unpublished accounts of firms available to labour leaders, purely to enable them to justify higher wage demands.[203] It was with evident unease that business spokesmen like Rudolf Blohm and Max Warburg bowed to the prospect of co-determination:

In order to shove the demands of the workers and clerks back to a tolerable level, it may well be necessary to allow [their] representatives a look at the

---

[199] On socialisation, K. Novy, *Strategien der Sozialisierung: Die Diskussion der Wirtschaftsreform in der Weimarer Republik* (Frankfurt, 1978); H. Habedank, *Um Mitbestimmung und Nationalisierung während der Novemberrevolution und im Frühjahr 1919* (Berlin, 1967); W. Honhart, 'The Incomplete Revolution. The Social Democrats' Failure to Transform the German Economy 1918–20' (Ph.D. thesis Duke University, 1972).

[200] StAH, FA AOM 1, Bd. 10, 136, Witthoefft to Eiffe, 14.12.18.

[201] WA, 'Jahresbericht 1920', Fritz Warburg to Anna Warburg, 14.11.18. Cf. the debate in *Wirtschaftsdienst*, Nr. 49, 6.12.18; Nr. 12, 21.3.19.

[202] BAP, RMfwD, 65/206–10, DMA Sitzung, 26.11.18; /194–200, DMA Sitzung, 30.11.18; HA, Holtzendorff to Cuno, 5.4.19.

[203] BAP, RMfwD, 65/178–287, DMA Sitzung, 10.12.18; RFM 46584 N. Reg. 328/246, MAV Bezirksleitung Hamburg to DMA, 27.2.19; RMfwD 25/137, DMA to MAV Bezirksleitung Hamburg, 27.3.19; HA, Holtzendorff Notizen, 26.4.19; StAH, SK II, III C Fasc. 1 Bd. 1, Sen. Prot. 13.8.19; FA B&V 1405, Bd. 1, Blohm to HKH, 26.8.19. Cf. Maier, *Recasting Bourgeois Europe*, pp. 160–4; P. von Oertzen, *Betriebsräte in der Novemberrevolution* (Düsseldorf, 1963).

accounts in private firms [. . .] Of course, this must not impede the entrepreneurial spirit.[204]

The demand that the responsible leaders of German economic life should work on the reconstruction of our economy in consultation with the nominated representatives of the workforce is a justified demand of the hour [. . .] The workers [. . .] must get some insight into the infinite difficulties with which an industrial concern in Germany now, more than ever, has to contend. [But] the workers' collaboration [. . .] must be confined [. . .] to those areas in which the workers' expertise can improve the profitability of the enterprise.[205]

'A look at the accounts' – meaning the published accounts – was indeed all that was ultimately conceded to the works' councils. However, it would be wrong to conclude from the limited extent of formal 'socialisation' that no permanent changes in industrial relations had been achieved by the revolution. The second factor which tended to erode the employers' advantage was the resurgence of collective organisation which began as real wages reached intolerably low levels and unemployment began to decline. With plans for socialisation and co-determination evidently stalled, employees in many branches of the economy began to turn back to the unions – a trend partly reinforced by the employers' own abortive attempt to bring back piecework by means of a workers' ballot. These, however, were the old ways writ large. The membership of the Hamburg branch of the General German Trade Union Federation (ADGB) stood at 240,000 by the end of the year, more than reversing the decline of the war years.[206] What was particularly striking was the spread of collective patterns of organisation to other employee groups. By the end of 1919, the Clerical Workers' Federation (the AfA-Bund, founded two years before) and the older German National Commercial Employees' Association had 25,800 and 6,000 members respectively.[207] In September 1919, the Hamburg state's civil servants established their own *Gewerkschaft der Bürobeamten*.[208] At the same time, there were efforts to increase the collective organis-

---

[204] WA, 'Jahresbericht 1919', Warburg to SS Schiffer [December 1918]. Compare Warburg's later comments on the role of his bank's *Angestellten- und Botenrat* in inducing a sense of 'joint responsibility for the overall performance of the firm': WA, 'Jahresbericht 1922', 'Erläuterungen zum Jahre 1922', 10.2.23.

[205] StAH, FA B&V 1203, R. Blohm, 'Wie gewinnen wir unsere Arbeiter zurück?', 11.12.19.

[206] Büttner, *Politische Gerechtigkeit*, p. 300 n. 207. Until 1921, the ADGB included the largest association of white-collar workers, the General Free Clerical Workers League (AfA-Bund). Cf. the national figures in Petzina, *Deutsche Wirtschaft*, p. 89; and the accounts in H. Pothoff, *Gewerkschaften und Politik zwischen Revolution und Inflation* (Düsseldorf, 1979); H.-A. Winkler, *Von der Revolution zur Stabilisierung. Arbeiter und Arbeiterbewegung in der Weimarer Republik, 1918–1924* (Berlin/Bonn, 1984).

[207] Lyth, 'Mittelstand', p. 125.

[208] *Ibid.*, pp. 208f.

ation of consumers by creating a Consumers' Chamber to put the cooperatives on an equal footing with the three business chambers.[209] The reason for this upsurge in collectivism was straightforward: as employment prospects improved and prices continued to rise, unionisation and other forms of collective organisation appeared the best way of defending individuals' living standards. There were some signs that this kind of bargaining could proceed along consensual lines: 1919 saw a significant increase in the number of workers covered by collective agreements to 6 million, compared with 1.4 million in 1913.[210] But the acceleration of inflation in 1919 tended to undermine such long-term agreements. Moreover, revolutionary measures such as the demobilisation decrees providing for arbitration through the Demobilisation Office encouraged employees to resort to strike action as a tactical device.[211] Certainly, the performance of the Arbitration Committee set up in Hamburg in February 1919 suggests that such institutions did little to promote harmony: of 5,332 cases it heard in the course of the year, only 972 were settled by a ruling which both sides accepted.[212]

The resumption of industrial unrest and the beginning of the wage–price spiral reflected the widened social base of collectivism. It was signalled by a successful two-week fishermen's strike in June.[213] In August, it was the turn of the bank clerks, after the five major Hamburg banks rejected an arbitration ruling.[214] Similar action by other clerical workers secured sharp rises in pay, for example from the Hamburg Electricity Works and the *Hochbahn*.[215] It was only a matter of time before this wage pressure manifested itself in industry. On Christmas Eve 1919, the floodgates opened when the ZAG ruled that the shipyard workers were entitled to a bonus of between 30 and 70 pfennigs to compensate for inflation. After two months, the Associ-

---

[209] StAH, DHSG III, Pr. IV Bd. 1, Mitteilungen für die Preisprüfungsstelle, 15.5.19; DHSG II, III C 53 (1919), 8. Sitzung, 22.7.19; C 54 (1920), 5. Sitzung, 2.3.20. Cf. Lyth, '*Mittelstand*', p. 354.

[210] Petzina, *Deutsche Wirtschaft*, p. 88.

[211] Feldman, 'Wirtschafts- und sozialpolitische Probleme', pp. 623–66; G. Mai, 'Arbeitsmarktregulierung oder Sozialpolitik? Die personelle Demobilmachung in Deutschland 1918 bis 1920/24', in Feldman *et al.*, *Anpassung*, pp. 202–36.

[212] BAP, RAM 34094/Nr. 3139, Schlichtungsausschuß Hamburg, Statistische Bericht, January 1920.

[213] StAH, DHSG II, Spez. XXX A 8 1 15, Fischereidirektion to DHSG, 19.6.19; 21.6.19. In fact, this strike was organised by the radical Seemannsbund, in spite of the efforts of the Transport Workers' Union. There was another strike in September: *Neue Hamburgische Zeitung*, 25.9.19; 13.10.19.

[214] BAP, RAM 333683/Nr. 2151, Deutscher Bankbeamtenverein to RAM, 8.8.19; *Der Tag*, 371, 10.8.19; RAM Notiz, 16.8.19, 19/20.8.19; Schlichtungsausschuß ruling, 20.8.19; Arbeitsgemeinschaft freier Angestelltenverbände to RAM, 22.8.19; Verband Hamburger Bankleitungen to RAM, 22.8.19; DMA Hamburg to RAM, 25.8.19.

[215] Lyth, '*Mittelstand*', pp. 130f., 149f., 154f., 172.

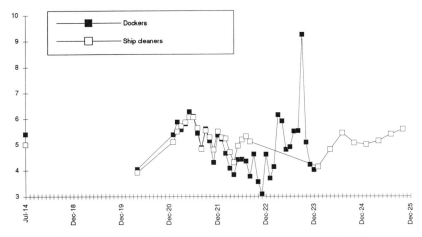

Figure 3.6 Dockers' real daily wages, 1914–1923 (gold marks)
Sources: *Hamburger Statistische Monatsberichte*, 1 Jg. (May 1924), p. 98;
Statistisches Handbuch 1925, p. 206; Büttner, *Staats- und Wirtschaftskrise*,
p. 707.

ation of Metal Industrialists gave way.[216] There was similar pressure
in the new year from civil servants, journeymen and even from tenants
in the face of a trifling rent increase.[217] The long wage freeze of 1919
ended with a torrent of wage demands in 1920, which led to substantial
increases in real as well as nominal terms (see figures 2.11, 2.12, 3.6
and 3.7).

The revolution of 1918/19 had its ideological roots in Hamburg in
a revitalised bourgeois liberalism. While some were cast down by the
collapse of the Prussian monarchy and the Bismarckian Reich, men
like Max Warburg, Franz Witthoefft and Carl Petersen were galvanised
into political activism. To some extent (as in their preservation of the
Financial Deputation), they acted defensively, aiming to contain popular radicalism. The *Hamburger Echo* was not entirely wide of the mark
when it later characterised Warburg as 'the cleverest spokesman of
the [. . .] party whose aim it is to accept political democracy in order
to stave off economic democratisation'.[218] But there was also a genuine
belief in the need to recast the Reich in such a way as to increase the
influence of the liberal bourgeoisie. Proposals for a united liberal
party, an Economic Council alongside the democratic parliament, the

---

[216] StAH, FA B&V 485; 249, Bd. I, Norddeutsche Gruppe des Gesamtverbands
Deutscher Metall-Industrieller, 4.2.20; 13, Bd. II, Firmenleitung, 5.2.20.
[217] Lyth, '*Mittelstand*', pp. 215f., 221, 253f., 302f., 427, 436.
[218] *Hamburger Echo*, 20.12.20.

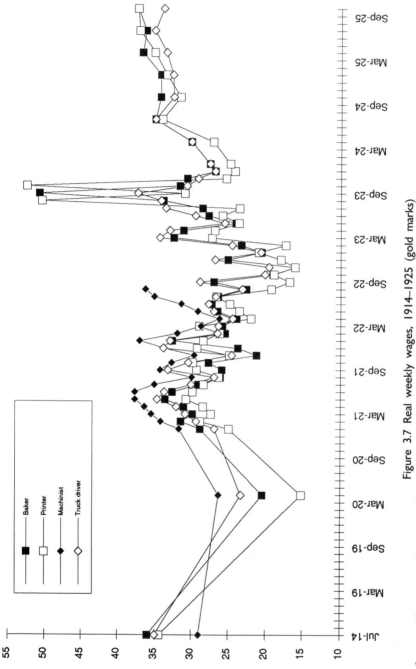

Figure 3.7 Real weekly wages, 1914–1925 (gold marks)

Sources: Hamburger Statistische Monatsberichte, 1 Jg. (May 1924), p. 98; Statistisches Handbuch 1925, p. 206; Büttner, Staats– und Wirtschaftskrise, p. 707; Statistische Mitteilungen, 13 (1922), pp. 32f.

break-up of Prussia and the creation of a Greater Hamburg were more than cynical gambits to preserve capitalism from the threat of socialism. As Max's brother Paul explained to a sceptical Mortimer Schiff in New York, it simply was not true 'that Germany [was] governed today by the same group as before the revolution [and] that the form of government was only a camouflage. [. . .] Every bit of news that we get from Germany gives a clear indication that the military spirit has been broken.'[219] However, the bourgeois political revolution was from the outset vulnerable, not only because a substantial body of bourgeois opinion rejected it, but also because it failed to satisfy all popular aspirations. The persistence of dearth in the first half of 1919 gave rise to a potent mixture of populist grievances – against the Allies, against capitalism, against trade union leaders and against Jews. Expressed by a rising level of violence, this exposed the inability of both the Majority Social Democrats and the bourgeoisie to maintain public order without the aid of the old military elites. Improved food supplies partly contributed to a diminution of such street protest. But the decisive shift which marked the end of the revolutionary phase occurred in the workplace. There the chances of a counter-revolution at first had seemed strong, as soaring unemployment and inflation undermined the gains made by workers' councils in the November days. Ultimately, however, the policy of financing demobilisation by increasing public sector deficits was bound to generate a backlash. Indeed, by rejecting workers' participation and openly inviting (as Blohm did) a return to the old confrontational labour relations, the employers succumbed to hubris. The combination of rising employment and accelerating inflation in the context of new legislation governing industrial relations led to a rapid revival and growth of collective organisation and action, which expressed itself in a renewed wage push in the second half of 1919. In this sense, the popular revolution had not been 'contained' in 1919; it had simply been shifted from the arena of the streets to that of the workplace. The battle for political power had been temporarily halted. But the price, paid in depreciating paper currency, was an escalating battle for purchasing power.

[219] Sterling Library, Yale University, Paul Warburg Papers, Series 1, Box 4, Folder 58, Warburg to Schiff, 21.3.19.

4

Versailles and Hamburg

It was a favourite phrase of Max Warburg's that Germany in the 1920s was 'an object, not a subject'; that is to say, its fate depended more on external forces than on the decisions of German policy makers. In particular, domestic politics were circumscribed by the burdens of the armistice and peace treaty imposed on the new Republic by the victorious Western Allies. For many years, historians influenced by such contemporary criticisms of the peace treaty echoed this view. Versailles had seen Wilsonian ideals and economic rationality sacrificed to traditional power politics and chauvinism; the price paid was the failure of democracy in Germany and a second European war.[1] However, since the 1970s, such arguments have fallen into disuse. New research in the French, British and American archives has led to substantial reappraisals of those countries' policies. French policy is now seen by a number of authors as a series of more or less rational strategems designed to increase France's leverage over her eastern neighbour, ranging from consensual proposals for economic cooperation to confrontational bids for control over the Rhineland and Ruhr.[2] American policy is portrayed as an attempt to achieve economic recovery in Europe (and arguably to arrest the spread of Bolshevism) by means of large-scale, though privately organised, capital export.[3] British

[1] See for example L. Zimmermann, *Deutsche Außenpolitik in der Ära der Weimarer Republik* (Göttingen, 1958).
[2] J. Bariéty, 'Les réparations allemandes après la première guerre mondiale. Objet ou prétexte à une politique rhénane de la France', *Bulletin de la Société d'Histoire Moderne* (1973), pp. 20–33; idem, *Les relations franco-allemandes après la première guerre mondiale. 10. novembre 1918–10. janvier 1925: de l'execution à la négociation* (Paris, 1977); W.A. McDougall, *France's Rhineland Diplomacy 1914–1924. The Last Bid for a Balance of Power in Europe* (Princeton, 1978); M. Trachtenberg, 'Reparation at the Paris Peace Conference', *JMH*, 51 (1979), pp. 24–55; idem, *Reparation in World Politics: France and European Economic Diplomacy 1916–1923* (New York, 1980); D. Stevenson, *French War Aims against Germany 1914–1919* (Oxford, 1982); J. Jacobson, 'Strategies of French Foreign Policy after World War I', *JMH*, 55 (1983), pp. 78–95. See also S.A. Schuker, *The End of French Predominance in Europe. The Financial Crisis of 1924 and the Adoption of the Dawes Plan* (Chapel Hill, 1976).
[3] A.J. Mayer, *Politics and Diplomacy of Peacemaking. Containment and Counter-revolution at Versailles 1918/19* (New York, 1967); C. Parrini, *Heir to Empire. United States*

policy is seen principally as an unrealistic effort to return to pre-war economic conditions and to abandon the 'continental commitment' in favour of a remoulded Empire.[4] It is possible to explain the failure of these policies to add up to anything more than 'the illusion of peace' by stressing the incompatible nature of the various national objectives, or by contrasting the position in 1919 with that in 1945, when Germany was defeated in the East as well as the West and suffered partition.[5] But more usually, the blame has been laid at the door of Weimar policy makers for refusing to accept the consequences of defeat. In post-war England, the belief in a continuum of German aggression and the folly of appeasement always inclined some historians to view with scepticism the complaints of Weimar revisionists.[6] More recently, economic historians have sought to demonstrate that the material burdens imposed by reparations were less onerous than the Germans claimed;[7] and the idea persists that, by taking a revisionist stance, democratic politicians were playing into the hands of the radical Right.

Without doubt, the makers of Weimar foreign policy tended to hope that, by instrumentalising Germany's still-intact economic power, it would be possible steadily to shed the burdens imposed at Versailles and to restore Germany's great power status.[8] Stresemann conceived of his task as Foreign Minister as being to 'take advantage of the world economic situation so as to conduct foreign policy by economic means, as this is the only respect in which we are still a great power'.[9]

Economic Diplomacy 1916–1923 (Pittsburgh, 1969); F. Costigliola, *Awkward Dominion. American Political, Economic and Cultural Relations with Europe, 1919–1923* (Ithaca, 1984); W. Link, *Die amerikanische Stabilisierungspolitik in Deutschland 1921–1932* (Düsseldorf, 1970).

[4] R. Bunselmeyer, *The Cost of the War, 1914–1918. British Economic War Aims and the Origins of Reparations* (Hamden, Conn. 1975); M.L. Dockrill and J.D. Gould, *Peace without Promise. Britain and the Peace Conference, 1919–1923* (London, 1981); A. Orde, *British Policy and European Reconstruction after the First World War* (Cambridge, 1990).

[5] S. Marks, *The Illusion of Peace: International Relations in Europe 1918–33* (New York, 1976); J. Jacobson, 'Is There a New International History of the 1920s?', *AHR*, 88 (1983), pp. 617–45; C.S. Maier, 'The Two Postwar Eras and the Conditions for Stability in Twentieth Century Western Europe', in *idem*, *In Search of Stability. Explorations in Historical Political Economy* (Cambridge, 1987), pp. 153–84; D.P. Silverman, *Reconstructing Europe after the Great War* (Cambridge, Mass., 1982).

[6] A.J.P. Taylor, *The Course of German History* (London, 1945), pp. 215–30.

[7] Marks, 'Reparations Reconsidered: A Reminder', pp. 356–65; *idem* 'The Myths of Reparations', pp. 231–55; Schuker, 'American "Reparations" to Germany, 1919–1933', in Feldman and Müller–Luckner (eds), *Nachwirkungen*, pp. 335–83. Cf. W.E. Wüest, *Der Vertrag von Versailles im Licht und Schatten der Kritik: Die Kontroverse um seine wirtschaftlichen Auswirkungen* (Zurich, 1962).

[8] See Schuker, 'Finance and Foreign Policy in the Era of the German Inflation', pp. 343–61; Holtfrerich, 'Die deutsche Inflation 1918 bis 1923 in internationaler Perspektive,' pp. 321–8; P. Krüger, 'Die Auswirkungen der Inflation auf die deutsche Außenpolitik', in Feldman and Müller-Luckner (eds.), *Nachwirkungen*, pp. 297–313.

[9] Quoted in Kolb, *Weimar Republic*, p. 58.

Brüning recalled setting out to 'make use of the world crisis [. . .] to put pressure on all the other powers [and] to turn our [economic] sickness into our weapon'.[10] As we shall see, such arguments originated in the inflation years and owed much to the arguments of the Hamburg business elite. Whether one should criticise the Allies for giving Germany room for manoeuvre or the Germans for manoeuvring is, however, debatable. Few historians would now dispute that, in Hillgruber's words, the Versailles Treaty was 'too weak to be a "Carthaginian" peace'; it did not, in fact, entirely reduce Germany to the status of 'an object'.[11] Nor can it be denied that paying reparations had a destabilising effect on German public finances at certain critical moments, even if the aggregate burden was smaller than used to be thought: it was not irrational to want revision.[12] As to the determination with which the Germans pursued revision, it is by no means clear that this worked to the advantage of the anti-democratic Right. Hostility to Versailles was common to Social Democrats, Democrats and Communists, as well as to conservatives, nationalists and radical *völkisch* parties;[13] and it can even be argued that Versailles was 'the unifying bracket that clamped German politics together'.[14]

Such arguments make it easier to understand why Weimar statesmen were revisionists. What they do not explain is why their revisionism failed. The strategy of revision by economic means was based on shrewd calculations about the likely economic consequences of the Versailles Treaty; calculations which, with certain modifications, continued to influence German diplomacy up until 1932. The unvarying

[10] Quoted in C.-L. Holtfrerich, 'Economic Policy Options and the End of the Weimar Republic', in I. Kershaw (ed.), *Weimar: Why did German Democracy Fail?* (London, 1990), p. 72.

[11] A. Hillgruber, 'Unter dem Schatten von Versailles – die außenpolitische Belastung der Weimarer Republik: Realität und Perzeption bei den Deutschen', in K.D. Erdmann and H. Schulze (eds.), *Weimar. Selbstpreisgabe einer Demokratie. Eine Bilanz heute* (Düsseldorf, 1980), p. 57; *idem*, 'Revisionismus – Kontinuität und Wandel der Außenpolitik der Weimarer Republik', *HZ*, 237 (1983), pp. 587–621; G.L. Weinberg, 'The Defeat of Germany in 1918 and the European Balance of Power', *CEH*, (1969), pp. 248ff.; W.A. McDougall, 'Political Economy versus National Sovereignty', *JMH*, 51 (1979), pp. 4ff.

[12] Felix, 'Reparation Reconsidered with a Vengeance', pp. 171–9; Krüger, 'Das Reparationsproblem der Weimarer Republik in fragwürdiger Sicht', pp. 21–74. See chapter 6 for a full discussion.

[13] See S. Miller, *Die Bürde der Macht. Die deutsche Sozialdemokratie 1918–1920* (Düsseldorf, 1978); J.C. Heß, *'Das ganze Deutschland soll es sein.' Demokratischer Nationalismus in der Weimarer Republik am Beispiel der Deutschen Demokratischen Partei* (Stuttgart, 1978); Schüddekopf, *Linke Leute von Rechts*; A. Thimme, *Flucht in den Mythos. Die Deutschnationale Volkspartei und die Niederlage von 1918* (Göttingen, 1969). Cf. U. Heinemann, *Die verdrängte Niederlage. Politische Öffentlichkeit und Kriegsschuldfrage in der Weimarer Republik* (Göttingen, 1983).

[14] H. James, 'Economic Reasons for the Collapse of Weimar', in Kershaw (ed.), *Weimar*, pp. 54f.

constant in these calculations was the idea that Germany could exert political leverage through trade. Increasing exports, it was believed, would put pressure on Germany's former enemies; blaming the increase on the peace terms would, in turn, bring about revision. Yet no matter how much this strategy succeeded in disrupting the collection of reparations, it did not achieve its objective. Such victories as it won – arguably, the Dawes Plan – were Pyrrhic; the ultimate cancellation of reparations was due more to exogenous factors. Moreover, the side effects of these policies within Germany were in all probability more damaging to the German economy than would have been a sincere attempt to comply with the treaty. It is this failure which needs to be explained.

The economic origins of revisionism

Historians have long been conscious of the unprecedentedly important role played by business interests in the diplomacy of the early 1920s. For successive stages of early Weimar foreign policy, it has been possible to demonstrate the influence, if not the primacy, of business interests: at Versailles, in the discussions over reparations in kind, in the 'preventive diplomacy' of the Rapallo treaty, in the Ruhr crisis and its aftermath.[15] There were two fundamental reasons for this. On the one hand, as has been suggested, politicians from Ebert to Stresemann were inclined to share the idea, explicit in the Stinnes-Legien agreement, that *die Wirtschaft* was 'the only power' left in Germany following the collapse of the Wilhelmine system. Only by exploiting the country's economic power, it was argued, could the damage to her international position be repaired. Ebert's little-known comment to Arndt von Holtzendorff at the time of the Ruhr occupation may be taken as typical: 'If France were to preserve power over the Ruhr in any form, there would be no possibility for Germany – even in the distant future – to rearm for a war of retaliation (*Vergeltungskrieg*).'[16] At the same time, the policy adopted by the Allies of demanding

---

[15] See P. Krüger, 'Die Rolle der Banken und der Industrie in den deutschen reparationspolitischen Entscheidungen nach dem Ersten Weltkrieg', in Mommsen *et al.* (eds.), *Industrielles System*, II, pp. 568–82; C.S. Maier, 'Coal and Economic Power in the Weimar Republic: the Effects of the Coal Crisis of 1920', in *ibid.*, pp. 530–42; G. Soutou, 'Der Einfluß der Schwerindustrie auf die Gestaltung der Frankreichpolitik Deutschlands', in *ibid.*, pp. 543–51; H. J. Rupieper, ' "Industrie und Reparationen"; Einige Aspekte des Reparationsproblems, 1922–1924', in *ibid.*, pp. 582–92; H. Pogge von Strandmann, 'Rapallo – Strategy in Preventive Diplomacy: New Sources and New Interpretations', in V. Berghahn and M. Kitchen (eds.), *Germany in the Age of Total War. Essays in Honour of Francis Carsten* (London/Totowa, NJ, 1981), pp. 123–46.

[16] HA, HB, Holtzendorff to Warnholtz, 8.9.23.

reparations from Germany meant that economic assets became not only objects of foreign policy, involving businessmen whether they liked it or not, but also instruments of policy. As early as 7 November, for example, Hugo Stinnes noted that 'despite the separation of Lorraine from the German Empire [. . .] Germany has a means of pressure in its possession of the coke needed for the running of the smelting plants [there]'.[17] German businessmen, it has been argued, 'exercised [a] veto-power over state economic policy, emasculating Berlin's ability to bargain abroad'. They were playing a double game, in that inflation not only gave business economic advantages, it also tended 'to wreck reparations'.[18]

However, it is somewhat misleading to identify *die Wirtschaft* in this context as a cohesive collective interest encompassing various branches of industry, commerce and banking.[19] In fact, the interests of heavy industry – on which much research has focused – were in some respects peculiar. Heavy industrial representatives kept a relatively low profile before and during the Paris peace conference and only came to the fore in 1920, when French policy increasingly became concerned with procuring reparations in the form of cheap German coal and coke.[20] It was other elements of German business which in fact set the pace of Weimar foreign policy in 1918/19. It is remarkable that, when the German peace delegation arrived in Paris at the end of March 1919, alongside three ministers, a politician and an academic, the Hamburg banker Carl Melchior was among its members; and that the delegation of 'experts' which accompanied them, which Melchior chaired, included his partner, Max Warburg, Eduard Rosenbaum and Franz Witthoefft, Secretary and President respectively of the Hamburg Chamber of Commerce, the head of the Hapag, Wilhelm Cuno, and his fellow director Richard Peltzer, as well as the head of the Bremen Norddeutsche Lloyd, Philipp Heineken. This was an unprecedentedly high representation for Hanseatic interests on a national body of such

---

[17] Feldman, *Iron and Steel*, p. 84.
[18] McDougall, 'Political Economy versus National Sovereignty', pp. 12, 16; B. Kent, *Spoils of War*, p. 382. See also Maier, *Recasting Bourgeois Europe, passim*.
[19] Krüger speaks of 'leading economic circles' and 'leading entrepreneurs of the Wilhelmine era': P. Krüger, *Deutschland und die Reparationen 1918/19. Die Genesis des Reparationsproblems in Deutschland zwischen Waffenstillstand und Versailler Friedensschluß* (Stuttgart, 1973), pp. 74f., 130f. Elsewhere he claims that Warburg 'spoke on behalf of industry and commerce': *idem*, 'Rolle der Banken', p. 572; *idem*, 'Die Reparationen und das Scheitern einer Verständigungspolitik auf der Pariser Friedenskonferenz im Jahre 1919', *HZ*, 221 (1975), pp. 326–75. See also Kent, *Spoils of War*, p. 80: 'All the German economic experts [. . .] were members of the old industrial, commercial and banking elite.'
[20] See G. Soutou, 'Die deutschen Reparationen und das Seydoux-Projekt 1920/21', *VfZ*, 23 (1975), pp. 237–70; P. Krüger, *Die Außenpolitik der Republik von Weimar* (Darmstadt, 1985), pp. 116–20.

importance. By comparison, there were only three representatives of heavy industry, and three of non-Hamburg banks.[21] Moreover, two of the most important ambassadorial posts in the period (London and Rome) were given to Hamburg men: Senator Friedrich Sthamer and John Berenberg-Goßler; while the Washington posting could have been Cuno's had he wanted it.

The leading role played by Warburg and Melchior in the peace preparations and at Versailles was partly determined by their wartime records as critics of government policy. The Ebert-Scheidemann government wanted as 'representatives of the new Germany' 'men who were politically unprejudiced and whose political outlook was known to be moderate' in order to 'facilitate the restoration of [. . .] international ties'.[22] This ruled out those businessmen – like Stinnes or the banker Salomonsohn – who had expressed support during the war for territorial annexation. Warburg, by contrast, had distinguished himself by his opposition to unrestricted submarine warfare and was clearly well connected in the United States. Moreover, his wartime conversion to the idea of a league of nations – and his political shift to the left in the course of 1918 – marked him out as someone likely to appeal to American tastes. Nor, as a letter to his son from Versailles in late April 1919 suggests, was his Wilsonianism insincere:

That will be the question for the next fifty years: how can we develop international economic agreements which will ultimately make the borders between peoples and nations [matters] of secondary importance, and which will lead, through the League of Nations, to the individual national parliaments sending delegates to a Super-parliament (*Überparlament*), in which the fundamental global questions can be solved in a more harmonious way than hitherto? [. . .] This task is far more important than grand statecraft [. . .] and I hope that through it we may succeed in killing off secret diplomacy, militarism, navalism and formalism, if not wholly, then largely.[23]

At the same time, from the point of view of those invited, representing Germany in the peace negotiations could be seen as a chance to put into practice lessons learnt during the war, where business interests had frequently suffered because of inadequate business influence over

---

[21] On the German delegation, see A. Luckau, *The German Peace Delegation at the Paris Peace Conference* (New York, 1941), pp. 188ff.; Haupts, *Deutsche Friedenspolitik.*, pp. 41, 51, 111, 397–404; *idem*, 'Zur deutschen und britischen Friedenspolitik in der Krise der Pariser Friedenskonferenz', *HZ*, 217 (1973), pp. 54–98; Warburg, *Aufzeichnungen*, p. 73. Cf. the comments in K. Schwabe, 'Versailles – nach sechzig Jahren', *Neue Politische Literatur*, 24 (1979), pp. 446–75.

[22] Schulze (ed.), *Kabinett Scheidemann*, pp. 64–96; Krüger, *Reparationen*, pp. 74f.

[23] WA, 'Jahresbericht 1919', Warburg to Eric Warburg, 24.4.19. Cf. Warburg, *Aufzeichnungen*, p. 77 (where the letter is described as addressed to his wife).

German foreign policy. Echoing the calls for increased domestic political engagement already discussed above, there was much talk in 1918
of the interdependence of economics and diplomacy:

Ultimately, we must abandon the unfortunate idea that [foreign] policy is to
be pursued for its own sake by the state; it must in future primarily act as
a basis and a support for economic policy [. . .] We neither can nor will have
politics without economics in the future.[24]

One expression of this new mood was the attempt by the Hanseatic
Chambers of Commerce to draft proposals to increase commercial
influence over future diplomacy – proposals which were not without
influence on the post-revolutionary Schüler reforms of the Foreign
Office.[25]

However, this does not wholly explain the delegates' decision to
accept what all of them realised was an onerous commission. Although
Warburg later admitted that he had 'laboured under deep misapprehen-
sions as to the terms which would be put to us', few of his circle had
expected to be treated lightly.[26] He himself had demurred when initially
asked to represent Germany at the peace negotiations because 'the
Entente conditions would doubtless be extremely hard'.[27] A week after
the signing of the armistice, Cuno, Heineken and Holtzendorff agreed
that 'at the coming peace negotiations, there is scarcely any chance
that we will be able to secure our objectives'.[28] Graf Bernstorff agreed
that the German delegation would 'achieve nothing [. . .] not the
slightest thing'.[29] Schiffer and Bergmann talked of reparations demands
of 20 bn. marks and 30 bn. marks; but Warburg warned them to
brace themselves for an 'absurdly high' figure. As he put it to Brockdorff-Rantzau in early April: 'We must be prepared for damned hard
conditions.'[30] Having once anticipated imposing reparations of up to
100 bn. marks on the Allies, he now assumed that Germany would

[24] Böhm, *Anwalt der Handelsfreiheit*, pp. 211f. Cf. Wiskemann, *Hamburg und die
Welthandelspolitik*, pp. 329–52.
[25] WA, 'Jahresbericht 1918', Anlage 14, 'Betr. amtliche Vertretung Deutschlands im
Auslande', pp. 1–10; Böhm, *Anwalt der Handelsfreiheit*, pp. 205–17; Haupts, *Friedenspolitik*, p. 148. Although the original Bremen proposal to transfer the consular
service to the new Economics Office was swiftly shot down by the Wilhelmstrasse,
the reforms did incorporate the Hamburg proposal for an international economic
news bureau. See in general K. Doß, *Das deutsche Auswärtige Amt im Übergang vom
Kaiserreich zur Weimarer Republik. Die Schülersche Reform* (Düsseldorf, 1977).
[26] Warburg, *Aufzeichnungen*, p. 75.
[27] *Ibid.*, p. 64.
[28] HA, HV, Bd. I, Holtzendorff to Vorstand, 18.11.18.
[29] Warburg, *Aufzeichnungen*, p. 71.
[30] Schwabe, *Wilson-Frieden*, pp. 526; Krüger, *Reparationen*, pp. 82, 119; Haupts,
Deutsche Friedenspolitik, p. 341.

be burdened with reparations for between twenty-five and forty years.[31] Witthoefft expected that, to pay for reparations, the tax burden would have to be 'increased to the maximum', to the point of 'a degree of socialisation of all sections of the population'.[32] Above all, Warburg was well aware that those who took responsibility for the peace would be likely to incur unpopularity at home – hence his reluctance to accept Max of Baden's invitation to lead the German peace delegation in October 1918.[33]

The most obvious practical reason for the involvement of Hanseatic business in the peace process was the extraordinary losses it had suffered during the war as a result of the disruption of trade, the sequestration of overseas assets and the seizure of German merchant vessels. As noted above, approximately 16.1 bn. marks of overseas investments totalling 20–28 bn. marks had been seized, to say nothing of around 1.9 bn. marks of short-term credits to foreign trading partners which had been frozen, and 1.34 m. tons of shipping which had been sequestrated. Although it is not certain what proportion of the total overseas assets were Hamburg owned, certainly, judging by the vehemence with which Hamburg interests insisted that 'our overseas assets' must 'fundamentally be exempted from any incursion aimed at the satisfaction of enemy financial demands on the Reich', it was not a trifling amount.[34] This helps to explain the anxiety of the Hamburg members of the German delegation to secure the restoration of Germany's colonies, where Hamburg firms had made significant pre-war investments.[35] It also clear that Hamburg was the biggest net overseas creditor of all the German states and major cities: the Hansestadt accounted for only 70.7 m. gold marks of the total 1.8 bn. marks owed to pre-war foreign lenders; but was owed an estimated 470 m. gold marks of the total 1.9 bn. marks due to German lenders from

---

[31] WA, Warburg Diaries, 4.1.19 (n.p.); Krüger, 'Rolle der Banken', p. 577. The position he took in a letter of 30 December to Graf Bernstorff was admittedly less realistic: 'For Germany, there can never be any talk of war compensation [. . .] Germany needs 50 to 100 years to restore its own land [. . .]': Akten zur deutschen auswärtigen Politik 1918–1945, Serie A, Bd. I (Göttingen, 1982), pp. 154f.

[32] StAH, FA AOM 24, Witthoefft Wahlrede, 31.12.18.

[33] Chernow, Warburgs, pp. 213–20.

[34] Warburg, Aufzeichnungen, p. 74; StAH, FA AOM 1, Bd. 10, 116, Witthoefft to State Secretary at the Economics Ministry, 26.11.18; 'Das Schicksal unserer Auslandseffekten', in Wirtschaftsdienst, 14, 4.4.19, pp. 275f.

[35] By comparison, Warburg was unconcerned about the prospect of formal cessions of territory on the European mainland, arguing that the continuing economic ties with any such peripheral areas would suffice to negate the impact of political separation: Haupts, Deutsche Friedenspolitik, pp. 335f.; Krüger, Reparationen, p. 128.

abroad.[36] This gave Hamburg firms a major interest in any decisions by the peacemakers affecting such pre-war liabilities. Finally, of the 1.3 m. gross tons of mechant shipping captured or confiscated during the war, a fifth belonged to Hamburg lines, as did a fifth of the 2.9 m. tons of merchant shipping still in German hands at the end of the war.[37] From the armistice negotiations onwards, it was clear that the Allies intended to lay claim to as much as possible of these assets as reparations; and it was readily discerned in Hamburg that the armistice provisions which continued the blockade and put the Allies in charge of German food imports could be used to justify placing the entire German merchant marine under Allied control.[38] It was therefore a fundamental objective of Hamburg business strategy to secure the return of as many of these assets as possible, and to avoid the loss of any more of them.

In short, the Hamburg group had strong economic motives for becoming involved in the peace process. As Max Warburg observed: 'There has never been as big a business transaction as the peace treaty.'[39] 'Credit and debit', rather than treaties, were the factors which now 'united' the nations, observed a senior Hapag official.[40] However, there were also political reasons for becoming involved. Those concerned aimed at more than merely increasing diplomatic awareness of commercial interests; influence over foreign policy, it was discerned, could also lead to influence over domestic politics. We have already seen how Hamburg's food supply – and hence its political stability – in 1918/19 came to depend on Allied decisions. Claiming that they could negotiate trade credits in the US, Warburg and Melchior set out to undermine the Economics Ministry's plans for trade control on the grounds that only free trade would be acceptable to the Americans. The committee of bankers which they persuaded the Ministry of Food

---

[36] StAH, DHSG II, II C 53, 16. Sitzung, 4.11.19. The comparable figures for Berlin were 804.3 m. marks and 880 m. marks, i.e., the capital's net creditor position was much less significant.

[37] GHH, 408213/0, 'Beteiligung der GHH an einer Schiffswerft', 17.3.18; Kohlhaus, 'Die Hapag', pp. 77f. Krohn, 'Zusammenbruch', pp. 218–22, gives a much lower figure for confiscations (535,000 tons); but there is also a much higher figure (2.04 m. tons) in BAP, RWM 764/268–301, 'Verluste der deutschen Handelsflotte'.

[38] HA, HV, Bd. 1, Holtzendorff to Vorstand, 16.11.18; 12.12.18; 16.12.18; 17.12.18; Holtzendorff to Cuno. 17.12.18. Hapag executives feared talk of socialisation within Germany principally because it might be used by the Allies to justify seizing the company's ships; and hurriedly sought undertakings from the government that compensation would be paid for any such confiscation: BAP, RFM 46579 N.Reg. 315/207, Holtzendorff to Schiffer, 9.12.18; /213–14, Waldstein to RWA, 10.12.18; HA, HV, Bd. 1, Holtzendorff to Vorstand, 11.12.18; 13.12.18; 14.12.18.

[39] WA, XIX Gesammelte Vorträge (Warburg speech before Economics Minister Scholz), 17.12.20.

[40] The Hapag Syndikus Hasselmann, quoted in Kohlhaus, 'Die Hapag', p. 76.

to set up in December 1918 then formed the basis for the Bureau (*Geschäftsstelle*) for the Peace Negotiations, through which Warburg was able to extend his influence over the Foreign Office.[41] In a similar fashion, the need to conciliate the Allies could be presented as an argument against radical political changes beyond parliamentarisation. Holtzendorff pointedly expressed the wish that 'Wilson's threat not to negotiate with any kind of dictatorship in Germany will ensure that the National Assembly will be called into being at an earlier stage than currently planned, so that we get orderly constitutional arrangements as soon as possible.'[42] Warburg likewise hoped 'that the present German constitution would be very similar to the American [. . .], anticipating that there would thereby arise a high degree of mutual understanding between the two countries'.[43] Indeed, he was still more specific when invited by Schiffer to represent the Treasury at the peace conference, only agreeing to let Melchior join the delegation on condition that 'the establishment of the Reich and the individual federal states on the broadest democratic basis is guaranteed, so that through the creation of a legally based parliament the legal procedure of budgetary approval is once again possible.'[44] In the same vein, Senator Carl Petersen argued before the DDP *Hauptvorstand* that, as soon as the workers' and soldiers' councils had been 'either rendered wholly harmless or, better still, got rid of completely', Germany would 'be treated quite differently by the Entente'.[45]

It would be misleading to argue that the Hamburg group's diplomatic strategy was based solely on considerations of economics and domestic politics. Warburg's experience during the war had, as we have already seen, significantly modified his view of international affairs. Yet the extent to which his policies constituted an 'alternative' to 'traditional' power politics should not be exaggerated.[46] Certainly, Warburg was no Pan German; but nor had the man who had supported German ambitions in Morocco in 1911 and colonisation of the Baltic states in 1918 entirely turned away from the pursuit of German national interests. He was, for example, fierce in his opposition to the idea of German 'war guilt'; not least because, as he pointed out to Eduard

---

[41] Haupts, *Deutsche Friedenspolitik*, pp. 196, 203, 254ff., 267n.; Krüger, *Reparationen*, pp. 74f., 78, 123; Krüger, 'Rolle der Banken', pp. 574f.; idem, *Außenpolitik*, pp. 70ff.

[42] HA, HV, Bd. I, Holtzendorff to Vorstand, 18.11.18.

[43] Warburg to Graf Bernstorff, 30.12.18, in *Akten zur deutschen auswärtigen Politik 1918–1945*, Serie A, vol. I (Göttingen, 1982), pp. 154f.

[44] WA, 'Jahresbericht 1914', Anlage 6, Warburg to Schiffer, 17.11.18; Warburg, *Aufzeichnungen*, p. 70.

[45] BAK, R45 III/15, DDP Hauptvorstand Sitzung, 4.2.19.

[46] Schwabe, 'Versailles nach 60 Jahren', p. 454.

Bernstein in March 1919, 'if the guilt question is unjustly passed to us alone [. . .] we will also suffer financial injustice'.[47] Warburg's view in 1918/19 was that Germany would best recover her status as a great power by appealing to the United States: 'traditional' national objectives had to be pursued in Wilsonian language. His views on self determination reveal this clearly:

If Wilson [. . .] remains true to [the idea of] the League of Nations, then it is still possible that a song will emerge that will strike a chord with us too. Personally, I am not over-optimistic, principally because Wilson does not know Germany well enough, and this method whereby one man, who cannot hope to know all the details, presides over the division of the world, is bound to lead to trouble.[48]

Rather than genuine ideological affinity, it was economic interest which Warburg believed could bring Germany and the United States together in the post-war world. At the end of December 1918 he recalled how, prior to the Revolution, he had envisaged 'close collaboration between America and Germany':

The field of action in which the Americans and Germans would [co]operate, would not be confined to South America, where the Germans would (alas) have to work under American financial dominance, but would, more importantly, include Russia, where the Americans can achieve nothing without the Germans. In both South America and Russia for the next fifty years, the Germans would be the natural extensions of the Americans [. . .] This follows not just from the fact that Russo-German collaboration would strengthen America's position in its rivalry with Japan, but also from purely commercial and financial interests making America reliant on Germany.[49]

Given that military defeat and the Revolution had undermined Germany's bargaining position, Warburg appreciated that such schemes would have to wait. Nevertheless, it remained likely that, in economic terms, America would be the decisive factor in the post-war period. As Warburg noted: 'The situation in which our [other] enemies find themselves, in particular France and Italy, [. . .] is just as bad as ours.'[50] The same calculations about the future role of American capital and Germany's pivotal position between East and West continued to provide the basic foundations for all Warburg's arguments about post-war German tactics.

---

[47] Krüger, *Reparationen*, pp. 148–51.
[48] *Ibid.* It is clear from his comments at around the same time on the future Reich constitution that Warburg had hopes of ultimately bringing about union with German Austria on the basis of self determination: see above p. 163.
[49] Warburg to Graf Bernstorff, 30.12.18, in *Akten zur deutschen auswärtigen Politik*, Serie A, I, pp. 154f.
[50] Haupts, *Deutsche Friedenspolitik*, p. 340; Krüger, *Reparationen*, p. 109.

This is most evident in his early arguments on the question of reparations. In an important series of debates, Warburg persuaded Schiffer and Bergmann that the best way to pay reparations was by means of an international (i.e. largely American) loan to Germany, which would allow her to pay a fixed capital sum in annuities spread over a period of twenty-five to forty years. The upper limit for reparations he summed up in the formula: 'Loans up to the limit of our ability to pay; and for the rest foreign participation [i.e., shareholdings] in German industry and in public enterprises; plus cession of colonies'.[51] By April, he was envisaging a loan of 100 bn. gold marks, 25 bn. of which would be ear-marked for the reconstruction of Northern France and Belgium.[52] Significantly, Warburg rejected the idea of reparations in kind on the grounds that the effect of paying compensation to industry would be inflationary. This is an important point in the light of future developments: for at the same time as he was insisting on restoring parliamentary budget procedures, Warburg was also arguing that 'the Reichsbank should as quickly as possible have its note issue monopoly restored, so that foreign confidence in our currency can return';[53] in other words, he envisaged halting the monetary expansion emanating from the state loan bank system. This suggests that Warburg initially saw the payment of reparations and monetary stabilisation as compatible objectives in the context of large-scale international lending, a liberal trade policy and a return to pre-war budgetary practices. To a large extent, this was a logical development of the arguments evolved in Hamburg during the previous year for a liberalised 'transitional economy'. As Ballin had perceived during the war, and as Witthoefft now reminded the politicians in Berlin, 'it is precisely our miserable currency which will indirectly facilitate our recovery'.[54] Provided no impediments were put in the way of trade, lost export markets would soon be recovered, thanks to the weakness of the German currency; and, after an initial slump, the mark would strengthen as the German economy revived. These arguments were clearly in direct contradiction to those being advanced by Moellendorff at the Economics Ministry; indeed, Warburg went still further in calling for the suspension of all exchange controls, which he argued

---

[51] Warburg, Diaries, 4.1.19 (n.p.); Warburg, *Aufzeichnungen*, p. 75; Krüger, 'Rolle der Banken', p. 577; Krüger, *Reparationen*, p. 119.

[52] Haupts, *Deutsche Friedenspolitik*, pp. 337–40. Optimistically, he toyed with the idea of denominating the bonds in paper marks, with the exception of those intended to pay off pre-war liabilities: Krüger, *Reparationen*, pp. 128f.

[53] WA, 'Jahresbericht 1918', Anlage 6, Warburg to Schiffer, 17.11.18; Warburg, *Aufzeichnungen*, pp. 7of.

[54] HA, HB, Holtzendorff to Cuno, 10.5.19.

were 'practically impossible to implement and incompatible with the need to obtain foreign credit'.[55] As he told Wissell:

Given the financial situation we currently find ourselves in, we shall have absolutely no interest – for at least the next decade – in restoring our currency even approximately to its old level. We must simply work towards a stabilisation [at the present level]. This stabilisation can only be achieved by lifting exchange controls.[56]

As has been suggested, Warburg was not optimistic about the chances of persuading the Allies to moderate their peace terms. However, even if the appeal to America failed, the German delegation had an additional card to play. Amid the prevailing anxieties about events in Russia, it could be argued that, if German economic recovery was impeded by the peace terms, 'the wave of Bolshevism' would sweep westwards through Germany. As Witthoefft noted, shortly after agreeing to join the Versailles delegation:

Bread and peace are the preconditions for order and work; otherwise we are headed for Bolshevism, and that will be the end of Germany. Yet I detect in this very danger of Bolshevism a certain safety valve with regard to the efforts of the Entente to checkmate us absolutely. If this malaise spreads from Hungary over Germany, neither France nor England will be immune; and that means the end for all Europe.[57]

Carl Melchior had made the same point the month before to a group of three British officers visiting Berlin; and it was a theme quickly taken up by Social Democrats.[58] There was more to this than mere scare-mongering. Significantly, during a meeting with ministers in Berlin in late April, Melchior argued that 'leanings towards Russia' must be contemplated as a future diplomatic strategy for Germany; a view which was endorsed by Ebert.[59] This was the alternative to Warburg's vision of Russo-German collaboration under the American aegis: Russo-German collaboration against the Allies.

Economic self interest, domestic political manoeuvring and power-political calculation all therefore played a part in the strategy evolved by the Hamburg group prior to the conference. Reparations could be paid provided, firstly, that Germany got back her overseas assets, her merchant fleet and the pre-war debts owing to her; secondly, that she received a loan; and, thirdly, that she was able to trade as freely as before the war, exploiting the advantages of a weak currency. If these

[55] Warburg, Diaries (January) 1919 (n.p.).
[56] Krüger, *Reparationen*, p. 183.
[57] StAH, FA AOM I, Bd. 10, 280, Witthoefft to Dr Niery, 24.3.19.
[58] Feldman, *Great Disorder*, pp. 99, 131, 136.
[59] HA, HB, Notizen, 27.4.19.

arguments were not heeded, the result might be a Red Germany, allied to Russia. This strategy was not based on naive optimism; as we have seen, those involved did not expect lenient terms from the victors. Rather, the objective of the Hamburg-inspired 'guidelines' was to create a basis for German counter-arguments in which commercial interests were accorded a crucial role; to establish in *German* minds as much as in American, British and French the idea that commerce was to be the linchpin of post-war economic recovery. Germany was not to revive behind a new tariff wall dressed up in the language of 'the common economy' and 'the protection of national labour', but through the pursuit of liberal economic policies.

The imagined consequences of the peace

One reason why it was difficult for the Hamburg group to be sanguine about the prospective treaty was the character of the renewed armistice agreed at Trier in January. Although Melchior secured modest amounts of grain and meat from the Allies, the price Erzberger was obliged to pay was to put all German merchant ships above 1,600 tons 'at the disposal' of the Allies 'for the duration of the armistice'.[60] There was little the shipping lines in Hamburg could do but to protest, accusing Erzberger of incompetence and the Allies of imposing 'Turkish arrangements' on Germany.[61] On the other hand, the subsequent disagreements between the British and French representatives over the financing of the food imports gave some grounds for hope on the German side. The peace conference convened at Paris in January was an extraordinarily unwieldy affair; and even after decision making had been concentrated in the hands of the Council of Four in late March there remained profound differences of opinion not only between the American, French, British and Italian leaders, but also within their respective delegations and domestic constituencies.[62] Keynes at the Treasury had suggested as early as October 1918 that 20 bn. gold marks was a realistic total figure for reparations – a figure similar to those mentioned in Berlin before Versailles.[63] Admittedly, the Treasury 'Memorandum on the Indemnity payable by the Enemy Powers for Reparation and other Claims' named a figure twice as high; but the Treasury's argu-

---

[60] Schwabe, *Wilson-Frieden*, pp. 355f.; Haupts, *Deutsche Friedenspolitik*, pp. 258–64, 300–20; Kent, *Spoils of War*, p. 62; Kohlhaus, 'Die Hapag', p. 9.

[61] Protests from the VHR in StAH, SK II, 1 c 2 a 5 Fasc. 4, VHR to Ebert, 19.1.19; SK to AA, 22.1.19; *Hamburger Fremdenblatt*, 20.1.19. Cf. Wilhelm Cuno, *Der Friedensvertrag und die deutsche Schiffahrt* (Hamburg, 1920), p. 2.

[62] Summarised in Kent, *Spoils of War*, pp. 66–9.

[63] E. Johnson (ed.), *The Collected Writings of John Maynard Keynes*. vol. XVI: *Activities 1914–19: The Treasury and Versailles* (Cambridge, 1977), pp. 338–43.

ments were in many ways close to those which the Germans intended to advance. It was acknowledged from the outset that even 'if every house and factory and cultivated field, every road and railway and canal, every mine and forest in the German Empire could be carried away and expropriated and sold at a good price to a ready buyer, it would not pay for half the cost of the war and of reparation added together'.[64] More importantly, the Treasury anticipated an argument which was to become central to German revisionist efforts, by distinguishing between 'two eventualities' which might arise from the attempt to collect reparations:

The first, in which the usual course of trade is not gravely disturbed by the payment, the amount of it being approximately equal to the sum which would accrue to the paying country abroad in any case, and would have been invested abroad if it were not for the indemnity; the second, in which the amount involved is so large that it cannot be paid without [. . .] a far-reaching stimulation of the exports of the paying country [. . .which] must necessarily interfere with the export trade of other countries [. . .] In so far as this country receives the indemnity, there is a heavy off-set to this injury. But, in so far as the indemnity goes into other hands, there is no such off-set.

Moreover, the same memorandum warned of the danger that a German fiscal crisis might lead to open debt repudiation or a break-up of the Reich.[65] This partly explains the strong sympathy which Keynes felt when he encountered Melchior for the first time in Paris. It may be that the former's subsequent declaration that he 'got to love' Melchior during the long negotiations at Trier obliquely alluded to a sexual attraction, but it seems more probable that Keynes was simply captivated by the sound of his own pessimism being articulated by another. As he later recalled, Melchior 'expected Germany to collapse and civilisation to grow dim; [. . .] it was the thought of the dark forces which might issue from the Eastwards which most obsessed him.'[66] The argument struck the intended chord. As the Foreign Office official Kurt von Lersner noted, following Lloyd George's anti-French intervention on the question of financing food imports: 'Thanks to Dr Melchior's clear explanation, Herr Keynes has realised that there is a danger for the Allies in delaying [matters] and is trying to find common

---

[64] *Ibid.*, p. 382 n. Cf. D. E. Moggridge, *Maynard Keynes. An Economist's Biography* (London, 1992), pp. 291ff.
[65] Keynes, *Collected Writings*, XVI, p. 379.
[66] J.M. Keynes, 'Dr Melchior, A Defeated Enemy', in *Two Memoirs* (London, 1949), reprinted in A. Robinson and D. E. Moggridge (eds.), *Collected Writings*, vol. X: *Essays in Biography* (Cambridge, 1972), p. 415. Cf. R.F. Harrod, *The Life of John Maynard Keynes* (London, 1951), pp. 231–4, 315, 394; R. Skidelsky, *John Maynard Keynes*, vol. I: *Hopes Betrayed, 1883–1920* (London, 1983), pp. 358–63.

ground with us.'[67] Significantly, in the immediate aftermath of the conference, Keynes warned that 'an immediate rapprochement between Germany and Russia' might be 'the only chance [of. . .] central Europe being able to feed itself'.[68]

There was a similar, though less sympathetic, appreciation of the probems raised by reparations within the American delegation. Although the financial experts Bernard Baruch and Norman Davis envisaged a higher burden than their British counterparts – around 84 bn. gold marks – they fully appreciated that 'the problem [was] not so much what Germany can pay but what the Allies can afford to have her pay' and warned against making 'Germany pay a certain indemnity and then making it impossible for her to pay'. Moreover, like Warburg, they sought to divide German obligations into hard currency and paper-mark portions.[69] However, the efforts of the German financial experts – who had arrived in France and been accommodated at the Château Villette on 28 March – to build on these American doubts were less successful than Melchior had been with Keynes. Once again, the spectre of Bolshevism was conjured up. At the first meeting of the Finance Commission on 3 April, Melchior warned the Americans: 'My colleagues and I are Germans of the old-fashioned type and we are now discredited. We have made promises which time and again have not come true and we are no longer able to persuade the masses, who listen to Russian agitators.'[70] Two weeks later Warburg privately approached the J.P. Morgan partner and US Treasury adviser Thomas Lamont to raise again 'the question of Bolshevism [. . .] He must say again that the situation was growing hourly worse; and that the populace was so affrighted at the alleged terms of the Treaty set forth in the newspapers [. . .] that no German delegation would dare to sign such a peace.'[71] The memorandum Warburg then handed Lamont set out the German case in detail. One hundred thousand people had already died in Germany because of the continuation of the blockade, and although some people had 'benefited by the changed conditions in Germany', it would be 'practically imposs-ible to extract the taxes' from them which would be necessary to pay

---

[67] Haupts, *Deutsche Friedenspolitik*, p. 340.
[68] Keynes, *Collected Writings*, XVII, p. 119.
[69] Rupieper, *Cuno Government and Reparations*, pp. 2–5. The figure of 84 bn. gold marks is obtained by deflating the 60 bn. paper marks portion of the total envisaged by the Americans using the exchange rate of March 1919, when their plan was drafted.
[70] Schwabe, *Wilson-Frieden*, p. 532 n.
[71] Baker Library, Harvard Graduate School of Business Administration, Thomas W. Lamont Papers 171–27, Memorandum by Max Warburg for Thomas Lamont, 16.4.19.

reparations. The Allies must establish the League of Nations as originally envisaged and entrust an independent court with the task of
determining the cause of the war; they must qualify the principle of
self determination to take account of 'economic interests' (for instance,
by requiring a 75 per cent majority in a referendum on the secession of
Alsace-Lorraine from the Reich); and they must secure 'the democratic
co-determination of the labouring classes in economic matters [. . .]
by means of international covenants'. If these 'new [. . .] fundamental
ideas' were adopted, the world could look forward to a period in
which 'international economic agreements' would make racial and
national boundaries a side-issue.[72] If not, the consequences would be
dire: either a 'militaristic reaction' would lead to a 'war of revenge'
or Germany would be 'driven into the arms of Bolshevism':

> The responsibility for the consequences which cannot be foreseen would fall
> on the victors. But the vanquished would carry the burden along with the
> sad consciousness that the [. . .] wrong which has been done will have to be
> righted one day. And then new terrors and sufferings would again come to
> the world.[73]

Two days later, Melchior issued a similar warning to Ellis Loring
Dresel, another member of the American delegation:

> He acknowledged freely that the result of refusing peace will be to plunge
> the country into Bolshevism but was quite clear that this was preferable to a
> dishonourable peace. He said if it were impossible to come to an understanding
> with the Western powers, obviously the only thing for Germany to do was
> to turn eastwards.[74]

With hindsight – bearing in mind particularly the events of 1939 –
much of this can be regarded as prophetic. Yet, in the immediate
circumstances of Versailles, it was badly misjudged, suggesting that
the Berlin government had overrated Warburg's insight into American
attitudes. True, Wilson came to believe that Melchior represented a
moderate group within the German delegation, distinct from the 'arro-
gant' aristocratic elements personified by Brockdorff-Rantzau. Perhaps
Lamont may also unwittingly have led Warburg on with his ambiguous
remark that Germany would 'have a "rigged" peace'.[75] However, the

---

[72] Warburg, *Aufzeichnungen*, p. 77.
[73] As note 71. Warburg was not entirely cynical in his pessimism: a telegram to Paul
Warburg which appears to be from him or his son and to date from around this
time also warned of 'the total collapse of Europe' if the Fourteen Points were not
'honestly adhered to': Sterling Library, Princeton, Paul M. Warburg Papers, Series
I, Box 4, Folder 58, 'Mason' to Paul Warburg (undated).
[74] NAW, RG 59, 862.00/800, Dresel memorandum, 20.4.19.
[75] Schwabe, *Wilson-Frieden*, pp. 562, 568, 582; WA, 'Jahresbericht 1919'. Certainly
Lamont was anxious to prevent Warburg from publishing in his memoirs details of
a conversation in which the American had allegedly said: 'You better sign, as there

Americans were privately sceptical of the German arguments. Lamont thought Warburg's memorandum 'an extraordinary document', commenting to Baruch: 'The nerve that these boche have is something terrible. I think you will agree with me that they are utterly lacking in insight into the real situation [. . .] The thing does not amount to anything.'[76] Not surprisingly, German requests for an informal meeting with President Wilson and his adviser Colonel House were denied.[77] It was primarily American opposition which scuppered Keynes's 'Grand Scheme for the Rehabilitation of Europe' which took up the German idea of a loan to Germany.[78]

When the peace terms were finally presented on 7 May, they were therefore severe – indeed, far more severe than even the pessimists in the German delegation had anticipated. There were, however, several ways of looking at the Allied terms. To many politicians and publicists in Germany, the 'war guilt' clause, the disarmament provisions and the loss of territory – twelve peripheral regions amounting to 13 per cent of the Reich's territory and 10 per cent of its population, as well as eight colonies in which 2.8 million Germans lived[79] – were the most objectionable features of the treaty. These could be denounced in emotively nationalistic terms, drawing on the rhetoric of the 'wars of liberation'.[80] Others, including the leader of the German delegation Brockdorff-Rantzau, preferred to adopt a legalistic position, pointing to the discrepancies between the Fourteen Points, the Lansing Note and the Versailles terms, and stressing the contractual and conditional nature of the original armistice.[81] From the standpoint of the economic experts, however, the crucial points of the Allied terms related to reparations – now, as a result of pressure from the British Dominions, to cover the costs of war-related pensions and allowances as well as civilian war damage.[82] One objection to the reparations terms was that, because of the wide differences of opinion among the Allies on the subject, they named no final sum, demanding only an initial 20 bn. gold marks plus occupation costs, and leaving the final figure to be

is a paragraph of revision': Baker Library, Harvard Graduate School of Business Administration, Thomas W. Lamont Papers 171–27, Memorandum, 30.4.45.

[76] *Ibid.*, Lamont to Baruch, 18.4.19.

[77] Warburg, *Aufzeichnungen*, pp. 73–8.

[78] Harrod, *Keynes*, pp. 228–51; Moggridge, *Keynes*, pp. 298–308.

[79] Petzina *et al.* (eds.), *Sozialgeschichtliches Arbeitsbuch*, III, p. 23. Cf. Kolb, *Weimar Republic*, pp. 23–33.

[80] See for example, G. Stresemann, 'Wilsons Frieden' (14.5.19), in *idem*, *Von der Revolution bis zum Frieden von Versailles* (Berlin, 1919), pp. 166–71.

[81] Krüger, *Reparationen*, pp. 41–51.

[82] Dockrill and Gould, *Peace without Promise*, pp. 45–56; Bunselmeyer, *The Cost of the War*, pp. 106–20; Kent, *Spoils of War*, pp. 67–77; Krüger, *Außenpolitik*, pp. 72–6; Trachtenberg, 'Reparation at the Paris Peace Conference', pp. 24–55.

decided in 1921: this created a potentially debilitating uncertainty.[83] But the most fundamental objections related to the immediate seizures of German assets on the reparations account: not only the permanent seizure of the ships handed over at Trier, but also substantial amounts of Germany's smaller vessels and rolling stock; all German overseas assets confiscated during the war (except those in the US, whose status was left undecided); German pre-war credits to foreigners, to be offset against money owed by Germans (at pre-war exchange rates) through the 'clearing' system; and deliveries of coal, up to around 40 m. tons a year. These expropriations meant, the experts argued, a chronic balance of payments deficit, made still worse by the loss of industrial capacity as a result of territorial changes and the stipulation limiting Germany's right to an independent trade policy, which entitled the world to raise tariffs against German exports, but obliged Germany to import on a most-favoured-nation basis.[84]

These diverse perspectives prompted very different responses to the treaty within the German peace delegation and government. Warburg noted Brockdorff-Rantzau's 'pathological nervousness' and increasingly 'grotesque persecution mania'; Dernburg was reported to be 'beside himself' and lachrymose.[85] Initially, even Warburg was caught up in the febrile mood:

To announce a new era to the world, to speak of love and justice, and then to perpetrate pillage on a global scale, to sow the seeds of future conflicts and kill all hope of better times, is to commit the greatest sin in the world. To experience this at first hand is appalling. One thing is certain: we can never seriously sign this peace.[86]

His first official response – 'dictated [. . .] in a prolonged rage' – also emphasised the 'shameless breaches of law' in the treaty.[87] However, within a matter of days, passions had subsided and economic considerations had once again come to the fore. As Warburg noted: 'Am prepared for the enemy to refuse all negotiation and to extend their occupation. [. . .] We must remain cool; that way we will reach an understanding.'[88] In shipping circles, the view was that the treaty could

---

[83] Maier, *Recasting Bourgeois Europe*, p. 233. On the decisive role of the British delegation in overruling American and French figures of between 100 and 180 bn. gold marks, see M.Trachtenberg, 'Reparation at the Paris Peace Conference', *JMH*, 51 (1979), pp. 24–55.
[84] H.-J. Schroeder, 'Die politische Bedeutung der deutschen Handelspolitik nach dem Ersten Weltkrieg', in Feldman *et al.*, (eds.) *Zwischenbilanz*, pp. 235–51.
[85] Haupts, *Deutsche Friedenspolitik*, p. 361; HA, Holtzendorff Notizen, 12.5.19.
[86] Warburg, *Aufzeichnungen*, p. 79, quoting letters to his wife of 8 and 9 May.
[87] Krüger, *Reparationen*, p. 187.
[88] Haupts, *Deutsche Friedenspolitik*, p. 361.

have been worse.[89] Nevertheless, the majority opinion on the Hapag board went against Huldermann, who argued stoically for writing off the line's losses and using the expected compensation money to build a new fleet; instead, it was agreed that the main objective must be to persuade the Allies to return the confiscated ships.[90] The economic argument for this was clearly spelt out by Cuno. Earnings from international carriage (which he estimated at 500 m. marks per annum in the years before the war) had been vital to the pre-war German balance of payments; and without her own merchant marine, Germany would have to pay 12.24 bn. paper marks per annum to foreign shippers. The implication was clear: no ships, no balance of payments surplus, no reparations.[91] Various possible alternatives to confiscation were discussed, such as offering to build new ships for the Allies; but the idea favoured was to offer the Allies shareholdings in the shipping lines and in other industrial concerns as an alternative to actual asset seizures. Erzberger was particularly enthusiastic at the prospect of 'a kind of bigger and better Morgan Trust':

[The Americans] would thereby gain a share not only in the ships, but also in all the German lines' dock facilities and their various connections; but from our point of view, with a single stroke the possibility would be created of getting back a share of the huge world transport [market].[92]

Indeed, the idea was given serious consideration for industry as a whole at a meeting of businessmen and Economics Ministry officials.[93]

Such direct participation in German business was, as we have seen, a form of reparations which Warburg had contemplated before leaving for Versailles. However, by this stage, he and Melchior had come to the conclusion that an altogether more radical counter-proposal was called for. They envisaged making an offer to the Allies of reparations totalling 100 bn. gold marks, in exchange for which they hoped to

---

[89] Although the terms of the treaty implied the loss of almost the entire remaining merchant fleet, at least there were to be no direct controls on coastal customs and waterways: HA, Holtzendorff Notizen, 14.5.19. The treaty envisaged that all ships above 1,600 tons would be handed over as reparations, as well as 50 per cent of those above 1,000 tons and 25 per cent of the rest. In the course of 1919, ships totalling 1.3 m. tons were handed over. By the end of 1922 – after further seques-trations imposed after the sinking of the German battle fleet at Scapa Flow – a total of 2.6 m. tons had gone. Altogether, war and peace had accounted for over 96 per cent of the pre-war German merchant fleet: BAP, RWM 764/302, Ablieferungskommissar Hamburg; Kohlhaus, 'Die Hapag', pp. 11ff.; Kent, *Spoils of War*, p. 62; Krohn, 'Zusammenbruch', pp. 218–22.

[90] HA, Holtzendorff Notizen, 16.5.19

[91] Kohlhaus, 'Die Hapag', p. 54; Kent, *Spoils of War*, p. 99.

[92] HA, HB, Cuno to Huldermann, 21.5.19; Notizen, 22.5.19; Notizen, 24.5.19; Notizen, 25.5.19.

[93] Feldman, *Great Disorder*, pp. 147–53.

secure major alterations in the peace terms: preserving some of the
merchant fleet, restoring colonies and overseas assets, and avoiding
the cession of Upper Silesia and the Saarland.[94] The proposal has been
described by one historian as 'astonishing', documenting as it did an
'honest will to pay' (Melchior's phrase) on the German side.[95] In fact,
the 100 bn. gold marks was not the 'present value' of the Warburg–
Melchior offer (which Keynes put at closer to 30 bn. marks), since
they envisaged the sum being paid over a prolonged period, beginning
in 1926, in annuities of which only a fifth would bear interest. Warburg
was, in effect, trying to dress up the estimated cost of reconstructing
the damaged areas of Belgium and Northern France (for which Germany had admitted liability) in such a way that it appeared sufficient
to cover the British claims too; and, in return for this offer, to 'rescue
large parts of the East, colonies (albeit only some of them)', 'to avoid
an economic and financial control by the Entente' and 'to protect
private property'.[96] His justification of the offer was at once calculated
and apocalyptic. To make a specific offer would, Warburg argued,
'make it difficult for [our enemies] to justify to their own countries
not negotiating with us':

We can compromise with regard to military, naval-technical and financial
questions; [but] on all other issues we must be, as far as is at all possible,
unyielding; because we will simply not be able to undo concessions of a
territorial, political, colonial and economic nature. If we do not force our
enemies to enter into negotiations with this kind of surprisingly good offer –
if all they hear from our side is criticism, rejection and [dire] forecasts – they
will simply break off the negotiations, occupy large areas of Germany, negotiate
if they can with individual federal states, and in two months the resistance
of the [. . .] population will be broken. What then? Then those who failed
to make peace [when they could] will be hounded out [of office] and any
available peace will be signed – and anyone who thinks that Germany will
quickly summon up the courage to reunite itself as a great power will, I fear,
be deceiving himself. It is my firm belief that it will all be over, not just for
decades but for ever. After five years of war the people have lost their nerve
so much that they simply cannot endure any further trial. Ten, fifteen or
twenty years [. . .] will do the rest. One [half] will seek union with the East,
the others with the West and thus it will be sealed: *finis Germaniae*.[97]

---

[94] On the origins of this proposal see WA, 'Jahresbericht 1919'; Haupts, *Deutsche
Friedenspolitik*, p. 17 n.; Krüger, *Reparationen*, p. 187; idem, 'Rolle der Banken',
p. 581. The idea may have originated with Keynes and Melchior, but it was Warburg
who added the various conditions.

[95] Haupts, *Friedenspolitik*, pp. 15f., 368.

[96] Warburg to Dernburg, 19.5.19, in *Akten zur deutschen auswärtigen Politik*, Serie A,
II, pp. 56–9; Schulze (ed.), *Kabinett Scheidemann*, p. 352 n., 355; Krüger, *Reparationen*, pp. 190f., 195, 198f.; Haupts, *Friedenspolitik*, pp. 16 n., 363, 370.

[97] Krüger, *Reparationen*, p. 195.

Like so much of Warburg's writing from this period, this vision of a divided Germany is more persuasive with hindsight than it was at the time. Although there was a faction in France which already thought in terms of detaching the Rhineland from the Reich, the other victorious powers at no stage seriously contemplated the partition of Germany.[98] Moreover, the government in Berlin – particularly the Finance Minister Dernburg – regarded the 100 bn. figure with great alarm. Dernburg was only prepared to regard Warburg's scheme as a provisional arrangement, to be maintained for three or four years until 'a turning point in the entire history of Europe frees Germany from the consequences of the obligations [thus] accepted' – a more optimistic, if vague, prognosis than Warburg's.[99] In a series of evidently heated meetings between members of the delegation and cabinet ministers at Spa, the Finance Minister sought to dissuade the peace delegation from specifying such a high figure.[100] Nevertheless, Warburg prevailed;[101] though, to appease Brockdorff-Rantzau, the final version of the German counter-proposal may have made more of the non-economic objections to the treaty than he and Melchior had intended.

The German counter-proposals[102] began with an attack on the legal basis of the Allied peace terms, and included a range of non-economic demands, notably for German membership of the League of Nations, and the retention (principally on the grounds of their German character) of Upper Silesia, the Saarland, Danzig and Memel. However, the central theme remained that the Allied terms implied 'the utter destruction of German economic life', condemning Germany politically to 'the fate of Russia'.[103] The critical arguments were presented in a Supplement on financial questions, probably drafted by Melchior and Warburg.[104] Given the economic constraints being imposed on Germany by the peace – in particular, the loss of industrial capacity, colonies, overseas assets and the merchant navy – the finance experts denied that Germany could pay war damages as defined by the Allies. Attempting to force her to do so by making the Reparations Commission 'absolute master of Germany' would have dire consequences:

[98] H.I. Nelson, *Land and Power. British and Allied Policy on Germany's Frontiers 1916–1919* (London/Toronto, 1963).

[99] Haupts, *Friedenspolitik*, pp. 16 n., 370; Krüger, *Reparationen*, pp. 193f., 198.

[100] Schulze (ed.), *Kabinett Scheidemann*, pp. 352 n., 355; Krüger, *Reparationen*, pp. 199, 203–8; Warburg, *Aufzeichnungen*, pp. 80–3; StAH, FA AOM I, Bd. 10, 350, Witthoefft to Warburg, 26.5.19.

[101] According to Warburg, the incensed Dernburg offered to resign and give him the post of Finance Minister: Warburg, *Aufzeichnungen*, p. 82.

[102] Text in Luckau, *German Delegation*, pp. 306–406 (Document 57).

[103] *Ibid.* pp. 319, 377.

[104] *Ibid.* pp. 378–91; P.M. Burnett, *Reparation at the Paris Peace Conference*, vol. II (New York, 1940), pp. 78–94.

There is a frightful danger that the only means of relief would be emigration on a huge scale, or if this should become impossible, death *en masse*. [. . .] German democracy [would be] destroyed at the very moment when the German people [. . .] were on the point of establishing it.[105]

Such rhetoric was by now familiar. Where the experts' Supplement broke new ground was in its explicit emphasis on the fiscal, monetary and commercial implications of reparations. To pay reparations from current government revenue, it was pointed out, would require that 'expenditures for the payment of interest on the war loans, for the allotments of the disabled German soldiers and for the pensions of the dependants of the fallen soldiers, must cease or be cut down, as well as the expenditures for cultural purposes, schools, higher education etc.'. This would simply 'destroy' German democracy: 'Any ability and inclination to pay taxes would disappear and Germany would be for decades to come the scene of uninterrupted social class struggles of the bitterest kind.' But the alternative – financing reparations by borrowing – posed equally grave problems:

In the immediate future it will be impossible to place German state loans in large amounts either at home or abroad, so that compensation [to the owners of assets expropriated for reparations] could be made only by means of large issues of notes. The inflation, already excessive, *would increase constantly if the peace conference as proposed should be carried out. Moreover, great deliveries of natural products can only take place if the state reimburses the producers for their value; this means further issues of notes.* As long as these deliveries last, there could be no question of the stabilising of the German currency even upon the present level.

Then came the crucial argument:

The depreciation of the mark would continue. The instability of the currency would affect not only Germany, however, but all the countries engaged in export, for Germany, with her currency constantly depreciating would be a disturbing element and would be forced to flood the world market with goods at ridiculously low prices.[106]

The 'assumptions' on which the German counter-offer was based were then set out:

That Germany shall be allowed to preserve that territorial integrity which the armistice promises; that we keep our colonial possessions and merchant ships [. . .]; and that all infringements of our economic rights in German private property, etc., which were suffered during the war, shall be settled according to the principle of reciprocity.[107]

---

[105] Luckau, *German Delegation*, p. 378.
[106] *Ibid.*, p. 384. Italics in original.
[107] *Ibid.*, pp. 388f.

Under these conditions, interest plus amortisation could be paid in the form of annuities on bonds worth 20 bn. gold marks between 1919 and 1926, and amortisation only in the form of annuities on bonds up to a maximum of 80 bn. gold marks – the annuities 'not [to] exceed a fixed percentage of the German imperial and state revenues' from 'direct and indirect taxes, excess profits and customs dues' – the limits being set by 'the total net budget, up to the present time, of the German empire in times of peace' (at most, including extraordinary expenditure, 2.67 bn. marks) and the tax burden 'of the most heavily-taxed of the states represented on the Reparations Commission'.[108]

The significance of the German counter-proposals has long been a subject of controversy. At the time, the 100 bn. gold marks figure was seized upon by the radical right as an example of the pusillanimity of Weimar's representatives at Versailles, and Warburg frequently had to defend himself in the 1920s by pointing out the extent of the conditions he had appended to the offer.[109] More recent writers have seen the concessions made in the offer as a basis for an 'alternative' liberal German foreign policy; or have at least been critical of the Allies for rejecting the proposal out of hand.[110] Certainly, the financial experts' argument succeeded where Warburg had initially failed in winning over the American delegation. Wilson himself expressed sympathy with Melchior's arguments for 'adjustments [. . .] from time to time' in the 'arrangements' for reparations.[111] The American financial experts, including Lamont, regarded a number of the German proposals – the need for a fixed sum, the need to limit the powers of the Reparations Commission and the need to leave Germany with adequate 'working capital', particularly merchant ships – as 'reasonable' and believed they 'held out a basis for getting together [. . .] with Germany very quickly'.[112] Yet when these arguments were rejected by the French and British,[113] Warburg was not suprised. He had from

[108] Ibid., pp. 389f.; figure for pre-war budget from Witt, Finanzpolitik, p. 380.

[109] WA, M. Warburg, 'Die notwendigen Vorbedingungen für die Gesundung der deutschen Währung', Vortrag, V. Allgemeiner Bankiertag, 26.10.20; Warburg, Aufzeichnungen, p. 79.

[110] Haupts, Friedenspolitik, pp. 15f.; Krüger, Reparationen, p. 208.

[111] Burnett, Reparation at the Paris Peace Conference, II, pp. 25f.

[112] Baker Library, Harvard, Lamont Papers, 169–1, Undated summary of, commentary on and draft reply to the German counterproposals, probably by Lamont; 169–3, T. Lamont, 'Suggestion as to the Manner of Meeting the Points as Stated', 31.5.19; J.F. Dulles (memorandum on German counterproposals), 1.6.19. Both felt it would be necessary to charge some interest on the 80 bn. gold marks and to increase the final figure to 120 bn. gold marks. See the six subsequent memoranda in 169–4 and 169–5.

[113] Baker Library, Harvard, Lamont Papers, 273, Lamont Diary, 4.1.19; 169–5, Reparations report to Supreme Council, 8.6.19; Draft reply to German Counter-Proposals, 10.6.19. For the final Allied and American reply of June 16, rejecting the 100 bn. gold marks figure as too 'small' see Luckau, German Delegation, pp. 411–72.

the early stages of drafting the German counterproposals expected 'nothing to come of it all', and expressed his growing fatalism with characteristic irony, by composing satirical verses on the peace conference with the title: 'The Villettiade (The First Part of A Tragedy)'.[114] Resigned to the fact that the Allies would not negotiate, Warburg's intention had simply been to make a public statement of what were, in his view, the decisive arguments for revision.[115] This is how the German counterproposals should be understood: not as a failed 'alternative' to subsequent revisionism, but as the first explicit assertion of the view that the economic consequences of the peace would necessitate its revision. It was in fact the origin of that strategy for revision by economic means to which Weimar governments would return repeatedly throughout the succeeding thirteen years – a strategy which above all revolved around the idea of inducing the Allies to revise the peace by artificially stimulating German exports.

In this light, the attitude of the financial experts to the question of whether or not Germany should sign the final peace treaty is less surprising than it appears if they are portrayed as the proponents of conciliation. Along with the German delegation itself, the financial experts argued that the German government 'must refuse to sign the treaty' since

the peace which menaces Germany would cut so deeply and lastingly into the roots of her energy; and the obvious consequences of a refusal to accept the treaty, such as the planned occupation of German territory and domestic unrest, are of minor importance, however terrible.[116]

Indeed, Cuno and Melchior argued that the government should tell the Allies 'that the conditions are impossible for us to accept because we cannot fulfil them; and we therefore recommend them to take over the German Reich [. . .and] take its government and administration in hand, in the way the League of Nations is taking charge of the [former German] colonies'.[117] Once again, this was rhetoric for Allied consumption, rather than a serious policy proposal. Warburg certainly did not need to be told by Groener that an occupation carried the

---

[114] Haupts, *Deutsche Friedenspolitik*, pp. 360f.; WA, 'Jahresbericht 1919', 'Labor et Constantia', Max M.W., Versailles, 5 June 1919, 'Die Villettiade' (Der Tragödie erster Teil). The German delegation had been accommodated in the Château Villette.

[115] Hence Melchior's view that, if the Allied peace had to be accepted, the German counterproposals should be published with it: Simons (statement), 4.6.19, *Akten zur deutschen auswärtigen Politik*, Serie A, II, pp. 86–8.

[116] Luckau, *German Delegation*, pp. 481–8, 489–95; Schulze (ed.), *Kabinett Scheidemann*, pp. 415–75; Warburg, *Aufzeichnungen*, p. 84.

[117] Kohlhaus, 'Die Hapag', p. 12; HA, HB, Notizen [meeting in Weimar of Noske, Erzberger, Dernburg, Witthoefft, Petersen, Albert, Sthamer and Gilsa (Noske's Chief of Staff)], 16.6.19; Notizen, 19.6.19.

risk of the disintegration of the Reich – that had been precisely his
own argument to Dernburg a month before.[118] The object of publicly
counselling rejection was merely to repeat, for the record, the ritual
prophecy of doom:

Germany's [. . .] industry will be condemned to stagnation [. . .] Germany
will collapse economically [. . .] and millons of Germans will die in civil
conflicts or will be forced to emigrate [. . .] The result will be an 'economic
Balkans' in the heart of Europe which will create endless unrest and constant
danger of its spreading to the rest of the world.[119]

Of course, there was a further reason for counselling rejection. On
their way back from Versailles to Weimar the German delegation's
train had been stoned – indeed, Melchior had been slightly injured;
and reactions in Hamburg itself were no less violent, as we have seen.
Clearly, there was no realistic alternative to signing the treaty; but
there was an understandable reluctance to take personal responsibility
for doing so, in view of the popular mood. This was the issue which
divided the Cabinet; drove Scheidemann to resign on 20 June; and
led his successor Bauer vainly to attempt conditional acceptance on
22 June. Warburg's attitude was typically candid: 'Dear God, if I
weren't a Jew, I really would take command now. But it's probably
just as well. It's not the first time that being a Jew has saved me from
folly.'[120] In short, the experts' report was not a manifesto for occupation
and domestic *Auflösung*, but rather, on the one hand, a first shot in
the revisionist propaganda campaign aimed at opinion in the Allied
countries – and, on the other, a domestic political insurance policy.
The gesture of defiance was not without its effect: Keynes was certainly
impressed by Melchior's denunciation of 'the insincere acceptance of
impossible conditions'.[121] But the real strength of the German experts'
argument lay in its apparent economic logic: Germany was willing to
pay an indemnity, but because of the effect of the treaty on the
German balance of payments, the country simply could not pay. As
Cuno put it, the aim now was to 'stress Germany's readiness to pay
an indemnity, but [to stress that] we must also [. . .] be allowed to

---

[118] Schulze (ed.), *Kabinett Scheidemann*, p. 480. Groener predicted that the Rhineland,
Hanover, 'Central Germany', the East and Hamburg would secede from the Reich.
Hamburg would 'immediately declare itself a *Räterepublik*'.
[119] Luckau, *German Delegation*, p. 492.
[120] WA, 'Jahresbericht 1919', Max Warburg to Alice Warburg, 20.6.19.
[121] Keynes, *Essays in Biography*, p. 428. 'The breach of discipline, the decay of honourable behaviour, the betrayal of undertakings by the one party and the insincere
acceptance by the other of imposssible conditions which it was not intended to carry
out – it was these offences against the Word which so much wounded him.' Cf.
Harrod, *Keynes*, p. 238.

work'; that there was, in short, 'a contradiction between the economic and the financial clauses' of the peace treaty.[122] The first phase of 'fulfilment' had begun: formally in order to preserve the defenceless Reich from partition;[123] informally to demonstrate in practice the economic impossibility of the treaty predicted by the experts.

In the months after the peace, the former finance delegates and their associates worked to refine and propagate this line of argument. Holtzendorff lobbied his nephew Sir Eyre Crowe, appointed as British representative to the Reparations Commission, and the British military attaché in Berlin.[124] Warburg wrote a widely publicised letter to Lord Parmoor of the 'Fight the Famine Council'.[125] Two developments conspired to lend force to the black forecasts made by the Hamburg delegates in June. Firstly, the mark slumped against the dollar from 14 marks to 99 marks between June 1919 and February 1920. The principal reason for this was the decision of the new Economics Minister Schmidt to lift exchange controls, thus enabling industry to take full advantage of the export premium created as the mark fell faster than domestic prices were rising.[126] The arguments of the Versailles delegates had not been wasted on Schmidt. As he put it bluntly:

The permanent need for Germany to export [. . .] makes it necessary that German products find their way abroad in the greatest possible amounts. This is more important than the immediate securing of the greatest possible return on their worth. [. . .] The tossing out of German goods abroad at slaughter prices [. . .] will compel the Entente to allow us to bring our exchange into order.[127]

The surge of depreciation appeared to confirm the assertion that the Versailles terms had created a balance of payments crisis and an export 'fire sale' which only, as Warburg now argued, a revision of the treaty and a large international loan could resolve:

The German people are [. . .] firmly resolved to fulfil the treaty as far as it is capable of doing so. If more is demanded, then a disaster will ensue that will affect not only Germany but will have repercussions for all other countries.

---

[122] W. Cuno, 'Friedensbedingungen die Schiffahrt betreffend', quoted in Rupieper, *Cuno Government*, pp. 2ff.

[123] The term 'fulfil' is first used in this sense in the 'Appeal of the German Government to the German People' of 24 June: Luckau, *German Delegation*, pp. 496f.

[124] HA, HB, Holtzendorff to Cuno, 17.7.19.; 13.12.19.

[125] WA, 'Jahresbericht 1919', Warburg to Lord Parmoor, 22.10.19; published in *Hamburgische Correspondent*, Nr. 570, 8.11.19; *Die Zukunft*, Nr. 7, 19.11.19; *Le Temps*, 11.11.19.

[126] See chapter 5; W. C. Matthews, 'The Continuity of Social Democratic Economic Policy, 1919 to 1920: the Bauer-Schmidt Policy', in Feldman et al. (eds.), *Anpassung*, pp. 485–512.

[127] Quoted in Feldman, *Great Disorder*, p. 172; Webb, *Hyperinflation*, p. 91.

The financial chaos already visible on the foreign exchange markets will spread.[128]

The second factor which lent force to the arguments of June was the dramatic success of the Red Army in Poland. This prompted renewed prophecies that the economic effects of the peace – 'poverty, hardship, unemployment' – would lead to 'insurrection' and the spread of 'the wave of Bolshevism over Poland into Germany'.[129] Melchior issued the calculated warning:

Now that Germany's economy has been smitten [. . .] by the loss of her colonies, her fleet and the confiscation of her overseas assets, she must to a far greater extent than hitherto turn her gaze eastwards [. . .] Perhaps there will develop [. . .] though without any culmination in aggression [. . .] a kind of League of the Vanquished [. . .] between Russia and Germany.[130]

An important, if only partially successful, initiative in the post-Versailles revisionist campaign came from Max's brother Paul Warburg, who was behind the invitation of a small group of bankers and financial experts to a conference in Amsterdam (hosted by the Governor of the Bank of the Netherlands, Vissering) in October 1919.[131] Initially, Warburg's principal concern seems to have been with the organisation of large-scale commercial credits for Germany to facilitate imports of raw materials.[132] But under Keynes's influence the discussion was broadened to include the question of reparations, war debts and the international loan requested by the German experts at Versailles; and he and Warburg jointly drafted an appeal to the League of Nations which effectively called for a reduction in reparations, the cancellation of war debts and a loan to Germany.[133] When a larger group, augmented

[128] WA, Jahresbericht 1920, II, Warburg to Lord Parmoor (Fight the Famine Council), 22.10.19

[129] StAH, FA B&V 1204, *Bürgerbund* to RWM/AA/RK 25.11.19; WA, Jahresbericht 1920, II, Warburg to A. Spitzer, 10.2.20.

[130] HA, HB, Carl Melchior, 'Zur auswärtigen Politik' (speech before Hamburg DDP) 20.2.20.

[131] Sterling Library, Yale, Paul M. Warburg Papers, Ser. II, Box 8, Folder 96, 'History of the European Memorandum'. Those who attended were: Keynes; van Vollenhove (Vice President of the Bank of the Netherlands); C.E. ter Meulen (of Hope & Co., Amsterdam); Georges Raphael Levy (a Parisian Senator); and Fred I. Kent, then acting as the temporary American representative on the Reparations Commission. Vissering also invited Benjamin Strong; but Strong, although sympathetic, could not attend: Federal Reserve Bank of New York, Benjamin Strong Papers, 1000.3, 'Diary of a Visit to Europe', pp. 111–15; 1150.0, Vissering to Strong, 21.8.19; Strong to Vissering, 23.8.19.

[132] Federal Reserve Bank of New York, Benjamin Strong Papers, 1000.3, Strong Diary, pp. 94f.; Sterling Library, Yale, Paul M. Warburg Papers, Ser. II, Box 8, Folder 96 (refers to an 'American credit organisation to finance essential exports from the US to European countries').

[133] Sterling Library, Yale, Paul M. Warburg Papers, Ser. II, Box 7, Folder 93, Minutes of Conference, 13.10.19; Keynes, *Collected Writings*, XVIII, pp. 128f., 'Notes on

by Scandinavian and Swiss bankers, reconvened in early November, this document was adopted and signed by numerous influential figures in the various European countries represented.[134] However, problems arose when Fred Kent, mindful of his official role at the Reparations Commission, sought the views of officials in the US Treasury, who insisted that the memorandum be addressed to national governments rather than the League, and who demanded the removal of four lines from the American version which referred to 'a deflation of the world's balance sheet'.[135] Even thus modified, the proposal for an international financial conference was still regarded as 'objectionable' in Washington since it risked awakening the hope 'that the American people through their Government will be called upon to assume the burdens of Europe by US Government loans'.[136]

This indication that the Americans were 'determined to do nothing' angered Keynes, who had already been unhappy with the modifications of the Amsterdam memorandum requested by Kent.[137] However, by the time the memorandum was published in January 1920, Keynes had managed to overshadow it almost completely with another publication of which he was the sole author. *The Economic Consequences of the Peace* was a brilliant polemic; but it is perhaps better remembered for its withering disparagement of the Allied leaders at Versailles than for its argument.[138] It would be an exaggeration to say that this was, in essentials, the argument put forward by Warburg, Melchior, Cuno and Witthoefft at the conference. But the resemblances to the Hamburg view are close; and it is not without significance that Keynes read a

Financial Conference at Amsterdam', pp. 136–48. Cf. Rosenbaum and Sherman, *M.M. Warburg & Co.*, p. 156; Golecki (ed.), *Kabinett Bauer* p. 627.
[134] WA, A. Vissering to Max Warburg and Carl Melchior, 10.1.20 (enclosing published versions of the appeal); Sterling Library, Yale, Paul M. Warburg Papers, Ser. I, Box 5, Folder 61, R.H. Brand to Warburg, 16.1.20.
[135] NAW, RG 59, 862.51/1237 1/2, Paul M. Warburg, Confidential Memorandum: 'Some Thoughts on Germany's Financial Future', 5.11.19; Sterling Library, Yale, Paul M. Warburg Papers, Ser. I, Box 5, Folder 59, Paul Warburg to Norman Davis, 17.11.19; Davis to Warburg, 26.11.19; Paul Warburg to Norman Davis, 26.11.19; and the versions of the document in Folder 61. See also the careful analysis of the German situation in the memorandum in *ibid.*, Ser. II, Box 7, Folder 91 (Memorandum on Europe), 5.12.19. It is striking that Benjamin Strong had contemplated similar measures as early as May 1919: Federal Reserve Bank of New York, Benjamin Strong Papers 1000.3, 'Draft Scheme for the Rehabilitation of Economic Life', 28.5.19. However, he declined to sign because of his 'intimate relations with our Treasury department': Federal Reserve Bank of New York, Benjamin Strong Papers, 1150.0, Strong to Vissering, 29.3.20.
[136] Sterling Library, Yale, Paul M. Warburg Papers, Ser. I, Box 5, Folder 60, Norman Davis to Paul Warburg, 7.1.20; Warburg to Davis, 12.1.20; Herbert Hoover to Warburg, 10.1.20; Carter Glass to US Chamber of Commerce, 28.1.20; Warburg to Leffingwell, 4.2.20; Box 61, Warburg to David Franklin Houston, 3.3.20.
[137] Keynes, *Collected Writings*, XVII, pp. 148–50.
[138] J.M. Keynes, *The Economic Consequences of the Peace* (London, 1919).

draft of the book to Paul Warburg and Melchior during the first of their meetings in Amsterdam.[139] Nor did Keynes deny the influence on him of the German experts.[140] Like them, he blamed the French for the 'Carthaginian' economic provisions of the Treaty and denounced the Reparations Commission as 'an instrument of oppression and rapine'.[141] Like them, he insisted that Germany 'had not surrendered unconditionally, but on agreed terms as to the general character of the peace' (the Fourteen Points and subsequent American notes).[142] And like them, he stressed that the loss of Germany's merchant marine, her overseas assets, her coal-rich territories and her sovereignty in matters of trade policy severely reduced her capacity to pay reparations. The Allies claimed compensation for damage and pensions amounting to 160 bn. gold marks, a sum which an asset-stripped Germany could only hope to pay out of her export earnings. Yet to turn the traditional German trade deficit into a surplus would put pressure on Allied business, while necessitating intolerable reductions in German consumption. Even leaving Germany with her essential assets (including the Silesian coal fields), 41 bn. gold marks was the most Germany could be expected to pay, three-quarters in the form of interest-free annuities spread over thirty years.[143] Nor did Keynes omit the apocalyptic warnings he had heard from Melchior at Versailles, conjuring up a vision of Malthusian crisis in Germany and the inflation-led destruction of capitalism in Eastern Europe:

The policy of reducing Germany to servitude for a generation, of degrading the lives of millions of human beings, and of depriving a whole nation of happiness [will. . .] sow the decay of the whole civilised life of Europe. [. . .] 'Those who sign this treaty will sign the death sentence of many millions of German men, women and children.' I know of no adequate answer to these words. [. . .] If we aim deliberately at the impoverishment of Central Europe, vengeance, I dare predict, will not limp. Nothing can then delay for very long the final civil war between the forces of Reaction and the despairing convulsions of Revolution, before which the horrors of the late German war will fade into nothing, and which will destroy, whoever is victor, the civilisation and the progress of our generation.[144]

---

[139] Keynes, *Collected Writings*, XVII, pp. 3–23.
[140] Keynes, *Economic Consequences*, p. 3: 'Those connected with the Supreme Economic Council [had. . .] learnt from the lips of the financial representatives of Germany and Austria unanswerable evidence of the terrible exhaustion of their countries.'
[141] *Ibid.*, pp. 25, 204.
[142] *Ibid.*, p. 51.
[143] *Ibid.*, pp. 102–200, 249f. These generous provisions make it hard to understand Keynes's dismissal of the German reparations counter-offer as 'somewhat obscure and also rather disingenuous' (p. 204).
[144] *Ibid.*, pp. 209, 212, 251.

Nothing short of 'a general bonfire' of international debts and a
German-led programme of economic reconstruction in Eastern Europe
would avert these calamities.[145]

In Hamburg, the publication of Keynes's book – and its enormous
success – was hailed as a breakthrough, auguring a sea-change in
British opinion. Melchior thought it 'magnetising' and 'a landmark for
a new development in [. . .] post-war history'.[146] Yet it was to prove
a false dawn. Quite simply, all the predictions of economic and political
disaster, which Keynes had imbibed from the German financial experts
at Versailles, turned out – in the all-important short run – to be
wrong. Instead of spiralling inexorably downwards, the mark – to the
dismay of the pessimists (including Keynes) who had been blithely
speculating against it – suddenly recovered. Instead of collapsing, the
German economy started to pick up. And instead of the wave of
Bolshevism sweeping into Germany, there was an attempted conservative *putsch*. The remainder of this chapter considers why the real
consequences of the peace were so at variance with the imagined
consequences.

The real economic consequences of the peace

In fact, the immediate economic significance of the Versailles Treaty
for Germany was far less than its critics claimed. Apart from the US,
all the combatant countries had emerged from the war with heavy
losses on their capital accounts. Britain had lost roughly 2.4 bn. gold
marks of investments and had sold off a further 16 m.; while French
investors had lost 16.8 bn. gold marks as a result of the Russian
revolution; a figure little different from the amount of overseas assets
taken away from Germans as a result of the war and the peace.[147]
Similarly, while Germany had lost the best part of her merchant fleet,
the total losses to world shipping during the war (the better part
of them inflicted by Germany) had totalled more than 15 m. tons.[148]
In any case, the significance of these lost assets should not be exaggerated:[149] shipping in particular was swiftly replaced, so that even as

---

[145] *Ibid.*, pp. 270–6. It is striking that Keynes here positively advocated a German
   eastward orientation, arguing that only German enterprise and organisation could
   reconstruct Russia: Germany's 'place in Europe' was 'as a creator and organiser of
   wealth for her Eastern and Southern neighbours'.
[146] Keynes, *Collected Writings*, X, pp. 427f.
[147] Hardach, *First World War*, p. 289.
[148] GHH, 408213/0 Karl Haniel, 'Das Problem des Schiffsraums', 19.5.19.
[149] The real annual losses in invisible income due to the peace terms have been estimated
   at just 200 m. gold marks: Kent, *Spoils of War*, pp. 98f. However, Kent's figure of
   40 m. gold marks for the annual income from German foreign securities surrendered
   to the Allies is too low; the correct figure must be in the region of 800 m. gold
   marks.

early as January 1919 total international capacity was only 9.5 per cent below its pre-war level, and by August of the same year that level had been surpassed.[150] Germany's total reparations burden had not yet been determined; but the money owed by the prospective recipients of reparations to the US already amounted to around 40 bn. gold marks.[151] In any case, reparations and inter-Allied debts were problems which could be postponed, pending diplomatic solutions; their impact on economic life in the year after Versailles was negligible. In the short run, the world economy boomed as businessmen rushed to replace inventories and plant run down during the war, and as trade links were restored which front lines, warships and submarines had disrupted. By 1920, international trade had recovered to 80 per cent of its pre-war level.[152] The monetary expansion generated by war finance, which had led to accumulations of cash balances in all the combatant economies, fuelled this up-swing.[153] Nor was economic recovery constrained by labour shortages. 9.8 million men had died in the conflict; but perhaps only in France did wartime mortality have serious economic consequences.[154] In Germany, because of pre-war demographic trends, there was, if anything, an excess of adult males in the post-war period.[155] True, wage costs had been pushed up by war and revolution;[156] but these were easily accommodated in the liquid monetary conditions of 1919/20. It was these underlying strengths which the Cassandras of Versailles had failed to take into account.

The war had left Hamburg's major firms with large liquid balances, and the government's policy of continued deficit spending to facilitate demobilisation served to boost these. In some cases – notably the compensation payments to the shipping industry – the process was direct. In October and November 1919 alone, Hamburg shipping lines applied for 1.8 m. marks of government funds, three-quarters of it to pay for contracts at Blohm & Voß; and by March 1920, a total of

[150] *Überseedienst*, Nr. 41, 23.7.19; *Weserzeitung*, Nr. 532, 16.8.19.
[151] Kindleberger, *Financial History*, p. 307; Henning, *Das industrialisierte Deutschland*, p. 45; D. Artaud, 'La question des dettes interalliées et la reconstruction de l'Europe', *Revue Historique*, 261 (1979), pp. 362–82.
[152] *Statistisches Jahrbuch für das Deutsche Reich*, 54. Jg. (Berlin, 1935), p. 118; I. Svennilson, *Growth and Stagnation in the European Economy* (Geneva, 1954), p. 292; League of Nations, *Memorandum on Production and Trade 1923–1926* (Geneva, 1928), pp. 29, 51.
[153] Aldcroft, *Versailles to Wall Street*, pp. 64ff.; C. P. Kindleberger, *The World in Depression, 1929–1939* (Harmondsworth, 1987), pp. 32ff.
[154] A. Sauvy, *Histoire économique de la France entre les deux guerres*, vol. I (Paris, 1965), p. 442.
[155] J. Reulecke, 'Veränderungen des Arbeitskräftepotentials im Deutschen Reich 1900–1933', in Mommsen *et al.* (eds.), *Industrielles System*, I, pp. 84–95.
[156] J.A. Dowie, '1919–20 is in Need of Attention', *EcHR*, 28, 3 (1975), pp. 429–50.

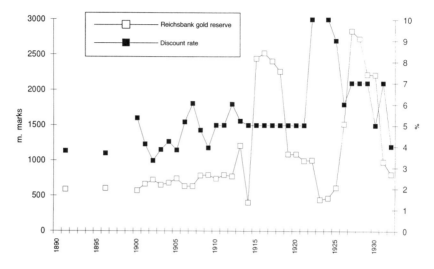

Figure 4.1 The Reichsbank: gold reserve and discount rate, 1890–1932
Sources: Kroboth, *Finanzpolitik*, pp. 490; Roesler, *Finanzpolitik*, pp. 208–14;
Holtfrerich, *Inflation*, p. 73; James, *Reichsbank*, pp. 358–63; Petzina et al.
(eds.), *Sozialgeschichtliches Arbeitsbuch*, III, pp. 71f.

20 m. marks had been requested, a third of the national aggregate.[157]
One set of government figures suggests that by the end of 1920, the
Hamburg lines had received a total of 1.15 bn. marks in the various
forms of compensation agreed by the government since the war.[158] For
the economy as a whole, the continued monetising of government
deficits by the Reichsbank provided liquidity indirectly. In the years
1919 and 1920, the volume of paper money in circulation and of
deposits at joint stock banks grew, in nominal terms, at annual rates
of around 70 per cent.[159] The money market was so easy that market
interest rates fell to between 3 and 3.5 per cent, despite the Reichsbank
discount rate remaining at 5 per cent (see figure 4.1).[160] A good
illustration of the position is provided by the Hapag. In 1913, the

---

[157] BAP, RFM 46580 N. Reg. 317/100, 'Übersicht betr. Anträge der Reedereien auf
    Erstattung von Überteuerungskosten'; 46583 N. Reg. 324/297–300, 'Übersicht betr.
    Anträge der Reedereien auf Erstattung von Überteuerungskosten'.
[158] BAP, RFM 46582 N. Reg. 322/275–85, 'Gutachten'. Figures up until April 1921
    for the shipping industry as a whole suggest that 1.652 bn. marks had been spent
    on compensation altogether; 46580 N. Reg. 319, 'Reichsausschuß für die Wiederher-
    stellung der Handelsflotte'. This indicates a much higher share of funds going to
    Hamburg than seems likely.
[159] Calculated from Holtfrerich, *Inflation*, pp. 50f.
[160] *Ibid.*, p. 73; Petzina et al. (eds.). *Sozialgeschichtliches Arbeitsbuch*, III, p. 71.

Hapag's liquid assets – cash, bank deposits, Treasury bills, commercial bills and other securities – had amounted to 54.4 m. marks: around 15 per cent of the firm's total capital value. In 1918, the figure was 164.1 m. marks; but by 1919, it had risen to 505.6 m. marks – 57 per cent of its total assets.[161] This meant that, despite having lost almost its entire fleet of ships, the Hapag was a fat potential investor. Blohm & Voß too managed to double its cash balances from 1917/18 to 1918/19, as it halved its workforce and collected its last war contract payments.[162] For such firms, financing investment from internal sources appeared a not unrealistic option. In addition, the banks had substantial liquid funds at the end of the war; and bank lending did much to fuel the investment upswing of 1919/20. Between 1919 and 1921, the balance sheets of the Hamburg joint stock banks all grew substantially in nominal terms, as they sought to channel increased deposits into new loans. The Commerz- und Diskontobank increased its lendings nearly fourfold between 1918 and 1920, 'dutifully' meeting the credit needs of its customers.[163] In 1920, both Blohm & Voß and Deutsche Werft issued debentures (largely taken up by their bankers) worth 20 m. marks and 30 m. marks.[164] The Shipping Loan Bank was especially open handed, lending 3.5 m. marks in 1919 and 7.7 m. marks in 1920 against existing ships. The stipulation that repayment be within twelve years gives a clear indication of the optimistic expectations about inflation then prevailing.[165]

Businessmen soon realised that money could be raised with equal if not greater ease on the stock market, which, with its promise of capital gains and inflated dividends, proved a magnet for savings once it was reopened in 1919.[166] There was a share boom in Hamburg, mainly reflecting the relative depression of the city's economy during the war and its alleviation by peace. The number of joint-stock companies rose by more than 50 per cent in Hamburg between the nadir of April 1919 and the end of 1920, compared with just 25 per cent for the Reich as a whole. The total share capital of Hamburg firms rose by roughly 170 per cent (from 763 to 2,069 m. marks); the national aggregate by only

[161] Calculated from Hapag, *Jahresbericht 1913; Jahresbericht 1914–1918; Jahresbericht 1919*.
[162] Blohm & Voß, *Jahresbericht 1917/18; Jahresbericht 1918/19*.
[163] See Commerz- und Diskontobank, *Jahresbericht 1919; Jahresbericht 1920*. The comparable increases for the Norddeutsche Bank and the Vereinsbank were closer to threefold. Figures calculated from Pohl, *Bankengeschichte*, pp. 119, 129.
[164] GHH, 300193012/5, Deutsche Werft (Bericht), 2.2.20; DW to Reusch 14.6.20; Blohm & Voß, *Jahresbericht 1920/21*. In addition, Deutsche Werft had short term borrowings totalling 4.35 m. marks from the Dresdner Bank.
[165] *50 Jahre Deutsche Schiffsbeleihungsbank*, pp. 62ff.
[166] Bresciani, *Inflation*, pp. 253–85.

75 per cent.[167] Contemporaries noted 'new firms springing up everywhere [while] the old firms increased their capital in proportion to the
fall of the mark'.[168] In the first quarter of 1921 alone, fourteen new
companies were floated with a total capital of 31 m. marks; and a further
twenty-four companies increased their share capital by 192 m. marks.[169]
Significantly, the big banks led the way: the Commerzbank, for example,
a leading light in the Shipping Loan Bank, raised its share capital from
85 m. marks to 200 m. marks in 1920.[170] Warburg's was heavily involved
in industrial share issues in 1920, organising major flotations for firms
like the oil company Stern-Sonneborn and the department store Karstadt.[171] Deutsche Werft trebled its capital.[172]

All these sources of cash could be tapped to finance post-war investment. However, it is important to distinguish between the various
forms of investment which businessmen could choose between. The
form associated in monetary theory with inflationary conditions is
investment in 'real values' – theoretically a rational response to currency
depreciation.[173] In fact, as the case of Hamburg shows, the expected
rate of depreciation was only one factor which businessmen took into
consideration when making investment decisions. Of more importance,
at least in the pre-hyperinflationary period, were assessments of future
market conditions. The Hapag contemplated a wide range of possible
investment opportunities in 1919 and 1920, including air travel (with
the AEG) and lignite production (with Warburg's).[174] However, given
the obvious shortage of shipping in Hamburg[175] and the willingness
of the government to finance reconstruction, it is perhaps not surprising
that the shipping lines concentrated their attention on their traditional
business. Because of obstacles to the simple purchase of existing vessels

---

[167] *Vierteljahreshefte zur Statistik des Deutschen Reiches* (1918), Ergänzungsheft II, p. 11;
      (1920), II, p. 106; (1921), III, p. 7; (1922), I, p. 151. Cf. the figures given by
      Webb for the Berlin stock exchange, Webb, *Hyperinflation*, p. 86. The corollary of
      this boom was an exceptionally low level of bankruptcy: *ibid.*, p. 99; Graham,
      Hyperinflation, p. 280.
[168] Rosenbaum and Sherman, *M.M. Warburg & Co.*, p. 158.
[169] NAW, RG 59, 862.00/1090, Stewart to State Dept., 30.4.21.
[170] Commerzbank, *Jahresbericht 1920*; Dresdner Bank, *Jahresbericht 1920*.
[171] WA, 'Jahresbericht 1920', pp. 22, 26.
[172] Claviez, *Deutsche Werft*, p. 41. For similar trends in industry, Feldman, *Iron and
      Steel*, p. 221.
[173] For a critical discussion of 'money demand'-based theories of inflation, see Lin-
      denlaub, *Maschinenbauunternehmen*, pp. 1–8, 48–57.
[174] HA, Cuno NL, material on Deutsche Luftschiffahrt AG, 1919/20; HA, HB, Holtzen-
      dorff to Cuno, 27.9.19, 28.9.19; GHH, 300193012/5, Scholz to Reusch, 14.4.20.
[175] As a result of the peace, the Hamburg lines had lost between 90 and 100 per cent
      of their vessels, with the Levant, Kosmos, German East African and Woermann Lines
      all wholly bereft: BAP, RFM 46582 N. Reg. 322/275–85, 'Gutachten: Aufstellung von
      Grundsätzen für die Fortsetzung der Zuschläge'.

abroad,[176] that meant orders for German yards. By April 1919, as we have seen, eighty-four orders had been placed by Hamburg lines. Blohm & Voß had fifteen orders in progress in July 1920, all from Hamburg lines; and by the end of the year Deutsche Werft had twenty-eight.[177] After the 40 per cent slump in 1919, the total of tonnage under construction rose by 110 per cent in 1920; while output reached nearly four times its 1918 level (see figures 1.2 and 2.2).

This high level of orders naturally raised the question of whether the shipyards themselves should invest in new plant. One clear decision to do so was taken by the companies who had set up Deutsche Werft. In July, 10 m. marks was made available to step up construction of the new yard.[178] Again, this decision was related less to money demand calculations than to projections about costs and orders; and illustrates the way manufacturing concerns – like banks – acted on the tacit assumption that the boom conditions would prevail for years, rather than months.[179] Despite warnings from Karl Haniel that a glut on the world shipping market would be swift in coming,[180] the management of the yard stuck to the wartime view that the post-war demand for light vessels would remain high for at least five years after the war, and around 60 m. marks was invested up until May 1921 in accommodation for workers and plant. The firm raised money from every source – its parent firms, the banks, the stock market – and embarked on a programme of long-term expansion.[181] Few of the existing shipyards were so sanguine, despite moderately good financial results in the year 1919/20.[182] At Blohm & Voß, for example, the belief that the company was suffering from excessive labour costs and overcapacity led instead to exceptionally high allowances for depreciation.[183]

In many ways a more rational form of investment in the immediate post-war period was the acquisition of existing companies to achieve

---

[176] BAP, RFM 46580 N. Reg. 319/99–108, Reichsausschuß für Wiederaufbau to RFM 1.6.20.

[177] Blohm & Voß, *Jahresbericht 1920/21*; Deutsche Werft, *Jahresbericht 1920*.

[178] GHH, 300193012/4, AEG to Reusch, 28.7.19.

[179] For the rationale of investing in ship-building from the GHH's point of view, GHH, 408213/0, 'Beteiligung der GHH an einer Schiffswerft', 17.3.18.

[180] For Haniel's pessimism, GHH, 408213/0 'Das Problem des Schiffsraums', 19.5.19; and similar criticisms of the high investment policy which prompted three members of the supervisory board to resign, GHH, 4001012012/39 (July 1920).

[181] Details of the investment programme in GHH, 300193012/4 (February/March, 1920); GHH, 300193012/6, Aufsichtsratssitzungen, 19.1.20; 9.9.20; Claviez, *Deutsche Werft*, pp. 29–41; GHH, *Denkschrift Nr. 30*, Bd. III (Oberhausen, 1930), pp. 29–43.

[182] NAW, RG 59, 862.00/1090, Stewart to State Dept., 16.7.20. Net profits on invested capital ranged from 2.9 per cent to 17.5 per cent.

[183] BAP, RFM 46582 N. Reg. 322/-, 'Referat über die Anträge auf Änderung des Normalwerkvertrages'; Blohm & Voß, *Jahresbericht 1919/20*.

increased concentration. There was a takeover and merger bonanza.[184] Although the most notorious style of concentration in the inflation years is that exemplified by the Siemens–Rhein–Elbe–Schuckert Union, which created unwieldy, vertically integrated concerns, it is important to stress that this was not the rule.[185] Vertical integration was a logical strategy for vulnerable economic sectors: thus a mine and foundry owner like Stinnes was prompted to invest in engineering and transport companies by his pessimism about heavy industry's long-term prospects.[186] Different calculations operated within the less crisis-ridden sectors which Stinnes wished to buy his way into. The Hapag had already had its period of vertical integration during the war, buying interests in land transport firms and travel agencies.[187] By the end of 1919, however, its objective was to rationalise the German shipping business. Throughout 1920 and 1921 vertical concentration in the shape of Stinnes battled with horizontal concentration in the shape of Cuno for control of the Hamburg lines – despite the fact that these lines scarcely existed other than on paper. In January 1920, the Hapag absorbed the Levant Line for 30 m. marks, at the same time issuing 5 m. marks of preference shares with multiple voting rights intended to give the firm 'the desired opportunity to secure [its] ties with other shipping lines [. . .] and to expand them in order to ensure mutual support against the influence of outsider concerns': a thinly veiled promise to oust Stinnes from the supervisory board positions he had built up by acquiring shares in the Hapag and the Woermann Lines.[188] Similar rationalisation went on in ship-building as the Deutsche Werft absorbed its prototype, the Hamburger Werft,[189] and in banking, where the Commerzbank absorbed over forty lesser banks, including the large Mitteldeutsche Privatbank (Magdeburg) in 1920 alone.[190]

The principal reason for optimism about Hamburg's economic future was the rapid recovery of German trade in 1919 and 1920. Such was the importance of the relationship between currency depreciation and merchandise flows in the minds of contemporaries that it merits closer empirical investigation; although it must be stressed that the data are

---

[184] Bresciani, *Inflation*, pp. 203–12.
[185] Feldman, *Iron and Steel*, pp. 210–79. Cf. idem, *Great Disorder*, pp. 272ff.
[186] Leckebusch, *Beziehung*, pp. 99ff.
[187] Hapag, *Jahresbericht 1914–18*.
[188] Hapag, *Jahresbericht 1920*; *Hamburgische Correspondent*, 3.1.20; 8.1.20. A cartoon in *Die Hamburger Woche*, No. 5 (1920), showed Cuno literally devouring three shipping lines served on a large plate. The issue of shares with multiple voting rights to friendly companies was a common device to reduce the risk of hostile takeovers.
[189] GHH, 300193012/1, Rathenau (proposal), 24.9.19; Claviez, *Deutsche Werft*, p. 35.
[190] Commerzbank, *Jahresbericht 1918; Jahresbericht 1919; Jahresbericht 1920*; Pohl, *Bankengeschichte*, p. 131.

perhaps the most problematical available for the period. German statistics do not record the substantial volumes of goods which passed
through the so-called 'Hole in the West', the customs-free frontier of the
occupied zone.[191] The statistics are also incomplete for the second half
of 1920 and the first half of 1921; and subsequent figures were often
called into question, for reasons discussed below.[192] Moreover, very different figures can be arrived at for the 'real' value of imports and exports
depending on which deflators are applied to the available paper mark
figures: if one uses the German wholesale price index on both import
and export figures, for example, no account is taken of the substantial
fluctuations in the terms of trade in the period. The distortion is still
greater if one simply converts volume figures into 1913 unit values on
the basis of pre-war price schedules.[193] Using the available monthly figures,[194] three different series of monthly trade figures can therefore be
provided: one expressed in terms of 1913 marks, simply deflating with
the wholesale price index; one adjusted to allow for the divergent tendencies of import and export prices; and one in volume terms.

Estimated annual figures from the first series show that in 1919 the
already wide wartime German trade deficit grew wider still, rising to
around 4.13 bn. gold marks, or 12 per cent of NNP; but fell close
to equilibrium in 1920 (see figure 4.2).[195] Monthly figures give a more
precise indication of the trend, showing the money trade deficit peaking
in July 1919, and thereafter narrowing until March and April 1920,
when a trade surplus was recorded (see figure 4.3). The surge in

[191] Witt, 'Staatliche Wirtschaftspolitik', pp. 177f.; Maier, *Recasting Bourgeois Europe*,
pp. 67–71; Feldman, *Iron and Steel*, p. 142; HKH, *Jahresbericht 1919*, pp. 19–22.
[192] See chapter 6.
[193] This explains why the annual figures calculated in this way in *Statistik des Deutschen
Reiches*, 317, p. 5, suggest such an improbably low trade deficit for the inflation
period as a whole (particularly 1922). The figures from this series cannot be reconciled
with the evidence discussed below for a substantial capital import during the inflation
years. This point is overlooked by Webb, *Hyperinflation*, pp. 89–92; Feldman, *Great
Disorder*, p. 600; and V. Hentschel, 'Zahlen und Anmerkungen zum deutschen
Außenhandel zwischen dem Ersten Weltkrieg und der Weltwirtschaftskrise', *Zeitschrift für Unternehmensgeschichte*, 31 (1986), pp. 95–9.
[194] Statistisches Reichsamt, *Monatliche Nachweise über den auswärtigen Handel Deutschlands 1920, 1921, 1922, 1923, 1924* (Berlin); Statistisches Reichsamt, *Das auswärtige
Handel Deutschlands in den Jahren 1920, 1921 und 1922 verglichen mit dem Jahre
1913 nach Warengruppen, Warengattungen und Ländern [Statistik des Deutschen Reiches,
Bd. 310]*, (Berlin, 1924); *Statistisches Jahrbuch für das deutsche Reich 1923*, pp. 189f.];
Bresciani, *Inflation*, p. 248.
[195] Annual goldmark figures for the inflation years are arrived at by interpolating the
missing months in the *Monatliche Nachweise* series. Slightly higher figures for the
trade deficit are given in: Keynes, *Collected Writings*, XVII, p. 251; XVIII, pp. 48,
54; Laursen and Pedersen, *Inflation*, pp. 69, 90, 101; Webb, *Hyperinflation*, pp.
76, 91.

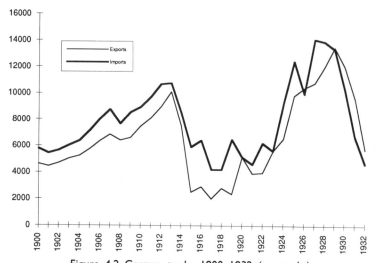

Figure 4.2 German trade, 1900–1932 (m. marks)
Sources: Hoffman et al., *Wachstum,* pp. 520f., 524f.; Hardach, *First World War,* p. 33; *Monatliche Nachweise;* Bresciani, *Inflation,* p. 248.

imports in the middle of 1919 was dammed partly by the imposition of customs in gold marks,[196] so that the value of German imports, which rose six-fold from 178 bn. gold marks in March 1919 to a peak of over 1 bn. gold marks in July 1919, fell to just 269 m. gold marks in February 1920; whereas the value of monthly exports fluctuated unsteadily between around 150 and 350 m. gold marks, before jumping to over 650 m. gold marks in July 1920. However, the gold mark figures disguise the significant fluctuations in the relative prices of imports and exports in the inflation years. Export prices did not rise as rapidly as import prices in 1919/20, reflecting above all the extent to which depreciation of the mark outstripped the rise in domestic prices; the deficit may therefore have been rather smaller in 'real' terms in 1919/20 (see figure 4.4). Such divergences are best measured by the real exchange rate (the nominal exchange rate divided by the ratio of German to foreign prices), which can be regarded as an index of German competitiveness (see figure 4.5).[197] Comparing this with the third series of trade figures – those for trade volumes – provides probably the clearest picture of the relationship between exchange

[196] StAH, DHSG II, III C 53 (1919), DHSG 10. Sitzung, 26.8.19; *Hamburger Fremden-blatt,* Nr. 458, 9.9.19; HKH, *Jahresbericht 1919,* pp. 19–22. Cf. C.-L. Holtfrerich, 'Deutscher Außenhandel und Goldzölle 1919 bis 1923', in Feldman et al. (eds.), *Anpassung,* pp. 472–84.
[197] See the details of computation in Holtfrerich, *Inflation,* pp. 22–5.

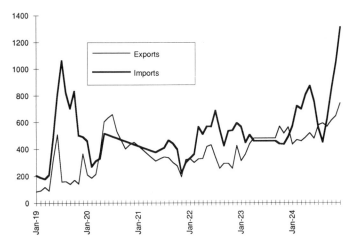

Figure 4.3 German trade in 1913 prices, 1919–1924 (m. gold marks)
Sources: Bresciani, *Inflation*, p. 248; Graham, *Hyperinflation*, p. 272; *Frankfurter Zeitung*; *Monatliche Nachweise*.

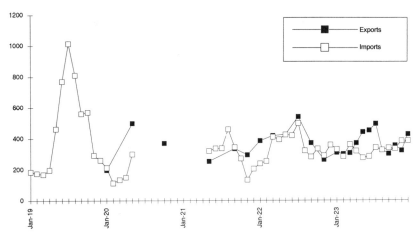

Figure 4.4 German trade: adjusted 1913 values, 1919–1923 (m. gold marks)
Sources: Bresciani, *Inflation*, p. 248; Graham, *Hyperinflation*, p. 272, table XVI; *Frankfurter Zeitung*; *Monatliche Nachweise*; Laursen and Pedersen, *Inflation*, pp. 133f.

rates, prices and merchandise trade (see figure 4.6).[198] It emerges that the volume of goods exported exceeded the volume of goods imported by some 2.3 m. tons in 1919 and 4.9 m. tons in 1920. Even in Hamburg, with its traditionally large volume deficit, the gap between

[198] Figures for trade volumes in Bresciani, *Inflation*, pp. 235, 448; Wagenführ, 'Die Industriewirtschaft', p. 26; Holtfrerich, *Inflation*, p. 212.

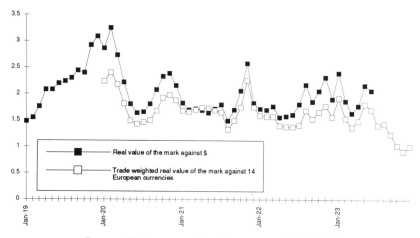

Figure 4.5 German real exchange rates, 1919–1923
Sources: Bresciani, *Inflation*, p. 446; Holtfrerich, *Inflation*, pp. 23f. Note:
1913 = 1. When index exceeds unity, competitiveness has increased.

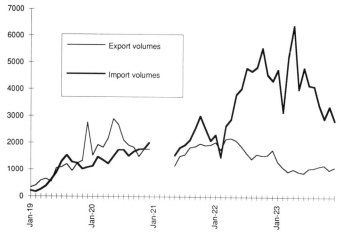

Figure 4.6 German trade volumes, 1919–1923 (000 tons)
Sources: Bresciani, *Inflation* p. 448; *Monatliche Nachweise*.

imports and exports quickly narrowed after the import surge of 1919.[199]
The figures are all the more remarkable in view of the very high
percentage of German imports which took the form of bulky food and
raw materials (76 per cent in 1920), and the high percentage (84 per

---

[199] See figure 2.1. Figures for the tonnage of *loaded* ships arriving and leaving suggest
that exports recovered more rapidly than imports in 1920/1, reaching 31 per cent
and 65 per cent of pre-war levels, compared with figures of 28 per cent and

cent) of German exports which took the form of compact finished goods.[200] It appears therefore that the weak mark did indeed lead to the 'dumping' of German exports at 'ridiculously low prices', as predicted by the German economic experts at Versailles.

It is clear that the majority of Germans assumed that this depreciation would continue. Max Warburg was not alone in seeking to pay off his firm's foreign currency liabilities, in the belief that they would only appreciate in mark terms.[201] At Deutsche Werft, optimism about orders from foreign shipping lines were based on the assumption that the mark would continue to fall, lowering the price of German goods to buyers from hard currency countries.[202] A number of textile firms also appear to have been banking on large export orders on the basis of this argument, with only a few lone voices nervously warning that 'the situation will be different if the mark rises, which is not out of the question'.[203] Moreover, the lifting of exchange controls in September 1919 meant that pessimistic Germans could 'flee' the mark in favour of foreign currency.[204] Heated objections to proposals by Erzberger to limit 'capital flight' suggest that this was being widely practised despite a supervisory board resolution to 'avoid speculation in foreign currency', Deutsche Werft elected not to repatriate 997,000 florins earned from the sale of four ships to a Dutch firm in 1920, leaving them in a Rotterdam bank account.[205] Pessimism about the mark manifested itself within Germany in falling demand for money: cash was moved from savings accounts into current accounts, and

---

62 per cent for imports: *Hamburger Statistische Monatsberichte 1924*, pp. 16, 238f.; *Statistisches Handbuch 1925*, pp. 157f.; *Statistisches Jahrbuch 1928/29*, p. 164.

[200] Figures for the structure of German post-war trade in Hentschel, 'Zahlen und Anmerkungen', p. 96; Keynes, *Collected Writings*, XVII, p. 251; Bresciani, *Inflation*, p. 194; Graham, *Hyperinflation*, pp. 214–25; Laursen and Pedersen, *Inflation*, p. 101.

[201] WA, 'Jahresbericht 1919', Melchior to Max Warburg, 5.8.19; Bresciani, *Inflation*, pp. 52f.; Feldman, *Great Disorder*, p. 178f. For similar expectations in industrial circles, see Feldman, *Iron and Steel*, pp. 132–8; Maier, *Recasting Bourgeois Europe*, p. 68.

[202] Claviez, *Deutsche Werft*, p. 32. See the accusation that Deutsche Werft was giving priority to foreign orders in BAP, RFM 46580 N. Reg. 317/38, Reichsausschuß für den Wiederaufbau der Handelsflotte, 26.11.19.

[203] Witthoefft was one of the few who anticipated the stabilisation of 1920; StAH, FA AOM 1, Bd. 10, 146, Witthoefft to Joesling, 20.12.19; Bd. 11, 136, Witthoefft to Chemnitzer Bank Verein, 21.2.20.

[204] Witt, 'Staatliche Wirtschaftspolitik', pp. 177f.

[205] On capital flight ordinances of September 1919, October 1919 and January 1920, see StAH, DHSG III, Pr. V 1, HKH to DHSG 29.9.19, 23.12.19. On Deutsche Werft, GHH, 300193012/4, Supervisory Board meeting, 24.9.19; 300193012/5, Deutsche Werft to Reusch, 14.6.20.

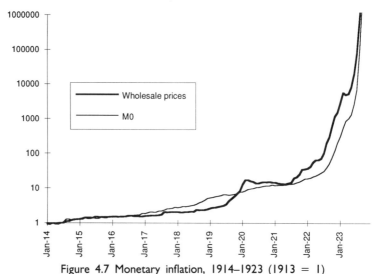

Figure 4.7 Monetary inflation, 1914–1923 (1913 = 1)
Sources: Bry, *Wages*, pp. 440–5; *Zahlen zur Geldentwertung*, p. 5; Holtfrerich,
Inflation, pp. 52ff.

transactions were increasingly made by giro transfers from one account to another.[206] This explains why, with a monetary growth rate of just 46 per cent in 1919, there was inflation of 228 per cent (see figure 4.7).[207] The effect of such pessimism on the exchange rate was even more pronounced – so long as it was shared by foreign currency speculators: by the end of 1919 the dollar had appreciated against the mark by around 465 per cent over the previous year. The more rapid rate of depreciation relative to domestic inflation explains why the price of German exports fell in real terms by around a third – confirming the point made above about the 'dumping' of German goods on the world market.[208]

Yet the expectation of further depreciation overlooked the strong countervailing tendencies being generated by Germany's economic recovery. According to one estimate, German NNP grew by 10 per cent in 1920 and 7 per cent in 1921.[209] Although German agriculture

---

[206] While savings deposits in Hamburg rose in nominal terms by just 22 per cent in 1919, giro transactions at the Hamburg branch of the Reichsbank went up by 129 per cent: *Statistisches Handbuch 1925*, pp. 235f. The velocity of circulation rose from 0.45 in December 1918 to 3.2 in March 1920: Bresciani, *Inflation*, p. 168, Graham, *Hyperinflation*, p. 105.

[207] Figures for the year December 1918–December 1919.

[208] Bresciani, *Inflation*, pp. 200, 248, 446f.

[209] See figure 2.3 Figures from Witt, 'Finanzpolitik', p. 424.

continued to languish,[210] indicators of industrial output show a sharp upward trend: up 46 per cent in 1920 and 20 per cent in 1921, with certain industries (notably ship-building and coal) experiencing especially rapid growth.[211] From a foreign point of view, this combination of rapid growth and a weak exchange rate appeared contradictory.[212]

To some extent, the recovery of foreign confidence in the mark was a side effect of Germany's immense appetite for imports in 1919. With export earnings at such low levels, the inward flow of food and raw materials could only be sustained by credits from foreign suppliers. In the first instance, this meant American suppliers: between 1919 and 1921, German imports from the United States totalled $776 m., according to US figures; Germany's trade deficit with the US rose from 246 m. gold marks in 1919 to 932 m. gold marks in 1920 and 1,226 m. gold marks in 1921 – almost equivalent to the entire German trade deficit given in the official German statistics (see figure 4.8).[213] As we have seen, the Hamburg commercial community hurried to make contact with American exporters after the signing of the armistice; and there was no shortage of interested American firms.[214] However, efforts to create large-scale channels for American import credits to Germany, such as the Deutsche Waren-Treuhand AG, a holding company set up by Hamburg firms in February 1920, tended to fall foul of the US Treasury.[215] The successful negotiation of a 200 m. florin

[210] Statistics for agricultural output in Bresciani, *Inflation*, p. 192; Graham, *Hyperinflation*, p. 285; Laursen and Pedersen, *Inflation* pp. 135f.; Holtfrerich, *Inflation*, p. 182; James, *German Slump*, pp. 250f.

[211] See figures 2.4, 2.5, 2.6 and 2.7. Figures from Wagenführ, 'Die Industriewirtschaft', pp. 23–8; Bresciani, *Inflation*, pp. 193f.; Graham, *Hyperinflation*, pp. 287, 292; Hoffmann *et al.*, *Wachstum*, pp. 358f., 383–5, 388, 390–3; Laursen and Pedersen, *Inflation*, p. 136; Feldman, *Iron and Steel*, pp. 474f.

[212] On the divergence of foreign and domestic expectations, reflecting partly the fact that foreign speculators were staking less than ordinary Germans, see Kindleberger, *Financial History*, p. 318; Holtfrerich, *Inflation*, p. 290.

[213] Cf. Holtfrerich, *Inflation*, pp. 214f.; Webb, *Hyperinflation*, p. 91. Twenty-one per cent of American cotton exports and 30 per cent of American copper exports went to Germany in 1921: cf. NAW, RG 39, G114.2, 17.

[214] HA, Holtzendorff to Vorstand, No. 973, 5.1.19; No. 976, 10.1.19; No. 979, 10.1.19; Holtzendorff to Cuno. 10.4.19; NAW, RG 39, G111, W.C. Tingle (Standard Oil) to Leffingwell, 13.8.19; Merchants National Bank to Secretary of State, 22.9.19; G114.1, Postau & Son to Glass, 29.9.19.

[215] WA, 'Jahresbericht 1920'; Warburg *Aufzeichnungen*, p. 93; StAH, FA AOM 1, Bd. 11, 220, Witthoefft to Lincke, 6.3.20. The Treuhand was intended to specialise in *Veredelungskredite* – advances of raw materials from foreign suppliers who would wait for payment until the materials had been turned into a finished product and exported. For official opposition in Washington (where any credits to Germany were seen as increasing the pressure for a government loan) see: NAW, RG 39, G114.1, State Department, War Trade Board Circular 802, 14.7.19; G111, Ass. Sec. at Treasury to Leffingwell and Davis, 5.8.19; Carter Glass to Secretary of State, 9.8.19; Lansing to Glass, 3.10.19; G114.1, Leffingwell Memorandum, 11.11.19. Leffingwell

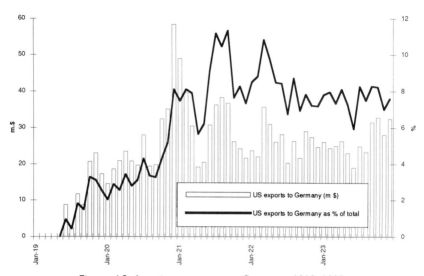

Figure 4.8 American exports to Germany, 1919–1923
Source: Holtfrerich, 'Germany and the International Economy', pp. 280–3.

credit from the Dutch state in January 1920 represented a drop in the ocean of the German trade deficit;[216] and even the International Acceptance Bank (IAB) – an ambitious venture set up in early 1921 by Warburg's and a consortium of Swiss, American, British, Dutch and Swedish banks – was only able to raise $9 m. to finance grain imports.[217]

In fact, the greater part of the German deficit in 1919/20 was financed not by large-scale foreign loans but by numerous, small-scale purchases of paper marks by foreigners. This was a speculative wave much remarked upon at the time. When Benjamin Strong visited Europe in August 1919, he was told by bankers in Amsterdam that 'every servant and carpenter in Belgium owned some marks, the poorer people carrying the actual Reichsbank notes, and those of larger means having

took the view that 'the best way to do business with Germany now and until the Reparations Commission shall have acted is on the basis of barter'.
[216] NAW, RG 39, GIII, American Embassy the Hague, to State Dept., 28.9.19; WA, 'Jahresbericht 1920'; Warburg, *Aufzeichnungen*, p. 93. Cf. Schröder, 'Handelspolitik'.
[217] On the IAB, which was first conceived of at a meeting beween Max Warburg, Paul Warburg and a group of Swiss bankers at St Moritz in the late summer of 1919: WA, 'Jahresbericht 1919'; 'Jahresbericht 1920', Warburg to Wirth, 6.12.20; NAW, RG 59, 862.00/1014, Stewart to State Dept., 23.8.20; Sterling Library, Yale, Paul M. Warburg Papers, Series 1, Box 5, Folder 62, Paul Warburg to N.M. Rothschild & Sons, London (n.d); Rosenbaum and Sherman, *M.M. Warburg & Co.*, p. 159. For the abortive 'Chandler' scheme for loans to Germany secured on frozen German assets in the US, see Kohlhaus, 'Die Hapag', pp. 82–5.

balances in German banks. The same thing has taken place in Scandinavia and, more striking still, [. . .] Americans were buying hundreds of millions of marks [. . .] for speculation.'[218] In October, Keynes heard that 'the aggregate foreign holding of marks has now reached the prodigious figure of 20 milliards'. 'The speculation,' he noted three months later, was 'on a tremendous scale and was, in fact, the greatest ever known.'[219] Recent research confirms these impressions. There was clearly a tendency for foreign visitors to Germany (of which there were many in the early 1920s) or people living in former occupied territory to retain marks in the hope of the currency's recovery. On a larger scale, foreign deposits at the seven Berlin great banks rose from 13.7 bn. marks in 1919 to 41.6 bn. marks in 1921, and accounted for almost a third of total deposits.[220] Purchases of marks in New York totalled 60 m. gold marks between July 1919 and December 1921.[221] At the same time, mark-denominated bonds became a popular investment, the state of Hamburg leading the way, as we have seen, with an unlimited issue of $4\frac{1}{2}$ per cent bonds which raised 48.6 m. marks in 1919 alone.[222] Some foreign investors were also attracted by German shares (for example, the Guggenheims bought 25 m. marks of AEG shares through Warburg's in May 1920), others by German real estate.[223] As far as can be established, there was a net capital inflow to Germany of around 13 bn. gold marks in the years 1919–23, with the lion's share coming in 1919, 1921 and the first half of 1922.[224]

[218] Federal Reserve Bank of New York, Benjamin Strong Papers, 1000.3, 'Diary of A Visit to Europe', pp. 65ff.

[219] J.M. Keynes, 'The Present State of the Foreign Exchanges', in *Collected Writings*, XVII, pp. 130f., 176. See also his later analysis, 'Speculation in the Mark and Germany's Balances Abroad', *Collected Writings*, XVIII, pp. 47–58.

[220] Holtfrerich, *Inflation*, p. 288.

[221] Webb, *Hyperinflation*, p. 57.

[222] Lippmann, *Leben*, p. 320. On Berlin's loan of 70.8 m. marks, see Feldman, *Great Disorder*, p. 204. For attempts by other municipalities to borrow abroad, see NAW, RG 39, GIII, Carter Glass to Secretary of State, 9.8.19; Leffingwell to American Mission, Paris, 13.10.19; Seasongood, Haas and Macdonald to Treasury Department, 17.11.19; First National Bank of Pittsburgh, 28.11.19. Paul Warburg was a strong proponent of such bond issues: Sterling Library, Yale, Paul Warburg Papers, Ser. II, Box 11, Folder 134, Paul Warburg, 'Investment of American Capital Abroad', Council on Foreign Relations dinner, 2.4.19.

[223] WA, 'Jahresbericht 1920', p. 15; Lyth, '*Mittelstand*', p. 448. For anxieties about the dangers of *Überfremdung* of national wealth, see StAH, SK II, III A I a 5, RWM Schmidt to Länder, 21.11.19; Senat to RWM, 9.2.21; HKH, HKHP, 20.2.20.

[224] Estimates of this capital inflow include Keynes's (12–15 bn. gold marks), Graham's (15.6 bn. gold marks) and Holtfrerich's (15 bn. gold marks). I arrive at the figure of 12.8 bn. gold marks by tallying my own extrapolated trade figures with the best available figures on reparations (and including Laursen and Pedersen's modest estimates for the service and gold balances): see table 2. Keynes and the McKenna committee sought to distinguish between purely speculative purchases of paper marks (2–3 or 0.7 bn. gold marks); foreign accounts in German banks (3 or 8 bn. gold marks); short-term business credits (0.5–1 bn. gold marks); and investment in

Perhaps the most striking instance of German-American economic reintegration brought together the Hapag and the Harriman concern – though the extent to which the Americans invested in the German firm is unclear. Adapting the idea which had been raised at Versailles of foreign participation in the German shipping lines, Cuno proposed a partnership between an American line and the Hapag to operate the Hapag's pre-war network of routes, insisting coolly that, although the Hapag had no ships at its disposal, the quality of its accumulated experience justified a strictly equal relationship.[225] In effect, Cuno wanted an American company to provide the Hapag with ships to operate half its old services until it had either recovered its confiscated vessels, or built new ones; in return for which the American company would get to operate the other half of the Hapag's pre-war routes. It was a bluff; but it appealed to the young Averell Harriman, and in June the outlines of the deal were made public.[226] The Hapag–Harriman deal was greeted in Germany as 'a step back to *Weltgeltung*'.[227]

Historians have tended to follow Keynes and other contemporaries in emphasising the net gain made by the German economy when these loans were rendered worthless by inflation.[228] However, in the short run, the effect of these capital inflows was to fund the German trade deficit, stabilise the German currency and stop inflation. In March

German securities and real estate (1 or 1.5 bn. gold marks). But these figures are little more than guesses. One of the many problems which arise is estimating the real value of any interest and dividend payments made to foreign lenders; cf. PA/ AA, Sonderref. W, Finanzwesen, 16A, Bd. 1, 3624/22, Reichswirtschaftsrat, 2. Sitzung, 17.10.22 (comments by Dauch).

[225] On the origins of the Hapag–Harriman agreement, see HA, HB, Holtzendorff to Cuno, 23.6.19; 1.8.19; 10.10.19; Holtzendorff Notizen, 29.3.20; Cuno to Holtzen-dorff, 7.5.20; Kohlhaus, 'Die Hapag', pp. 66–8; Hapag, *Jahresbericht 1920*; and the extensive press cuttings in Hamburg Weltwirtschaftsarchiv.

[226] Kohlhaus, 'Die Hapag', pp. 74, 171; *Hamburger Fremdenblatt*, 1.7.20.

[227] *Schiffahrt Zeitung*, 7.6.20; *Hamburgische Correspondent*, 7[?].6.20. See also Krohn, 'Zusammenbruch', pp. 233f.; H. Priester, *Der Wiederaufbau der deutschen Handels-schiffahrt. Ein Beitrag zur Wirtschaftsgeschichte der Gegenwart* (Berlin, 1926), pp. 97–110.

[228] For early comments to this effect, see NAW, RG 39, G110 (20–4), F.A. Vanderlip to C.A. Stone, 8.9.21; Keynes, 'Record Depreciation of the Mark', 9.11.21, *Collected Writings*, XVIII, p. 10; Keynes, 'Speculation in the Mark and Germany's Balances Abroad', 28.9.22, *Collected Writings*, XVIII, pp. 47–58. Cf. C.-L. Holtfrerich, 'Ameri-kanischer Kapitalexport und Wiederaufbau der deutschen Wirtschaft 1919–1923 im Vergleich zu 1924–1929', *VSWG*, 64 (1977), pp. 497–529; Schuker, 'American "Reparations" to Germany', *passim*. Schuker probably exaggerates the net gain when he attempts to compare reparations with foreign lending wiped out by inflation (and later by depression). Once allowance is made for German capital flight and repay-ments, the total 'gain' over the whole period (1919–32) is only slightly more than total reparations: 21 bn. gold marks compared with 19 bn. gold marks. Such neo-mercantilist calculations tend to obscure the American economy's gain from the high German demand for American exports, and the low cost to Americans of German exports; cf. Lindenlaub, *Maschinenbauunternehmen*, pp. 103–19.

1920, the mark suddenly ceased falling against the dollar and rallied, rising from a rate of 99.11/$ to a peak of 30.13/$ in June. In the months after March, all the trends of the previous eight months were reversed: export prices rose, and the gap between German prices and world market prices abruptly closed.[229] This development came as a shock in Hamburg, as elsewhere in Germany: Warburg, hastily rearranging his bank's portfolio, confessed that he could 'not understand the exchange rate movement at all' and attributed it to the speculations of 'an extraordinarily powerful group'.[230] Nor were the losses confined to German pessimists. Keynes himself lost around £13,125 of his own money and £8,498 of his friends', invested on the assumption that the economic consequences of the peace would be as he had forecast.[231] It was not until some time later that he and Warburg fully grasped what had happened:

The mark is viewed with such incredible confidence abroad – which is more than we can feel. We are living off the credit of earlier decades. The foreigners persuade themselves that we Germans have the industrious character to emerge from all this misery. It is the only explanation for the high mark exchange rate.[232]

Or as Keynes put it in September 1922:

[From] itinerant Jews in the streets of the capitals [. . .to] barber's assistants in the remotest townships of Spain and South America [. . .] the argument has been the same. [. . .] Germany is a great and strong country; some day she will recover; when that happens the mark will recover also, which will bring a very large profit. So little do bankers and servant girls understand of history and economics.[233]

'History and economics' – and hindsight – might well point to the possibility of further depreciation, irrespective of economic 'fundamentals', but those who had ignored history and economics had been right about the mark in the short run. The reality was that anyone visiting Hamburg in 1920 saw little sign of the calamities predicted by Keynes after Versailles. In May, Harry Graf Kessler marvelled at

the Alster alive with hundreds of boats making pleasure trips to and fro [. . .] Thousands of people going in and out of the boat house, looking for places

---

[229] *Zahlen zur Geldentwertung*, p. 10; Bresciani, *Inflation*, pp. 200, 248, 446f.

[230] WA, 'Jahresbericht 1920', I, Max Warburg to Fritz Warburg, 11.4.20. Other evidence of surprise in GHH, 300193012/5, Deutsche Werft to Reusch, 27.5.20; Reusch to Deutsche Werft, 31.5.20; Lindenlaub, *Maschinebauunternehmen*, pp. 52f.

[231] Keynes, *Collected Writings*, XVII, p. 131; Harrod, *Keynes*, pp. 288–95; R. Skidelsky, *John Maynard Keynes*, vol. II: *The Economist as Saviour* (London, 1993), p. 41.

[232] WA, X, 'Pol. Corr. 1921', Warburg (speech before RWM Scholz), 17.12.20.

[233] Keynes, 'Speculation in the Mark', p. 48.

to sit, families enjoying chocolate ices and raspberry juice at five marks a
throw. You would think El Dorado had been discovered.[234]

Five months later a French visitor, who expected to find the
place 'dead', instead found 'in the harbour, the warehouses, docks
and wharfs [there are] crates and food in abundance [. . .] Swarms
of workers work methodically and with discipline [. . .and] there
is food from every corner of the globe to be found in the shops.
One looks in vain for any sign of Germany's defeat.'[235] Indeed it
had been, as Warburg admitted, 'a year of crass contradictions';
but the contradictions lay principally in his and Keynes's earlier
analysis.[236] A trade deficit did not necessarily mean continual,
inexorable depreciation of the currency; it simply meant depreciation
to the point at which Germany achieved an export surplus, or a level
of deficit which foreign lenders were willing to fund. Ironically, it was
precisely the policies of liberalisation which Warburg had advocated
which had ensured that the economic situation stabilised. Where
Warburg had erred had been in exaggerating the importance of
Germany's lost assets in the context of the post-war boom; and in
assuming that American capital could only have a stabilising effect on
the German situation if lent to Germany through a formal international
loan.

The political consequences of the peace

Having argued that the impact of Versailles on the German economy
would be calamitous, the Hamburg group thus found themselves over-
taken by economic stabilisation. But what of the second argument they
had advanced against the peace treaty – namely that its economic
consequences would drive Germany to the Left, into the arms of
Bolshevism? We have already seen how inflationary policies in 1919
had the effect of shifting the conflicts of the revolutionary period from
the streets to the workplace. As employment levels rose after the lifting
of the blockade, the battle for political power of November 1918–July
1919 was transformed into a battle for purchasing power, with employee
groups growing increasingly confident in their use of collective action
to adjust nominal wage rates upwards in step with inflation. The
success they had in this regard does much to explain the relative
decline in influence of the radical Left in the course of 1920. The

---

[234] Harry Graf Kessler, *Tagebücher. 1918 bis 1937* (Frankfurt am Main, 1982), p. 230.
[235] PA/AA, Po. 5 s. I, German ambassador in Paris to AA, 11.10.20.
[236] Warburg, *Aufzeichnungen*, p. 93.

failure of other social groups to compensate for inflation with equal success, on the other hand, does much to explain why, contrary to the predictions made at Versailles, it was the radical Right which flourished in 1920.

It is true that, by comparison with the lean years between mid 1916 and mid 1919, the two years after the signing of the Versailles treaty were times of prosperity for most Germans. In nominal terms, the cost of living did not significantly increase between February 1920 and May 1921; indeed rents continued to lag significantly behind inflation.[237] Despite a dramatic 19 per cent increase in the population of Hamburg – caused not only by demobilisation and a recovery of the birth-rate, but above all by a significant amount of in-migration[238] – unemployment fell rapidly from its peak of around 24 per cent (of the employed population) in the middle of 1919 to around 7 per cent in 1920/1.[239] From their nadir in February 1920, real wages and salaries rose sharply over the rest of the year, generally reaching peaks around the middle of 1921.[240] Food consumption indices were depressed by pre-war standards; but per capita consumption of sugar, rice, salt, cocoa and, above all, tobacco, had fallen less than per capita real income between 1913 and 1921, suggesting that Germans were beginning to increase their propensity to consume in response to inflation.[241] Available indicators of public health (with the exception of infant mortality) also improved after the low-point of 1917/18, the mortality rate falling from 19.2 per 1,000 in 1918 to 12.0 in 1921; while there was a marked increase in marriages and births – a common

---

[237] See figure 3.5.
[238] See figure 1.3. Cf. *Statistisches Handbuch 1927*, pp. 8f.; *Aus Hamburgs Verwaltung und Wirtschaft*, 4. Jg. (April 1927), p. 104. Between 1919 and 1925, 72 per cent of the net increase in population was due to in-migration, compared with just 28 per cent due to natural increase. Note also the exceptionally low level of emigration from Germany in the years 1919 and 1920: Petzina *et al.* (eds.), *Sozialgeschichtliches Arbeitsbuch*, III, pp. 35, 62.
[239] See figures 3.1 and 2.10 for the parallel national trend. Additional data on employment in Laursen and Pedersen, *Inflation*, pp. 136f.; Scholz, 'Lohn und Beschäftigung'. Note the depressed levels of productivity, suggesting a degree of overmanning in German industry: Laursen and Pedersen, *Inflation*, pp. 136ff.; Bry, *Wages*, pp. 403ff.; Graham, *Hyperinflation*, p. 295.
[240] See figures 2.11, 2.12, 3.6 and 3.7. Cf. the figures in Scholz, 'Lohn und Beschäftigung', p. 286; Lindenlaub, *Machinebauunternehmen*, p. 235. Per capita real incomes rose by 9 per cent in 1920 and 8 per cent in 1921: Witt, 'Finanzpolitik und sozialer Wandel', pp. 424f.
[241] Graham, *Hyperinflation*, p. 305; Bry, *Wages*, p. 233. This may also be inferred from the fall in a very rough ratio of new savings to pay increments in 1921 (5 per cent) relative to 1920 (7 per cent), calculated from figures in *Hamburger Statistische Monatsberichte*, 13 (1922), p. 24; *Statistisches Handbuch 1920*, pp. 364f., *Statistisches Handbuch 1925*, pp. 201, 236.

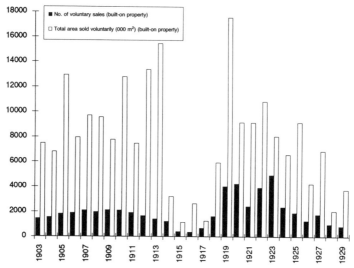

Figure 4.9 The Hamburg property market, 1903–1929
Source: *Statistisches Handbuch 1929/30*, p. 125.

phenomenon in the aftermath of wars, but also a sign of relative economic optimism.[242]

Yet these aggregate benefits of economic recovery were more evenly distributed than was traditional in German society. For the educated and propertied bourgeoisie, the sense of relative deprivation which had been so strong in the war persisted despite economic recovery. There is good reason to think that the exceptionally high level of property sales in 1919 reflected not only the desire of landlords to get rid of investments on which the real return (frozen rents) was constantly diminishing, but also the more general pressure on middle-class families to liquidate fixed assets in order to maintain established patterns of consumption (see figure 4.9). When a friend advised Franz Witthoefft against selling his 123 hectare estate at Luetjensee, he made the point that 'land is in many respects better than German money'; but Witthoefft evidently needed the cash.[243] It was also around this time that the first discussions were heard of the 'proletarianisation' of bourgeois

---

[242] National figures in Petzina *et al.* (eds.), *Sozialgeschichtliches Arbeitsbuch*, III, pp. 32f.; Hamburg figures in *Statistisches Handbuch 1929/30*, pp. 51, 61. The number of marriages as a percentage of Hamburg's population was higher in 1920 than in any other year between 1841 and 1929. It is striking that so many new households were being formed, despite a serious shortage in housing: Lyth, *Inflation*, p. 103.

[243] StAH, FA AOM 1, Bd. 10, 146, Witthoefft to Joesling, 20.12.18.

groups, particularly senior civil servants like judges.[244] In the private sector, established firms complained of the competition from men like the 'apprentice of nineteen years' described to the American consul, 'who before the war earned no wages, but after a time in the army became a lieutenant and later captain and was paid more money than he ever dreamed of earning': such men were now opening 'their own offices and are doing business for their own account with very little capital and no credit'.[245] The very high numbers of students at German universities from 1920 until the end of the inflation can, on the other hand, be seen as an indicator of concealed bourgeois unemployment – a flight into *Bildung* in the face of economic uncertainty;[246] though other elements of the traditional bourgeois education had to be sacrificed. As Max Warburg noted:

Periodicals, learned societies, cultural enterprises of every kind that were nurtured for decades have had to be given up. [. . .] Sons and daughters can no longer be educated to the standard that had formerly been taken for granted. Fine houses and old family heirlooms must be sold. There is a silent poverty [. . .] developing which, in the case of pensioners, rentiers and all those dependent on fixed incomes, is proving utterly hopeless.[247]

Even bourgeois pleasures such as travel were curtailed. The 10,000 marks which Percy Schramm inherited during the war, which was intended to finance a trip to Brazil, sufficed only to get him to Italy; while his parents suffered the indignity of running out of money during a trip less far afield, to Mecklenburg.[248]

Yet arguably of more importance than the material difficulties experienced by bourgeois groups in this period was the crisis of values which appeared to accompany post-war recovery. For Percy Schramm's uncle, speculating against the mark was simply 'not the done thing'.[249] Similarly, the increase in consumption detectable in economic statistics manifested itself in a hedonism which those inculcated with nineteenth-century precepts of frugality and abstemiousness found repellent. One British officer in 1919 was struck by the way a combination of 'apathy' and 'nervous excitability' gave rise to 'a desire for distraction at any cost' and an 'anomalous outburst of dancing and reckless extravagance

[244] See, e.g., Oberamtsrichter Hertz, 'Die Proletarisierung des Richterstandes?', *Hamburger Fremdenblatt*, 10.2.20; Landrichter Denmer, 'Rechtspflegegarantien und Richterbesoldung', *Hamburger Nachrichten*, 23.3.20.
[245] NAW, RG 59, 862.00/807, Stewart to State Dept., 12.2.20.
[246] Petzina *et al.* (eds.), *Sozialgeschichtliches Arbeitsbuch*, III, p. 169.
[247] Rosenbaum and Sherman, *M.M. Warburg & Co.*, pp. 125f. Cf. WA, 'Jahresbericht 1920', Blatt 30, for Warburg's own support for various educational and charitable foundations.
[248] Schramm, *Neun Generationen*, II, pp. 371, 512.
[249] *Ibid.*, 407.

in other amusements'. Other foreign observers seeking 'civic con-
science' found only 'profound moral degeneration':

Idle women go to prostitution; idle men agitate or drift into crime. Men have
lost the sense of responsibility for their families, their trade or for the state;
the whole situation represents a storm-and-stress period.[250]

The American consul noted a typical affront to traditional values in
1920: 'On Good Friday dancing parties were permitted and the prohib-
ition against the many picture theatres for the same day was lifted.
[. . .] Not to be wondered at in a socialistic city, but [. . .] a source
of annoyance and mortification to many.'[251] The post-war dance craze
too had, in some eyes, an apocalyptic aspect:

> Soon we shall be the world's beggars and slaves;
> What's that to us?
> We'll keep dancing so long as the fiddle still plays;
> We'll dance and we'll dance by the fiery abyss;
> With blindfolded eyes we'll go down like this –
> Still dancing.[252]

The same connection between hedonism and national decline was
widely made with respect to changing sexual mores, though the notorious Weimar 'wave of eroticism' is not easily quantified.[253] Criminality
certainly appeared to be on the increase. The number of criminal
prosecutions in Hamburg in 1919 was 77 per cent above that of the
previous year, with the trend continuing upwards in 1920. As national
figures for convictions indicate, the increase was mainly accounted for
by crimes against property: clearly, if inflation allowed the state to
expropriate wealth by legal means, many people felt less compunction
about making their own, small-scale expropriations (see figure 4.10).[254]
The theft in March 1920 of 600,000 marks intended to pay unemployment benefit was seen as 'a climax to the numerous robberies reported
daily'.[255] Moreover, the proliferation of petty economic regulations
since the war – for example, against smuggling – tended to diminish

---

[250] Offer, *Agrarian Interpretation*, pp. 390f. See in general Bessel, *Germany*, pp. 220ff.,
246f., 249f.

[251] NAW, RG 59, 862.00/911, Stewart to State Dept., 5.4.20.

[252] Lippmann, *Leben*, p. 240.

[253] There was clearly a sharp increase in the divorce rate in Hamburg from around 9
per 10,000 inhabitants before the war to a peak of 22.6 in 1920: *Statistisches Handbuch
1929/30*, p. 42; but the evidence is less clear-cut on prostitution, homosexuality and
abortion, all of which were said by conservative commentators to have increased:
cf. Usborne, *Politics of the Body in Weimar Germany*, pp. 69ff.

[254] Figures for Hamburg in NAW, RG 59, 862.00/952, Stewart to State Dept., 9.5.20; /
1044, 22.11.20.

[255] NAW, RG 59, 862.00/824, Stewart to State Dept., 23.3.20. A spate of suicides in
the same week was seen as another 'sorrowful sign of the times'.

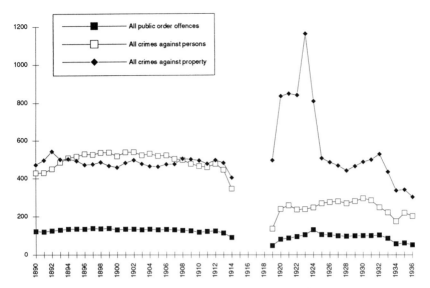

Figure 4.10 Crime rates, 1890–1936 (per 100.000 citizens)
Source: Hohorst *et al.* (eds.), *Sozialgeschichtliches Arbeitsbuch*, II, pp. 168ff.;
Petzina *et al.* (eds.) *Sozialgeschichtliches Arbeitsbuch* III, pp. 137ff.

since the war – for example, against smuggling – tended to diminish
respect for the law, since these were so difficult to enforce, and
created opportunities for bribery.[256] In October 1919, Keynes voiced
the widespread view that there had been an increase in official corruption since the war: 'Everybody in Germany [. . .] who is concerned
with the movement of goods now takes bribes, and Germany, which
was formerly quite incorruptible in this respect, is getting down to
the Russian level.'[257] The American Consul in Hamburg echoed this:

A great deal is heard among businessmen about the lack of honor and integrity
among the official classes as well as working men, a trait that prior to the
war was the pride of all Germans. Among the railway operatives, customs
employees and many other branches of the Government service, conditions
exist that parallel those in Mexico. Formerly no one would think of offering
a bribe to any railway or customs employee, but now [. . .] each and every
one has his price and bribes must be paid in order to do business.[258]

Even the customary social manners of bourgeois society appeared to
be under attack. Schramm's uncle regarded it as an affront to his

[256] See the reports of smuggling in GStA, Rep. 84a Justizministerium, 4878/1a, Sitzung
[. . .] betreffend Kontrolle des Küstenverkehrs durch die Kriegsmarine, 30.10.19.
[257] Keynes, *Collected Writings*, XVII, pp. 134f.
[258] NAW, RG 59, 862.00/807, Stewart to State Dept., 12.2.20.

'merchant's honour' when a revolutionary sailor barged into him in the Rathausmarkt.[259] Keynes related a similar confrontation in the German delegation's quarters at Trier, after he had asked to speak privately with Melchior:

He led me along the passage and entered one of the rooms. At the further end of it were three young Germans; one was strumming loudly on a piano, a fat ungainly creature in his shirt-sleeves bellowed a raucous tenor, the third sprawled on a table. 'Excuse me,' said Melchior, 'but I'd be much obliged if for a few minutes I could have this room for a private conference.' They roared at him vulgarly. Did he not know that this was the hour of the day when music was permitted in that place? And had he forgotten – pointing to his cigarette – that smoking was prohibited there before five o'clock? We went further down the passage. With a shrug of his shoulders, 'Here,' he said, 'you have a picture of Germany in revolution. These are my clerks.'[260]

It was experiences of this sort, in the context of a generalised challenge to the traditional values of bourgeois society, which tended to alienate middle-class Germans from the Weimar Republic. As we have seen, the revolution which began in October 1918 had in many ways been a bourgeois revolution, enjoying the support of many liberally inclined men like Melchior. But by early 1920, the economic and social costs of the revolution had, in the eyes of many, come to outweigh the benefits of political liberalisation. When the American Consul took soundings in the business community in February 1920, he heard a succession of calls for 'strong government':

The present form of government was not the right one, for now every man wanted to be boss and nobody wanted to obey, and Germany would only exist with a government where one man was boss and all others had to obey, though he did not think the Kaiser was that man. He was quite convinced that the coming election would result in Hindenburg being elected President and in his opinion the best government would be composed of Hindenburg, Ludendorff and Lettow-Vorbeck. When his attention was called to this being a military government pure and simple he answered that such a government was needed [. . .] that the people had been educated to live under such a government and could not exist under any other.[261]

In his diary, a Hamburg lawyer was still more passionate in his condemnation of Weimar's new society: the working class, he wrote, was 'shamelessly [pursuing] the programmatic enslavement and dis-orientation, the fleecing and impoverishment of the *Bürger*'. In a

---

[259] Schramm, *Neun Generationen*, II, p. 407.
[260] Keynes, *Collected Writings*, X, p. 414.
[261] NAW, RG 59, 862.00/807, quoting a businessman 'of the average class but a real Prussian type'.

striking contrast with the renunciation of Wilhelmine unpoliticism made by Franz Witthoefft a year before, the diarist now branded middle-class acceptance of Weimar as a symptom of bourgeois political immaturity:

[The *Bürger* has] failed. [He] has entirely failed to grasp the imperatives of self-preservation; and in doing so has shown that his day is at an end. He lacks the great sense of sacrifice which the worker possesses; [. . .and] is without a common goal. [He] has shown himself to be politically immature; and will only be able to think of the future when he quite consciously restores the barrier between himself and the proletariat.

Once again, there was no mistaking the political means he envisaged to that end:

When the spiritual means fail, obstructed by deliberate political strangulation, [it is a] matter of self-defence to switch to the test of physical strength. [. . .] But who can awaken the class with the giant night-cap? Who can make the danger so clear in its mind that even the most wretched dreamer wakes up in terror and sees that, truly, sleeping on is the greater evil? Who will finally drive the *Bürger* to pull himself together? Where is the man to take the lead, deliberately, intelligently and ruthlessly?[262]

This revulsion against Weimar went hand in hand with antipathy towards the Versailles treaty and all the attendant aspects of Germany's international subjugation. It has been suggested that hostility to Versailles was so universal that it acted as a 'bracket' holding Weimar Germany together;[263] but this understates the very deep division which emerged between those (like Warburg and his associates) who were prepared to accept the realities of Germany's position, in order to pursue revision by economic means, and those who adopted a stance of outright rejection, regardless of the consequences. We have already seen how Warburg and Witthoefft were attacked in the summer of 1919 for their role in the armistice and peace negotiations. This gap between advocates of 'fulfilment' (i.e., formal acceptance of the peace terms as a starting point for a realistic revisionism) and advocates of rejection and confrontation grew wider in the succeeding months. Demands for the extradition of German 'war criminals' prompted a surge of 'rejectionism' in Hamburg and renewed calls for Germany to 'join hands with Russia' against the Allies. Indeed, one businessman bluntly assured the American Consul that 'Germany would one day

---

[262] H.-D. Loose, 'Abwehr und Resonanz des Kapp-Putsches in Hamburg', *ZVHG*, 56 (1970), p. 78.
[263] James, 'Economic Reasons for the Collapse of Weimar', in Kershaw (ed.), *Weimar*, p. 54.

have revenge upon France and Poland';[264] while Richard Krogmann
hoped that an Allied occupation of Germany would force Germany to
'find a Minister like Bismarck, who will weld the people together
again and rouse them to great deeds'.[265] In the same vein, the radical
nationalist *Hamburger Warte* called for 'a man [. . .] to make the
enslaved, defenceless Germany once again truly free'.[266] A revealing
indication of the public mood in early 1920 were the exceptional profits
made by a public hall which had been 'in great demand for meetings
of workmen, unemployed and demonstrations against the terms of the
peace treaty'.[267]

A further sign of bourgeois political radicalisation was the growth
of anti-Semitism. Again, it was no coincidence that this increased
markedly in Hamburg at the time of the signing of the Versailles
treaty. By early 1920, organisations like the *Deutschvölkische Bund* and
the *Schutz- und Trutzbund* were sufficiently well organised to unite as
the *Deutschvölkische Schutz- und Trutzbund*, with the stated objective
of making Jews 'lightning conductors for all injustice'.[268] True, the
modus operandi of the radical Right was not sophisticated: their principal
activities were the publication of crude anti-Semitic tracts such as the
one denouncing Warburg's role at the 'Jewish' peace conference, and
the staging of rowdy demonstrations like the one which disrupted a
performance by the actor Alexander Moissi in February 1920.[269] However, the involvement in such activities of Gymnasium and university
students, as well as former members of the Bahrenfelder troop, suggested that anti-Semitism was no longer confined to petty bourgeois
groups.[270] This was an impression confirmed by the evolving character
of the Hamburg DNVP. The British Consul General noted 'among
the merchant classes at Hamburg [. . .] a fairly strong element of the
Deutsch-National (*sic*), who include not only merchants and the wealthier classes, but also some of the smaller employees such as tailors,
smiths etc. [and] a considerable sprinkling of ex-officers who

---

[264] NAW, RG 59, 862.00/807, Stewart to State Dept., 9.2.20; 12.2.20.
[265] Pohlmann, *Richard Krogmann*, pp. 247ff.
[266] Ullrich, 'Arbeiterbewegung', p. 710.
[267] NAW, RG 59, 862.00/884, Stewart to State Dept., 8.3.20. For a typical meeting
organised in February to protest against further seizures of German shipping see
StAH, FA B&V, 1204, *Bürgerbund* to Reich Chancellor *et al.*, 25.11.19; Vorstand,
5.2.20
[268] Jochmann, *Nationalsozialismus*, p. 26; *idem*, 'Ausbreitung des Antisemitismus', pp.
410ff., 440–3; Krause, p. 29. Cf. Lohalm, *Völkischer Radikalismus*. By October 1920,
the *Bund* claimed a national membership of 100,000.
[269] Lorenz, *Juden in Hamburg*, II, pp. 1014f.
[270] StAH, NL Lamp'l, No. 8a, *Der Mittag*, 8, 9.5.19.

are now engaged in commerce'.[271] In ideological terms, this meant a convergence of *völkisch* elements from the *Schutz- und Trutzbund* and conservative elements from the Nationalklub of 1919;[272] while in practice, it meant tacit support by members of the business elite for anti-Semitic comments such as those directed against Leo Lippmann by the DNVP Bürgerschaft deputy Henningsen.[273] When Warburg appealed to Friedrich von Loebell, founder of the *Reichsbürgerrat*, to resist anti-Semitism in the DNVP, he was told with regret that 'a clear position against anti-Semitism could easily call forth opposition and division [. . .] among us'.[274] Nor were the other bourgeois parties entirely immune to anti-Semitism. Although the Hamburg DVP – the party in which businessmen were most strongly represented – was prepared openly to disavow anti-Semitism, Warburg could not get Stresemann to make a similar statement at the national level, because of anti-Semitic tendencies in the party's South German branches.[275] Even the DDP experienced difficulties of the same sort, despite the efforts of Carl Petersen.[276]

The growth of hostility to Weimar, repudiation of Versailles and anti-Semitism put the leaders of the Hamburg business community in an extremely difficult position. DVP members involved in the peace talks were perturbed to find their own party trying to distance itself from the *'Schmachfrieden'*.[277] 'Nationally-minded' Jews like Max

[271] PRO, FO 371/8797/C18990, Consul General Oliver, 'Development of Political Tendencies at Hamburg', 31.10.23.

[272] R. Behrens, 'Die Deutschnationalen in Hamburg' (Diss. Hamburg, 1973), pp. 80–6, 340–64; Büttner, *Staats- und Wirtschaftskrise*, pp. 66–75.

[273] Lippmann, *Leben*, p. 253.

[274] BAK, von Loebell NL, Max Warburg to von Loebell, 23.12.19; WA, 'Politische Correspondenz 1920', von Loebell to Warburg, 17.8.20. By 1923, the anti-Semite Henningsen was a regular speaker at meetings of the Hamburg *Bürgerbund*, which three years before had declared itself 'not party-political, but at the same time not unpolitical': StAH, FA B&V, 'Jahresbericht 1923'; Büttner, *Staats- und Wirtschaftskrise*, pp. 75f.

[275] Lorenz, *Juden in Hamburg*, II, pp. 1014f.; Vagts, 'M.M. Warburg & Co.', pp. 378ff. On the composition of the Hamburg DVP in the early 1920s, BAK, R45 II, 60, list of members of DVP Reichsausschuß für Handel und Industrie, 1921; and list of occupations of 40 Bürgerschaft candidates, February 1921. Even within the Hamburg DVP, there was a division between a right wing, around the former Fatherland Party member Heinrich Bagge, and a left wing around Warburg and Witthoefft: StAH, FA AOM 1, Bd. 12, Witthoefft to Warburg, 7.10.21; Comfort, *Revolutionary Hamburg*, p. 60.

[276] BAK, R45 III/ 15, Hauptvorstand Sitzung, 28.10.19; WA, 'Politische Correspondenz 1920', Warburg to Petersen, 25.1.20. For details of the Hamburg DDP, Büttner, *Staats- und Wirtschaftskrise*, pp. 30f.

[277] L.E. Jones, *German Liberalism and the Dissolution of the Weimar Party System, 1918–1933* (Chapel Hill, 1988), pp. 55–61. For Warburg's dismay at the DVP's protest resolution against the German counter-proposals at Versailles, StAH, FA AOM I, Bd. 10, 407, Witthoefft to Warburg, 6.6.19.

Warburg might insist that it was possible at once 'to uphold German national identity [*das nationale Deutschtum*]' while at the same time 'striving for a cosmopolitan bourgeoisie, compatible with this national identity'; but even he felt obliged to 'make a clear distinction between the German Jews resident here' and the unpopular immigrant '*Ostjuden*'.[278] It was futile for non-party organisations like the Hamburg *Bürgerbund* to attempt to ignore these difficulties in the name of 'the totality of the German bourgeoisie' by rejecting 'party politics' in favour of the 'great, shared ideals [of] resistance to radicalism, the transcendence of class conflicts [and] upholding of the national ideal'.[279] The *Bürgerbund*, along with other notionally 'unpolitical' organisations like the Nationalklub, the Hamburg Red Cross and even the Hamburg Racing Club, found it increasingly difficult to 'emphasise the national ideal' without absorbing the more radical – and more divisive – politics espoused by the Hamburg DNVP.[280] The choice appeared stark: for or against Weimar and Versailles, with the middle ground of qualified acceptance constantly shrinking.

This ideological polarisation increased dramatically as a result of the events of March 1920. In raising the possibility of a shift to authoritarianism while at the same time triggering a powerful working-class defensive strike, the Kapp *putsch* presented middle-class Germans with an uncomfortable choice between renegade army officers and radicalised strikers.[281] For those involved in the maintenance of order, the crisis revealed clearly how little the military occupation of Hamburg the previous summer had done to resolve the question of maintaining public order in the wake of revolution. Dissension had persisted over who should lead the Security Police established by Lettow-Vorbeck after the Senate replaced its original commander Völckers with a more politically sympathetic officer named Meyn in December 1919; nor had there been any clarification of the role of the other defence forces like the Bahrenfelder and the various part-time volunteer forces based in nearby Mecklenburg.[282] The first instruction received in Hamburg from the Kapp 'government' on 13 March was an order placing the

[278] WA, 'Jahresbericht 1919', Max Warburg, 'Rede gehalten vor den hamburgischen kaufmännischen Vereinen am 5.3.19'; Warburg to Hermann Samson, 13.7.20; Warburg to von Loebell, 7.8.20. For official investigations of the alleged role of Galician Jews in smuggling, StAH, DHSG III, Pr. V 1.

[279] StAH, FA B&V 1204, *Bürgerbund* Vorstand, 5.12.19.

[280] See Rohrmann, *Max von Schinckel*, pp. 212f.; Büttner, *Staats- und Wirtschaftskrise* pp. 74f.

[281] See in general J. Erger, *Der Kapp-Lüttwitz Putsch. Ein Beitrag zur deutschen Innenpolitik 1919/20* (Düsseldorf, 1967); H. Hürten, *Der Kapp-Putsch als Wende. Über Rahmenbedingungen der Weimarer Republik seit den Frühjahr 1920* (Opladen, 1989).

[282] HA, HB, Cuno to Holtzendorff, 30.1.20; Jochmann, *Nationalsozialismus* pp. 38f.; Danner, *Ordnungspolizei*, pp. 34–45.

Security Police under a new commander, von Menges, backed up by the Reichswehr garrison at Schwerin; an order which a Kappist officer named von Wangenheim attempted to enforce by arresting Meyn.[283] By 16 March, the city appeared on the brink of civil war, with thousands of rifles being distributed by the Senate to members of the MSPD, DDP and USPD, hurriedly drafted into the Home Guard to counter Kappist troops from the Baltic; while numerous students evidently left their studies to join 'military forces in Mecklenburg [. . .] whose loyalty is questioned'.[284] The confusion was complete when the commander of the 18th Reichswehr regiment, Ledebur, pledged its support for the Senate in defiance of his superiors in Schwerin.[285] By April it was clear that the restored government had made its peace with the Reichswehr, so that the Senate's attempts to prosecute the military supporters of the coup came to nothing.[286] There was similar confusion among the civil authorities. The Senate itself had been quick to pledge loyalty to the 'old' government in Dresden; but matters were confused by the evident sympathy of the Hamburg representative in Berlin, Albrecht, for some kind of compromise with the putschists, and by disagreements within the civil service about whether to obey the orders from Schwerin or the strike call from Dresden, which led to a number of senior officials being suspended.[287] In the Bürgerschaft, the loyalty of the MSPD and DDP to Bauer was unequivocal, while the DNVP backed Kapp; but concern at the arming

---

[283] StAH, SK II, I A 1 a 21/3, Ministry of the Interior to Senate, 13.3.20; /4, Generalmajor Ribbentrop to Senate, 13.3.20; /10, Wangenheim Proclamation to the population of Greater Hamburg; Senate (telegram to Noske), 13.3.20; /27, von Lettow to Senate, 16.3.20; Lamp'l NL 12, Zeller to Lamp'l, 16.3.20; NAW, RG 59, 862.00/905, Stewart to State Dept., 29.3.20.

[284] NAW, RG 59, 862.00/880, Stewart to State Dept., 16.3.20; *Hamburger Fremdenblatt*, Nr. 137, 16.3.20; StAH, SK II, I A 1 a 21/32, Wolff Telegraph Bureau, 17.3.20. Around thirty people died when the two sides clashed. For subsequent attempts to recover the arms distributed, GStA, MdI 77, 7329/4, Hamburg garrison commander, 'Lagebericht für Reichskommissar für die Überwachung der öffentlichen Ordnung', 20.3.20; 7329/38, 'Lagebericht', 24.3.20. For the efforts of the Senate to disband the Freikorps, NAW, RG 59, 862.00/905, Stewart to State Dept., 29.3.20.

[285] StAH, SK II, I A 1 a 21, Schwerin garrison to Senate, 21.3.20, 27.3.20; Reich Defence Ministry to Senate, 28.3.20.

[286] See the material in StAH, SK II, I A 1 a 21/55–79. For subsequent attempts to purge the Security Police, NAW, RG 59, 862.00/905, Stewart to State Dept., 29.3.20.

[287] StAH, SK II, I A 1 a 21 (anonymous note of events, citing:) Senate to Reich Chancellor Bauer, 13.3.20 and Diestel to Oberpostdirektion, 14.3.20; /11, Minister of the Interior Koch to Senate, 14.3.20; /12, Senate to Albrecht, Sieveking, 15.3.20; Albrecht (telephone message), 16.3.20; Minister of the Interior Koch to Senate, 16.3.20; Senate to Gollnow prison (requesting the release of Laufenberg), 24.3.20; Albrecht to Senate, 15.3.20; 16.3.20; 17.3.20; 18.3.20; 19.3.20; 20.3.20; 22.3.20; /37, Koch to SK, 19.3.20; /38, SK to Koch, 19.3.20; Koch to Senate, 29.3.20; Senate to Giesberts, 18.3.20; Giesberts to Senate, 1.4.20. On the civil service, Lyth, '*Mittelstand*', pp. 139, 219f.

of USPD members by the Senate (to say nothing of the reappearance on the scene of erstwhile revolutionaries like Laufenberg) may have sufficed to make the DVP opt for neutrality, despite its expressed objections to the seizure of political power by the 'reactionaries of the extreme Right'.[288] The fact that strike action and other popular demonstrations persisted even after the collapse of the *putsch* added weight to bourgeois fears of a 'second revolution' from the Left.[289] The shipyard workers in particular seized the opportunity presented by the official general strike call to press for higher wages from the employers.[290] In the aftermath of the failed *putsch* there were violent demonstrations of the unemployed in April, renewed strikes in May, food riots and looting in June and further disturbances in October.[291]

Under these circumstances, the reluctance of the business community to align itself with either side is far from unintelligible. Their dissatisfaction with the Weimar *status quo* was as legitimate as their scepticism about the viability of a conservative coup; their inaction as much a reflection of impotence as conviction.[292] Certainly, there was some enthusiasm for Kapp within the Hamburg bourgeoisie. Warburg recalled how the Bahrenfelder – 'in which a great many young people from good Hamburg families were active' – wanted 'to join Kapp right away', while 'some very experienced Hamburg businessmen and academics [. . .] were also really delighted at the first news of the Kapp *putsch* and naively believed it to be a solution'.[293] But none of those business spokesmen who had played a leading role in the politics and diplomacy of the 1918/19 period had wanted a coup. In August 1919, Holtzendorff had poured scorn on the idea of a counter-revolutionary *putsch*, dismissing talk of such a thing as 'a sign of how little the conservatives understand the times'. Such a *putsch*, he argued, would be 'pure madness. It would only smooth the

---

[288] *Sten. Ber. d. Bürgerschaft*, 1920, p. 420; Loose, 'Abwehr', pp. 74–6.
[289] StAH, SK II, I A 1 a 21/39, Albrecht to SK, 19.3.20; HG to SK, 20.3.20; /44, HG Abschrift.
[290] *Ibid.*, Völckers to Schramm, 13.3.20; NAW, RG 59, 862.00/880, Stewart to State Dept., 16.3.20; /896, 22.3.20; /897, 22.3.20; /824, 23.3.20; GHH, 300193012/5, Deutsche Werft to Reusch, 16.3.20; HKH, HKHP, 17.3.20; GStA, Rep. 77, MdI, 7329/77, Hamburg garrison commander, 'Lagebericht' for RKfdÜöO, 6.4.20.
[291] NAW, RG 59, 862.00/926, Stewart to Dresel, 17.4.20; /925, Stewart to State Dept., 19.4.20; /934, 26.4.20; /951, 3.5.20; /950, 18.5.20; /960, 21.5.20; /985, 28.6.20; /987, 4.7.20; /1039, 25.10.20; /1041, 1.11.20; GStA, Rep. 77, MdI, 7329/143, 'Lagebericht', 23.4.20; /155, 27.4.20; /145, 27/28.6.20; GStA, Rep. 84a, 936/220, Reichstag, Drucksache Nr. 152, 'Bekanntmachung betr. Verhängung des Ausnahmezustandes', 27.6.20; BAP, RMI, 13360, 36, Senate Abschrift, 27.6.20; Verordnung 1, 27.6.20; Verordnung 2, 28.6.20; Chef der Sicherheitswehr to RMI, 'Die Lehren des 26. Juni, 1920', 9.8.20.
[292] Loose, 'Abwehr', pp. 76, 78. For reactions in the Ruhr, see G.D. Feldman, 'Big Business and the Kapp Putsch', *CEH*, 2 (1971), pp. 99–131; Maier, *Recasting Bourgeois Europe*, pp. 168f.
[293] WA, 'Jahresbericht 1920', Blatt 13.

path for the extreme left-wing parties.'[294] Carl Melchior had taken a
similar view, but with an eye to the international implications of a coup:

Any overthrow of the democratic system, any move to an absolutist, dictatorial
form of government, whether through a communist revolution or a reactionary
restoration, would greatly reduce the possibilities of reaching an understanding
with those nations which are currently dominant.[295]

On the evening when news of the *putsch* reached Hamburg, Warburg,
Melchior, Cuno and Carl Petersen met and discussed whether to 'send
a delegation from Hamburg to Berlin to dissuade Kapp from his insane
conduct'. There was also discussion in the Chamber of Commerce of a
possible emergency meeting of the Honourable Merchants' Assembly;
and the *Bürgerbund* considered whether to initiate its 'defensive strike',
originally intended to counter a coup from the Left.[296] However,
Holtzendorff's advice from Berlin, based on a conversation with Carl
Fürstenberg, was to 'stand still [. . .since] no one knew whether a step
forwards or a step backwards would be the right thing'.[297] It seems clear
that inertia was generally a matter of prudence rather than a sign of tacit
support for Kapp. John Foster Dulles, who was in Berlin between 15
and 18 March, probably captured the prevailing mood in financial and
commercial circles when he reported that 'leading bankers [who. . .]
before the revolution [. . .] had seemed to me reactionary in their tendencies and sympathetic with the monarchy were outspoken and obviously
sincere in their denunciation of Kapp's coup'.[298] But the news reaching
Warburg on the 13th and 14th was that 'Kapp had the German military
in his hands': 'It looked,' he later recalled, 'anything but harmless.'[299]
It is possible to infer sympathy for Kapp from the refusal of Blohm &
Voß to recognise the strike action in their yards; but for strictly economic
reasons the management had every right to 'emphasise explicitly that
politics must under no circumstances be brought into the workplace'.
There was an element of truth in Rudolf Blohm's later complaint that
the decision of the *Zentralarbeitsgemeinschaft* to award pay for the days
of the anti-Kapp strike had whetted his employees' appetite for industrial
action.[300]

[294] HA, HB, Notizen, 7.8.19.
[295] WA, C. Melchior, 'Der Friedensvertrag und die deutschen Finanzen'. Vortrag am
     15. November 1919 in der Gesellschaft Hamburger Juristen, p. 33.
[296] WA, 'Jahresbericht 1920', Blatt 12ff., 13.2.20; HKH, HKHP, Plenarsitzung, 15.3.20;
     StAH, FA B&V 1204, *Bürgerbund* Sitzung, 14.3.20, 16.3.20, 18.3.20.
[297] HA, HB, Holtzendorff to Huldermann, 14.3.20.
[298] Mudd Library Princeton, John Foster Dulles Papers, Box 3, Statement for the
     Secretary of State, 24.3.20.
[299] WA, 'Jahresbericht 1920', Blatt 15.
[300] StAH, FA B&V 13, Bd. 2, Firmenleitung 18.3.20; B&V 485, Rudolf Blohm to
     HKH, 7.7.21.

Blohm's desire to keep politics out of the workplace in some ways epitomised the response of the Hamburg business community to the political polarisation of 1919/20. It is striking that, whether Jewish or Christian, liberal or conservative, businessmen reacted to the Thermidorean trend by retreating from direct participation in politics. Efforts by both Bauer and his successor Müller to persuade Cuno to become Finance Minister (which dated back to February) finally came to nothing, as Cuno – who only a few months before had urged Melchior to accept the post of State Secretary at the Economics Ministry – demurred with reference to 'the party-political and extra-parliamentary influence of the unions [. . .] on the running of the Cabinet'. 'The party-political way of looking at things in our parliament', he argued, would make it 'impossible [for] a reactionary as crass as me' to achieve the 'huge task of restoring our finances to health'.[301] Melchior likewise turned down the post of Reconstruction Minister.[302] Even activity within the political parties was now shunned. Witthoefft refused to stand again as a national candidate for the DVP, giving no reason;[303] Warburg withdrew his name from the list of alternative candidates, clearly because of the growth of anti-Semitism;[304] and Cuno too resisted pressure to stand for both the DVP and the Centre, arguing that 'it would be impossible to reconcile the interests of the shipping lines with a party programme', and that he would prefer to use his influence to bring about cooperation between the bourgeois parties.[305] Similarly, Arndt von Holtzendorff turned down an invitation to join the DDP national committee, arguing that his role in Berlin required him to be 'doubly careful' to offer 'neutral territory to all parties': 'I have to avoid any kind of prominence, and remain as far as possible one of *"die Stillen im Lande"*.'[306] Dismayed by such reticence, the industrialist Albert Vögler remonstrated with Rudolf Blohm:

[301] HA, HB, Cuno to Holtzendorff, 19.7.19; Anon. note, possibly by Cuno, 28(?).3.20; Holtzendorff to Cuno, 31.3.20; Kohlhaus, 'Die Hapag', pp. 64–7; WA , 'Jahresbericht 1920', Blatt 13; Jahresbericht 1920, III, Cuno to Warburg, 26.2.20; Warburg to Cuno, 27.2.20; Cuno to Warburg, 27.3.20; Golecki (ed.), *Kabinett Bauer*, pp. 755f., 764–7; M. Vogt (ed.), *Das Kabinett Müller I* (Boppard am Rhein, 1971), p. 1.
[302] WA, Jahresbericht 1920, III, Melchior to Koch, 30.3.20. For Warburg's scathing comments about Chancellor Müller after meeting him and other members of his Cabinet at Holtzendorff's, see *ibid.*, Max Warburg to Fritz Warburg, 11.4.20. Cf. HA, HB, Holtzendorff to Cuno, 12.4.20.
[303] StAH, FA AOM 1, Bd. 10, 407, Witthoefft to Rose, 28.7.19.
[304] BAK, R45 II/53, DVP Geschäftsführender Ausschuß, 19.4.20.
[305] HA, HB, Cuno to Holtzendorff, 23.1.20; Kohlhaus, 'Die Hapag', p. 172. For Cuno's efforts to revive the Navy League as the *Deutsche Seeverein* see HA, HB, Holtzendorff Notizen, 24.4.19; Holtzendorff to Cuno, 1.10.19; Holtzendorff to Cuno, 3.4.21. Cf. Böhm, *Flottenbau*, p. 181.
[306] HA, HB, Holtzendorf to Cuno, 10.10.19. The 'silent ones in the land' was a phrase used of the late eighteenth- and nineteenth-century Pietists.

If it were to prove possible to secure occupational [i.e. as opposed to democratic] representation with appropriate [voting] rights, then perhaps we could leave direct parliamentary activity to the secretaries of associations as we used to. But that will only come about if, by first achieving a strong representation in the political parliament, we can bring the National Assembly round to support [such a reform]. There is therefore simply no alternative but to make full use of the time between now and the new elections to ensure that as large a number of industrialists as possible is elected in all the parties [. . .particularly] the DNVP, which has so far shown little sign of sympathy for the representation of industry.[307]

But, despite this classic exposition of the tactics of 'unpolitical politics', Blohm too decided not to stand, pleading business commitments.[308] Similarly, neither Max von Schinckel nor Richard Krogmann was willing to lend active support to the DNVP.[309] The most Hamburg businessmen were willing to do for parties after 1919 was to provide funding.[310]

In the wake of the Kapp *putsch*, Warburg expressed the forlorn hope that both the extreme Left and the extreme Right had now 'shot their bolts';[311] but this hope was shattered by the elections of June 1920. The campaign itself was fought in an intense and sometimes violent atmosphere unprecedented in German electoral history. As the American consul in Hamburg observed:

No individual concedes the right of any other individual to possess a different opinion from his own and instead of the so-called 'mud-throwing' that often characterises elections in the US, there has been a great deal of throwing of clubs and bricks at the various rallies held in Hamburg [. . .] The most unscrupulous wild-cat bill-poster of some Broadway theatre would have opened his eyes in wonder would he have seen how faithfully the workers of the various candidates had plastered the city with every available sort of poster [. . .] No available space was missed.[312]

The results saw gains by both political extremes (see figure 4.11).[313] In his frustration, Warburg lashed out at Karl Helfferich, who had headed the DNVP list in Hamburg:

If he now significantly increases the power of the DNVP, a parliamentary situation will arise which will simply be impossible. [. . .] He should either have bided his time or worked to strengthen the middle parties by emphasising

---

[307] StAH, FA B&V 1203, Vögler to Blohm, 18.11.19.
[308] *Ibid.*, Blohm to Dr Arnold Lienau, 10.1.20.
[309] Rohrmann, *Max von Schinckel*, pp. 243f.; Pohlmann, *Richard Krogmann*, pp. 252f.
[310] StAH, FA AOM 1, Bd. 11, Witthoefft to Otto Harms, 6.5.20, for contributions by Hamburg firms to the DVP in 1920. Warburg's provided 50,000 marks, Heinrich Traun 20,000 marks. Cf. Vagts, 'M.M. Warburg & Co.', p. 378. In February 1921, Blohm & Voß contributed 10,000 marks: StAH, FA B&V 1207.
[311] HA, HB, Holtzendorff to Cuno, 12.4.20.
[312] NAW, RG 59, 862.00/968, Stewart to State Dept., 31.5.20; /974, 6.6.20.
[313] Cf. Comfort, *Revolutionary Hamburg*, p. 161; Maier, *Recasting Bourgeois Europe*, p. 171.

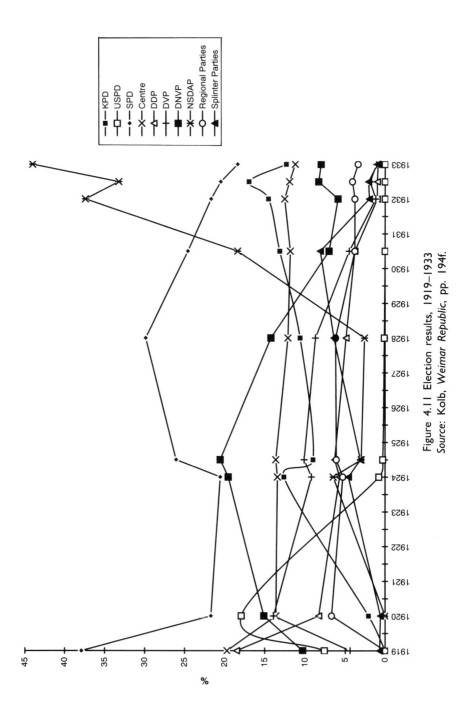

Figure 4.11 Election results, 1919–1933
Source: Kolb, *Weimar Republic*, pp. 194f.

their major differences with the radical right [. . .] But Helfferich, Westarp & Co. [. . .] can't see beyond their own shadows [. . .He is] working for short-term success.[314]

Yet 'biding time', if that was what Warburg and his colleagues were doing, was a recipe for political impotence. The decision of both Melchior and Cuno once again to refuse office in a government composed of precisely those 'middle parties' they supported hardly served to fortify the centre ground.[315] There was an air of defeatism about this retreat from the political fray which stands in marked contrast to the relative optimism which had characterised Warburg's attitude in the first months after the Revolution. It was typical of the new mood that, when Warburg heard in December 1920 that Cuno was 'coquetting' with the idea of one day becoming President of the Reich, he noted dryly: 'I regard the Hapag as a better firm.'[316]

International consequences

In short, not only had the economic consequences of the peace proved to be quite different from those predicted by the German experts at Versailles; so too had the political consequences. Instead of a chronic balance of payments crisis, the mark had stabilised thanks to an influx of foreign capital; and instead of a wave of Bolshevism, the radical Right had profited from bourgeois disenchantment. Here lies the explanation for the stagnation of the Hamburg group's revisionist offensive in 1920. Efforts continued to be made to persuade American and British opinion of the economic and political reasons for revision. But with the British demanding the surrender of yet more merchant shipping in retaliation for the scuttling of the German navy at Scapa Flow and the American Senate refusing to ratify the Versailles Treaty, the international loan which had been the keystone of Warburg's approach at Versailles now seemed a remote prospect: 'We will [. . .] experience exactly the same financially as we have already experienced politically. America will play the *cunctator* and perhaps eventually do the right thing, but practically to no effect, because it will come too late.'[317] Such pessimism was reinforced by a meeting with the American

---

[314] WA, Jahresbericht 1920, III, Warburg to Lucius von Stoedten, 11.6.20; and the unsigned article by Warburg in the *Hamburger Fremdenblatt* [?].6.20. Precipitating an open breach, he accused Helfferich of 'demagogy' (*Hetzen*) to his face in October: WA, 'Jahresbericht 1920', Blatt 25.

[315] *Ibid.*, Melchior Notiz, 21.6.20, 22.6.20; *Neue Hamburger Zeitung*, 22.6.20. Stinnes, Vögler and Wiedfeldt also refused office in the Fehrenbach Cabinet.

[316] *Ibid.*, Warburg to Melchior, 10.12.20; cf. HA, HB, Holtzendorff to Cuno, 18.12.20, for Stresemann's attempts to lure Cuno into office.

[317] WA, Jahresbericht 1920, II, Warburg Notizen, 14.1.20, 30.1.20.

ambassador Dresel, who accused Warburg of simply wanting 'the
country with the best exchange rate to make the biggest sacrifices' and
warned him that 'the American man in the street had no interest in
Europe; which would make it difficult to pull off a big financial
transaction in America just now'.[318] Some American converts were
certainly made: John Foster Dulles expressed sympathy with the arguments for revision in the light of his visit to Germany;[319] but when
Dresel met Max Warburg again in July, he was struck by his 'complete'
pessimism.[320] Significantly, Keynes too was 'much too pessimistic at
the present stage of affairs to be of the slightest practical use to
anyone'.[321]

A clear indication that the Hamburg group was losing the initiative
in the formulation of German policy came in the spring of 1920, when
the government asked Warburg and Melchior to join a committee of
twenty-two economic experts charged with drawing up a new German
proposal for reparations.[322] After prolonged discussions in which Warburg ruled out any repeat of the 100 bn. gold marks offer (on the
grounds that the conditions he had envisaged in 1919 had not been
granted) and Melchior argued for an annuity of 1 bn. gold marks tied
to an index of economic prosperity, the committee produced a report
on 'Germany's Ability to Pay' which was so far removed from the
figures being discussed by Lloyd George and Millerand that the
government invited the economist Moritz Bonn to produce an alterna-

---

[318] WA, 'Jahresbericht 1920' (notes of meeting with Dresel), 20.1.20. For details of
Dresel's meeting with Rathenau ten days later, and a second meeting with Warburg,
see NAW, RG 59, 862.00/781, Dresel to State Dept., 30.1.20; /788, Dresel Memorandum, 30.1.20; /782, Dresel to State Dept., 1.2.20. The similarities in their
arguments make it seem likely that Rathenau and Warburg were acting in concert.
[319] Mudd Library, Princeton, John Foster Dulles Papers, Box 3, Dulles, 'An Economic
Conference?' (May?) 1920: 'I do not know the precise condition of Mr Stinnes's
wardrobe now that he has become a billionaire, but I do know that his increased
purchases are insignificant compared to the number of shirts and suits which the
Germany (sic) worker has had to go without. [. . .] Europe, by inflating, is destroying
its ability to buy from us, and is increasing its ability to compete with us. [. . .]
As the primary cause lies the Reparation unsettlement. Germany cannot balance her
budget because the present schedule of payments required of her is so excessive.'
See also his speech 'What America should know about Germany', Council of Foreign
Relations, 11.1.21; and the pro-German article by Paul Warburg published after his
visit to Germany: Sterling Library, Yale, Paul M. Warburg Papers, Series II, Box
11, Folder 136, Paul M. Warburg, 'Europe at the Crossroads', Political Science
Quarterly, 35, 4.12.20.
[320] NAW, RG 59, 862.00/1074, Dresel to Secretary of State Colby, 12.7.20.
[321] Keynes, Collected Writings, XVII, p. 197. Cf. Skidelsky, Economist as Saviour,
pp. 46f.
[322] For the origins of the committee, see Vogt (ed.), Kabinett Müller I, p. 43; Feldman,
Great Disorder, pp. 206ff.

tive version.[323] In the weeks preceding the conference with the Allies at Spa in July, further modifications produced a scheme for a thirty-year schedule of annuities of around 2 bn. gold marks.[324] However, the Allies refused to discuss the proposal – hardly surprising, since at Boulogne the previous month they had discussed a figure of 269 bn. gold marks, payable over forty-two years.[325]

A further sign of the Hamburg group's relative decline was the 'intense discussion' required to persuade the industrialists Otto Wiedfeldt, Carl Duisberg and Richard Merton to sign the memorandum: for the first time since the end of the war, the Ruhr was beginning to assert itself.[326] Moreover, Wiedfeldt, Stinnes and Ewald Hilger, the Silesian coal magnate, were invited to advise the German delegation to Spa. The main reason for this higher industrial profile was straightforward: coal, not commerce or cash reparations, was the key issue to be discussed at Spa, reflecting the temporary but acute coal shortage which was afflicting post-war Europe.[327] Germany's failure to fulfil the deliveries of coal required by the Allies had given the French an opportunity to take the first step in the direction of further territorial encroachment on Germany. Once differences between France and Britain over the pricing of German coal had been settled, the question arose whether to accept the Allied demand for two million tons of coal a month, or face the occupation of the Ruhr.[328] To the consternation of Melchior, Rathenau and Dernburg, Stinnes argued for rejection, on the grounds that the proposed level of deliveries would increase unemployment by 2 million; and that the consequences of a French occupation – 'Bolshevism in Germany and chaos in Europe' – would be preferable.[329] Superficially, Stinnes's arguments resembled those which Melchior himself had used to persuade Keynes of the dangers of reparations. But Melchior had merely wished to alarm the Allies;

---

[323] *Ibid.*, pp. 126f., 158; WA, 'Jahresbericht 1920', Blatt 16, 'Deutschlands wirtschaftliche Leistungsfähigkeit'; Mudd Library, Princeton, John Foster Dulles Papers, Dulles to Norman Davis, 1.4.20.

[324] GFM (Spa Allg.), 3242/D715974, Melchior, 'Taktisches Vorgehen', 21.6.20; WA, Warburg 'Diaries', 5.7.20. Cf. Kent, *Spoils of War*, p. 110.

[325] Vogt (ed.), *Kabinett Müller I*, pp. 319–25; Kent, *Spoils of War*, p. 95.

[326] WA, Warburg 'Diaries', 10.5.20; GFM (Spa Allg.), 3243/D715933, Stinnes to U.S.S. Müller, 29.4.20.

[327] Maier, *Recasting Bourgeois Europe*, pp. 195–225; Kent, *Spoils of War*, pp. 82–110.

[328] P. Wulf (ed.), *Das Kabinett Fehrenbach* (Boppard am Rhein, 1972), pp. 1–5, 14–16, 63ff.; Maier, 'Coal and Economic Power', pp. 530–4; Krüger, *Außenpolitik*, pp. 103–11; Kent, *Spoils of War*, pp. 82–110; C. Bergmann, *Der Weg der Reparationen. Von Versailles über den Dawesplan zum Ziel* (Frankfurt am Main, 1926), pp. 32–43.

[329] Warburg, *Aufzeichnungen*, p. 90; HA, HB, Notizen, 12.7.20; Maier, *Recasting Bourgeois Europe*, p. 206. For Stinnes's defence of his position at a subsequent DVP meeting; BAK R45 II/53, Geschäftsführender Ausschuß, 21.7.20.

whereas, with the Ruhr still reverberating with the after-shocks of the anti-Kapp strike, Stinnes appeared to be in earnest in advocating a 'policy of catastrophe'. Moreover, it was revealing that Stinnes subsequently made a thinly veiled anti-Semitic attack on the 'racial vote' and 'alien psyche' of those – Melchior, Rathenau, Dernburg and Bonn – who had overruled him.[330] Stinnes was a political weather-vane, and his brief foray into the rhetoric of rejectionism and racialism reflected the political swing to the Right which occurred in 1920 – just as his conversion to 'corporatism' in the autumn of 1918 had been a response to the opposite trend.

The failure of the League of Nations international financial conference which convened in Brussels in the autumn of 1920, and the subsequent reparations conference, also held in Brussels, set the seal on the Hamburg group's disillusionment. The Amsterdam memorandum had called for just such a conference to resolve the post-war monetary and financial tangle, and delegates arrived with a plethora of pet schemes of varying degrees of ingenuity. The French representative Seydoux put forward a far from unrealistic proposal for increasing the proportion of reparations paid in kind (i.e., in the form of German goods provided free of charge for French reconstruction); and Warburg had an opportunity to add his proposal for a tax-free international 'Economic Renaissance' loan to the pile of reconstruction schemes produced for the Committee on International Credits.[331] However, opposition in Paris and delaying tactics by the industrialists' representatives in Berlin stymied the Seydoux Plan; and the American Treasury's refusal to give its blessing to any scheme for international loans (for fear that they might take precedence over the repayment of war debts) ensured that even the compromise devised by the Dutch banker ter Meulen came to nought.[332] All that remained were seemingly unbridgeable gaps: one between what Britain, France and Belgium wanted from Germany and what the Germans were willing to pay; the other between what the same countries wanted from the United States, and

[330] Warburg, *Aufzeichnungen*, pp. 90f.; WA, Jahresbericht 1920, II, Warburg Notiz, 1920. For Melchior's later protest, see *ibid.*, Melchior to Stinnes, 11.2.21; and Stinnes's unrepentant reply, Stinnes to Melchior, 14.2.21. Cf. Mosse, *German-Jewish Economic Elite*, pp. 261–4.

[331] Soutou, 'Einfluß', pp. 543–52; WA, 'Jahresbericht 1920', Blatt 32; 'Politische Correspondenz, 1921', Universal Service radio interview transcript, January 1921; PA/AA, SRW, FW, 16 I, II, III. Cf. Wulf (ed.), *Kabinett Fehrenbach*, pp. 338, 341, 379–86.

[332] Eichengreen, *Golden Fetters*, pp. 153ff.; Kent, *Spoils of War*, p. 119. For Max Warburg's frustration with the American attitude see WA, 'Politische Correspondenz 1921', Max Warburg to Paul Warburg, 13.2.21; and Paul Warburg's agreement that 'the American point of view at this time [. . .] mean[s] the pt. of view of a provincial and purely self-centred grocery store, [rather than. . .] a world affair': NAW, RG 59, 862.50/441, Paul Warburg to Henry P. Fletcher, State Dept., 23.2.21.

what the Americans were willing to write off or lend.[333] At Paris in January 1921, under pressure from an impatient Lloyd George, the Allies agreed on a scheme for reparations totalling 226 bn. gold marks, to be collected by annuities rising from 2 to 6 bn. gold marks, and an additional payment equivalent to 12 per cent of German exports.[334] Melchior and Cuno promptly resigned from the German delegation at Brussels and returned to Berlin to join the 'small circle' of experts charged with formulating a response;[335] but Simons's counter-offer of 30 bn. gold marks, payable partly by a loan and partly by annuities over twenty-five years struck even Lloyd George as risible.[336] Sanctions were duly imposed in the form of the occupation of the Rhine ports and the imposition of the Reparations Recovery Act (a duty on German exports to Britain initially levied at 50 per cent).[337] Simons's effort to avert the threatened occupation of the Ruhr by appealing to President Harding and suggesting a reparations total with a present value of 50 bn. gold marks achieved nothing.[338] On 27 April, the Allies set a definitive total bill of 132 bn. gold marks; demanded a first payment of 1 bn. gold marks by September; and threatened to occupy the Ruhr if Berlin did not accede.[339]

The failure of the revisionist strategy devised by Warburg, Melchior, Cuno and others in the course of 1919 was inevitable. Having become involved in the peace process partly to defend their own private economic interests, the Hamburg group had come to argue that the destruction of Germany's principal commercial assets would have catastrophic consequences not merely for Germany but for the international economy. Unarrestable currency depreciation caused by a chronic balance of payments deficit would lead to the dumping of German exports, social turmoil within Germany and the spread of Bolshevism

---

[333] For the inconclusive discussions on the shipping question, see HA, Cuno NL, Notes (of meeting with Lord D'Abernon), 18.12.20, and related material; Kohlhaus, 'Die Hapag', pp. 32–4.

[334] Maier, *Recasting Bourgeois Europe*, pp. 237–40; Kent, *Spoils of War*, pp. 119, 125ff.; Feldman, *Great Disorder*, pp. 327f.

[335] HA, NL Cuno, Cuno Notes, 29.1.21; Melchior and Cuno to Simons, 31.1.21; HA, HB, Holtzendorff Notizen, 20.2.21, 21.2.21; Kohlhaus, 'Die Hapag', pp. 36f., 52f., 56; Wulf (ed.), *Kabinett Fehrenbach*, p. 485; Feldman, *Great Disorder*, pp. 329f. The other members of this 'small circle' were Wiedfeldt and Bergmann.

[336] Kent, *Spoils of War*, pp. 125ff.; Maier, *Recasting Bourgeois Europe*, pp. 239f. Simons and his experts fell out when he refused to allow them to negotiate directly with the British government: HA, HB, Holtzendorff Notizen, 20.2.21, 21.2.21; WA, 'Politische Correspondenz 1921', Warburg to Kurt Hahn, 15.5.21.

[337] Maier, *Recasting Bourgeois Europe*, p. 240. For reactions in Hamburg; StAH, DHSG III, Pr. III 39, HKH to DHSG, 22.2.21, *Hamburgische Correspondent*, Nr. 127, 17.3.21.

[338] Kent, *Spoils of War*, pp. 129f.; Maier, *Recasting Bourgeois Europe*, pp. 240–8.

[339] See chapter 6.

into Central Europe. However, these predictions were belied by the evident economic recovery which took place in Germany after Versailles, which caused the mark to stabilise, and by the premature attempt by Kapp and Lüttwitz to realise bourgeois aspirations for authoritarian rule. These unexpected developments undermined the political position of the Hamburg group, leading to reverses in the sphere of foreign policy, and a new reticence in domestic politics. The question which now had to be answered was whether the 'natural' economic stabilisation of early 1920 could be made permanent by a change in domestic economic policy – at the risk of demonstrating a greater capacity to pay reparations than had hitherto been admitted.

5

Relative stabilisation

If one is to question the inevitability of the mark's collapse, the fourteen months between March 1920 and May 1921 are of critical importance. This period must be seen in the context of the general international slump which began in early 1920 as the restoration of trade links ended shortages in Europe, and as the British and American monetary and fiscal authorities began to take steps to settle the bills run up during the war and to end inflation by raising taxes and restricting credit. 1920/1 saw severe deflation in both countries, with prices and production slumping and unemployment sharply rising;[1] and this deflation tended to spread to their trading partners.[2] In Germany too, prices stopped rising, falling by around 20 per cent from a peak in March 1920 to a trough in July, and then oscillating at around thirteen to fourteen times their pre-war level until July 1921.[3] This reflected not only the fall in import prices caused by British and American deflation, but also the recovery of the mark exchange rate and the increase in domestic production described in the previous chapter. The question is whether anything could have been done to make this 'relative stabilisation' last. It is clear that any attempt to restore the mark to pre-war parity on the British pattern was out of the question; a drop in output of at least 4.8 per cent and unemployment of 11.3 per cent (the effect of British deflationary policies in 1920/1) would almost certainly have been politically intolerable.[4] But why was the mark not stabilised at, say, 50–60 marks/$ or 8–10 per cent of its pre-war value – as some contemporary economists suggested?[5] Such a stabilisation would certainly not have entailed a British-style slump.

[1] D.H. Aldcroft, *The Inter-War Economy. Britain 1919–1939* (London, 1970), pp. 34–7; Friedman and Schwartz, *Monetary History of the United States*, pp. 229–32.
[2] Eichengreen, *Golden Fetters*, pp. 100–24. Cf. Aldcroft, *Versailles to Wall Street*, pp. 66ff.; Kindleberger, *World in Depression*, pp. 16f.
[3] See figure 3.4.
[4] Haller, 'Rolle der Staatsfinanzen', pp. 140f., 152; Holtfrerich, *Inflation*, p. 125–31.
[5] Feldman, *Great Disorder*, pp. 151f., 215ff. Cf. Aldcroft, *Versailles to Wall Street*, pp. 126f., 145–9; Kindleberger, *Financial History*, pp. 312–14.

For Graham and, more recently, Holtfrerich and Eichengreen – as for the majority of contemporary German observers – the answer is that the imposition of the London schedule of reparations in the summer of 1921 made a resumption of inflation inevitable, irrespective of the policies pursued in Germany. The stabilisation of 1920/1 was therefore an illusory lull due to diplomatic factors.[6] However, other writers have laid more stress on the contribution of domestic economic policies. Criticism has been levelled at the failure of fiscal policy to reduce or even eliminate government deficits,[7] and at the continuing laxity of monetary policy, which has been variously characterised as 'unbelievable', 'shocking' and 'senile'.[8] Admittedly, since credit restriction would clearly have led to some measure of recession and unemployment, historians who accept that this was undesirable are hard-pressed to suggest an alternative path for monetary policy. Feldman has nevertheless tried to do so, suggesting that it was not the policy of easy money which was wrong, so much as the refusal of the Reichsbank, and the banking world generally, to acknowledge that the credit system had become dependent on 'hot' foreign money, speculatively invested in the expectation that the mark would recover. Had the bankers accepted, instead of intransigently opposing, Hirsch's scheme for a Reich Economic Bank, the credit system might have been better insulated against the sudden fall of foreign confidence in the mark following the London Ultimatum in May 1921.[9] Maier has also emphasised the inadequacy of exchange controls in the face of this danger.[10] The question of responsibility for these various policy failures has been addressed most directly by Witt, who has argued that early Weimar governments were in fact attempting 'something like counter-cyclical policy' (*Konjunkturpolitik*) or 'welfare economics'. They had an 'integrated, economic, social and financial policy with the explicit goal of securing [. . .] democracy' by means of subsidies to industry to maintain employment levels, progressive, redistributive taxation, trade and

---

[6] Graham, *Hyperinflation*, *passim*; Holtfrerich, *Inflation*, pp. 137–55; Eichengreen, *Golden Fetters*, pp. 125–51. The question of the role of reparations in causing inflation to resume is discussed in chapter 6.

[7] Bresciani, *Inflation*, pp. 47–54, 64f.; Webb, 'Government Revenue and Spending', pp. 46–82; *idem*, 'Fiscal News and Inflationary Expectations' *idem*, *Hyperinflation*, pp. 31, 36ff., 41ff., 54, 110.

[8] Bresciani, *Inflation*, pp. 75–82, 155–82, 398f.; Czada, 'Ursachen und Folgen', pp. 15ff.; Feldman, *Iron and Steel*, pp. 315f.; C.-D. Krohn, *Stabilisierung und ökonomische Interessen. Die Finanzpolitik des Deutschen Reichs, 1923–1927* (Düsseldorf, 1974), pp. 17f.

[9] G. D. Feldman, 'The Political Economy of Germany's Relative Stabilisation during the 1920/21 Depression', in Feldman *et al.* (eds.), *Zwischenbilanz*, pp. 180–206. This argument is significantly less explicit in *idem*, *Great Disorder*, pp. 255–72. Feldman now seems to see mid 1922 as a more opportune time for stabilisation.

[10] Maier, *Recasting Bourgeois Europe*, p. 69.

exchange controls, and workers' participation through works' councils. However, 'capitalist economic interests more or less deliberately engineered the destruction of the foundations' of this 'integrated' policy, 'in that, in every political area, they made at least some of the more important measures ineffective through their opposition and thus produced the bogus proof that the whole concept was unviable'.[11] To take a single example: Erzberger's tax reform programme was fundamentally sound, but was watered down by opposition from the bourgeois parties in the Reichstag, the Reichsbank and economic interest groups, and then 'sabotaged' by business tax evasion.[12]

While acknowledging the importance of business opposition, this chapter questions the inherent viability of government policy. Far from being 'integrated', economic policy from July 1919 until May 1921 was *dis*integrated: the unworkable product of a Byzantine process of decision making which combined most of the established weaknesses of the Wilhelmine system with a plethora of new ones. The problem was not merely that governments kept changing, or leading ministers resigning. As we have seen, even before the war there had been weak central control over German fiscal and monetary policy, because of the federal structure of the Reich, the weakness of the Treasury Office, the tension between executive and Reichstag and the limited powers of the Reichsbank; and the war had added a further tier of 'corporatist' institutions representing economic interests and wielding considerable power over the allocation and pricing of resources. The responses of the new regime to these problems were far from coherent. Socialist and non-socialist ministers alike had widely varying tastes in economic management: some were attracted to the liberalising remedies proposed by businessmen, others to the schemes for planning concocted by bureaucrats. Some politicians were principally concerned with maximising production and employment, others with redistribution; some with public ownership, still others with the balance of trade. At the same time, they were under pressure from a host of representative bodies and pressure groups, all claiming a say in economic policy. The favoured solution to any problem was the creation of yet more decision-making bodies, usually designed in such a way that they could not come to a decision. The year 1920 saw this process reach its nadir,

[11] Witt, 'Staatliche Wirtschaftspolitik, pp. 151ff.
[12] Witt, 'Finanzpolitik', *passim*; *idem*, 'Tax Policies, Tax Assessment and Inflation: Towards a Sociology of Public Finances in the German Inflation, 1914 to 1923', in *idem*, *Wealth and Taxation in Central Europe. The History and Sociology of Public Finance* (Leamington Spa/Hamburg/New York, 1987), pp. 137–60; *idem*, 'Reichsfinanzminister und Reichsfinanzverwaltung. Zum Problem des Verhältnisses von politischer Führung und bürokratischer Herrschaft in den Anfangsjahren der Weimarer Republik (1918/19–1924)', *VfZ*, 23 (1975), pp. 1–61.

with the creation of such cumbersome organs as the Reich Economic Council (RWR), the Iron Economic League (EWB), the foreign trade boards and the second Socialisation Commission, all of which were designed according to the principle of 'parity'. If any of these bodies reached a clear-cut decision, it was generally regarded as an indication that parity had not been achieved. In a speech in October 1920, Max Warburg summed up the problem:

Positioned between the old western and the new eastern world views, our mission will be to find the right foundations for the new economic and state structures. [. . .But] today a trial councils-system; tomorrow an experimental socialism, simultaneously decapitalisation by taxation: no people can prosper in this fashion.'[13]

It was this situation which made many individuals, particularly businessmen, begin yearning for some kind of 'dictatorship' which would cut through the knots of economic 'polycracy'. Although the importance of this critique of Weimar in the development of National Socialist ideology is obvious, not everyone who voiced it necessarily was sympathetic to Hitler's proposed remedies in the way that its most sophisticated advocate, Carl Schmitt, later became. It was the DVP ministers in the Fehrenbach cabinet who, in August 1920, argued that 'an active [economic] policy' was prevented by

the parliamentary system, [. . .] which fits Germany like a fist in the eye. [It is] this system [which] forces us into see-saw politics. It will in all likelihood finish us off if we do not alter it. [. . .] The people yearn for activity, energy and a master.[14]

The significance of such sentiments should not be distorted by hindsight. To businessmen like Max Warburg or Franz Witthoefft, a 'dictatorship' meant simply an emergency device to implement what they saw as 'necessary' financial reforms; it bore very little relation to the idea of a strong, demagogic 'leader' which was taking shape on the political fringe. 'The question arises,' wrote Witthoefft in November 1919, as inflation was spiralling, 'whether at this moment a personality can be found who would be willing to take over the position of Finance Minister with dictatorial powers, to haul the cart out of the mud.'[15] Warburg came to sympathise with this view, arguing, for example, that there was an insuperable conflict of interests between the Finance Ministry and the Reichsbank which made stabilisation of the currency

[13] WA, XIX, Gesammelte Vorträge, 'Die notwendigen Vorbedingungen für die Gesundung der deutschen Währung', 26.10.20.
[14] GFM, Kabinettsprotokolle 3242, Pf. XVII, D 712703, Sitzung 9.8.20.
[15] StAH, FA AOM 1, Bd. 11, 58, Witthoefft to Eschenburg (HK Lübeck), 18.11.19.

impossible.[16] Yet it was an irony typical of the period that among the institutional brakes on decision making was one of Warburg's and Witthoefft's own devising. The idea of an Economic Council had been intended as a pro-business counterweight to democratic parliaments and workers' councils – a forum to represent 'all the productive circles' alongside the parliamentary system 'which, at least in its present form has not proved a success in all countries'.[17] But when put into practice at both the local and the national level it proved a double-edged weapon, adding as much to the power of the unions as to that of business organisations.[18] Doubly ironic was the reaction of Max von Schinckel to Erzberger's financial reforms: the man who admired Mussolini for restoring the nine-hour day in Italy fulminated against 'the tax dictator of the German Reich'.[19] It might be argued that, had Erzberger only fitted this description, Witt's 'integrated policy' could have been saved from subversion by vested interests. The point is that to look for 'integrated policies' in a system as excessively pluralistic as Weimar's is to wish for dictators; and to blame 'capitalist' interest groups for sabotaging those policies is simply to echo contemporary frustrations at the way the early Weimar system worked. A distinction must clearly be drawn between alternative economic policies which, viewed in narrowly economic terms, might have achieved a lasting stabilisation at a lower cost than was subsequently incurred in 1923/ 4, and alternative economic policies which would have been politically feasible, given the Weimar system. While the former are conceivable, the latter are all but impossible to imagine.

The dilemmas of deficit finance

As noted above, a central charge against businessmen in the period 1919/21 is that they subverted the programme of financial reforms introduced by Erzberger in 1919, in order to avoid paying the high direct taxes which were its centrepiece.[20] However, to argue that Erzberger failed because interest groups in the Reichstag voted against some of his measures, or because businessmen evaded tax, is to ignore

---

[16] WA, XIX, Gesammelte Vorträge, Warburg, 'Die notwendigen Vorbedingungen', 26.10.20.
[17] WA, Jahresbericht 1920, Max Warburg, 'Niederschrift zum Währungselend' (February/March, 1920).
[18] Hamburg representatives had fifteen places when the Reich Economic Council first convened on 30 June 1920, among them Witthoefft and Cuno; HA, HB, Cuno to Holtzendorff, 17.11.19; StAH, FA AOM 1, Bd 11, 380, Witthoefft to HKH, 29.6.20.
[19] Rohrmann, *Max von Schinckel*, p. 218.
[20] Witt, 'Staatliche Wirtschaftspolitik', pp. 177f.; Webb, 'Government Revenue and Spending', p. 64; Maier, *Recasting Bourgeois Europe*, p. 82.

the other, decisive side of the financial equation: expenditure. Although
businessmen certainly disliked Erzberger's taxes, they hardly needed
to subvert his financial policy: for the failure of Erzberger and his
colleagues to control expenditure ensured that the programme subverted itself.[21] It was not opposition to high taxes which caused the
continued budget deficits and monetary expansion of the years 1920
and 1921, but the still higher spending undertaken by the various
Weimar ministries in pursuit of various 'social' objectives; and to
call this Konjunkturpolitik is to exaggerate the sophistication of those
responsible. As we have seen, with the high levels of liquidity left
from the war in 1919, and the influx of foreign capital in 1920, the
German economy was set fair to expand; the government's policy of
adding to the monetary fuel simply led to 'over-heating'. The net
effect of government policy, in other words, was to increase the
susceptibility of the economy to inflation – to reduce rather than
increase the chances of permanent stabilisation.

From an early stage, Hamburg businessmen had in fact anticipated
high taxation as part of a programme of retrenchment and price
stabilisation, unhesitatingly rejecting the idea of a simple repudiation
of the Reich debt ('state bankruptcy') as a recipe for economic 'debili-
tation'.[22] In March 1919, Holtzendorff discussed the financial question
with Schiffer, who told him of his hope that

prices [could be] stabilise[d], raising the purchasing power of money accordingly, [through] a confiscation of [. . .] property, whether directly or in the
form of an interest-free forced loan. He believes that in this way he will be
able to bring order to our finances and that we may thus extricate ourselves
from the mire without reaching the point of state bankruptcy.[23]

This confirmed Holtzendorff's earlier forecast of 'a large property levy
and an enormous income tax'.[24] The prospect of a high reparations
bill only made such heavy taxation seem more inevitable. When Warburg tabled the idea of the 100 bn. gold marks offer at Versailles he
declared his awareness that it

pronounced the death sentence for me and my family from a pecuniary point
of view, because the raising of such a sum will entail a property tax on the
one hand and an income tax which will reach 75 per cent for those [. . .] on
large incomes. It will also entail an inheritance tax which will almost certainly

---

[21] Webb, 'Government Revenue', p. 55; idem, Hyperinflation, pp. 41ff.
[22] Haupts, Deutsche Friedenspolitik, p. 336. Given the widespread distribution of war
bond holdings, state bankruptcy would have had the effect of a general capital levy;
but the effect on the Reich's future creditworthiness would have been disastrous.
[23] HA, HV, Holtzendorff to Cuno, 26.3.19.
[24] Ibid., Holtzendorff to Cuno, 27.2.19.

make it impossible to [. . .] leave one's children anything significant. Those
who may reckon themselves among the *beati possedentis* will feel this blow the
hardest; yet I do not give this a second's thought.[25]

Nor did the failure of the 100 bn. gold marks counter-offer change
Warburg's mind on this subject. In a detailed analysis of the currency
crisis in early 1920, he acknowledged that the budget deficit was as
much to blame for inflation as the balance of payments deficit, arguing
for retrenchment by means of the highest possible taxes, cuts in public
spending (notably in unemployment benefit), the levying of all taxes
at source without delays in payment, a forced loan to reduce the note
circulation, and reform of the Reichsbank Law to free it from having
'Treasury bills forced upon it'.[26] These were not isolated views: the
Reichsbank itself said much the same in its memorandum to the
government of 1 July 1919.[27] There was nothing unexpected, therefore,
about the reforms announced by Erzberger a week later, which were
intended to consolidate the floating debt and balance the budget by
issuing a new 'premium loan', raising a progressive property levy (the
Reichsnotopfer), transferring substantial shares of direct taxation from
the states to the Reich, raising the level and steepening the progressive
slope of income tax, and increasing the turnover tax.[28]

Why then were business spokesmen so vociferous in their criticisms
of the Erzberger reforms? Witthoefft predicted the reduction of
business capital by half; while the Chamber of Commerce insisted
that, taking all the new imposts together, some business incomes would
now be taxed at 100 per cent.[29] More emotively, Max von Schinckel
denounced the 'terror of tax legislation which borders on confiscation'
and labelled the reforms 'the last stab in the back against the independent [. . .] German *Staatsbürger*'.[30] Such criticism is traditionally dismissed as the special pleading of vested interests. Yet it was not
entirely specious; for, in putting into practice his maxim that 'a good
Finance Minister is the best Socialisation Minister', Erzberger had
certainly attempted a drastic increase in direct taxation. The National

---

[25] Warburg to Dernburg, 19.5.19, in *Akten zur deutschen auswärtigen Politik*, Serie A,
II, pp. 56–9
[26] WA, Jahresbericht 1920, I, 'Niederschrift zum Währungselend'.
[27] Feldman, *Great Disorder*, pp. 158f.
[28] Specht, *Politische und wirtschaftliche Hintergründe*, pp. 21–9; Witt, 'Finanzpolitik',
pp. 414–21; Webb, 'Government Revenue and Spending', p. 47; *idem, Hyperinflation*, pp. 18, 31ff.; Petzina, *Deutsche Wirtschaft*, p. 85; Feldman, *Great Disorder*,
pp. 159–65. Cf. A. Möller, *Reichsfinanzminister Matthias Erzberger und sein
Reformwerk* (Bonn, 1971); K. Epstein, *Matthias Erzberger and the Dilemma of German
Democracy* (Princeton, 1959).
[29] HA, HB, Holtzendorff Notizen, 12.7.19; Holtzendorff to Cuno, 7.10.19; HKH,
Jahresbericht 1919.
[30] Rohrmann, *Max von Schinckel*, p. 237.

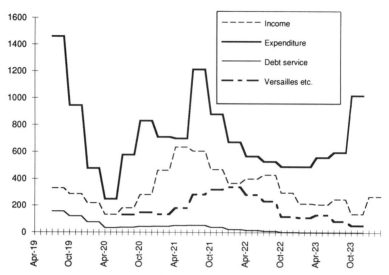

Figure 5.1 Real monthly Reich finances, 1919–1923 (m. gold marks)
Source: Webb, *Hyperinflation*, pp. 33, 37.

Assembly had already passed substantial levies on wartime increases in personal wealth and income, with increases in property above 375,000 marks taxed at 100 per cent; now the 'Reich Emergency Levy' (*Reichsnotopfer*) taxed property above 10,000 marks at rates rising from 10 per cent to 65 per cent, while the Reich income tax envisaged a top rate of 60 per cent on income above 500,000 marks. Erzberger also transferred taxes on profits and land sales to the Reich, while deliberately avoiding increases in taxation of consumption to mollify the Social Democrats. As a result, the share of Reich tax revenue coming from direct taxation rose to around 60 per cent in 1920/1 and 75 per cent in 1921/2, compared with just 14.5 per cent (including stamp taxes) before the war.[31] Moreover, although the transfer of revenue to the Reich was counterbalanced by the *Finanzausgleich* which transferred much of the revenue back to the states, there was a temptation for the states and local authorities to increase the taxes they still controlled directly. Around half of the Hamburg state's traditional revenues were taken by the Reich in 1920, which the Finance Deputation sought to counterbalance by increasing those taxes which remained, including those on real estate and businesses.[32] By

---

[31] Figures calculated from Witt, 'Tax Policies', pp. 156f. Pre-war figures in Witt, *Finanzpolitik*, p. 379.

[32] Brandt, *Hamburgs Finanzen*, pp. 25f. Taxes on 'luxuries' (entertainment, pleasure vehicles, pet dogs) were also introduced; but clearly had much less fiscal significance. Cf. F. Menges, *Reichsreform und Finanzpolitik. Die Aushöhlung der Eigenstaatlichkeit Bayerns auf finanzpolitischem Wege in der Zeit der Weimarer Republik* (Berlin, 1971).

comparison with traditional levels of direct taxation, this did indeed seem like fiscal 'socialisation'.

Tax evasion by business has been portrayed as 'sabotage' of Erzberger's reforms; but in the sense that it reflected a perception among taxpayers that the new taxes were excessive, evasion was to some extent inevitable. The second serious defect of the reforms was that, besides asking for too much, they did little to prevent such evasion. For example, the *Reichsnotopfer* could be paid in instalments over periods ranging from twenty-five to forty-seven years, with interest charged at only 5 per cent after December 1920.[33] So long as inflation remained above 5 per cent, delayed payment was clearly advantageous. Moreover, those whose incomes were not paid as wages could easily defer payment of the Reich income tax, unlike those whose tax was deducted at source. This meant that wage earners in fact paid a rising share of this supposedly progressive tax.[34] In mid 1921, Warburg privately estimated the level of avoidance of the *Notopfer* alone at 1 billion gold marks;[35] and the records of the Hamburg regional tax authorities confirm the impression that richer taxpayers were taking advantage of loopholes in the legislation in order to delay payment.[36] To portray this as capitalist sabotage is misleading. Evasion was by no means irrational, given the extent of redistribution envisaged by Erzberger and the legal opportunities to postpone payment. Better-designed taxes would have raised more revenue: as Webb has suggested, if the revenues from the income tax had not been eroded by renewed inflation after mid 1921, the real primary deficit (net of debt service) for the period July 1920 to June 1921 would have been just 1.31 bn. gold marks, as opposed to over 5 bn gold marks.[37]

In any event, opposition to, and evasion of taxation were less important than the government's continued spending policies in ensuring the persistence of deficits and hence of inflation. Despite the new taxes, the 1920/1 budget was expected (in December 1920) to show a deficit of 83 bn. marks, with tax revenues covering just over a third (36 per cent) of total spending. That figure was only slightly improved (to 44 per cent) in 1921.[38] As a proportion of NNP, total public

---

[33] Webb, *Hyperinflation*, pp. 33f.; Flemming et al., 'Sozialverhalten', p. 259.
[34] Witt, 'Tax Policies', *passim*.
[35] WA, X, Pol. Corr. 1921, Max Warburg to Paul Warburg, 4.6.21.
[36] BAP, RFM 47055 N.Reg. 2574/19, Finanzamt Unterelbe, Geschäftsbericht, Anlage: 'Umsatzsteuer', November 1920; RFM 47047 N. Reg. 2574, Finanzamt Unterelbe, Geschäfts- und Verwaltungsbericht, November 1920; RFM 47055 N.Reg. 2574/47, Landesfinanzamt Unterelbe, Geschäftsbericht, March 1921; 72–89, Landesfinanzamt Unterelbe, Geschäftsbericht, December 1921.
[37] Webb, *Hyperinflation*, pp. 52ff. See also Eichengreen, *Golden Fetters*, pp. 139–42.
[38] Feldman, *Great Disorder*, pp. 322ff.

spending in 1920 was unchanged on the previous year (around 42 per cent), and fell only slightly (to 37 per cent) in 1921. The Reich deficit fell only slightly from around 18 per cent of NNP in 1919 to 12 per cent in 1921.[39] There were, it is true, moments when equilibrium seemed within reach; but Bresciani's deflated monthly data clearly show the erratic trend of spending in real terms, with large increases in June and December 1920 and again in February 1921; while Webb's deflated quarterly figures point to sharp real increases in spending in the second quarters of 1920 and 1921 (see figure 5.1).[40]

Why did it prove impossible to bring government spending down to a level compatible with tax revenue? The German government put the blame on the burdens imposed by the Treaty of Versailles; and although many historians have argued that the government was deliberately understating Germany's capacity to pay, there is no question that reparations payments constituted a very substantial burden when expressed as a fraction of the revenue the German government was able to raise via taxation. For the years 1920 and 1921, three different sets of figures suggest that payments relating to the peace treaty amounted to between 50 and 65 per cent of Reich tax revenue (see figures 5.2 and 5.3).[41] However, as a percentage of *total* public spending in those years, reparations amounted to no more than 15 per cent. Even if one subtracts reparations payments, German public spending in those years was still running at around 33 per cent of NNP, compared with around 18 per cent before the war.[42]

The real cause of the continuing deficits was domestic 'social' policy. This included higher spending on public sector pay (an additional 3.9 bn. marks in March 1920), doles for the unemployed, of which the Reich paid half, subsidies for housing construction (4.35 bn. marks between 1918 and 1920 and 3.7 bn. marks in 1921), and subsidies to keep down the costs of food (7 bn. marks in 1920).[43] The most notorious 'hole' in the budget was the deficit run by the rail and post system, which totalled 18 bn. marks in 1920, nearly 12 per cent of total Reich spending. Before the war, the railways had been run by the states and had been relatively profitable. After the war, having been taken over by the Reich, they rapidly ran out of financial control. In part, this was a consequence of new and costly purchases of

---

[39] Calculated from Webb, *Hyperinflation*, pp. 33, 37. Cf. figure 0.4.
[40] See figure 3.3.
[41] Calculated from Bresciani, *Inflation*, pp. 437f.; Graham, *Hyperinflation*, pp. 44f.; Holtfrerich, *Inflation*, p. 148 and Witt, 'Tax Policies', pp. 154–9; Webb, *Hyperinflation*, pp. 33, 37.
[42] Calculated from figures in Webb, *Hyperinflation*, p. 37; Witt, 'Finanzpolitik', pp. 425f.
[43] Feldman, *Great Disorder*, pp. 214–39.

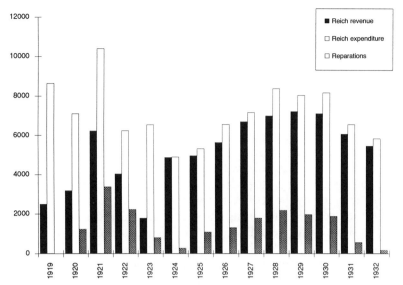

Figure 5.2 Reparations and finance, 1919–1932 (m. gold marks)
Sources: Bresciani, *Inflation*, pp. 437f.; Holtfrerich, *Inflation*, p. 147; Webb,
Hyperinflation, pp. 33, 37, 108; Schuker, 'Reparations', pp. 378f.; Balderston,
Economic Crisis, pp. 226, 239.

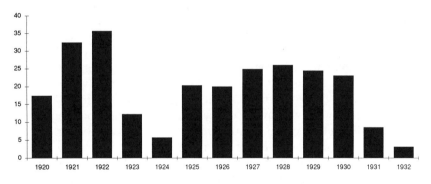

Figure 5.3 Reparations as a percentage of Reich expenditure, 1920–1932
Source: As for figure 5.2.

rolling stock, as well as uneconomically low fares and freight rates.[44]
But as Carl Melchior explained to an English correspondent, the
government's principal concern was to maintain employment levels
and thus avoid unrest. The railway deficit was necessary to avoid

[44] Bresciani, *Inflation*, p. 71n.; Webb, *Hyperinflation*, pp. 33, 37.

putting 100,000 superfluous employees on the dole, 'and thus leaving them to political radicalism'.[45]

A less well-known case of government subsidy is that of the merchant marine. Formally, the payments made to rebuild the merchant marine were compensation payments to private owners of assets which had been handed over to the Allies, as required by Article 297 of the Versailles Treaty. However, in practice the Reich authorities could regard compensation payments as discretionary rather than mandatory, not least because of the discrepancy between the claims of the German firms concerned and the sums which the Reparations Commission (set up in February 1920) was willing to count as having been received.[46] It soon became clear that the amounts of money actually paid would be determined by the relative bargaining power of the firms concerned, with the decisive factor being the degree to which compensation payments would generate employment and hence dampen down working-class radicalism.[47] Thus the smaller merchant houses whose assets had been sequestrated got short shrift;[48] while the shipping industry was treated generously. As we have seen, this order of priority had become apparent within months of the November Revolution, when the new government had agreed to supplement the existing wartime compensation due to the shipping lines, after more or less explicit threats from the shipyards to lay off workers.

The negotiations between the shipping industry and the government which followed the further depletion of the merchant fleet at Versailles provide a perfect illustration of the fiscal consequences of corporatist politics. No sooner was the ink on the treaty dry, than Cuno was seeking a commitment from the government to pay compensation, conjuring up a figure of 4 bn. gold marks as the capital value of the lost merchant fleet – a figure which subsequently doubled.[49] The shipping lines were well aware of the weakness of their position, and certainly did not expect to recoup such a large sum. Indeed, as Cuno acknowledged, the possibility existed that the National Assembly might simply resolve to pay compensation in paper marks to save money, or might make any payment conditional upon socialisation or nationalis-

---

[45] WA, Pol. Corr. 1921, Melchior to S. Japhet & Co. Ltd., London, 15.1.21; Warburg, *Aufzeichnungen*, p. 94.

[46] See Holtfrerich, *Inflation*, p. 147.

[47] Cf. Mai, 'Arbeitsmarktregulierung oder Sozialpolitik?', pp. 202–36.

[48] For efforts to persuade the government to grant compensation to smaller commercial firms: BAP, RFM 46580 N. Reg. 317/9–16, Bund der Auslandsdeutschen to RFM, 25.8.19; RWM to RFM, 1.9.19; HA, HB, Holtzendorff Notizen, 10.7.19; 12.7.19; HKH, HKHP, Sitzung 1.8.19.

[49] HA, HB, Cuno to Holtzendorff, 18.7.19; Kohlhaus, 'Die Hapag', pp. 13–19; BAP, RWM 764/247, Hapag to RWM, 23.4.20.

ation.[50] In the event, it proved relatively easy to strike a deal with the key government department, the Finance Ministry, thanks to the readiness of Erzberger to acknowledge the strategic and economic importance of the merchant marine. By August 1919, it had been agreed to advance the shipping lines 1 bn. marks, with 9 bn. marks as the planned total – a settlement so generous that it prompted Holtzendorff to wish fervently 'that the enormously detested Erzberger will remain at the top of the Finance Ministry'.[51] However, as with all aspects of early Weimar economic policy, ministers could propose; but other institutions disposed. When the first Compensation Bill reached the National Assembly, the SPD inserted a clause effectively obliging the ship-builders to spend the money on the construction of new ships in German shipyards.[52] This was a severe blow to Cuno, who believed that new ships would not be ready quickly enough for the Hapag to stake its claim to a share of the post-war market. Now the compensation money looked like being diverted into a fund whose principal function would be 'to guarantee the shipyards that they can pay their shareholders dividends for decades to come'.[53] Typically, the shipping lines responded by appealing to another government department, the new Reconstruction Ministry, but retreated when the Minister, Gessler, began talking of some kind of direct Reich control over shipping.[54]

Nevertheless, the combination of wartime assistance (*Beihilfe*), revolutionary excess cost payments (*Überteuerung*) and now reparations compensation (*Entschädigung*) appeared to place German shipping on a secure post-war footing. On the strength of this legislation, a vast programme of ship-building was begun, with orders at the German shipyards totalling 2.86 m. tons (484 ships) by December 1920 – roughly a third of pre-war tonnage.[55] The ultimate cost of this programme to the Reich was expected to reach between 10 bn. and 17 bn. marks – between a fifth and a third of total Reich tax revenue in 1920 – of which around 3 bn. marks had been paid by November

[50] HA, HB, Holtzendorff to Cuno, 31.7.19; Cuno to Holtzendorff 31.7.19; 5.8.19.
[51] *Ibid.*, Cuno to Holtzendorff, 5.8.19; Holtzendorff Notizen, 7.8.19; Kohlhaus, 'Die Hapag', p. 39.
[52] HA, HB, Holtzendorff to Cuno, 12.8.19, 20.8.19, 22.8.19; Kohlhaus, 'Die Hapag', pp. 13f., 40. For the Gesetz über Enteignungen und Entschädigungen aus Anlaß des Friedensvertrages of 31 August 1919, see *RGB*, 1919, Nr. 171, pp. 1530–8. Although a special bill for the merchant marine was envisaged it did not materialise.
[53] HA, HB, Holtzendorff Notizen, 25.11.19; 26.11.19; 30.11.19.
[54] *Ibid.*, Holtzendorff to Cuno, 5.12.19; 10.12.19; Cuno to Holtzendorff, 23.1.20; Holtzendorff to Cuno, 29.1.20; Kohlhaus, 'Die Hapag', pp. 13, 19, 40–5.
[55] StAH, FA B&V 264, Kriegsausschuß der deutschen Werften, 4.12.20; 31.12.20. Of these orders, eleven had been completed, 141 were under construction and 159 had had materials purchased.

1920.[56] Yet even this did not suffice to satisfy the needs of the shipping industry, prompting complaints from the shipyards about delays in the payment of funds.[57]

Once started, the practice of subsidies proved difficult to stop. In an attempt to halt this seemingly unarrestable spiral, the new Finance Minister Joseph Wirth brought forward a proposal to wind up the various schemes of compensation in late 1920. 'The situation of the Reich was grave,' Wirth told the shipyards: 'Up until now it had provided the money by using the printing press. That could not go on.'[58] Not surprisingly, the news that the Reich was about to welsh on its commitments caused dismay in the shipyards. Already, in October, Deutsche Werft had been obliged by a shortfall in government payments to liquidate some of its reserves of foreign currency (earned on a series of contracts for Dutch lines).[59] Then, in December, the GHH-owned Oldenburgische-Portuguesische Line cancelled two orders at the yard because of lack of government money.[60] *Direktor* Stahl of the Hamburg Vulkan yard summed up the position bluntly:

If state bankruptcy is not declared, then the printing press can go on smoothly running and everything can stay as it is. If the state does declare itself bankrupt, however, then the shipyards will be enormously over-extended. If the programme stops, we will be worse off than ever.[61]

Blohm was no less appalled at the prospect: 'The situation is extraordinarily serious. [. . .] The Reich is declaring itself bankrupt [and] wants to take private industry down with it.'[62] One possible solution to the problem was put forward by Max Warburg, who argued that the shippers should try to raise a domestic 'reconstruction loan' to complete

---

[56] BAP, RMfW 1835/105–26, 'Denkschrift des Reichsausschusses für den Wiederaufbau der Handelsflotte', 24.11.20; RMfW 1835/190–211, RMfW to Strandes, 25.1.21; Präsidialkanzlei 19777/84–9, Kriegsausschuß der deutschen Reederei, 'Aufzeichnung über den Stand der Verhandlungen über die Gewährung einer Gesamtabfindung', 17.2.21; Reichstag Drucksache, 1. Wahlperiode, 1920/21, Nr. 526, 8.3.21. Inevitably, the shipping lines put the total figure for payments received lower still at 1.65 bn. marks: BAP, RFM 46582 N. Reg. 322/275–85, 'Gutachten'; 46580 N. Reg. 319, Reichsausschuß für die Wiederherstellung der Handelsflotte.

[57] BAP, 46586 R. Reg. 333/100–102, Cuno to RFM, 8.10.20.

[58] StAH, FA B&V 264, 'Aktennotizen über die außerordentliche Hauptversammlung der Kriegsausschuß der deutschen Werften' (Nawatski), 3.12.20. For the origins of the *Abfindung*, see; HA, HB, Holtzendorff to Cuno, 15.10.20; Kohlhaus, 'Die Hapag', p. 45. Cf. the retrospective memoranda in HA, HB, Holtzendorff Bericht, 26.1.21; and BAP, Präsidialkanzlei 19777/84–89, Kriegsausschuß der deutschen Reederei, February 1921.

[59] GHH, 300193012/5, Deutsche Werft to Reusch, 21.10.20; 23.10.20.

[60] GHH, 300193012/6, Oldenburgische-Portuguesische Dampfschiffsrhederei to Deutsche Werft, 9.12.20

[61] StAH, FA B&V 264, KDW Hauptversammlung (Stahl), 4.12.20.

[62] *Ibid.* (Blohm), 4.12.20.

the work that had been undertaken.[63] However, neither the shipyards nor the lines had any desire to increase their indebtedness by the 10–15 bn. marks the banker envisaged. That, as Stahl put it, would be 'fearful'; and he added a pointed reminder of the implications for employment: 'My firm today employs around 18,000 clerical and manual workers. In the event of state bankruptcy, I would rather work with 6,000 men than overstretch my borrowing.'[64] Instead, the shipping lines argued that the Reich should have a 'last' resort to the printing press in order to make a one-off settlement (*Abfindung*) payment to the shipping industry, rejecting a Reich proposal for an additional 10 per cent top-up of the excess costs agreement.[65] Cuno started the bidding with 15 bn. marks (as a final total, including the sums already paid), which he believed would suffice to reconstruct a third of pre-war tonnage; but the yards pushed the figure up to 17.27 bn. marks, and inserted the inevitable clause that 90 per cent of the money must be spent in German yards.[66] Wirth naturally wanted to pay less; and a compromise figure of 12 bn. marks was eventually agreed in February 1921, under the condition that there should be only minimal government control over its disbursal through a new bank, the *Schiffbau-Treuhand*, to be set up by a consortium of all the interested companies. This meant, in effect, 4.7 bn. marks of 'new' money.[67]

From the point of view of the shipping lines, this settlement was once again advantageous. It removed the earlier threat of government control; and provided a final capital sum on which to base long-term plans for reconstruction. Cuno's first acts following the conclusion of the agreement were to announce his intention of restoring the Hapag fleet to a third of its pre-war level within five years; and to oust Stinnes from the Hapag board.[68] However, the shipyards were less sanguine. As Blohm had put it, 'We are simply relying on the Reich printing more notes [. . .] Let us not stick our heads in the sand.

[63] GHH, 300193012/5, M.M. Warburg & Co. to Deutsche Werft, 19.10.20; Scholz to Reusch, 20.10.20; StAH, FA B&V 264, Aktennotiz, 23.11.20. Significantly, Warburg stressed that such a loan would be non-inflationary.

[64] StAH, FA B&V 264, KDW Hauptversammlung, 4.12.20; Kohlhaus, 'Die Hapag', pp. 21ff.

[65] *Ibid.*, p. 23

[66] StAH, FA B&V 264, KDW Hauptversammlung, 4.12.20, Abschrift; Auszug aus der Sitzung zwischen Stahlwerken, Regierung und Werften in Essen, 20.12.20; KDW to Zetzmann, 31.12.20; Kohlhaus, 'Die Hapag', pp. 25–7.

[67] HA, Cuno NL, Cuno to Bergmann, 25.1.21; HA, HB, Holtzendorff Aktennotizen, 18.2.21; Kohlhaus, pp. 27, 46–8; BAP, RMfW 1835/11–14, Abschrift Wa 3, Nr. 2903, 28.3.21.

[68] Hapag, *Jahresbericht 1921*; HA, 'Stinnes' Akten (May 1921); *Deutsche Bergwerks Zeitung*, 3.5.21; *Vorwärts*, 31.7.21; *Vossische Zeitung*, 1.8.21. For Stinnes's anger at Cuno's conduct, HA, HB, Stinnes to Max von Schinckel, 28.4.21.

That will only last half a year and then the catastrophe will be upon us.'[69] It would be hard to improve on this assessment. The case of shipping compensation perfectly illustrates why the Reich failed to stabilise its finances in 1920. The expenditure of 12 bn. marks in the financial years 1919 and 1920 represented around 6 per cent of total Reich expenditures – a remarkable amount for a subsidy to a branch of the economy which remained (unlike the railways) largely in private ownership.[70] Such open-handedness effectively wiped out the increased revenue generated by Erzberger's tax reforms, ensuring the persistence of deficits.

This continuation of inflationary finance was by no means inevitable. The Hamburg state, for example, turned a deficit of 110 m. marks in 1920 into a surplus of 1 bn. marks in 1921.[71] What was lacking at the Reich level was a more rapid collection of income and other direct taxes, and some corresponding reductions in public expenditure. It would not have been necessary to balance the budget in 1920 to have increased the chances of an enduring stabilisation; merely to have reduced the Reich deficit below the excessive level of around 16 per cent of NNP. To have halved that figure would have required tax increases of around 1.5 bn. gold marks and spending cuts of the same order – which, in the relatively buoyant economic circumstances of 1920, would surely not have had devastating effects.[72] The puzzle is that Erzberger himself seemingly saw no contradiction in simultaneously introducing unprecedented levels of direct taxation and paying out such generous subsidies. Publicly, he boasted that his policy of fiscal 'socialisation' would 'make good the injustices of the war'. Privately – at Holtzendorff's table – he talked of staffing the Finance Ministry with ex-officers to ensure that subsidies did not simply 'make life easy for layabouts'.[73] Was this an 'integrated policy'? It seems, at best, doubtful.

The momentum of monetary growth

'Ultimately,' Max Warburg told the *Hamburger Nachrichten* in February 1920, 'the present situation is like a contest between the note issuing

[69] BAP, Reichstag Drucksache, I. Wahlperiode 1920/21, Nr. 526, 8.3.21; StAH, FA B&V 264, KDW Hauptversammmlung (Blohm) 4.12.20.
[70] Total nominal spending in 1919 and 1920 calculated from figures in Witt, 'Tax Policies', pp. 154–9.
[71] Brandt, *Hamburgs Finanzen*, pp. 25ff.
[72] I have not attempted to estimate exactly the kind of contraction which such a fiscal squeeze would have caused. Suffice to say that it would have been less severe than the contraction experienced in 1923, when NNP fell by around 10 per cent.
[73] HA, HB, Holtzendorff Notizen, 7.8.19.

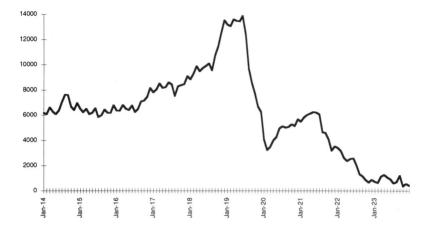

Figure 5.4 The real value of currency in circulation, 1914–1923 (m. gold
marks)
Source: Holtfrerich, *Inflation*, pp. 52ff.

banks of the various countries to see who can issue the most notes.
Unfortunately, Germany is rather far in front.'[74] At first sight, monetary
policy was as much to blame as fiscal policy for the failure of stabilisation to endure. Whether one measures narrow money (currency in
circulation) or high-powered money, the rate of monetary growth was
higher in 1920 (respectively, 4.1 per cent and 3.8 per cent per month)
than it was in either 1919 (3.5 per cent and 3.2 per cent) or 1921
(3.5 per cent and 3.4 per cent).[75] Because of the relative price stability
of 1920, the rate of growth of money in real terms was therefore even
higher (see figures 0.5 and 5.4). This expansion was only partly due
to the continuation of government deficits, since a rising share of
Treasury bills was held outside the Reichsbank (from 53.4 per cent
in March 1920 to 66.8 per cent in February 1921).[76] It reflected above
all the high liquidity of the money markets and the static discount
rate policy of the Reichsbank, which kept market interest rates at
around 3.5 per cent and the discount rate at 5 per cent until 1922.[77]

[74] *Hamburger Nachrichten*, 18.2.20.
[75] Calculated from Holtfrerich, *Inflation*, pp. 50f.
[76] Holtfrerich, *Inflation*, pp. 67f. Cf. S.B. Webb, 'The Supply of Money and Reichsbank
Financing of Corporate Debt in Germany 1919–1923', *JEcH*, 44 (1984), pp. 499–
507.
[77] See figure 4.1; interest rates for the years 1919, 1920 and 1921 in Holtfrerich,
Inflation, p. 73; Petzina *et al.* (eds.), *Sozialgeschichtliches Arbeitsbuch*, III, p. 71. Cf.
O. Pfleiderer, 'Die Reichsbank in der Zeit der großen Inflation, die Stabilisierung
der Mark und die Aufwertung von Kapitalforderungen', in Bundesbank (ed.), *Währung und Wirtschaft*, pp. 157–201; Holtfrerich, 'Reichsbankpolitik 1918–1923 zwischen
Zahlungsbilanz und Quantitätstheorie' pp. 193–214.

Although the Reichsbank went so far as to threaten to stop discounting Treasury bills in 1919,[78] it at no time showed any sign of wanting to tighten credit conditions for the private sector. Indeed, at the first sign of such a tightening, it stepped in to maintain business liquidity: in the mild squeeze caused by the strengthening of the mark in the spring of 1920, there was a marked increase in the volume of commercial bills discounted as a fraction of total note circulation from 3.1 per cent in March to 9.0 per cent in May.[79] This explains why banks found themselves able to satisfy 'most willingly' a 'rising demand for bank credits [which. . .] would, under normal circumstances, have led to a sharp tightening of the money market'.[80] The Reichsbank not only opposed Erzberger's plan for an administered reduction in the money supply (whether by means of a loan, or by the withdrawal or 'stamping' of certain banknotes), it also industriously maintained and increased the supply of new notes emanating from the *Reichsdrückerei*.[81]

The question remains whether the Reichsbank had any alternative. Holtfrerich has argued that, before May 1921, there was a discrepancy between the Reichsbank's public explanation for monetary expansion and inflation, which blamed the balance of payments deficit and reparations, and the *Direktorium*'s confidential advice to the government, which clearly blamed the growth of the Reich's floating debt. The government, however, was under no obligation to heed Reichsbank advice on financial matters. The only option open to the bank was therefore to use its discount rate in the hope of increasing the appeal of government bonds to the public and attracting foreign capital to Germany; yet in practice such an interest rate increase would have worsened the fiscal position, without necessarily increasing investor confidence.[82] On the other hand, if the government had so wished, an alternative monetary policy could have been adopted. Prior to May 1921, the Reichsbank's traditional reserve requirements remained in force. True, these continued to be perverted by the wartime decision to treat *Darlehnskassenscheine* as equivalent to gold in the reserve, and Reich Treasury bills as equivalent to commercial bills. But by the end of 1920, the total volume of *Darlehnskassenscheine* had fallen by 12.5 per cent compared with the previous year; the amount of Treasury

---

[78] Specht, *Politische Hintergründe*, pp. 28, 51f.; Holtfrerich, *Inflation*, p. 165; Feldman, *Great Disorder*, pp. 158f.
[79] Graham, *Hyperinflation*, p. 64.
[80] Dresdner Bank, *Jahresbericht 1919*; *Jahresbericht 1920*.
[81] Specht, *Politische Hintergründe*, pp. 51f.; *Deutsche Allgemeine Zeitung*, 28.4.21, 'Ein Besuch in der Reichsdrückerei'.
[82] Holtfrerich, 'Reichsbankpolitik', *passim*; idem, *Inflation*, pp. 155–80. Cf. Habedank, *Reichsbank in der Weimarer Republik*, *passim*.

bills in the Reichsbank's portfolio had risen by only 16.3 bn. marks; while its gold reserve was almost exactly at its 1913 level at 1,091.6 m. gold marks – 19 per cent of the real value of currency in circulation, compared with 18 per cent in 1913.[83] In other words, a reform of the currency could in theory have been undertaken in 1920 without necessarily causing a significant real monetary contraction if the paper mark had simply been devalued to around 5 or 10 gold pfennigs. This was the course of action which had been recommended by the economist Richard Häuser in July 1919.[84]

There were several arguments advanced against this course during a long and wide-ranging debate.[85] Firstly, it was argued, those firms and individuals with foreign currency debts (like the Hapag's 20 m. kronen loan dating back to 1917) would be deprived of the theoretical possibility of some longer-term recovery of the mark if devaluation were formalised.[86] Secondly – and contrariwise – exporters currently benefiting from the depreciation of the currency would lose their advantage. In October 1919, Erzberger had argued that Germany would 'lose the possibility of exports' in the event of a stabilisation of the mark; a view echoed with hindsight by Felix Deutsch a year later:

Our good fortune in the midst of misfortune is our poor currency, which enables us to export on a large scale. If the currency improves externally at a rapid rate, as we saw a few months ago, our exports stop entirely, and our industry is ruined.[87]

It was for this reason that the Economics Ministry took the remarkable step of intervening *against* the mark between March and June 1920,

---

[83] Holtfrerich, *Inflation*, p. 50; Bresciani, *Inflation*, p. 448; Kroboth, *Finanzpolitik*, p. 494.

[84] R. Häuser, 'Zur Währungsfrage', *Bank-Archiv*, 19 Jg., pp. 197–99.

[85] F. Bendixen, 'Devalvation. Eine Richtigstellung', *ibid.*, pp. 163–9; C. Weill, 'Betrachtungen zum Devalvationsproblem', *ibid.*, p. 183. See also *Berliner Börsenzeitung*, 'Gegen eine Devalvation!', 19.10.19; 26.10.19; *Die Welt am Montag*, 'Devalvation?', 20.10.19; 10.11.19; *Hamburger Correspondent*, 'Devalvation?', 22.10.19; *Hamburger Fremdenblatt*, 'Handel: Selbsthilfe', 15.11.19; *Weltwirtschaftszeitung*, 'Davalvation', 30.1.20; *Deutsche Allgemeine Zeitung*, 'Die Kehrseiten einer Devalvation', 26.3.20; 'Devalvation', 18.4.20; 'Grundsätzliches zur deutschen Devalvationsproblem', 15.11.20; *Der Tag*, 'Rückkehr zur Friedenswährung oder Devalvation?', 26.10.20; 'Eine abstufende Devalvierung', 30.11.20; 'Nochmals zum Devalvationsproblem', 18.12.20; 'Abermals die Devalvation', 30.12.20; 'Eine abstufende Devalvation', 31.5.21; *Kreuz-Zeitung*, 'Keine Devalvation der deutschen Währung', 9.2.21; 10.2.21; *Frankfurter Zeitung*, 1.6.21.

[86] BAP, RMfW 1835/44–51, Abschrift, 21.1.21; RWM, 764/245–8, Hapag to RWM, 23.4.20; RMfW 1835/253–7, 'Niederschrift über die Besprechung im RWM', 30.4.20; /265, Hopff to RWM, 23.6.20; StAH, DHSG II, Spez. XXXIV 215 5, Senate to DHSG, 9.3.20, HKH to DHSG, 21.4.20; SK II, III A 1 a 7, Heidecker to SK, 12.3.20; HKH, HKH P, 21.5.20; 23.7.20; 29. Plenarsitzung, 20.8.20.

[87] Specht, *Politische Hintergründe*, pp. 30, 43n.

buying substantial amounts of foreign currency to limit the appreciation of the mark.[88]

The most important reason why no serious attempt was made to stabilise the monetary system, however, was the fear of a liquidity crisis or 'credit shortage'. The most plausible evidence for this is that there were around two and a half times as many bankruptcies in the first half of 1921 as in the first half of 1920.[89] The experience of Deutsche Werft was not untypical. To finance a programme of investment in 1920, which involved spending 48.1 m. marks (approximately 3.2 m. gold marks) on new plant,[90] Deutsche Werft had accrued substantial debts (12.9 m. marks), including 10 m. marks from its parent company GHH. By reducing the mark value of its export earnings, the stabilisation of the exchange rate in early 1920 created an acute cash-flow crisis which the company could only solve by borrowing a further 25 m. marks at $4\frac{1}{2}$ per cent from Oberhausen.[91] The result was that almost all of the 37.8 m. marks the firm received in April 1921 from the *Treuhand* went to pay off its debts to the GHH; and when the next compensation payments were delayed, the yard had to begin 'letting suppliers wait'.[92] When Reusch baulked at this, the yard was forced to turn to its banker, the Dresdner Bank, which was now charging substantial commissions to compensate for the negative real interest rates on its loans.[93] Similar experiences throughout the economy inevitably led to calls for the government to intervene to alleviate the credit crisis.

In fact, the possibility of a 'credit *Planwirtschaft*' had been bruited in the Economics Ministry as early as September 1919.[94] By early 1920, two basic ideas had been devised by the Ministry, one typical of the Moellendorff-inspired 'corporatist' approach to economic problems; the other indicative of the more *dirigiste* outlook of his successor Hirsch. The former (associated with the RdI Presidium member Hans Jordan) envisaged the creation of compulsory credit syndicates, which would coordinate the allocation of foreign and domestic credits to particular economic branches. The Hirsch plan envisaged the creation

---

[88] Feldman, 'Relative Stabilisation', pp. 180ff.; Webb, *Hyperinflation*, p. 31; StAH, SK II, III A 1 a 7, HG to SK, 7.6.20.

[89] Graham, *Hyperinflation*, p. 280; Webb, *Hyperinflation*, p. 99. See figure 7.3.

[90] GHH, 300193012/6, Aufsichtsratssitzungen, 19.1.20; 9.9.20; 30.5.21.

[91] GHH, 300193012/5, Deutsche Werft to Reusch, 14.6.20; 19.6.20; 10.7.20; 4.9.20; Deutsche Werft to Deutsch, 29.7.20; GHH, 300193012/6, Deutsche Werft to Reusch, 11.12.20.

[92] GHH, 300193012/6, Deutsche Werft to Reusch, 29.4.21; 28.7.21; Reusch to Deutsche Werft, 30.7.21.

[93] *Ibid.*, Reusch to Deutsche Werft, 22.11.21; Deutsche Werft to Reusch, 25.11.21.

[94] See the retrospective memorandum on the origins of the *Reichswirtschaftsbank* in BAK, R38, 70, RWM Scholz to RFM Wirth, 20.10.20.

of a state 'Economic Bank', which would direct and allocate credit to 'firms of essential importance to the national economy [. . .] according to the needs of the national economy', irrespective of 'private economic considerations'.[95] When the complaints about a 'credit crisis' began to increase in volume in the late summer of 1920, it was the second idea to which the Economics Minister Scholz turned.[96]

Although Feldman has portrayed the failure of the scheme as a missed opportunity to consolidate 'relative stabilisation',[97] in fact the Economic Bank was essentially a device to keep inflation going. The Economics Minister Scholz claimed that the Bank would conscript the savings banks, giro institutions and unspecified foreign lenders into providing credit to industry; but the implicit objective – since these sources would clearly not reach the 100 bn. marks target set by Scholz – was the continuation, in some form, of the wartime *Darlehnskassen* system, allowing liquidity to be injected into the economy without reference to the Reichsbank.[98] This is clear from the 'lively debate' on the subject between Warburg and Rathenau when they met at Holtzendorff's in October 1920:

Rathenau put forward the argument that Germany could well endure a further inflation [i.e., monetary expansion], since in his opinion the mark's value would never fall to nil; but on the contrary would rise back to its [former] heights, so long as production was maintained in Germany. Warburg, by contrast, was very pessimistic, and said we could not endure a further increase in our debts.[99]

Rathenau repeated this view three months later:

He was not afraid of the inflation. [. . .] If the crisis which has already broken out to its full extent in England were now to come over to us, we should allow the printing press to do a bit more work and begin rebuilding the country. This activity would enable us to build a dam against the crisis. It is simply wrong to say that the printing press would render us *kaputt*.[100]

It was, however, Warburg who prevailed. In a speech before Wirth at the Hamburg Chamber of Commerce he denounced the Economic

[95] *Ibid.*; Feldman, 'Relative Stabilisation', pp. 199f.; *idem*, *Great Disorder*, pp. 258–62.
[96] Wulf (ed.), *Kabinett Fehrenbach*, pp. 164–6, 168, 205.
[97] Feldman, 'Relative Stabilisation', p. 199.
[98] For the hostility of the Finance Ministry on these grounds, see BAK, R38, Wirth to Scholz, 27.10.20. Scholz envisaged 'a great credit institution which, under the most accommodating conditions, would place the needed means at the disposal of the cash-starved factories'. The Finance Ministry official Moesle retorted that the plan was merely an 'attempt to bring about an improvement in our economic situation through further inflation': Feldman, *Great Disorder*, p. 262.
[99] HA, HB, Holtzendorff Notiz, 16.10.20. The industrialists were not wholly convinced of the viability of the Economic Bank plan; but clearly rejected the bankers' fatalism; see BAK, R38 70, RdI to RWM, 4.8.20; 20.9.20.
[100] Quoted in Holtfrerich, *Inflation*, p. 210.

Bank as an attempt 'to win [. . .] political applause'. It was absurd
to speak of a shortage of credit when 'today everyone who has money
is only too eager to change it from note form to real values or credits'.[101]
He followed this with a wide-ranging and highly influential lecture at
the German Bankers' Conference in Berlin on 26 October, in which
he systematically dismissed not only the Economic Bank but all other
schemes for monetary reform currently being discussed in Germany,[102]
and with a speech 'against state economic planning' to Scholz when
the latter visited Hamburg in December 1921.[103] The *coup de grace*
was delivered in his testimony to the Reich Economic Council in
January and February 1921.[104] An Economic Bank, he argued, would
simply be a glorified 'holding company', distributing funds to industry
on behalf of blind investors – a superfluous institution since the banks
had already provided industry with 11.3 bn. marks in 1920. The real
problem was not credit shortage, but excess liquidity: because of the
government's inflationary policies, the extent of the structural economic
crisis was being – literally – papered over in Germany. With heavy
irony he told the RWR committee: 'I do not know of any occasion
when, providing the firm was creditworthy, it could not obtain credit
[. . .] With the aid of our greatest helper, the Reichsbank, which
indefatigably prints notes, we will always be in a position to grant any
credit request (laughter).'[105] And he added:

The credit crisis will only begin when the financial system of the Reich, and
thus the currency, become solid (hear, hear!) and we no longer have a
continually increasing inflation. [. . .] The individual debt-relationships have
grown so enormously that the banks are obliged to prop up those firms
which find themselves in payments difficulties. We are therefore at present
experiencing the greatest latent world crisis. (Interjection by Georg Bernhard:
So much the better!) Quite so [. . .] and so much the worse will be the
consequences for us.[106]

---

[101] WA, XIX, Gesammelte Vorträge (untitled speech), October 1920.
[102] For the unabridged text of the speech, 'Die notwendigen Vorbedingungen für die
Gesundung der deutschen Währung', see *ibid.* For the shorter version delivered in
Berlin, see *Berliner Börsen Zeitung*, Nr. 473, 27.10.23; *Deutsche Wirtschaftszeitung*,
Nr. 23, 1.12.20; WA, 'Jahresbericht 1920', Bl. 24; Warburg, *Aufzeichnungen*, p. 93.
Scholz and the Foreign Minister Simons were present; see BAK, R43 I/644, Pro-
gramm des V. Deutschen Bankiertages, 25.-27.10.20. For the 'well-nigh frenetic
applause' the speech received, see HA, HB, Holtzendorff to Cuno, 27.10.20.
[103] WA, XIX, Gesammelte Vorträge, 17.12.20; *Hamburger Echo*, 20.12.20.
[104] WA, Jahresbericht 1920, III (undated copy). For a sceptical view of the bankers'
argument, see Feldman, *Great Disorder*, pp. 265–72.
[105] WA, X, Politische Correspondenz, Warburg, depositions before RWR (29.1.21,
11.2.21).
[106] *Ibid.* (11.2.21). Bernhard, editor of the magazine *Plutus*, was an early supporter of
the Economic Bank idea.

The implication was quite clear: the choice was between monetary stabilisation and continuing to defer the inevitable crisis. The only purpose of the Economic Bank proposal was to put off the hour of reckoning:

I regard it as impossible to give credits simply so that firms can build up their stocks. [. . .In other words,] to keep the poor workers employed, certain industries will be kept afloat! But that is simply to grow hothouse flowers! If you want to keep industries going, working to stockpile, purely because you lack the courage to close industries which are no longer viable, then we are heading for a calamity which will simply be irreparable.[107]

Warburg's success in defeating the Economic Bank scheme prevented the creation of yet another source of paper liquidity for the German economy. However, the arguments put forward on both sides revealed the strength of opposition to a stabilisation of the existing monetary arrangements. Few – if any – industrialists or officials shared the view of the banker Jakob Goldschmidt 'that an elemental crisis [should] occur as soon as possible'; most – if not all – agreed with Hans Kraemer that 'everything had to be done to avoid the catastrophe'.[108] Rather than cement the natural stabilisation which began in early 1920 by an early currency reform, policy makers agreed to continue a policy of easy money. Warburg's best argument against the Economic Bank was that the Reichsbank was already doing the job of maintaining liquidity at any price.

Mismanaged trade

If monetary policy continued to drift during the period of 'relative stabilisation', the same could not be said of trade policy. As we have seen, there had been a clear move in the direction of trade liberalisation after the resignation of Wissell and Moellendorff in mid 1919, based on the belief that the rapid depreciation of the mark would provide a strong stimulus for exports.[109] As predicted by the German delegates at Versailles, this did indeed lead to a 'flood' of German goods on to the world market, often at extremely low prices in terms of foreign currency; but it also led to a substantial widening of the trade deficit in money terms, as the expanding domestic economy sucked in imports through the customs-free 'hole in the West'. The previous chapter considered some of the international consequences of these develop-

[107] *Ibid.* (29.1.21).
[108] Feldman, *Great Disorder*, pp. 262f.
[109] HKH, *Jahresbericht 1919*, p. 23.

ments. It is time to consider now their domestic impact, and the backlash they provoked.

In essence, Schmidt's free trade policy had two domestic consequences. Firstly, it led to shortages of those goods which were diverted into exports. Secondly, it caused the prices of some imported commodities and products to soar. On both counts, this ran counter to the Social Democrats' desire to keep down the cost of living to ordinary consumers, and provoked loud denunciations from the Left of the party of the so-called 'sell out' (*Ausverkauf*) of Germany. It was not surprising that the attack on 'hunger profits' and 'the intolerable consequences of the free market' was led by the man whose earlier arguments now appeared to have been vindicated, Rudolf Wissell.[110] However, what the proponents of free trade had not bargained for was the defection of leading figures in industry to the side of trade regulation. The industrial *volte face* was partly the work of Jakob Reichert of the RdI, whose influential pamphlet 'Rescue from the Currency Crisis' argued for a combination of export controls and increased prices – a compromise between his own enthusiasm for the wartime system of central trade boards and the desire of Hugo Stinnes to close the gap between German export prices and world market prices.[111] Equally important was the intervention of the electrotechnical industry on the side of trade controls. This reflected the belief of Rathenau and Deutsch of AEG that trade control would advance their interests in 'direct' exports, i.e., the integration of overseas marketing into the structure of industrial firms, thus freeing them from dependence on the commercial middle man.[112] Nor did the revulsion against free trade stop there. Even traditionally friendly voices in Hamburg were raised against the policy of liberalisation. The *Hamburger Fremdenblatt*, for example, expressed a widespread sense of disillusionment, pointing out that the supposedly beneficial consequences of 'the sell out of Germany' had failed to manifest themselves, and alleging that exporters were not only selling 'too cheaply' but also failing to repatriate their foreign currency earnings.[113] Within the Hamburg state bureaucracy too, there was a revulsion against the 'egoistical selfishness and criminal profit-mania' which deregulation

---

[110] See, e.g., R. Wissell, 'Hungergewinn?', *Hamburger Echo*, 28.12.19. Cf. D.E. Barclay, 'The Insider as Outsider: Rudolf Wissell's Critique of Social Democratic Economic Policies 1919 to 1920', in Feldman *et al.* (eds.), *Anpassung*, pp. 451–71.

[111] See Feldman, *Iron and Steel*, pp. 132–6.

[112] For Rathenau's views on the obsolescence of Hamburg commerce, see the interesting letters by ex-Colonial Minister Solf in StAH, DHSG III, Pr. III 34 Bd. 1 61, Solf to Petersen, 11.2.20; VHEx to HKH, 26.3.20; BAK, Solf NL, 63, Schüler (AA) to Solf, 12.2.20; Weidenfeld to Solf, 19.2.20.

[113] *Hamburger Fremdenblatt*, 15.11.19; 10.12.19; 10.1.20.

had unleashed.[114] Under these circumstances, the proponents of *laissez faire* were increasingly isolated. The Chamber of Commerce continued to insist that 'only through high exports can the balance of payments be improved [. . .] In the interests of the improvement of the mark, [the government] can do no more than see to it that as many goods as possible are exported'.[115] But these arguments no longer carried weight in the Economics Ministry, where Hirsch was increasingly convinced of the need for regulation. In any case, it was hard for Hamburg interests to deny the need for some control of trade, given the loss of business the city evidently suffered as a consequence of 'the hole in the West'.[116]

The system of trade control which took shape between December 1919 and April 1920 partly incorporated Moellendorff's plan for the extension of the wartime system of licensing boards. However, instead of pure self regulation, there were to be two committees per board: one official, and one representing the interests involved (e.g., primary production, processing, trade) on the now *de rigueur* basis of employer–employee parity.[117] These committees were to start from the assumption that 'imports are fundamentally prohibited', with the exception of 'precisely listed raw materials and semi-finished goods'; while exports were 'fundamentally permitted', with the exception of specified foods and raw materials.[118] In addition, the decrees introduced the idea for an export levy, intended to tax the profits allegedly being made from the difference between German and world market prices – though instead of the high duty wished for by the Finance Ministry, only a minimum levy of 5 per cent was introduced for the specific purpose of paying supplements to pensions.[119] The result was bureaucratic

[114] Lippmann, *Leben*, pp. 240–3. This partly reflected the vested interests of bureaucrats employed in wartime organisations like the Hamburg War Provisions Office, who stood to lose their jobs if the economy was wholly deregulated.

[115] For the Chamber of Commerce's vain rearguard action, which the Senate supported, see: StAH, Sen. Cl. 1 Lit. T No. 9c vol. 38b, HKH to DHSG 17.11.19; SK II, III A I C 3 Bd. 1, Albrecht to SK, 17.11.19; SK to RFM, 26.11.19; SK to RWM, 29.11.19; 'Ein Aufruf zur Solidarität der Handelsvertreter', *Hamburgische Correspondent*, 22.11.19; DHSG III, Pr. III 34 Bd. 1, HKH to DHSG, 18.12.19; DKH to DHSG, 23.12.19; Albrecht, Bericht, 20.12.19.

[116] In volume terms, only around 4 per cent of German exports passed through Hamburg in 1919, compared with 10.6 per cent in 1913.

[117] See Reichsrat Drucksache Nr. 277, 11.12.19; and the decree of 20 December 1919, in *RGB* 1919, No. 247, pp. 2128f. Cf. G. Krämer, 'Die deutsche Außenhandelskontrolle in der Nachkriegszeit' (Diss. Frankfurt, 1928); Matthews, 'Continuity of Social Democratic Economic Policy', pp. 485–512.

[118] StAH, DHSG III, Pr. III 38 Bd. 1, RWM to Länder, 16.10.19; SK II, III a 1 a 7, HG, 10.3.20.

[119] StAH, DHSG III, Pr. III 34 Bd. 1, Ausführungsbestimmungen der Verordnung über die Außenhandelskontrolle vom 20.12.19, 8.4.20; Feldman, *Iron and Steel*, pp. 163, 191–3.

hypertrophy. In addition to some sixteen wartime 'central boards', there were added five foreign trade boards (for chemicals, wood, leather, paper and cork), three 'sub-boards' for transactions which defied sectoral categorisation, one 'umbrella association' for metal, one 'Reich board for the textile economy', and so on, as new categories of international transaction came to the notice of the Economics Ministry.[120] The only concession to Hamburg interests was that 'control board for the export trade' (known as the 'Afex' for short) was set up under the control of a hastily created Committee of German Import and Export Trade Associations.[121] By April there were forty-two such boards in existence; by October, no less than fifty-six, supposedly processing 30,000 applications for trade licences every day. By January 1921, the number of boards had reached 170.[122]

The irony was that this effort by the government to control inflation by controlling the balance of trade came into effect almost exactly at the same time as the equilibrating forces described in the previous chapter brought the original surge of currency depreciation, cheap exports and expensive imports to an end. As we have seen, from its nadir against the dollar in February 1920, the mark unexpectedly recovered. However, the German price level, although it fell, did not fall as far as the dollar against the mark, so that Germany's competitive advantage was reduced.[123] This meant that, at the very moment that a small army of officials set about levying a tax on the gap between foreign and domestic prices, the gap was closed by appreciation of the mark. Confusion reigned as the profit margins on export deals concluded before the stabilisation of the mark were wiped out; while the foreign trade boards began demanding their percentage of nothing.[124] An acrimonious battle ensued as exporters, struggling to revise prices

---

[120] Details from: StAH, DHSG III, Pr. III 38 Bd. I, Hirsch to Länder, 16.10.19; DHSG III, Pr. III 34 Bd. 1, Mitteilungen für die Preisprüfungsstelle, 1.4.20.
[121] StAH, DHSG III, Pr. III 34 Bd. I, Petersen (interpolation at National Assembly), 24.12.19; DHSG III, Pr. III 37, Strandes to SK, 4.7.19; DHSG III, Pr. III 38 Bd. I, HKH to DHSG, 5.8.19; 9.9.19; SK to RWM, 12.9.19; HKH to DHSG, 23.9.19; 6.10.19; RWM to SK, 6.10.19; HKH to DHSG, 11.10.19; 27.10.19; 14.11.19; Hamb. Bev. to SK, 17.11.19; Hamb. Bev. to SK, 8.11.19; HKH to DHSG, 14.1.20; Hamb. Bev. to SK, 15.1.20; DHSG III, Pr. III 34 Bd. I, Witthoefft to Strandes, 10.2.20.
[122] StAH, DHSG III, Pr. III 34 Bd. I, Mitteilungen für die Preisprüfungsstellen, 1.4.20; DHSG III, Pr. III 38 Bd. II, HKH to DHSG, 8.10.20.
[123] See figure 4.5.
[124] The RWM did not actually publish the detailed rates for the export levy until 22 April 1920. They were due to become effective on 1 May (later 10 May), and only trade transactions *completed* by 1 July were exempt; see Feldman, *Iron and Steel*, p. 192. For the anger in Hamburg at this procedure, StAH, DHSG III, Pr. III 34 Bd. I, HKH to DHSG, 31.3.20; HKH to DHSG, 10.4.20; RWM to VHEx, 17.4.20; SK to RWM, 23/26.4.20; HKH to RWM, 28.4.20; RWM to SK, 28.4.20.

upwards (which incensed foreign customers) or to cancel contracts altogether (which incensed domestic suppliers), vented their frustration on the Economic Ministry and its 'mistaken measures'.[125] As the Chamber of Commerce put it:

Export has practically ground to a halt [. . .] as a consequence of the economic downturn and the improvement in the exchange rate, but especially because of the high export prices [caused by] government export policy and the export levy.[126]

The protracted battle over foreign trade control perfectly illustrates how unmanageably 'polycratic' the system of economic policy making had become by 1920. It was in some ways true, as the Hamburg Commerce Deputation said, that 'the decision [had] become a question of power in the economic and political struggle';[127] but it was a struggle conducted over too many battlefields and involving too many feuding forces to produce a decisive outcome. Typically, the Bavarian and Hanseatic representatives in the Reichsrat both tabled motions against the levy, but proposed wholly incompatible alternatives to it, the former arguing for a sliding scale system to link the levy to the exchange rate; the latter urging a greatly reduced flat rate.[128] Antagonism to the levy flared up within the industrial associations, with Stinnes himself expressing dissatisfaction; but at the same time motions were introduced in the Hamburg Bürgerschaft complaining that industry itself was exploiting the system to the detriment of small commercial firms – and here Stinnes's name was cited as a beneficiary of trade control.[129] The Association of Hamburg Exporters sought to portray the conflict as one between business and the burgeoning Weimar welfare state. Controls should be lifted, 'even at the risk that in isolated cases we sell goods abroad too cheaply', since the important thing was 'to win back and hold onto temporarily lost markets':

Without doubt our social responsibilities have grown beyond all measure; but there can scarcely be said to be a connection between the export industry and the welfare of widows and children. [. . .] It seems equally wrong-headed to

---

[125] 'Verfehlte Maßnahmen', *Hamburger Nachrichten*, Nr. 242, 17.5.20; 'Der neueste Schlag gegen den deutschen Außenhandel', *ibid.*, Nr. 246, 20.5.20; *Deutsche Allgemeine Zeitung*, Nr. 94, 20.2.20. For a list of complaints from fifty-one commercial firms, see StAH, DHSG III, Pr. III 34 Bd. I, HKH to DHSG, 11.6.20.

[126] StAH, DHSG III, Pr. III 34 Bd. I, HKH To DHSG, 11.6.20.

[127] StAH, Krg. B II b 121 i vol. I, DHSG to Heidecker, 22.10.20.

[128] StAH, DHSG III, Pr. III 34 Bd. I, Reichsrat Drucksache No. 169, 18.5.20; HG to DHSG, 2.6.20; 4.6.20; 5.6.20; 23.6.20; HG Abschrift, 24.6.20; RWM to HG, 5.7.20.

[129] Feldman, *Iron and Steel*, pp. 194–202; 'Die soziale Ausfuhrabgabe', *Hamburger Fremdenblatt*, Nr. 392, 13.8.20; *ibid.*, No. 485, 7.10.20; *Sten. Ber. d. Bürgerschaft*, 41. Sitzung, 8.9.20.

try to use a portion of the profits from exports to stabilise the domestic price level.[130]

Yet not all business interests took this robust line. As one weary Social Democrat observed: 'in the same industry, some [are] for keeping the limits, others for getting rid of them, some [. . .] for the rationing of new materials, others against it – always of course from their own personal interest'.[131] There was a brief moment in late 1920 when the key ministers in the new Fehrenbach cabinet – Wirth, Scholz and Hermes – appeared to indicate their lack of commitment to trade control.[132] But the socialist supporters of control were able to mount a highly effective rearguard action against the winding down of the system on the new Reich Economic Council.[133] Indeed, no sooner had the commercial spokesman Hugo given Reichert a drubbing on the Reichstag Economic Committee than he himself was driven to resign from the Afex by the supporters of control on the Economic Council.[134] Pressure on ministers led to reductions in the export levy; but it then transpired that the trade boards were – as Moellendorff had originally intended – developing a self-regulatory will of their own, and had begun insisting on their own initiative that export contracts be exclusively in foreign currency.[135] Thus, by the spring of 1921 – after which point the question of trade controls became inextricably bound up with the reparations issue – a bizarre impasse had developed. The problem of a German 'sell-out', which the trade boards had been set up to solve, had evaporated; but the boards themselves remained, employing yet more bureaucrats, at the cost of yet more public money. There can be few better illustrations of the endemic confusion of early Weimar economic policy.

Labourism and cost-push inflation

A common anxiety linked Erzberger's insufficient fiscal reforms, the failure to stabilise monetary policy, and the futile attempt to regulate

[130] *Hamburger Fremdenblatt*, Nr. 462, 23.9.20.
[131] *Ibid.* Reichert, for example, continued to defend the system in his testimony to the Reichstag Committee for the Economy: StAH, DHSG III, Pr. III 34 Bd. 2, HG to SK, 23.11.20; *Hamburger Fremdenblatt*, Nr. 565, 24.11.20.
[132] HKH, HKHP, 29.9.20 (visit by Wirth); 5.2.21 (visit by Hermes); StAH, DHSG III, Pr. III 39, Sen. Prot. 9.2.21; HKH, HKB and HKL to RK, 12.2.21; HG to SK, 17.3.21.
[133] StAH, DHSG III, Pr. III 34 Bd. 2, HG to SK, 12.11.20.
[134] *Hamburger Fremdenblatt*, Nr. 565, 24.11.20. Cf. Hugo's speech at the third DVP conference in Nuremberg in December 1920, BAK, R45 II 26. For the attack on Hugo in the RWR, StAH, DHSG III, Pr. III 39, HG to SK, 11.1.21; 27.1.21; 10.2.21; 16.2.21; *Hamburger Fremdenblatt*, Nr. 118, 11.3.21.
[135] VHEx, *Jahresbericht 1920*; *Hamburger Fremdenblatt*, Nr. 462, 23.9.20.

foreign trade – namely, a profound fear of social unrest. The politicians who governed the Reich in the period of 'relative stabilisation' were reluctant to adopt any policy which might have the effect of increasing the level of unemployment or lowering real wages (that is, raising the cost of living). It was this, more than any other consideration, which ruled out policies which might have consolidated the relative stabilisation of early 1920. As the trade unionist Paul Umbreit put it: 'If economic and social effects are set in opposition to one another, then the social interests have to be given precedence.' Any attempt at stabilisation, noted the industrialist Richard Merton, 'in our situation would have extremely dangerous consequences'.[136] Most historians have tended to accept this analysis.[137] Yet this assumption that policies of retrenchment would trigger a 'second revolution' merits reassessment. There is a sense in which, just as later Weimar governments feared inflation when it had ceased to be a threat, so early Weimar governments continued to fear revolution when it too had ceased to be a threat. The result in both cases, it can be argued, was the adoption of inappropriate policies.

It is true that the coincidence of the relative stabilisation of the mark and the Kapp *putsch* in the spring of 1920 had a traumatic impact on the German labour market. In the first instance, the success of the general strike as a weapon against the counter-revolutionary coup boosted the confidence of the German trade unions, and to some extent healed that breach between rank-and-file and leadership which the war had opened up. In Hamburg, the shipyard workers and dockers went on strike within hours of news of the *putsch* reaching the city, followed by most of the public sector workforce, so that by Monday, 15 March, the entire urban economy (with the exception of the fire, gas, water and electricity services) was at a standstill.[138] Although the unions called the strike off the following day, not all groups returned to work at once; and while there was nothing approaching the militancy witnessed in the Ruhr, there were sporadic outbreaks of violence as the authorities attempted to recover the rifles that had been distributed at the height of the crisis.[139] The reaction to Kapp certainly represented a revival of popular radicalism, after the seven

---

[136] Feldman, *Great Disorder*, pp. 249, 253.
[137] See esp. Haller, 'Rolle der Staatsfinanzen', p. 151.
[138] NAW, RG 59, 862.00/880, Stewart to State Dept., 16.3.20; StAH, SK II I A 1a 21, Völckers to Schramm, 13.3.20; GHH, 300193012/5, Deutsche Werft to Reusch, 16.3.20
[139] NAW, RG 59, 862.00/897, Stewart to Dresel, 19.3.20; Stewart to Dresel, 22.3.20; Stewart to State Dept., 23.3.20. On events in the Ruhr, see E. Lucas, *Märzrevolution im Ruhrgebiet*, 2 vols. (Frankfurt am Main, 1970, 1973); J. Gorlas and D. Peukert (eds.), *Ruhrkampf 1920* (Essen, 1987).

months of relative docility which had followed the Sülze riots. However, the revival coincided with a significant drop in the demand for labour, occasioned by the world slump and the loss of Germany's depreciation-induced export advantage. Unemployment, which had fallen steadily from its peak of 75,000 (around 18 per cent of the labour force) in the first half of 1919 to 32,000 in April 1920, rose by 15 per cent and remained at around 38,000 throughout the summer.[140] At around 9 per cent of the workforce, this was comparable with unemployment in Britain in the same period; and it was significantly higher than in other German cities, reflecting the disproportionate impact of falling export orders on Hamburg.[141] In the volatile atmosphere of the post-Kapp months, it is hardly surprising that those affected reacted violently. There was a spate of ill-tempered demonstrations involving unemployed men, the worst of which led to an outbreak of looting so widespread that the authorities were forced to declare a state of emergency.[142]

It is not clear how politically organised the rioters were, compared with those of the previous summer. The year 1920 was one of great upheaval within the KPD and USPD in Hamburg. In February 1920 the former revolutionary leader Laufenberg had quit the KPD to set up the German Communist Workers' Party (KAPD), a 'national-bolshevist' organisation which went so far as to support Kapp. At around the same time, the Hamburg USPD was being led by Ernst Thälmann towards fusion with the KPD under the umbrella of the Third International, a process completed in November 1920.[143] These party-political divisions coincided with divisions within the workplace between advocates of a return to traditional trade union organisation and syndicalists, who established rival unions such as the Seamen's League,[144] as well as divisions within the working class between the

---

[140] See figure 3.1.

[141] NAW, RG 59, 862.00/1041, Stewart to State Dept., 8.11.20.

[142] NAW, RG 59, 862.00/926, Stewart to Dresel, 17.4.20; /925, Stewart to State Dept., 19.4.20; /934, Stewart to State Dept., 26.4.20; /951, Stewart to State Dept., 3.5.20; /960, Stewart to State Dept., 21.5.20; /985, Stewart to State Dept., 28.6.20; /987, Stewart to State Dept., 4.7.20; GStA, Rep. 77, MdI, 7329/143, RKfdÜöO Lagebericht, 23.4.20; 7329/155, RKfdÜöO Lagebericht, 27.3.20; 7330/145, RKfdÜöO Lagebericht, 27/28.6.20; GStA, Rep. 84a, 936/220, Reichstag Drucksache Nr. 152; BAP, RMI 13360, 36, Senate Abschrift, 27.6.20; 13359, 36, Chef der Sicherheitswehr to Reichsministerium des Innern, 'Die Lehren des 26. Juni 1920', 9.8.20.

[143] Ullrich, 'Arbeiterbewegung', pp. 720–6. By 1921, KPD membership in the Wasserkante region reached 40,000, around 11 per cent of the national total: A. McElligott, 'Mobilising the Unemployed: the KPD and the Unemployed Workers' Movement in Hamburg-Altona during the Weimar Republic', in R.J. Evans and D. Geary (eds.), The German Unemployed (London/Sydney, 1987), p. 242.

[144] See, e.g., Die Freiheit, 18.9.20. Cf. R. Rettig, 'Die Gewerkschaftsarbeit der KPD von 1918 bis 1925' (Diss. Hamburg, 1954).

employed and the unemployed. When rioters looting a truckload of boots were told that they were taking boots destined for workers at the Vulkan yard, they tersely replied that 'the unemployed want boots too'.[145] Yet despite these signs of division and disorganisation, the authorities at the national and the state level took the threat of social unrest extremely seriously; and, as in the wake of the revolution, economic policies were to a large degree determined by the fear that unrest could lead to political instability. As we have seen, not only were substantial subsidies made available to expand employment, particularly in the transport sector, but considerable sums were expended on unemployment relief. A decree was issued in November 1920 restricting the right of employers to shut down uneconomic factories.[146]

The scale of the stimulus to employment in the ship-building industry – and to employment in Hamburg as a whole – was enormous.[147] Figures for October 1920 indicate that over half those employed at the big Hamburg yards were working on compensation contracts. From its low point in February 1920 of 5,371, the Blohm & Voß workforce increased virtually without interruption until April/June 1921, when it reached 9,800, of whom three-quarters were employed on reconstruction contracts. Deutsche Werft raised its workforce from 1,163 in November 1919 to 6,600 in July 1921, as did Vulkan, from 4,388 in November 1919 to 8,320 in April 1921.[148] Total employment in Hamburg rose by 21 per cent in 1920 and around 8 per cent in 1921, attracting a surge of migrants to the city; unemployment fell by 70 per cent to just 11,000 at the end of 1921.[149]

The problem with this strategy was that it tended to stoke up wage pressure by strengthening the bargaining position of labour. Clearly, both the Bauer and Fehrenbach governments hoped that it would be possible to limit such pressure by reimposing controls on prices, following the rapid inflation of late 1919. This was clearly signalled by the revival of the wartime Ministry for Food and Agriculture; the imposition on the iron producers of the Iron Economic League (EWB) in December 1919; and the revival of the wartime system of price

---

[145] BAP, RMI 13359, 36, Chef der Sicherheitswehr to RMI, 9.8.20; RWM 7569/4–5, HKH Abschrift, 'Organisation der Arbeitgeber und Arbeitnehmer auf dem Gebiet der Seeschiffahrt', 26.9.19.

[146] Feldman, *Great Disorder*, pp. 242f.

[147] It was calculated that around 46 per cent of 1.4 bn. marks of contracts given by the German shipyards to other firms in 1920 as a result of the reconstruction programme went to firms in the Hanseatic cities: BAP, RFM 46580 N. Reg. 317/102–15; 46583 324/297–300.

[148] See figure 3.2; other figures from material in StAH, FA B&V 264, Schiffbau-Treuhand, 19.7.21.

[149] Büttner, *Politische Gerechtigkeit*, p. 145. On net in-migration, see figure 1.3; on unemployment, see figure 3.1.

control boards in November 1920.[150] In each case, attempts were made to increase the representation of workers or consumers on bodies charged with price regulation, on the grounds that they would tend to oppose price increases. However, because of extensive smuggling and black marketeering, price controls were even less effective than they had been in wartime. Indeed, it may even be that reimposing controls prevented German consumers from feeling the full benefit of the international deflation of 1920/1: wholesale prices did not fall by as much as import prices, and food prices continued to rise in 1920.[151] At any event, price controls alone did not compensate for the reductions in real wages which had occurred in the course of 1919.[152]

The inflationary danger inherent in the government's policy of employment creation had not gone unnoticed. At an early stage in the negotiations over shipping compensation, Erzberger had offered to include a clause in the legislation prohibiting the use of compensation funds for wage increases.[153] However, as a spokesman for the shipyards pointed out, if the money were obviously coming from the Reich it would be almost impossible 'to exercise restraint on unreasonable wage demands': 'Already the only thing we ever hear from the workers is: "But the Reich will pay for everything", and their wage demands keep rising immeasurably.'[154] A clear nexus had been established between government spending and the demand for labour at the shipyards; and the shipyard workers drew the obvious conclusion that, if the Reich cared enough about them to provide them with jobs, then it would have no objection to paying them higher wages into the bargain. This was more or less confirmed in April 1920, when the Labour Ministry imposed a 50 per cent wage increase on the shipyards, an increase accepted by the employers only 'under protest', given its significance in real terms at a time of falling prices.[155]

As chapter 3 concluded, there had already been strong indications of wage pressure at the end of 1919, after over a year during which real wages had been steadily depressed. The anti-Kapp strike stoked up this pressure, by revealing not only the strength of the strike weapon, but also that the employers could be overruled by the government – first on the issue of strike pay, then on the issue of a large increase. Given that this breakthrough coincided with a major increase in the demand for labour in the shipyards, it is hardly surprising that

[150] Feldman, *Iron and Steel*, pp. 160–87; idem, *Great Disorder*, pp. 181–98, 223ff.
[151] See figure 3.4.
[152] See chapter 3.
[153] Kohlhaus, 'Die Hapag', p. 40; HA, HB, Holtzendorff Notizen, 7.8.19.
[154] HA, HB, Holtzendorff Notizen, 25.11.19.
[155] StAH, FA B&V 13, Bd. II, Firmenleitung, 15.4.20; 29.4.20; NAW, RG 59, 862.00/ 925, Stewart to State Dept., 19.4.20.

there was a burgeoning of labour militancy. In the wake of the April pay award, the shipyard electricians downed tools, a dispute which lasted until the end of June.[156] In May, the shipyard clerical employees struck, leading to an ill-tempered confrontation between the management and the entire workforce of Blohm & Voß.[157] Infectiously, the unrest spread throughout the Hamburg economy: 'Everyone else is striking,' workers were heard to argue, 'So why don't we?'[158] In September, the metalworkers, fishermen and dockers all struck.[159] In October, it was the turn once again of the shipyard workers, this time demanding a 30 per cent increase in the piecework rate.[160] Like the shipyard workers, the public sector employees were quick to recognise the implications of government fiscal laxity: the state rail and tram workers won a 50 per cent wage increase in April 1920, and struck again in August 1920 and January 1921; while the postal employees were said to work 'only when the mood takes them'.[161] But even groups with little experience of collective action were drawn into the wage spiral. Harry Graf Kessler was struck by the way relative prosperity and endemic labour trouble seemed to go hand in hand: 'At the moment the musicians are on strike; a few days ago it was the waiters.'[162] Even the ships' cooks established their own union.[163]

The wage spiral has to be seen in the context of the structural arrangements for collective bargaining and arbitration which had emerged from the Revolution.[164] The formal basis for these had been in existence since the demobilisation decrees of November 1918; but there was a lag of over a year before arbitration began to function on a significant scale. By 1920, union membership was at an unprecedented level (nearly 9.2 million nationally); in addition, works' councils had acquired clearly defined if limited powers under the

---

[156] GHH, 300193012/5, Deutsche Werft to Reusch, 25.6.20.

[157] *Ibid.*, Deutsche Werft to Reusch, 12.5.20; StAH, FA B&V 1368, Abschrift (Norddeutsche Gruppe), Rundschreiben des Gesamtausschusses der Angestellten deutscher Seeschiffswerften, 15.5.20; Niederschrift über die Sitzung der NDG, Abteilung Seeschiffswerft, 20.5.20.

[158] NAW, RG 59, 862.00/950, Stewart to State Dept., 18.5.20.

[159] NAW, RG 59, 862.00/1015, Stewart to State Dept., 6.9.20; /1018, 13.9.20; /1021, 23.9.20.

[160] StAH, B&V 1368, Niederschrift über die Sitzung der NDG, Abt. Seeschiffswerft, 19.10.20; NDG to members, 1.11.20; NAW, RG 59, 862.00/1037, Stewart to State Dept., 18.10.20; /1039, 25.10.20

[161] GStA, Rep. 77, MdI, 7329/77, Garrisonkommando Hamburg to RKÜöO, 6.4.20; NAW, RG 59, 862.00/1004, Stewart to State Dept., 11.8.20; 16.8.20; /1051, 10.1.21; WA, 'Jahresbericht 1920', Bl. 21.

[162] Kessler, *Tagebücher*, p. 230.

[163] BAP, RWM 75665/18–20, HKH Abschrift, 4.8.20.

[164] See in general J. Bähr, *Staatliche Schlichtung in der Weimarer Republik. Tarifpolitik, Korporatismus und industrieller Konflikt zwischen Inflation und Deflation, 1919–1932* (Berlin, 1989).

legislation of January 1920,[165] and there was an increasing tendency for national and local bodies to intervene in wage disputes. The Reich Labour Ministry, for example, intervened in the shipyard clerical workers' strike of May 1920, in the dockers' strike four months later, and again in the two-month long fitters' strike which began in October of the same year.[166] The Hamburg authorities also took a hand, notably in the strike of the railway workers of August 1920, which the Senate sought to resolve by giving the post-revolutionary Economic Council an arbitrating role. Interestingly, the Deputation for Commerce now claimed that the Council had been set up 'specifically [. . .] to avoid difficulties for workers in the transitional period'.[167] In fact, this represented a significant departure from Warburg and Witthoefft's original conception of the Council as a means of integrating the revolutionary Workers' Council into the city's established corporative system of chambers. Now, as Rudolf Blohm pointed out, the Council was acting against the interests of employers by awarding the railway workers a pay increase only slightly below what they had demanded. In a strongly worded letter, Blohm denounced the whole principle of arbitration, arguing that:

there would not be so many strikes if the arbitrating bodies did not exist. Those making wage demands reckon with certainty on the intervention of an arbitration round, at which they will be able to push through at least a part of their demands. [. . .] The arbitration bodies do not heal wounds, but merely patch them over, so that they open up still more widely the next time.[168]

Although there were one or two employers in other sectors who did not share this view, Blohm clearly had the majority on his side.[169] Why this was so becomes clear from the available figures for real wages. Despite a slight dip when the cost of living temporarily increased in the winter of 1920, the overall trend of real wages in the period

---

[165] Maier, *Recasting Bourgeois Europe*, pp. 217–22. Details of the implementation of the works' council legislation in the shipyards in StAH, B&V 1368, NDG, Anweisungen zum Betriebsrätegesetz, 12.4.20; Abschrift, Vorschläge des Zentralrates der Werftarbeiter über Aufgaben der Betreibsräte, 15.5.20.

[166] StAH, FA B&V 1368, Abschrift, Rundschreiben des Gesamtausschusses der Angestellten deutscher Seeschiffswerften, 15.5.20; Niederschrift über die Sitzung der NDG, 20.5.20; 10.12.20; NAW, RG 59, 862.00/960, Stewart to State Dept., 21.5.20; /964, 24.5.20; /1021, 23.9.30; /1047, 16.12.20; GHH, 300193012/5, Deutsche Werft to Reusch, 25.10.20; 24.12.20.

[167] NAW, RG 59, 862.00/1004, Stewart to State Dept., 11.8.20;/ 1010, 30.8.20; StAH, DHSG III, Pr. IV 10 Bd. I, DHSG to Senate, 26.8.20. On the Council's origins, see chapter 3.

[168] StAH, FA B&V 1249, Rudolf Blohm to Rudolf Sieverts, 21.8.20.

[169] *Ibid.*, Sieverts to Blohm, 22.8.20; Arbeitgeberverband Hamburg Altona to Rudolf Blohm, 25.8.20; Arbeitgeberverband to HKH/DKH/GKH, 27.8.20.

of relative stabilisation was unmistakably upwards (see figure 5.5).[170] Whereas for most of 1919 wages had been stagnant when prices had been rising; now in 1920, with prices stagnant, it was wages which rose. Between March 1920 and May 1921, real hourly wage rates rose by between 30 per cent and 130 per cent, weekly rates by between 43 per cent and 97 per cent, and monthly salaries in the public sector by between 103 per cent and 130 per cent.[171] These gains were clearly the rewards of labour militancy in the context of binding arbitration: typically, in the wake of the railway workers' award, the shipyard workers demanded an additional 25 pfennigs per hour, which the Labour Ministry's arbitration committee immediately granted.[172] The significance of this 'wage-push' is most obvious if one compares the trend in nominal wages with the trend in steel prices within the ship-building industry: while steel prices actually fell by 16 per cent in 1921, wages rose by 81 per cent, a reversal of the tendency in 1919 and 1920, when prices had outstripped wages (see figure 5.6). Employer allegations that it was wage pressure which was preventing a further fall of prices were therefore to some degree justified: a call from the Economic Council for 'first price cuts, then wage cuts' provoked a tirade against bourgeois pusillanimity from Rudolf Blohm.[173] All this sheds interesting light on the charge made by some contemporaries and now widely accepted by historians that employers and employees were raising prices and wages in collusion.[174]

A further grievance raised by Blohm was the low productivity of workers. The evidence for this is not unambiguous. Aggregate output in German industry rose significantly in 1920 and 1921: Wagenführ's index shows a 45 per cent increase in ouput in 1920 and a 20 per cent increase in 1921, substantially more than the comparable increase in employment.[175] But by comparison with pre-war norms, there is no question that productivity remained low, particularly in sectors like coal which experienced declines in output during 1920.[176] As might

---

[170] See also figures 2.11, 2.12, 3.6 and 3.7.
[171] For additional data on real wages indicating similar pressures in other sectors and regions, see Laursen and Petersen, *Inflation*, p. 76; Scholz, 'Lohn und Beschäftigung', p. 286; Lindenlaub, *Maschinebauunternehmen*, p. 235.
[172] StAH, FA B&V 1249, R. Blohm, Entwurf, 3.9.20.
[173] StAH, FA B&V 1249, Arbeitgeberverband Hamburg-Altona to HKH/DKH/GKH, 27.8.20; HKH Mitteilungen, No. 18, 28.8.20; Blohm to Arbeitgeberverband, 28.8.20; Blohm to HKH 30.8.20; Blohm, Entwurf, 3.9.20; HKH to Arbeitgeberverband, 4.9.20.
[174] See, e.g., von Raumer quoted in Feldman, *Iron and Steel*, p. 173.
[175] See figure 2.4.
[176] Cf. Laursen and Pedersen, *Inflation*, pp. 136ff.; Bry, *Real Wages*, pp. 403ff.; Roesler, *Finanzpolitik*, p. 222; Graham, *Hyperinflation*, p. 295; Balderston, *Economic Crisis*, pp. 63, 73. On the coal industry, A. Gladen, 'Der Ruhrbergbau in der Inflationszeit', in Büsch and Feldman (eds.), *Historische Prozesse*, pp. 188–96.

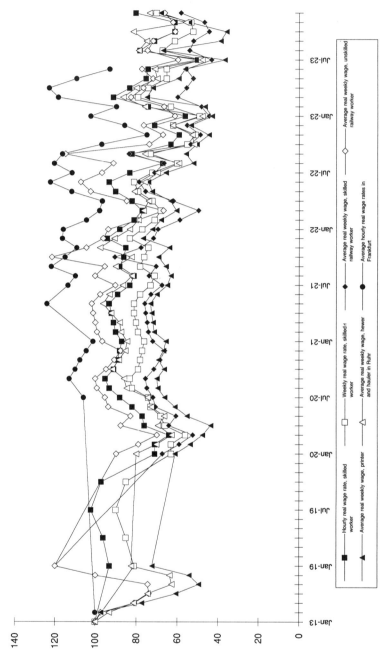

Figure 5.5 Real wages in Germany, 1913, 1919–1923 (1913 = 100)
Sources: Bry, *Wages*, pp. 453ff.; Holtfrerich, *Inflation*, pp. 233f., 243.

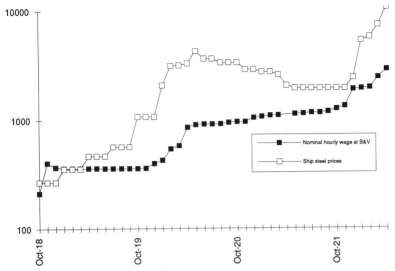

Figure 5.6 Costs in ship-building, 1918–1922 (1914 = 100)
Sources: StAH, FA B&V 139; 249, Bd. 2; BAP, RFM 46586 N.Reg. 333/29,
RMfW, October 1920; *Deutsche Bergwerks-Zeitung*, 8.6.1922.

be expected, given the scale of government subsidy, output in ship-building rose substantially: by between 35 per cent and 60 per cent in 1920 and between 50 per cent and 65 per cent in 1921 – perhaps even exceeding the level of 1913.[177] The shipyards' consumption of German produced steel rose from around 6,000 tons per month (January–March 1920) to a peak of 49,608 tons in April 1921.[178] However, figures for total employment in the Hamburg shipyards suggest a level 35 per cent above that of 1913 – a larger increase than that suggested by output figures.[179] Indeed, annual output per man at the newly established Deutsche Werft fell from around 34,000 tons in 1919 to just 13,000 in 1921 – though other factors besides poor productivity clearly played a role in this decline.[180] The problem facing the shipyards can also be expressed with reference to profits. Gross profits at Blohm & Voß rose by 200 per cent in nominal terms between 1919 and 1921; wage rates by 340 per cent.[181] In order to meet

---

[177] Differing estimates for output in *SJfdDR 1921/2, 1924/5*; Hoffmann *et al.*, *Wachstum*, p. 358. Cf. figure 1.2.

[178] *Deutsche Bergwerks Zeitung*, 8.6.22. Cf. the figures for Deutsche Werft's annual consumption of steel from GHH, which reached a peak of 37,743 tons in 1920, compared with an average for the remainder of the decade of around 20,000; GHH, *Denkschrift Nr. 30* (Oberhausen, 1930), Bd. III, 43.

[179] Figures in StAH, FA B&V 249, Bd. 1; 268; 264.

[180] Calculated from figures given in Deutsche Werft, *Jahresbericht 1919, Jahresbericht 1920, Jahresbericht 1921* and data in GHH archive.

[181] Calculated from the figures given in Blohm & Voß *Jahresbericht 1918/19, Jahresbericht 1919/20, Jahresbericht 1920/21, Jahresbericht 1921/22*. See figure 3.2, which clearly shows the simultaneous rise in employment and real wages at Blohm & Voß.

increased orders, firms were forced to increase employment disproportionately, while at the same time being forced to pay excessive
wages. From a purely economic standpoint, this was unsustainable –
particularly for those firms which, like Deutsche Werft (or the South
German engineering firms studied by Lindenlaub), had seen the period
of relative stabilisation as an opportune time to embark on new investments.[182] In order to accommodate wage pressure, firms were forced
either to cut net profits and dividends, as Deutsche Werft did, or to
cut investment and even, as Blohm & Voß did, to reduce their
depreciation allowances below the minimum necessary to avoid 'substance loss'. In other words, the problem of wages rising ahead of
productivity and eroding profitability – which has come to be associated
with the period after 1924 – was already making itself felt in the
period of relative stabilisation.

   The wage push was not only economically unsustainable, it was
also politically unsustainable. The government's policy of boosting
employment and real wages had been intended to diminish the radicalism of groups like the shipyard workers. In practice, however,
expanding the numbers and wage-packets of the shipyard workers only
served to bolster the position of the more radical elements in the
unions and the works' councils, to antagonise employers, and hence
to exacerbate industrial friction. As early as June 1920, a Prussian police
official reported to the Economics Ministry that Hamburg employers,
including Blohm & Voß, were deliberately fomenting industrial conflict
in the hope of extricating themselves from the pressures generated by
relative stabilisation:

The business community [. . .] would have nothing against it if the mark
were to fall again, and they would not complain if the desired depreciation
of the currency were to come about as a result of internal unrest, in particular
Bolshevik uprisings. Therefore a part of the business community is not paying
as much attention as it ought to avoiding difficulties with the workforce; on
the contrary, certain circles are calculating that, by laying off large numbers
of workers, they could bring about economic difficulties and thus a fall in the
currency, which would lead to an improvement in their economic position.[183]

This was probably somewhat exaggerated; but Blohm certainly made
no secret of his desire for a showdown:

It has become usual in Hamburg since the Revolution to ensure that one does
not tread on the Majority Socialists' toes, as the phrase goes. It tends to be

---

[182] Lindenlaub, *Maschinenbauunternehmen*, pp. 40–5, 226 (table 2). Cf. Webb, *Hyperinflation*, pp. 84f., 100f.
[183] StAH, DHSG III, Pr. IV 10 Bd. I, Landespolizeiamt beim Staatskommissar für
Volksernährung to RWM, 9.6.20.

forgotten that there is no more a pact with the Majority Socialists on the question 'private economy or socialisation' than there is with the other social-democratic parties. The Majority Socialists may pursue their goals more quietly, but they pursue them all the more determinedly. In my view, there can never be a compromise with them. The gulf cannot be bridged. [. . .] The notorious catch-phrase that one must adapt oneself to the given circumstances has already done great damage here. Did the Social Democrats adapt themselves to the given circumstances before the war? They stuck to their objectives with stubborn determination and never shirked a conflict. Regrettably, the same cannot be said for the bourgeoisie today in Hamburg.[184]

The desire for confrontation manifested itself in November, when Deutsche Werft succeeded in defying a ruling by the Demobilisation Office and breaking the fitters' strike.[185] Four months later, Senator Stubmann was attacked by Blohm & Voß as a 'well-meaning and prominent ignoramus' for suggesting that striking engineering workers be offered an 'Easter gift' to resume work.[186] The invitation by Blohm of Hindenburg and Ludendorff to attend the launching of the *Hindenburg* in February 1921 did nothing to dampen the mood of antagonism on the waterfront, where workers regarded even the flying of the black, white and red flag by merchant vessels as a sign of support for Kapp.[187]

The showdown was not long in coming; for, whatever ill-conceived plans for a national coup had been hatched by the KPD leadership in Berlin, the 'March Action' in Hamburg must be seen as the culmination of months of industrial friction, if not the deliberately provoked crisis which the Prussian police had predicted nine months before.[188] On 23 March, after a demonstration on the Heiligengeistfeld, Communist-organised gangs of unemployed men attacked the labour exchange at Landungsbrücken and the main Hamburg shipyards, occupying office buildings, setting up 'action committees' and hoisting the red flag.[189] Similar events occurred at the Vulkan yard and, three days later, at the dynamite factory at Geesthacht, though the scale of the

---

[184] StAH, FA B&V 1249, Blohm, Entwurf, 3.9.20.
[185] GHH, 300193012/5, Deutsche Werft to Reusch, 25.10.20; 24.12.20.
[186] StAH, FA B&V 228, Bd. 2, Firmenleitung to Blohm, 5.3.21.
[187] *Ibid.* Firmenleitung to Blohm, 12.2.21; NAW, RG 59, 862.00/1037, Stewart to State Dept., 18.10.20.
[188] On the March Action, see PA/AA, Po. 5, No. 3, Bd II, Reichskommissar für die Überwachung der öffentlichen Ordnung, *Denkschrift über die Märzunruhen im Jahre 1921* (Berlin, 1921); S. Koch-Baumgarten, 'Zum Problem der Theorie und Politik der "Offensive": Die Märzaktion der KAP 1921 unter besonderer Berücksichtigung Hamburgs und Rheinland-Westfalens', (Diss., Freie Universität Berlin, 1983).
[189] PA/AA, Po. 5 No. 3, Bd. II, RKfdÜöO, *Denkschrift*; Wolf Telegraph Bureau, Nr. 568, 23.3.21; Nr. 571, 24.3.21; GHH, 300193012/6, Deutsche Werft Bericht 23.3.21; Deutsche Werft to Reusch, 24.3.21.

enterprise did not approach that undertaken in Saxony.[190] Yet it would be difficult to view the March Action as a serious revolutionary threat. A year previously, the Kapp *putsch* had exposed the divisions within the Hamburg security forces and the unity of the organised working class. In 1921, however, it was the workers who were divided, with many non-Communists opposing the action; while Danner's reformed *Ordnungspolizei* proved ruthlessly effective. The initial demonstration was forcibly dispersed; the shipyards were swiftly cleared; and, in addition to numerous arrests, around twenty-six Communists were killed in exchanges of fire.[191] It was precisely the kind of confrontation which the employers had yearned for since November 1918. In the aftermath, hundreds of workers who had taken part in the action were fired, twenty radicals on shipyard works' councils were purged and a determined effort was made to resist renewed attempts at arbitration by the Economic Council.[192]

This victory for the employers was only superficial. The structural problems of direct subsidies, union-led wage pressure, and over-sympathetic arbitration persisted. Yet the failure of the March Action does suggest that the authorities had rather more political room for manoeuvre than they realised in the period of relative stabilisation. In theory, as has been suggested above, more might have been done to reduce the fiscal deficit and reform the currency; less might have been done to interfere with the 'natural' stabilisation of trade, prices and wages. The argument against such policies was always that their social costs would be excessive, and would lead to fresh political instability. Yet it is by no means clear that this threat was as great in 1920/1 as it had been in 1918/19. In their exaggerated fear of sparking off a 'second revolution', policy makers in 1920 and 1921 may thus have missed the opportunity to implement more effective policies of fiscal and monetary stabilisation.

Schumpeter argued that the post-war German economy 'could not be rationalised in either the socialist or the capitalist sense'; and described the compromise as a kind of 'crippling labourism'.[193] The

---

[190] BAP, RMI 13360, 36, Chef der Ordnungspolizei to RMI, 29.3.21; Wulf (ed.), *Kabinett Fehrenbach*, p. 609; *Deutsche Allgemeine Zeitung*, Nr. 139, 24.3.21.

[191] PA/AA, Po. 5 No. 3, Bd. II, RKfdÜöO, *Denkschrift*; NAW, RG 59, 862.00/1088, Stewart to State Dept., 4.4.21; /1089, 11.4.21.

[192] StAH, FA B&V 1368, Blohm & Voß to NDG, 31.3.21; Niederschrift über die Verhandlungen über die Wiederherstellung der Arbeiterschaft, 31.3.21; Niederschrift über die Sitzung, 7.4.21; Anlage zum Rundschreiben an die NDG: Betr. Befreiung der Betriebsratsmitglieder von der Arbeit, 27.5.21; B&V 264, Blohm Aufzeichnung, 20.6.21; Norddeutsche Gruppe des Gesamtverbands deutscher Metallindustriellen, Protokolle 27.5.21; B&V 485, Blohm to HKH, 7.7.21; Arbeitgeber-Verband Hamburg-Altona, 8.7.21; HKH to Wirtschaftsrat 19.7.21.

[193] J. Schumpeter, *Business Cycles*, vol. II (New York/London, 1939), p. 702.

contradictions of the policies pursued in the period of relative stabilisation bear his critique out. Certainly, it is possible to imagine a 'rationalisation' of the Weimar economy in a 'capitalist sense' in 1920/1. Fiscal stabilisation could have been achieved by collecting new taxes on incomes and capital more efficiently, and by cutting subsidies and doles. Monetary stabilisation could have been achieved by pegging the mark at a devalued exchange rate against the dollar and establishing a realistic discount rate. The liberal trade policy of the second half of 1919 could simply have been continued, allowing the trade gap to narrow as export prices rose and the demand for imports levelled off. Together, these policies would probaby have sufficed to eliminate the distortions in the labour market which were giving rise to wage-push inflation in 1920/1, since they would have resulted in an increase in unemployment – though by no means as large an increase as in England. But 'under the given circumstances' – to use Blohm's bitter phrase – a continuation of inflation was, in practice, the line of least resistance. By abandoning any attempt at fiscal retrenchment, subsidies could continue to be paid to industries like ship-building. By keeping the printing presses rolling in the Oranienstrasse, the credit squeeze so feared by industrialists like Rathenau could be postponed. By allowing the mark to depreciate again, exporters believed they would be able to escape from the constraints of a firm mark and trade control. And renewed inflation offered – on the experience of 1919 – the easiest means of reducing real wages. As Rathenau had said in October 1920: 'Germany could well endure a further inflation'; and so it seemed. True, there had been some, like Max Warburg, who had disagreed, arguing against any further postponement of the inevitable credit crisis. However, even he could discern an argument for a return to inflationary policies. It is to that argument that we must now turn.

6

The failure of 'fulfilment'

The rationale of 'fulfilment'

At no time in the period of 'relative stabilisation' between March 1920 and May 1921 did Max Warburg explicitly advocate a return to inflationary fiscal and monetary policies. However, in his influential speech at the German Bankers' Conference in October 1920, he was careful to stress that there were circumstances in which such a return to inflation might be impossible to avoid. Unlike some commentators, notably Rathenau,[1] Warburg did not at this juncture blame the inflation solely on the impact of the peace terms on the balance of payments. Monetary factors, he conceded, also played an important role.[2] However, he insisted that no 'financial–technical' policy to halt inflation could be effective if the balance of payments remained in deficit, repeating the now-familiar Hamburg call for a lifting of restrictions on trade:

Even at the risk of sometimes selling our own products too cheaply abroad, the current policy must be abandoned. The world must be made to understand that it is impossible to burden a country with debts and at the same time to deprive it of the means of paying them [. . .] The most complete collapse of the currency [. . .] cannot [. . .] be avoided if the peace treaty is maintained in its present form [. . .] We are on the edge of the abyss.[3]

This line of argument had, of course, been heard before. As we have seen, even before the end of the war, Ballin had pointed out the advantages which Germany would be able to derive from the weakness of her currency, and at Versailles Warburg and Melchior had forecast

---

[1] See for example W. Rathenau, 'Der Kern des Ubels', *Vossische Zeitung*, 1.1.21.
[2] 'In all cases we see increases in note circulation without simultaneous increases in the production of goods; disruptions of the international money and credit system and, resulting from all of this, disruptions to international balances of payments. It is hard to say which of these factors works most strongly. . .': WA, XIX, Gesammelte Vorträge, 'Die notwendigen Vorbedingungen', 26.10.20.
[3] *Ibid.* Cf. Bresciani's comment, *Inflation*, p. 46.

the unarrestable depreciation of the mark and a glut of German exports. Warburg's 1920 speech revealed that the argument had not been abandoned, despite the embarrassing recovery of the mark at the beginning of the year. Speaking at Brussels two months later, Cuno backed up his demand for the return of part of the confiscated merchant fleet with similar reasoning:

A factor which was formerly one of our strongest pillars in the balance of trade [i.e., payments] has now been changed from the active to the passive side [. . .As a result] Germany [. . .] is a bad buyer and the foreign countries with a high level of their exchange are bad sellers [. . .] Political power does not do away with economic facts. If you ignore these facts, Germany must of necessity remain a constant danger for those countries who think they can get on without us.[4]

In short, currency depreciation continued to be regarded as the secret economic weapon of German revisionism because of its stimulating effect on German exports: if the Allies could be persuaded that the peace terms were the root cause of both, then a revision of the treaty might be possible. Quite apart from the domestic economic advantages of renewed inflation discussed in the previous chapter, it was this calculation which persuaded Warburg and others to abandon any idea of stabilisation when confronted by the Allies' definitive demand for reparations in 1921.

The London Ultimatum demanded that, beginning at the end of May 1921, Germany pay interest and amortisation on 'A' and 'B' bonds totalling 50 bn. gold marks in the form of a 2 bn. gold marks annuity, due quarterly. It also specified that, beginning in November 1921, a payment equal to 26 per cent of the value of German exports should be made. As German exports in 1920 had been estimated at around 5 bn. gold marks, this implied a total annual payment of around 3 bn gold marks.[5] When German exports had reached a level sufficient to pay off the 'A' and 'B' bonds, non-interest-bearing 'C' bonds with a face value of 82 bn. gold marks would be issued. The 12 bn. gold marks still outstanding from the 20 bn. gold marks demanded at Versailles were tacitly included in this total, while sums

---

[4] HA, Cuno NL, Cuno speech at Brussels, 18.12.20. Similarly, Warburg based his case for an international loan and the restoration of the sequestrated property on the point that 'its liquidation, for which Germany has to indemnify owners' made it 'impossible for [the] exchange rate to improve'; WA, X, Pol. Corr. 1921, Universal Service radio interview transcript, January 1921.

[5] Maier, *Recasting Bourgeois Europe*, pp. 241f.; Kent, *Spoils of War*, pp. 132–8. Webb suggests that altogether 4 bn. gold marks was being demanded because of occupation costs and 'clearing' payments; Webb, *Hyperinflation*, pp. 104f.

due to Belgium were not, so that the sum outstanding was around
125 bn. gold marks.[6] In nominal terms, this was certainly less than
had originally been envisaged by some on the Allied side (for example,
the Cunliffe Committee's 480 bn. gold marks, or Klotz's 8 bn. gold
marks annuity). Moreover, it can be argued that the 'C' Bonds were
unlikely ever to be collected; or, at least, that their real value would
be significantly reduced if German trade were slow to recover.[7] In
terms of national income too, the annuity was less of a burden than
Keynes and others claimed at the time: recent estimates of the potential
burden on national income of the annuity vary from 5 per cent to 10
per cent.[8] True, this far outstrips the burdens imposed on developing
countries by international debt in the 1980s, let alone the sums paid
by Western countries in the form of aid to the Third World; but
France's initial annual burden in 1872 was arguably higher.[9]

Taking the period during which Germany continued to pay reparations as a whole (1919–32), it is clear that the Allies received far less
than the 125 bn. gold marks demanded at London. Around 19 bn.
gold marks would seem to be a reasonable figure for the total value
of unrequited transfers from Germany to the Allies, a relatively small
proportion (2.4 per cent) of total national income over the period.[10]
This has given rise to a large literature on the question of whether
Germany 'could have paid a good deal more if she had chosen to do
so'.[11] A view frequently expressed is that – as many French observers
alleged at the time – German politicians deliberately set out to sabotage
an economically feasible scheme by 'working systematically towards
bankruptcy'.[12]

[6] Marks, 'Reparations Reconsidered: A Reminder', pp. 356f. Cf. Felix, 'Reparation
Considered with a Vengeance', pp. 171–9; and S. Marks, 'Rejoinder', *CEH*, 5, 4
(1972), pp. 358–61.
[7] Marks, 'Reparations Reconsidered', *passim*; Maier, *Recasting Bourgeois Europe*,
pp. 241f. One contemporary estimate of the present value of the London schedule
put it as low as 49 bn. gold marks.
[8] C.S. Maier, 'The Truth about the Treaties', *JMH*, 51 (1979), pp. 56–67; Holtfrerich,
Inflation, pp. 148f.; Schuker, 'Finance and Foreign Policy in the Era of the German
Inflation, p. 351; Webb, *Hyperinflation*, pp. 54, 104; Eichengreen, *Golden Fetters*,
pp. 129f.
[9] Webb, *Hyperinflation*, p. 107; Holtfrerich, *Inflation*, pp. 151, 154f.
[10] See table 2. For other recent attempts to compute total payments, see Holtfrerich,
Inflation, pp. 147–50; Schuker, 'American "Reparations" to Germany, 1919–1933',
pp. 364–71, 382f.
[11] Marks, 'The Myths of Reparations', pp. 231–55. But see Krüger, 'Das Reparationsproblem der Weimarer Republik in fragwürdiger Sicht', pp. 21–47.
[12] Quoted in Feldman, *Great Disorder*, p. 377. Cf. Maier, 'Inflation and Stabilisation',
p. 127; Schuker, 'Finance and Foreign Policy', *passim*; Schroeder, 'Handelspolitik',
passim; Rupieper, *Cuno Government*, pp. 32f.; Specht, *Politische Hintergründe*,
pp. 33, 38.

In fact, the extent of the effort *initially* made by Germany should not be underestimated. At least 8 bn. gold marks (and perhaps as much as 13 bn. gold marks) were handed over in the period before the Dawes Plan: between 4 per cent and 7 per cent of total national income.[13] There were, however, two fundamental reasons why such a level of unrequited transfers could not be sustained without recourse to inflationary policies. In the first place, the annuity demanded in 1921 put an intolerable strain on the state's finances. As we have seen, it is possible to devise a 'counterfactual' scenario in which, with cuts in spending and more efficient tax collection, the Reich deficit could have been reduced in the period of 'relative stabilisation'. But to have generated a surplus sufficient to pay reparations over a prolonged period would have required an inconceivably drastic policy of retrenchment. In fiscal terms, total expenditure under the terms of the Versailles treaty in the years 1920 to 1923 amounted to at least 50 per cent of Reich revenue, 20 per cent of total Reich spending and 10 per cent of total public spending.[14] As Webb has shown, reparations accounted for the lion's share of the Reich deficit in 1921 and 1922 (68 per cent and 56 per cent respectively); they were thus, in Eichengreen's words, 'ultimately responsible for the inflation', in as much as no Weimar government could have raised taxes or cut spending sufficiently to pay reparations *and* balance the budget.[15] Such austerity could only have been achieved by a regime of the sort which was able to extract comparably heavy reparations from the Soviet zone of occupation between 1945 and 1953, or the substantially greater sums transferred from occupied France to the Third Reich between 1940 and 1944.[16] By contrast, the Reparations Commission and the Committee of Guarantees could only threaten and impose limited sanctions, the effect of which was to reduce rather than increase the reparations collected.[17]

Even if one imagines a fiscal solution to the problems discussed above, there remained a second obstacle to the payment of reparations,

---

[13] Cf. estimates in Bresciani, *Inflation*, p. 457; Holtfrerich, *Inflation*, pp. 147–50; Schuker, 'American "Reparations"', pp. 364–71. I follow Eichengreen in using national income figures in 1913 goldmarks: *Golden Fetters*, p. 129 n.

[14] Calculated from the various figures (ranging between 6.5 and 7.6 bn. gold marks) in Bresciani, *Inflation*, pp. 53, 358, 437f.; Graham, *Hyperinflation*, pp. 44f.; Witt, 'Finanzpolitik', pp. 425f.; Witt, 'Tax Policies and Tax Assessment', pp. 156f.; Holtfrerich, *Inflation*, pp. 148f.; Webb, *Hyperinflation*, pp. 33, 37, 108; Eichengreen, *Golden Fetters*, p. 146. See also Webb, 'Government Revenue and Spending', pp. 67ff.; Kent, *Spoils of War*, p. 113.

[15] Webb, *Hyperinflation*, p. 37; Eichengreen, *Golden Fetters*, p. 141; Feldman, *Great Disorder*, pp. 428, 451.

[16] Webb, *Hyperinflation*, p. 112; A. Milward, *War, Economy and Society, 1939–1945* (Harmondsworth, 1977), pp. 137–44.

[17] Kent, *Spoils of War*, p. 145.

namely the means whereby reparations in cash could be converted, as the Allies required, into gold or foreign currency.[18] The most straightforward way this could have been achieved was by Germany running a balance of payments surplus, which, in view of the impact of the Versailles treaty on German overseas investments and shipping, effectively meant a trade surplus. Clearly, this did not happen. Trade surpluses were recorded in only five years (1920, 1926 and 1930–2) during the Weimar period, and only twice (in 1931 and 1932) exceeded reparations paid.[19] To have turned an average annual deficit of 0.7 bn. gold marks into an average annual surplus of 3 bn. gold marks would have required either a severe contraction in German consumption, implying an acute domestic distributional conflict, or a phenomenal increase in German exports, implying a no less acute international conflict of interests. Of course, the transfer of reparations might notionally have been reconciled with persistent trade deficits if there had been sustained foreign lending to Germany;[20] and as we have seen this did happen on a substantial scale.[21] But this was not a sustainable process. War debts and American domestic politics ruled out large-scale government-guaranteed lending; and the economic and political consequences of reparations – whether of paying them or trying to avoid paying them – tended to erode the confidence of private investors.[22] Moreover, even in an imaginary world without inflation, it seems unlikely that lending to finance reparations would have been sustainable, because of the tendency for the rising burden of debt service on such loans to outweigh their benefits. As it was, the government had increasing difficulty in persuading foreign lenders to provide it with funds, precisely because the London schedule undermined confidence in the Reich's creditworthiness.

[18] Not all reparations had to be paid in this way: cash reparations only accounted for around a quarter of total treaty expenses between 1920 and 1922, compared with around 45 per cent paid in the form of free goods. However, the net effect on the balance of payments was the same, even if the method of transfer was different: cash transfers required foreign currency to be earned and then handed back, whereas payments in kind simply entailed exporting for nothing. Only treaty expenses such as occupation costs and the loss of state property in ceded territory had no influence on the balance of payments: see Webb, *Hyperinflation*, p. 108.

[19] See table 2.

[20] W. Fischer, 'Die Weimarer Republik unter den weltwirtschaftichen Bedingungen der Zwischenkriegszeit', in Mommsen *et al.* (eds.), *Industrielles System*, I, pp. 26–50.

[21] The net capital movement into Germany in the years 1919 to 1923 must have been in the region of 12–13 bn. gold marks: see table 2. Cf. the estimates in C.-L. Holtfrerich, 'Internationale Verteilungsfolgen der deutschen Inflation', in *Kyklos*, 30 (1977), pp. 271–92; *idem*, 'Amerikanischer Kapitalexport und Wiederaufbau der deutschen Wirtschaft 1919–1923 im Vergleich zu 1924–9', pp. 497ff.; *idem*, 'Die deutsche Inflation 1918 bis 1923 in internationaler Perspektiv', pp. 321–8; Schuker, 'American "Reparations"', pp. 365–8.

[22] Holtfrerich, *Inflation*, pp. 154f.; Kindleberger, *Financial History*, pp. 306ff.

Reparations, as envisaged in 1921, *were* therefore excessive – as the German government claimed. However, it does not necessarily follow from this that the German government was therefore right not to *attempt* to pay them; or that, as Holtfrerich and others have argued, 'the progressive depreciation of the mark' was the most effective way of 'persuading the rest of the world of the need for a reduction of the reparations burden'.[23] The principal question addressed in this chapter is not whether the transfer was impossible, but whether the strategy adopted by the German government after May 1921 was the best way of convincing the Allies that this was so. In fact, this strategy – of instrumentalising depreciation to secure revision – was fundamentally flawed; and whatever illicit gains the German economy may have made at the expense of foreign lenders, a more sincere attempt to pay the sums due might well have been a better way of demonstrating the impossibility of the task.

Although all three declined ministerial office in it,[24] Warburg, Melchior and Cuno played leading roles in formulating the initial revisionist strategy of the Wirth government. In a speech drafted in July, Warburg set out once again the central German argument:

Only through the greatest trade crisis that there has ever been [. . .] will we arrive at rational economic conditions. [. . .] By the end of August it will be clear that this method of pumping us dry is giving rise to an impossible situation in Germany and in the world. As a consequence of the appreciation of foreign currency [and] the depreciation of the mark, the danger exists that we will once again have an export premium, which could call forth an artificial boom in Germany and lead to a flooding of the whole world with [German] goods [. . .].[25]

At a dinner a week later with Wirth, Rathenau and the British ambassador D'Abernon, Melchior and Cuno made the same point, though they did not predict such rapid results as Warburg. According to Melchior, Germany could:

get through the first two or three years with the aid of foreign loans or possibly of further bank note issues. By the end of that time, foreign nations will have realised that these large international payments can only be made by huge German exports,

---

[23] Holtfrerich, 'Die deutsche Inflation 1918–1923 in internationaler Perspektive', p. 327. Cf. Graham, *Hyperinflation*, pp. 4, 7–9, 11, 30–5, 248, 321; Keynes, *Collected Writings*, XI, p. 365; Borchardt, 'Wachstum und Wechsellagen', p. 700.

[24] WA, XI, Pol. Corr., Warburg Notiz, 7.6.21; Kohlhaus, 'Die Hapag', p. 63; Maier, *Recasting Bourgeois Europe*, p. 247; E. Laubach, *Die Politik der Kabinette Wirth 1921/22* (Lübeck, 1968), p. 34. Cuno also declined the post of US ambassador: HA, HB, Holtzendorff to Cuno, 28.8.21.

[25] WA, XIX, Gesammelte Vorträge, Warburg, 'Entwurf einer nicht gehaltene Rede anläßlich der Pressetagung in Hamburg', 4.7.21. Cf. Warburg, *Aufzeichnungen*, p. 98.

and these German exports will ruin trade in England and America, so that the creditors themselves will come to us to require modification.[26]

Similar warnings of the international consequences of 'the progressive
decomposition of German economic life' and 'cheap German competition' were directed at the English bankers Goodenough and Grenfell,
as well as at Herbert Hoover.[27] As Paul Warburg put it, 'Every new
slump in the reichsmark results in a large volume of foreign orders
[. . .and hence] is a menace to competing industrial countries.'[28] By
the end of 1921, the argument had been taken up by the Hamburg
Chamber of Commerce and the RdI. The Allies, it was argued, would
only realise 'the impossibility of what they demand as a result of their
own sufferings'; already 'millions of unemployed' in Britain and America were looking 'with sad comprehension at Germany, where almost
all factories work in unhealthy activity to earn foreign exchange to pay
for reparations'.[29] The Reichsbank too insisted that 'the deterioration of
the exchange rate [. . .] was the explanation for the world economic
crisis, i.e., for the production difficulties and unemployment in England
and America'.[30] The argument was repeated by Melchior in London
in February 1922 at a meeting with Sir Robert Horne, the Chancellor
of the Exchequer,[31] and by Max Warburg in a lengthy memorandum
entitled 'The German Problem' which was widely circulated among
business leaders and politicians when he visited the United States in
the autumn of 1922.[32]

[26] Lord D'Abernon, An Ambassador of Peace. Pages from the Diary of Viscount D'Abernon
Berlin 1920–1926 (London, 1929–30), vol. I, pp. 193f.
[27] StAH, FA Sthamer 7, Melchior to Goodenough, 22.7.21; WA, 32, Pol. Corr. 1921,
Warburg to Grenfell, 22.10.21; Sterling Library, Yale. Paul Warburg Papers, Ser.
1, Box 5, Folder 63, Melchior Memorandum, 23.8.21; Kohlhaus, 'Die Hapag', pp.
57, 64.
[28] Paul Warburg Papers, Ser. 1, Box 5, Folder 63, Paul Warburg to Hoover, 29.8.21.
[29] HKH Jahresbericht 1921, p. 8. Cf. H. Bücher, 'Die internationale Wirtschaftslage
in ihren Beziehungen zu Deutschland', in Die deutsche Industrie und die Wiedergutma-
chungsfrage. Bericht über die dritte Mitgliederversammlung des RdI in München, September
1921 (Berlin, 1921), pp. 21–32. Cf. Specht, Politische Hintergründe, p. 47 n.
[30] Cit. Specht, Politische Hintergründe, p. 62.
[31] WA, Allgemeines 1922, Melchior Report, 18.2.22; Melchior Memorandum, 20.2.22:
Depreciation of the mark was leading to 'cheap conditions of labour and great
industrial activity, which simultaneously disturbs the industries of competing
countries.' Cf. Melchior to Warburg, 6.4.22.
[32] WA, Allgemeines 1922, 'The German Problem': 'The mark in foreign countries falling
so much more rapidly than the purchasing power of the mark in Germany, the latter for
four years has been selling her goods much below the price in world markets. . .' Cf. the
correspondence between Paul Warburg and Parker Gilbert in NAW, RG 39, 6110 (20–
4). For details of Warburg's visit, which included meetings with Hughes, Mellon and
Hoover, see WA, Allgemeines 1922, Warburg to M.M. Warburg & Co., 22.9.22; F.I.
Kent to Warburg, 28.9.22; Warburg to M.M. Warburg & Co., 3.10.22; Warburg to
Bendix, 4.10.22; Warburg, 'Aide de Memoire' ('Alternative Fourteen Points'), 6.10.22;
Warburg to Wiedfeldt, 6.10.22; Warburg to Wiedfeldt, 9.10.22; Warburg to Alice War-

There were certainly some individuals in Britain and America who were persuaded. Keynes, of course, was already a convert. Considering the fiscal challenge confronting the Germans, he doubted whether 'the whips and scorpions of any government recorded in history [would] have been potent enough to extract nearly half (*sic*) their income from a people so situated'.[33] The need to increase German exports, on the other hand, posed a direct threat to the recipients of reparations themselves:

If Germany could compass the vast export trade which the Paris proposals contemplate, it could only be by ousting some of the staple trades of Great Britain from the markets of the world. [. . .] I do not expect to see Mr Lloyd George fighting a general election on the issue of maintaining an Army to compel Germany at the point of the bayonet to undercut our manufactures.[34]

Nor was Keynes now the lone voice he had been in 1919. One of Franz Witthoefft's British contacts quoted Reginald McKenna as saying that: 'If Germany could keep up the reparations payments for six months, unemployment in England and America would lead to intolerable conditions.'[35] When Havenstein visited London in November 1921, he too detected a change in mood.[36] On the other side of the Atlantic, Herbert Hoover argued that, if the United States did not 'interest itself in the countries struggling with fiscal [. . .] problems, we must expect to pay many thousand fold in the loss of export markets and in the employment of our people'.[37] Yet such considerations did not suffice to persuade the Allied governments to accede to the twin German requests for a moratorium and an international loan. Wirth's first bid for a moratorium of two or more years at the end of 1921

burg, 25.10.22; Warburg, Notes 11.11.22; Warburg to Wirth, 23.11.22; Warburg to Cuno. 26.11.22; 'Jahresbericht 1922', Diktat, 1940 (meeting with Hoover); Warburg, *Aufzeichnungen*, pp. 109–12; Rosenbaum and Sherman, *M.M. Warburg & Co.*, p. 162. Warburg's hopes of persuading American business leaders to take an interest in the German crisis were disappointed: he could not even persuade the American Chamber of Commerce to send a sympathetic telegram to the German Chambers of Commerce: see the material in WA, File XX.

[33] J.M. Keynes, 'New Reparations Settlement: Can Germany Pay?', 21.8.21, in Keynes, *Collected Writings*, XVII, pp. 242–9.

[34] J.M. Keynes, 'The Economic Consequences of the Paris Settlement', 31.1.21/1.2.21, in Keynes, *Collected Writings*, XVII, pp. 207–13; *idem*, 'The New Reparations Proposals', 6.5.21, in *ibid.*, p. 234; *idem*, 'The New Reparations Settlement: Effect on World Trade', 28.8.21, in *ibid.*, pp. 249–56. Cf. Skidelsky, *Economist as Saviour*, pp. 48, 54, 90. See also Keynes, *A Revision of the Treaty*, (London, 1921), in which he proposed a reduction of reparations to 21 bn. gold marks.

[35] PA/AA, SRW FW 16 II, 1105/11, (report of RWR finance policy committee), 15.10.21. See also the letter from an anonymous 'British employer' making a similar point in *The Times*, 20.10.21.

[36] Feldman, *Great Disorder*, pp. 377ff.

[37] Eichengreen, *Golden Fetters*, p. 161n.

won only a very limited breathing space: at Cannes, the Allies agreed
to postpone the full January and February payments, but still insisted
on a continuing transfer of 30 m. gold marks every ten days.[38] Indeed,
the more doggedly German spokesmen adhered to the 'balance of
payments theory', the more Allied representatives insisted that the
problem lay in German fiscal and monetary laxity.[39] When a reduction
in the 1922 cash payment to 720 m. gold marks was provisionally
agreed in March 1922, the Germans were required to agree to raise
taxes by 60 bn. paper marks; and an extension of that agreement in
May was made conditional on eliminating the deficit altogether.[40]
Doubts about the German government's fiscal credibility in turn diminished the chance of the international loan. Although the German
financial delegates at Genoa won some sympathy from their British
counterparts when they argued for a 4 bn. gold marks loan, the
committee of bankers set up under J.P. Morgan to report on Germany's
creditworthiness rejected the idea after two months of deliberation.[41]
It was possible, as Rathenau did, to see the Morgan committee's
verdict – that a loan to Germany was impossible 'unless and until the
reparations question was settled' – as 'the greatest step forward for the
government's policy since the London Ultimatum'.[42] But reparations
remained, and with them the possibility of increased sanctions rather
than revision. A renewed request for a moratorium in July was rejected
by the French government in the absence of 'productive guarantees'.[43]
By the time Wirth made his last desperate plea for a three-year
moratorium on 14 November 1922, it was clear that French patience
had run out.

[38] Laubach, *Kabinette Wirth*, pp. 120–4; Specht, *Politische Hintergründe*, pp. 74f.; Maier,
Recasting Bourgeois Europe, pp. 249f., 265ff.
[39] Kent, *Spoils of War*, pp. 158–65; Maier, *Recasting Bourgeois Europe*, pp. 276ff.
[40] Laubach, *Kabinette Wirth*, pp. 157–68, 228–36; Kent, *Spoils of War*, pp. 174–9;
Specht, *Politische Hintergründe*, pp. 77f.; Maier, *Recasting Bourgeois Europe*,
pp. 282f.; Feldman, *Great Disorder*, pp. 340–5.
[41] Kent, *Spoils of War*, p. 177; Maier, *Recasting Bourgeois Europe*, p. 284; Rupieper,
'Industrie und Reparationen', p. 591. The delegation at Genoa included Melchior
and Cuno: I. Schulze-Bidlingsmaier (ed.), *Die Kabinette Wirth I und II* (Boppard
am Rhein, 1973), vol. II, pp. 655ff. Cf. C. Fink, *The Genoa Conference: European
Diplomacy, 1921–1922* (Chapel Hill, 1984). On the bankers' committee, see Kent,
Spoils of War, p. 182; Link, *Amerikanische Stabilisierungspolitik*, pp. 122–35. Significantly, even Keynes was not wholly persuaded by the German case, rejecting the
idea of an international loan as 'an illusion (as big) as reparations on a grand scale':
Keynes, 'The Reparations Problem at Genoa', 24.4.22, *Collected Writings*, XVII,
pp. 398–401; 'A Moratorium for War Debts', *Collected Writings*, 5.8.22, XVIII, pp.
12–31; 'Is a Settlement of the Reparation Question Possible Now?', 28.9.22, *ibid*,
32–43.
[42] Thomas Lamont Papers, 176–1, J.P. Morgan & Co. Statement, July/August 1922;
Specht, *Politische Hintergründe*, p. 78.
[43] *Ibid.* p. 82; Kent, *Spoils of War*, p. 185.

It is, of course, possible to attribute the failure of fulfilment to factors beyond the control of German policy makers. When Briand appeared to waver in early 1921, domestic political forces in France toppled him in favour of Poincaré, who was more willing to risk a confrontation with Germany. Lloyd George was perhaps over-ambitious in proposing a 'grand design' for East European reconstruction at Genoa.[44] Above all, it can be argued that so long as the United States remained intransigent on the question of inter-Allied debts, the likelihood of a breakthrough on reparations was nil.[45] Yet if the revisionist calculation had been correct, these factors would have mattered less. The depreciation of the mark was supposed to lead to a significant boost in German exports at the expense of Allied economies. The German calculation was that this immediate economic pressure would overrule other political considerations, forcing Allied politicians to reduce reparations as a matter of self interest. In order to understand why this did not happen, an analysis of the macroeconomic impact of fulfilment is necessary.

The fulfilment of expectations

The starting point for the strategy for revision through currency depreciation was fiscal imbalance. In order to demonstrate Germany's incapacity to pay in the intended way, the budget deficit had to be maintained; for to attempt to balance it would amount to a step towards genuine fulfilment of the London schedule. As Wirth himself put it in arguing against a property levy (or 'seizure of real values', in the contemporary catch phrase): 'The goal of our entire policy must be the dismantling of the London Ultimatum. It would therefore be a mistake if, by initiating a seizure of real values at this moment, we were [in effect] to declare the Ultimatum to be 80 per cent possible.'[46] The domestic debate on financial reform between May 1921 and November 1922 was therefore to some extent a phoney debate, as the Chancellor himself was not in earnest about trying to balance the budget. This explains why proposals like that for the 'seizure of real values' – which was initially conceived as a compulsory mortgage on all immobile property, then as a capitalised corporation tax – ultimately came to nothing. Such measures had to be discussed partly in order

---

[44] Orde, *British Policy and European Reconstruction after the First World War* pp. 160–207.
[45] Artaud, 'La question des dettes interalliées et la reconstruction de l'Europe', C.A. Wurm, 'Frankreich, die Reparationen und die interallierten Schulden in den 20er Jahren', in Feldman *et al.* (eds.), *Nachwirkungen*, pp. 315–33.
[46] Specht, *Politische Hintergründe*, p. 75.

to appease the Reparations Commission and partly to mollify those (notably the officials at the Economics Ministry) who disapproved of the return to inflation; but they were never intended to 'close the hole in the budget'.[47] The State Secretary at the Foreign Office, Fischer, captured the prevailing mood when he described the Reparations Commission's 'wish for a further increase in taxes' as implying a 'wish for the economic destruction of Germany'.[48] Even local tax collectors believed that 'it is in the interests of our people [. . .] that we do not yet extract all that we can to throw into the mills of the Entente'.[49] Significantly, Max Warburg's principal anxiety on the eve of the Genoa conference was that an attempt might be made to impose a 'financial control' on Germany.[50]

The Wirth governments succeeded, it is true, in cutting the level of real monthly expenditure from a peak of over a billion in the summer of 1921 to between 400 and 500 m. gold marks during most of 1922.[51] Indeed, at 24 per cent of NNP, total public spending in 1922 was at its lowest level since before the war.[52] But despite a host of new tax measures, real revenue from taxation also fell in the second half of 1921, and rose only slightly in the first half of 1922; so that although the Reich deficit was falling as a percentage of NNP (from 16 per cent in 1920 to 12 per cent in 1921 and 9 per cent in 1922), it remained excessive by modern standards.[53] Typically, the 1 bn. gold marks graduated 'forced loan' – devised in response to the Allies' demand for financial reforms at Cannes – raised only 50 m. gold marks because the Finance Ministry fixed the multiplier for converting paper marks into gold at too low a level.[54] By the time he visited Berlin in November 1922 as one of Wirth's committee of foreign experts,[55] even

---

[47] *Ibid.*, pp. 69–71; Laubach, *Kabinette Wirth*, pp. 61–6, 145f.; Maier, *Recasting Bourgeois Europe*, pp. 247–55; Kent, *Spoils of War*, p. 147.

[48] GFM, 3243/D713267, Kabinettsprotokolle, Chefbesprechung, 23.3.22.

[49] Feldman, *Great Disorder*, p. 349.

[50] WA, Allgemeines 1922, Warburg to Melchior, 20.3.22; Rosenbaum and Sherman, *M.M. Warburg & Co.*, p. 158. He instructed Melchior to 'leave the conference hall at once' if such a control was proposed.

[51] See figures 3.3 and 5.1.

[52] See figure 0.4. This partly reflected economies on the railways and cuts in food subsidies: Feldman, *Great Disorder*, pp. 354–76, 577–80. However, the cost of grants to increasingly insolvent municipal authorities continued to rise: *ibid.*, pp. 561ff., 625f.

[53] See table 1. Figures calculated from Webb, *Hyperinflation*, pp. 33, 37 and Witt, 'Finanzpolitik', pp. 425f.

[54] Bresciani, *Inflation*, pp. 57ff.; Specht, *Politische Hintergründe*, p. 76; Laubach, *Kabinette Wirth*, pp. 145–8; Kent, *Spoils of War*, p. 173; Holtfrerich, *Inflation*, p. 135. See the comments of the Hamburg representative on the Bundesrat: StAH, SK II, II A 4 Fasc. 16, Strandes to SK, 8.3.22; Strandes to SK, 19.5.22

[55] Keynes, *Collected Writings*, XVIII, pp. 61ff.; Laubach, *Kabinette Wirth*, pp. 298–306; Specht, *Politische Hintergründe*, pp. 88–91; Kent, *Spoils of War*, pp. 192f.

Keynes had become disillusioned with the government's financial policy. In the majority report which he signed, and in a subsequent letter to Havenstein, Keynes explicitly repudiated 'the point of view which looks first to the balance of trade, and seeks for an improvement there first of all, or alternatively to the support of a foreign loan'. 'If I felt confident that I could control the budgetary position,' he added pointedly, 'I should not doubt my capacity [. . .] to control the exchanges. As soon as the supply of new currency is limited, I do not see how it is possible that the balance of trade should be adverse.'[56]

In the absence of radical fiscal reform, clearly, the German government could only pay reparations in cash by borrowing foreign currency.[57] However, as immediately became clear, few investors were willing to lend foreign currency to a government with a notional external debt of 125 bn. gold marks. The first instalment of reparations under the London schedule – 1 bn. gold marks, due by 31 August – was only paid with difficulty. Although it proved possible to negotiate short-term credits of around 300 m. gold marks from Holland and Italy, the Reichsbank reserves of foreign currency (accumulated during the 1920 intervention against the mark) were almost entirely used up.[58] When Havenstein turned to the Bank of England for 500 m. gold marks to help pay the second instalment, he was politely refused.[59] Wirth was no more successful when he appealed to German industry to undertake some kind of 'credit action' on the Reich's behalf.[60] It was in itself a watershed in relations between the state and the economy that the Association of German Industry should offer to borrow 1.5 bn. gold marks abroad on behalf of the Reich, provided the SPD abandoned the idea of a 'seizure of real values'. The fact that Stinnes and others (including Rudolf Blohm) went on to propose the privatisation of the railway system as a further *quid pro quo* merely underscored the point: inflation was diminishing not only the Reich's credit but also its authority.[61] A similar point could be made about Rathenau's attempt

[56] Skidelsky, *Economist as Saviour*, pp. 116f., 120.
[57] Graham, *Hyperinflation*, p. 134. Even if the Reichsbank's entire gold reserve had been handed over as reparations, it would not have sufficed to pay for a single year's annuity. In any case, there was strong opposition to such a sacrifice of the Reichsbank's gold. Although the last remaining reserve rules were abandoned in May 1921, it was assumed that Germany would ultimately return to the gold standard.
[58] Bresciani, *Inflation*, pp. 93ff.; Kent, *Spoils of War*, p. 142.
[59] *Ibid.*, pp. 157f.; Specht, *Politische Hintergründe*, pp. 74f.
[60] Bergmann, *Reparationen*, pp. 102f., 109–13, 130–2; Schulze-Bidlingsmaier (ed.), *Kabinette Wirth*, I, p. 266; Maier, *Recasting Bourgeois Europe*, pp. 264ff.; Kent, *Spoils of War*, p. 151; Specht, *Politische Hintergründe*, pp. 72–4; Feldman, *Great Disorder*, pp. 358–76.
[61] GFM, Stresemann NL, 6992/H140554, Kurt Sorge to Stresemann, 17.10.21; PA/ AA, SRW, FW 16 II, 1119, RWR Arbeitsausschuß für die Beratung des Problems der Devisen-Beschaffung für die Reparationen, 18.10.21; 1119/21, Unterausschuß

at Wiesbaden to reduce the Reich's need for hard currency by increasing the share of reparations in kind – direct transfers of goods – in the total reparations bill. Diplomatically, the bilateral arrangement with France irritated Britain, without reducing the burden of reparations in the short run.[62] Economically, it replaced real exports with unrequited transfers, without evading the tariffs on French imports from Germany. And financially, it was only advantageous if industry were willing to accept less from the government in paper marks than it would earn from conventional exports – one of a number of reasons why Stinnes regarded Wiesbaden as 'thoroughly bad'.[63] In fact, reparations in kind only became attractive to industry after mid 1922 when the gap between German and world prices had closed (making conventional exports less easy), and the system had been effectively 'privatised' by the Cuntze–Bemelmans and Gillet–Ruppel Agreements.[64]

In short, whether to finance government deficits, buy foreign currency or pay for deliveries in kind, paying reparations meant printing paper marks. The critical question was what effect this inflationary fiscal policy would have on the exchange rate, and what effect the exchange rate would have on trade.[65] The link between the transfer of reparations and the depreciation of the mark was a complex one.[66] The exchange rate depends in the long run upon relative international economic competitiveness, in that this determines the balance of trade

des RWR, 13.10.21; 1120, Reparationsausschuß des RWR, 19.10.21; 1147, Aufzeichnung über die beabsichtigte Kreditaktion der Deutschen Gewerbe, 29.10.21; 1202, RWR Sitzung, 4.11.21. See also the material in PA/AA, SRW, FW 16 I, 1045/21. Stinnes's new condition effectively torpedoed the plan, although Schacht tried in vain to revive the scheme in March 1922: Mudd Library, Princeton, John Foster Dulles Papers, Box 4, Schacht to Dulles, 20.3.22.

[62] The agreement envisaged reparations in kind being paid over five years up to a total of 7 bn. gold marks, but no more than 1 bn. gold marks was to count towards the annual sums before 1926. See in general, Maier, *Recasting Bourgeois Europe*, pp. 262–7; Specht, *Politische Hintergründe*, pp. 93ff.; Kent, *Spoils of War*, p. 148; Feldman, *Great Disorder*, pp. 356f. For Keynes's critical comments, WA, Pol. Corr. 1921, Keynes to Melchior, 22.8.21; Melchior to Rathenau, 26.9.21; Melchior to Keynes, 17.10.21; Keynes, *Collected Writings*, XVII, pp. 282f.

[63] GFM, Stresemann NL, 6992/H140574, Stinnes to Rathenau, 19.10.21; /H140576, Rathenau to Stinnes, 20.10.21.

[64] Lindenlaub, *Maschinebauunternehmen*, pp. 153–64; Specht, *Politische Hintergründe*, p. 95. These formed the basis for the more famous Stinnes–Lubersac Agreement: Feldman, *Iron and Steel*, pp. 329, 447; idem, *Great Disorder*, pp. 460ff., 479ff.

[65] As Warburg and others realised, Rathenau saw the problem differently, seeing the balance of trade as an 'unalterable fact', unaffected by monetary factors. WA, Allgemeines 1922, Warburg Note (on Wiesbaden); D'Abernon, *Ambassador of Peace*, I, pp. 289f.

[66] C.-L. Holtfrerich, 'Erwartungen des In- und Auslandes und die Geldnachfrage während der Inflation in Deutschland 1920–1923', *Bankhistorisches Archiv*, 6 (1980) pp. 3–19; Webb, 'Fiscal News and Inflationary Expectations'. Cf. Holtfrerich, *Inflation*, pp. 75f.; Kindleberger, *Financial History*, p. 319; Webb, *Hyperinflation*, pp. 44–64.

(and hence the demand for foreign currency to pay for imports and the supply of foreign currency from export earnings), and capital flows (purchases of foreign and domestic assets). In the short run, however, it can fluctuate far more rapidly than is justified by changes in competitiveness because of the rapidity with which the expectations of investors change. The post-First World War period was especially volatile in this regard because knowledge and experience of floating exchange rate systems was evolving rapidly from a low point, political instability was very great, and the number of economic agents involved in foreign currency speculation grew rapidly.[67] Thus the very sharp depreciation of the mark against the dollar between May (62.30) and November 1921 (262.96) was principally due to German flight from the mark: the difficulty of paying the first instalment of the London schedule and the loss of Upper Silesia evidently caused more alarm in Germany than abroad, where holders of marks continued to believe in an ultimate recovery of the exchange rate.[68] As Max Warburg observed, it was not necessary to believe in a conspiracy of 'influential circles [. . .] trying forcibly to weaken the currency in order to draw attention to an insolvency that Germany does not actually suffer from, and to force an export that would not otherwise take place'.[69] The German speculation against the mark was spontaneous, and required no coordination, because the insolvency was real.[70] Typically, Paul Reusch advised Deutsche Werft not to sell foreign currency in December 1921 because

at present there is no evidence available to justify an expectation of a permanent improvement in the mark. [. . .] There will doubtless be an increased need for foreign currency to pay for food imports in the new year; and in addition it is to be feared that the substitution of deliveries in kind for gold marks

[67] Webb has attempted to construct a model relating expectations to government deficits, arguing that 'Inflation [. . .] resulted from the accumulation and the anticipation of government deficits. Inflationary expectations depended therefore on fiscal news. [. . .] Political events were fiscal news as they changed the chances for the government to balance the budget': Webb, 'Fiscal News', pp. 769f. This may exaggerate the extent to which contemporaries appreciated the link between government deficits and inflation.

[68] On the speculation against the mark in Berlin in September, Bresciani, *Inflation*, pp. 61, 96f., 100.

[69] WA, Politische Correspondenz 1921, Warburg to Major Sequin, Zürich, 29.9.21. See the similar comment made by Keynes in November 1921: 'I do not believe a word of the silly stories that the German government could be so bold or so mad as to engineer on purpose what will in the end be a great catastrophe for their own people. . .': Keynes, 'Renewed Depreciation of the Mark', 9.11.21, *Collected Writings*, XVIII, p. 10.

[70] The role of numerous new 'banks' which had sprung up since the end of the war was widely commented upon; see, e.g., BAK, R43 I/2433, Hansabund to RK, 10.10.21.

payments will lead to an increased inflation in Germany, which must inevitably have a further unfavourable influence on the mark exchange rate.[71]

Stinnes was not the first to comment that 'all business today has by and large become an exchange insurance business and otherwise a speculation business'; the Hamburg Chamber of Commerce had made the same point as early as April 1921.[72] It is impossible to know exactly how much capital flowed out of Germany in this way; but clearly there was a movement amounting to several billion gold marks at around this time.[73] By contrast, Keynes's pessimism about the mark was exceptional among foreign investors, judging by the forward exchange rate against the mark in London, and figures for purchases of marks in New York.[74] A last flicker of foreign hope (ignited by the Cannes conference) accounts for the temporary halt to depreciation in December–February 1922.[75]

In short, apart from that brief lull, the mark did depreciate rapidly during Wirth's period as Chancellor. What effect did this then have on German trade? The theory was that depreciation would, as it had in the second half of 1919, create a gap between German domestic prices and world market prices, because the mark would lose value faster abroad than it did at home. It would thus boost German exports, because hard currency countries would be able to buy German goods at bargain-basement prices. Moreover, it would impede German imports, because German importers would find the prices of foreign goods

---

[71] GHH, 300193012/7, Kroll to Reusch, 18.12.21; DW to Reusch, 4.1.22.
[72] Feldman, *Iron and Steel*, pp. 312f.; StAH, DHSG III, Pr. III 34 Bd. 2, HKH to RKEAB, 6.4.21.
[73] In August 1922, *The Times* estimated German foreign investments at close to their pre-war level, but Keynes dismissed this as a gross overestimate, suggesting 1–3 bn. gold marks as a plausible figure; Keynes, 'Speculation in the Mark and Germany's Balances Abroad', 28.9.22, *Collected Writings*, XVII, pp. 56ff. He later revised this upwards to 1.7–3.8 bn. gold marks; *The Nation and Atheneum*, 19.4.24. The McKenna committee ultimately opted for a figure of 5.7–7.8 bn. gold marks for total German capital abroad at the end of the inflation period, but this figure was little more than an educated guess: Schuker, 'American "Reparations"', p. 366. Cf. *The Economist, Reparations Supplement*, 12.4.24.
[74] Keynes, 'Will the German Mark be Superseded?', in *Collected Writings*, XVIII, pp. 1–6. Keynes had of course been wrong to speculate against the mark a year previously. On the forward exchange rate and foreign holders of marks, see Holtfrerich, *Inflation*, p. 73. On foreign purchases of marks in New York, see Webb, *Hyperinflation*, p. 57. Webb errs in arguing that monetary expansion led to a capital outflow and hence to a trade surplus in 1921/2; *ibid.*, p. 94. In fact, it is possible to derive a time-path for foreign confidence using (a) the forward exchange rate (*ibid.*, p. 73), (b) data on foreign purchases of marks abroad (*ibid.*, p. 57) and (c) data on foreign deposits in German banks (Holtfrerich, 'Die deutsche Inflation in internationaler Perspektive'). These indicate that confidence only fell in 1922 – and indeed not until July.
[75] See figure 6.1.

impossibly high in paper mark terms.[76] For a time, the theory appeared
to be working. The Economics Ministry reported that 'the fall of the
mark [. . .] though in itself deplorable' was 'an unmistakable factor
behind the improvement in exports'.[77] In Hamburg the shipyards
celebrated an influx of foreign contracts due to the 'poor level' of the
mark.[78] As if to bear this out, the available export statistics point to
a 35 per cent increase in the gold marks value of monthly exports (83
per cent in volume terms) in the year after May 1921.[79] Annual figures
suggest a two-thirds increase of exports in volume terms, with Hamburg
enjoying particularly rapid export growth.[80] Graham's calculations for
forty-three categories of commodity also point to increases in exports.[81]
Indeed, it may even be that all these figures are slight underestimates.
The Allies claimed that the German government was understating
exports to reduce the amount of reparations due; while the Economics
Ministry itself accused German firms of understating their foreign
sales, in order 'to leave the surplus profit abroad'.[82] There was also a
good deal of smuggling at this time.[83]

However, this tells only a part of the story. In fact, imports substantially outstripped exports – a vital point, since only a trade surplus
would have had the intended effect of exerting economic pressure on
the Allies. Estimated annual figures point to a trade deficit of around
690 m. gold marks in 1921 and over 2,200 m. gold marks in 1922,

[76] Graham, *Hyperinflation*, pp. 117–33, 174–97, 209, 248.
[77] StAH, SK II, III 1 a 1, Bd. I, RWM to RK, 'Die Wirtschaftslage', 21.7.21.
[78] Deutsche Werft in particular secured valuable contracts in England, Italy and Scandinavia: GHH, 300193012/7, Deutsche Werft to Reusch, 29.10.21; Deutsche Werft to
Reusch, 11.3.22; Deutsche Werft, *Jahresbericht 1924*.
[79] See figure 4.3.
[80] Figures from Bresciani, *Inflation*, pp. 194, 235; Wagenführ, 'Die Industrie wirtschaft',
p. 26. See figure 2.1 for Hamburg's foreign exports, which trebled between 1920
and 1922. Hamburg's share of total German exports rose to 23–24 per cent, compared
with a pre-war figure of just 10 per cent.
[81] Graham, *Hyperinflation*, pp. 214–38, 261. In fact, Graham's results are less convincing
than he asserted. Only sixteen of his forty-three commodities showed an upward
export trend, and only ten showed a downward import trend. Moreover, there was
a clear correlation to exchange-rate and price movements in only eight cases. In any
case, his use of May 1921–December 1923 without reference to preceding or succeeding periods took the second depreciation phase out of context. His estimate that
Germany suffered a net loss of 10 bn. gold marks selling exports too cheaply is
curious, since at higher prices fewer exports would presumably have been sold;
ibid., pp. 260–76.
[82] Keynes, *Collected Writings*, XVIII, pp. 48, 54; J.M. Williams, 'German Foreign
Trade and the Reparations Payments', *Quarterly Journal of Economics*, 36 (1922);
Graham, *Hyperinflation*, pp. 214f.; Feldman, *Great Disorder*, pp. 349, 354ff.
[83] On smuggling, see the material in GStA, Rep. 84a, 4878/88–93, Wirtschaftsausschuß
der deutschen Reederei to Min. Dir. Jonquières, RMfW, 20.8.21; Rep. 84a, 129/
196, Zentralverein deutscher Rheder, Rundschreiben, 11.9.22; /249–53, Zentralverein
deutscher Rheder, 'Schmuggel und Ladungsberaubungen durch der Schiffsmannschaft'
(1922).

compared with a tiny surplus in 1920.[84] Monthly figures provide a more precise record: the trade gap widened between May and September 1921; narrowed to record a small surplus in December 1921; and then widened again to reach a peak of 348 m. gold marks in July 1922.[85] The figures for trade volumes tell the same story, but suggest an even more dramatic widening of the deficit after February 1922, despite the fact that by this stage the proportion of semi-finished and finished goods had risen to a third of all imports.[86] Of the most successful German exports – vehicles, machinery, electrical goods, chemicals, leather goods, silk goods, paper and wood – only vehicles and wood exceeded their 1913 volumes in 1922. By comparison, thirteen categories of import did so: not only foodstuffs and raw materials, but also iron goods (four times the pre-war volume) and cotton goods.[87] What is more, these figures may understate the extent of the trade gap. Although Hirsch and others continued to claim that exports were being underestimated and that the deficit in 1922 was negligible, there was 'complete consensus' in the Reich Statistical Office 'that the balance of trade deficit was being significantly underestimated'.[88]

The striking point is that, in diametric opposition to the predictions of the architects of the strategy of fulfilment, the trade deficit widened at times of most rapid nominal exchange rate depreciation (the second half of 1919, May to October 1921 and March to July 1922), and narrowed when the mark stabilised (March 1920 to April 1921 and

---

[84] See table 2. There are a number of quite different calculations to choose from, beginning with Keynes's estimates in *Collected Writings*, XVIII, pp. 48, 54; *Statistik des Deutschen Reiches*, 317, p. 5; Laursen and Pedersen, *Inflation*, pp. 68f., 83, 89–91; Holtfrerich, *Inflation*, p. 212; *idem*, 'Germany and the International Economy', p. 276; Webb, *Hyperinflation*, p. 91; and Feldman, *Great Disorder*, p. 600 (citing estimates by R. Pilotti for the Reparations Commission). Though all clearly indicate an increased deficit in 1921, Holtfrerich, Webb and Feldman follow the *Statistik des deutschen Reiches* in arguing that there was a near balance in 1922. However, the relevant figures are arrived at by converting volume figures into 1913 unit values using the customs schedule of 1913, which makes no allowance for the 'dumping' of German exports. My own calculations based on monthly data for value as well as volume suggest that the deficit grew to around 2 bn. gold marks in 1922, close to the estimate given by Laursen and Pedersen.

[85] See figure 4.3.

[86] See figure 4.6. Data on the structure of trade in Hentschel, 'Zahlen und Anmerkungen', p. 96; Laursen and Pedersen, *Inflation*, pp. 99–107; Bresciani, *Inflation*, p. 194. For evidence of the trade deficit in yarn and cloth, see Außenhandelsstelle für Ein- und Ausfuhr von Wolle, 'Valutagewinn und Substanzverlust' (1923). A substantial part of the volume deficit in 1922 and 1923 was accounted for by the need to import coal, which intensified during the Ruhr crisis: Graham, *Hyperinflation*, pp. 214–25; Feldman, *Great Disorder*, p. 447.

[87] Calculated from Hentschel, 'Zahlen und Anmerkungen', pp. 103–8.

[88] Feldman, *Great Disorder*, p. 484 n.

November 1921 to February 1922).[89] Hence, paradoxically, at a time when Germany was supposed to be putting the Allied economies under pressure from cheap German exports, in reality it was relieving the pressure on them by providing them with an outlet for their exports.[90] In May–September 1921 and March–April 1922 – i.e., at critical moments in the diplomacy of fulfilment – Germany's share of American exports rose to peak levels of nearly 12 per cent, so that Germany temporarily eclipsed Britain as the largest single foreign market for American raw materials.[91] The total US trade surplus with Germany between 1919 and 1923 amounted to around $770 m.[92] Similarly, whereas between 1904 and 1913, Britain had had a trade deficit with Germany, in the years 1920–3 British exports to Germany exceeded imports from Germany by £83 m. – close to 0.5 per cent of UK GNP. The percentage of British exports going to Germany rose from 2.3 per cent in 1919 to 6.7 per cent in 1923.[93] In fact, it was in politically irrelevant weak-currency countries in the Mediterranean, Scandinavia and the Far East that German exports were most successful.[94] Fully 37 per cent of German exports went to these countries in 1920, compared with 13.6 per cent before the war. By contrast, Britain, France, Belgium, Italy and the US accounted for 26.3 per cent of

[89] Compare figures 3.4, 4.3, 4.6 and 6.1. Cf. Bresciani, *Inflation*, pp. 83–92, 100–54.

[90] Holtfrerich, *Inflation*, pp. 213f. For an opposing view, see Schuker, 'Finance and Foreign Policy', p. 353; Webb, *Hyperinflation*, pp. 89–94. Webb attempts to show that the trade balance narrowed between July 1919 and March 1920, becoming a surplus between December 1919 and March 1920; then returned to deficit during the rest of the period of relative stabilisation; and turned positive again from May 1921. This implies that depreciation *did* boost exports. However, Webb's figures are arrived at by applying different deflators to import and export data, hence eliminating changes in the terms (and composition) of trade since 1913. Following the same procedure, I also arrive at a narrow surplus for the period November 1921 to November 1922 (see figure 4.4). But what this shows is only that *had German imports and exports been valued at 1913 prices*, there would have been a surplus in the fulfilment period. The important point, as the remainder of this section argues, is that even although German exports were to some extent undervalued in historic terms, the gap between German and foreign prices was less pronounced than in 1919/20 because Germany's economy was booming while those of her trading partners were deflating. It was this divergence in economic performance which gave rise to the deficit in dollar (or gold mark) terms; and for the purposes of the reparations question, it was the current dollar value of trade which mattered. Webb is in error to conclude that 'Germany's efforts to pay reparations punched the mouth they were supposed to feed' (*ibid.*, p. 94); the contrary was true.

[91] See figure 4.8. Cf. Holtfrerich, 'Germany and the International Economy', pp. 278ff.; *idem, Inflation*, pp. 214f.; and on American cotton exports to Germany – the single largest item in German–American trade – see NAW, RG 39, G114.2, (17).

[92] Webb, *Hyperinflation*, p. 91.

[93] Calculated from *The Economist, Economic Statistics 1900–1983* (London, 1981). Even the Reparations Recovery Act could not wholly exclude German exports from the British market, as the £4 bn. raised in 1921/2 confirms.

[94] Balderston, *Economic Crisis*, pp. 86–93.

German exports in 1922, compared with 38.5 per cent in 1913, but 44.8 per cent of German imports, compared with 35.3 per cent in 1913.[95]

All of this, as Holtfrerich has pointed out, was good for the world economy, helping to lift it out of a slump which might otherwise have become a depression; but it was also (and this he overlooks) bad for revisionism.[96] Warburg and others had predicted that if the mark were allowed to depreciate, the pressure of German exports would force the Allies to abandon the London schedule of reparations. Instead, Germany had provided the Allied economies with a booming market for their own exports. The argument that fulfilment failed because French and American attitudes did not change is therefore inadequate, since the objective had been precisely to change Allied attitudes by exerting economic pressure. The point is that by doing the opposite – by relieving economic pressure on the Allies – fulfilment removed any need for them to revise the London schedule. As Wirth himself came to realise in October 1922, the Germans had 'robbed themselves of one of the most effective propaganda tools in the struggle to relieve our reparations burdens [. . .] in that the horrifying situation of German foreign trade has remained unknown at home and abroad'.[97]

What had gone wrong? According to Balderston, continuing hostility to Germany on the part of her former foes may have negated the price advantage of depreciation; whereas the former neutrals, as Hentschel has noted, had accumulated large paper mark balances during the war which they were eager to exchange for German goods.[98] But a further economic explanation is that, although in nominal terms the mark clearly depreciated against the other major currencies, in real terms – allowing for changes in relative prices – there was no significant improvement in German competitiveness.[99] Compared with the gap which had opened up between German prices and world market prices from July 1919 until the relative stabilisation of the mark, the gap which opened up after May 1921 was far less significant, all but

---

[95] Hentschel, 'Zahlen und Anmerkungen', p. 113.

[96] Holtfrerich, *Inflation*, pp. 206–20; *idem*, 'Germany and the International Economy', pp. 265f. Holtfrerich estimates that, if Germany had adopted deflationary policies, imports from the US would have been reduced by 60 per cent, and imports from the UK by 44 per cent. In effect, he suggests, German inflation averted a world depression of the sort experienced a decade later. This point is hard to reconcile with his assertion that inflation was the only way to persuade the Allies of the need for revision after 1921.

[97] Feldman, *Great Disorder*, pp. 484f.

[98] Balderston, *Economic Crisis*, pp. 82ff.; Hentschel, 'Zahlen und Anmerkungen', pp. 99–112.

[99] See figure 4.5.

vanishing in February 1922.[100] The underlying reasons for this can be considered under foreign and domestic headings. Among the former, the most important was the prevailing international economic slump, as a result of which prices, particularly of British and American goods, had fallen sharply since 1919/20. Between 1920 and 1922, British prices fell by 50 per cent, American prices by 40–45 per cent.[101] Equally important, however, were the domestic factors at work. From one point of view, 1921 and (to a lesser extent) 1922 were among the 'golden years' of the Weimar economy. Estimates for NNP suggest growth rates of around 7 per cent and 4 per cent; indeed, taken together, the years 1920–2 witnessed the most impressive period of growth of the Weimar years.[102] Industrial production rose by around 20 per cent in 1921 and 8 per cent in 1922, with strong growth in iron and steel production, and especially in ship-building.[103] The output of German shipyards rose by perhaps as much as 150 per cent.[104] Moreover, there is evidence of substantial investment by businesses in new plant, evidently in anticipation of sustained expansion. Of course, it is well known that the aggregate capital stock fell by around 10 per cent between 1913 and 1924.[105] But such fragmentary data as are available suggest that in the years 1920–2 there was a significant effort to compensate for a much deeper depreciation caused by the war years.[106] Deutsche Werft, for example, 'relentlessly' turned its profits from 'liquid assets' into new dock facilities.[107] In 1921 all but 100,000 marks of gross income totalling 14.6 m. marks were invested in 'real values' – including 6.6 m. marks in accommodation for its growing workforce.[108] Similarly, in April 1922, an investment programme costing 68.8 m. marks was drawn up, which was later increased to 136 m.

---

[100] This had been predicted by Hilferding: 'With the increase of the issues [of notes] the balance of trade necessarily becomes passive. In effect, the issues increased internal prices, and that stimulated imports and impeded exports'; Bresciani, *Inflation*, p. 44 n.; Maier, *Recasting Bourgeois Europe*, p. 251.

[101] *The Economist, Economic Statistics*.

[102] See figure 2.3.

[103] See figures 2.4 and 2.5.

[104] See figure 1.2. Hoffmann et al., *Wachstum*, p. 358, suggest growth of just 55 per cent, with virtually no increase in output in 1922. However, figures for Deutsche Werft suggest that this is too low: output grew by 50 per cent in 1921 and 20 per cent in 1922: Deutsche Werft, *Jahresbericht 1921*; *Jahresbericht 1922*; Blohm & Voß, *Jahresbericht 1921/2*; *Jahresbericht 1922/3*.

[105] Hoffmann et al., *Wachstum*, p. 253.; Petzina, 'Was there a Crisis before the Crisis?' in Kruedener (ed.), *Economic Crisis*, pp. 9–12.

[106] See figure 2.6.

[107] GHH, 4001012012/0, Deutsche Werft, Bericht, 8.5.24.

[108] Deutsche Werft, *Jahresbericht 1921*; GHH, 300193012/6, Aufsichtsratssitzung, 30.5.21. The annual report appears to understate this investment.

marks – compared with reported earnings of just 115 m. marks.[109] The ships produced by firms like Deutsche Werft can also be regarded as investments by the shipping lines which purchased them. Considering the devastation of the merchant marine, the fact that it was restored to 58 per cent of its pre-war tonnage by 1924 must be acknowledged as one of the greatest feats of investment of the inflation years.[110] The Hapag, for example, initiated its reconstruction programme in March 1921 with a pledge to restore a third of its pre-war tonnage within five years. In the first year of this programme, it purchased nine old ships, twenty-seven new ones and placed orders for a further forty-three; in the second, three old ships were acquired, twenty-six new ones and a further fourteen ordered. Altogether, the Hapag purchased vessels weighing 143,000 reg. tons in 1921 and 120,000 reg. tons in 1922, with the result that its five-year target was achieved within just two.[111] Nor was such investment confined to shipping. There was increased mechanisation in some sectors, notably coal mining;[112] and there were substantial investments in the railway system. The average number of new locomotives put into service annually in the inflation years (1919–23) was 1,725, compared with 956 before the war (1910–13) and just 391 in the stabilisation period (1924–5). More than 2,000 were purchased in 1921, a peak also reflected in the railway budgets for new plant and repairs.[113] Likewise, the number of road vehicles in Hamburg more than doubled between 1921 and 1924;[114] while the number of telephones in Germany rose by 60 per cent in the five post-war years, compared with 9 per cent in the preceding six years and 36 per cent in the succeeding six.[115] There is also some evidence of investment in bricks and mortar: for Germany as a whole, the number of new dwellings totalled 240,000 in the inflation years, and some statistics suggest an increase in the stock of non-residential buildings.[116] At first sight, this would seem to suggest that at least

---

[109] Deutsche Werft, *Jahresbericht 1922*; GHH, 300193012/8, Deutsche Werft to Reusch, 15.3.22; 25.4.22; 31.8.22.

[110] Hoffmann *et al.*, *Wachstum*, p. 409; Bresciani, *Inflation*, p. 194.

[111] Hapag, *Jahresbericht 1921*; *Jahresbericht 1922*; *Hamburgische Correspondent*, 16.6.24. Although published accounts from the inflation years must be read with scepticism, it is not implausible to deduce an increase in 'real values' (real estate, buildings, inventories and ships) of around 70 m. gold marks for the Hapag between 1921 and 1924.

[112] Balderston, *Economic Crisis*, pp. 66, 73f.

[113] Graham, *Hyperinflation*, pp. 307f.

[114] *Hamburger Statistische Monatsberichte* [1.] Jg. 1924 (June), p. 120.

[115] Hohorst *et al.* (eds.), *Sozialgeschichtliches Arbeitsbuch*, II, p. 83; Petzina *et al.* (eds.), *Sozialgeschichtliches Arbeitsbuch*, III, p. 69.

[116] Laursen and Pedersen, *Inflation*, p. 138; Bresciani, *Inflation*, p. 382; Graham, *Hyperinflation*, p. 311. See also the figures for domestic cement consumption in figure 2.6.

some firms did act as money-demand theory predicts – taking refuge in 'real values' rather than be left holding depreciating cash and paper assets.[117] Even Max Warburg admitted to having done so.[118]

Finally, employment figures provide the most frequently cited evidence that the era of fulfilment was an era of economic prosperity. Having averaged 3.8 per cent for most of 1920, the percentage of trade union members out of work fell from 4.7 per cent in February 1921 to just 0.6 per cent in June and July 1922, with only a brief increase in January and February of 1922.[119] This meant that, while Britain and the United States struggled with unemployment of 10–15 per cent, Germany effectively enjoyed full employment.[120] Because such a large percentage of German exports and imports passed through Hamburg, the city did especially well. Unemployment fell from around 30,000–35,000, where it had hovered for most of the period of relative stabilisation, to the extraordinarily low level of 8,000 in June 1922.[121] The Hapag, for example, increased its workforce from 3,575 to 8,740 during the fulfilment period.[122] At Blohm & Voß, the workforce rose by 15 per cent from 9,675 in May 1921 to 11,113 in early 1923; while employment at Deutsche Werft increased by more than a quarter (from 5,301 to 6,758).[123] By January 1922, labour shortages were developing, particularly in engineering: as the British Consul-General noted, 'Hundreds of situations for boiler-smiths, copper-smiths [. . .] and locksmiths remain[ed] unfilled.'[124]

Yet in a number of vital respects this boom was phoney, so that any idea that renewed inflation was beneficial to the German economy should be viewed with suspicion. Firstly, it should be noted that, at 10 per cent and 46 per cent respectively, the growth rates of NNP and industrial output were higher in 1920, the year of relative price stability, than in the succeeding two years; and both were clearly

[117] See on this point Abelshauser, 'Inflation und Stabilisierung', p. 168; Abelshauser and Petzina, 'Krise und Rekonstruktion', pp. 62f.; Laursen and Pedersen, *Inflation*, pp. 82f.; Petzina, *Deutsche Wirtschaft*, p. 14; Stolper, *German Economy*, pp. 86–9; Holtfrerich, *Inflation*, pp. 204ff.

[118] WA, 'Jahresbericht 1919' (wrongly filed), 'Erläuterungen zum Jahre 1922', 10.2.23. 'In the past years we have spent money on new fittings in a more casual way than we would allow ourselves in normal times. Sometimes this represented a flight from the sliding mark into [more] valuable object(s).'

[119] See figure 2.10. Cf. Bresciani, *Inflation*, p. 449; Graham, *Hyperinflation*, pp. 281, 317; Laursen and Pedersen, *Inflation*, p. 110; Bry, *Wages*, p. 432; Holtfrerich, *Inflation*, p. 199; Scholz, 'Lohn und Beschäftigung', *passim*; Petzina *et al.* (eds.), *Sozialgeschichtliches Arbeitsbuch*, III, p. 119.

[120] Abelshauser, 'Rekonstruktion', p. 165; Petzina, *Deutsche Wirtschaft*, pp. 16f.

[121] See figure 3.1.

[122] Hapag, *Jahresberichte 1914–20, 1921, 1922*.

[123] See figure 3.2; StAH, FA B&V 264; GHH, 300193012/7.

[124] PRO, FO 371/7514, British Consul-General Quarterly Report, 23.1.22.

slackening in 1922.[125] Secondly, there is reason to question the thesis of a 'flight into real values' leading to increased investment. Most of the instances of investment cited above – shipping, the railways, the telephone system and building – were at least partly, if not wholly financed by the public purse and had little basis in economic rationality.[126] For example, the rail and telegraph services made immense losses during the inflation, not least because fares and charges for public services were kept at absurdly low real levels.[127] As the American Vice-Consul in Hamburg noted in a shrewd commentary on the firm's published accounts in June 1923, the Hapag's investment programme was largely financed through massive tax evasion based on systematic falsification of income and asset values.[128] By contrast, it is exceedingly hard to find cases of firms in the private sector undertaking investments above the pre-war or post-stabilisation levels without government subsidies: the industrial concerns Krupp, Mannesmann, Haniel, Siemens, MAN, Maschinenfabrik Esslingen and Carl Schenk all without exception reduced investment in the period 1921–3.[129] In the case of Deutsche Werft, it is striking that the biggest *real* investment in plant came in 1920 – the year of relative stability – when the company invested 48.1 m. marks (3.2 m. gold marks – around two-thirds of the total real increase in plant achieved during the inflation).[130] In practice, 'flight into real values' was not a response to accelerating inflation much favoured by businesses. On the contrary, the case of Deutsche Werft illustrates clearly the way rising inflation could lead to the abandonment of planned investments: only 16.6 m. marks of the planned 136 m. marks was actually spent on new plant in 1922 –

---

[125] See figures 2.3 and 2.4.

[126] This important point has largely been passed over in the literature, with the rare exception of P.-C. Witt, 'Anpassung an die Inflation. Das Investitionsverhalten der deutschen Staatsbahnen/Reichsbahn in den Jahren 1914 bis 1923/24', in Feldman *et al.* (eds.), *Anpassung*, pp. 392–432.

[127] Bresciani, *Inflation*, p. 71 n. It is a striking indication of the illusory nature of the inflation boom that volume of freight traffic remained substantially below pre-war levels (1913: 100, 1922: 68), while the volume of passenger traffic was substantially higher (1913: 100, 1922: 182): Hohorst *et al.* (eds.), *Sozialgeschichtliches Arbeitsbuch*, II, p. 82; Petzina *et al.* (eds.), *Sozialgeschichtliches Arbeitsbuch*, III, p. 68; Bresciani, *Inflation*, p. 194; Graham, *Hyperinflation*, pp. 297ff., 300.

[128] NAW, RG 59, 862.512/143, Vice-Consul Walk, 'An analysis of the financial statements of the leading German shipping companies with special reference to the undervaluation of taxable assets', 6.6.23. According to Walk's careful calculations, the Hapag had invested over $4 m. on new shipping in 1922, but declared its profits to be just $100,000 and its fleet to be worth $400,000. It paid no more than $14,000 in tax in that year.

[129] Lindenlaub, *Maschinenbauunternehmen*, esp. p. 95; and Webb, *Hyperinflation*, p. 87; Feldman, *Great Disorder*, pp. 604ff.

[130] Calculated from Deutsche Werft, *Jahresberichte 1919, 1920, 1921, 1922, 1923, 1924*.

equivalent to just 400,000 gold marks.[131] New machinery and new buildings were not, after all, the only assets which were proof against inflation; and some of the alternatives were far more liquid. Thus the inflation years witnessed heightened activity on the German real estate market, as investors sought to buy existing houses with their cash. The Hamburg property market was peculiarly distorted: on the one hand, there was an acute shortage of housing, with over 30,000 persons classified as homeless in 1922; on the other hand, rent controls meant that the real value of rents continued to fall: from 10 per cent of their pre-war level in June 1921 to less than 1 per cent in December 1922.[132] Under these circumstances, many landlords evidently chose or (particularly in 1922) were forced to sell their property to speculative buyers who were willing to acquire a physical asset irrespective of the poor return on it in the short term.[133] There was even greater activity on the stock markets as companies issued new shares and debentures which, although they did not appreciate in price as rapidly as the cost of living, nevertheless offered large nominal capital gains in the short run, and the possibility of acquiring cheaply an enduring stake in a profitable concern.[134] Altogether, around 4.1 bn. gold marks was raised on the Berlin bourse between 1919 and 1923.[135] Better still, firms could invest in foreign currency, often by leaving export earnings in accounts in London or Amsterdam.[136] This was a facet of the 'capital flight' already alluded to above.

A further peculiarity of the fulfilment 'boom' – and one that was of great importance in widening the trade deficit – was the increased alacrity with which Germans responded to inflationary signals. Between July 1919 and March 1920, as chapter 3 described, the exchange rate of the mark had plummeted; but domestic prices had lagged some way behind, and wages had altogether stagnated. Thus foreign buyers had been able to buy German goods and German labour at 'fire sale' prices, subsidised, in effect, by ignorance and uncertainty. However, things were different when the mark began to slide again in May

[131] Deutsche Werft, *Jahresbericht 1922*.
[132] On the housing shortage, Lyth, *'Mittelstand'*, p. 419; PRO, FO 371/5976/C19805, British Consul-General at Hamburg, Quarterly Report to 30.9.21; NAW, RG 59, 862.502/17, US Vice-Consul Maurice Walk to State Dept., 27.8.22. On rent controls, Lyth, *'Mittelstand'*, pp. 428, 431, 434, 441–7.
[133] See figure 4.9.
[134] Bresciani, *Inflation*, pp. 260–71, 452ff. A share with a nominal value of 100 marks in 1913 was worth 25 gold marks at the end of 1921; whereas a 100 mark note was worth 2.86 gold marks.
[135] Webb, *Hyperinflation*, p. 86. Once again, however, it was in 1920/1 that the biggest real sums were raised.
[136] J. Houwink ten Cate, 'Amsterdam als Finanzplatz Deutschlands', in Feldman *et al.* (eds.), *Consequences*, pp. 149–80.

1921, as producers, wholesalers and retailers all struggled to pass on the '*schwarze Peter*' of higher prices. From November 1921, Stinnes and Silverberg pressed for 'semi-automatic' adjustment of iron and steel prices via the so-called 'coal clause', with the result that by the summer of 1922, steel prices were subject to fortnightly revision.[137] This was not enough for some companies (for example, Rheinstahl) which sought to insert 'price-on-delivery' clauses into contracts, to the great ire of the Hamburg shipyards.[138] Exporters also found themselves struggling with suppliers who sought to 'avoid fulfilling their contractual obligations' when prices rose.[139] Those most adversely affected were retailers, who found themselves charged realistic prices by wholesalers but prevented by law from charging 'replacement cost' prices to consumers.[140] Figure 6.1 clearly shows how rising import prices, pushed upwards by the depreciating currency, were closely shadowed by wholesale prices and export prices, with the cost-of-living index (i.e., retail prices) lagging behind – a quite different picture from that shown in figure 3.4 for 1919–20, when the gap between import prices and all domestic prices persisted.

Similar tendencies were detectable in the movement of wages. While retailers and landlords were prevented from trying to maintain the real value of their incomes, no such constraint bound workers. Between July 1919 and March 1920, employees had experienced drops in real wages of between 50 and 60 per cent. However, the advances in collective organisation made in 1920, combined with the rising demand for labour in Hamburg, meant that almost as soon as depreciation

---

[137] Feldman, *Iron and Steel*, pp. 286ff. The effect of accelerating price adjustment was compounded by a more fundamental cost pressure: shortage. The loss of parts of Upper Silesia in October 1921, followed by rail strikes at the beginning of 1922, led to general coal shortages, with Hamburg once again particularly hard hit; PRO, FO 371/5976/C19805, British Consul-General at Hamburg, Quarterly Report to 30.9.21; HA, HB, Cuno to Groener, 1.2.22.

[138] StAH, FA B&V 1301, Blohm (speech before RdI meeting in Hamburg), 23.5.22; B&V 62, Blohm to HKH, 19.9.22; Auszug, Industriekommission Sitzung, 20.9.22; Auszug aus der Hauptversammlung des Vereins deutscher Seeschiffswerften, 21.11.22. Cf. Feldman, *Iron and Steel*, pp. 289, 297f.

[139] Verein Hamburger Exporteure, *Jahresbericht 1921*.

[140] The revival of inflation in mid 1921 threw into bold relief the anomalies in the price-regulating system, much of which dated back to the war; see StAH, DHSG III, Pr. IV 11 Bd. 1, Mitteilungen der Handelskammer, Nr. 11., 28.5.21; Kammer der Vereinigungen nicht-gewerblicher Verbraucher to DHSG, 11.10.21; DKH to DHSG, 17.10.21; HKH to DHSG, 2.11.21. However, the Supreme Court and the Economics Ministry ruled that 'replacement cost prices' were illegal: Feldman, *Great Disorder*, pp. 566–8; Büttner, *Politische Gerechtigkeit*, p. 168; Lyth, '*Mittelstand*', p. 369. For efforts to enforce the legislation in Hamburg, StAH, Bürgerschaft I C1138, Senatskommission für die Justizverwaltung, 11.11.21; *Hamburger Fremdenblatt*, Nr. 510, 14.11.21; *Hamburger Nachrichten*, 16.11.21; 19.11.21; *Hamburger Echo*, Nr. 527, 10.11.21. It was not until December 1922 – i.e., after the onset of hyperinflation – that the Reichsgericht sanctioned 'replacement cost prices': Lyth, '*Mittelstand*', pp. 371–6.

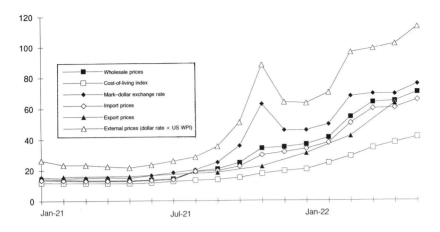

Figure 6.1 Inflation and fulfilment, 1921–1922
Sources: Bry, *Wages*, pp. 422–9, 440–5; *Zahlen zur Geldentwertung*,
pp. 16ff.; Holtfrerich, *Inflation*, p. 17; Laursen and Pedersen, *Inflation*,
pp. 133–5; Graham, *Hyperinflation*, table XVI.

resumed in mid 1921 there was a spate of wage demands. In July 1921, the Hamburg trade unions called on the Economic Council to coordinate a general increase in wages, a move which employers on the waterfront attempted in vain to resist. In the course of the second half of 1921 and early 1922, wage increases became increasingly frequent and indeed, as Rudolf Blohm complained, came to be regarded as 'self-evident', especially once the responsibility for arbitration in disputes passed from the Economic Council[141] to the Labour Ministry.[142] Particularly marked at this stage was the radicalisation of clerical workers: the shipyards in particular became embroiled in a protracted dispute over the right of their white-collar employees to engage in collective bargaining – a dispute settled once again in the employees'

[141] *Hamburger Echo*, 6.7.21; StAH, FA B&V 485, Rudolf Blohm to HKH, 7.7.21; HKH to Wirtschaftsrat, 19.7.21; Rudolf Blohm to Vereinigung der deutschen Arbeitgeberverbände, 8.8.21; B&V 1368, Norddeutsche Gruppe, Niederschrift über die Sitzung, 14.9.21; 21.9.21; 22.12.21.
[142] StAH, FA B&V 1368, Norddeutsche Gruppe, Niederschrift über die Sitzung, 28.1.22; 15.2.22; 28.2.22; 6.3.22; 7.4.22; 26.4.22; 20.6.22; B&V 1259, Blohm (Note), 17.5.22; B&V 228, Bd. 2, Firmenleitung to Rudolf Blohm, 29.7.22. In March, Blohm resigned the chairmanship of the Norddeutsche Gruppe in frustration at having to accept an arbitration ruling, having failed to organise a lock-out in the shipyards. By October 1922, wage increases were being agreed by arbitration on a fortnightly basis.

favour by the intervention of the Labour Ministry.[143] There were similar pressures from workers and civil servants in the public sector.[144] Of course, in real terms, pay rates still fell – by 30 per cent on average between May 1921 and December 1922 – so that employers were effectively freed from the upward pressure which had built up during 1920, and could afford to be accommodating. But repeated increases in nominal pay did mean that real wages followed a saw-tooth path, preventing a collapse of real wage costs such as had occurred in the second half of 1919.[145]

Two further behavioural changes further reduced the benefits to the economy of currency depreciation. Firstly, it is clear that high levels of employment, although made possible by falling real wages, went hand in hand with falling productivity.[146] In 1920–2, productivity in mining stood at just two thirds of its 1913 level, the lowest level for the entire period 1890–1935.[147] Secondly, there was what might be described as a poor man's consumer boom. In the period 1916–19, indicators of consumption had lagged behind figures for national income, reflecting the extent to which the war had diverted resources from 'butter' into 'guns'. However, in the years 1920–2, at a time when real wages were falling for many groups and real national income increased by no more than 12 per cent, consumption appears to have risen sharply. For example, per capita consumption of beer rose by 35 per cent, of sugar by 51 per cent and of spirits by 184 per cent. Significantly, consumers' associations attracted new members in droves, increasing national membership by almost 50 per cent between 1919 and 1922. The Hamburg based *Produktion* expanded its operations boldly, so that by 1921 it controlled 267 shops (mostly bakeries and

[143] GHH, 300193012/7, Deutsche Werft to Reusch, 26.11.21; StAH, FA B&V 1368, Norddeutsche Gruppe, Sitzung, 6.3.22; 15.3.22; 30.3.22; B&V 1255, ZAG (hearing), 31.3.22; B&V 1368, Norddeutsche Gruppe, Sitzung, 11.5.22; Abschrift, RAM Ausschuß Schiedsspruche, 5.7.22; Abschrift, RAM to Norddeutsche Gruppe, 22.7.22; B&V 228, Bd. 2, Firmenleitung to Rudolf Blohm, 22.7.22; B&V 1368, Norddeutsche Gruppe to members, 26.7.22; B&V 228, Bd. 2, B&V to Rudolf Blohm, 5.8.22; B& V 1368, Norddeutsche Gruppe, Sitzung, 25.8.22; 7.9.22; 16.9.22; 29.9.22; 16.10.22; 27.10.22; 24.11.22; 28.12.22; 26.1.23; B&V 1255, ZAG Kommission zur Behebung von Tarifstreitigkeiten, 25.10.22. Cf. in general Lyth, '*Mittelstand*', pp. 131f., 140–4, 161f.

[144] BAP, RMI 33946/Nr. 2702, Verband der Staats- und Gemeinde-Arbeiter Hamburg to Senate, 6.10.21 (and subsequent correspondence, chronicling wage negotiations to March 1922); Lyth, '*Mittelstand*', pp. 227–38; Kunz, 'Variants of Social Protest', esp. pp. 329–39; Büttner, *Politische Gerechtigkeit*, p. 158. On strikes by railway workers, Laubach, *Kabinette Wirth*, pp. 145–8.

[145] See figures 2.11, 2.12, 3.6 and 3.7. Cf. Feldman, *Great Disorder*, pp. 609–21.

[146] StAH, SK II, A4 Fasc. 29, Inv. 1, HG, 18.10.22 (report of RWR Working Committee on Currency Question).

[147] Petzina et al. (eds.), *Sozialgeschichtliches Arbeitsbuch*, III, p. 62; Graham, *Hyperinflation*, p. 295; Balderston, *Economic Crisis*, pp. 63, 73.

butchers) and employed over 125,000 members.[148] In the absence of proper national accounts, it is hard to know just how far there was an increase in consumption as a proportion of national income: as Alfred Lansburgh commented, 'the large attendance at places of amusement, the great consumption of alcohol' may have reflected 'a shifting and coarsening rather than an increase of consumption'.[149] But it certainly suggests that, even if businessmen hesitated to plough liquid resources into 'real values', consumers did respond to accelerating inflation by seeking to minimise their cash balances, turning savings into money and money into goods with increasing rapidity. There are numerous contemporary references to this practice. The American Consul in Hamburg noted 'a vast amount of retail buying' as early as November 1921; and by July 1922, the *Hamburgische Correspondent* was referring in shocked tones to the 'monstrous lust for goods throughout society, from the bare necessities of life to the most expensive luxury articles'. There was, the paper went on, 'such a craving for the good life and for pleasure – for dancing and playing – that one could begin to doubt the sincerity of the German people's desire to get back to stable conditions'.[150] This phenomenon – which can be traced on the monetary side in the rising velocity of circulation and the falling real value of savings accounts – had implications for demand. Spending of this sort inevitably tended to favour consumer goods, since individuals seeking to spend their weekly wage in a hurry could hardly invest in machinery. The statistical evidence confirms that consumer goods production rose faster than that of capital goods: beer production rose by 33 per cent, brandy by 53 per cent and sugar by 86 per cent.[151] An American banker was startled to learn that a Krupp arms factory he visited had gone over to manufacturing cream separators.[152] All of these points cast further doubt on the thesis that inflation boosted investment.

These, then, were the various economic forces underlying the German economy's failure to generate a trade surplus in 1921/2. On the one hand, foreign prices and demand were depressed, while foreign capital sought a profitable outlet in an apparently booming Germany. On the other, prices and wages within Germany adjusted more rapidly than hitherto to currency depreciation, while productivity fell and

---

[148] NAW, RG 59, George D. Hopper to State Department, 14.6.23. See figure 2.13.
[149] NAW, RG 39, G110 (20–4), A. Lansburgh, 'Das große Problem' [translation of article in *Die Bank* (1922)].
[150] NAW, RG 59, 862.50/436, J. Klahr Huddle to State Dept., 2.11.22; F.W Grote, 'Unsere Krankheit: Die Inflation', *Hamburgische Correspondent*, 7.7.22; cf. Lyth, '*Mittelstand*', pp. 82, 368. Cf. Feldman, *Great Disorder*, pp. 851f.
[151] See figure 2.7.
[152] NAW, RG 39, G110 (20–4), F.A. Vanderlip to Charles A. Stone, 8.9.21.

income was increasingly diverted into unproductive value-retaining assets or consumption. The cumulative effect was to erode the competitiveness of German exports and stimulate imports. By May 1922, Deutsche Werft was losing orders to British companies which, as Scholz noted, had been much more successful in reducing wages than the German yards;[153] and the firm was reduced to breaking up sailing ships and manufacturing rubbish bins for the Hamburg state.[154] The Economic Ministry's report on the period June to November 1922 effectively admitted the bankruptcy of the fulfilment strategy. Previously, it was true, 'the depreciation of the mark had had a stimulating effect on domestic manufacturing activity, [. . .] because the domestic flight from the mark into real values stimulated demand and the gap [between domestic and foreign prices] acted as [. . .] an export premium'. But

today a fall in the mark leads, as a rule, to bottlenecks, because what little available capital there is, given the present tightness of money, has learnt to flee directly into foreign currency, rather than into goods; and because [. . .] the adjustment of the internal value [of the mark] to its external value happens so quickly that scarcely any time remains to make sustained use of it.[155]

The reference to 'the tightness of money' is significant. None of this, after all, could be sustained without monetary accommodation; and it was the Reichsbank's inability to provide the economy with sufficient liquidity which threatened to end the fulfilment 'boom'. Three factors were responsible for the credit crisis of mid 1922. Firstly, as a result of the various tax reforms initiated to appease the Reparations Commission, as well as significant real reductions in public spending, the Reich deficit contracted: the monthly increase in the floating debt fell from nearly 700 m. gold marks in December 1921 to just 100 m. gold marks in June 1922.[156] Secondly, the last vestige of foreign hope for an eventual stabilisation of the mark evaporated, beginning with the failure of the Genoa conference, and culminating with the assassination of Rathenau and the failure of all efforts to achieve French approval for a moratorium.[157] As foreigners frantically sought to sell German currency, the mark's premium on the forward exchange markets vanished and foreign deposits at German banks fell from 35 per cent to just 11 per cent of total deposits.[158] Above all, the changes in inflationary

---

[153] GHH, 300193012/7, Scholz to Reusch, 10.5.22. See also the anecdote in D'Abernon, *Ambassador of Peace*, I, p. 283.
[154] Claviez, *Deutsche Werft*, p. 36.
[155] Specht, *Politische Hintergründe*, p. 87 n.
[156] See figure 5.1.
[157] Webb 'Fiscal News and Inflationary Expectations', p. 786.
[158] Holtfrerich, *Inflation*, p.73; *idem*, 'Germany and the International Economy', p. 288.

expectations outlined above had the effect of causing a real monetary contraction. Certainly, the monthly rate of growth of cash in circulation increased from 2.7 per cent in the period of relative stabilisation to 6.3 per cent between May 1921 and June 1922; but, whereas in the previous period prices had actually fallen (at an average monthly rate of −0.7 per cent), now prices rose at 13.8 per cent; with the result that the real value of cash in circulation plummeted from 6.25 bn. gold marks (compared with 6.32 in June 1914) to just 2.02 bn. gold marks, a fall of more than two-thirds.[159] The pressure on liquidity manifested itself in various ways. First, the velocity of circulation rose: a diminishing proportion of money was held in the form of time deposits.[160] Second, the liquidity ratio of joint stock banks fell by 40 per cent.[161] And, third, the proportion of Treasury bills which the private sector was willing to hold fell from 64 per cent to 42 per cent as banks sold their holdings in exchange for cash.[162]

The 'crunch' came in the late summer of 1922, as the collapse of the mark pushed the monthly inflation rate for the first time past 50 per cent – the threshold of hyperinflation. The banking system in Hamburg cracked under the strain. The Vereinsbank informed Blohm & Voß that it could provide only half of the cash necessary to meet its wage bill of 22 bn. marks.[163] The following month, the Vulkan yard found itself in the same predicament.[164] On 18 August, the Hamburg banks went on to a three-day week in an attempt to keep the already overburdened system of giral payments from collapsing.[165] When Keynes visited Hamburg in late August, he encountered monetary chaos:

The prices in the shops change every hour. No one knows what this week's wages will buy at the end of the week. The mark is at the same time valueless

---

[159] Calculated from Holtfrerich, *Inflation*, pp. 17, 55; Graham, *Hyperinflation*, p. 101. See figure 5.4.

[160] Bresciani, *Inflation*, pp. 168; Graham, *Hyperinflation*, p. 105f.; Holtfrerich, *Inflation*, pp. 58f.

[161] I.e., the ratio of liquid assets to deposits; see Holtfrerich, *Inflation*, p. 72.

[162] *Ibid.*, pp. 67f.

[163] StAH, FA B&V 228, vol. 2, Firmenleitung to Rudolf Blohm, 15.7.22. The firm had long since exhausted the 137 m. marks which it had set aside as a cash reserve in early 1921; *Jahresbericht 1921/22*.

[164] Büttner, *Politische Gerechtigkeit*, p. 158. For similar problems in other sectors of industry, see Feldman, *Iron and Steel*, p. 257; Lindenlaub, *Maschinenbauunternehmen*, p. 54.

[165] Büttner, *Politische Gerechtigkeit*, p. 154. As the real value of notes in circulation contracted, individuals and firms had increasing resort to direct debit payments. However, as only seven banks provided this service, the system came under increasing strain, with transactions taking as long as two weeks. On the collapse of the Hamburg branch of the Schleswig-Holsteinische Girozentrale; see PA/AA, SRW 20 1 K520/K149321–437, CVDBB, *Jahresbericht 1922*.

and scarce. On the one hand, the shops do not want to receive marks, and some of them are unwilling to sell at any price at all. On the other hand, in Hamburg yesterday the banks were so short of ready cash that the Reichsbank advised them to cash no cheques for more than 10,000 marks [. . .] and some of the biggest institutions were unable to cash their customers' cheques for payment of weekly wages.[166]

As one businessman put it, it had become necessary to 'abandon long-term projects and simply live from hand to mouth'.[167] The German economy had become, in Walther Dauch's phrase, like 'a twenty horse-power steam engine coupled to a transmission mechanism requiring 60 h.p. The effect is that, [since] we cannot move it, the machine runs empty and goes bust.'[168] For the first time since early 1920, there was a rise in unemployment: between June 1922 and February 1923, the number out of work in Hamburg trebled; and there was a sharp increase in the number of workers on short time.[169]

The German inflation could – and perhaps should – have ended with a financial collapse in the summer of 1922.[170] The fact that it did not was due to important changes in fiscal and, in particular, monetary policy. On the fiscal side, the government simply abandoned any pretence of seeking to reduce the deficit, allowing a slight increase in real expenditure even as real revenues contracted. One especially flagrant use of fiscal policy to bale out business was the payment of a further 18 bn. marks to the shipping lines. Since the supposedly definitive 4.7 bn. marks payment of 1921, 2.5 bn. marks had been paid out by the Schiffbau-Treuhand; but the shipping lines now claimed that insufficient allowance had been made for inflation, and warned of high unemployment if additional cash were not made available.[171] Although the matter was referred to the law courts, this appears to have been a formality to preempt criticism by the Reparations Commission and the Reichstag.[172] The shipping industry, however,

---

[166] Keynes, *Collected Writings*, XVIII, pp. 27f., 'Fluctuations of the Mark', 26.8.22; 'German People Terrified by Uncertainty', 28.8.22. Cf. Moggridge, *Keynes*, pp. 379f. In an effort to provide temporary relief, the Hamburg state issued illegal 'emergency money'; Lippmann, *Leben*, p. 318.

[167] StAH, SK II, II A 4 Fasc. 29, Inv. 1, Karl Jenckel to SK, 28.10.22.

[168] BAK, R45 II/27, Protokolle, 4. Parteitag der DVP, Stuttgart, 25.10.21.

[169] See figures 2.10 and 3.1.

[170] Feldman, *Great Disorder*, p. 838.

[171] StAH, FA B&V 264, Schiffbau Treuhand Bank (report to Reich government), 31.7.22; Wirtschaftsausschuß der deutschen Werften, 20.9.22.

[172] GHH, 30013012/8, Schiedsgericht (judgement), 22.8.22; StAH, FA B&V 264, Schiffbau–Treuhand Bank, Aufsichtsratsitzung, 28.9.22; HA, Cuno NL, Cuno to Warburg, 16.10.22. It was agreed to pay a further 18 bn. marks between September 1922 and March 1923, which was supposed to cover 75 per cent of the increased costs of completing ships under construction. Cf. Kohlhaus, 'Die Hapag', p. 49; 'Die Grossreeder und das Reich', *Deutsche Allgemeine Zeitung*, 19.10.22.

was a special case. For the economy as a whole, it was the Reichsbank's monetary policy which came to the rescue. The formal position of the Reichsbank had been altered twice since the start of fulfilment: first in May 1921, when the vestigial reserve requirements linking its assets to its note issue were suspended, and again a year later when it was made legally independent of the Reich government.[173] However, Reichsbank policy had largely remained unchanged: Havenstein confined himself to discounting Treasury bills as usual and warding off attempts to use the Reichsbank's gold reserve as security for a 'stabilisation loan'.[174] The liquidity crisis of August 1922 gave him an opportunity to use his new statutory freedom. Faced with the prospect of a financial collapse, Havenstein began generously discounting commercial bills, instruments which had all but disappeared in the years of easy money. The value of such bills in the Reichsbank's portfolio rose from 1 bn. marks in December 1921 to 422 bn. marks a year later, or from less than 1 per cent of total note circulation to almost a third.[175] In addition, the war-time loan bureaus were allowed to resume their activities, increasing their total lending from 13.9 bn. marks at the start of 1922 to 252 bn. marks in December.[176] At the same time, it is true, the discount rate was increased – for the first time since the outbreak of war – from 5 per cent to 10 per cent in fortnightly steps beginning on 28 July; but this was little more than a symbolic nod in the direction of orthodox banking practice.[177] A new phase of inflation was initiated, in which the Reichsbank's printing presses would keep stabilisation at bay by discounting corporate paper in a race to outstrip inflationary expectations.

Were the German authorities right to flee from stabilisation? As we have seen, the strategy of revising the London schedule of reparations by means of depreciation failed not solely because of French and American obstinacy, but because it was a misconceived strategy which relieved rather than increased the pressure on the American and British economies. It therefore seems legitimate to ask whether an attempt to stabilise the German economy would have been more effective as a diplomatic lever. Higher taxes, bigger cuts in government spending,

---

[173] Feldman, *Great Disorder*, pp. 349, 445, 450ff.
[174] *Ibid.*, pp. 473ff.
[175] Graham, *Hyperinflation*, pp. 63f.; Feldman, *Iron and Steel*, pp. 316f.; Holtfrerich, *Inflation*, pp. 78f.; Feldman, *Great Disorder*, pp. 581–94. A 51.4 bn. marks lombard credit to the Reich Grain Corporation added to the monetary expansion.
[176] *Ibid.*, p. 585.
[177] Holtfrerich, *Inflation*, pp. 73ff.; Webb, *Hyperinflation*, p. 30. Nominal daily money rates remained around 0.75 per cent below the discount rate; but most bank lending rates were in real terms closer to 50 per cent by the last quarter of 1922 because of provisions and other charges.

a financial 'clear-out': none of this would have sufficed to pay the London schedule. But the braking effect of such measures on the German economy would, if nothing else, have curtailed the enormous influx of imports into Germany and thereby closed the export 'ventilator' which fulfilment provided to the Atlantic economies. As events in 1931 were to prove, the combination of an international slump and deflationary German fiscal and monetary policies was fatal to reparations. Might that not have been the case ten years earlier?

The road to confrontation

The principal objection to this argument remains that, by leading to high levels of unemployment, a bursting of the inflationary bubble would have been socially painful and hence politically destabilising.[178] Yet inflation was destabilising too. 'I did not appreciate until I came here,' wrote Keynes from Hamburg in August 1922, 'how near Germany is to a nervous breakdown. The effect of the crashing fall of the mark on the sentiment of the general public is terrifying and disintegrating. [. . .] The public is pessimistic and depressed and has lost all confidence. [. . .] I find widespread apprehension [. . .] that a new Putsch from the Right or from the Left might overwhelm the government in Berlin.'[179] Writing at around the same time, Max Warburg decribed Germany as

a country divided into three classes of society: one that suffers and goes under in decency; another that profiteers cynically and spends recklessly; and another that writhes in desperation, and wishes to destroy in blind fury whatever is left of a government and a society that permits such conditions.[180]

It is important not to understate the social consequences of the economic processes described above. Full employment coincided with the highest level of industrial unrest since 1919.[181] But industrial workers were faring relatively well. The year 1922 brought middle-class immiseration which extended from the lower ranks of the *Mittelstand* to the elites of the *Bildungsbürgertum*.[182] Contemplating the effects of price regulation, the American Consul found it 'difficult to understand how [the retailers] kept their heads above water'.[183] A Hamburg fishmonger

---

[178] Haller, 'Die Rolle der Staatsfinanzen', pp. 140f.
[179] Keynes, *Collected Writings*, XVIII, pp. 28f.
[180] Sterling Library, Yale, Paul M. Warburg Papers, Ser. II, Box 9, Folder 10, Max M. Warburg, 'The German Problem'.
[181] See figure 7.2.
[182] Eulenberg, 'Die sozialen Wirkungen der Währungsverhältnisse', esp. pp. 773ff., 784, 789.
[183] NAW, RG 59, 862.50/469, J. Klahr Huddle to State Dept., 4.11.22.

explained the problem succinctly: 'We of the middle class are not organised against the wholesalers, while the workers are organised against us.'[184] Property owners forced to sell their real estate felt much the same: 'The exploitation of the workers in former times,' complained the journal of the Hamburg property owners typically, '[was] nothing compared with the privileges that these workers have claimed for themselves since they have held power.'[185] Professionals too were suffering: lawyers, doctors and academics faced unprecedented hardship.[186] The 'plight of the mental workers' (*Not der geistigen Arbeiter*) extended to actors, writers and artists.[187]

The most obvious political manifestations of this reversal were confusion among the so-called 'bourgeois parties',[188] and a proliferation of new bourgeois political associations, some concerned with narrow economic interests,[189] others modelling themselves on traditional nationalist *Vereine*, still others adopting the model of the secret, conspiratorial society.[190] Although the majority of these associations remained in the familiar public sphere of bourgeois politics, holding public meetings and publishing flysheets, a number resorted to secrecy and violence, their most notorious achievements being the assassinations of Erzberger in August 1921 and of Rathenau ten months later. It is not without significance that the peak of full employment in Hamburg coincided with a rash of terrorist bombings by an organisation called the Sprengkolonne Warnecke. There were further violent clashes between police and demonstrators in the wake of Rathenau's murder. Any attempt to justify the inflationary policies of 1921/2 on social or political grounds must founder in the face of such evidence.

The party politics of fulfilment were ambiguous from the outset. The architects of the government's revisionist strategy initially expressed frustration at the refusal of the DVP to join the Wirth coalition; yet the failure of the government to achieve a decisive breakthrough on reparations justified Stresemann's caution. Wirth's unspoken objective might be revision, but outwardly he was obliged to conciliate the Allies, and that in turn entailed compromise with the Social Democrats on fiscal issues. The longer this continued – the more 'genuine' fulfilment became – the more tempting it became to adopt a confron-

---

[184] Webb, *Hyperinflation*, p. 17.
[185] Lyth, '*Mittelstand*', p. 467 n.
[186] Feldman, *Great Disorder*, pp. 528–31, 542–55.
[187] *Ibid.*, pp. 533–42.
[188] See esp. Jones, *German Liberalism*, pp. 148–83.
[189] Jones, 'Dying Middle'; Jones, 'Rückwirkungen der Inflation'; Hughes, 'Economic Interest'.
[190] H. Mommsen, 'Die Auflösung des Bürgertums seit dem späten 19. Jahrhundert', in Kocka (ed.), *Bürger und Bürgerlichkeit*, pp. 288–315.

tational stance and leave responsibility to others. In May 1921, Warburg and Melchior urged the DVP to support Wirth in the hope of achieving a 'coalition ministry of the centre, excluding the right-wing and left-wing chauvinists', an objective broadly shared by Carl Petersen.[191] But they themselves refused Wirth's offers of ministerial office; while the liberal party leaders encountered strong resistance from their rank-and-file to such a move.[192] A succession of emotive 'national' issues exacerbated the problem. Melchior himself joined an organisation to protest against the so-called 'schwarze Schmach' – the stationing of French colonial troops from North Africa in the occupied Rhineland.[193] The continued use of the old imperial flag by the merchant fleet provided a similar focus for bourgeois 'patriotic' feeling, with displays of the black, white and red colours on the Alster and in shop windows provoking street violence in August 1921.[194] The breaking point for many came in October, when the League of Nations ruled that parts of Upper Silesia should be ceded to Poland, despite the majority's vote to remain in the Reich. Since December 1920, Warburg and Melchior had seen this as a crucial issue; indeed, they had justified fulfilment as necessary precisely to avoid the loss of Upper Silesia.[195] They therefore saw no alternative but that Wirth should resign following the League's ruling; and were strongly critical of Wirth and Rathenau's decision to form a new cabinet.[196] 'Economically a great deal that is practical; politically things that are impossible' – this was how Hermes, the Finance Minister, described Stinnes's counsel at this

---

[191] WA, Politische Correspondenz 1921, Warburg to Melchior, 15.5.21; Warburg, Aufgabe, 28.5.21; Warburg to Melchior, 4.6.21; BAK, Koch-Weser NL, 74, Warburg to Koch-Weser, 17.5.21; BAK R 45 III/17, DDP Vorstand Sitzung, 11.9.21. Cf. Warburg, Aufzeichnungen, pp. 97ff.

[192] Maier, Recasting Bourgeois Europe, p. 247; Büttner, 'Liberale', p. 17. For Walther Dauch's opposition to Wirth, GFM, Stresemann NL, 6992/H140591, Rose to Stresemann, 21.10.21; Stresemann to Rose, 22.10.21.

[193] BAP, RMI 13360, 36, Hamburgische Landesverband gegen die Schwarze Schmach to RMI, 3.5.21. The committee's membership is revealing: besides Melchior there were two Protestant ministers, a judge, two academics, a doctor and the former Kappist head of the Hamburg Einwohnerwehr, Hermann Vering; cf. Jochmann, Nationalsozialismus, p. 39.

[194] StAH, FA B&V 1204, Bürgerbund Sitzung, 30.7.21; SK II, VI D 1 Fasc. 15, Senate Anlage, 6.9.21; Hamburger Fremdenblatt, 1.8.21. For the debate on the merchant fleet's use of the old flag, see esp. Sten. Ber. Reichstag, 125. Sitzung, pp. 4163–89; Kohlhaus, 'Die Hapag', pp. 99–107.

[195] WA, 'Jahresbericht 1920', Bl. 28 (Notes), 22.12.20; Politische Correspondenz 1921, Melchior to Dauch, June 1921.

[196] WA, Politische Correspondenz 1921, Warburg to Wirth, 25.10.21; Rathenau to Koch-Weser, 31.10.21; Melchior to Rathenau, 1.11.21; Rathenau to Melchior, 31.11.21; Warburg, Aufzeichnungen, pp. 101ff.; Laubach, Kabinette Wirth, pp. 86–9. Cf. L. Albertin, 'Die Verantwortung der liberalen Parteien für das Scheitern der großen Koalition im Herbst 1921', HZ, 205 (1967), pp. 566–627.

juncture.[197] Yet in October 1921 this judgement could just as well have been applied to Warburg. As Rathenau pointed out to Melchior, he and Warburg had been the first to criticise Simons for inflexibility earlier in the year, when a higher reparations offer might have averted the London Ultimatum, and inflexibility now could bring far worse consequences.[198]

If the strategy of fulfilment survived the crisis of October 1921, it was for two reasons. Firstly, it was still possible to believe that the slow process of economic attrition in the West might yield results. As Warburg put it in February 1922:

> If you consider that three years ago Cunliffe demanded 28 bn. gold marks a year; two years ago Klotz demanded 18 bn. gold marks; one year ago the Reparations Commission wanted around 8 bn. gold marks; and the London Ultimatum demanded [. . .] around 4 bn., then the trend is clear. We are not so far removed from [achieving] what can ultimately be fulfilled, namely no cash payments.[199]

As late as December 1921, Warburg was still working on new proposals for the holy grail of an international loan to Germany.[200] Secondly, there seemed to be a possibility of increasing Germany's diplomatic room for manoeuvre in the East – again, by economic means. One idea which the Hamburg group toyed with was the possibility of a currency union with Austria as a means of achieving '*Anschluß*'; another, more realistic tactic was the signing of bilateral trade treaties with the successor states.[201] But the most plausible avenue of opportunity seemed to lead towards Moscow. It was not only German industry which saw economic opportunities in the Soviet Union, as civil war gave way to the New Economic Policy.[202] Hamburg businessmen thought in the same terms. In April 1921, the Hapag set up the German–Russian Transport Co. ('Derutra') to act as conduit for

---

[197] WA, Politische Correspondenz 1921, Hermes to Warburg, 21.10.21.
[198] *Ibid.*, Rathenau to Melchior, 31.10.21.
[199] BAK, Solf NL, 137, Warburg to Solf, 17.2.22.
[200] WA, Politische Correspondenz 1921, Warburg to Melchior, 30.12.21. See also HA, Cuno NL, Warburg to Spiegelberg, 26.4.21.
[201] WA, Politische Correspondenz 1921, Warburg Aufgabe, 4.2.21; Melchior to Rosen, 11.8.21; Melchior to Warburg, 18.8.21; Allgemeines 1922, Warburg (Note), 30.8.22. Cf. S. Suval, *The Anschluß Question in the Weimar Era* (Baltimore, 1974).
[202] See H. Pogge von Strandmann, 'Großindustrie und Rapallopolitik. Deutsch-sowjetische Handelsbeziehungen in der Weimarer Republik', *HZ*, 222 (1976), pp. 265–341; idem, 'Rapallo – Strategy in Preventive Diplomacy'; Krüger, *Aussenpolitik*, pp. 166–83. See also W. Beitel and J. Woettzold, *Deutsch-sowjetische Wirtschaftsbeziehungen in der Zeit der Weimarer Republik. Ein Bilanz in Hinblick auf gegenwärtige Probleme* (Baden-Baden, 1979); H.-J. Perrey, *Der Russlandausschuß der deutschen Wirtschaft. Die deutsch-sowjetischen Wirtschaftsbeziehungen der Zwischenkriegszeit* (Munich, 1985).

trade between the USSR, Germany and the USA, a project which culminated in an agreement signed in February 1922.[203] Deutsche Werft secured the celebrated contract for the conversion of 700 locomotives to the Russian gauge.[204] Blohm & Voß also renewed its pre-war links to Russia, winning a number of repair contracts.[205] Warburg's also became involved in attempts to renew financial ties.[206] It is true that in economic terms, German–Soviet relations remained of minor significance: the USSR accounted for only around 2.5 per cent of total exports through Hamburg and 1.9 per cent of total imports in 1924.[207] But it was hoped that such contacts would have a disproportionate political significance. On this point, Hamburg and industry certainly agreed. In a speech in February 1920, Melchior had argued that Germany 'must turn its gaze eastwards to a far greater extent than hitherto':

Admittedly, it must not presume to seek there a new field of activity in the colonial sense. It will be Germany's role to appear as the friend and adviser to the economically and technically less developed eastern countries, particularly Russia, [. . .] in the spirit of cooperation rather than exploitation. [. . .] Perhaps there will then emerge a kind of League of the Vanquished [between Germany and Russia], albeit without any offensive goal.[208]

The American banker George McFadden heard very similar arguments from Felix Deutsch and Max Warburg in July 1921, who left him in 'no doubt that the hopes of Germany are turned towards Russia, as in Russia lies her emancipation politically and economically'.[209] Such congruence was hardly surprising, given the close economic ties which had developed between the AEG and Hamburg since 1914.[210] In any

---

[203] HA, HB, Cuno, Wiedfeldt, Alexander, Melchior and Deutsch to Hermes, 9.1.22; Cuno NL, Warburg to Cuno, 11.1.22; Kohlhaus, 'Die Hapag', pp. 89–98; Hapag, *Jahresbericht 1921*.

[204] GHH, 300193012/7, Deutsche Werft to Reusch, 29.8.21; Reusch to Deutsche Werft, 16.9.21; Deutsche Werft to Reusch, 19.9.21.

[205] StAH, FA B&V 1104, Amstea to B&V, 15.10.21; B&V to Amstea, 17.10.21; B&V 446, Rudolf Blohm to Verein deutscher Seeschiffswerften, 2.1.22.

[206] HA, HB, Holtzendorff to Cuno. 17.5.22; Holtzendorff to Vorstand, 30.1.23; Hapag to Holtzendorff, 3.2.23; WA, Allgemeines 1922, Warburg to Hammer, 7.2.23.

[207] Calculated from *Statistisches Handbuch 1925*, pp. 134f., 145f. Cf. H. Eckhardt, 'Deutschland und der Wiederaufbau Rußlands', *Hansa*, 59. Jg., 18, 29.4.22, pp. 533f.

[208] HA, HB, Carl Melchior, 'Zur auswärtigen Politik', speech at DDP Versammlung, Hamburg, 20.2.20.

[209] Mudd Library, Princeton, John Foster Dulles Papers, Box 3, G. McFadden, Memoranda of interview with Mr Deutsch, 31.7.21. 'D. realised that the exploitation of Russia by Germany at present would not be permitted by the Allies, and therefore he hoped to accomplish the same purpose under the camouflage of international [. . .] or interallied protection, but he realised that Germany would be the principal beneficiary.'

[210] See for example HA, Cuno NL, Warburg to Cuno, 6.10.22. Deutsche Werft was, of course, part-owned by the AEG, the Hapag and GHH.

case, it had become something of a truism in diplomatic circles that (in Wirth's words), 'a good relationship with Russia [. . . could] reduce Western political pressure'.[211]

Yet when such thinking bore diplomatic fruit in the form of the Treaty of Rapallo, signed after Rathenau's notorious 'pyjama party' with the Russian delegation at Genoa, Melchior and Cuno publicly distanced themselves; and Warburg expressed vigorous criticism. This breach reflected the differing tactical views in Hamburg and Berlin of how 'the Russian card' should be played. Aside from any desire for a diplomatic coup, Rathenau's principal concern appears to have been that German industry might be preempted by British industry in the event of an agreement between the Allies and Russia over Tsarist debts and reparations – a fear which Lloyd George had done much to stimulate.[212] In Hamburg, by contrast, it was hoped that German economic influence in Russia might be used as a lever in the main campaign for revision of the London system of reparations; in particular as a way of luring the United States out of isolation. This reflected the role being played by Hamburg firms as mediators between Russia and the United States – a role which Warburg had anticipated as early as December 1918. For example, part of the bait which Cuno had used in negotiating his agreement with Harriman in June 1920 had been the prospect of access to East European markets; and the Derutra was clearly intended to provide this.[213] Similarly, Blohm & Voß was seeking to establish a Russian partnership with the American engineering concern Amstea. This had its political dimension in Warburg's attempts to advance the idea of an American loan to Germany during 1921. Reviving arguments he had first used in 1919, Warburg warned that without a loan, German economic malaise would infect its neighbours:

Instead of being stabilised by Germany, Russia would find in Germany a new focus of unrest, and – without in any way wanting to raise the spectre of Bolshevism – [I anticipate that] their common misfortune must quite naturally lead to rapprochement between the two impoverished countries. Ultimately it is a struggle between Bolshevism and capitalism.[214]

---

[211] Pogge, 'Rapallo', p. 130.
[212] For an early expression of this anxiety from a German industrialist, see GHH, 300193012/5, Hermann Michaelson (Eisen und Stahl Gießerei), Abschrift, 16.7.20. See in general Pogge, 'Rapallo', passim; Kent, Spoils of War, pp. 158–65. Cf. R. Himmer, 'Rathenau, Russia and Rapallo', CEH, 9 (1976), pp. 146–83. It is interesting that Stinnes was pursuing his own separate goal of an Anglo-German 'Central European Transport Plan': Warburg, Aufzeichnungen, p. 104.
[213] Vossische Zeitung, 18.6.21.
[214] HA, Cuno NL, Warburg to Spiegelberg, 26.4.21.

This argument ('We are drifting towards Russo-German union [despite] our national mission as the bulwark of the West') was used again at the time of the London conference to persuade English bankers to back the loan; while Cuno made it clear that his interest in Genoa related to Germany's role as 'a psychological bridge' between Russia and America.[215] It was a theme which Warburg embellished when he visited the United States in late 1922:

Germany has been the bulwark against Bolshevism. Her liberal and constructive elements hold out their hands to the democracies in the West. If no response is [forth]coming from that direction, either the leaders of the reaction or of communism or both together will succeed in turning Germany to the East. In this amalgamation the Slavic race might easily become the dominant element. With Mahommedan pretorian guards conscripted in Africa and carried across the Mediterranean by France in order to be taught how to overlord [sic] the white men and white women, and with the Turk back in Europe, one cannot view with calm indifference the prospect of seeing Asiatic civilisation advance [. . .] from the Vistula to the Rhine.[216]

With the Anglo-American perspective so much to the fore, it is not surprising that Warburg saw no reason for precipitate action at Genoa. Although Melchior was aware of the rumours of an agreement between Russia and the Allies, Warburg and Cuno both counselled patience: their priority remained reparations.[217] On the eve of the Rapallo agreement, Melchior was evidently far more interested in the revival of the Amsterdam memorandum by the conference's Currency, Credit and Exchange Commission than in the Russian question.[218] He was apparently surprised by Rathenau's revelation about Rapallo on 16 April, and annoyed when Rathenau brushed aside the reassurances he had obtained from Keynes and the Italian delegate Jung concerning the terms of the mooted Allied agreement with Russia.[219] Convinced that

---

[215] WA, Politische Correspondenz 1921, Warburg to Melchior, 30.12.21; Kohlhaus, 'Die Hapag', p. 178.

[216] WA, Allgemeines 1922, 'The German Problem'.

[217] WA, Politische Correspondenz 1921, Melchior Aufgabe, 2.12.21; Kohlhaus, 'Die Hapag', p. 93. Warburg and Melchior were pessimistic about what could be achieved at Genoa. Warburg declined to attend, predicting that nothing would be achieved on 'the currency question and the international loan [which] are all that interest me'; and only asked of Melchior, who agreed to go but expected only 'window dressing', that he 'leave the hall' if any further attempt were made to impose financial controls on Germany; WA, XVII, Allgemeines 1922, Warburg to Melchior, 20.3.22; Melchior to Warburg, 20.4.22. Cf. Feldman, Great Disorder, p. 436.

[218] WA, XVII, Allgemeines 1922, Melchior Notiz, 25.4.22; Melchior to Paul Warburg, 25.4.22. Cf. Warburg, Aufzeichnungen, p. 105; Rosenbaum and Sherman, M.M. Warburg & Co., p. 161; Schulze-Bidlingsmaier (ed.), Kabinette Wirth, I, pp. 655–7; 683–725.

[219] Warburg, Aufzeichnungen, p. 105.

Rapallo was jeopardising the progress they had been making with the British delegation, he and Cuno went so far as to dissociate themselves publicly from the treaty, in order, as they said, to preserve the 'bridge to the West' they had been building.[220] Rathenau – as he himself had anticipated – was regarded by Warburg as an 'ass'. There had been no real threat of a Russian reparations claim against Germany, maintained Warburg, so that the Russians gained more – the waiving of pre-revolutionary financial claims – from the agreement than Germany. The decision to secure an agreement had not only undermined the progress being made on the reparations question, but positively strengthened the hand of the 'hawks' in France.[221]

The symbolic importance of Rapallo in arousing 'old suspicions' (in Keynes's phrase) continues to the present day to obscure its immediate practical significance. Certainly, it demonstrated the possibility of bilateral cooperation between Germany and the Soviet Union, something which would prove of no small importance in the coming twenty years; but, in the short term, Warburg was probably right that Rapallo brought scant benefit. Then again, his alternative strategy was yielding just as little. Rapallo's true significance was probably as an expression of the frustration felt by German diplomats with fulfilment. It was a gesture, giving the illusion of autonomy. In reality, Germany's economic ties to Russia provided as little political leverage as did the ties with the United States which Warburg and Melchior sought to exploit.

The price of diplomatic failure was high indeed. No matter that those responsible for German foreign policy in 1921/2 were pursuing 'national' objectives; the fact that they had to base their revisionist strategy on economic calculation and cloak it in the language of conciliation sufficed to damn them in the eyes of more radical – or less realistic – nationalists. Nearly four years had passed since the end of the war, and as the image of the external enemy receded in all but the occupied territories, the image of the enemy within grew sharper. Wholly lacking in practicable economic or diplomatic alternatives, the demagogues and terrorists of the Right sought to personify their grievances – Erzberger stood for surrender, Thälmann for revolution, Rathenau for fulfilment – or even to symbolise them by attacking

---

[220] For Keynes's disapproval, WA, XVII, Allgemeines 1922, Keynes to Melchior, 23.4.22; Keynes, *Collected Writings*, XVII, p. 394. Melchior and Cuno denied all knowledge of the Rapallo agreement in an interview with a Dutch newspaper, and shortly afterwards left the conference.

[221] Warburg, *Aufzeichnungen*, pp. 100f. For Warburg's criticisms, WA, Allgemeines 1922, Warburg to Lucius von Stoedten, 1.5.22; Warburg to M.M. Warburg & Co., 25.7.22. However, in a letter to the American banker Mortimer Schiff, Warburg defended Rathenau; Warburg to Mortimer Schiff, 4.5.22. Another critic of Rapallo was Moritz Bonn; see BAK, R45 III/ 11, DDP Parteiausschuß, Sitzung, 28.5.22.

revolutionary edifices. In Hamburg, the Sprengkolonne Warnecke directed their aggression against the Ohlsdorf revolutionary monument, the offices of the Communist newspaper, and Thälmann's house.[222] The Deutschvölkische Schutzbund, meanwhile, renewed its published attacks on eminent Jews, notably Rathenau.[223] Radical nationalist students were involved in the Bismarckbund, which combined anti-Communist and anti-Semitic rhetoric;[224] while a handful of petty-bourgeois malcontents organised themselves into the Hamburg branch of a new fringe party, the National Socialist German Workers' Party.[225] Such organisations posed acute problems for the Hamburg state. First, prior to June 1922, there was uncertainty about the extent of police authority over political meetings.[226] Second, there were numerous personal links between the security forces and unofficial organisations like the Organisation Escherich, the Nachrichtenkopf Hamburg and the Heimschutz Blankenese.[227] A pro-republican rally held after Rathenau's assassination ended in bloodshed when the police opened fire on demonstrators defacing the Bismarck memorial.[228] Under these circumstances, it proved impossible to enforce the new legislation banning radical right-wing organisations which was introduced in June and July. They simply renamed themselves: the Wanderbund, the Bund der Aufrechten, the Junglehrerbund Baldur, the Bund der Niederdeutschen, the Blücher Turn-, Sport- und Wandervereinigung.[229]

The efforts of Max Warburg to counter these tendencies were no less in vain. Ever since Versailles, Warburg had been conscious of

---

[222] BAP, RMI 13359 36, RKfdÜöO to RMI, 2.6.22; Jochmann, *Nationalsozialismus*, p. 36; T. Krause, *Hamburg wird braun. Der Aufstieg der NSDAP von 1921 bis 1933* (Hamburg, 1987), p. 27.

[223] BAP, RKfdÜöO 67174, Bl. 329, Deutschvölkische Schutzbund (collection of pamphlets): A. Roth, *Das sollt Ihr tun!* (Hanover, 1921); *idem, Unser Wollen – unsre Arbeit. Eine Antwort auf die Frage nach Zweck und Ziel des Deutschvölkischen Schutz- und Trutzbundes* (Hamburg, 1921); *idem, Rathenau: Der Kandidat des Auslandes* (Hamburg, 1922).

[224] *Deutsche Tageszeitung*, 27.1.21; Krause, *Hamburg wird braun*, p. 43; Behrens, 'Deutschnationalen', pp. 106ff. See also Lorenz, *Juden in Hamburg*, II, p. 1016.

[225] Krause, *Hamburg wird braun*, p. 24. The founder members of the NSDAP were Karl Teichelmann, a petty official in the police department, Alfred Koch, a St Pauli shopkeeper, and Josef Klant, a cigar dealer.

[226] StAH, SK II, VI D 1 Fasc. 15, SK Anlage, 17.5.21; RMI to SK, 5.1.22.

[227] BAP, RKfdÜöO 67104, Bl. 42, Polizeibehörde Hamburgs to RKfdÜöO, 21.3.22; StAH, SK II, VI B 1 Fasc. 2, RMI to SK, 15.4.22; Jochmann, *Nationasozialismus*, p. 39; Krause, *Hamburg wird braun*, pp. 24, 31ff., 50.

[228] *Hamburger Echo*, Nr. 293, 27.6.22. This illustrates the importance of monuments in the politics of the period; see the interesting comments made by Max Warburg on the use of old monuments as 'symbols which serve to glorify the old days and to ignore and ridicule the present': WA, Allgemeines 1922, Warburg to Freiherr Bernhard von Rechenberg, 17.6.22.

[229] Schulze-Bidlingsmaier (ed.), *Kabinette Wirth*, II, pp. 908, 918; Jochmann, *Nationalsozialismus*, pp. 36f.; Krause, *Hamburg wird braun*, pp. 31ff.

the need to defend the strategy of revisionism as he conceived of it against attacks from the Right. To that end he had established the Institute for Foreign Affairs in Hamburg under Albrecht Mendelssohn-Bartholdy, an organisation principally concerned with the origins of the war and the legitimacy of the peace treaty.[230] But scholarship offered no protection against the attacks of anti-Semites. Increasingly after May 1921, Warburg felt constrained by such attacks to lower his public profile. He gave up attending the synagogue, confining himself to private worship.[231] When Rathenau offered him and Melchior ministerial or ambassadorial positions, they declined, arguing that acceptance would be grist to the anti-Semites' mill.[232] Such reticence was justified: Warburg's name appeared on a list of prominent Jews drawn up by the Deutschvölkische Schutzbund which also included Rathenau and Maximilian Harden, who had narrowly survived an assassination attempt.[233] In the wake of Rathenau's assassination, Warburg was advised by the police to move house and was provided with a bodyguard; but thought it best to withdraw from public life altogether and go abroad, first to Holland (under an alias) and then to the United States for a period of several months.[234] It had been easy for Paul Warburg in New York to argue that domestic instability – 'strikes, unrest, overthrow of the government and food shortages' would act as 'an excellent means to convince the Allies [. . .] of the impossibility of implementing the London Ultimatum';[235] but for his brother, the consequences came close to being fatal.

Max Warburg's response to the growth of anti-Semitism was far from evasive, however. In the immediate aftermath of Rathenau's murder, he struggled to make sense of the phenomenon:

---

[230] WA, Allgemeines 1922, Melchior to Mendelssohn-Bartholdy, 7.12.21; Mendelssohn-Bartholdy to Melchior, 2.12.21; Warburg to Mendelssohn-Bartholdy, 18.6.22. Cf. Warburg, *Aufzeichnungen*, p. 125; Vagts, 'M.M. Warburg & Co.', p. 370; G. Gantzel-Kress, 'Zur Geschichte des Instituts für Auswärtige Politik. Von der Gründung bis zur nationalsozialistischen Machtübernahme', in K.J. Gantzel (eds.), *Kolonialrechtswissenschaft, Kriegsursachenforschung, Internationale Angelegenheiten* (Baden-Baden, 1983), pp. 23–88.
[231] WA, Politische Correspondenz 1921, Warburg to Alice Warburg, 28.8.21.
[232] WA, Allgemeines 1922, Melchior to Warburg, 15.2.22; Warburg, *Aufzeichnungen*, p. 107; Rosenbaum and Sherman, *M.M. Warburg & Co.*, pp. 161f.
[233] BAP, RKfdÜöO 67174, Bl. 329, Deutschvölkische Schutz- und Trutzbund Abschrift 1922; Vagts, 'M.M. Warburg & Co.', p. 377.
[234] WA, Allgemeines 1922, Max Warburg to Paul Warburg, 1.7.22; 'Jahresbericht 1922', Warburg, Diktat (1940). Ironically, the bodyguard transpired to be a Nazi. Characteristically, Warburg made light of giving up his various public posts: 'Anti-Semitism has so far prevented me from wearing myself out prematurely in certain directions. I wasn't an officer; a corps student; a Senator; nor an ambassador. Had I done all these things, I would have been kaputt long ago.'
[235] PA/AA, SRW FW 16 III 1430, Carl Bergmann, Abschrift, 28.11.21.

All the dissatisfied, indeed desperate circles, in whom only need and hopelessness are visible, are becoming desperados. It is this desperation [. . .]
which brings forth such acts. In the parental home, hatred is preached; the
family has ceased to be a place of tranquility, but [has become] the source
of false doctrine. Into all this anti-Semitism comes naturally, since the mis-
guided desire to help [matters], to change [matters] and to agitate all too
readily turns on the minority. Finally of course there is the Peace of Versailles –
but that is merely a secondary factor – [and] the demagogy of Helfferich and
comrades, who turn the heads of the young.

In an attempt to vent his feelings, he sought to organise a collective
protest against anti-Semitism in conjunction with Lili du Bois-
Reymond. It was not, he told her, 'the security of the individual
which is at stake, but the danger that, unless there is not now a
decided change, Germany will sink permanently into the second class,
the class of pogrom countries'.[236] His own draft of the proposed protest
stressed the link between anti-Semitism and 'the barbarity of the East',
warned against 'the mentality of civil war', and painstakingly sought
to dispel anti-Semitic myths – the 'stab in the back' legend, the belief
that Jews were profiting from the inflation, the idea that Jews had not
made a significant contribution in the war, and so on.[237] Yet such
arguments were unlikely to have much impact. The problem was
exemplified by the refusal of other businessmen – notably Heinrich
Otto Traun and Rudolf Blohm – to observe the national day of
mourning for Rathenau.[238] They argued that they were simply keeping
'politics' out of the workplace; but increasingly such neutrality could
be construed as tacit approval of anti-Republicanism, if not of anti-
Semitism.

The economics of confrontation

The failure of fulfilment to exert economic pressure on the Allies and its
consequent loss of domestic political legitimacy made an international
confrontation more or less inevitable – as Rathenau realised when, on
the eve of his murder, he accused Stinnes of wanting to put Germany

---

[236] WA, Allgemeines 1922, Warburg to Lili du Bois-Reymond, 15.7.22; Fritz Warburg
to Max Warburg, 20.7.22; Lili du Bois-Reymond to Max Warburg, 21.7.22; Warburg
to Melchior, 25/28.7.22; Lili du Bois-Reymond to Max Warburg, 30.7.22; Max
Warburg to Fritz Warburg, 12.8.22. Cf. Lorenz, *Juden in Hamburg*, I, p. cxli.
[237] WA, Allgemeines 1922, 'Aufruf' (draft), August, 1922. Cf. the critical comments
from Kurt Hahn and Ernst Spiegelberg. For Warburg's relations with Hahn and
his interest in the school at Salem, see esp. the correspondence of 20/21.7.21.
[238] StAH, B&V 228, Bd. 2, Firmenleitung to Rudolf Blohm, 1.7.22; Firmenleitung to
Rudolf Blohm, 8.7.22; Büttner, *Politische Gerechtigkeit*, p. 165.

on a 'collision course with France'.[239] Yet whatever its emotional attractions, confrontation was fraught with risk for German business – particularly for those businessmen with interests in the Ruhr, where French sanctions were most likely to strike. Why then did so many of them support confrontation – to the extent that it was a businessman who became Chancellor on the eve of the occupation of the Ruhr? The fundamental answer lies in the business community's refusal to contemplate stabilisation when any possibility remained of prolonging the inflationary boom. However, this was dressed up in the assertion that, if only businessmen could take over from the politicians, the elusive diplomatic breakthrough might be achieved. Although highly improbable from an international perspective, this was a proposition which neatly expressed the shift in the domestic balance of power which had occurred during the period of fulfilment. In fiscal terms, the state was shrinking; in monetary terms, it was being supplanted by business as the Reichsbank's main customer. The great corporations, by contrast, were never more bloated, their payrolls and nominal profits never bigger. It was not entirely surprising that, at the very moment when hyperinflation and invasion threatened the very integrity of the Reich, businessmen should seek to assert the primacy of *Wirtschaft* over *Politik*.

From an early stage, there had been elements within the Wirth government which had opposed the strategy of revision through depreciation. Warburg had feared that the Finance Ministry would be the main source of dissent, because of the link between exports and reparations payments established by the London schedule.[240] In fact, the principal opponent of the strategy proved to be the Economics Ministry, just as it had been the main source of opposition to the 1919 '*Ausverkauf*'. In March 1922, the Reich Commissioner for Import and Export Licensing Trendelenburg openly attacked 'those who are of the opinion that, in the absence of controls on prices, Germany's increased export-opportunities will force England to a solution of the reparations problem':

An aggressive export policy, aimed at exerting strong pressure on the world market with a view to moderating reparations [. . .], is not compatible with the policy of fulfilment, [. . .] but is more aggressive than Germany is able to sustain in the general political situation [. . .] The side-effect of the convergence of domestic prices and world market prices cannot be overlooked. The

[239] Maier, *Recasting Bourgeois Europe*, p. 288. Cf. Feldman, *Great Disorder*, pp. 447ff.
[240] As he observed, 'The more we export [. . .] the better it goes for us in certain regards, so much the worse for the Finance Ministry, which has to pay ever more because of the improvement'; WA, Politische Correspondenz, Max Warburg to Paul Warburg, 4.6.21.

question is whether the financing of the state can be maintained [under these conditions] or whether the currency and the state will collapse financially.[241]

Once again, he and Hirsch sought to counter the effects of depreciation by reviving the system of foreign trade control. There had been hopes in early 1921 that the system might be dismantled; instead, it was extended, so that by 1922 50,000 export transactions involving nearly 1,000 different types of goods were being processed every day by trade control bureaus employing over 4,000 people.[242] Moreover, the bureaus' powers to impose fines on exporters were increased and the exemption enjoyed by importers from the turnover tax was suspended.[243] Finally, the Economics Ministry was able to use the London Ultimatum's requirement that 25 per cent of export earnings be transferred as reparations to justify maintaining the export levy and to require all exporters to invoice their business in foreign currency.[244]

The reaction to these last efforts to control trade began in Hamburg,[245] but quickly spread to encompass industry. Throughout the first half of 1922, the Chamber of Commerce waged a campaign against the Economics Ministry which was unprecedented in its virulence: Franz Witthoefft and other Chamber spokesmen accused the trade control boards of being not only inefficient and economically malign, but also corrupt.[246] It is true that until May 1922, the

---

[241] StAH, DHSG III, Pr. III 39, HG to SK 22.3.22. Cf. Feldman, *Great Disorder*, pp. 386–92.

[242] StAH, DHSG III, Pr. III 39, Auszug, *Sten. Ber. d. Bürgerschaft*, 11. Sitzung, 8.3.22; DHSG III, Pr. III 34 Bd. 2, HG to SK, 2.7.22. For hopes of reform in early 1921, see *Hamburgische Correspondent*, Nr. 127, 17.3.21; DHSG III, Pr. III 39, HKH to DHSG, 30.3.21; SK II, III A 1 c 3 Bd. 2, SK to Scholz, 31.3.21; DHSG III, Pr. III 39, HG to SK, 8.4.21; HG to SK, 11.4.21; HG to SK, 14.4.21; RWM to SK, 27.4.21.

[243] StAH, DHSG III, Pr. III 34 Bd. 2, HG to SK, 3.2.22; Auszug, Sen. Prot., 6.2.22; SK II, II A 3 12, Bd. IV, SK to RFM, 31.12.21.

[244] StAH, DHSG III, Pr. III 39, Heidecker to Stolten, 8.6.21; HKH, HKHP, 26.5.21; StAH, FA B&V 446, Verein deutscher Seeschiffswerften to members, 20.6.21; DHSG III, Pr. III 34 Bd. 2, RWM Entwurf, 20.8.21; Auszug, Sen. Prot., 2.9.21; HG to SK, 12.9.21; HKH to DHSG, 5.9.21; SK II, III A 1 a 1 Bd. 1, Senate to SK, 7.12.21; HG to SK, 14.12.21; PA/AA, SRW FW 16 II 1322, RWR, Reparationsausschuß, Sitzung, 7.12.21; StAH, DHSG III, Pr. III 40, HKH to DHSG, 9.1.22; Böhm, *Anwalt der Handelsfreiheit*, p. 229.

[245] StAH, FA B&V 446, Wirtschaftsausschuß der deutschen Werften, 18.6.21; DHSG III, Pr. III 34 Bd. 2, HKH to DHSG, 11.2.21; HKH to DHSG, 21.4.21; HKH to DHSG, 5.11.21; *Hamburger Fremdenblatt*, Nr. 335, 221.7.21; *Hamburger Fremdenblatt*, Nr. 382, 17.7.21; *Deutsche Allgemeine Zeitung*, Nr. 311, 6.7.21; BAK, R45 III/11, DDP Partieausschuß Sitzung, 11.11.21; II/27 (Hugo speech at DVP party conference 4/5.10.21), pp. 389–453.

[246] For details of the campaign, which was precipitated by the decision to give the foreign trade controls quasi-judicial powers, see HKH, *Jahresbericht 1921*, p. 71; StAH, DHSG III, Pr. III 39, RWM to Senate, 27.1.22; HKH to RWM, 23.3.22; *Sten. Ber. d. Bürgerschaft*, 10. Sitzung, 1.3.22; 11. Sitzung, 8.3.22; PA/AA, SRW FW 16 III, Rechenberg to AA 23.2.22; 1.3.22; StAH, DHSG III, Pr. III 39,

Chamber frequently identified the industrial associations as the villains of the piece, since it was they which effectively controlled the trade boards.[247] However, these criticisms were increasingly echoed within industrial circles, where dissatisfaction with the associations' role in the *Zwangswirtschaft* had been growing for some time.[248] A rapprochement was not long in coming. Indeed, it perfectly illustrated the way the power of the state was crumbling in the economic sphere: while the Economics Ministry attempted to bring the Chamber of Commerce to account over its allegations of corruption, an understanding on the trade issue was arrived at 'privately' between commerce and industry.[249] It was no coincidence that this agreement was reached in Hamburg, at a special meeting of the RdI held at the end of May.[250] This was the occasion for a general settling of disputes between trade and industry – a settlement so comprehensive in scope that it resembled a united business political platform.

The main planks of this platform were laid down in a speech by Max Warburg which combined an open declaration of opposition to stabilisation measures (particularly exchange controls) with a careful technical exposition of how firms could cope with hyperinflation by adopting gold mark calculation in accounting, utilising the forward exchange market and avoiding hostile takeovers. Given the remoteness of the moratorium and international loan for which Warburg continued to call, the speech amounted to a counsel of defiance:

The Reichsbank can no more stop inflation than the Bürgermeister of Hamburg can tell the patients in the hospitals to stop being ill (laughter) [. . .] As long as it is possible for the French to invade Germany, there can be no talk of a stabilisation of our currency [. . .] The recovery of the mark should not

---

RKEAB to Senate, 8.3.22; HKH to RWM, 23.3.22; RWM to SK, 29.3.22; HG to SK, 1.4.22. A Hamburg Committee for the Freedom of Foreign Trade was set up to coordinate the campaign.
[247] StAH, DHSG III, Pr. III 34 Bd. 2, John Schütt & Co. to HKH, 3.3.22; HKH to DHSG, 3.3.22; VHEx to HKH, 9.3.22; DHSG III, Pr. III 39, HG to SK, 22.3.22.
[248] Feldman, *Iron and Steel*, pp. 205–8.
[249] StAH, DHSG III, Pr. III 39, RWM to HKH, 10.5.22; HKH to DHSG, 15.5.22; Cohn Bericht, 17.5.22; HG to SK, 18.5.22; Arnoldi, Abschrift, 1.6.22; HG to SK, 2.6.22; HKH to DHSG, 27.9.22; SK to DHSG, 18.9.22; *Hamburger Fremdenblatt*, 20.9.22; HKH to DHSG, 27.9.22; Auszug, Sen. Prot., 4.10.22; HG to SK, 4.10.22; HG to SK, 2.11.22; HG to SK, 7.11.22; HKH to DHSG, 14.11.22; HG to SK, 17.11.22; HG to SK, 23.11.22; HG to SK, 5.12.22; *Deutscher Großhandel*, Nr. 23, 15.12.22; HG to SK, 17.11.22; HG to SK, 22.12.22; HKH to DHSG, 5.1.23; *Hamburger Nachrichten*, 25.1.23; *Hamburger Fremdenblatt*, 25.1.23; *Deutsche Allgemeine Zeitung*, Nr. 42/43, 27.1.23.
[250] See the material in StAH, FA B&V 1301; *Mitteilungen der HKH*, Nr. 11, 8.6.22; HKH, HKHP, 16.6.22; VHEx, *Jahresbericht 1922*.

occur suddenly, but only gradually (Quite right!) [. . .] We must reject the
Turkification of Germany, the introduction of a *dette publique*, in any form.[251]

The significance of this becomes clear in the light of the subsequent
policy debate among the leading members of the RdI. Kurt Sorge was
honest enough to admit after a series of lively debates that 'we ourselves
don't really know what we want';[252] but Warburg had put his finger
precisely on what everyone in business did not want: stabilisation,
least of all at the behest of the Reparations Commission. Perhaps the
most striking thing about this essentially negative posture was the
reckless overconfidence which underlay it. Bücher's comments not long
after the Hamburg conference epitomised the growing arrogance of
the German business community at this time: 'The solution will only
be found with the help of the leading *Wirtschaftler* of the whole world;
not through the Finance Ministers of [. . .] indebted nations.'[253] Quite
what the *Wirtschaftler* were going to do if the French occupied the
Ruhr was nor clear; but such considerations were brushed aside in a
general fit of contempt for the established political processes.

Because of the traditional concentration of historians on the machi-
nations of the heavy industrialists, the extent to which this defiant
attitude emanated from Hamburg is not generally recognised. In fact,
as Sorge admitted, industry was rather unsure how to proceed at
this point: while Bücher favoured a diplomatic initiative, Stinnes and
Silverberg preferred to force a showdown with the Left, and Reusch
and Duisberg adopted a middle position.[254] By comparison, there was
clarity of purpose in Hamburg. In the wake of the RdI meeting, there
was a flurry of activity in Hanseatic business circles, centring around
the staging of a Hamburg Trade Fair – the *Überseewoche*. This had
been discussed sporadically since as early as 1919, but had been
rejected as premature in its first incarnation as an export fair.[255]

---

[251] WA, XIX, Gesammelte Vorträge, Max Warburg 'Deutsche und internationale Finanzprobleme in ihrer Bedeutung für die deutsche Industrie' (speech before fourth
members' meeting of RdI), 22.5.22. At Keynes's request Melchior outlined a similar
loan and moratorium scheme in the *Manchester Guardian*'s 'Reconstruction Supplements'; Skidelsky, *Economist as Saviour*, p. 103; cf. Blohm's criticism of Warburg's
loan scheme, StAH, FA B&V 1301, Blohm to Hugenberg, 6.5.22; and press reports
in *Deutsche Bergwerkszeitung*, 16.5.22; 24.5.22; *Hamburger Fremdenblatt*, 27.5.22;
Kölnische Volkszeitung, 13.6.22. For subsequent discussion of gold mark accounting,
Frankfurter Zeitung, Nr. 621, 3.9.22; StAH, SK II, II A 4 Fasc. 29, Inv. 1, HG
to SK, 18.10.22.
[252] Feldman, *Iron and Steel*, p. 319.
[253] Rupieper, 'Industrie und Reparationen', p. 584.
[254] For the deliberations of the 'Special Committee for an Economic Programme', see
Feldman and Homburg, *Industrie und Inflation*, pp. 328–43.
[255] StAH, DHSG II, III C 54, 23. Sitzung, 2.11.20; SK II, III A 1 a 13, DHSG
to SK, 3.11.20; StAH, FA AOM 1, Bd. 11, Witthoefft to Riedel; B&V 1205,

However, the scheme was revived two years later by Warburg, Cuno, Dauch as well as the Dresdner Bank director in Hamburg, Anton Hübbe,[256] and in the summer of 1922 invitations began to be sent to politicians and foreign diplomats.[257] At around the same time, a new *Überseeklub* was established. Club and Fair alike had an ulterior motive. Ostensibly an English-style club for the entertainment of visiting businessmen and the provision of funds for economic research,[258] the Overseas Club in reality had a political purpose, as the speeches made at its opening indicate. Warburg's (delivered by a proxy because of fears for his safety) set the tone with a call to end the division between business and politics – between *'Nur-Politiker'* and *'Nur-Kaufleute'*:

For too long we have lived in the belief that trade policy and politics in the narrower sense are separate matters. The same manufacturer who could become incensed over the smallest alteration in the tariff rates affecting him took no part whatever [. . .] in high politics. [. . .] The businessmen failed to see the clouds which were gathering in politics, and the politician overlooked economic questions, the vital importance of which [. . .] only became clear to him in the war.[259]

This familiar theme, first heard in the early phase of the revolution, was taken up by Witthoefft: 'It is time [. . .] finally to give precedence to the men of business over the diplomats and politicians in all questions of world economics.'[260] Unlike the industrialists, the leaders of commerce were quite clear about their objectives: calling for 'a new free trade' policy, Warburg once again urged the lifting of trade controls, and repeated the fundamental point he had made at the RdI meeting:

Until the burdens [imposed by] the Versailles-Diktat and our own budget are so arranged that our income can match them and the balance of payments can be stabilised, it is useless to think about a currency reform. As long [as

Blohm to Norddeutsche Hansabund, 12.1.21; Böhm, *Anwalt der Handelsfreiheit*, p. 273.

[256] WA, XVII, Allgemeines 1922, Willy Sick to Warburg, 11.10.21 and subsequent correspondence; StAH, FA AOM 1, Bd. 12, 465, Witthoefft to Warburg, 17.5.22.

[257] See the material in StAH, SK II, III A 1 a 13, Gesellschaft zur Förderung der Überseewoche Hamburg.

[258] WA, Allgemeines 1922, Programme of the Überseeklub; L. Gelder, 'Die Überseeklub 1922–1972', in *Kommerz und Kultur im Amsinck-Haus am Neuen Jungfernstieg* (Hamburg, 1972); Freudenthal, *Vereine in Hamburg*, pp. 455f. The Club was formally called the Hamburg Society for the Economic Reconstruction of Germany and Foreign Affairs and used rooms in the building of the old Patriotic Society. Its Präsidium included Warburg, Cuno and Witthoefft.

[259] WA, Allgemeines 1922, Max Warburg, 'Zur Gründung des Überseeklubs'.

[260] F.H. Witthoefft, 'Überseehandel und Wiederaufbau', *Hamburger Überseejahrbuch*, I (1922), p. 6.

this has not been done . . .] advice to bring the inflation under control is as useless as the advice to the drowning man not to swallow water.[261]

The process of mobilising the 'men of business' began at once, with Cuno seeking out the American ambassador Houghton, Fritz Warburg lobbying the British commercial attaché Thelwell, Warburg travelling to Holland to meet Otto Kahn of Kuhn, Loeb & Co., and Cuno, Melchior (and Wiedfeldt, who was in close touch with Cuno) pressing Ebert and Hermes for official backing.[262] The culmination of all this activity was the Overseas Week, which began on 17 August: on the surface, an exercise in civic pomp attended by President Ebert, the Ministers Groener and Köster, various diplomats and numerous Reichstag deputies; behind the scenes, an unofficial conference on German foreign policy, with Keynes as the guest of honour.[263] It is clear that the Hamburg group had intended to concentrate the private discussions on yet another scheme for an international loan.[264] However, this agenda was overshadowed by Poincaré's speech calling for 'productive pledges' at Bar-le-Duc on 21 August,[265] and by the remarkable response this elicited from Keynes in his address which concluded the week on 26 August. Keynes's reception in Hamburg was not unlike that bestowed on Cobden when he had visited Hamburg in 1847. Introduced by Cuno as 'the man most responsible for the changed attitude of the English-speaking world towards Germany', he was cheered to the echo; and it is tempting to wonder how far the applause influenced the content of his speech. Having expressed the hope that 'the day of scientific, administrative and executive skill is at hand [. . .] not this year, indeed, but next year,' Keynes made a fateful prediction:

I do not believe [. . .] France may actually carry into effect her threat of renewing war. [. . .] One or two years ago France might have acted thus with the necessary inner conviction. But not now. The confidence of the Frenchmen in the official reparations policy is utterly undermined. [. . .] They know in their hearts that it has no reality in it. For many reasons they are reluctant to admit the facts. But they are bluffing. They know perfectly well that illegal acts of violence on their part will isolate them morally and sentimentally, ruin

[261] Warburg, 'Zur Gründung'.
[262] Rupieper, *Cuno Government*, p. 29; WA, Allgemeines 1922, Fritz Warburg, Memorandum, 30.6.22; Max Warburg, Memorandum, 13.7.22; Kohlhaus, 'Die Hapag', p. 111.
[263] StAH, SK II, III A 1 a 13 (programme), 17.8.22. The former President of the Board of Trade, Walter Runciman, also appears to have attended.
[264] WA, Allgemeines 1922, Melchior Memorandum, 5.8.22. Melchior now envisaged a three to five year 'pause' in reparations, along with a loan to be issued up to a maximum of 20 bn. gold marks.
[265] Maier, *Recasting Bourgeois Europe*, p. 284; *Hamburger Fremdenblatt*, 26.8.22.

their finances and bring them no advantage whatever. M. Poincaré [. . .] may make harsh speeches and inflict futile minor outrages [. . .] but he will not act on a big scale. Indeed, his speeches are an alternative not a prelude to action. The bigger he talks the less he will do. [. . .] The Germans will do well to keep cool and not be too much alarmed.[266]

To cap this, he dismissed the idea that inflation was causing 'the disintegration of German life':

One must not lose sight of the other side of the balance sheet [. . .] The burden of internal debt is wiped off. The whole of Germany's payments to the Allies so far [. . .] have been entirely discharged by the losses of foreign speculators. I do not believe that Germany has paid a penny for these items out of her own resources. The foreign speculators have paid the whole of these liabilities and more too.[267]

His conclusion amounted to an endorsement of the Hamburg proposals for a moratorium, a loan and a reduced reparations burden.[268] In private, it is true, Keynes was rather less rash. His argument for rejecting demands that the Reichsbank's reserve be used to guarantee future reparations payments was that 'if the French actually have political plans (occupation of the Ruhr area [. . .] etc.), then a concession would be worthless: the conflict would only come a few months later'. His advice on monetary policy likewise acknowledged the imminence of the liquidity crisis.[269] But it was the public remarks which had the greatest impact; not least because he was telling the Germans what they wanted to hear. Poincaré's 'bluff' should be called: this was the message relayed to Wirth from Hamburg. The fact that Wirth promptly offered the Foreign Ministry to Melchior and then Cuno was a sign that the much-vaunted fusion of business and politics was drawing nearer.[270]

The corollary of confronting Poincaré was confronting the Economics Ministry. Hirsch's response to the collapse of the exchange rate in July of 1922 was to propose an ambitious 'total system' for shoring up the mark, beginning with a proposal for a domestic 'gold loan',

---

[266] Keynes, *Collected Writings*, XVIII, pp. 18–26.
[267] *Ibid.*
[268] Keynes suggested a total of 40 bn. gold marks to be paid in annuities of no more than 1 bn. gold marks before 1930. Cf. the reports of the American Consulate: NAW, RG 59, 862.607/44, Huddle to State Dept., 30.8.22; Walk to State Dept., 1.9.22. The significance of this speech is not appreciated by Keynes's biographers: see Harrod, *Keynes*, pp. 316, 325; Skidelsky, *Economist as Saviour*, p. 115.
[269] WA, Allgemeines 1922, Melchior Notiz, 28.8.22. Also present at this meeting, which was held at Cuno's house, were Cuno, State Secretary Schröder (Finance Ministry) and the reparations expert Bergmann.
[270] WA, Allgemeines 1922, Melchior Notiz, 30.8.22. Cf. Warburg to Max of Baden, 25.8.22.

intended to tempt Germans into parting with their hard currency.[271] Exchange controls, which had been reintroduced in a mild form in February were now to be extended to include a ban on the use of foreign currency in domestic transactions.[272] There was also renewed talk of intervention on the foreign exchange markets and even the creation of some kind of hard currency (or 'value-retaining unit') alongside the paper mark.[273] All of these proposals were opposed by business spokesmen, with the support of the Finance Ministry and the Reichsbank President Havenstein. Havenstein dismissed the gold loan idea as 'carrying with it severe dangers for our economy, for our entire monetary system and for our political situation'; the scheme was abandoned.[274] The exchange controls were widely criticised, with the result that numerous exemptions were introduced.[275] The culmination of this opposition was a session of the *Reichswirtschaftsrat*, at which Melchior gave evidence. Without exception, he rejected all the proposed measures for stabilisation, dismissing the gold loan idea as 'a huge speculation in dollars'.[276] In frustration, Hirsch accused Melchior of having nothing to say but (in Fritz Reuter's words) '*Dat bliwwt all, as dat west ist*'. Melchior promptly replied with another Reuterism: '*In der Fixigkeit bist du mir über, aber in der Richtigkeit bin ich dir über.*' [277] What this meant was that Hirsch had no alternative but to abandon the idea of an active policy.

That the Wirth government was living on borrowed time was by now obvious. However, it was not clear who would replace Wirth, particularly in view of the party-political impasse which seemed to

[271] StAH, SK II, II A 4 Fasc. 29, Inv. 1, HG Abschrift (RWR Wirtschaftspolitisch- und Reparartionsausschüsse, Sitzung), 29.8.22. See Feldman, *Great Disorder*, pp. 466–75.
[272] The earlier *Devisenverkehrsgesetz* placed all foreign currency transactions under the control of banks; *RGB* (1922), I, pp. 195–7. For the later 'Verordnung über die Spekulation mit ausländischen Zahlungsmitteln', *RGB* (1923), I, pp. 795–7.
[273] StAH, SK II, II A 4 Fasc. 29, Inv. 1, HG Abschrift (Sozialisierungskommission, Sitzung), 17.10.22; 18.10.22; 20.10.22; *Deutsche Allgemeine Zeitung*, Nr. 452, 18.10.22; *Hamburger Echo*, 7.10.22; Specht, *Politische Hintergründe*, pp. 81, 83ff., 86f.
[274] StAH, SK II, II A 4 Fasc. 29, Inv. 1, HG Abschrift (RWR Wirtschaftspolitisch- und Reparartionsausschüsse, Sitzung), 29.8.22.
[275] *Hamburger Fremdenblatt*, Nr. 421, 9.9.22; StAH, DHSG III, Pr V 2, HG to SK, 15.9.22; SK II, II A 4 Fasc. 29, Inv. 1, HG to SK, 18.10.22; 20.10.22; 26.10.22; NAW, RG 59, 862.5151/1026, Walk to State Dept., 21.10.22; Böhm, *Anwalt der Gewerbefreiheit*, pp. 229f.
[276] PA/AA, SRW FW 16A, Bd. I, 3624/22, RWR Arbeitsausschuß für die Währungs- frage, 18.10.22 (Melchior); StAH, SK II A 4 Fasc. 29, Inv. 1, HG to SK, 18.10.22; 20.10.22. Cf. the detailed notes by Max Warburg for Melchior's guidance: WA, Allgemeines 1922, Warburg (replies in note form to RWR questionnaire), 18.10.22.
[277] PA/AA, SRW FW 16A Bd. I 3624/22, RWR Arbeitsausschuß für die Währungs- frage, 18.10.22 (Melchior).

rule out cooperation between the SPD and the DVP.[278] Indeed, it is still far from clear to historians why it was Wilhelm Cuno – the head of a Hamburg shipping line – who emerged as Wirth's successor. In most accounts, Cuno is little more than the 'fat cigar' whom Ebert decided to try 'on account of the attractive label' (his celebrated American connections); a Chancellor whose lack of party affiliation merely reflected the bankruptcy of the Weimar parties.[279] But this picture is misleading. In fact, it is clear that Cuno had been preparing to take a direct political hand for some time. In September, it is true, he had refused the post of Foreign Minister, insisting that it was futile to try to 'bridge the distance between Germany and France by political discussions and conferences'. However, he had added that he believed 'economic approaches' stood more chance of success; and had not ruled out the possibility that his own 'connections in America and England' might help to pave the way to a 'real solution' at an 'impending, decisive reparations conference'. It had been the present 'composition of the cabinet and its current head' which had disinclined him to accept the post, since these seemed to offer 'no basis for objective work'.[280] He made his position still clearer at the RdI meeting of 6 September, repeating the now-familiar rhetoric of the Overseas Club:

Recovery internally depends on recovery externally. [. . .] We should in general demand a separation of economics from politics. [. . .] Our economic freedom of movement should not be constrained by politics. So long as we are dependent on a government in which there is no one who knows the economy, we cannot expect a recuperation to take place.[281]

This was a thinly veiled bid for power; and a month later, when he was offered the Foreign Office again, the veil was thinner still. Cuno now saw evidence that 'the franc was beginning its downward slide' and believed that the time was right for Germany to put forward 'a positive programme'. However, he continued to feel that 'a sensible economic policy is not possible [. . .] given the present composition of the cabinet, with the wholly overbearing influence of the unions (of socialist and Catholic observance) in economic matters'. He therefore 'declare[d] that he [would] not enter the government until homogeneity,

---

[278] Maier, *Recasting Bourgeois Europe*, p. 300.
[279] The 'fat cigar' phrase was Rathenau's; Kessler, *Tagebücher*, p. 361. For accounts which portray Cuno as a 'last resort', see Rupieper, *Cuno Government* pp. 13f.; Laubach, *Kabinette Wirth*, pp. 293–8, 307–31; Maier, *Recasting Bourgeois Europe*, pp. 300f. For another sceptical contemporary view see the comic verses about 'Ritter Cuno' in *Hamburger Nachrichten*, 20.11.22.
[280] Kohlhaus, 'Die Hapag', pp. 112f.
[281] Feldman, *Great Disorder*, pp. 479f.

encompassing the Economics Ministry too, ha[d] been established'.[282] This was a more or less open challenge to Ebert to allow the formation of a government untrammelled by Social Democrat influence over economic policy, and clear evidence that Cuno was now aiming beyond the Wilhelmstraße. Certainly, the extent of Cuno's ambitions was not apparent from Max Warburg's vantage point in America.[283] But the American ambassador in Berlin saw much more clearly the movement towards a pro-business government. On 30 October, Stinnes assured him that Wirth was 'at the end of his rope' and implied that he had suggested Cuno's name to Ebert as a possible minister. He also let Houghton see his own draft proposals for a reparations settlement, the corollary of which would be radical reforms of the German economy – to include the abolition of the eight-hour day, the end of government regulation 'in all branches of domestic and foreign business intercourse', a five-year ban on strikes in 'any industrial undertaking that is of vital importance', cuts in public sector ownership and employment, and 'extremely severe punishment' for 'crimes against property'.[284] Just four days later, Houghton met Cuno and his American business partner Harriman to discuss the possibility of Cuno becoming Chancellor.[285] Thus, when Wirth finally resigned, following the refusal of the SPD to agree to the DVP's Stinnes-inspired conditions for joining a Great Coalition, and with the Centre unwilling to support the appointment of Adenauer or Stegerwald, Cuno was already waiting in the wings.[286]

There was no doubt about the kind of cabinet Cuno wished to form. Even Keynes in England could see that this would be 'a govt. a little more to the right than was Wirth's, and a little more under industrial influences'.[287] It was, Cuno told Ebert, to be 'a cabinet of Labour, composed according to the necessity for the objective management of business' – meaning, of course, a cabinet which would exclude the influence of organised labour.[288] Between 16 and 22 November, he

---

[282] WA, Allgemeines 1922, Cuno to Melchior, 25.10.22; Melchior to Warburg, 28.10.22; Kohlhaus, 'Die Hapag', p. 112.

[283] WA, Allgemeines 1922, Warburg to Firma, 27.10.22; Warburg to Melchior, 30.10.22; HA, NL Cuno, Warburg to Cuno, 28.10.22. Warburg regarded the idea of Cuno as Foreign Minister as 'nonsense', preferring Wiedfeldt as a candidate.

[284] NAW, RG 59, 862.00/1192, Houghton to Secretary of State, 30.10.22; enclosed memorandum from Stinnes; Feldman, *Great Disorder*, pp. 481f. Cf. S.A. Diamond, 'Ein Amerikaner in Berlin. Aus dem Papieren des Botschafters Alanson B. Houghton 1922–1925', *VfZ*, 27 (1979), pp. 431–70.

[285] Rupieper, *Cuno Government*, p. 29.

[286] Laubach, *Kabinette Wirth*, pp. 293–8, 307–31; Maier, *Recasting Bourgeois Europe*, p. 300; Rupieper, *Cuno Government*, pp. 13f.; Kohlhaus, 'Die Hapag', pp. 115–20; Feldman, *Great Disorder*, pp. 487f.

[287] Keynes, *Collected Writings*, XVIII, pp. 64f.

[288] K.H. Harbeck (ed.), *Das Kabinett Cuno* (Boppard am Rhein, 1968), p.1 n.

doggedly held out for a mandate to govern without the socialists, in the face of determined efforts by the SPD to veto specific ministerial appointments.[289] The result was not quite the gallery of business leaders which Warburg appears to have contemplated, but with a shipping magnate as Chancellor and a former Director of Rheinische Stahlwerk (Becker) as Economics Minister, it was without question more economically conservative than any previous Weimar government.[290]

The formation of the Cuno government was the culmination of a process of political realignment set in train by the diplomatic failure of the strategy of fulfilment, the economic crisis precipitated by the onset of hyperinflation, the increasingly confrontational mood of bourgeois politics, and the attempt by the Economics Ministry to reassert government control over the economy. Its immediate origins can be traced back to the rapprochement between commercial and industrial interests in the summer of 1922, the rhetoric of business politics aired at the launch of the Overseas Club, and the counsel of defiance provided by Keynes at the Overseas Week. Arguably, its roots can be traced back further, to that gradual convergence of business and the state which had been brought about by the war and its aftermath. Cuno had begun life as a civil servant, had gravitated into business through the war economy, and had established early on a relationship with Ebert through the Hapag's agent, Holtzendorff. His appointment as Chancellor was in many ways the logical conclusion of this symbiosis between the corporate and the public sectors. Yet, as Warburg appears to have appreciated, it was in some ways illogical for *die Wirtschaft* now to take upon itself the burdens of political office. The tendency of events in 1922 had been to weaken the power of the state. Not only had it begun to lose its grip over public order, but its control over the economy had dwindled to a minimum. At the same time, no coherent diplomatic alternative to fulfilment had been put forward, other than to 'call Poincaré's bluff'. In these circumstances, there was little the new government could hope to do but to repeat the apologetics of the previous year, and hope that Keynes had been right. As events soon revealed, this amounted to a leap in the dark. The catastrophe of 1923 gave the lie to the claims of Cuno that he stood for 'objectivity' and a 'sober and businesslike' approach to government, and laid bare the contradictions underlying the idea of government by business.

---

[289] Rupieper, *Cuno Government*, pp. 21, 26; Kohlhaus, 'Die Hapag', pp. 115, 117, 120.

[290] For the list of 'ministerial candidates' (including Wiedfeldt, Stinnes, Urbig, and Vögler), see WA, Allgemeines 1922, Warburg Aufgabe, 26.11.22. The final list of ministers is given in Rupieper, *Cuno Government*, p. 22. Although it included a number of prominent members of the Centre, DVP, DDP and Bavarian People's Party, they were seen as acting as individuals, without formal responsibility to their parties – hence the phrase 'party-free cabinet'; *Vossische Zeitung*, Nr. 560, 26.11.22.

7

Dissolution and liquidation

The bankruptcy of business politics

There had been much rhetoric during 1922 about the need to increase the influence of 'men of business' over German policy making. Now that a businessman was Chancellor, the theory of 'business politics' could be put into practice. The experiment can scarcely be judged a success. In the course of the nine months during which Wilhelm Cuno held office, the German Reich was brought closer to the brink of dissolution than at any time since its foundation. A Franco-Belgian force occupied the Ruhr. To finance 'passive resistance' to this occupation, the production of paper currency was expanded to the limit of the printing presses' capacity. Attempts to arrest its consequent international depreciation failed, as did the strategy of passive resistance itself. Moreover, the increasingly rapid adjustment of prices and wages meant that the process of real monetary contraction which had begun in 1921/2 accelerated, leading to a *de facto* stabilisation crisis – long before deliberate steps were taken to end inflation. Although the continuing monetary chaos made it possible for firms to avoid overt bankruptcy, lack of liquidity forced many to curtail production and employment. Diminishing economic returns led in turn to political fragmentation. In Bavaria, the state government pursued an increasingly independent course; in Saxony and Thuringia, the Communists steadily increased their influence; while the secession of the occupied Rhineland became a distinct possibility. But these were only the most overt regional responses to the bankruptcy of the national polity. So great were the centrifugal forces at work, that even Hamburg, the Chancellor's own state, contemplated economic secession from the Reich. Two weeks before his resignation, the Treasury Minister Hans Albert and the industrialist Otto Henrich confronted the Chancellor with a grim analysis of his achievement:

What we have to fear is that the war of all against all for daily bread will begin in the city and that, for the maintenance of order in their own regions, the different parts of the Reich will proceed independently and the Reich will thus fall apart. That state which is no longer in the position to halt the collapse of its currency [. . .] necessarily loses its authority and ultimately its right to existence.[1]

Four years earlier, Keynes had cited Lenin to the effect that the best way to undermine the capitalist system was to debauch the currency. The effect of hyperinflation on the nation state was much the same.

For many contemporaries inside and outside Germany, the fact that this débâcle occurred while a capitalist was Chancellor had a sinister significance. The hope had been fostered by Cuno himself that, as Chancellor, he would be able to make use of his international business contacts to achieve a solution to the reparations question. When that hope proved illusory, Cuno's business connections took on a different hue. Trade union leaders had warned as early as February that the popular belief in 'an unbroken chain between high finance and the government' was spreading; and by June, trade unionists in Hamburg were speaking openly of government 'by the economic organisations'.[2] The *Hamburger Echo* noted that 'in the recent enormous rise in German industrial shares, above all in shipping, the Hapag has taken an outstanding place', and wondered: 'What would the Pan Germans have said if the shares of the AEG had performed so outstandingly while Rathenau was in office?'[3] Similar questions were raised by the SPD economic expert Hilferding and the liberal journalist Georg Bernhard about the relationship between the Reichsbank and industry.[4] The message was still more explicit in the Communist Georg Grosz's *Abrechnung Folgt!*, published in April 1923, which portrayed Stinnes as Ebert's puppet master, and the policy of passive resistance as a capitalist fraud.[5] Nor were such views confined to the Left. Writing shortly before Cuno came to power, a minor Hamburg businessman had advanced an explanation for the onset of hyperinflation which perfectly illustrates the appeal of the capitalist conspiracy theory:

Economic power and hence control over the mark lie in the hands of the [. . .] cartels of the united mining and related industries, the chemical industry and the great banks. These are dumping the mark. For them it is no longer a means of payment but a political weapon against the present regime.

In his view, it was clear that 'the desire of big business for political power' coincided with the the desire of 'leading American business

---

[1] Harbeck (ed.), *Kabinett Cuno*, pp. 682–8; Rupieper, *Cuno Government*, pp. 207ff.; Maier, *Recasting Bourgeois Europe*, p. 372.
[2] Harbeck (ed.), *Kabinett Cuno*, Nr. 68; Büttner, *Politische Gerechtigkeit*, p. 159.
[3] *Hamburger Echo*, 17.6.23.
[4] StAH, SK II, II A 4 Fasc. 29 Inv. 1, HG to SK, 16.1.23; HG to SK, 30.1.23.
[5] G. Grosz, *Abrechnung Folgt!* (Berlin, 1923), esp. p. 41, 'Stinnes und sein Präsident'.

circles' to give Germany a loan. Only France stood in the way of this scheme; and the dumping of the mark must therefore be a device to undermine the French position, because the franc tended to fall in the wake of the mark.[6] Similarly convoluted theories appeared in the British popular press, which portrayed Cuno as merely a 'front-man' for still more powerful figures like Stinnes or, sometimes, Warburg.[7] French and American observers took the same view.[8] It is hardly surprising that such allegations have frequently been echoed in the work of historians.[9]

Both Cuno and Warburg disputed such charges. As Cuno put it in December 1922: 'The government leads and industry supports the government. There is no authority, no centre of power in industry, which would be strong enough to seize the initiative from the government.'[10] For his part, Warburg denied that he had 'overturned Wirth's politics' or 'made Cuno Chancellor':

I am not active in politics, neither directly nor indirectly. I restrict my activity to business and to expressing, when consulted, my opinion as an expert on purely financial and technical questions. [. . .] The gentlemen [in Berlin] often take my advice, but invariably do the opposite of what I advise. If only they did not, the world would be in a much better state than it presently is. [. . .] My main occupation is as a philosopher. In my spare time I am a family man and a banker; nothing more.[11]

Certainly, there is no evidence that Cuno consciously misused his political position in order to advance the interests of the Hapag or any other firm.[12] Having accepted the office of Chancellor, he conscientiously put the interests of the Reich above those of the Hapag. Yet Warburg's claim that he had no political influence is far from easy to reconcile with, for example, the memorandum he presented to Cuno on 2 July 1923, entitled 'If I were Chancellor', which combined general suggestions for government policy with detailed recommendations on exchange controls, in which Warburg clearly had a private interest.[13] As this chapter demonstrates, it was no coincidence that Cuno's government witnessed the nadir of the state's authority and the zenith of the

---

[6] StAH, SK II, II A 4 Fasc. 29, Inv. 1, Karl Jenckel to SK, 28.10.22.
[7] *Daily Mail*, 18.1.23; *Daily Express*, 10.2.23.
[8] WA, 32, Pol. Corr. 1923, Lucius von Stoedten to Warburg, 6.6.23.
[9] See, e.g., Specht, *Politische Hintergründe*, pp. 102, 107.
[10] Rupieper, *Cuno Government*, p. 57.
[11] WA, 31, Pol. Corr. 1923, Warburg to *Daily Express*, 12.2.23; WA, 32, Pol. Corr. 1923, Warburg to von Stoedten, 11.6.23.
[12] See, e.g., HA, HB, Holtzendorff to Hapag Vorstand, 7.4.23; Hapag to AA, 19.5.23; Kohlhaus, 'Die Hapag', pp. 3, 6f., 100; Rupieper, *Cuno Government*, pp. 17, 28.
[13] WA, Pol. Corr. 1923, Warburg, 'Wenn ich Kanzler wäre', 30.6.23; Warburg to Cuno, 2.7.23.

business 'veto-power'. Cuno's anti-French policy required material
sacrifices by business to be effective; but when it became apparent
that his former colleagues in the private sector were unwilling to make
these, Cuno proved incapable of compelling them to do so. The idea
of a government of *die Wirtschaft* was exposed as a contradiction in
terms, because, in the crisis of 1923, business invariably put its own
interests before those of the state; and a former businessman was of
all people the least able to stop them doing so.

Despite the initial enthusiasm of Keynes, who urged the new government to 'call [. . .] out in a clear voice', and confessed to 'envy[ing]
Cuno his job',[14] the limitations of trying to base government on business
quickly became apparent. The first month of Cuno's Chancellorship
was frittered away in desultory haggling about last-ditch reparations
offers and loan schemes; and the final offer hammered out by his
unofficial 'cabinet' of businessmen was so derisory that it was decided
not to put it forward in Paris.[15] Clearly, dispensing with the parties
did not make the process of policy making any simpler; the *Wirtschaftler*
appeared to have just as much difficulty reaching agreement as the
party leaders. As the hopelessness of the diplomatic position became
increasingly obvious, Warburg and others began to distance themselves.
Both Wiedfeldt and the Hapag agent in New York noted that the
chances of a decisive American intervention – Cuno's supposed trump
card – were nil;[16] while Warburg bitterly concluded that no positive
help was to be expected from 'perfidious Albion' either, and demurred
when Cuno requested his presence in Berlin on 28 December.[17] This
was the background to Cuno's speech at the Hamburg stock exchange
on 31 December, when he told his audience that he intended to 'direct

[14] PA/AA, SRW FW 16A II 4392, Warburg to Cuno, 24.11.22; Keynes, *Collected Writings*, XVIII, pp. 85, 90, 97, 105f., 116; WA, 32, Pol. Corr. 1923, Keynes to Melchior 5(?).1.23; Skidelsky, *Economist as Saviour*, pp. 121f. Cf. G.F. Bravo, '"In the name of our mutual friend." The Keynes-Cuno Affair', *JCH*, 24 (1989), pp. 147–68.
[15] Rupieper, *Cuno Government*, pp. 25, 43, 46f., 49f., 59–67, 70–5; idem, 'Industrie und Reparationen', p. 587; Harbeck (ed.), *Kabinett Cuno*, pp. 37f.; Maier, *Recasting Bourgeois Europe*, pp. 302f.; Specht, *Politische Hintergründe*; Feldman, *Disorder*, pp. 490–507. For Keynes's advice, PA/AA, SRW FW 16A II 4392, Warburg to Cuno, 24.11.22; BAK, R43 I/185, Keynes to Melchior, 1.12.22; Melchior to Cuno, 5.12.22; Keynes, *Collected Writings*, XVIII, pp. 97, 116f.
[16] WA, XVII, Allg. 1922, Pierre Schrumpf-Pierron to Melchior, 29.11.22; Melchior to Schrumpf-Pierron, 2.12.22; Wiedfeldt to Warburg, 12.12.22; Kohlhaus, 'Die Hapag', p. 124. On Cuno's abortive appeal to J.P. Morgan for a loan, see Feldman, *Great Disorder*, p. 498.
[17] Vagts, 'M.M. Warburg & Co.', p. 379; WA, 32, Pol. Corr. 1923, Warburg to Alice Warburg, 22.11.22; Melchior Notiz, 24.11.22; Warburg to Melchior, 28.12.22. This verdict on Bonar Law's proposal of 9 December seems unduly harsh, since, under Keynes's influence, the British now accepted the idea of a four-year moratorium and a reduced reparations total: cf. Skidelsky, *Economist as Saviour*, pp. 123f.

the negotiations of the Reich according to the methods which flow from the spirit of the Honourable Merchant'.[18] The truth was that these methods were unequal to the situation; and when, in early January 1923, the Paris conference ended in the inevitable deadlock and the Reparations Commission pronounced Germany in default on coal deliveries, Cuno seems to have welcomed the opportunity to abandon his role as cool man of business in favour of the still potent patriotic rhetoric of 1914.[19]

However, he could not escape so easily from the contradictions of the business politics he himself had once idealised. In order to be effective, Cuno's new strategy of 'passive resistance' to the French occupation required not only a revival of the 'spirit' of 1914, but also a major economic effort.[20] It was now that the full extent of the incompatibility of national and private interests became manifest. Essentially, the hastily formulated strategy had four main components. First, Cuno wanted to make the occupation as costly as possible for Poincaré by subsidising a coal strike in the Ruhr – which meant paying both owners and workers. At the same time, output had to be maintained in the rest of Germany by providing industry with imported British coal. Thirdly, it was hoped that the strain of the occupation on French finances would place the franc under pressure on the foreign exchanges. Finally, Cuno continued to cling to the hope that British and American doubts about Poincaré's strategy could be translated into effective diplomatic pressure.[21] Clearly, however, the first and second of these objectives entailed substantial increases in government expenditure, which would tend to undermine the German currency, rather than the French, unless stringent monetary and fiscal measures were adopted.[22] Moreover, the chances of a diplomatic breakthrough in the short term were negligible. The encouragement proffered by Keynes or Houghton was always couched in terms of Germany 'holding

[18] Harbeck (ed.), *Kabinett Cuno*, pp. 103–10; WA, 32, Pol. Corr. 1923, Warburg to Cuno, 2.1.23.
[19] For Cuno's appeals to wartime patriotism, see Harbeck (ed.), *Kabinett Cuno*, pp. 322–6; Specht, *Politische Hintergründe*, p. 100, 103n. For Warburg's approval, BAK, NL Solf, 137, Warburg to Solf, 19.3.23. See also Keynes, *Collected Writings*, XVIII, p. 120 (Melchior).
[20] On the Ruhr occupation, see Rupieper, *Cuno Government*, pp. 112–19; idem, 'Industrie und Reparationen', pp. 588ff.; McDougall, *France's Rhineland Diplomacy, 1914–1924*, pp. 241f., 244–9, 251–9; Trachtenberg, *Reparation in World Politics. France and European Economic Diplomacy*, chapter 7; K. Schwabe (ed.), *Die Ruhrkrise, 1923* (Paderborn, 1985).
[21] Rupieper, *Cuno Government*, pp. 98–107; Maier, *Recasting Bourgeois Europe*, pp. 356f.; Feldman, *Iron and Steel*, pp. 351–5; idem, *Great Disorder*, pp. 631–40; Specht, *Politische Hintergründe*, p. 101.
[22] WA, 33, Pol. Corr. 1923, Melchior Aufgabe, 12.1.23; Melchior to Cuno, 13.1.23; Warburg, *Aufzeichnungen*, p. 112.

out to the limit of her endurance' and the government 'keeping its nerve'.[23] The problem was that, under the economic pressure of sustaining passive resistance, 'German endurance' quickly reached its limits; while, as Holtzendorff and others who visited London discovered, official British opinion was still far less sympathetic than Keynes.[24] The friction between Cuno and his supposed allies in business increased with each new expedient adopted by the government to prolong passive resistance.

This was most immediately obvious in the fiscal sphere, where virtually nothing was done to compensate for the increases in expenditure occasioned by passive resistance, which cost the Finance Ministry around 5.2 trillion marks between January and June. In real terms, total public spending rose by more than 75 per cent in 1923 compared with the previous year, with monthly Reich spending rising from 433 m. gold marks in January 1923 to nearly 1.5 bn. in August. Yet revenue plummeted to as little as 70 m. gold marks in July, giving rise to an unprecedented surge in government borrowing.[25] The total deficit in 1923 was equivalent to around 22 per cent of NNP, the highest since 1918.[26] In part, this reflected the automatic impact of rising inflation on real revenues.[27] But it also reflected the complete breakdown of 'tax morality' at both the microeconomic and the political levels. Tax evasion, made easy by the complexity of tax legislation, was rife.[28] At the same time, the very idea of paying tax was challenged by business spokesmen. Typically, a spokesman for the RdI argued that it was more important that 'industry should continue to produce than that the deficit should be reduced';[29] and even a small increase in the turnover tax elicited vehement protests from the Hamburg Chamber of Commerce.[30] Some taxes were even reduced in response

[23] WA, 32, Pol. Corr. 1923, Keynes to Melchior, 17.1.23; Oswald Falk to Melchior, 20.1.23; Melchior to Falk, 25.1.23; Falk to Melchior, 30.1.23; 30.1.23; Melchior to Falk, 6.2.23; HA, HB, Holtzendorff to Vorstand, 30.1.23; Keynes, Collected Writings, XVIII, pp. 119f.

[24] WA, 32, Pol. Corr. 1923, Holtzendorff to Warburg, 4.3.23; Richter to Melchior, 4.2.23; Kohlhaus, 'Die Hapag', pp. 127–30; Rupieper, Cuno Government, pp. 130f.; Kessler, Tagebücher, pp. 377–403.

[25] See figures 3.3 and 5.1. On the precise way in which passive resistance was financed, see Feldman, Iron and Steel, pp. 358–74; Maier, Recasting Bourgeois Europe, p. 357.

[26] See table 1.

[27] Aldcroft, Versailles to Wall Street, p. 134.

[28] BAP, RFM 47055 N. Reg. 2574/91–112, Landesfinanzamt Unterelbe Bericht, 14.12.22; /113–35. The tax office listed thirteen different ways in which firms in Hamburg were seeking to avoid tax, including simple falsification of accounts, the transfer of profits to bogus foreign companies, undervaluation of assets, bogus allowances for depreciation, the inclusion of personal tax liability in company overheads; and the use of out-dated exchange rates on foreign earnings or payments.

[29] Specht, Politische Hintergründe, p. 109.

[30] StAH, SK II, Gen B XX Nr 1 vol. 1a Fasc. 1, HKH to DHSG, 30.12.23; 10.1.23.

to business pressure.[31] Attempts to compensate for the effect of inflation on direct tax revenues were half hearted.[32] As an American observer put it: 'It is certainly no secret [. . .] that German business is not paying taxes. The government knows it; the newspapers know it; and the businessmen brag about it.'[33]

The link between political events, fiscal policy and the exchange rate was now sufficiently obvious for this to precipitate an unprecedented fall in the mark. Between December 1922 and February 1923, the dollar rose by a factor of around 3.6 against the mark.[34] Clearly, the pressure on the mark was greater than that on the franc. However, when the government sought to counter this with other policy devices, it encountered still greater business resistance. Commercial interests continued to campaign vigorously against the use of trade controls to regulate the balance of payments.[35] This left only monetary policy. As we have seen, Havenstein had responded to the private sector liquidity crisis of mid 1922 by generously discounting commercial bills, increasing the output of the Reichsbank's printing presses in a fashion which, had he been producing any other commodity than banknotes, would have been most impressive. After December 1922, public sector borrowing once again swelled the monetary flood. As a result, the monthly rate of growth of M0 (notes in circulation) rose from 12.4 per cent in July 1922 to 76.8 per cent in February 1923, having never previously risen above 20 per cent (and only rarely exceeded 10 per cent; see figure 7.1). At this point, Havenstein came under growing pressure to alter monetary policy. He increased the discount rate from 10 per cent to 12 per cent in January, and then to 18 per cent in April, mainly in the hope of increasing the credit banks' willingness to hold Treasury bills, while at the same time pressing the banks to restrict

---

[31] The coal tax was reduced and then suspended in May; postal and rail rates were frozen; and in June the export levy was lifted; Specht, *Politische Hintergründe*, pp. 108f., 110.

[32] Specht, *Politische Hintergründe*, p. 102, 122; Rupieper, *Cuno Government*, pp. 174–80; Maier, *Recasting Bourgeois Europe*, pp. 363f. Taxation under the Cuno government became increasingly regressive simply because the government failed to alter the income tax legislation which deducted tax directly from wages, but allowed other taxpayers to delay payment.

[33] NAW, RG 59, 862.512/143, Vice-Consul Walk, 'An analysis of the financial statements. . .', 6.6.23.

[34] Holtfrerich, *Inflation*, p.17.

[35] For business pressure on the government to abolish the controls outright, StAH, DHSG III, Pr. III 39, HKH Mitteilung, 10.1.23; HKH to Becker, 16/17.3.23; HG to SK, 27.3.23; Heidecker to SK, 17.4.23; DHSG III, Pr. III 34 Bd. II, HKH to DHSG 13.6.23; GHH, 400101290/119, Reusch to Cuno, 11.7.23; Sen Cl I Lit T No. 9c vol. 52 Fasc. 13, HKH to RK/RWM/RFM, 21.7.23; DHSG III, Pr. III 39, HKH to RWM, 13.8.23. Critics of the system of control were vindicated in droll fashion when English translations of a speech by Cuno were impounded by Hamburg customs officials because they lacked the requisite export licence: *The Times*, 23.5.23.

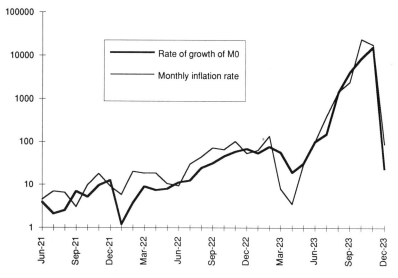

Figure 7.1 Monthly growth rates of money and prices, 1921–1923
Sources: Bry, *Wages*, pp. 422–9, 440–5; Holtfrerich, *Inflation*, pp. 52ff.

their own lending.[36] This had at least some effect: monetary growth slowed to just 19 per cent in April.[37] Secondly, he was prevailed upon by Cuno to use the Reichsbank's reserves of gold, silver and foreign currency to intervene on the foreign exchange markets on an unprecedented scale.[38] This 'support action' was intended to take advantage of the fact that, relative to the Reichsbank's reserves of around $250 m., the mark was undervalued. Purchases of paper marks totalling 178 m. gold marks pushed the mark up from a nadir of 49,000 against the dollar to around 20,000, where it was held throughout March.[39] Thirdly, it was decided to try to 'flush out' foreign currency held in Germany by offering, at a generous discount, dollar-denominated three-year Treasury bills to a value of $50 m.[40]

[36] StAH, SK II, II A 4 Fasc. 29, Inv. 1, HG to SK, 16.1.23. Cf. Feldman, *Great Disorder*, p. 641.
[37] See figure 7.1.
[38] StAH, SK II, II A 4 Fasc. 29, Inv. 1, HG to SK, 30.1.23; 8.2.23; 9.2.23; WA 32, Pol. Corr. 1923, Melchior Angabe, 15.2.23.
[39] Holtfrerich, *Inflation*, pp. 308f.; Rupieper, *Cuno Government*, pp. 107–12; Specht, *Politische Hintergründe*, pp. 105f.; Maier, *Recasting Bourgeois Europe*, p. 367; Feldman, *Great Disorder*, pp. 642–6. Cf. Keynes, *Collected Writings*, XVIII, pp. 127f.
[40] Rupieper, *Cuno Government*, p. 109; Harbeck (ed.), *Kabinett Cuno*, pp. 276f., 400n.; Feldman, *Great Disorder*, pp. 647–55. Further details in WA, 34, Pol. Corr. 1923, Melchior Angabe, 19/20.2.23; *Berlin Börsen-Courier*, 1.3.23; *Deutsche Allgemeine Zeitung*, Nr. 134/5, 22.3.23.

The government's objective in shoring up the mark was, as one official put it, to demonstrate Germany's 'capacity to resist' while at the same time eroding its 'capacity to pay' by throwing away the Reichsbank's reserves and creating an enduring burden of hard currency Reich debt.[41] Once again, however, the strategy foundered because of a fundamental conflict of interest between the government and the private sector. Even before the onset of hyperinflation, some firms had begun conducting business in foreign currency and building up foreign currency reserves.[42] In Hamburg, firms like Deutsche Werft had been keeping export earnings in foreign accounts since 1919; while others, including Blohm & Voß, had begun demanding payments in sterling and dollars from German customers, despite the introduction of prohibitions on its use in domestic transactions.[43] Max Warburg subsequently maintained that he had felt unable 'to preserve our holdings in foreign currency when it meant indirectly damaging our own currency', and heatedly denied allegations that his firm had sold marks for francs in February; but he himself had taken the decision in January to convert German industrial shares into foreign currency, because of the 'greater security' it offered.[44] Likewise the shipping lines began looking for ways to mortgage ships for foreign currency; while exporters simply hung on to their foreign earnings.[45] Indeed, foreign currency was increasingly carried by individuals for use in everyday transactions.[46] Thus the government's desire to support the mark was contradicted directly by the desire of businessmen to minimise their holdings of marks; a desire which growing pessimism about Cuno's chances of success only whetted.

---

[41] Harbeck (ed.), *Kabinett Cuno*, p. 112.

[42] On industrial foreign currency holdings, see Feldman, *Iron and Steel*, pp. 312–14; Lindenlaub, *Maschinenbauunternehmen*, p. 171.

[43] In March 1923, Deutsche Werft had over 3 m. gold marks in seven different accounts, some in pounds, some in dollars, as well as small amounts of Italian, Dutch and Scandinavian currency; GHH, 3001930012/8. On Blohm & Voß's illegal sterling contract, StAH, DHSG XIX A 3 Nr. 41, Bd. 1, Devisenbeschaffungsstelle v. Blohm & Voß, 22.8.23. See also the dollar and sterling figures for the Hapag's earnings in HA, NL Cuno, Cuno to Warburg, 16.10.22.

[44] Warburg, Aufzeichnungen MSS, pp. 74ff.; *Hamburgische Correspondent*, 14.2.23; WA, 32, Pol. Corr. 1923, Warburg to Müller, 12.2.23; 13.2.23; Warburg to Melchior, 28.12.22; Warburg to Louis Hagen, 6.1.23; Melchior to Warburg, 20.1.23. Cf. the detailed 'Jahresbericht 1923', which shows that at the end of the financial year Warburg's had foreign assets totalling 1.5 m. gold marks; although it is true that, 'from a sentimental standpoint', the bank had held on to some mark-denominated assets.

[45] HA, HB, Holtzendorff Notiz, 20.2.23; StAH, FA AOM, Bd. 15, 400f., Witthoefft to Warburg, 6.7.23. Behn, Meyer & Co. had reserves of $1 m. at the end of the financial year 1922. See also BAP, RFM 47055 N.Reg. 2574/91–112, Landesfinanzamt Unterelbe Bericht, 14.12.22; /113–35, Landesfinanzamt Unterelbe Bericht, 15.6.23.

[46] See, e.g., Lippmann, *Leben*, p. 316.

The reluctance of businessmen to part with foreign currency doomed the $50 m. loan to failure. So low was the Reich's credit that, despite the theoretical attractions of the bonds (interest was paid in advance), the issue was a flop, with only around a quarter of the total ($12.6 m.) being taken up of the initial issue, and around $15 m. still unsold by the end of July.[47] The result was especially bad in Hamburg: of $2.5 m. which it sought to place, Warburg's was only able to sell $400,000.[48] Typically, Deutsche Werft was willing to give up no more than a paltry £1,000, pleading 'very strong demands on our liquid reserves'.[49] Although Warburg attempted to place the blame on various technical shortcomings of the issue, Cuno bitterly accused business, and in particular commerce, of having let him down.[50] Moreover, the failure of the dollar loan precipitated a fresh run on the mark and the collapse of the 'support action',[51] prompting furious claims by the Reichsbank and the government that Stinnes had undermined the currency by making large-scale purchases of sterling.[52]

All this made the diplomatic failure of Cuno's strategy inevitable: it was increasingly clear in business circles that the mark would collapse long before any diplomatic breakthrough. As early as February 1922, Stinnes was trying to persuade Warburg that passive resistance should be abandoned in favour of 'reconciliation with France'.[53] Two months

[47] BAK, R43 I/2435 172–204, 205–39; Harbeck (ed.), *Kabinett Cuno*, pp. 399–402, 678, 710 n.; Maier, *Recasting Bourgeois Europe*, p. 367; Rupieper, *Cuno Government*, pp. 110, 199f.

[48] WA, 32, Pol. Corr. 1923, Warburg to Cuno, 30.3.23. Warburg informed Cuno that he 'had never received so many refusals, or been sent packing so often. Only a French officer could fare worse.' With hindsight, Warburg felt the limits placed on the bonds as security for lombard credits had put off investors; Warburg, 'Das Ergebnis der Dollarschatzanweisungsanleihe des Deutschen Reiches', *Bank-Archiv*, 15.4.23. Cf. StAH, SK II, II A 4 Fasc. 29, Inv. 1, HKH Abschrift, 30.4.23.

[49] GHH, 300193012/8, Deutsche Werft to Reusch, 23.3.23; Reusch to Deutsche Werft, 31.3.23. The yard in fact had £13,798 in one of its London accounts; GHH, 300193012/8, Bilanz, 10.3.23.

[50] Harbeck (ed.), *Kabinett Cuno*, pp. 403f.; WA, 33, Pol. Corr. 1923, Melchior, Notiz, 27.4.23.

[51] Harbeck (ed.), *Kabinett Cuno*, pp. 424f.; Bresciani, *Inflation*, pp. 63, 78; Feldman, *Great Disorder*, pp. 655ff.

[52] Bresciani, *Inflation*, p. 63; Rupieper, *Cuno Government*, p. 111; Lindenlaub, *Maschinenbauunternehmen*, pp. 170f. Stinnes was alleged to have purchased £115,000 in a series of private transactions in April 1923. In fact, he had purchased £60,000 to finance coal imports authorised by the Transport Ministry. For Melchior's defence of Stinnes before the Reichstag Currency Committee, see *Berliner Börsen Courier*, 20.6.23; *Deutsche Allgemeine Zeitung*, 21.6.23. Intervention to support the mark continued until the end of July, at a total cost of around 660 m. gold marks; Feldman, *Great Disorder*, pp. 647, 688.

[53] WA, 32, Pol. Corr. 1923, von Stoedten to Warburg, 20.1.23; Warburg to Cuno, 10.2.23; 'Jahresbericht 1923', pp. 12f.; Warburg, Aufzeichnungen MSS, p. 264. See

later, Paul Reusch, Melchior and others advised him to make new over-tures to Britain, following Curzon's speech on 20 April.[54] However, it was one of Max Warburg's American contacts who finally persuaded Cuno to break his diplomatic silence. Fred Kent of the Bankers' Trust Co. had made a speech at the International Chambers of Commerce conference in Rome calling for an end to the Ruhr conflict, and arrived in Berlin convinced that he could broker a compromise with Paris.[55] Bergmann and Melchior worked out a draft proposal offering 30 bn. gold marks as a final sum, which alluded to securities as well as to the familiar combination of loan and moratorium; but Cuno, Becker and Rosenberg preferred a less generous version of the earlier January note, offering around half as much in real terms and omitting any reference to securities.[56] Inevitably, the note was rejected by Poincaré, and Kent departed in disgust.[57] A second initiative, this time directed at British opinion, was urged on Cuno by Melchior and Keynes;[58] but this too came to nothing. After consultations with the new Prime Minister, Bald-win, and McKenna (whom he wrongly expected to be the next Chancellor), Keynes travelled to Berlin; and, largely as a result of his influence, the new note made no mention of a total sum.[59] But Keynes continued to underestimate the weakness of the German position:

also Mudd Library Princeton, Fred I. Kent Papers, Box 24, Kent to Paul de Vallanbresa, 4.4.23, citing the views of 'high-class German business interests'.
[54] WA, 32, Pol. Corr. 1923, Melchior Diary Notes, 27.4.23; Harbeck (ed.), *Kabinett Cuno*, pp. 384–91, 412f.; Rupieper, *Cuno Government*, pp. 145ff.; Kohlhaus, 'Die Hapag', p. 133. Cf. Feldman, *Great Disorder*, pp. 658–69.
[55] Mudd Library, Princeton, Fred I. Kent Papers, Box 28, Max Warburg to Kent, 28.3.23; Kent to Paul Warburg, 31.3.23; Box 24, Kent to Cuno. 27.4.23; Rupieper, *Cuno Government*, p. 139. Warburg had got to know Kent during his visit to the US in 1922, when they had initially discussed the possibility of using the International Chambers of Commerce as a channel for a diplomatic initiative.
[56] WA, 32, Pol. Corr. 1923, Entwurf, 27.4.23; Harbeck (ed.), *Kabinett Cuno*, pp. 440–55, 474–9; Rupieper, *Cuno Government*, pp. 147–52; Specht, *Politische Hintergründe*, pp. 113ff.
[57] Mudd Library, Princeton, Fred I. Kent Papers, Box 28, Kent to Paul Warburg, 9.5.23. 'The Germans,' commented Kent, 'spend all their time [. . .] saying what they want to do and what they can't do and what it is impossible to do. [. . .] It is beyond my comprehension how men of intelligence and real desire to help their country could possibly have been so foolish as to have sent the kind of note that was put out last week.'
[58] WA, 33, Pol. Corr. 1923, Melchior Notes, 11.5.23; Keynes, *Collected Writings*, XVIII, pp. 134–41; Skidelsky, *Economist as Saviour*, pp. 121–5; Bravo, 'Keynes-Cuno Affair', pp. 147–58, 163. In suggesting that this initiative 'paved the way' for the Dawes plan, Skidelsky and Bravo exaggerate its significance.
[59] WA, 33, Pol. Corr. 1923, Keynes to Cuno, 16.5.23; Warburg to Holtzendorff, 17.5.23; Melchior to Keynes, 22.5.23; Keynes to Melchior, 24.5.23; Holtzendorff to Warburg, 25.5.23; Melchior to Keynes, 26.5.23; Keynes to Melchior 26.5.23; Melchior to Keynes, 28.5.23; Melchior Angabe, 4.6.23; Warburg, *Aufzeichnungen*, p. 116; Keynes, *Collected Writings*, XVIII, pp. 143–90; Skidelsky, *Economist as Saviour*, pp. 126f.; Bravo, 'Keynes-Cuno Affair', pp. 159ff.

Let Germany, instead of making moan about how badly she is being treated, insist rather on her capacity of indefinite resistance and even introduce a slight note of menace. Her present propaganda [. . .] produces the impression that she will break down before long. *In the long run*, firmness and a proud bearing will produce more effect on opinion than conciliations and moans.[60]

Such fighting talk overlooked the fact that the impression of imminent collapse was not a tactical device but a true representation of the German situation: 'indefinite resistance' was not a realistic option. Although the final draft, with its guarantees of state revenues and a mortgage on private property, went significantly further than the first note, it brought no immediate relief, since the British Foreign Secretary declined to reply and Poincaré refused to negotiate until passive resistance was suspended.[61] Meanwhile the crumbling of the German state had advanced a step further in the course of discussions about the assets Germany might offer as guarantees for reparations, with both the RdI and the Reich Agrarian League blatantly demanding political concessions in return for their cooperation.[62] A final attempt by John Foster Dulles to mediate between Berlin and Brussels (again initiated by Warburg) came to nothing, mainly because Rosenberg refused to contemplate suspending passive resistance.[63]

To the despairing Rosenberg, French intransigence was the insuperable obstacle:

They were satisfied that France did not want a financial settlement [. . .] He was certain that if he should go to Poincaré today and say that out of a newly discovered gold mine they had extracted 132 bn. gold marks which would be delivered tomorrow, Poincaré would say, it is due *today*, you are in default and I seize your railroads so that you cannot make delivery tomorrow. France was determined to humiliate and crush Germany and any new German step [. . .] would merely be a sign of weakness.[64]

---

[60] WA, 33, Pol. Corr. 1923, Keynes to Melchior, 24.5.23.
[61] Rupieper, *Cuno Government*, pp. 159–63; Skidelsky, *Economist as Saviour*, pp. 127ff. Cf. the successive drafts in WA, 35.
[62] Harbeck (ed.), *Kabinett Cuno*, pp. 508–15; Rupieper, *Cuno Government*, pp. 154–9, Maier, *Recasting Bourgeois Europe*, p. 370.
[63] Mudd Library, Princeton, John Foster Dulles Papers, Box 5, Paul Warburg to Max Warburg, 16.5.23; Memorandum of Conference with Mr Cuno, 2/5.7.23; Memorandum of Conference with M. Barthou, 7.7.23; Memorandum of Conference with M. Theunis, 10.7.23; Memorandum of Conference with Melchior, 12.7.23; Memorandum of Conference in Germany, 13/16.7.23; Draft Memorandum, 16.7.23; Memorandum, 17.7.23; Memorandum of Conference with Benes and Masaryk, 19.7.23; Memorandum of Conference with Theunis, 19.7.23; Melchior to Dulles, 27.7.23; Dulles to Melchior, 3.8.23; Melchior to Dulles, 27.8.23; Dulles to Cartier, 17.9.23; Dulles to Warburg (1942); WA, 34, Pol. Corr. 1923, Melchior Diary, 25.6.23; Melchior Angabe, 17.7.23; Melchior Notiz, 27.7.23; Warburg, Aufzeichnungen MSS, pp. 292–5; Rupieper, *Cuno Government*, pp. 164–73.
[64] Mudd Library, Princeton, John Foster Dulles Papers, Memorandum, 17.7.23.

In reality, it was Rosenberg and Cuno who were being unreasonable.
It was one thing to say that 'Germany would not submit to humiliation
by France' and that 'its people would prefer to die or be submerged
for twenty years', but the limit of German endurance could be measured
not in years but in days, so long as business refused to make the
economic sacrifices necessary to sustain the *Ruhrkampf*. When Cuno
requested new measures 'to avert the complete collapse of our mark
for the time being', Hermes replied bluntly that 'the complete collapse
of the mark is already underway'.[65] This was underlined after the
failure of the second note, when Cuno adopted a new device to prop
up the mark (now down to around 100,000 against the dollar): strict
exchange controls, based on an officially pegged exchange rate.[66] The
possibility of such a measure had been bruited as early as April,
though it had been decided simply to tighten the existing system of
supervision by the banks. Even this had aroused opposition from those
parts of the economy which were now heavily reliant on foreign
currency, notably Hamburg's banking, shipping and trading sectors;
and the idea of 'foreign currency centralisation' which the Economics
Ministry now suggested was viewed with horror, not least because it
would inevitably lead to undervaluing of German firms' foreign currency holdings, allowing customers to pay off importers in overvalued
paper marks.[67] Along with the representatives of the Berlin great banks,
Melchior and Warburg argued that no measure could counter a 'world
speculation' and that a fixed rate would simply give rise to a black
exchange market.[68] Nevertheless, Cuno informed his erstwhile business
colleagues that 'these reservations' would have to be 'subordinated to
the general interest of the German people'.[69] It proved a short-lived
experiment. Cuno was bombarded with protests from Hamburg as
firms laid off workers and suspended imports, which included vital

---

[65] Specht, *Politische Hintergründe*, pp. 116–20.
[66] Harbeck (ed.), *Das Kabinett Cuno*, pp. 598–602; Rupieper, *Cuno Government*,
pp. 180–5.
[67] StAH, SK II, II A 4 Fasc. 29, Inv. 1, HKH, HKBremen and Bremer Baumwollbörse
to Trendelenberg, 24.4.23; HG to SK, 9/12.5.23; DHSG III, Pr. V 2, 'Verordnung
[. . .] Maßnahmen gegen die Valutaspekulation', 8.5.23; 'Die neue Devisenverord-
nung', *Hamburger Fremdenblatt*, Nr. 130, 12.5.23. Cf. Warburg, Aufzeichnungen
MSS, pp. 215, 272.
[68] WA, 34, Pol. Corr., Warburg Angabe, 2.6.23; Melchior to Warburg, 19.6.23;
Melchior Notiz, 21.6.23.; WA, 32, Pol. Corr. 1923, Warburg, 'Wenn ich Kanzler
wäre', 30.6.23; Warburg, Aufzeichnungen MSS, p. 286; *idem, Aufzeichnungen*, p. 117.
Cf. Harbeck (ed.), *Kabinett Cuno*, pp. 598–602; Rupieper, *Cuno Government*, p. 185.
[69] StAH, SK II, II A 4 Fasc. 29, Inv. 1, Cuno to Hamburg Senate, 23.6.23; *RGB*,
Nr. 50, (1923), 'Verordnung [. . .] gegen Valutaspekulation und Kapitalflucht',
29.6.23.

food supplies.[70] On 4 August, a little over a month after it had been enacted, the *Einheitskurs* was lifted.[71]

There was now no mistaking the severity of the economic and political crisis and the urgency of the need for action.[72] Pointing out (in terms reminiscent of Keynes's *Economic Consequences*) that 'a capitalist economy which eliminates the idea of money from the economy [. . .] prepares the ground for Bolshevist chaos', Cuno for the last time 'ask[ed] *die Wirtschaft* whether it was ready to make possible an attempt to save the state from ruin'.[73] However, his request for an additional loan of 50 m. gold marks in foreign currency as part of an emergency fiscal programme merely brought business politics to its nadir.[74] Brushing aside Cuno's desperate threat of resignation, his unofficial cabinet of bankers and industrialists coolly debated what conditions to set in return for their cooperation. Should taxes be levied on private automobiles as well as on the total number of employees per firm? Stinnes in particular seemed anxious to avoid what might be seen as a tax on 'war profiteers'. Could the abolition of trade controls be part of the bargain, wondered Vögler? Another voice suggested a 'foreign exchange amnesty'. There was a brief moment when the impropriety of the discussion struck Warburg, who 'half jokingly' characterised Vögler's suggestion as 'immoral';[75] but Warburg too was inclined to drive a hard bargain, opposing the limits Havenstein wished to place on the lombardability of the new gold bonds and criticising, in a heated exchange, the Reichsbank's decision to raise the discount rate to 30 per cent.[76]

[70] StAH, SK II, II A 4 Fasc. 29, Inv. I, Auszug, Senatsprotokolle, 25.6.23; HKH Abschrift, 11.7.23; DHSG Abschrift, 12.7.23; Abschrift der Firma Georg Plange, 18.7.23; Abschrift der Vereinbarung der am Kaffeehandel Beteiligten, 17.7.23; Kriegsversorgungsamt Abschrift, 21.7.23; Senate to Cuno, 1.8.23; HKH to DHSG, 6.8.23; FA B&V 228, Bd. II, Firmenleitung to Rudolf Blohm, 30.6.23; GHH, 300101290/119, Reusch to Cuno, 11.7.23; BAK, R43 I/2435, HKH (telegram) to Cuno, 12.7.23; NAW, RG 59, 862.5151/1673, George D. Hopper (US Consul) to State Dept., 27.7.23.
[71] StAH, SK II, II A 4 Fasc. 29, Inv. I, HG to SK, 7.8.23.
[72] Harbeck (ed.), *Kabinett Cuno*, pp. 575–81, 652–79; Rupieper, *Cuno Government*, pp. 192, 201–5.
[73] Harbeck (ed.), *Kabinett Cuno*, pp. 697–702; Rupieper, *Cuno Government*, p. 209.
[74] Harbeck (ed.), *Kabinett Cuno*, pp. 639–8; Rupieper, *Cuno Government*, pp. 207–10; Webb, *Hyperinflation*, p. 18. The programme was based on the memorandum drawn up by Henrich and Albert on 27 July.
[75] WA, 34, Pol. Corr. 1923, Warburg Aufgabe, 1.8.23; Warburg Notiz, 2.8.23. See also StAH, FA B&V 4511, RdI to Blohm. 3.8.23; Siemens circular, 6.8.23; Blohm to Bücher, 9.8.23, 11.8.23; HKH to DHSG, 15.8.23; Blohm & Voß to Reichsbank Direktorium, 24.8.23. The Hamburg shipyards raised $63,500 in response to the government's appeal. See also Lindenlaub, *Maschinenbauunternehmen*, p. 176.
[76] WA, 34, Pol. Corr. 1923, Warburg Notiz, 2.8.23; Warburg, Aufzeichnungen MSS, pp. 299f.

Under these circumstances, it was only a matter of time before disillusionment with the so-called 'discountable' (i.e., creditworthy) government drove Cuno from the Chancellery. The liberal and the Catholic press launched a series of scathing attacks on the government, disparaging the 'Cuno legend':

The man with the American connections stood revealed [in his nationalistic speeches] as a politician after the heart of the German *Hausfrau* [. . .But] what was the point of having Dr Becker in the cabinet, the functionary of leading industries, or Dr Hermes, Klöckner's son-in-law? Why did we bother with the whole 'discountable' government if the industrialists and bankers sabotaged the loan?[77]

To this, Cuno and his advisers responded by complaining about the central government's lack of domestic political power:

Unfortunately, industry and the banking world had left him in the lurch. He greatly regret[ted] that he had so little power as Chancellor to act domestically in the way that he wanted to. In foreign policy, he would yet achieve his objective; but in domestic politics the Reich government had damned little influence. In Prussia there was a socialist government, in Bavaria a far Right one, in Saxony a Communist government, and in Thuringia another socialist one. That naturally made things enormously difficult for the government. [. . .] The only way to improve matters would be a dictatorship.[78]

Although Cuno added that such a remedy was 'obviously impossible at the present time', it is clear that such authoritarian yearnings were growing more prevalent in government circles. In conversation with the Chancellor, Melchior too attacked the 'current *Länder-Wirtschaft* [. . . whereby] the Reich has the legislative power, the *Land* the executive, and what is decided at the Reich level is either ignored in Bavaria, Saxony and Prussia, or done quite differently'. His proposed solution, the establishment of the Rhineland and Westphalia as separate *Länder*, implied nothing less than the break-up of Prussia:

It is quite clear to me, that this could lead to the transition to a unitary state and perhaps the secession of Bavaria, or at least Old-Bavaria (without Franconia and Swabia); for if the Rhine and the Ruhr were to become independent, [then] Hanover, probably also East Prussia – as well as, in Cuno's view, Upper Silesia – would constitute themselves as independent [. . .] *Länder*. Prussia would thus disintegrate. I put forward my view that a transition [. . .]

[77] Thomas Wehrlin, 'Nachruf auf Cuno', *Das Tagebuch*, 19.5.23, pp. 700–4; Georg Bernhard, 'Fünf vor Zwölf', *Vossische Zeitung*, Nr. 309, 3.7.23. The most sustained attacks were in *Germania*, Nr. 205, 27.7.23; Nr. 206, 28.7.23; Nr. 217, 8.8.23; Nr. 218, 9.8.23.
[78] HA, HB, Holtzendorf to Hapag, 7.4.23.

to a unitary state [. . .] would mean an enormous strengthening of Germany.[79]

In a similar vein, the Justice Minister Heinze called for a simplification of the decision-making process at the centre:

Whereas there were only two institutions under the Bismarckian constitution – the united governments in the Bundesrat and the Reichstag – today the minister has to deal with the Reich cabinet; the governments of the *Länder*, with their democratic peculiarities, the *Reichswirtschaftsrat* – in all around eight institutions before whom he must appear.[80]

Warburg too was thinking in terms of centralisation. In August he discussed with Stinnes 'giving dictatorial blanket powers to a Finance Minister along with a few other men', thus creating a '*Finanzdirektorium*', '*Consilium*' or '*Kuratorium*', composed (in Warburg's version) of the Chancellor, Bergmann, Graf Roedern (the wartime State Secretary at the Treasury) and Otto Henrich.[81] Similar daydreams might have been been understandable in the face of the institutional paralysis of the relative stabilisation period. In 1923, however, they represented a disingenuous attempt to shift the blame for the political crisis away from business. It was significant that, at the same time, Warburg called for the 'depoliticisation of the money supply, so that the economy [could] function, independently of the current state-form and holders of power' and 'the old world view of work, pay and parsimony' could be preserved.[82] In some ways, his vision of independent monetary authorities, freed not only from the constraints of gold but also from the inflationary instincts of governments, was ahead of its time – like Melchior's vision of the break up of Prussia. In the context of 1923, however, such views more truly reflected the cavalier attitude businessmen had developed towards the authority of the state. 'The parliamentary system in this form is at any event not the right solution for difficult times,' wrote Warburg in November 1923.[83] It would not be the last time that an economic crisis drove German businessmen to draw such conclusions.

In fact, the idea that Cuno and his colleagues might now attempt some kind of dictatorship was probably never more than a fantasy born of impotence; as Houghton noted on 24 July, 'the government seems [. . .] largely without initiative or power'.[84] Hilferding provided

[79] WA, 34, Pol. Corr. 1923, Melchior Notiz, 22.5.23; Melchior Angabe, 24.5.23.
[80] *Hamburger Nachrichten*, 5.6.23.
[81] WA, 34, Pol. Corr. 1923, Warburg to Holtzendorff, 5.8.23; BAK, R43 I/2357, Holtzendorff to Cuno, 6.8.23; Rupieper, *Cuno Government*, p. 212. Cf. Maier, *Recasting Bourgeois Europe*, pp. 382–4.
[82] WA, 34, Pol. Corr. 1923, Warburg (memorandum on currency), 12.8.23.
[83] *Ibid.* Warburg to Alice Warburg, 21.11.23,
[84] NAW, RG 59, 862.00/1272, Houghton to Hughes, 24.7.23.

the best rejoinder to the authoritarian fantasies of Cuno and his colleagues:

Each ministry says: it has nothing to do with me; it has to do with the other ministry. Financial policy and currency policy have to do with the Finance Ministry. Foreign exchange policy has to do with the Economics Ministry. [. . .] The entire question of wage negotiations belong[s] to the Labour Ministry. [. . .] The Finance Ministry has nothing to say about the financial administration of the government enterprises [because] the Railroad Minister [and] the Postal Minister forbid it. [. . .] Besides that, we have no relationship between this Cabinet and the Reichsbank, and that is the basis of all the evils.[85]

Even his own advisers had by now lost patience. At a DDP *Vorstand* meeting in July, Melchior, along with Moritz Bonn, Schacht and Dernburg, called for the 'reform of the currency' and the creation of a new *'Festmark'* (sound mark);[86] and it was the resolution drafted at this meeting for *Festmark* taxes, wages and savings certificates, which, when it was adopted by the DDP-DVP-Centre *Arbeitsgemeinschaft*, effectively served notice on Cuno that the parties were ready to resume control.[87] Cuno denounced the proposal as 'gunpowder, given the present conflicts of interest', and sought to preempt the parties with a belated programme of tough fiscal measures;[88] but when the Centre declared its willingness to form a Great Coalition with the SPD, he had little option but to resign.[89]

Like Brüning in 1932, Cuno could console himself that he had been within yards of success.[90] The reality was that politics by businessmen had been a disaster. This was not just because Cuno was a bad politician; though he certainly became a somewhat absurd figure in later years. It was because the kind of 'party-less', 'objective' politics which he sought to embody was riven with contradictions. Partly, the

---

[85] Feldman, *Great Disorder*, p. 691.
[86] BAK, R45 III/17, DDP Vorstand, 28.7.23. The DDP had been moving towards this position for some time; see *Hamburger Fremdenblatt*, 11.4.23; Warburg, *Aufzeichnungen*, p. 117. Significantly, both Petersen and Schacht spoke out against the idea of a dictatorship at this meeting; though Petersen later proposed uniting the Finance Ministry and the Economics Ministry; Rupieper, *Cuno Government*, p. 212.
[87] WA, 34, Pol. Corr. 1923, Melchior Angabe, 30.7.23; *Hamburger Fremdenblatt*, 30.7.23. See also Petersen's speech two weeks later, *Hamburger Fremdenblatt*, 17.8.23.
[88] WA, 34, Pol. Corr. 1923, Melchior Angabe, 30.7.23; Harbeck (ed.), *Kabinett Cuno*, Nr. 211, n.3; Feldman, *Great Disorder*, pp. 695ff.
[89] Rupieper, *Cuno Government*, pp. 211–17; Harbeck (ed.), *Kabinett Cuno*, pp. 733–43; Maier, *Recasting Bourgeois Europe*, p. 373.
[90] This was Warburg's view, based on the coincidence of Cuno's fall and a note from Curzon to Poincaré criticising the Ruhr occupation; WA, 34, Pol. Corr. 1923, Warburg to Cuno, 13.8.23; Warburg to Paul Warburg, 14.8.23. For Cuno's own version of events, *ibid.*, Melchior Angabe, 16.8.23; HA, HB, Cuno to Gildemeister, 22.1.24.

problem was that Cuno overestimated the international power of business: with hindsight, his desire to draw American and British economic interests into a solution of the reparations problem tended in the right direction; but the breakthrough could not come as quickly as he had hoped. The main weakness of Cuno's position, however, was that the strategy of passive resistance, intended to weaken the French position, required significant material sacrifices from business, which he was incapable of exacting. Time and again, private interests prevailed over the national interest, preventing the necessary fiscal and monetary policies from being implemented. As a result, the 'discountable' government could only finance its nationalistic policy of passive resistance by printing money, a strategy which, paradoxically but inevitably, tended to undermine the integrity of the nation itself.

Dissolution

Cuno's fall was not merely the result of party-political manoeuvring in Berlin. The parties were galvanised into action by the acute economic, social and political crisis precipitated as the hyperinflation reached its climax. Moreover, the same crisis began to undermine the ability of business interests to exercise their 'veto-power' against stabilisation. By the end of August 1923, any remaining economic benefits of inflation had almost disappeared, leading to illiquidity and sharp falls in output, exports and employment. Having effectively abandoned the sinking ship of the state, in other words, businessmen found that their own enterprises were foundering. Moreover, the social crisis caused by this *de facto* stabilisation threatened the capitalist economic order itself: political authority threatened to be swept away by the centrifugal tendencies which Cuno had blamed for his impotence as Chancellor. Certain aspects of this phenomenon are familiar – the Bavarian government's defiance of central government, the increasing influence of the Communists in Saxony, the separatist drift in the Rhineland, the tendency of the Ruhr industrialists to negotiate independently with the French forces. Yet these were only the most politically striking manifestations of a general process of dissolution. The disintegrative forces unleashed by hyperinflation proved hard to resist, even when there was no radical political inclination – or foreign pressure – to break with Berlin.

As we have seen, the Reichsbank's credit policy in late 1922 and the financing of the *Ruhrkampf* had led to a dramatic increase in the rate of monetary growth. However, the trend of prices and the exchange rate in hyperinflation did not directly correlate to monetary expansion. On the contrary, it was the relative sluggishness of money supply growth which prevented the public's pessimistic expectations about the currency from pushing prices to infinity. Expectations of the complete collapse of the currency expressed themselves in bouts of rapid depreciation of the mark against the dollar; and in roughly synchronised leaps in domestic prices.[91] But the growth rate of currency in circulation consistently lagged behind. For example, in August 1922, the mark fell by 130 per cent against the dollar; wholesale prices rose by 91 per cent; the cost of living by 44 per cent; but narrow money by just 24 per cent, leading to a slowing in depreciation and inflation the following month. The same happened in November 1922, January 1923 and May 1923. On each occasion, the upward surge of prices was braked by monetary forces, and in March 1923 actually reversed.[92] Only from June 1923 did monetary growth rates match and even outstrip the rates of depreciation and inflation.[93] This can be expressed another way: up until this point, the real money supply was subject to bouts of contraction.[94]

Moreover, although the trend of real wages and salaries was downwards over the year of hyperinflation, increasingly frequent nominal increases coupled with occasional slackening in inflation periodically drove real pay levels upwards, notably in March and August/September 1923.[95] The position of public sector employees improved as a result of ageements which extended indexation and introduced quarterly payment in advance.[96] In the private sector, once again, the system of arbitration expedited wage demands. In December 1922 the management of Blohm & Voß was obliged to grant pay claims of 60–70 per cent on the previous month, as well as uniform bonus payments which had the effect of eroding still further the wage differentials separating skilled from unskilled workers.[97] By June 1923, wage increases of 30–

---

[91] August Behrmann, a senior figure at Warburg's, recalled how employees in the neighbouring Hapag building used binoculars to follow the hourly fluctuations in the exchange rate as they were recorded in the bank; they then ran to the Karstadt department store in their lunchbreaks 'to change wages into goods', or went to the harbour to buy dollars from newly arrived sailors; Rosenbaum and Sherman, *M.M. Warburg & Co.*, p. 163.

[92] The comparable figures for November 1922 are 126 per cent, 104 per cent, 102 per cent and 59 per cent; for January 1923, 137 per cent, 89 per cent, 63 per cent and 54 per cent; and for May 1923, 95 per cent, 57 per cent, 29 per cent and 31 per cent. Price controls also continued to play a part in restraining prices, but were of diminishing importance.

[93] See figure 7.1.

[94] See figure 5.4. The real value of Reichsbank notes in circulation sank to 170 m. gold marks at the inflationary peaks of January 24–31 and July 24–31; 80 m. gold marks in the first week of August; and below 50 m. gold marks in mid October; Webb, 'Fiscal News', p. 788.

[95] See figure 2.12.

[96] Lyth, '*Mittelstand*', pp. 241f., 249f.; Feldman, *Great Disorder*, pp. 679f.

[97] StAH, B&V 228, Bd. 2, Blohm & Voß to Rudolf Blohm, 9.12.22; 23.12.22.

40 per cent per week were the norm; and, by the following month, the Labour Ministry was imposing 55–70 per cent increments.[98] As the firm's negotiators noted, they and the other North German employers had come to accept such increases with 'equanimity, not to say fatalism'.[99]

Inevitably, this tendency for wages and prices to surge ahead of monetary growth placed intolerable strains on the financial system which, as noted above, had already broken down once in the summer of 1922. As the big Hamburg employers' weekly wage bills soared upwards, the banks struggled to provide the necessary cash.[100] The final collapse seems to have been precipitated by the attempt to peg the exchange rate, which artificially reduced the demand for foreign currency. In August, the Hamburg banks operating giral payments were forced to adopt a three-day week, subsequently refusing to process transactions smaller than 50 m. marks,[101] while firms like Blohm & Voß and the Hapag found that their weekly delivery of Reichsbank notes no longer sufficed to meet the wages bill in full.[102] In a vain attempt to fill the monetary gap, the main Hamburg banks announced the issue of 'emergency money' in the form of 2 m. and 5 m. mark notes; while the Hapag illegally printed 600 bn. marks of its own *Gutscheine*, warning that if the Reichsbank could not satisfy its requirements, it could not be held responsible for 'the further development of the situation'.[103] In rural areas, local authorities did the same, inscribing suitably melancholy mottos after the rows of noughts: '*Zarte Sehnsucht, süßes Hoffen; So leben wir, so leben wir*'; or: '*Und sut et ut ok noch so schlecht, dat treckt sich allens wedder torecht*'.[104] According to one estimate, there were around seventy different forms of money in circulation in Hamburg in August 1923, including money made of

[98] *Ibid.*, Blohm & Voß to Rudolf Blohm, 23.6.23; 7.7.23; 14.7.23; 21.7.23; B&V 1368, NDG Sitzung, 5.7.23; 6.8.23.
[99] StAH, FA B&V 228, Bd. 2, Blohm & Voß to Rudolf Blohm, 7.7.23.
[100] See for example *Ibid.*, Blohm & Voß, transactions at Vereinsbank, 2–8.12.22; 9–15.12.22; 16–22.12.22. One symptom of the pressure on the financial system was the unprecedented level of clerical employment in the banking sector, which rose to around 8,000, more than double the number in 1907; Lyth, '*Mittelstand*', p. 166.
[101] *Hamburger Nachrichten*, 30.7.23; 7.9.23; F. Rittstieg, 'Der Zusammenbruch des Hamburger Giroverkehrs und seine Ursachen', *Der Zahlungsverkehr*, 5. Jg., 11/12 (1923), pp. 221ff.
[102] BAK, R43 I/666; Strandes to Geheimrat Kempner (?).8.23.
[103] *Hamburgische Correspondent*, 11.8.23; HA, HB, Warnholtz to Holtzendorff, 20.8.23; Hapag to Holtzendorff, 22.8.23; Holtzendorff to Warnholtz, 24.8.23; Holtzendorff to Hapag, 27.8.23. Such *Notgeld* could only be issued if equivalent sums were deposited at the Reichsbank; Lindenlaub, *Maschinenbauunternehmen*, p. 193; Webb, *Hyperinflation*, pp. 14f.; Holtfrerich, *Inflation*, p. 310. Cf. Karl Lund, *Das Papiernotgeld von Schleswig-Holstein und Hamburg*, 1914–23 (Berlin, 1971).
[104] Lippmann, *Leben*, pp. 318f.; Warburg, Aufzeichnungen MSS, p. 307.

porcelain, iron, cork and leather.[105] Yet such expedients did not suffice. Even if one includes all the various forms of emergency money (1.1 bn. gold marks) and foreign currency (2–3 bn. gold marks) which were being used as domestic cash in late 1923, the total real value of currency in circulation was still substantially less than in 1914.[106]

The effect of this real monetary contraction, in the context of the dislocation caused by the *Ruhrkampf*, was that the deflationary crisis arrived well in advance of any currency reform. Total industrial production fell by 34 per cent in 1923, with mining (45 per cent) not surprisingly taking the lead and ship-building production falling by around a third.[107] There were sharp falls in all investment indicators.[108] The Hapag, for example, halted its building programme and concentrated instead on hoarding foreign currency and paying off debts in worthless paper marks.[109] Moreover, although exports fell, imports fell further, so that the money trade deficit all but vanished in 1923 in real terms – another sign of *de facto* deflation.[110] This contraction soon had its effect on employment levels. The national unemployment rate for trade union members rose from around 2 per cent in mid 1922 to over 25 per cent at the end of 1923; and although this was lower than the peak of unemployment in 1932, the much higher proportion of workers on short time in 1923 suggests that the severity of the earlier crisis was not incomparable.[111] The rise in unemployment in Hamburg was rather less than at the national level: the number of registered unemployed rose from its trough of 8,000 (around 2 per cent of the labour force) in June 1922 to a peak of 57,000 (13 per cent) in December 1923; but at least 10,000 workers were on short time.[112] As might be expected from the output data, it was the capital

[105] Büttner, *Politische Gerechtigkeit*, p. 155.
[106] Holtfrerich, *Inflation*, p. 312.
[107] See figures 1.2, 2.4 and 2.5. As in 1922, consumer goods industries benefited from the stimulus to demand provided by the flight into goods; see figure 2.7. Agricultural production was actually higher than in 1922. On ship-building, see NAW, RG 59, 862.00, Hopper reports January–June 1923; Deutsche Werft, *Jahresbericht 1923*.
[108] See figure 2.6. Cf. Graham, *Hyperinflation*, pp. 306–12; Webb, *Hyperinflation*, pp. 253f.
[109] Hapag, *Jahresbericht 1922*; *Hamburgische Correspondent*, 1.4.23.
[110] See figures 4.2, 4.3 and 4.4. In volume terms, however, the deficit remained wider: see figure 4.6. The Economics Ministry was oblivious to this, continuing to argue that depreciation would make German exports more competitive; StAH, SK II, II A 4 Fasc. 29, Inv. 1, HG to AK, 19.12.22; Specht, *Politische Hintergründe*, pp. 107n., 110n. Because of the distorting effect of the Ruhr occupation, the volume of Hamburg's trade expanded in 1923. Almost 50 per cent of German exports passed through Hamburg in 1923; calculated from *Statistisches Handbuch 1920*, p. 153; Büttner, *Politische Gerechtigkeit*, p. 687; Brandt, *Hamburgs Finanzen*, p. 92; Meyer, *Hamburg*, p. 107.
[111] See figure 2.10.
[112] See figure 3.1; NAW, RG 59, 862.504/144, Theodore Jaeckel to State Dept., 7.11.23.

goods industries which were first to shed labour: Deutsche Werft began to lay off workers in March 1923, and by October had reduced its workforce more than 50 per cent.[113] Employment at Blohm & Voß reached a belated post-war peak in February 1923 (11,113 workers), only to slump rapidly thereafter to just over 8,000 in October 1923.[114] Smaller businesses, by contrast, encountered difficulties as early as November 1922, when it was reported that 12–15 per cent of artisans had closed their workshops.[115]

This crisis precipitated a new wave of popular unrest: rising unemployment was as destabilising in the summer of 1923 as the onset of hyperinflation had been a year before. In the first instance, there was an upsurge of strike action, as workers sought to defend their crumbling position: in all there were eighty-eight strikes in Hamburg during 1923, involving 100,000 workers.[116] The culmination came in August 1923, after workers at Blohm & Voß had for the first time tabled a demand for 'stable-money wages' (*wertbeständige Löhne*).[117] A lock-out by the company triggered a rash of wildcat strikes along the Hamburg waterfront – part of the nationwide bout of industrial action which was one of the decisive factors in Cuno's fall.[118] Yet this flaring of unrest was a sign more of the increasing weakness of the workers' position than of their strength: *de facto* deflation tended to undermine the collective power of labour, reducing trade union membership and eroding the bargaining power of labour (see figure 7.2). Significantly, Deutsche Werft was able to make the resumption of work conditional upon the sacking of 200 'trouble makers', including eight members of the works' council.[119] Moreover, a distinctive feature of the strife in 1923 was the friction within the labour force between unionised and 'wild' strikers.[120] And, as the dramatic increase in the number of crimes against property suggests, more and more individuals were being driven to illegal forms of 'self help' as they struggled to weather the economic storm – one of a number of symptoms of social malaise

---

[113] GHH, 300193012/8, Deutsche Werft to Reusch, 10.3.23; Deutsche Werft to Reusch, 24.8.23; Deutsche Werft Report, July–October 1923. Cf. NAW, RG 59, 862.504/ 82, Malcolm C. Burke to State Dept., 24.2.23.

[114] See figure 3.2.

[115] Lyth, '*Mittelstand*', pp. 310f.

[116] *Ibid.*, p. 84.

[117] StAH, B&V 228, Bd. 2, Blohm & Voß to Rudolf Blohm, 21.7.23. Cf. Büttner, *Politische Gerechtigkeit*, p. 147; Feldman, *Great Disorder*, pp. 673–7.

[118] GHH, 300193012/8, Deutsche Werft to Reusch, 14.8.23, 17.8.23; WA, 34, Pol. Corr., Warburg to Alice Warburg, 13.8.23. Cf. W. Ersel, *Aktionseinheit stürzt Cuno: Zur Geschichte des Massenkampfes gegen die Cuno Regierung 1923 in Mitteldeutschland* (Berlin, 1963).

[119] GHH, 300193012/8, Deutsche Werft to Reusch, 17.8.23.

[120] BAP, RMI 13360 36, SK to RMI, 12.9.23.

35000000
30000000
25000000
20000000
15000000
10000000
5000000
0
1900
1902
1904
1906
1908
1910
1912
1914
1916
1918
1920
1922
1924
1926
1928
1930
1932
Total membership of 'Big Three' unions
Duration of strikes (working days)
Duration of lockouts (working days)
Numbers covered by collective agreements

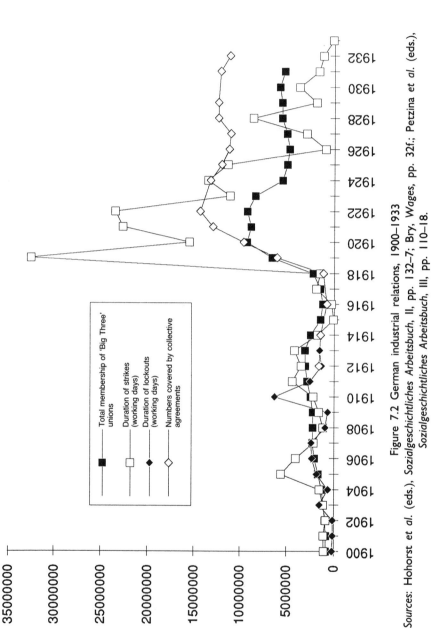

Figure 7.2 German industrial relations, 1900–1933

Sources: Hohorst *et al.* (eds.), *Sozialgeschichtliches Arbeitsbuch*, II, pp. 132–7; Bry, *Wages*, pp. 32f.; Petzina *et al.* (eds.), *Sozialgeschichtliches Arbeitsbuch*, III, pp. 110–18.

peculiar to the crisis of 1923.[121] This breakdown of collectivism clearly worked to the advantage of the more radical elements in the KPD, whose membership rose by 7,000 to 18,000 in the eighteen months after April 1922.[122] Although the party's official policy was now to promote a 'united front' with the SPD, with a view to establishing leftist *Länder* governments like the ones which emerged in Saxony and Thuringia in October, there was mounting pressure on the Berlin *Zentrale* to adopt a more overtly revolutionary strategy. A leading proponent of insurrection was the Hamburg radical Ernst Thälmann, who was preparing for revolutionary action even as his superior, Hugo Urbahn, was attempting to strike a bargain with the SPD.[123] The way ahead was pointed by the KPD's attempt to turn the August strikes into a general strike, which led to violent clashes with police and the imposition of a week-long state of emergency.[124]

There were similar developments on the extreme Right, however. Like the conflict over Upper Silesia in 1921, the *Ruhrkampf* provided ideal conditions for nationalist, para-military organisations like the Bismarckbund and the Stahlhelm. Not only was the public mood favourable to their 'patriotic' demonstrations; the Reichswehr regarded them as 'black' (unofficial) units and provided them with arms and ammunition.[125] The Hamburg authorities sought to ban right-wing demonstrations, but were quite powerless to combat the Reichswehr's activities.[126] At the same time, the *völkisch* anti-Semitic associations continued to operate covertly, despite the bans imposed on them in 1922.[127] Max Warburg was stung into legal action by a series of libels in anti-Semitic journals like the *Hammer* and the *Völkische Beobachter*.[128]

---

[121] See figure 4.10. Note the far lower increase of crimes against property in 1929–32.

[122] A. Voß, 'Der Hamburger Aufstand im Oktober 1923', in A. Voß, U. Büttner and H. Weber, *Vom Hamburger Aufstand zur politischen Isolierung. Kommunistische Politik in Hamburg und im Dritten Reich* (Hamburg, 1983), pp. 24f.; Büttner, *Politische Gerechtigkeit*, pp. 158ff.; *idem, Staats- und Wirtschaftskrise*, p. 522 n. 41; Rettig, 'Gewerkschaftsarbeit der KPD von 1918 bis 1925'. The big shipyards and the outlying 'rent barrack' areas of Barmbek and Schiffbek provided many of the new recruits. For KPD penetration of the Deutsche Werft works' council, see GHH, 300193012/8, Deutsche Werft to Reusch, 3.10.23.

[123] Voß, 'Aufstand', pp. 16, 28–33.

[124] BAP, RMI 13360 36, Polizeibehörde Hamburg to RMI, 16.8.23; Voß, 'Aufstand', pp. 15f.

[125] *Hamburger Echo*, 16.1.23; 23/24.1.23; 15/16.5.23; *Hamburger Volkszeitung*, 26.6.23; Jochmann, *Nationalsozialismus*, pp. 38–46.

[126] BAK, R43 I/2730, Stolten to RK, 12.5.23; Harbeck, *Das Kabinett Cuno*, pp. 551f., 603–5; BAP, RMI 13359 36, Reichswehrministerium to Senate, 25.7.23.

[127] StAH, Staatliche Pressestelle, *Mitteilungen*, Nr. 217, 10.7.23.

[128] See WA, 33, Pol. Corr. 1923, for material relating to Warburg's lawsuit in Hamburg against Theodor Fritsch in February 1923 for articles in *Der Hammer*, Nr. 471, 473 and 475 alleging (among other things) that Warburg had financed the Russian revolution; also the article 'Bankjude und "Arbeiterführer"', *Völkische Beobachter*, Nr. 23, 22.2.23. Cf. Lorenz, *Juden in Hamburg*, II, p. 1019; Chernow, *Warburgs*,

Yet the courts provided less redress to the litigant than publicity to the defendants; while a measure of respectability was lent to anti-Semitism by the decision of the Hamburg DNVP (in advance of the national party) to exclude Jews from party membership.[129]

As the crisis deepened, anxious observers likened the situation in October 1923 to that before the revolution five years before.[130] Yet there was a fundamental difference: in 1918 it was the dearth of food and other essentials which did most to undermine stability, whereas the problem in 1923 was the absence of a functioning currency. This was more manifestly a failure of the Reich than the crisis of 1918 had been. Although attempts had been made, there had been no realistic possibility of individual regions circumventing the Allied blockade; but in 1923 the possibility of self help by the *Länder* was a real one. As Cuno's advisers had rightly said, a state incapable of providing a functioning currency was bound to forfeit its authority; and it is in these terms that the centrifugal tendencies of mid 1923 should be understood. The various regional attempts to challenge the authority of the Reich government all to some extent represented attempts to overcome the economic dysfunction of the German state, of which the worthlessness of the mark was merely the most obvious symptom. In Bavaria or Saxony, the solutions contemplated were based on a political critique of the Weimar system. Others – such as those tried in the Rhineland and the Ruhr – simply reflected the occupation of those regions by a more credible national authority with which it made sense to deal. By contrast, the response of Hamburg to the collapse of the currency was narrowly economic, rather than political. While Hamburg state foundered and the Reich neared collapse, the Hamburg business community took it upon itself to create a viable dollar-based currency and to set up a central bank for the eventuality of the collapse of the Reich. Moreover, unlike a comparable project in the Rhineland, the Hamburg currency actually came into being.[131]

p. 270. For renewed attempts by Warburg to combat anti-Semitism by persuasion, WA, 33, Pol. Corr. 1923, Warburg to Stinnes, 3.1.23; Warburg to Dr H. Samson, 30.3.23; Warburg to Rabbiner, 1.4.23; Warburg to Mortimer L. Schiff, 7.6.23.

[129] WA, 34, Pol. Corr. 1923, Warburg to Holtzendorff, 9.6.23; cf. *Sten. Ber. d. Bürgerschaft*, 5. Sitzung, 31.1.23, for DNVP's attacks on the Institut für auswärtige Angelegenheiten. The *reductio ad absurdum* of such allegations was the claim that the Organisation Escherisch, which had been responsible for the assassination of Rathenau, was 'a judified association, [and] received regular funding from Jewish sources, including Max Warburg'; BAP, RKfdÜöO 67104, Bl. 42, Nachrichtenkopf Schleswig to RKfdÜöO, 8.10.23.

[130] PRO, FO 371/8795/C15712, British Consul General in Hamburg, Report, 4.9.23: 'The well-to-do classes are chiefly concerned [. . .] lest the looting that went on at the time of the revolution should be repeated.' For Melchior's more sanguine view, Keynes, *Collected Writings*, XVIII, pp. 212f.

[131] M. Vogt, 'Ansätze für eine rheinische Währung im Spätsommer und Herbst 1923', in Büsch and Feldman (eds.). *Historische Prozess*, pp. 432–42; McDougall, *France's*

The roots of this highly successful expedient can be traced back to the growing demand among Hamburg firms for the creation of some kind of 'value-retaining' currency. This went further than the idea of 'gold mark calculation' (i.e., the use of a dollar deflator in private business calculations) which Warburg and others had begun propagating since mid 1922.[132] By March 1923, there was increasing support for the idea (first advanced by the Economics Ministry official Rudolf Dalberg) of allowing gold mark accounts, similar to the 'mark banco' accounts used for commercial transactions in the mid nineteenth century.[133] Such a step was opposed by the Reichsbank and the banking establishment (including Warburg), mainly on the grounds that the new accounts would have the effect of irreparably undermining the paper mark, thus forfeiting prematurely 'the advantage of cheap wages and salaries' and leading to intolerable levels of unemployment.[134] All attempts to replace the paper mark before a reform of the Reich's finances, argued Warburg, would simply 'emancipate [the] private sector from the Reich's misfortune, giving rise to confusion, price fluctuations and desperation on such a scale that a collapse of the Reich into revolution would occur'.[135] Yet the bankers were attempting to resist what was (as Warburg himself admitted) an 'elemental movement'.[136] As the monetary crisis became more acute, commercial and industrial firms simply took matters into their own hands. It is clear, for instance, from the arguments put forward by Walther Dauch in a long memorandum to Cuno that his firm had gone over to using gold (i.e., dollar) accounts by July 1923. Dauch argued for the creation of a *Neumark* equivalent to 10 cents, and stressed not only the politically stabilising effects of such a step but also the historic precedent for it:

Here in Hamburg alone, we would pull at least 30,000–40,000 people back out of the radical current and turn them into reliable citizens. Just as Hamburg

Rhineland Diplomacy, pp. 202f.; Maier, *Recasting Bourgeois Europe*, pp. 398–403. See in general H.O. Schötz, *Die Kampf um die Mark 1923/24. Die deutsche Währungsstabilisierung unter dem Einfluß der nationalen Interessen Frankreichs, Großbritanniens und der USA* [*Beiträge zur Inflation und Wiederaufbau in Deutschland und Europa, 1914–1924*, Bd. 9] (Berlin/New York, 1987).

[132] WA, 19, Gesammelte Vorträge, Max Warburg, 'Deutsche und internationale Finanzprobleme in ihrer Bedeutung für die deutsche Industrie' (speech at RdI members' meeting) 22.5.22; and his article in the *Hamburger Fremdenblat*, 3.1.23. However, Warburg opposed the complex system of calculation proposed by the economist Eugen Schmalenbach: WA, 31, Warburg Angabe, 28.2.23; Warburg, Aufzeichnungen MSS, 28.3.23.

[133] *Bank-Archiv*, Nr. 13, 1.4.23, pp. 165f.

[134] WA, 31, Pol. Corr. 1923, Warburg Notiz, 'Goldmark-Besprechung', 1.3.23; *Hamburger Fremdenblatt*, 1.3.23; Warburg, Aufzeichnungen MSS, p. 264; Max von Schinckel, 'Zur sog. Bankowährung', *Bank Archiv*, Nr. 12, 15.3.23, pp. 153f. Cf. Rupieper, *Cuno Government*, p. 193; Feldman, *Great Disorder*, pp. 690ff.

[135] WA, 31, Pol. Corr. 1923, Warburg Aufgabe, 15.7.23.

[136] *Ibid.*

once played a ground-breaking role in Germany with its banco-mark, so [it] should now [. . .] set [a similar] example for the whole Reich.[137]

Dauch was not alone in going on to the dollar of his own accord. As early as April 1923, Blohm & Voß was investigating the possibility of establishing gold mark 'savings' accounts for its employees, with the intention of reducing the amount of paper that had to be found for wage packets each week.[138] The first accounts were set up in early July.[139]

By the beginning of August 1923, the 'possibility of a disintegration of the Reich' was being openly discussed in Hamburg business circles; the pressure 'to isolate Hamburg from the general disintegration of Germany and from the further collapse of the currency' was becoming increasingly difficult to resist.[140] On 12 September, Franz Witthoefft informed Warburg, the Director of the Commerzbank, Lincke, and a representative of the cooperative *Produktion*, that the Hamburg Economic Council now supported the idea of establishing some kind of gold note bank – the first time the possibility of note issue had been broached.[141] The proposal was seconded by Dauch at a Chamber of Commerce meeting two days later;[142] and by 16 September Warburg had grudgingly delegated his employee Spiegelberg to draw up the statutes of such a bank.[143] It was already clear that the foreign currency necessary to create a Hamburg hard currency was readily available: Warburg himself had already succeeded in raising substantial foreign currency loans for both the Hapag ($2 m.) and the Hamburg state (£1 m.).[144] Nevertheless, he and the other bankers remained hesitant.[145] From the outset, Warburg stipulated that any bank should only provide facilities for gold mark-denominated accounts, and should not formally issue notes. Moreover, although Spiegelberg's report was submitted to

[137] BAK, R43 I/2435 Walther Dauch to Cuno, 12.7.23.
[138] StAH, FA B&V 491, Schlubach, Thiemer & Co. to Blohm & Voß, 25.4.23; Carl Dörner to W. Blohm, 26.6.23.
[139] StAH, FA B&V 228, Bd. 2, Blohm & Voß to Rudolf Blohm, 7.7.23; B&V 491, Noltenius to Rosenstiel, 8.8.23; Rosenstiel to Noltenius, 14.8.23; NDG (draft plan), 22.8.23.
[140] HA, HB, Hopff to Holtzendorff, 25.8.23; Warburg, Aufzeichnungen MSS, p. 302. Cf. StAH, FA B&V 1286, Bd. 2, Blohm & Voß to RdI, 5.9.23.
[141] WA, 34, Pol. Corr. 1923, Spiegelberg Notiz, 12.9.23.
[142] HKH, HKHP, 14.9.23. The Chamber itself was on the brink of insolvency and had to be baled out by Warburg's five days later with a loan of 10 bn. marks; WA, 35, Pol. Corr. 1923, HKH to Warburg, 19.9.23; Warburg, *Aufzeichnungen*, p. 118.
[143] WA, 34, Pol. Corr. 1923, Warburg Aufgabe, 16.9.23. Again the rate of 10 gold marks to the dollar was envisaged.
[144] WA, 'Jahresbericht 1923', p. 32; Warburg, Aufzeichnungen MSS, p. 315; *idem, Aufzeich-nungen*, p. 73. Cf. NAW, RG 59, 862.51/1725, Jaeckel to State Dept., 27.10.23.
[145] WA, 'Ansprache anläßlich der Bilanzbesprechung für das Geschäftsjahr 1923', 27.8.24; Warburg, Aufzeichnungen MSS, p. 315.

the Chamber of Commerce on 1 October, three weeks later still nothing concrete had emerged.[146] In the meantime, the city's economy teetered on the brink of collapse. The Senate struggled to bridge the widening gap between welfare payments to the unemployed and the price of bread; but the funds made available to its Emergency Commission were constantly eroded by inflation.[147] Despite continued issues of emergency money, more and more firms found themselves simply unable to carry on business for want of functioning money.[148] It was only the breakdown of public order which persuaded the bankers to stop dragging their feet.

The Communist *Aufstand* of October 1923, though bloody, probably never posed a serious threat to the Hamburg authorities.[149] Either in ignorance or in defiance of the Berlin *Zentrale*'s decision to abandon a nationwide coup attempt, Thälmann and his associates took as their cue a new bout of strike action on the Hamburg waterfront; but they lacked the manpower and the popular support to overcome the city's *Ordnungspolizei* outside the KPD strongholds of Barmbek and Schiffbek.[150] Once again, the fear of revolution, so often invoked as an argument against stabilisation measures, proved exaggerated. The rising merely provided conclusive proof that the time for a Hamburg currency had come. As the *Hamburgische Correspondent* put it:

If we succeed in creating a new currency within three days, so that the people know how they are going to pay for their bread, all political issues will immediately lose their intensity [. . .] Stubborn adherence to the currency unit of the Reich poses the greatest threat of all to the unity of the Reich.[151]

---

[146] M. Försterling, 'Die Hamburgische Bank von 1923 Aktiengesellschaft', in *Hamburger Wirtschaftschronik*, 3 (1965), pp. 22ff. Cf. Pohl, *Bankengeschichte*, pp. 136–8; T. Plaut, 'Die Hamburgische Bank von 1923: ihre Organisation, Entwicklung und Bedeutung', *Deutsche Bergwerks Zeitung*, 2/3.2.24.

[147] Büttner, *Politische Gerechtigkeit*, pp. 156–9. In a humiliating change of tune, the Hamburg SPD was reduced to pleading that 'if all else fails' the government should 'use the Reichswehr to provide the people with the necessities of life'.

[148] Försterling, 'Hamburgische Bank', pp. 23f.; *Hamburger Fremdenblatt*, 13.10.23; HA, HB, Holtzendorff to Hopff, 24.10.23.

[149] Details in Voß, 'Aufstand', pp. 9–43; H. Habedank, *Zur Geschichte des Hamburger Aufstandes 1923* (Berlin, 1958), pp. 92–187; W.D. Hund, *Der Aufstand der KPD 1923* (Opladen, 1983), pp. 32–61.

[150] BAP, RMI 13359 36, Chef der Ordnungspolizei Hamburg to RMI, 'Bericht über die Unruhen in Hamburg vom 20.-26.10.23'. Cf. K.D. Erdmann and M. Vogt (eds.), *Die Kabinette Stresemann I und II* (Boppard am Rhein), II, p. 701. See also L. Reissner, *Hamburg at the Barricades and other Writings on Weimar Germany* (London, 1977), pp. 41–110; L. Peterson, 'A Social Analysis of KPD Supporters. The Hamburg Insurrectionaries of October 1923', *International Review of Social History*, 28, 2 (1983), pp. 200–39. On the strike at Deutsche Werft, GHH, 300193012/8, Deutsche Werft to Reusch, 29.20.23.

[151] *Hamburgische Correspondent*, Nr. 495, 23.10.23.

Even before the police had reestablished order, Melchior, Spiegelberg, Kaemmerer (for the Norddeutsche Bank) and Hübbe (for the Dresdner Bank) met Bürgermeister Diestel to put the finishing touches to the statutes of the Hamburg Bank of 1923 – 'forced' into action, as Warburg put it, 'by revolution'.[152] The bank (which formally came into being on 25 October) was a direct descendant of the Hamburg Bank of 1914 set up to weather the liquidity crisis precipitated by the war, and once again it was dominated by the established Hamburg banks. In theory, it was to provide, as Warburg had insisted, only deposit and direct debit facilities to its 103 founder firms, using a reserve of $3 m. (a quarter of which was paid in at once). However, almost at once, it began issuing 'certificates' against foreign currency deposits which were obviously gold mark notes in all but name.[153] By the end of October, most of the major employers, including the Hamburg state itself, were able, thanks to the bank, to pay their employees at least partly in these gold mark notes.[154]

The Hamburg dollar was more than a hasty response to social unrest. Although the leading figures on the bank's board insisted that the 'certificates' were only intended as a temporary device for the 'interim period [. . .] until the appearance of the expected new Reich currency', this was not entirely sincere.[155] As the one commentator put it: 'A sound Hamburg currency, based not on the state but on the economy, is possible; a sound Reich currency under the present circumstances is not.'[156] Indeed, the real rationale underlying the new bank was, as Spiegelberg put it

the general conviction that Hamburg must prepare itself for the danger of a further fragmentation of the German Reich as a result of the separatist movement in Bavaria, the forcible removal of the Rhineland and the Communist government in Saxony; and in this event would need a central bank.[157]

---

[152] Warburg, Aufzeichnungen MSS, p. 315; Försterling, 'Die Hamburgische Bank', pp. 24ff.

[153] Försterling, 'Die Hamburgische Bank', pp. 25ff. It is interesting that the bank was established on a dollar basis, rather than a sterling basis, and that the idea of a new gold mark–dollar exchange rate was abandoned in favour of the pre-war rate of 4.20 gold marks to the dollar.

[154] Försterling, 'Die Hamburgische Bank', pp. 44–8; StAH, FA B&V 530, Rudolf Blohm to Hamburgische Bank von 1923, 31.10.23. See aso NAW, RG 59, 862.515/ 64, US Consul in Hamburg to State Dept, 2.11.23.

[155] *Hamburgische Correspondent*, Nr. 497, 24.10.23; *Hamburger Börsen-Halle*, Nr. 504, 28.10.23.

[156] *Hamburger Börsen-Halle*, 1.11.23.

[157] Försterling, 'Die Hamburgische Bank', pp. 44f. It is not without significance, in this context, that the Hapag had elected to quit the RdI at around this time, in the belief that any attempt to reestablish the national currency would be accompanied by a heavy 'burdening of industry'; HA, HB, Hopff to Holtzendorff, 10.9.23; Holtzendorff to Warnholtz, 3.10.23.

Such fears were far from exaggerated. Throughout October, events in Bavaria were viewed with increasing alarm in Hamburg; and although there was little local support for the Hitler-Ludendorff *putsch* launched on 8 November,[158] Warburg was sufficiently concerned to leave Hamburg until it blew over; and was finally persuaded by friends and family to spend the rest of the year in New York.[159] As it happened, Warburg was right to think that the *putsch* had 'a whiff of Kapp' about it and was unlikely to last; but it undoubtedly added to fears that the Reich was falling apart. Under these circumstances, it was not surprising that the Hamburg Bank's dollar-based notes proved such a signal success. There was soon a considerable demand for the notes outside Hamburg; prompting one commentator to wonder whether 'perhaps the Hamburg currency might become the German currency, or even an international currency, as the Hamburg Girobank [i.e., the mark banco] once was'.[160]

Such aspirations indicate that the Hamburg business community remained fundamentally committed to the principle of German unity. The most radical political changes to be advocated in Hamburg continued to be concerned with reforming, rather than abandoning the federal system.[161] Nevertheless, as its founders and admirers discerned, the bank of 1923 did have an anti-national character in practice. In many ways, it was an institution which was at once particularist and cosmopolitan, recalling the days when the city had been more economically independent of the hinterland – and more international in its outlook. The effect of the *Ruhrkampf* and the ensuing hyperinflation on the German economy had been to recreate those conditions, throwing the hinterland into disarray and Hamburg back on its own resources. In short, events of 1923 in Hamburg confirmed that, to hold the Reich together, appeals to patriotic feeling were not enough. The federal state could not long survive without the prosaic economic bonds provided by a stable currency.

The liquidation of the inflation

The inflationary crisis of 1919–23 stands in the shadow of the deflationary crisis which occurred ten years later. This is hardly surprising:

[158] Jochmann, *Nationalsozialismus*, pp. 49ff.; T. Krause, 'Von der Sekte zur Massenpartei. Die Hamburger NSDAP von 1922 bis 1933', in M. Bruhns *et al.* (eds.), *'Hier war doch alles nicht so schlimm.' Wie die Nazis in Hamburg den Alltag eroberten* (Hamburg, 1984), p. 32.
[159] WA, 34, Pol. Corr. 1923, Warburg Notiz, 5.11.23; Warburg to Alice Warburg, 9.11.23; Warburg Aufzeichnungen MSS, p. 311; *idem, Aufzeichnungen*, pp. 120–5.
[160] T. Plaut, 'Dollargeld', *Hamburger Fremdenblatt*, 301, 31.10.23. See also StAH, FA B&V 530, Rudolf Blohm to Senator Berenberg-Goßler, 5.11.23.
[161] See, e.g., *Hamburger Fremdenblatt*, 26.10.23.

the principal casualty of the former was merely the established currency; while the latter crisis claimed the established constitution as its victim. Moreover, whereas the paper mark was replaced, ultimately, by a reichsmark that was little different in essentials from its pre-war predecessor, the Weimar constitution itself was replaced in 1933 by a radically different political system. Nevertheless, these contrasting outcomes should not blind us to the comparable severity of the earlier crisis. The collapse of the currency was simply one symptom of a political breakdown which was no less severe than the one which brought Hitler to power. On both occasions, it was necessary to invoke the Presidential powers under Article 48 and to pass Enabling Acts in order to free the executive from the constraints of both parliamentary parties and economic interest groups. And on both occasions, force had to be used to quell opposition to the new regime.

Contemporaries tended to look back on the creation of a new currency, the *Rentenmark*, in November 1923, as the watershed marking the end of the inflation; 'the saviour of Germany'.[162] This is misleading. The evaporation of the economic advantages of inflation clearly made the creation of a new currency inevitable; but if nothing more had been done, those forces which had been responsible for the collapse of the paper mark might easily have reasserted themselves, causing the new currency to go the way of the old. In order to prevent this, major institutional and political changes were required: amounting to what has been called a 'regime change'.[163] Firstly, and most importantly, a political change was necessary to replace the impotent and discredited Cuno government with one capable of overcoming the resistance of interest groups to essential monetary and fiscal reforms. Secondly, it was necessary to reform, if not replace, the Reichsbank, which since 1914 had relentlessly debased the currency in response to the alternating demands for credit of the private and public sectors. Thirdly, the chronic imbalance between income and expenditure in the Reich finances had to be brought to an end. Reform in these two areas inevitably had important implications for the economy as a whole, which had become attuned to setting prices and wages on the assumption of continuing inflation. Finally, a change in the international situation was needed, to bring about some kind of consensus on reparations. None of these was easily or quickly achieved.

---

[162] See, e.g., Warburg, *Aufzeichnungen*, p. 118.
[163] Sargent, 'The Ends of Four Big Inflations', pp. 41–97; H. James, 'Die Währungsstabilisierung 1923/4 in internationaler Perspektive', in Abelshauser (ed.), *Weimarer Republik als Wohlfahrtsstaat*, pp. 63–79; Maier, 'Inflation and Stabilisation', pp. 106–29; Holtfrerich, *Inflation*, pp. 301–30; Webb, *Hyperinflation*, pp. 65–74.

The resignation of Cuno on 12 August did nothing to end the crisis of the parliamentary system which had begun with the breakdown of Wirth's coalition. Stresemann's first Great Coalition ministry lasted little more than six weeks, during which time the Reichstag scarcely met, and fell when the Social Democrat Fraktion refused to support an Enabling Act which might infringe the revolutionary settlement on working hours.[164] The second Stresemann Cabinet secured an Enabling Act on 13 October, adjourned the Reichstag until 20 November, but fell three days after it reconvened when the Social Democrats once again withdrew their support.[165] From late September until mid November, there seemed a more than even chance of a military dictatorship being established – much as happened in Spain in 1923, Lithuania in 1924 and Poland in 1926. The state of emergency declared on 27 September (in respose to the Bavarian government's appointment of Gustav von Kahr as State Commissar) empowered General von Seeckt and the regional military commanders to take whatever measures they thought necessary to avert the break-up of the Reich; and this encouraged renewed speculation that the time had come for some kind of dictatorship – or 'Directory', as Seeckt preferred to call it.[166] Indeed, this might very well have been the outcome, had it not been for the hesitation of Seeckt himself, divisions within the Reichswehr and disagreements between the various businessmen (notably Stinnes and Friedrich Minoux) who favoured a dictatorship. Seeckt ousted the Socialist–Communist coalition which had been formed in Saxony; but hesitated to challenge the position of von Kahr in Bavaria, since the latter enjoyed the support of the local Reichswehr commander. When the attempted putsches in Hamburg and Munich failed without his intervention, Seeckt's moment had passed.[167] Nevertheless, the fall of the second Stresemann ministry revealed the continuing impossibility of parliamentary government. Eventually, after much prevarication by the parties and persuasion by President Ebert, a minority government

---

[164] H.A. Turner, *Stresemann and the Politics of the Weimar Republic* (Princeton, 1963), pp. 115ff.; Krohn, *Stabilisierung*, pp. 1–20; Maier, *Recasting Bourgeois Europe*, pp. 373–84; Feldman, *Great Disorder*, pp. 698f., 740f., 744.

[165] *Ibid.*, p. 800.

[166] See, e.g., NAW, RG 59, 862.00/1292, Houghton to State Dept., 4.10.23. In general, M. Vogt, 'Seeckt und die Vorbereitungen zur Stabilisierung der Mark', in Büsch and Feldman (eds.), *Historische Prozesse*, pp. 309–20; Feldman, *Great Disorder*, pp. 740f.. 775ff., 800.

[167] There is evidence that Warburg was in touch with Seeckt shortly before the intervention in Saxony and prior to the Munich *putsch*; WA, 34, Pol. Corr. 1923, Warburg Notiz, 19.10.23; Melchior Notiz, 3.11.23; but there were no direct appeals by business for Reichswehr intervention in Hamburg of the sort there had been in 1918/19.

was formed by the Centre leader Marx, empowered with an Enabling Act passed on 12 December, to run until 15 February. Yet even this can hardly be regarded as the moment of political stabilisation, for the Reichstag elections of 4 May saw the vote of the principal anti-Republican parties more than double.[168] Not until the elections of December 1924, when the anti-republican vote fell by 6.1 per cent to 32.5 per cent, could political stabilisation be spoken of with any confidence.

The steps towards monetary stabilisation were equally slow and tentative.[169] A superficially important breakthrough came on 18 August, when Havenstein informed the new Chancellor Stresemann that the Reichsbank would cease to discount government Treasury bills at the end of 1923; but although this was accompanied by a further tightening of credit conditions for the private sector, its immediate impact was negligible and the printing presses continued to roll.[170] Indeed, a number of monetary measures introduced under Stresemann – notably the restoration of the fixed exchange rate for the paper mark on 21 October and its subsequent extension to cover gold-denominated bonds – significantly worsened matters.[171] As had happened before, the impact of the artificially overvalued paper mark exchange rate led to a payments crisis in those parts of the economy which had effectively gone on to the dollar, as holders of gold mark-denominated money (such as the Hamburg Bank's notes) withdrew them from circulation.[172]

---

[168] See figure 4.11. If the DNVP, the National Socialists and the KPD are regarded as anti-Republican, their share of the vote more than doubled from 17.2 per cent to 38.6 per cent compared with the last national elections in June 1920. In addition, the share of the vote going to small splinter parties rose from 3 per cent to 8.6 per cent.

[169] 'Währungsgesundung und Wirtschaftssanierung', *Frankfurter Zeitung*, Nr. 962, 25.12.24; Bresciani, *Inflation*, pp. 334–56; James, 'Währungsstabilisierung' pp. 63ff.; Holtfrerich, *Inflation*, pp. 298–327; Webb, *Hyperinflation*, pp. 65–74. Cf. H. Schacht, *The Stabilisation of the Mark* (London, 1927); K.B. Netzband and H.P. Widmaier, *Währungs- und Finanzpolitik der Ära Luther 1923–1925* (Tübingen, 1964).

[170] Rupieper, *Cuno Government*, p. 195; Webb, *Hyperinflation*, p. 61. By this stage the Reichsbank was providing work for around 130 printworks, thirty paper mills and twenty-nine galvanised plate manufacturers: Feldman, *Great Disorder*, pp. 782ff.

[171] 'Verordnungen über den Handel mit ausländischen Zahlungsmittel und Dollarschatzanweisungen zum Einheitskurs, 22.10.23', *RGB*, Nr. 106, 22.10.23; 'Verordnung über den Handel mit wertbeständige Anleihe', *RGB*, 2.11.23. There was also a decree making it illegal to refuse payment in paper marks; 'Verordnung über die Verpflichtung zur Annahme von Reichsmark bei Inlandsgeschäften', *RGB*, 7.11.23. Cf. Feldman, *Great Disorder*, pp. 781–9.

[172] StAH, DHSG, Pr. V 3, Preisprüfungsstelle to Hamburgische Bank, 3.11.23; HKH to DHSG, 6.11.23; Senate to DHSG, 12.11.23; *Hamburger Echo*, 5.11.23; 17.11.23; *Hamburger Fremdenblatt*, 6.11.23; 7.11.23; 9.11.23; 13.11.23; 15.11.23; 22.11.23; *Hamburgische Börsen-Halle*, 10.11.23; *Hamburgische Correspondent*, 12.11.23; WA, Pol. Corr. 1923, Melchior to Luther, 12.12.23; Försterling, 'Die Hamburgische Bank', pp. 47–50. On the Senate's attempt to fill the resulting monetary gap with emergency money, Lippmann, *Leben*, p. 318; Büttner, *Politische Gerechtigkeit*, pp. 174f.

The futility of such measures increased the pressure for a more radical step: the creation of a new currency. Schemes for currency reform were many and various in the second half of 1923;[173] but they generally fell into one of two groups – those which assumed a return to gold, and those which envisaged some other form of reserve asset. As Finance Minister, Hilferding favoured some version of the former. But while he dithered, the initiative passed to Karl Helfferich, who proposed a new money based on a mortgage of the national capital-stock (i.e., a capital levy) and denominated in rye.[174]

Previous experiments with non-metal money, from John Law to the *assignat*, did not offer much encouragement to the proponents of this latter scheme.[175] Moreover, it was obvious that Helfferich intended to secure generous concessions for his agrarian and industrialist friends in return for the proposed mortgage; and to establish a 'rye bank' (*Roggenbank*) which would be under their direct control.[176] For these reasons alone, one can sympathise with the scepticism of the German banking establishment. Warburg was quite right to argue that such a currency would present severe problems to companies engaged in international trade, since it would create a double exchange rate: in terms of dollars on the one hand and paper marks on the other.[177] And it was true, as other Hamburg critics noted, that a new currency would quickly go the way of the old if the Rentenbank were as overgenerous with its credit to the government and the private sector as the Reichsbank had been.[178] But the bankers' counter-proposal for issuing more gold- (i.e., dollar-) denominated bonds of the sort which had been issued by the Cuno government in August 1923 hardly constituted an adequate alternative.[179] The only realistic option was

---

[173] See the collection of sometimes bizarre proposals in BAK, R43 1/2433, 2435, for example, W.A. Gantzen ('Berater in der Spezialwissenschaft des Wert-Meßwesens'), *Gullivers Währungssanierung*. For another example, see S. Gesell, *Die Natürliche Wirtschaftsordnung durch Freiland und Freigeld* (1920).

[174] Elster, *Von der Reichsmark*, pp. 215–26; Schacht, *Stabilisation*, pp. 54–63; Maier, *Recasting Bourgeois Europe*, pp. 375–9.

[175] Kindleberger, *Financial History*, pp. 326f.

[176] Feldman, *Great Disorder*, pp. 707–11, 715ff., 720–5.

[177] Erdmann and Vogt (eds.), *Kabinette Stresemann*, II, p. 160 n. (letter from Keynes to Melchior, 21.8.23); WA, Pol. Corr. 1923, Warburg Aufgabe, 6.9.23; Spiegelberg to M.M. Warburg & Co., 8.9.23; Warburg Aufgabe, 17.9.23; Warburg Notiz, 18.9.23; Erweiterte Ausschuß-Sitzung der CVDBB, 18.10.23; Warburg to Urbig, 31.10.23; Warburg (Notes), 5.11.23; Warburg (Notes of meeting of CVDBB), 8.11.23; CVDBB to Luther, 7.11.23. See also his retrospective comments in Warburg, *Aufzeichnungen*, pp. 118f.; Aufzeichnungen MSS, pp. 300–6. Cf. Maier, *Recasting Bourgeois Europe*, p. 378.

[178] 'Die Handelskammer zum Plan einer Währungsbank', *Wirtschaftsdienst*, 8 (1923), pp. 941–3; *Handelskammer Mitteilungen*, 13.10.23; T. Plaut, 'Dollargeld', *Hamburger Fremdenblatt*, Nr. 301, 31.10.23.

[179] Warburg's argument was that to acknowledge the need for a new currency would render the paper mark worthless, ruling out the possibility of an ultimate revaluation

Hilferding's gold-based currency, which the Cabinet in fact adopted on 10 September. But pressure from a variety of different quarters forced Stresemann to reverse this decision, leaving it to the increasingly influential Hans Luther to devise a modified version of Helfferich's plan.[180]

The new rentenmark promised in the decree of 15 October was formally to have the same relationship to the paper mark as the gold mark (i.e., the dollar), but would not be internationally tradable; while the new Rentenbank, with its mortgage-based reserve, would be able to lend no more than 1.2 bn. of the new currency to the government. This looked like a moral victory for Helfferich and his associates. However, it was not until a month later that the new currency became available, and then only in very limited quantities, so that the monetary chaos continued.[181] In fact, the opponents of the roggenmark/rentenmark ultimately got their way, largely thanks to Hjalmar Schacht, who was appointed to the new post of 'Currency Commissioner' on 12 November. Schacht had no doubt that the rentenmark should be replaced as soon as possible by a real gold-based currency as it was obvious to him that other peripheral states – particularly the Rhineland – would follow Hamburg's lead in setting up their own convertible currencies if this did not happen.[182] Accordingly, his first act was to peg the paper mark against the dollar by allowing it to fall to the level of 4.2 trillion marks to the dollar – a trillion times the old gold standard exchange rate – paving the way for a simple conversion of the old mark. At the same time, the printing of paper money began

of paper mark assets other than by means of a legal fiat. However, as such small-denomination bonds (around 300 m. gold marks of which were in fact issued in October) effectively performed the role of money, despite being interest bearing, their impact was essentially the same as a new currency – as with the notes of the Hamburg Bank of 1923; WA, Pol. Corr. 1923, Warburg to Melchior, 18.9.23; Warburg to Frisch, 26.9.23; Warburg Notiz, 3.10.23; Spiegelberg Notiz, 7.10.23; Urbig, Goldschmidt, Loeb, Aschaffenburg, Hermann, Pilster, Frisch, Jeidels and Warburg to Luther, 10.10.23; Warburg Notiz, 9.10.23; Warburg to Luther, 11.10.23; Bernstein report to M.M. Warburg & Co., 13.10.23 (meeting between representatives of the economy and government officials held at the Finance Ministry). For Warburg's refusal to accept a place on the Rentenbank Executive Council, WA, Pol. Corr., Warburg to Bernstein, 16.10.23; Bernstein to Warburg, 16.10.23.

[180] Feldman, *Great Disorder*, pp. 725–36, 751–3. Cf. Maier, *Recasting Bourgeois Europe*, p. 379; Sommariva and Tullio, *Macroeconomic History*, p. 130; Holtfrerich, *Inflation*, p. 317 n.

[181] See the comments in *Hamburger Fremdenblatt*, Nr. 322, 21.11.23; 23.11.23; O. Schoele, 'Die technischen Schwierigkeiten der Einführung des Rentenmarkverkehrs', *Der Zahlungsverkehr*, 5. Jg., N. 11/12 (1923), p. 224. Cf. Feldman, *Great Disorder*, pp. 781–93.

[182] Schacht, *Stabilisation*, p. 99. The Hamburg Bank's total circulation of notes and coins had reached 29 m. gold marks by the end of 1923; and through Warburg it had obtained a $2.5 m. rediscounting facility in New York.

to be wound up by Reichsbank announcements ending the legality of 'emergency money' and 'valorising' further paper mark credits.[183] The next decisive step was taken on 22 December, with the government's decision to appoint Schacht as Reichsbank President in place of Havenstein, who had died on 20 November, intransigently printing money to the last.[184] Schacht at once set about establishing a German Gold Discount Bank, to apply at the national level the principle underlying the Hamburg Bank, thus laying the foundation for a gold-based reform of the Reichsbank. In fact, a similar plan had been devised by the ex-Chancellor Cuno as early as September.[185] But Cuno lacked serious foreign support; and it was this which clinched Schacht's success. Montagu Norman in London was enthusiastic when Schacht visited him at the beginning of 1924: seeing an opportunity to reassert British financial power, he offered a £5 m. credit to assist the foundation of the new bank. The Dawes Committee was more hesitant when it heard Schacht's scheme in Paris two weeks later; but by 10 February, Schacht had been given the green light.[186] On 7 April the *Golddiskontbank* came into being, based on Norman's loan and £5 m. advanced by around 150 German firms.[187] The Americans, at Paul Warburg's initiative, then matched Norman by offering a $20 m. credit.[188]

The Gold Discount Bank made around £14 m. available in credits to German firms with international interests. Yet this was only a fraction of the monetary expansion being generated by the polycentric monetary system in the first quarter of 1924. With the discount rate held at just 10 per cent, total credits by the Reichsbank, the Rentenbank and the other note-issuing banks rose from just 609 m. gold marks at the end of 1923 to over 2 bn. gold marks at the end of March 1924 – a monthly growth rate of close to 50 per cent.[189] Significantly, after a 'very long

---

[183] *Ibid.*, pp. 64–87. Cf. Feldman, *Great Disorder*, pp. 792–8.

[184] *Ibid.*, pp. 821–35. The Reichsbank Central Committee had wanted Helfferich: cf. Warburg, *Aufzeichnungen*, pp. 121f.

[185] On Cuno, PA/AA, SRW FW 16 Bd. 8, Lang to Stresemann, 24.9.23; Stresemann to Cuno, 30.9.23; Cuno to Stresemann, 4.10.23; Stresemann to Cuno, 7.10.23; Cuno to Stresemann, 11.10.23; Wiedfeldt to Ritter, 13.10.23; Kohlhaus, 'Die Hapag', pp. 137–43; Feldman, *Great Disorder*, p. 826. See also the plan advanced by the former Warburg's employee Regendanz, on the basis of the Austrian experience, in *Hamburger Fremdenblatt*, 1.11.23.

[186] Schacht, *Stabilisation*, pp. 95–110; James, 'Währungsstabilisierung', pp. 66f.; Feldman, *Great Disorder*, pp. 827ff., 823ff.

[187] Schacht, *Stabilisation*, p. 111.

[188] Federal Reserve Bank of New York, Benjamin Strong Papers, 120.0 2, M.M. Warburg & Co. to Paul Warburg, 10.3.24; Paul Warburg to Max Warburg, 10.3.24; Paul Warburg to Owen D. Young, 21.3.24; Strong to 'P.J.', 4.4.24. Cf. Feldman, *Great Disorder*, p. 831.

[189] Bresciani, *Inflation*, pp. 334ff.; Webb, *Hyperinflation*, p. 70; Eichengreen, *Golden Fetters*, pp. 145–7.

discussion', the managing committee of the Hamburg Bank 'adopted the standpoint that the Reich Gold Note Bank should not be sabotaged, but that one should not wait for it' either, and continued to expand the bank's note issue.[190] The old inflationary pressures were reasserting themselves, pushing up wholesale prices at nearly 2 per cent per month between January and April, and causing the unofficial rentenmark exchange rate to fall by around 10 per cent.[191] It was therefore only when Schacht introduced an effective credit freeze on 7 April that real monetary stabilisation was achieved: in the succeeding four months, the money supply stabilised, short-term interest rates rose to 45 per cent; prices fell by 7 per cent, the demand for foreign currency abated, and the Reichsbank's reserve of gold and foreign currency doubled.[192] A last spasm of currency speculation – this time against the franc – ended with heavy losses for the speculators, including many in Hamburg.[193] Even so, it took several more months of haggling before Schacht succeeded in marginalising the Hamburg Bank. When the various laws were passed confirming the restoration of the national monetary system in August 1924, the note issue of the Hamburg Bank was at its peak of 46.25 m. gold marks; and it was not until the end of the year that the bank's note-issuing role had effectively ceased.[194]

Hamburg's scepticism about the national monetary reform was not unjustified. In itself, the reform of the monetary system was not enough to guarantee stability. Only if the credit restriction was seen to be effective in both the public and private sectors could confidence in the new currency take root. Fiscal reforms were therefore as important as monetary reforms in the stabilisation process. Steps in the direction of serious reform had in fact been taken by the Cuno government just before its fall; Hilferding merely had to implement a raft of measures including new taxes on factory payrolls and accelerated payment of existing income and consumption taxes.[195] But these did not suffice to balance the budget so long as the *Ruhrkampf* had to be financed. After more than a month of drift, his successor Hans Luther took matters further with his First and Second Emergency Tax Decrees of 7 and

---

[190] Försterling, 'Die hamburgische Bank', pp. 55–62.
[191] Schacht, *Stabilisation*, p. 113; Pohl, *Bankengeschichte*, p. 126; Sommariva and Tullio, *Macroeconomic History*, pp. 130f.; James, 'Währungsstabilisierung', pp. 131f.
[192] Schacht, *Stabilisation*, p. 116; Balderston, *Economic Crisis*, pp. 136f.; Feldman, *Great Disorder*, p. 833.
[193] WA, 'Jahresbericht 1923', 31.7.24; *Frankfurter Zeitung*, Nr. 962, 25.12.24; Warburg, *Aufzeichnungen*, p. 124; Pohl, *Hamburger Bankengeschichte*, pp. 139f.
[194] Försterling, 'Die Hamburgsiche Bank', p. 78.
[195] M. Vogt, 'Rudolf Hilferding als Finanzminister im ersten Kabinett Stresemann', in Büsch and Feldman (eds.), *Historische Prozesse*, pp. 127–60; Maier, *Recasting Bourgeois Europe*, p. 381; Feldman, *Great Disorder*, pp. 700–13.

19 December, which established all taxation on a gold mark basis.[196] Taken together, the various measures brought the inflationary tax 'holiday' to a painful end for business, imposing effective income and corporation taxes, and inevitably prompted anguished protests.[197] On the expenditure side, the government faced still greater resistance as it set about reducing the burden of public sector pay, cutting salaries and laying off surplus employees. The *Personalabbau* decree of 27 October cut the number of Reich employees by 25 per cent, eliciting anguished protests at the violation of civil service tenure.[198] There were also cuts in Reich contributions to the health insurance system, and an end to the *ad hoc* contributions to the states and communes to assist with local unemployment relief and public sector pay. Relations between Reich, state and communes, thrown into disarray by the hyperinflation, were rearranged, roughly along the lines envisaged by Erzberger in 1919/20. The Reich remained dominant; but the new *Ausgleich* gave the states and, through them, the communes a new source of revenue, the *Mietzinssteuer* (in effect, a tax on rented property), a substantial share (initially 90 per cent) of income tax receipts, and 20 per cent of revenue from the turnover tax.[199] Consequently, the states and communes were forced to set their houses in order: in Hamburg, the number of public sector employees fell to 9,850, a third lower than at the peak in mid 1920, as spending was cut.[200] The net result of all these reforms was effectively to balance the Reich budget, and to reduce total public spending in real terms by some 4.3 bn. gold marks, from around 47 per cent to 31 per cent of NNP.[201]

Of critical importance for stabilisation was the decision partially to revalue some paper mark assets. Had nothing of this sort been done, the total value of public debt would have stood at just 2 gold pfennigs; that of private debt at around 1 gold pfennig – an immense gain for

[196] James, *Slump*, pp. 42f.; C.-D. Krohn, 'Steuerpolitik und Industrie in der Stabilisierungsphase: Von den Steuernotverordnungen im Winter 1923 zur Finanzreform im August 1925', in Mommsen *et al.* (eds.), *Industrielles System*, I, pp. 426–38; Feldman, *Great Disorder*, pp. 815f.; Netzband and Widmaier, *Währungs- und Finanzpolitik der Ära Luther*, p. 149.

[197] See, e.g., StAH, Sen. Cl. 1 Lit. T No. 1b Vol. 7 Fasc. 48 Inv. 1, HKH to RFM, 6.9.23.

[198] On the *Personalabbau*, A. Kunz, 'Stand versus Klasse. Beamtenschaft und Gewerkschaften im Konflikt um den Personalabbau 1923/4', in *G&G*, 8 (1982), pp. 55–86; James, *Slump*, p. 44; Feldman, *Great Disorder*, pp. 758f., 807f.

[199] Balderston, *Economic Crisis*, pp. 231–44.

[200] Brandt, *Hamburgs Finanzen*, pp. 32f. The number of state employees of all kinds fell by as much as 8,000; see Lyth, '*Mittelstand*', pp. 247, 252; Büttner, *Politische Gerechtigkeit*, p. 172; Krause, 'Hamburger NSDAP', p. 62.

[201] See table 1.

debtors.[202] The government had already ducked the issue of mortgage revaluation in March, and Luther clearly wished to avoid any kind of revaluation, concentrating on taxing 'inflation profits'. But in November the Supreme Court ruled that a nominalist treatment of debts – the 'mark–equals–mark' principle – violated the 'equity and good faith' (*Treu und Glauben*) paragraph of the civil code.[203] Reluctantly, under pressure from Stresemann and the Justice Minister Emminger, Luther agreed to include in his Third Emergency Decree of 14 February a 15 per cent benchmark for the revaluation of private mortgages and debentures contracted after 1917, but postponed a decision on public sector bonds.[204] It was not until July 1925 – after much heated debate – that the position was finally clarified by legislation. In the end, mortage and debenture creditors did slightly better than Luther had initially envisaged; but holders of public bonds, particularly those (around 60 per cent of the total) who had purchased them before July 1920, did less well, regaining at most only 12.5 per cent of their investment.[205] Other assets, such as savings accounts, pension funds and insurance policies, were revalued on more or less generous lines, with only bank accounts left worthless.[206] The fiscal effect of all this was to reduce drastically the public sector debt burden – making the reduction in public expenditure overall less impressive.[207] As for the political effect, a coherent critique of revaluation proved hard to sustain because of the way the burdens of balancing the budget were distributed. Disgruntled creditors could be mobilised by the DNVP and special-interest groups; but business groups whose grievance was high taxation were naturally disinclined to favour the idea of higher levels of revaluation: at least in the short term, the tax issue and the revaluation issue cancelled one another out.[208]

[202] Hughes, *Paying for the German Inflation*, pp. 5ff. Hughes estimates that around 25–30 per cent of the electorate were net paper mark creditors.

[203] D.B. Southern, 'The Revaluation Question in the Weimar Republic', *JMH*, 51 (1979), pp. 1029–53; *idem*, 'The Impact of Inflation: Inflation, the Courts and Revaluation', in R. Bessel and E.J. Feuchtwanger (eds.), *Social Change and Political Development in Weimar Germany* (Totowa, NJ, 1981), pp. 56–76; O. Pfleiderer, 'Das Prinzip "Mark=Mark" in der deutschen Inflation 1914–1924', in Feldman *et al.* (eds.) *Zwischenbilanz*, pp. 157–201; Holtfrerich, *Inflation*, p. 319; Feldman, *Great Disorder*, pp. 682ff., 812.

[204] Holtfrerich, *Inflation*, p. 321–3; Feldman, *Great Disorder*, pp. 816–21. In fact, the provisions for repayment meant that the present value of such revalued debts was rather less than 15 per cent.

[205] Holtfrerich, *Inflation*, pp. 321–3, 325–30. Cf. Bresciani, *Inflation*, pp. 318–26.

[206] Hughes, *Paying for the German Inflation*, p. 190.

[207] James, *Slump*, p. 48. Hamburg's debt was reduced to just 70 m. reichsmarks; Lippmann, *Leben*, pp. 317ff., 362–72.

[208] For a typical anti-revaluation protest, see StAH, Bürgerschaft I C1139, Reichsverband der Besitzer deutscher Anleihen to Aufwertungsausschuß der Hamburgischen Bürgerschaft, 10.6.25.

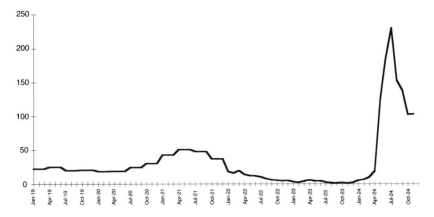

Figure 7.3 Bankruptcies and receiverships, 1919–1924 (monthly average, 1913 = 100)
Sources: *Frankfurter Zeitung*, Nr. 966, 28.12.24; Graham, *Hyperinflation*, p. 280; Webb, *Hyperinflation*, p. 99.

The monetary and fiscal reforms achieved by Schacht and Luther completed the economic 'shake-out' which had been deferred throughout the post-war years, but which had begun to occur piecemeal as a consequence of the real monetary contraction caused by hyperinflation. Schacht's credit squeeze emerges as the decisive factor from the statistics on bankruptcy and receivership, which soared to a peak between April and July 1924 (see figure 7.3). Not without cause did the financial press speak of a *'Generaldirektordämmerung'*.[209] Ship-building output fell by at least 15 per cent in 1924 as Luther ended the reconstruction subsidies.[210] Yet in many respects the process of stabilisation was less severe in the private sector than might have been expected. The total number of bankruptcies in Hamburg in 1924 was only slightly more than in 1913.[211] Similarly, national figures suggest that industrial output increased in most sectors after the trough caused by hyperinflation and the Ruhr crisis,[212] while unemployment fell rapidly from its peak in December 1923/January 1924.[213]

[209] *Frankfurter Zeitung*, Nr. 962, 25.12.24. The most celebrated victim was Stinnes's empire, the disintegration of which followed hard on the heels of his death; see Feldman, *Iron and Steel*, pp. 454ff.; *idem*, *Great Disorder*, p. 844.

[210] See figure 1.2. This principally reflected the cut in subsidies implemented by Luther; BAP, RFM 46580 N. Reg. 317/250, Aktenvermerk über eine Besprechung im Reichsministerium für Wiederaufbau, Abteilung Schiffahrt, 13.11.23. Blohm & Voß cut its workforce from 8,755 in July 1923 to just 6,718 twelve months later.

[211] Lyth, *Hyperinflation*, p. 165.

[212] See figures 2.4, 2.5, 2.6 and 2.7.

[213] See figures 2.10 and 3.1.

From the point of view of many employers, stabilisation was an opportunity to turn the clock back in industrial relations, undoing the gains made by labour in the revolution. However, the hopes which some had expressed of a major 'turning of the tables' proved over-optimistic.[214] After much pressure from industry throughout 1923, the Marx government finally allowed the post-war demobilisation decree on working hours to lapse on 17 November and on 21 December it recognised the possibility of exceptions to the eight-hour day 'on economic grounds'. This effectively signalled the end of the post-war 'working community' between industry and labour.[215] However, the Labour Ministry had already taken steps to increase its influence over the anticipated wave of wage disputes by a decree of 30 October, which empowered it to impose legally binding resolutions on employers and employees.[216] Taken together, these measures were a recipe for industrial strife in Hamburg: for if workers regarded the eight-hour day as sacrosanct, employers were determined to combat the system of binding arbitration on wages 'with all means'.[217] The result was a protracted three-month strike on the waterfront, recalling the great shipyard strikes of the pre-war years.[218] It was not until the end of May 1924 that both sides had agreed on a compromise based on longer working hours and higher wages.[219]

Throughout 1921 and 1922, it had been argued by German spokesmen that there could be no domestic stabilisation without a stabilisation of Germany's international situation. The events of 1923/4 to some extent belied this claim. On the other hand, it could be argued that it was the relative generosity of international settlement worked out in London in 1924 which ensured that the domestic stabilisation achieved in that year lasted as long as it did. As with every aspect of stabilisation, the process of ending Germany's diplomatic crisis was by no means swift or smooth. The last months of 1923 saw a confusing range of private and uncoordinated German initiatives, with Adenauer and

---

[214] Maier, *Recasting Bourgeois Europe*, pp. 404f. For the argument that this in fact took place at the national level, see *idem*, 'Inflation and Stabilisation', p. 115.

[215] Feldman, *Iron and Steel*, pp. 430–44; *idem*, *Great Disorder*, pp. 742f., 748, 755f., 798, 807. Cf. G.D. Feldman and I. Steinisch, 'Die Weimarer Republik zwischen Sozial- und Wirtschaftsstaat: Die Entscheidung gegen den Achtstundentag', *AFS*, 18 (1978), pp. 353–75.

[216] James, *Slump*, pp. 219–23.

[217] StAH, B&V 228, Bd. 2, Blohm & Voß to Rudolf Blohm, 29.12.23, 5.1.24; B&V 1368, Norddeutsche Gruppe Sitzung, 5.2.24.

[218] StAH, B&V 1368, Norddeutsche Gruppe to members, 14.2.24; Norddeutsche Gruppe Sitzung, 31.3.24; GHH, 4001012012/0, Deutsche Werft to Reusch, 28.2.24; Claviez, *Deutsche Werft*, p. 37.

[219] StAH, B&V 1368, Norddeutsche Gruppe Sitzung, 7.5.24; GHH, 4001012012/0, Deutsche Werft to Reusch, 25.4.24; Deutsche Werft to Reusch 12.5.24; 20.5.24; GHH, *Denkschrift*, Nr. 30, Bd. III, pp. 29–43.

Hagen discussing the possibility of a semi-autonomous Rhineland Republic with Tirard;[220] the Ruhr coal owners resuming coal deliveries to the Inter-Allied Commission controlling Factories and Mines (MICUM);[221] and Melchior holding meetings with British representatives in London aimed at winning support for a stabilisation loan to Germany.[222] The turning point came at the end of October 1923 with the British proposal for the creation of two committees to review the German situation – one on reparations, chaired by Charles Dawes, the Director of the US Bureau of the Budget, and one chaired by the former British Chancellor of the Exchequer Reginald McKenna, to investigate the extent of German capital flight. French acceptance of this proposal was cheaply purchased by the abandonment of the unsustainable policy of passive resistance.[223] Of course, there remained the possibility that the experts might judge Germany harshly. As late as October 1923, Max Warburg still feared that the British objective was to establish 'an administration *de la dette publique*, in order to keep us down permanently'.[224] In fact, it was Montagu Norman who quashed an American idea for a direct foreign control of the Reichsbank's note-issue department; and the final extent of foreign control over German fiscal and monetary policy was limited compared, for example, with the conditions which had earlier been imposed on Austria by the League of Nations.[225] Although half the Reichsbank's new General Council were to be foreigners, and an American Reparations Agent was charged with ensuring that the transfer of reparations did not undermine the exchange rate, in practice the principal constraint on German monetary policy was the 40 per cent gold-exchange reserve requirement imposed on the reformed Reichsbank. Similarly, although certain indirect taxes were earmarked for the payment of

[220] Maier, *Recasting Bourgeois Europe*, p. 395; McDougall, *France's Rhineland Diplomacy*, pp. 202f. Cf. WA, 34, Pol. Corr., Melchior Notiz, 21.22.23.

[221] Feldman, *Iron and Steel*, pp. 418–58; Maier, *Recasting Bourgeois Europe*, pp. 390ff., 416f.; Eichengreen, *Golden Fetters*, p. 147.

[222] WA, 34, Pol. Corr. 1923, Melchior Aufgabe, 25.10.23; Melchior Memorandum, 29.10.23 (for General Smuts); Melchior Aufgabe, 2.11.23 (meetings with General Smuts, Dudley Docker, Reginald McKenna); Melchior Notes, 2.11.23 (meeting with Anthony and Lionel Rothschild); Melchior Notiz für Herrn Wahlen, 5.11.23 (meeting with Brand of Lazard's); Warburg Notiz, 7.11.23 (discussion of draft reparations plan with Goldschmidt); cf. Keynes, *Collected Writings*, XVIII, pp. 221, 233. See also Holtzendorff's visit to Munich, intended to win Bavarian backing for these efforts, as well as those of Cuno and Warburg in the United States; HA, HB, Aktennotiz, 7.11.23; Kohlhaus, 'Die Hapag', p. 142.

[223] James, 'Währungsstabilisierung', pp. 66–70; Eichengreen, *Golden Fetters*, pp. 150f.; Schuker, *End of French Predominance*, pp. 171–231, 272–83; Feldman, *Great Disorder*, pp. 736ff., 747–50.

[224] WA, 31, Pol. Corr. 1923, Warburg statement at expanded committee of Bankers' Association, 18.10.23.

[225] James, 'Währungsstabilisierung', p. 71.

reparations, as well as the interest on over 16 bn. reichsmarks of debentures issued by the railways and industry, the fiscal burden was mitigated by a loan of 800 m. gold marks, similar to that given to Austria in 1922.[226] Finally, there was a quasi-moratorium, which envisaged the reparations annuity rising gradually from 1 bn. gold marks to 2.5 bn. gold marks over five years.[227] In many ways, it was this relative 'room for manoeuvre' which ensured that stabilisation endured. Politically, it took the sting out of radical revisionism. It gave German monetary policy international credibility. And the huge influx of foreign lending (around 2.9 bn. reichsmarks net in 1924 alone) which followed the Dawes loan greatly eased the pain of stabilisation in both the public and the private sector. The Hamburg state was one of many public bodies to issue large foreign loans in the mid 1920s; many firms like Deutsche Werft were saved from bankruptcy by foreign lending.[228]

The republican system had survived. The currency had been reformed. A budget surplus had been achieved. The wage–price spiral had come to an end. And the reparations problem had been resolved. Judged in these simplistic terms, the Weimar Republic had indeed been stabilised by the end of 1924. Perhaps, however, it would be more appropriate to speak of 'liquidation' rather than 'stabilisation'. The end of the inflation had been forced on the German economy as much by hyperinflation's diminishing returns as by a political 'regime change'. To the last, business interests had obstructed the reforms that were needed to end the inflation – most blatantly when it was one of their own number, Cuno, who was trying to introduce them. It was only economic collapse and the threat of the disintegration of the Reich which made possible a reassertion of public authority. When Moritz Bonn defended the choice of Schacht as Reichsbank President he made an important point:

He [Schacht] has [. . .] not spared the special interests even if they come from his own professional circles. [. . .] The fact that there is resistance [to his appointment] is not an argument against but rather an argument for his appointment. The German business community must learn to obey, not to command.[229]

[226] *Frankfurter Zeitung*, Nr. 962, 25.12.24; Petzina, *Deutsche Wirtschaft*, p. 79; Kolb, *Weimar Republic*, pp. 6of.
[227] Kindleberger, *Financial History*, p. 302.
[228] Lippmann, *Leben*, pp. 323–54; GHH, 4001012012/0, Deutsche Werft to Reusch, 28.3.24; Reusch to Deutsche Werft, 29.3.24; Deutsche Werft Bericht, 8.5.24; Reichsbankhauptstelle Hamburg to Dresdner Bank, 10.5.24; Deutsche Werft to Reusch, 12.5.24; GHH to Deutsche Werft, 20.6.24; Deutsche Werft to GHH, 20.6.24; Reusch to GHH, 25.6.24; Deutsche Werft to Reusch, 31.7.24, 30.8.24.
[229] Feldman, *Great Disorder*, p. 823.

But it had little option but to do so after the catastrophic failure of government by *die Wirtschaft*.

The inflation had been liquidated then – or, rather, it had liquidated itself. As a result, it had been possible to change the regime. Yet the reassertion of the state's authority over private interests in 1924 was not, by itself, enough to ensure that stability would endure. Liquidation did not mean that the new regime started with an entirely clean slate. People did not think of it as especially new. Nor did they speak of a '*Stunde Null*', as they would after the second great currency reform of modern German history. On the contrary, the inflation left behind it a legacy of profound economic, social and political disruption which continued to burden the Republic long after the last paper mark had vanished from circulation. It is to this legacy that we must now turn.

8

The legacy of the inflation

In the early days of October 1933, two small boats, the *Hermia* and the *Jessica*, set sail from Hamburg, bound for London. Their cargo, packed into 531 crates, consisted of 60,000 books and 20,000 photographs – the complete library of Aby Warburg, who had died in 1929.[1] Just months before, Max Warburg's brother-in-law Moritz Oppenheim had committed suicide with his wife in Frankfurt; and by the end of 1934 his daughter Renate, his would-be-successor Siegmund, his niece Ingrid and his cousin's son Karl would all have left Germany for England.[2] He himself would endure a further four years of discrimination, beginning with his exclusion from the Hapag supervisory board,[3] before finally leaving Germany. Yet almost exactly two decades before the departure of the *Hermia* and the *Jessica*, Warburg had been celebrating, along with the rest of the Hapag board, the launch of the *Imperator*, the leviathan liner created by that other great Hanseatic entrepreneur – and fellow-Jew – Albert Ballin. These contrasting events symbolise the alteration which Hanseatic bourgeois society had undergone between 1913 and 1933; for if the launch of the *Imperator* epitomised the inflated aspirations which had characterised North German capitalism on the eve of the First World War, then the departure of the Warburg library was a symptom of that crisis of bourgeois culture which lay at the root of Weimar's failure. To portray the one as hubris and the other as nemesis would, of course, understate the complexity of the events described here, and the intricacy of the connections between the economy, society, politics and diplomacy. But the central argument should by now be clear enough. It was inflation which led from Wilhelmine grandeur to Weimar collapse.

Balances

As chapter 1 suggested, inflationary pressures in the pre-1914 period were in many ways a reflection of Germany's economic dynamism. But

---

[1] Chernow, *Warburgs*, pp. 408–19; Attali, *Siegmund Warburg*, p. 119.
[2] Chernow, *Warburgs*, pp. 372–83, 401–19; Warburg–Spinelli, *Erinnerungen*, pp. 95ff.
[3] Warburg, *Aufzeichnungen*, p. 149.

the war brought the golden years to an end. International movements of capital and goods were abruptly halted and German production had to be diverted to military ends. Partly as a result of Allied action and partly as a result of maladministration, German output slumped; while the removal of the monetary ceiling imposed by the gold standard and the growth of government deficits led to inflationary pressures which were only held in check by crude controls. All of this had an especially detrimental effect on Hamburg's economy. Nowhere was the collapse of sea-borne trade so devastating in its impact; nowhere was the loss of overseas assets – especially merchant shipping – so keenly felt; nowhere was manufacturing so hard hit. In the light of this, it is hardly surprising that Hamburg businessmen hoped for a rapid revival of trade and investment in the post-war period; and that they generally supported policies such as trade deregulation, the floating of the exchange rate, low taxation, low interest rates and subsidies to boost production.

In the immediate post-war period, their hopes appeared to be fulfilled. Once the blockade had been lifted, trade boomed and companies rushed to invest liquid funds, taking advantage of negative real interest rates, falling real wages and low real tax burdens. Indeed, inflation even appeared to have beneficial effects for the economy as a whole, since Germany's average annual growth rate in the years 1920–2 compares very favourably with the recessions experienced at that time in the US and the UK. However, these benefits largely proved ephemeral, and were outweighed by the negative side effects of inflation.

This can be shown first in the case of exports. Because of a substantial influx of foreign speculative funds, the depreciation of the mark came to a sudden stop in the spring of 1920; and the German export advantage was further eroded by the imposition of government trade controls and foreign tariffs. Moreover, that advantage was never subsequently recovered, despite the resumption of currency depreciation in 1921, because the gap between foreign and domestic prices was never again as wide as in 1919. Overall, German trade volumes throughout the inflation years remained substantially below pre-war levels; and, contrary to the expectations of those who had assumed that exports would benefit from currency stimulation, it was import volumes which grew most rapidly. Moreover, exports grew in volume and value far more rapidly in the years *after* stabilisation, increasing at an average rate of 15.5 per cent between 1924 and 1929 (32 per cent in volume terms), compared with a figure of 7.6 per cent for imports.[4] Overall,

---

[4] See figure 4.2. Even in Hamburg, where exports grew more rapidly than at the national level during the inflation, the available figures show that import volumes grew faster still; and in any case the level of foreign exports from Hamburg rose still higher in 1926: see figure 2.1. Cf. the data on shipping in *Hamburger Statistische*

German trade grew less rapidly than world trade during the inflation years and more rapidly after stabilisation – even if neither the absolute volume of trade, nor its share of national income, nor its share of world trade ever recovered to their 1913 levels.[5] Of course, many non-economic factors unquestionably played a part in this: notably the post-war discrimination against German goods in the markets of former enemy states, and the more generally protectionist climate of the 1920s.[6] But what is certain is that the stimulus to exports which German businessmen expected from currency depreciation was insufficient to overcome such barriers, and was more than outweighed by the stimulus to imports provided by inflation.[7] Currency stability proved better for German exports, which grew rapidly after 1924 *despite* an apparent decline in competitiveness as measured by unit export values.[8]

Nor does the argument that inflation stimulated investment in 'real values' stand up to close inspection. For a start, it would appear that the highest levels of investment occurred in the year of relative stabilisation, and that inflation in fact tended to deter large-scale expansion of capacity by leading to cash-flow crises. Secondly, many firms preferred to convert liquid funds into securities or foreign currency rather than plant. Thirdly, much of the finance for investment came from the public purse, and therefore does not illustrate a flight by entrepreneurs from money into real values, since the public sector was not necessarily concerned with profit maximisation. Fourthly, many firms allowed large nominal balance sheets to blind them to real 'substance loss' caused by inadequate allowances for depreciation. Fifthly, real wages actually rose at certain times, while productivity almost certainly fell due to overmanning, further reducing profitability. Sixthly, the inflation stimulated consumption as much as investment,

---

Monatsberichte (1924), pp. 16, 238f.; *Statistisches Handbuch 1925*, pp. 157f.; *Statistisches Jahrbuch 1928/9*, p. 164.

[5] James, *German Slump*, p. 13; Balderston, *Economic Crisis*, pp. 43–6, 53, 95–125.

[6] For example, trade between Hamburg and North America, which had accounted for 17 per cent of the city's sea-borne imports and 21 per cent of its exports before the war fell to 11 per cent and 12 per cent respectively. Other overseas markets – Africa, Asia, Latin America and the Pacific – had also become less important; while Hamburg's trade with European markets had recovered or exceeded pre-war levels by 1924. Yet these trends had largely been reversed by 1927. Structurally, the long-term trends continued: a still larger share of Hamburg's imports were primary products than before the war; and a still larger share of her exports were finished goods. Apart from the collapse of trade in saltpetre, there was no radical change in the character of the principal commodities passing through Hamburg; *Statistisches Handbuch 1925*, pp. 134–6, 144–6; *Statistisches Jahrbuch 1928/29*, pp. 130–43, 145–59; Meyer, *Güterumschlagsplatz*, pp. 95ff., 108.

[7] The decline in Hamburg's imports between 1924 and 1926, as well as the setback to exports in 1927, contrasted with the rapid growth of the inflation years; Büttner, *Staats- und Wirtschaftskrise*, p. 100; Meyer, *Güterumschlagsplatz*, p. 107.

[8] Balderston, *Economic Crisis*, pp. 95ff.

since there was a disincentive to save at a time of negative real interest rates, and since rents, heating and transport costs were held down by state controls and subsidies. And finally, where investment in 'real values' did occur, it was often misallocated, in structurally obsolescent sectors.

The condition of Hamburg's capital stock after the inflation underlines many of these points. Even if one regards the purchase of other companies as a form of investment, the degree of concentration brought about by the inflation was very limited. The percentage of employees in firms employing more than ten people was only slightly higher in 1925 (64 per cent) than it had been in 1907 (57 per cent); the percentage of firms employing more than 200 had risen only slightly.[9] In 1924 there were 154 joint-stock companies quoted on the city's bourse with a share capital of 205.4 m. reichsmarks; compared with 182 on the eve of the war, with a share capital of 904.6 m. marks.[10] This 77 per cent contraction compares very unfavourably with Reich statistics which suggest an average shrinkage in share capital of 6.6 per cent for the economy as a whole, and significant expansion in most industrial sectors.[11] Evidence for the expansion of physical capacity is sparse, but gives a similar picture.

The one possible exception to the rule was the shipping industry, often cited as the classic case of inflation investment. By 1924 the German merchant fleet had been restored to around 58 per cent of its pre-war tonnage; the Hamburg fleet to around a third.[12] However, this was the result not only of private investment but also of public subsidies, to the tune of 30 bn. paper marks disbursed between 1920 and 1923 under various compensation schemes. The real value of these payments can, unfortunately, only be estimated. Deflating the payments according to approximate times of payment, the sums paid may have amounted to around 1 bn. gold marks; but since the final tonnage built under the compensation scheme amounted to only 1.85 m. tons, this implies that the taxpayer was paying around three times the market rate per ton. It seems more likely that delays in allocation eroded the real value of the payments to something closer to 380 m. gold marks.[13] From the point of view of the shipping lines, this money certainly

[9] Cf. Lyth, 'Mittelstand', pp. 280ff, 341f.
[10] Vierteljahreshefte zur Statistik des Deutschen Reiches, Ergänzungsheft II (1914), p. 11; III (1924), p. 78.
[11] Lindenlaub, Maschinenbauunternehmen, p. 34; Krohn, Stabilisierung, p. 21.
[12] Figures from Statistisches Jahrbuch für das Deutsche Reich 1921/2, 1924/5; Kohlhaus, 'Die Hapag', pp. 11–13; Lippmann, Leben, p. 313; Büttner, Staats- und Wirtschaftskrise, pp. 100f.
[13] StAH, FA B&V 264, Schiffbau Treuhand Bank (final balance), 1923. Information on German market rates per ton from GHH, 300193012/7, Scholz to Reusch, 10.5.22.

helped mitigate a severe loss of assets, enabling the Hapag to restore
a third of its tonnage within just three years. For the shipyards, the
government was providing contracts which would otherwise have been
scarce, accounting for around a quarter of Deutsche Werft's total
output between 1919 and 1923;[14] and perhaps as much as two-thirds
of Blohm & Voß's.[15] However, the most that can be said is that these
contracts prevented post-war profits from being disastrous, and simply
made them low. Real net profits at Blohm & Voß were significantly
below wartime levels (1–2 m. gold marks), and slightly worse than
post-stabilisation profits (0.5–1 m. reichsmarks);[16] while at Deutsche
Werft, net losses were recorded. Moreover, profits at Blohm & Voß
were evidently 'illusory', failing adequately to allow for 'substance loss'
of close to 20 m. gold marks.

A further, if limited insight into the question of inflation investment
can be gleaned from the 'goldmark opening balances' published by
most firms in 1924.[17] Although the valuations of plant and inventories
acquired during the inflation must be viewed with some scepticism,
it is nevertheless important to notice how the inflation allowed firms
to wipe substantial levels of debt off the slate. Holders of Blohm &
Voß debentures, who had lent the company around 8.35 m. gold
marks in the years before 1921, lost around 5.65 m. gold marks of
their money. On the other hand, the firm valued its assets in July
1924 at 34.9 m. reichsmarks, which suggests that since at least 1921/
2 the firm's accounts had contained major understatements.[18] Unlike
Blohm & Voß, Deutsche Werft had, as we have seen, invested substantial amounts in plant during the inflation: the real value of its plant
increased by around 5 m. gold marks between 1918 and the 'opening
balance' of January 1924, and its total assets were valued at 16.43 m.
reichsmarks against liabilities of just 11.11 m. reichsmarks. Again,
however, it was the holders of debentures who lost out, suffering a
net loss of around 1.43 m. gold marks (around 80 per cent of the
total lent).[19] By contrast, shareholders were given relatively generous

---

[14] StAH, FA B&V 264, Schiffbau Treuhand Bank (final balance), 1923.
[15] StAH, FA B&V 264, Schiffbau Treuhand Bank (report on work in progress), 19.7.21.
[16] Büttner, *Staats- und Wirtschaftskrise*, p. 537 n.
[17] Bresciani, *Inflation*, pp. 274ff.
[18] Calculated from Blohm & Voß, *Jahresbericht 1921/22*; *Jahresbericht 1922/23*; *Eröffnungsbilanz 1924*. The undervaluation of its plant (valued at 12.6 m. reichsmarks in 1924) clearly dated back even further.
[19] Calculated from Deutsche Werft, *Jahresbericht 1918*; *Jahresbericht 1919*; *Jahresbericht 1920*; *Jahresbericht 1921*; *Jahresbericht 1922*; *Jahresbericht 1923*; *Eröffnungsbilanz 1924*. Cf. GHH, 300193012/8, Reusch to Deutsche Werft, 3.12.23.

treatment by both shipyards.[20] A similar picture emerges in the case of the Hapag. Although the firm had acquired ships with a total tonnage of around 300,000 gross tons between 1919 and 1923, the total fleet was still only around 30 per cent of its pre-war size at the end of the inflation period, so that the values attached to it (26 per cent of the pre-war figure) and to its shares (35 per cent of the pre-war figure) were probably not gross underestimates. The Hapag's most creative piece of accounting had in fact preceded stabilisation, and once again affected debenture holders: the holders of 69.5 m. marks of such bonds had been repaid in depreciated marks, suffering a net loss (inclusive of interest payments) of 48.2 m. gold marks (70 per cent).[21]

Events after 1924 again put the inflationary investment into perspective: the Hamburg fleet grew by considerably more between 1924 and 1928 (by 97 per cent) than between 1920 and 1924 (by 38 per cent), so that, even ignoring the government's role, the idea of an exceptional level of investment in the inflation years cannot be sustained.[22] Yet this raises a further question: how economically rational was the reconstruction of the merchant marine? Given the enormous growth of ship-building outside Europe after 1914, there was already a problem of global overcapacity even in 1919, which German reconstruction exacerbated. It could therefore be argued that the entire rebuilding project represented a misallocation of resources, encouraged by government subsidies: a classic attempt to return to pre-war conditions, rather than to seek new technological opportunities. Certainly, that is the impression gained from the subsequent experience of the Hamburg shipping industry, which experienced chronic structural problems in the later 1920s. Even before the onset of the Slump, capacity was only being utilised at around 38–50 per cent in the shipyards; while cargo ships were arriving in Hamburg only 60–80 per cent full, and leaving only 40–60 per cent full.[23] According to one estimate, German ship-building capacity had expanded by around 50 per cent during the

---

[20] On Blohm & Voß, which reduced its total nominal capital by 30 per cent and converted preference shares at revaluation rates of 25–33 per cent, see the material in StAH, FA B&V 523 (especially the letter from Walther Blohm to Erwin Hauers, 24.7.24, pointing out that the company was under no legal obligation to revalue its shares); Blohm & Voß, *Jahresbericht 1924*. On Deutsche Werft, whose shares issued in 1918, 1920 and 1922 largely retained their real value, see Deutsche Werft, *Eröffnungsbilanz 1924*.

[21] Calculated from Hapag, *Jahresbericht 1913*; *Jahresbericht 1914–1918*; *Goldmark-Eröffnungsbilanz 1924*. Cf. the analysis on *Hamburgische Correspondent*, 16.6.24.

[22] Figures from Büttner, *Staats- und Wirtschaftskrise*, pp. 100f.

[23] Krohne, 'Der Zusammenbruch', pp. 224f., 230–2; Wiskemann, *Welthandelspolitik*, pp. 339f.; Büttner, *Staats- und Wirtschaftskrise*, pp. 532 n. 65, 535 n.

inflation; but as a Deutsche Werft report of December 1924 noted, Blohm & Voß alone could virtually satisfy the total world demand for German-built ships, and capacity utilisation was consistently below 50 per cent.[24] These difficulties were not properly alleviated by attempts at 'rationalisation' – mergers such as the Hapag's takeover of the German–Australian Line and the Kosmos Line in 1926, or the fusion of Deutsche Werft with the Reiherstieg yard in 1927.[25]Athough the British General Strike brought a boost to the shipping lines, which placed a large number of new orders in 1926, the upturn proved ephemeral. Blohm & Voß typified the malaise: with its fifty-one hectares of docks and capacity to employ 12,500 workers, it struggled to record average net profits of 5.5 per cent on its reduced share capital between 1926 and 1928.[26] Deutsche Werft, which was rather more profitable, nevertheless had to be baled out by the Hamburg state, which bought its Tollerort yard for 3 m. reichsmarks to encourage the proposed merger with Reiherstieg.[27] Indeed, without some 50 m. reichsmarks made available to the shipping industry by the Reich in 1924 to finance job creation, it is hard to see how any of the major yards would have survived stabilisation.[28]

Investment during the inflation, then, was limited; where it did occur it was publicly subsidised and often economically unjustifiable. This partly explains the relatively limited enthusiasm for new investment by German business in the period after 1924.[29] On the other side of the investment balance sheet were the losses suffered by the creditors of companies like the Hapag, Deutsche Werft and Blohm & Voß – in particular, bond-holders. Without question, these losses were responsible for the weakness of the German capital market in the post-stabilisation period: as Balderston has observed, high bond yields

[24] Leckebusch, *Beziehung*, p. 97; GHH, 4001012012/0, Scholz to Reusch, 'Die Lage der deutsche Seeschiffswerften', 27.12.24.

[25] Büttner, *Staats- und Wirtschaftskrise*, p. 101; *Frankfurter Zeitung*, 1, 1.1.25. For efforts to 'rationalise' the Hamburg shipping industry, see GHH, *Denkschrift No. 30*, Bd. III, pp. 29–43; R. Erdmann, 'Die Krise im deutschen Schiffbau', *Wirtschaftsdienst* (1928), pp. 1502–5; W. Greiling, 'Die Hamburger Schiffahrtsfusion', *ibid.* (1926), pp. 1553–5. On the limits of industrial 'rationalisation', see R. Brady, *The Rationalisation Movement in German Industry* (Berkeley, 1933) and the recent case studies: H. Homburg, 'Die Neuordnung des Marktes nach der Inflation. Probleme und Widerstände am Beispiel der Zusammenschlussprojekte von AEG und Siemens, 1924–1933, oder "Wer hat den längeren Atem?", in Feldman and Müller–Luckner (eds.), *Nachwirkungen*, pp. 117–54; T. von Freyberg, *Industrielle Rationalisierung in der Weimarer Republik. Untersucht am Beispielen aus dem Maschinenbau- und der Elektroindustrie* (Frankfurt am Main, 1989).

[26] Blohm & Voß, *Jahresbericht 1924*; Büttner, *Staats- und Wirtschaftskrise*, p. 537 n.

[27] GHH, *Denkschrift Nr. 30*, Bd. III, pp. 29–43; Büttner, *Staats- und Wirtschaftskrise*, p. 537 n.; Leckebusch, *Beziehungen*, p. 108.

[28] Krohne, 'Zusammenbruch', pp. 223–49.

[29] Balderston, *Economic Crisis*, p. 364.

clearly reflected investors' bitter experiences of inflation and revaluation.[30] Moreover, the biggest institutional bond-holders – the banks –
were left in a seriously weakened state by the inflation, with aggregate
banking sector reserve ratios at unprecedentedly low levels throughout
the post-stabilisation period (1.5–2.5 per cent, compared with around
4–4.5 per cent before the war) (see figure 8.1).[31] Compared with the
depreciation suffered by industrial concerns like the shipyards, the
balance sheets of the principal Hamburg joint-stock banks had shrunk
dramatically compared with their pre-war levels. The merchant bank
Schuback & Söhne was a typical case, with its capital fixed in its
stabilisation 'gold mark opening balance' at around 25 per cent of the
pre-war figure; while the joint-stock Vereinsbank fared only slightly
better (29 per cent), and the Norddeutsche Bank slightly worse (24
per cent).[32] A more spectacular disaster was the Schiffsbeleihungsbank,
whose paid-up capital of 1.23 m. paper marks was reduced to a 'gold
balance' of just 15,000 gold marks.[33] Worst affected were the Hamburg
savings banks, whose total deposits in 1924 were equivalent to 3.3 per
cent of their pre-war level.[34] By contrast, the Commerzbank fared
better than average, its capital being depleted by around 50 per cent,
compared with the 57 per cent figure for the seven 'great' banks.[35]
But even Max Warburg could not deny the severity of the impact of
stabilisation: although the bank's balance sheet at the end of 1924 had
returned to a healthy 72 per cent of its pre-war level, his confidential
report on the previous year admitted that substantial sums of money
had been lost as a result of commodity speculation during the credit
squeeze.[36] A clear indication of the weakness of the banks was the

---

[30] Balderston, 'Links between Inflation and Depression: German Capital and Labour
Markets 1924–1931', pp. 157–85; idem, 'The Origins of Economic Stability in Germany, 1924–1930: Market Forces versus Economic Theory', VSWG, 69 (1982), pp.
488–514; idem, Economic Crisis, pp. 184ff. See also James, 'Economic Reasons for
the Collapse of Weimar', in Kershaw (ed.), Weimar: Why did German Democracy
Fail?, p. 34; Holtfrerich, 'Economic Policy and the End of the Weimar Republic',
in ibid., pp. 81–4.
[31] Cf. Bresciani, Inflation, pp. 280f., 294; James, German Slump, pp. 132–9; Feldman,
Great Disorder, pp. 846–9; Pohl, 'Die Situation der Banken in der Inflationszeit';
Holtfrerich, 'Auswirkungen der Inflation auf die Struktur des deutschen Kreditgewerbes', pp. 187–208; Feldman, 'Banks and Banking in Germany after the First World
War', pp. 243–62.
[32] Möring, Schuback & Söhne; Pohl, Bankengeschichte, pp. 119, 127ff.; Statistisches
Handbuch 1920, pp. 262f.
[33] Pohl, Bankengeschichte, p. 140.
[34] Statistisches Handbuch 1920, pp. 364f.; Lyth, Inflation, p. 147.
[35] Ibid., pp. 119, 127f.
[36] Such details as are available for the firm's accounts reveal how the bank was able
to balance losses due to 'the bankruptcies of second- and third-class firms' in the
hyperinflation crisis with substantial profits from commodity-, share- and foreign
currency-dealing; and indicate that, by 1923, it had accumulated foreign currency

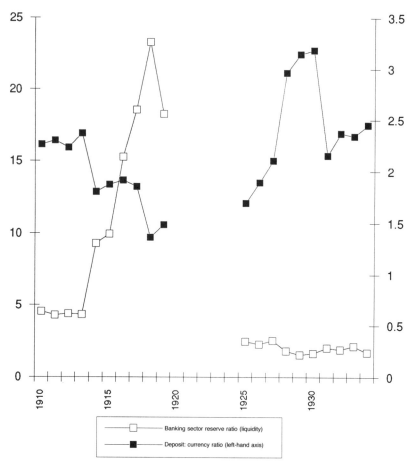

Figure 8.1 Banking liquidity before and after the inflation, 1910–1934
Sources: Holtfrerich, *Inflation*, pp. 50f.; James, *Reichsbank*, pp. 364–8.

major reductions in staff which followed stabilisation: the Commerzbank's payroll shrank from 26,000 (1923) to a mere 7,000 in 1925,
while even Warburg's cut its much smaller staff from 535 to 358.[37]
True, as in other sectors of the economy, there were attempts at
rationalisation. The Norddeutsche Bank became a branch of the Disconto-Gesellschaft in 1929, while the Commerzbank fused with the
Mitteldeutsche Creditbank in the same year.[38] Warburg's meanwhile

accounts and assets worth over 10 m. gold marks. WA, 'Jahresbericht 1923' contains
rare details of the firm's inflation balances.
[37] Pohl, *Bankengeschichte*, p. 126; WA, 'Jahresbericht 1924'.
[38] Pohl, *Bankengeschichte*, pp. 142–6.

continued to develop its role (already established during the inflation) as a conduit for American investment in Germany, as well as seeking new fields of activity in Central Europe and playing an important role in industrial mergers.[39] Yet none of this could make good the damage that had been done in the inflation. On the whole, the main Hamburg banks suffered from the same 'shortness of breath' and lack of dynamism that characterised the German banking system as a whole after 1924.[40]

In short, it is difficult to see the economic benefits of the inflation outweighing the costs – particularly the structural costs of misinvestment and a weakened money and capital market. The undeniably rapid growth of 1920–2 was paid for not only in the postponed stabilisation crisis in 1923–4, but also in the subsequent weak performance of the economy.[41] The recession of 1925/6 gave notice of the fragility of post-inflation stability; and the German economy turned down in 1927/8, well before the onset of the world depression.[42] True, so long as export markets remained buoyant, there was some respite for Hamburg; but with the collapse of trade after 1930, the city's commercial economy imploded. Numerous merchant houses were driven into bankruptcy. Ships lay idle or sailed empty; and the Hapag was only saved from insolvency by emergency payments of 77 m. Reich marks from the Reich. Blohm & Voß was forced to reduce its workforce from 10,700 in 1929 to just 4,879 in December 1930, and less than 2,500 two years later.[43] Amid the general collapse, perhaps the most dramatic failure was that of Warburg's. The bank had survived hypertrophic monetary growth between 1919 and 1923; it had survived stabilisation, and even appeared to prosper in the mid 1920s; but when the German money supply contracted sharply between June 1930 and June 1931, it was shipwrecked. Max Warburg had evidently anticipated a crisis, travelling to New York to enlist Paul's assistance in October 1930. But the bank's overexposure was irrepar-

---

[39] For Warburg's performance in the post-stabilisation period, see Warburg, *Aufzeichungen*, pp. 130ff.; Rosenbaum and Sherman, *M.M. Warburg & Co.*, pp. 133–43; Pohl, *Bankengeschichte*, pp. 141f.; James, *German Slump*, p. 145; Attali, *Siegmund Warburg*, p. 91. Of particular importance were the American and Continental Corporation and European Shares Inc., which existed to channel dollars into the German stock market.

[40] James, *German Slump*, pp. 139f., 294, 420.

[41] Cf. Borchardt, 'A Decade of Debate', in Kruedener (ed.), *Economic Crisis*, pp. 126–47. For an opposing view, see esp. Abelshauser and Petzina, 'Krise und Rekonstruktion'; Petzina, 'Was there a Crisis before the Crisis?', in Kruedener (ed.), *Economic Crisis*, pp. 1–20.

[42] Compare P. Temin, 'The Beginning of the Depression in Germany', *EcHR*, 24 (1971), pp. 240–8; Balderston, *Economic Crisis*, pp. 212, 332f.

[43] Büttner, *Politische Gerechtigkeit*, pp. 238ff.

able. In the last week of 1930, a run on the bank forced the repayment
of 80 per cent of its foreign and 50 per cent of its domestic monies;
and the collapse of the Austrian Creditanstalt five months later proved
the last straw.[44] When James Warburg arrived in Hamburg in June
1931, he found a cumulative deficit of $3.53 m. and numerous bad
debts including loans to the virtually bankrupt Karstadt department
store.[45] Although the American was inclined to let his uncle sink,
blaming him for irresponsible management, Max's brothers Felix and
Paul agreed to put up $9 m. in loans and guarantees to save the family
bank; while the Reich intervened with a payment of 30 m. reichsmarks
to avoid a collapse of the Hanseatic banking system.[46] However, when
the extent of the Danat Bank's insolvency came to light, the government
refused to act – to the amazement of James Warburg.[47] The German
banking crisis therefore began with the collapse of the Danat on 13
July; but it might equally well have begun with the failure of Warburg's
the previous month.[48]

The links from inflation to depression should not be exaggerated.
Other factors – to be discussed below – clearly played a role in the
collapse of the German economy after 1928. But there undoubtedly
were connections between the attempt to postpone stabilisation in the
post-war years and the peculiar severity of the depression in Germany.
Since around 1897, German business had grown accustomed to a
measure of inflation as an accompaniment of economic expansion.
Apart from fleeting episodes (price stability in 1913/14, currency reform
in 1924), prices had risen every year for three decades. This was true
even between 1924 and 1929: although wholesale prices stagnated, the
cost of living continued to rise at an annual rate of 3.3 per cent.[49] As
a result, when prices collapsed between 1929 and 1933 – falling, in
the case of wholesale prices, at an average rate of 11 per cent each
year – German business was, for all the talk of rationalisation, wholly
unprepared. Its assumptions continued to be inflationary even in the

---

[44] Warburg was on the bank's supervisory booard; Pohl, *Bankengeschichte*, p. 147.
[45] John F. Kennedy Memorial Library, Boston, James P. Warburg Papers, Box I,
  'Skizze zu den Richtlinien für eine Reorganisation', 31.5.31; James Warburg to Paul
  Warburg, 8.6.31; 9.6.31; 10.6.31; 15.6.31; James Warburg, 'A Book. . .', pp. 52–
  65; Pohl, *Bankengeschichte*, pp. 145f.; Attali, *Siegmund Warburg*, p. 100.
[46] James, *German Slump*, p. 311; Büttner, *Staats- und Wirtschaftskrise*, pp. 217–33;
  Chernow, *Warburgs*, pp. 323, 327–36. A temporary arrangement was then reached
  with the Berliner Handelsgesellschaft, at the suggestion of Siegmund Warburg, newly
  appointed a partner; Rosenbaum and Sherman, *M.M. Warburg & Co.*, p. 153.
[47] James P. Warburg, 'A Book. . .', pp. 55–60.
[48] K.E. Born, *Die deutsche Bankenkrise 1931* (Munich, 1967); H. James, 'The Causes
  of the German Banking Crisis of 1931', *EcHR*, 37 (1984), pp. 68–87; idem, *German
  Slump*, pp. 315, 387f.
[49] See figure 0.2.

teeth of deflation – as witness the assumption of some firms that the banking crisis would lead to devaluation and increased export orders.[50] Certainly, it was the Slump which finally discredited Weimar's system of corporatist capitalism, opening the way for a far higher level of state intervention in the mid 1930s. But the combination of structural weakness and banking overexposure, which were among the main reasons for the intensity of the Slump in Germany, were legacies of the inflation.

The crisis of bourgeois society

The economic costs of the inflation may have outweighed its short-term benefits, but can the same be said of its social consequences? It has often been suggested that the inflation was fundamentally the product of sociological forces: of an 'inflationary consensus', whereby capital and labour – big business and organised labour – united to pass on the costs of the lost war to other, less organised social groups. Writing in the last days of the inflation, Keynes acknowledged that this had meant 'the impoverishment [. . .] of the middle class, out of which most good things have sprung'; but maintained that this was a reasonable price to pay for the stimulus to employment which the inflation had brought the much larger working class.[51] This is a conclusion which has often been echoed in more recent writing.

However, such a class-based view takes too narrow a view of the social effects of the inflation. To begin with, it is important to see the inflation in the context of rapid demographic change, dating back to the 1890s. As chapter 1 made clear, pre-war Hamburg society was characterised by rapidly changing rates of mortality and fertility and high levels of migration. The war abruptly reversed some of these trends and accelerated others. Where young men had once poured into Hamburg to seek work, now they poured out to make war, many never to return. As a consequence, the birth rate fell sharply; while poor nutrition drove up the rates of still birth, illegitimate infant mortality and lung disease. Although, when the war ended, the level of in-migration soared and there was a spate of marriages, the optimism which underlay these phenomena proved ephemeral, and the inflation years saw no significant improvements in health or mortality.[52] Yet the fact that Weimar Germany had fewer children than Wilhelmine Germany mattered less than the fact that it had a larger proportion

[50] Borchardt, 'Das Gewicht der Inflationsangst in den wirtschaftspolitischen Entschei-dungsprozessen', in Feldman and Müller–Luckner (eds.), *Nachwirkungen*, pp. 235ff.
[51] J.M. Keynes, *A Tract on Monetary Reform*, in *Collected Writings*, IV, pp. 3, 29.
[52] See figure 1.3.

of young, employable men – the generation born too late to fight in
the war, which reached adulthood in the 1920s.[53] The proportion of
the male population aged between sixteen and sixty rose from 62.6
per cent in 1907 to 69.3 per cent in 1925 in Hamburg.[54] The post-war
economy thus had to absorb not only the returning soldiers, but also
their elder sons and younger brothers.[55] In addition to these demographic trends, it is important to bear in mind secular changes in the
structure of employment. By 1925, the proportion of manual workers
in the working population had declined from the 1907 level of 53 per
cent to 43 per cent; while the proportion of 'self-supporting' individuals
(i.e., mostly self-employed small businessmen) had also declined from
21 per cent to 16 per cent. By contrast, white-collar workers accounted
for around 32 per cent of the working population in 1925, compared
with 14 per cent in 1907.[56] This increase was due in part, it is true,
to changes in classification, but mainly reflected the expansion of
employment in Hamburg's service sector.[57] The inflation thus took
place at a time when manual work and self-employment were declining
relative to forms of clerical employment.[58]

In view of these constraints, the immediate post-war economy tri-
umphantly succeeded in creating full employment. The statistical evidence confirms that inflationary policies maintained employment levels
substantially above those in countries which stabilised sooner.[59] From
a post-war peak of around 18 per cent of the workforce, unemployment
in Hamburg followed a general (though not uninterrupted) downward
trend until mid 1922, reaching a post-war trough of 1.9 per cent in
June 1922. However, from July 1922 onwards, unemployment tended
upwards, reaching a peak of around 13 per cent in December 1923.[60]
It then fell during the stabilisation period, levelling off at around 5–
6 per cent in 1924/5. In 1926, however, unemployment rose sharply,
approaching in absolute terms the peak of 1923; and it remained at

[53] J. Reulecke, 'Veränderung des Arbeitskräftepotentials im Deutschen Reich, 1900–
1933', in Mommsen, et al. (eds.), Industrielles System, I, p. 86; K. Bade, 'Arbeitsmarkt, Bevölkerung und Wanderungen in der Weimarer Republik', in M. Stürmer
(ed.), Die Weimarer Republik. Belagerte Civitas (Königstein, 1985), pp. 160–87.
[54] Aus Hamburgs Verwaltung und Wirtschaft, 4. Jg. (1927), pp. 105, 106.
[55] On the increase in the 'participation ratio', see Bry, Wages, p. 25; Petzina, Deutsche
Wirtschaft, p. 179; Reulecke, 'Veränderungen', p. 88.
[56] Hamburger Statistische Monatsberichte (June 1926), 'Die berufliche und soziale Gliederung der Bevölkerung Hamburgs nach den Zählungen von 1925 und 1907'. Cf.
Büttner, Politische Gerechtigkeit, p. 145; idem, Staats- und Wirtschaftskrise, pp. 91ff.;
Lyth, Inflation, p. 36.
[57] See figure 1.1.
[58] Lyth, 'Mittelstand', passim.
[59] D. Petzina, 'Arbeitslosigkeit in der Weimarer Republik', in idem (ed.), Die Weimarer
Republik als Wohlfahrtsstaat, pp. 239–59; Abelshauser, 'Rekonstruktion', p. 165.
[60] See figure 3.1.

levels significantly higher than for most of the inflation period through-out 1927, 1928 and 1929, before soaring to disastrously high levels in 1930–3.[61] At its peak in 1933, more than 176,000 people were registered as unemployed, or 38 per cent of the workforce.[62] In the light of these figures, there therefore seems little reason to question the accepted view that, in the years from 1919 to 1922, inflation was indeed better for the majority of people than would have been a less expansionary policy such as was adopted in Britain. On the other hand, this merely postponed an inevitable recession. To be sure, outright unemployment in 1923/4 did not reach the levels of 1931/2; but the percentage of trade union members on short-time work did.[63] Moreover, if – as has been suggested in the previous section – the inflation fundamentally weakened the German economy, then it must take at least some of the blame for the subsequent levels of unemployment, which were higher than those experienced in other countries between 1924 and 1932.[64]

As Keynes observed, the post-war boost to employment was achieved at the cost of a substantial redistribution of income and wealth. Esti-mates for national income suggest a rapid recovery of per capita real incomes between 1920 and 1922, following general immiseration during the war and revolution;[65] but not all social groups fared the same. In Hamburg, as elsewhere, the war began a process of levelling which tended to narrow the income gap between manual workers in certain industries and other social groups, such as clerical workers and civil servants, who were unaccustomed to defending their real incomes by collective action. This was accelerated by the Revolution, which sharply increased nominal wages for manual workers. True, the combination of high unemployment and rising prices (due initially to the continuance of the blockade, and later to the depreciation of the mark) swiftly wiped out these gains, pushing real wages down to a nadir in early 1920. But revived labour militancy from early 1920, along with a steadily rising demand for labour, led to upward pressure on wages – and, as white-collar groups became increasingly willing to resort to collective action, on salaries as well. Government fiscal policies and state intervention added to this pressure, so that between March 1920 and May 1921, most wages and salaries rose significantly in real terms; and in the case of some manual workers actually outstripped pre-war

---

[61] Büttner, *Staats- und Wirtschaftskrise*, pp. 538, 679; Lipmann, *Leben*, pp. 314, 374f.
[62] Büttner, *Politische Gerechtigkeit*, pp. 241f.
[63] See figure 2.10.
[64] Balderston, *Economic Crisis*, pp. 8–18.
[65] See the estimates in Witt, 'Finanzpolitik', pp. 424f.; Henning, *Das industrialisierte Deutschland*, p. 49; Holtfrerich, *Inflation*, pp. 148f.

wage rates. This trend was continued after an initial setback when inflation resumed in mid 1921, as workers' expectations of inflation adjusted more swiftly. Only the onset of hyperinflation after July 1922 ended this upward pressure, causing sharp drops in real wages and salaries between July and November 1923 – though there is evidence of overcompensation for inflation in the public sector.[66] Finally, stabilisation led to a realignment of wages which initially suggested a significant drop relative to pre-war levels, and a partial restoration of differentials.

It would, of course, be wrong to conclude that upward pressure on real wages implied improvements in living standards. Despite the relative sophistication of the Hamburg cost-of-living index, statistics for real wages and salaries do not always take into account the effects of shorter working days, or higher taxation; nor do they tell us about the incomes of self-employed groups like shopkeepers; nor do they adequately reflect factors such as food shortages, the poor quality of available consumer goods, or the chronic shortage of housing, which one contemporary claimed led to homelessness for up to 36,000 individuals in Hamburg at the height of the inflation.[67] But, by the same token, nor do they fully reflect the increased social-welfare provision of the early Weimar period. Rent and price controls are taken into account, but not the value of subsidised education and health provision. Certainly, the impression that the inflation pushed up wages at the expense of other forms of income seems to be confirmed by comparing income tax figures for 1925 with those for 1913. At the national level, there appears to have been a significant levelling, though the available figures are not easily comparable.[68] Adjusted for inflation to create roughly equivalent tax bands, the figures for Hamburg suggest a similar picture: the percentage of income accruing to those in the top two tax bands fell from nearly 49 per cent in 1913 to 22 per cent in 1925.[69]

It is, of course, possible to view this flattening of the income pyramid positively, on the simple grounds that greater equality is always desirable. Yet this seems questionable on three grounds. Firstly, by shifting income from the *rentier* to the worker, the inflation discouraged saving, and thus was partly responsible for the subsequent weakness of the German money and capital markets.[70] Secondly, it can be argued that,

---

[66] Data summarised in figures 2.11, 2.12, 3.6 and 3.7.
[67] Lyth, '*Mittelstand*', p. 419.
[68] Holtfrerich, *Inflation*, p. 272. Cf. Hoffmann et al., *Wachstum*, pp. 512ff. for Pareto coefficients for Prussia, showing increased equality in 1925 compared with 1913.
[69] Lippmann, *Leben*, pp. 384f.; *Statistisches Handbuch 1920*, pp. 244f.
[70] This point has been acknowledged by Holtfrerich in his suggestion that after the inflation workers should have been forced to save via 'a compulsory investment of parts of wage income into capital formation funds owned by the workers or employees': Holtfrerich, 'Economic Policy', in Kershaw (ed.), *Weimar*, p. 84.

if they exceeded increases in productivity, rising real wages may have eroded profitability and thus reduced aggregate economic growth. This is a point that has frequently been made with regard to the years after 1924, when excessive real wages allegedly contributed to a 'crisis before the crisis'; an economic malaise which made the Slump inevitable.[71] Certainly, there is evidence to support Borchardt's thesis in the case of Hamburg after the inflation. Immediately after stabilisation, wages began once again to creep upwards.[72] Nominal weekly wages for eleven different occupational groups in Hamburg rose by between 80 and 180 per cent between 1924 and 1928.[73] Within two years of the currency reform, a bank clerk's monthly salary had risen by 70 per cent.[74] Of course, such figures have to be adjusted not only for the renewed rise in the cost of living, which in Hamburg averaged 5.3 per cent per annum between 1924 and 1928, but also for the higher tax and insurance burdens on wage earners (which had risen to around 10 per cent of gross pay, compared with 6 per cent before the war).[75] On this basis, the evidence suggests that, while public sector pay was somewhat reduced in real terms between mid 1924 and 1927, and then remained more or less steady during the Slump, real wages in the private sector showed a pronounced upward trend, interrupted only by the downturn in 1926/7, and reaching a peak in the spring of 1931. For example, real hourly wages for six manual occupations rose by between 63 per cent and 145 per cent between the first quarter of 1924 and the first quarter of 1931; while dockers' daily wages rose by 59 per cent in real terms, and bakers' weekly wages by 51 per cent (see figure 8.2). These increases clearly exceeded average productivity growth, which was around 30 per cent overall according to Holtfrerich's figures,[76] lending credence to the idea advanced by Borchardt and others of a deteriorating 'real wage position'.

The question is whether this also happened *before* 1923. Admittedly, it is hard to prove that inflation wages rose ahead of productivity or

---

[71] K. Borchardt, 'Zwangslagen und Handlungsspielräume in der grossen Wirtschaftskrise der frühen dreißiger Jahre', *Jahrbuch der Bayerischen Akademie der Wissenschaften* (1979), pp. 87ff.; C.-L. Holtfrerich, 'Zu hohe Löhne in der Weimarer Republik? Bemerkungen zur Borchardt-These', *G&G*, 10 (1984). pp. 122ff.; A. Ritschl, 'Zu hohe Löhne in der Weimarer Republik? Eine Auseinandersetzung mit Holtfrerichs Berechnungen zur Lohnposition der Arbeiterschaft, 1925–1932', *G&G*, 16 (1990), pp. 375–402; Borchardt, 'A Decade of Debate', in Kruedener (ed.), *Economic Crisis*, pp. 137–47; Holtfrerich, 'Economic policy', in Kershaw (ed.), *Weimar*, pp. 75–84.

[72] Scholz, 'Lohn und Beschäftigung', in Feldman *et al.* (eds.), *Anpassung*, pp. 293f..

[73] Calculated from *Aus Hamburgs Verwaltung und Wirtschaft*, 4. Jg. (Juni 1927), Sonderbeitrag 2.

[74] Pohl, *Bankengeschichte*, pp. 126f.

[75] Scholz, 'Lohn und Beschäftigung', pp. 298f. Cf. J. von Kruedener, 'Die Überförderung der Weimarer Republik als Sozialstaat', in *G&G*, 11 (1985), pp. 358–76.

[76] Holtfrerich, 'Economic Policy', p. 76.

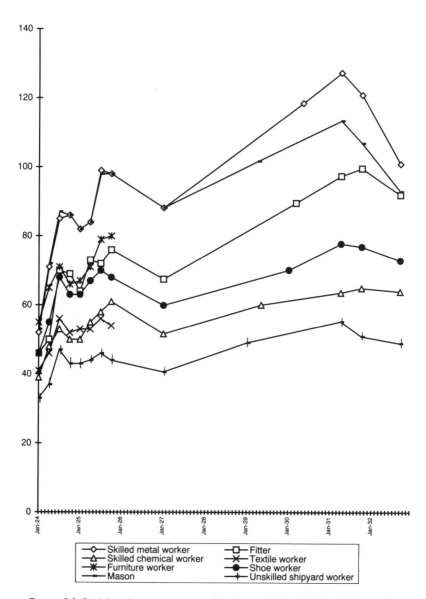

Figure 8.2 Real hourly wage rates in Hamburg, 1924–1932 (gold pfennigs)
Sources: *Statistisches Handbuch 1925*, p. 206; Büttner, *Staatskrise* pp. 707ff.

eroded profits, because of a paucity of reliable data. Nor can we be sure that the share of wages in national income increased gradually between 1914 and 1924, in the absence of reliable aggregate data; it might conceivably have fallen during the inflation and only risen in stabilisation. However, the evidence presented above suggests that rising real wages did cause employers in the ship-building industry difficulties, and partly contributed to the abandonment of investment projects in 1922. A tentative conclusion might be that the experience of accelerating inflation taught German workers to keep a vigilant eye on prices when bargaining about wage levels; while at the same time establishing the various institutional mechanisms whereby labour demands for higher wages could easily be realised.[77] To be sure, Balderston has persuasively argued that rising real wages after 1924 were necessary to increase the participation ratio, and did not diminish the competitiveness of German exports – or, for that matter, the rate of profit.[78] But it is difficult to make the same defence of rising real wages in 1920/1.

The third objection to the levelling effect of inflation on income distribution is that it did not lead to greater social stability, as has often been claimed by proponents of the inflationary 'consensus' between business and labour. In reality, the inflation years saw unprecedented industrial strife. Businessmen and politicians may have set out to diminish revolutionary sentiment after 1918 by boosting employment and nominal wages; but rising employment led to increased labour militancy, with waves of strikes in early 1919 and 1920, mid 1921, late 1922 and mid 1923. Despite an increase in the number of workers covered by collective agreements, the number of days lost through industrial disputes was higher in the inflation years than at any other time between 1900 and 1933, exceeding 20 m. in 1921 and 1922.[79] The state's efforts to keep shipyard workers in employment were rewarded not by political loyalty, but by recurrent 'actions' and 'risings', such as those in Hamburg in March 1921 and October 1923. In short, there are reasons to doubt that the greater equality of incomes achieved in the inflation period was either economically efficient or socially functional.

The inflation not only narrowed income differentials; it also brought about a radical reduction and redistribution of wealth.[80] There was a dramatic depletion of total nominal capital: according to the returns of the December 1923 property tax, total wealth in Hamburg had

[77] Balderston, 'Links between Inflation and Depression', pp. 168–78.
[78] *Idem, Economic Crisis*, pp. 20–42, 49–61, 80f.
[79] See figure 7.2.
[80] Maier, 'Political Economy', p. 72.

been reduced by more than two-thirds in the space of ten years; while
the number of people with capital exceeding 10,000 marks had fallen
by half, to just over 20,000.[81] However, the degree of redistribution is
less easily established. In common with many contemporaries, Keynes
believed that Germany had been 'the scene of the most extreme
redistribution of national wealth from the many to the few', citing
Stinnes as the archetypal 'debonair freebooter' who had seized on the
'glorious chances' of the inflation.[82] Yet there is little to support this
view in the statistics. On the contrary, the available figures suggest
that inflation levelled the wealth pyramid as much as it levelled the
income pyramid. Between 1913 and 1923, the percentage of taxpayers
with wealth exceeding 500,000 marks fell from 1.5 per cent to 0.7 per
cent and their share of total taxable wealth from a third to a fifth;
while there were corresponding gains within the lowest tax-bracket
(10,000–20,000 marks).[83] True, the evidence from savings banks
appears to suggest that small savers lost heavily: total deposits at the
five main Hamburg savings banks were down to around 3 per cent
of their pre-war level in 1924, and we know that the majority of savers
were clerical employees and small businessmen.[84] But much of this
'loss' may have been due to cash withdrawals during the phase of
hyperinflation: the number of depositors fell from 909,000 in 1922 to
just 40,000 in 1923.[85] By contrast, the picture is more clear-cut in the
case of property owners, a rather more elite group. It is clear that the
exceptional level of activity on the Hamburg real estate market in 1919
and 1922 reflected at least in part the detrimental impact of rent
controls on established landlords, who found themselves forced to sell
out – often to foreign purchasers or local authorities.[86] At the same
time, surprisingly few property owners appear to have taken advantage
of the hyperinflation to pay off their mortgages.[87] It is hard to disagree
with the verdict of the Property Owners' Association that, in purely

---

[81] Lippmann, *Leben*, pp. 383f. The comparison of 1913 marks with 1924 reichsmarks
is not entirely satisfactory, particularly since estimates of the real value of certain
types of property (e.g., real estate) were undoubtedly too low at this early stage in
the stabilisation process. However, the figures provide a rough guide to the redistributive effect of inflation.

[82] Keynes, *Collected Writings*, XVIII, pp. 245f.

[83] Holtfrerich, *Inflation*, p. 277.

[84] *Statistisches Handbuch 1920*, pp. 364f.; Lyth, *Inflation*, p. 147; Büttner, *Staats- und
Wirtschaftskrise*, p. 701.

[85] Lyth, '*Mittelstand*', pp. 88–90.

[86] *Ibid.*, pp. 431–57. Rent controls had the effect of reducing landlords' incomes to
30 per cent (1919), 9 per cent (1920), 8 per cent (1921), 2.6 per cent (1922) and
4.1 per cent (1923) of their pre-war levels. Figures on property sales in *Statistisches
Handbuch 1925*, pp. 126f.; *Hamburg Statistische Monatsberichte* (1924), Sonderbeitrag
3, pp. 118f.

[87] Lyth, '*Mittelstand*', pp. 451ff.

material terms, they had fared worse than most in the inflation years.[88] As in the case of income distribution, of cour~~ it can be argued that this redistribution of wealth represented social progress; but, again, the means – hyperinflation – were so drastic that lasting damage was done to the capital market, and particularly the market for personal savings. The extent to which people lost confidence in financial intermediation should not be exaggerated, of course: there was a revival of saving after the inflation, as broad money supply figures indicate.[89] But even Holtfrerich has conceded that low rates of saving after the inflation were partly responsible for depressed investment in the mid 1920s.[90]

On balance, then, the relative material beneficiaries of inflation included those who had fared worst in pre-war bourgeois society: the unskilled, poorly paid workers. In real terms, the gap between their incomes and those of the unskilled worker, the clerical employee and the professional narrowed; whereas, if stabilisation had been attempted sooner, they would have experienced unemployment sooner – as their British counterparts did. The material losers in Germany were *rentiers* and landords, who saw the gap widen between themselves and other sections of the bourgeoisie – in particular, some businessmen. Such an outcome does indeed make it tempting to analyse the inflation in class terms: in Britain (and Italy), the propertied classes united against the working classes to impose the cost of the war on them, in the form of unemployment; in Germany, as in most of Central Europe, revolutionary regimes pursued full employment at the expense of middle-class savings and incomes, with industrialists preferring to appease labour rather than safeguard the interests of shareholders and other creditors. Yet this purely materialistic analysis tells only half the story – and perhaps less. The inflation had contradictory effects on class consciousness: it stimulated it when it encouraged manual workers to strike or expropriated bourgeois savers; but diminished it by promoting social mobility and an individualistic war of all against all. On balance, it probably shrank 'objective' social collectivities from the large-class coalitions of the late Wilhelmine and war period to the more fragmented interest groups of mid Weimar. But in any case, attitudes were not shaped solely by the distribution of income and wealth. To grasp the true impact of the inflation on German urban society, it is necessary to look at its impact on values other than those denominated in marks.

---

[88] Freudenthal, *Vereine in Hamburg*, p. 533.
[89] See, e.g., figure 0.5, showing the rapid growth of M3 after 1925.
[90] Holtfrerich, 'Economic Policy', in Kershaw (ed.), *Weimar*, pp. 80–4.

As chapter 1 suggested, Wilhelmine Hamburg relied on a shared set of cultural values for its stability: the harsh imperatives of economic individualism were mitigated by the values of the family, the religious community, the school, the voluntary association and the court. It was these which inculcated the ethics of bourgeois society: not only the virtue of industry and thrift, the sanctity of property rights and contractual obligations, but also ideas of morality, piety, honour and cultivation. Although it is not easy to distinguish the effects of inflation from other secular trends, a fundamental argument of this book is that the inflation undermined the institutions which upheld these values, and hence the values themselves. It was thus as much a cultural crisis as a material crisis for the German bourgeoisie – perhaps more so.

To take a simple example: the large family, as we have seen, had been the fundamental unit of nineteenth-century capitalist society. It is true that demographic and socal forces had begun to erode this familial culture even before 1914, as family size began to decline and educational opportunities lured sons and daughters away from the family firm. But the process was dramatically accelerated by the upheavals of 1914–24. In 1910, 42.5 per cent of German households had had five or more members (i.e., including parents); and 10.1 per cent – around 1.4 million households – had had upwards of eight. By 1930, however, only 19.1 per cent of families still had four or more children; while the percentage settling for two or less had risen from 29.3 per cent to 65.4 per cent.[91] Nor was the new family merely a reduced version of the old. Middle-class women were freed from – or sometimes forced out of – the gilded cage of domesticity, aided by greater access to contraception, education and employment, impelled by economic necessity. For example, the proportion of women in employment in Hamburg increased from 24.8 per cent in 1907 to 29.9 per cent in 1925; one in ten married women now worked, compared with one in twenty before the war.[92] A girl like Ingrid Warburg could enjoy an education as good as any man's – indeed, it is hard to imagine a more sophisticated education than hers: the Mary Henkel Girls' School in Hamburg, Salem under Hahn, Heidelberg under Jaspers, Oxford under Isaiah Berlin.[93] Divorce increased.[94] For men, by contrast, patriarchal power appeared threatened, as did the bond

---

[91] Jaide, *Generationen eines Jahrhunderts. Wechsel der Jugendgeneration im Jahrhunderttrend.* p. 44; Hentschel, *Wirtschaft und Wirtschaftspolitik im wilhelminischen Deutschland.* p. 64 n. Cf. figures for the fall in average household size between 1910 and 1925 in *Aus Hamburgs Verwaltung und Wirtschaft*, 4. Jg. (1927), p. 104.
[92] *Ibid.*
[93] Warburg–Spinelli, *Erinnerungen*, pp. 63–88.
[94] *Aus Hamburgs Verwaltung und Wirtschaft*, 4. Jg. (1927), p. 105.

of brotherhood, so important in the culture of the nineteenth century. German society had entered the Freudian era of the 'nuclear family' – an essentially introverted, even claustrophobic unit dominated by sexual complexes, generational conflict and sibling rivalry. The volume of conservative social criticism directed against sexual laxity, 'the sickness of youth' and the decline of *gute Sitten* is a testament to the neuroses triggered by this transformation.[95] Certainly, these too were social changes which antedated the war and continued after stabilisation. But the case of the Schramm family illustrates the way material pressures accelerated the decline of the traditional grand bourgeois family. Precisely because of their father's status as a Senator, the family found the inflation years a succession of humiliations: having to queue for food during the war, agonising over whether to break the price regulations by buying on the black market, being reduced to taking in lodgers, running out of money while on holiday – these were the tribulations of bourgeois society in microcosm.

This 'crisis of the family' was only part of a more general crisis of bourgeois culture. For example, the 1920s witnessed a crisis of faith. In 1910, 0.9 per cent of the Hamburg population had been identified as without religious affiliation; in 1925 that figure was above 6 per cent.[96] This was not only reflected in declining religious observance, but also in the blurring of the barriers between religious communities. Increasingly, Jews married outside the Jewish community; by the mid 1920s, 50 per cent of all marriages involving at least one Jewish partner were mixed, and only 66 per cent of Jewish marriages were ritually celebrated: a marriage like Aby Warburg's, once shocking, was becoming normal.[97] Once again, it would be absurd to deny that such trends antedated the inflation years. But again, the inflation acclerated them by directly undermining the churches' economic foundations, obliged as they had been to invest in government bonds.[98] Traditional education was also detrimentally affected by the inflation. As we have seen, Max Warburg was struck by the way that inflation eroded the value of the various charitable foundations as well as the fees on which education traditionally depended,[99] and numerous private schools went bankrupt in 1923, notably the girls' *Realgymnasium* and *Lyzeum*.[100] Voluntary

---

[95] See for example, H. Hass, *Sitte und Kultur in Nachkriegsdeutschland* (Hamburg, 1932). Cf. Usborne, *Politics of the Body*, pp. 69ff.
[96] *Hamburger Statistische Monatsberichte* (1926).
[97] Lorenz, *Die Juden in Hamburg*, I, pp. liii, cxxix.
[98] Feldman, *Great Disorder*, p. 818. See for example Lorenz, *Die Juden in Hamburg*, I, pp. cvi, cxi, cxv, cxvi.
[99] WA, 'Jahresbericht 1920'; also quoted in Rosenbaum and Sherman, *M.M. Warburg & Co.* pp. 125f.
[100] Büttner, *Politische Gerechtigkeit*, p. 217.

associations, those pillars of bourgeois society, found their assets too
reduced to worthlessness. A case in point is the German Union of
Women's Suffrage, which held a well-attended meeting on the subject
of 'Inflation' in 1912, only to find twelve years later that its funds,
held in government bonds, were worth just five marks and fourteen
pfennigs.[101] Even the Hamburg Racing Club's assets were decimated;
while the venerable Patriotic Society, that product of Enlightenment
social activism, was reduced to letting out its building, the Amsinck
House.[102] True, inflation also wiped out foundations for poor relief
with assets worth 134 m. gold marks, to say nothing of the national
social insurance funds;[103] but the state showed more readiness to make
good these losses than it did when only bourgeois savings were affected.
Finally, inflation played havoc with those essential institutions of civil
society, the law courts. Not only were the lawyers and judges who
ran the courts impoverished. The courts were also overburdened by
the wave of civil and criminal cases unleashed by the inflation. As we
have seen, the level of crime against property doubled at the height of
the inflation;[104] but the efficiency of the courts suffered a corresponding
decline. Moreover, the civil courts brought themselves into disrepute
by continuing for most of the inflation period to apply the principle
'mark equals mark' with respect to the settlement of debts – effectively
sanctioning the expropriation of creditors.[105] The lawyer and DDP
politician Carl Petersen was prepared to accept Rathenau's argument
that the the inflation had been 'an absolute [. . .] necessity [. . .] to
maintain the German economy and [avoid] immense unemployment';
but insisted that it had not been necessary to maintain 'the fiction that
mark equals mark' or 'to brand the honourable merchant a profiteer
with legislation'.[106]

The impact of this institutional crisis on bourgeois culture was
profound. If the nineteenth century had witnessed a 'silent bourgeois
revolution', based on the free market, the sanctity of private property,
the rule of law and the creation of a public sphere, then the inflation

---

[101] Evans, *Feminist Movement*, pp. 97, 248.
[102] Freytag, *Geschichte des Hamburger Rennclubs und seiner Rennen*, p. 7; W. Sieveking,
  'Die Patriotische Gesellschaft in den letzten 50 Jahren', in *Die Patriotische Gesellschaft
  zu Hamburg 1765–1965*, pp. 114f.
[103] Büttner, *Politische Gerechtigkeit*, p. 210; G.D. Feldman, 'The Fate of the Social
  Insurance System in the German Inflation, 1914 to 1923', in *idem et al.* (eds.),
  Anpassung, pp. 433–47.
[104] See figure 4.10.
[105] Pfleiderer, 'Das Prinzip "Mark=Mark" in der deutschen Inflation, 1914–1924', in
  Büsch and Feldman, *Historische Progesse*, pp. 157–201; Southern, 'The Impact of
  the Inflation: Inflation, the Courts and Revaluation', in Bessel and Feuchtwanger
  (eds.), *Social Change and Political Development*, pp. 56–76.
[106] *Hamburger Fremdenblatt*, 17.8.23. Cf. Feldman, *Great Disorder*, pp. 515–27.

undid the achievements of that revolution. Bourgeois society upheld industry; the inflation broke the link between pay and productivity, profit and diligence. Bourgeois society believed in thrift and parsimony; the inflation expropriated savers and benefited those who borrowed to the hilt and consumed. Bourgeois society was a hierarchy resting on the ownership of property; the inflation precipitated a radical reshuffle of wealth, rendering bonds and other paper assets worthless. Bourgeois society's civil law code was based on the binding nature of contract – on equity and good faith; the inflation subverted this principle by allowing debtors to pay creditors in depreciated marks. Bourgeois society upheld the rule of law; the inflation unleashed a crime wave and discredited the courts. Above all, bourgeois society craved *Ruhe und Ordnung*; the inflation was a time of disorder and violence.

The traumatic experience of this inversion of the bourgeois world is easily illustrated in contemporary art and literature.[107] Elias Canetti, who was a young student in Frankfurt in 1923, recalled:

> It was more than disorder that smashed over people, it was something like daily explosions. [. . .] The smallest, the most private, the most personal events always had one and the same cause: the raging plunge of money. [. . .] I [had] regarded money as something boring, monotonous [. . .] But now I suddenly saw it from a different, an eerie side – a demon with a gigantic whip, lashing at everything and reaching people down to their most private nooks and crannies.[108]

Cultural values had indeed rested on material values, and when money collapsed, intellectuals and artists were thrown into confusion. Georg Grosz is remembered for the unequivocally revolutionary message of his caricatures of grotesque profiteers, unreconstructed militarists and emaciated war orphans; but he relied on the patronage of an aristocrat, Graf Kessler, to make ends meet.[109] Otto Dix is another artist often seen as having 'captured' the amoral atmosphere of post-war Germany with his Expressionistic visions of violence and brutalised sexuality; but he too had to survive economically, churning out watercolours to order for the Düsseldorf art dealer who had explained to him that oil paintings were not cost effective.[110] The corrupting effect of inflation

[107] G.D. Feldman, 'Weimar Writers and the German Inflation', in G. Brude-Firnau and K.J. MacHardy (eds.), *Fact and Fiction. German History and Literature, 1848–1924* (Tübingen, 1990), pp. 173–83. See for Hamburg, E. Oppens, *Der Mandrill, Hamburgs Zwanziger Jahre* (Hamburg, 1969); R. Jaeger and C. Steckner, *Zinnober. Kunstszene Hamburg, 1919–33* (Hamburg, 1983).
[108] E. Canetti, *The Torch in my Ear* (London, 1990), pp. 51f.
[109] Kessler, *Tagebücher*, pp. 122, 159ff. Cf. M.K. Flavell, *George Grosz. A Biography* (New Haven, 1988).
[110] P. Barth, *Otto Dix und die Düsseldorfer Künstlerszene, 1920–1925* (Düsseldorf, 1983). Cf. O. Conzelmann, *Der andere Dix* (Stuttgart, 1983).

provided a central theme in plays like Georg Kaiser's *Nebeneinander*
or Mehring's *Der Kaufmann von Berlin*, about a Galician Jew who
becomes a millionaire, and in films like Fritz Lang's *Dr Mabuse – der
Spieler*.[111] Indeed, in Dr Mabuse, gambling not just with money but
with life, Lang personified the link between economic devaluation and
moral devaluation.[112] Nor was the crisis perceptible only among the
modernists. It is surely not without significance that Aby Warburg's
period of mental collapse began in 1914, intensified in October 1918,
and continued for the next four and half years, his recovery coinciding
almost exactly with Germany's economic and political stabilisation.[113]
After 1923, Warburg made a number of explicit allusions in his work
to the economic upheaval which had coincided with his illness. In a
1928 lecture, for example, he drew a parallel between the inflation
and the baroque – a cultural inflation in which the 'gold reserves of
suffering' inherited through images from the art of antiquity, were
devalued by the printing press.[114] It could be argued plausibly that at
least part of Warburg's cultural crisis – his sense that the irrational
might triumph within him – was related to what he perceived as its
triumph around him after 1914. As Carl Melchior put it in October
1923, with pardonable exaggeration:

> As a result of these privations, social dislocation through the submersion of
> our best circles, namely the educated middle class, and finally through the
> feeling of hopelessness and national despair, a condition of general nervous
> excitement has set in [. . .] Among us, eight or nine of every ten men is
> suffering from nervous illness.[115]

Of course, not every German bourgeois suffered such a spiritual
crisis: Max Schramm, who had also read his Nietzsche and Schopenhauer,[116] survived the war more or less unruffled. Not all early Weimar
art was Expressionist. Yet even for less culturally sophisticated members of the *Bürgertum*, this was a period in which inner values were
threatened. The experience of the Schramms, again, reveals how
inflation represented as much a moral as well as a material shock:
'Should I use my money on [. . .] the black market?' Ruth Schramm
asked her brother; 'Or do the principles which held firm for me before

---

[111] J. Willett, *The Theatre of the Weimar Republic* (New York, 1988), pp. 53–92.
[112] Feldman, 'Weimar from Inflation to Depression', in *idem* and Müller–Luckner (eds.),
Nachwirkungen, pp. 385–401. Gambling was indeed rife in the inflation years; see
BAP, RFM 47047 N. Reg. 2594, Geschäftsbericht, Landesfinanzamt Unterelbe,
November 1920.
[113] Gombrich, *Aby Warburg*, pp. 7, 206–24.
[114] *Ibid.*, pp. 250, 266f.
[115] Feldman, *Great Disorder*, p. 772.
[116] Both, by his own admission, 'without understanding'; he preferred Goethe and
Schiller, Ranke and Treitschke, Hauptmann and Fontane: Schramm, *Neun Generationen*, II, pp. 445–53.

1914 still hold?' As we have seen, their uncle Alfred inveighed against
those who speculated against the mark.[117] Before the war, lamented
the Property Owners' Association, 'Everyone [had known] what was
his own'; now, as Lord D'Abernon heard, 'real poverty' appeared to
coincide with 'champagne at 30 marks a bottle and the clearest signs
of extravagance'.[118]

The point is clear: any theory of the inflation which portrays its
distributional levelling in a positive light overlooks the severity of the
cultural crisis this provoked. From 'war socialism' to the collectivist
excesses of the revolution, from the corporatism of 1920 to the war
of all against all in 1923 – the inflation years imposed severe material
burdens on broad sections of the German bourgeoisie. But it was the
psychological disruption as much as the materal disruption which
caused the lasting damage. Those who suffered were not merely the
economic laggards; they were the people who had continued to keep
faith with the values of the pre-war world. The inflation in this sense
was Germany's anti-bourgeois revolution: Bebel's prophecied 'twilight
of the gods of the bourgeois world'. The danger lay in the political
darkness that threatened subsequently to descend. For the legacy of
this crisis of values was a volatile combination: on the one hand, a
reactionary desire among many older people to see traditional values
restored; on the other, a diminished fidelity among the next generation
to those values. This is the essential background to the paradox of
the later Weimar years: that so many believers in the values of bourgeois society came to support a political movement that was bent on
their negation. In fact, the crumbling during the inflation of the
traditional pillars of bourgeois culture – the family, religious community, voluntary association, school and court – made the restoration
of that culture unlikely. More probable was a continuation of the
secular transitions: from social hierarchy to social homogeneity; from
kith and kin to the nuclear family; from piety to state religion; from
voluntarism to mass mobilisation; from the work ethic to consumerism.
The challenge after the inflation was not to turn back this modernist
tide, but to filter and channel it in ways that would make it acceptable
to bourgeois Germany. It was this that Weimar failed to do.

The 'modernisation' of the urban polity

Was this political failure inevitable? Historians of Hamburg have traditionally tended to portray their state's political development in terms

---

[117] *Ibid.*, pp. 407, 495.
[118] Freudenthal, *Vereine in Hamburg*, p. 533; D'Abernon, *Ambassador of Peace*, III,
pp. 8of.

of continuity and stability, emphasising the institutional links from the
Kaiserreich to Weimar, and – in the case of Ursula Büttner's work –
emphasising the degree to which a 'social–liberal' consensus emerged
in the early 1920s. Even before the war, it is argued, there had been
a gradual convergence of left-liberalism and reformist social democracy
in Hamburg, which the war had done much to accelerate; and although
the November Revolution had threatened to disrupt the gradual democratisation of the Hamburg polity, it was successfully 'contained' by
the compromise struck between the old Senate and the MSPD, and
by the inflationary boom. After stabilisation, Hamburg enjoyed a
golden age of 'political justice and the social spirit' which was only
brought to an end by exogenous forces: the Slump and Brüning's
policy of deflation.[119] This picture of smooth transition and stability is
an attractive one, chiming as it does with the traditional notion of
Hanseatic exceptionalism: if nowhere else, Weimar worked here –
nearly. Yet this view exaggerates the strength of the social–liberal
partnership, and overlooks the alienation of important groups who had
fared relatively better under the older system. Tempting though it is
to see the Slump – or Brüning – as a *deus ex machina*, in reality
Weimar Hamburg was a city built on foundations of paper.

The transformation of the nineteenth-century polity had begun in
the 1890s, with the emergence of the fractious 'Hamburg system' of
industrial relations on the waterfront; the creeping democratisation of
the Bürgerschaft franchise, thanks to inflation; and the increasing
bureaucratisation of urban administration. In this process, shocks like
the cholera epidemic of 1892 and the strike of 1896 played an important
role; but neither had an impact as great as the First World War.
Dearth and de-skilling undermined the power of both unions and
employers, forcing the authorities to rely on a combination of price
controls and military policing to maintain order; and when mutiny
eliminated the latter in November 1918, revolution swept the old order
aside. True, Hamburg's business community moved swiftly to stabilise
the situation by offering financial assistance to the new government as
well as representation on an Economic Council to the unions. But the
reconstruction of the Senate to incorporate the Majority Social Democrats in 1919 did not represent a definitive compromise. On the
contrary, urban order broke down annually thereafter, beginning with
the Sülze riots of 1919, and continuing with the Kapp crisis in 1920,
the Communist 'Action' in 1921, the right-wing violence of mid 1922
and the Communist 'Rising' of October 1923. What is striking is
the pendulum-like quality of instability. In 1919, 1921 and 1923,

---

[119] Büttner, *Staats- und Wirtschaftskrise*, *passim*; idem, *Politische Gerechtigkeit*, *passim*.

working-class elements took to the streets to protest against dearth and unemployment; in 1920 and 1922, bourgeois groups resorted to violence to express their dissatisfaction with the post-war regime. Those involved never numbered more than a few thousand, it is true – sometimes less. Indeed, the reality of the revolutionary threat never lived up to the dire warnings of those who claimed to fear it. Nevertheless, these challenges to the new regime exposed its fundamental weakness: the fragmentary character of the two classes on which the social–liberal compromise was supposed to rest.

Even before the war, it had been clear that the Hamburg bourgeoisie lacked a coherent response to the rise of working-class organisations like the unions, the cooperatives and the SPD. Within the business community, big employers like the Blohm brothers had tended to pursue their own, unsuccessful strategy of trying to stamp out the free trade unions. At the other extreme, legally trained liberals like Carl Petersen, had adopted a more integrative approach, based on a fundamental sympathy with the Social Democrat reformists' aspiration to expand the role of the state as a provider of health care, education and housing. The disagreeable implications of this for groups like shopkeepers and property owners became clear during and after the war, as the authorities used price and rent controls to subsidise working-class real incomes; while at the same time narrowing the differentials between the salaries of civil servants and the wages of dustbin men. All this might just have been tolerable had it delivered the promised social peace. Yet, as we have seen, far from appeasing the working class, these policies tended to radicalise elements within it, particularly those younger men who were employed more casually, and tended to protest more violently and spontaneously. In short, the social–liberal coalition antagonised important middle-class groups, without satisfying all working-class groups.

It can, of course, be argued that matters improved in the period after the inflation. The governing coalition of SPD, DDP and DVP which emerged after stabilisation under Max Schramm and governed the state from March 1925 to September 1931 steadily improved its electoral showing from 53 per cent to 62 per cent in the succeeding four years.[120] But this view surely underestimates the trauma of the 1914–24 period; and overestimates the economic and political health of the post-inflation regime. In reality, the coalition was always a frail thing. The Hamburg DDP was anti-business and wary of pre-1918 patriotism; the DVP was pro-business and distinctly *schwarz-weiß-rot*

---

[120] Büttner, *Politische Gerechtigkeit*, pp. 186–9; Comfort, *Revolutionary Hamburg*, pp. 148f., 161f.

in complexion; the SPD was a party of ageing union functionaries.[121] In practice, the only way Schramm could govern was by making the familiar 'unpolitical' distinction between administration and politics: in Carl Petersen's words, making more *städtisch* than *staatlich* policy.[122] It has been argued that this was a coded call for conservatism, which allowed Wilhelmine civil servants discreetly to undermine the efforts of reforming SPD Senators.[123] But in practice, little was done to obstruct the expansion of welfare provision and urban infrastructure which were the main Social Democrat objectives. Two Welfare Bureaus, one Old People's Home; a Youth Hostel, a state hospital, a mental asylum, a Health Department, a swimming pool, a waterworks, a university, forty new secondary schools, more than 58,000 new homes and the electrification of the city's rail network – to say nothing of free primary education, the highest supplementary benefits in the Reich and a motorised refuse-collection service: such were the achievements of the Hamburg welfare state of the 1920s.[124] It was impressive; as one enthusiastic labour functionary put it: 'You can tell the democratic consciousness of the people of Hamburg in the [very] architecture of the city.'[125] Unfortunately, it was unaffordable.

Between 1924/5 and 1929/30, the state payroll grew by 20 per cent, to nearly 50,000; total state expenditure more than doubled, from 240 m. reichsmarks to 508.3 m. richsmarks. The three biggest budget headings were for housing, education and welfare, which together accounted for around 45 per cent of ordinary expenditure. Between 1924/5 and 1930/1, the state spent a total of 298 m. reichsmarks on housing alone.[126] Clearly, if this increase in spending had been translated directly into increases in taxation, middle-class toleration of the new regime would have been sorely tried, since around 30 per cent of ordinary revenue came from taxes on income, property or business turnover.[127] However, in common with other municipal authorities – and continuing its practice before and during the inflation – the

---

[121] Büttner, 'Vereinigte Liberalen', pp. 15–18; *idem*, *Staats- und Wirtschaftskrise*, pp. 31f., 50, 58ff.; Comfort, *Revolutionary Hamburg*, p. 143.

[122] Büttner, *Staats- und Wirtschaftskrise*, p. 41. Cf. Walther Dauch's call for 'less party politics, more objectivity'; *ibid.*, p. 44.

[123] *Ibid.*, p. 45.

[124] For Hamburg's social policies, see Lippmann, *Leben*, pp. 323–54, 390–6, 439–57, 482–7; Büttner, *Politische Gerechtigkeit*, pp. 191–9, 202f., 210, 213–22.

[125] Herzig, 'Einleitung', in *idem et al.* (eds.), *Arbeiter in Hamburg*, pp. 29f. See also H. Hipp, 'Wohnungen für Arbeiter', in *ibid.*, pp. 471–81; *idem*, *Wohnstadt Hamburg. Mietshäuser der zwanziger Jahre zwischen Inflation und Weltwirtschaftskrise* (Hamburg, 1982).

[126] *Statistisches Handbuch 1926/27*, pp. 254–7; Büttner, *Staats- und Wirtschaftspolitik*, pp. 90, 692f.; Lippmann, *Leben*, pp. 439–57.

[127] Lippmann, *Leben*, pp. 390–6.

Hamburg state was able to finance a considerable part of its spending by borrowing. Foreign investors had already lost once on Hamburg state bonds, as a result of inflation; but when, as in 1923, the state was willing to borrow in dollar or sterling terms at attractive rates of interest, investors were tempted back. Under the direction of Senator Carl Cohn (and against the advice of the city's financial expert Leo Lippmann), the city floated a second series of 6 per cent bonds in 1926: £2 m. at 93.5 through Schröder's in London and $10 m. at 91.75 through Kuhn, Loeb & Co. in New York. However, even the 70 m. reichsmarks this brought in did not suffice; and by 1931, the city had accumulated short-term debts abroad totalling 120 m. reichsmarks. A breakdown of the city's total liabilities two years later reveals that more than 30 per cent of the 389 m. marks total owed was short term.[128] Fritz Schumacher's new building for the Finance Deputation at Gänsemarkt may have suggested stability; economically, it was a house of cards. When foreign lenders refused to renew bonds worth $400,000 in August 1931, the house collapsed.[129]

The SPD–DDP–DVP coalition had already shown signs of strain during the fourteen-week shipyard strike of October 1928; but the need to make drastic cuts in public expenditure – demanded by the Reich government as the price of financial assistance – proved fatal to it.[130] Between 1929/30 and 1932/3, total spending was slashed by 30 per cent, at a time when unemployment was already rising rapidly.[131] For the SPD, it was a suicidal policy: by 1932, 41 per cent of trade union members were unemployed in the Hamburg region and nearly two-thirds of unionised metal workers; and as union membership collapsed, so did the SPD vote.[132] The Democrats too were ship-

---

[128] *Ibid.*, pp. 297ff., 482–7.
[129] Büttner, *Politische Gerechtigkeit*, p. 248; *idem*, 'Die Finanzpolitik des Hamburger Senats in der Weltwirtschaftskrise, 1929–32', *ZVHG* (1978), pp. 181–226.
[130] *Ibid.*, p. 178; F.-W. Witt, *Die Hamburger Sozialdemokratie in der Weimarer Republik. Unter besonderer Berücksichtigung der Jahre 1929/30–33* (Hanover, 1971). See also U. Büttner, 'Das Ende der Weimarer Republik und der Aufstieg des Nationalsozialismus in Hamburg', in U. Büttner and W. Jochmann (eds.), *Hamburg auf dem Wege ins Dritte Reich. Entwicklungsjahre 1931–3* (Hamburg, 1983), pp. 7–37; *idem*, 'Rettung der Republik oder Systemzerstörung', in U. Büttner and W. Jochmann (eds.), *Zwischen Demokratie und Diktatur. Nationalsozialistische Machtaneignung in Hamburg. Tendenzen und Reaktionen in Europa* (Hamburg, 1984), pp. 41–65.
[131] Büttner, *Staats- und Wirtschaftskrise*, p. 692.
[132] *Ibid.*, p. 269. Cf. U. Büttner, 'Die Politik der Hamburger SPD in der Endphase der Weimarer Republik', in Herzig *et al.* (eds.), *Arbeiter in Hamburg*, pp. 457–69; *idem*, 'Die politische Haltung der Hamburger Freien Gewerkschaften in der Weltwirtschaftskrise, 1928–31', in *ibid.*, pp. 517–28; A. Schildt, 'Hanseatische Vernunft kontra Extremismus? Zum antifaschistischen Kampf der Hamburger Sozialdemokratie, 1929–1933', in Berlin (ed.), *Das andere Hamburg*, pp. 263–82. See also Projektgruppe Arbeiterkultur Hamburg, *Vorwärts und nicht vergessen. Arbeiterkultur in Hamburg um 1930. Materialien zur Geschichte der Weimarer Republik* (Berlin, 1982).

wrecked, with the majority of the Hamburg party opposing the national leadership's support for Brüning and agreeing only reluctantly to the merger with the Young German Order. This left the junior partner in the coalition, the DVP, whose commitment since 1925 had appeared to rest principally on the absence of acceptable alternatives. Its participation in an 'above-party' meeting 'of the *Bürgertum* against Marxism' in March 1931 was the first sign that such an alternative was emerging.[133]

It is clear that there was never an alternative to the left of the Weimar coalition. Although the KPD temporarily revived its 'united front' tactic in 1927, calling for a 'Workers' Senate', this was never a credible proposition;[134] and the anti-SPD position adopted after the VIth Comintern Congress of 1928 set the party on a course for destruction.[135] Although successful in attracting the votes of unemployed workers, it was incapable of making an effective electoral appeal to middle-class voters.[136] Admittedly, this reflected the confusion of middle-class aspirations, which was evident in the notorious fragmentation of bourgeois politics. For example, significant numbers of businessmen – like Karl Gottfried Gok of Blohm & Voß – continued to withhold their support from the Republic, aligning themselves with the DNVP. Other interests – including artisans and urban property owners – temporarily rallied to the flag of the *Wirtschaftspartei* in November 1926, in an attempt to distinguish themselves from the big business interests represented in the DVP.[137] And on the periphery were the various paramilitary organisations, like the Stahlhelm and the Wehrwolf; and the *völkisch* groups like the Schutz- und Trutzbund, the German Popular Freedom Party (DVFP) and the National Socialist German Workers' Party. It proved extremely difficult to unite these disparate elements in a single, right-wing front. The *völkisch* 'block'

[133] Büttner, 'Liberalen', pp. 33f.

[134] J. Berlin, W.D. Hund et al., *Arbeiterregierung in Hamburg. Die Verhandlungen zwischen ADGB, KPD und SPD nach den Bürgerschaftswahlen 1927* (Hamburg, 1983).

[135] Büttner, *Staats- und Wirtschaftskrise*, pp. 6of., 255; Herzig, 'Einleitung', in *idem et al.* (eds.), *Arbeiter in Hamburg*, p. 27.

[136] McElligott, 'Mobilising the Unemployed: the KPD and the Unemployed Workers' Movement in Hamburg-Altona during the Weimar Republic', in Evans and Geary (eds.), *German Unemployed*, pp. 228–60. See also Voß et al. (eds.), *Vom Hamburger Aufstand zur politischen Isolierung*; H. Caspar, 'Die Politik der RGO. Dargestellt am Beispiel der Arbeitslosenpolitik in Hamburg', in *Deutsche Arbeiterbewegung vor dem Faschismus* (Berlin, 1981), pp. 50–79.

[137] Büttner, *Staats- und Wirtschaftskrise*, pp. 65; *Hamburger Nachrichten*, 30.8.24; *Hamburger Anzeiger*, 18.11.26; 19.11.26; Lyth, '*Mittelstand*', p. 462; Hauschild-Thiessen, *Grundeigentümer-Verein*, p. 262; F. Domurad, 'The Politics of Corporatism: Hamburg Handicraft in the late Weimar Republic', in Bessel and Feuchtwanger (eds.), *Social Change*, pp. 174–206. Cf. M. Schumacher, *Mittelstandsfront und Republik. Die Wirtschaftspartei – Reichspartei des deutschen Mittelstandes, 1919–1932* (Düsseldorf, 1972).

formed in 1924 managed to unite the various anti-Semitic groups with the Pan Germans and the German National Commercial Employees and achieved electoral success in May 1924; but this proved ephemeral,[138] and signs of a united front of veterans' associations and paramilitary groups in 1928 proved equally transient.[139] Before 1929, there was certainly no indication that the elusive goal of unity on the right would be achieved by a party based in Southern Germany, whose Hamburg branch numbered at best a few hundred members.

The history of the NSDAP in Hamburg between its reestablishment in 1925 and 1929 was, to say the least, unpromising.[140] It was led by quarrelsome cranks like Josef Klant and his successor, the former teacher and hack writer Albert Krebs.[141] Its membership rose only slowly from around 135 in 1925 to just 600 three years later; and, although its share of the vote did rise from just 1.5 per cent in the Bürgerschaft elections of 1927 to 2.6 per cent in May 1928, it remained in absolute terms insignificant.[142] However, there followed a dramatic improvement. Party membership rose to over a thousand in June 1929, nearly two thousand in September 1930 and close to 15,000 in July 1933. Membership of the paramilitary *Sturmabteilung* increased by a factor of ten between June 1929 and October 1932. In the September 1930 Reichstag elections, the Nazi vote in Hamburg soared to 19 per cent, reached 26 per cent in the Bürgerschaft elections a year later, exceeded 31 per cent in the Bürgerschaft elections of April 1932, and reached a peak of 34 per cent in the first Reichstag election of July 1932.[143] This did not make Hamburg a Nazi stronghold by national standards, of course. But it did enough fatally to undermine the legitimacy of the governing coalition.

The question 'Who voted for Hitler?' has not always been satisfactorily answered in the case of Hamburg. By adopting oversimplistic sociological profiles of the city's districts, Hamilton concluded that the NSDAP had done disproportionately well among the city's *Großbürgertum* in the crucial elections of 1930 and 1932.[144] In fact, the above

[138] Krause, *Hamburg wird braun. Der Aufstieg der NSDAP von 1921 bis 1933*, pp. 33, 41, 54f., 57.

[139] *Ibid.*, p. 82; Büttner, *Staats- und Wirtschaftskrise*, p. 73.

[140] Krause, 'Von der Sekte zur Massenpartei. Die Hamburger NSDAP von 1922 bis 1933', in Bruhns *et al.* (eds.), *'Hier war doch alles nicht so schlimm'*. See also H. Anschütz, 'Die Nationalsozialistische Deutsche Arbeiterpartei in Hamburg. Ihre Anfänge bis zur Reichstagswahl vom 14. September 1930' (Diss. Hamburg, 1955).

[141] W.S. Allen (ed.), *The Infancy of Nazism: the Memoirs of ex-Gauleiter Alfred Krebs, 1923–1933* (New York, 1976).

[142] Krause, *Hamburg wird braun*, pp. 36ff., 72–7, 84–90.

[143] *Ibid.*, pp. 118, 122–7, 143, 174; Büttner, *Staats- und Wirtschaftskrise*, pp. 260f., 268.

[144] R.F. Hamilton, *Who Voted for Hitler?* (Princeton, 1982).

average Nazi vote in Rotherbaum reflected the popularity of the party in the less prosperous western side of the district.[145] This, like the other Nazi strongholds of Hohenfelde, Eilbek, St Georg and Eimsbüttel, was a predominantly *kleinbürgerlich* neighbourhood.[146] Similarly, the overrepresentation of *Selbständige* among Nazi party members reflected the high number of small businessmen and artisans who joined the party. Still more markedly overrepresented were clerical employees (42 per cent of members in 1930) and civil servants (7 per cent).[147] The key to Nazi success was not the mobilisation of the middle-class as such, but the discreet penetration of existing middle-class interest groups and professional associations, a strategy of 'synchronisation from below' explicitly adopted in 1932.[148] Clerical employees, the police, doctors, lawyers and students, all acquired their National Socialist sub-organisations in Hamburg between 1928 and 1933.[149] In this way, the Nazis pioneered a system of 'niche-mobilisation', establishing further off-shoots to mobilise women and, above all, youth. Indeed, the Nazis' success in mobilising the younger generation was arguably the single most important factor in the party's breakthrough in 1930.[150]

Yet, as the work of Falter and others has shown, even these qualified sociological correlations between Nazism and the middle class understate the breadth of the Nazis' social appeal. The key to the party's success was precisely that it did not portray itself as the party of the *Mittelstand*, but as a *Volkspartei*.[151] True, the Nazis' campaign to capture working-class votes in Hamburg never achieved the gains in this area hoped for by the party's more socialist and self-consciously '*abürgerlich*' elements like Klant and Krebs.[152] Nevertheless, there clearly were many manual workers in other sectors – handcrafts, public transport, seamen – who were attracted by the party's pro-worker rhetoric, and the increase in the percentage of worker members from

---

[145] Krause, *Hamburg wird braun*, p. 174. Cf. T. Childers, 'Who, Indeed, did Vote for Hitler', *CEH*, 17 (1984), pp. 45–53; W.S. Allen, 'Farewell to Class Analysis in the Rise of Nazism: a Comment', in *ibid.*, pp. 54–62.

[146] Krause, *Hamburg wird braun*, pp. 104–7.

[147] *Ibid.*, pp. 101, 190; Büttner, *Staats- und Wirtschaftskrise*, p. 525. Cf. T. Childers, *The Nazi Voter. The Social Foundations of the Fascism in Germany* (Chapel Hill, North Carolina/London, 1983), p. 246.

[148] Krause, *Hamburg wird braun*, p. 181.

[149] Büttner, *Politische Gerechtigkeit*, pp. 246, 266f.; Krause, *Hamburg wird braun*, pp. 100, 160–3. On the role of the SS as a channel for the more socially elite activists, see *ibid.*, p. 152.

[150] *Ibid.*, pp. 96, 107f., 162ff., 184f. In 1928, nearly a third of those aged between twenty and thirty in Hamburg did not vote; in 1930, 42 per cent of the Nazi vote came from that age group.

[151] See J. Falter, T. Lindberger and S. Schumann, *Wahlen und Abstimmungen in der Weimarer Republik: Materialien zum Wahlverhalten, 1919–1933* (Munich 1986).

[152] Krause, *Hamburg wird braun*, pp. 92–5, 182–4.

21 per cent in 1925 to 26 per cent in 1933 was no mean achievement.[153] In no other party were working-class and middle-class groups so evenly represented. Moreover, it was precisely the party's commitment to uniting German society in a *Volksgemeinschaft* which middle-class Germans found so attractive, playing as it did on a traditional aversion to socio-economic divisions in politics. The diary of Luise Solmitz, a Hamburg schoolteacher and ex-officer's wife illustrates this point: her description of a Hitler rally in Hamburg in April 1932 captures not only the impressive combination of 'immaculate order and discipline' and technical special effects (aeroplanes, loudspeakers, cine cameras), but also the carefully crafted message of a Hitler speech:

Main theme: out of parties shall grow a nation. He censured the 'system' ('I want to know what there is left to be ruined by this state!') [. . .] Otherwise, he made no personal attacks, nor any promises, vague or definite. [. . .] How many look up to him with touching faith! as their helper, their saviour, their deliverer from unbearable distress – to him who rescues the Prussian prince, the scholar, the clergyman, the farmer, the worker, the unemployed, who rescues them from the parties back to the nation.[154]

She echoed these sentiments two months later:

Not only the desperate but also those who purposely contract debts in our neighbourhood are enthusiastic Hitler people – as are all those who hope for something to the Left or Right or anywhere. [. . .] Nevertheless, every person who thinks or feels as a German, the bourgeois, the farmer, the aristocrat, the prince and the intelligentsia stands by Hitler. It is the nationalist movement.[155]

Ironically – in view of the large Marxist-inspired literature on the role played by 'big business' in Hitler's rise – the middle-class group which was probably least susceptible to Nazi penetration was the economic elite.[156] Although one or two obscure businessmen have been identified as having financed or joined the NSDAP before 1932, the Nazis had great difficulty in persuading Hamburg business that they were not 'more social than national' and bent on 'all possible measures of expropriation'.[157] There were efforts by the party to gag radicals like Krebs and Hüttmann; to portray itself as a supplier of anti-socialist labour to major employers like the Hapag; to stress the anti-Marxist themes of Hitler's

---

[153] *Ibid.*, pp. 155f., 160, 190.
[154] Quoted in J. Noakes and G. Pridham (eds.), *Nazism, 1919–1945*, vol. I (Exeter, 1983), p. 74.
[155] *Ibid.*, pp. 8of. The significance of the reference to debt is unclear, but suggests the continuing importance to bourgeois culture of moral behaviour in creditor–debtor relations – in deflation as in inflation.
[156] Cf. H.A. Turner, *German Big Business and the Rise of Hitler* (Oxford, 1985).
[157] Krause, *Hamburg wird braun*, pp. 82 n., 128, 147f., 150f., 173, 198–206.

ideology, as when he addressed the Nationalklub of 1919 in 1926, or
when Heß paid a visit three years later; and to propose alternative economic policies in the Slump.[158] There were some who acknowledged the
possibility that the Nazis might be useful political partners: Cuno, the
failed Chancellor, toyed with the idea that he might be able to use Hitler
to revive his own political career; while even Siegmund Warburg
detected in the movement 'valuable, typically German strengths, which
[. . .] show strong feeling for social and economic duties'.[159] But it seems
clear that many middle-class observers were alarmed by persistence of
socialist rhetoric in Nazi propaganda; by the recurrence of anti-Semitic
hooliganism;[160] and by the policy of violent confrontation with the
Communists, particularly when it reached its bloody climax in Altona
on Sunday 17 July 1932, when around eighteen people died in street
violence.[161] Such activities may have attracted petty-bourgeois voters and
members, like the unemployed artisans and clerical workers who joined
the SA;[162] but they evidently put off the 'valuable bourgeois element'
personified by Luise Solmitz, who by December 1932 saw the Nazis as
'a party sliding more and more into a dubious future'. 'The Nazis [. . .]
want to expel every employer from their ranks who lowers wages,' she
had lamented in September: 'Can an employer remain a Nazi at all?'[163]
Such anxieties help to explain the fall in the Nazi vote in the second
Reichstag elections of 1932.

On the other hand, such reservations were far too weak to prompt
positive action against the Nazis: Aby S. Warburg's attempt to persuade
the Evangelical and Catholic Churches to join the Jewish communities
in a joint condemnation of anti-Semitism produced only anodyne
'unpolitical' cant: 'Every man and woman should continually strive to
make their belief fully effective, within whichever circle they are able

---

[158] *Ibid.*, pp. 90, 95, 101, 135f., 150, 170, 189, 192, 197ff., 204; W. Jochmann (ed.),
Im Kampf um die Macht: Hitlers Rede vor dem Hamburger Nationalklub von 1919
(Frankfurt am Main, 1960), pp. 28–44; *idem, Nationalsozialismus*, p. 238; Büttner,
Staats- und Wirtschaftskrise, pp. 50, 54f.

[159] Kohlhaus, 'Die Hapag', pp. 173, 176; Krause, *Hamburg wird braun*, p. 196–205;
Chernow, *Warburgs*, pp. 365f. Max Warburg seems also to have underestimated the
threat, regretting that 'this movement, which has so much good in it, is encumbered
by so much rubbish, and that the anti-Semitism makes it impossible to line up in
formation with it': *ibid.*, pp. 372–83. Cf. Warburg, *Aufzeichnungen*, p. 146; Vagts,
'M.M. Warburg & Co.', p. 387; Mosse, *German-Jewish Elite*, p. 293.

[160] On anti-Semitic actions between 1930 and 1932, which were largely confined to
defamatory literature, intimidation of Jews and vandalism of religious sites, see
Lorenz, *Die Juden in Hamburg*, I, pp. cxliv–cxlviii.

[161] A. McElligott, 'Street Politics in Hamburg', *History Workshop Journal* (1983), pp.
83–90; Krause, *Hamburg wird braun*, pp. 78–82, 137ff.; Büttner, *Politische Gerechtigkeit*, p. 263.

[162] Krause, *Hamburg wird braun*, pp. 160, 190.

[163] Noakes and Pridham (eds.), *Nazism*, I, pp. 108f.

to influence.' No charges were brought against the Nazis who vandalised the Rentzelstraße cemetery.[164] Clearly, with the feeling that some kind of Nazi participation in government was possible, if not inevitable, calculations of self preservation and opportunism supervened. In this respect, there is perhaps a similarity between the response of the Hamburg business community to the revolution of 1918/19 and their response to the revolution of 1932/3. On each occasion, a group of merchants, bankers and industrialists moved swiftly to make contact with the leaders of the revolutionary masses, in order to preserve, as far as possible, Hamburg's economic freedom. In 1918, it had been Max Warburg and Franz Witthoefft who had taken the lead; in 1932 it was the shipping heir Carl Vincent Krogmann, along with Emil Helfferich, Kurt Woermann, Erwin Merck – and the same Franz Witthoefft.[165] For Krogmann, the political choice in November 1932 was between 'dictatorship based on the bayonet, i.e., reaction' and 'the counter-revolution from the Right' based on Hitler. Given the greater popularity of the latter option, it was vital to teach the Nazis that 'socialist government [of the economy] is impossible, regardless of what form the socialism takes'. As the Blohm & Voß manager Gok put it:

This is something which our National Socialist friends will have to learn, in addition to the[ir] strong wave of nationalism, which in many ways outdoes ours, and the strong national will, which they share with us. And they will have to learn it from us.[166]

In association with the South German businessmen Wilhelm Keppler, Krogmann, Woermann, Helfferich, Merck and Witthoefft sought to steer Hitler's economic thinking in the direction of overseas trade and colonies, and in late 1932 they publicly called for his appointment as Reich Chancellor.[167]

As in 1919, the advocates of compromise sought to secure the formal continuity of the institutions of the urban economy and polity in the face of an ultimately irresistible revolutionary pressure. When the Nazis had won forty-three seats in the Bürgerschaft elections of September 1931 (increased to fifty-one seven months later), the social-liberal Senate had not resigned, but had continued governing without a majority: as at the national level, democrats could only resist Nazism by undemocratic means. But the appointment of Hitler as Chancellor

---

[164] Lorenz, *Juden in Hamburg*, I, p. cxlviii.
[165] *Ibid.*, pp. 202–9; Büttner, *Politische Gerechtigkeit*, pp. 266f. With the exception of Witthoefft, all were members of the younger generation in the *Handelskammer*.
[166] Krause, *Hamburg wird braun*, p. 202; Behrens, *Deutschnationalen*, p. 370.
[167] Turner, *German Big Business*, pp. 239–46.

of a Nazi–Nationalist coalition in January 1933 made this situation more or less unsustainable, for two reasons. Firstly, it reassured middle-class voters that conservative elements could hold Hitler in check: Luise Solmitz described the new Cabinet ecstatically as a combination of 'National Socialist drive, German National reason, the non-political Stahlhelm, not to forget Papen'.[168] It was a point vividly illustrated by the torch-lit parade which took place in Hamburg on the night of 6 February, which was led by '20,000 brownshirts', followed by field-grey-clad Stahlhelm members playing Prussian military marches, and students in the regalia of the *Burschenschaften*. The implicit historical sequence – 1933–1914–1813 – was complicated only by the fact that the SS brought up the rear.[169] Secondly, it put the Nazis in a position to squeeze the Senate from above and below, demanding on the basis of the Decree for the Protection of People and State of 28 February that it take repressive action against the Left. Although the SPD and *Staatspartei* Senators were willing to arrest seventy-five KPD members – especially in the wake of the Reichstag fire – they could hardly authorise the suppression of the SPD's own *Hamburger Echo*, and duly resigned on 3/4 March.[170] Yet even after this the belief in accommodation persisted, as a new Senate 'of the Right' was elected under the DVP Senator Paul de Chapeaurouge. That too collapsed within days in the face of the demand from Berlin that the SA Standartenführer Alfred Richter be made chief of police – a demand delivered in unmistakably revolutionary style by Gauleiter Kaufmann while a group of Nazi policemen hoisted the swastika flag over the Rathaus.[171] But once again, a compromise was attempted. Chapeaurouge having resigned, protesting in anachronistic tones about 'interference in Hamburg's sovereignty', another more pro-Nazi representative of the 'old families', Carl Krogmann, was given the office of Bürgermeister in a Nazi-dominated Senate.[172]

It is clear that Krogmann and his associates were seeking to replicate the achievement of 1919, when the revolution from the Left had been contained by a combination of economic lobbying and urban coalition building. Yet their hopes were in vain. In reality, the National Socialists

---

[168] Noakes and Pridham, *Nazism*, I, pp. 129f.
[169] *Ibid.*
[170] Büttner, *Politische Gerechtigkeit*, p. 277. For a credulous, not to say hysterical, reaction to the official version of the Reichstag fire, see Luise Solmitz's diary for 1 March, quoted in Noakes and Pridham, *Nazism*, I, pp. 142f.
[171] Noakes and Pridham, *Nazism*, I, pp. 144f.
[172] W. Johe, 'Institutionelle Gleichschaltung in Hamburg 1933: Revolutionäre Umgestaltung oder Wiederherstellung traditioneller Ordnungen?', in Büttner and Jochmann (eds.), *Zwischen Demokratie und Diktatur. Nationalsozialistische Machtaneignung in Hamburg*, pp. 66–90.

were infinitely more revolutionary in their objectives and more ruthless in their methods than had been the revolutionaries of 1918. Moreover, the established order was at each level – economic, social and political – far weaker in 1933 than it had been fourteen years before; while the international constraints, which had so hampered the November revolutionaries, had all but vanished. His senior partner, Max Warburg, may have initially been complacent about the new government, but Carl Melchior saw with clarity how much more dangerous the National Socialists were than the Social Democrats of 1918. As he had written to the firm's Amsterdam agent as early as August 1932:

I am occupied at the moment less with economic affairs than with matters of public *mores*, for it is in these matters that I see the most dangerous developments for us. [. . .] The leaders of our largest political party declare their solidarity [. . .] with men who [. . .] have committed murder in the usual sense of the Penal Code. [. . .] This problem, which lies entirely outside the economic and technical-political sphere, has become the most important for us.[173]

Even Luise Solmitz had become aware by February 1933 that she and other conservatives had struck a Faustian pact: 'The black–white–red front represents responsibility, represents the solid citizens, morality, protection of individuality, property, free enterprise, without experiments, without the use of force – [but] it is a powerless little group outside Hitler's mighty shadow.'[174] Hitler, in short, clearly did *not* stand for the essential bourgeois values; and vestiges of institutional continuity at the state level were to prove worthless under a national government bent on radically expanding the power of the Reich at home and abroad, without the slightest regard for those values.

From inflation to deflation

There had, of course, been repeated attempts to achieve greater centralisation and greater international leverage for the German Reich before 1933. Without question, the political development of Hamburg was more influenced by events in Berlin in the 1920s and 1930s than it had been in the 1870s and 1880s, when it had been precisely the limited nature of the Reich's power which made it acceptable to traditionally 'egoistical' Hamburg. But the degree of centralisation brought about after 1914 should not be exaggerated. Indeed, it is one of the main arguments of this book that at no time before the 1930s were the powers of the Reich satisfactorily defined and consolidated

[173] Rosenbaum and Sherman, *M.M. Warburg & Co.*, p. 175.
[174] Noakes and Pridham, *Nazism*, I, p. 134.

relative to the states and the communes, nor relative to the private sector of the economy. Whatever the value of the various structural theories of inflation, it was this political defectiveness that was the main cause of inflation, in that it led to fiscal laxity and excessive monetary expansion. The external corollary of this internal weakness was balance of payments instability.

Although a single German fiscal and monetary system had been created in the 1870s, the Reich's political responsibilities from the outset tended to exceed its fiscal resources. Despite politically tortuous attempts at fiscal reform before 1914, the Reich remained confined to around a third of total public revenues, mostly indirect taxation; while its share of public sector borrowing was also limited. At the same time, there were limits to the central government's control over monetary policy. The Reichsbank lacked effective leverage over the rapidly expanding banking system; while the decision to put Germany on the gold standard meant that the Reich's monetary policy was subject to international capital movements, which the Reichsbank could influence only in conjunction with the Bank of England and the Bank of France. Successive governments after 1890 strove to increase Germany's international power and prestige; but precisely because of the Reich's domestic political weaknesses, they were never able to translate as large a proportion of its GNP into actual military power as the Reich's international rivals. As men like Albert Ballin and Max Warburg came to realise, attempts to challenge English naval supremacy or to pressurise the French into making colonial concessions were therefore bound to be frustrated. Increased spending on arms precipitated domestic-political conflict as the democratic Reichstag sought to increase its share of total taxation; or pushed up interest rates as public borrowing increased. International crises led to damaging outflows of capital from Germany; while protective tariffs did not significantly reduce German dependence on imports from overseas.

The war was in many ways a product of these weaknesses; for the decision to risk a military confrontation with Russia rested at least in part on the assumption that the Reich was fiscally deadlocked, and could not hope to win a sustained arms race with its eastern neighbour. Yet even the pressures of war failed to bring about an effective restructuring of the Reich. On the contrary, despite the high-flown notions of economic planning which the war encouraged in Berlin, the extent and efficiency of central control over the war effort was very limited. The government bungled the supply side, leaving the allocation of contracts and raw materials to private industrial interests whose prime concern was to maximise profits, not output. Worse still, it allowed demand to run out of control as a result of defective fiscal and monetary policies. Total public expenditure soared from 18 per cent to 77 per cent of NNP; but ordinary tax revenues covered only 14 per cent of Reich expenditures. This meant that, despite a twenty-fold increase in the funded debt, the floating debt exceeded 50 bn. marks by the end of the war. This, in turn, fed a spiral of monetary expansion (see figure 8.3). Only the system of price controls kept the annual average rate of inflation down to between 20 per cent and 30 per cent; but these were at once unfair and inefficient, contributing to a growing popular dissatisfaction with the *Kaiserreich* as a political system. Under these circumstances, Germany stood only a slim chance of achieving victory. The involvement of Britain exposed the full extent of the Reich's external vulnerability: German trade was debilitated and her overseas assets wiped out. The main puzzle is why the German government was unable to cut its losses and seek a negotiated peace while it had a strong bargaining position. Even in economically stricken Hamburg, no consensus emerged in favour of a compromise settlement. There was a disastrous failure to appreciate the fragility of the German war effort's foundations, and the possible consequences of domestic crisis and defeat. Businessmen opposed any continuation of economic controls into peacetime, resisted all but the most limited constitutional reform, and optimistically assumed that the weakness of the mark and Germany's strategic position between East and West would quickly overcome 'the hatred felt abroad towards Germany'.

The storm which broke over Germany when the military leadership admitted defeat therefore came as a profound shock. Some businessmen – notably Max Warburg – had, it is true, been moving in the direction of a negotiated peace and domestic reform. However, with the Americans refusing to negotiate with the liberal government of Prince Max and the British continuing the economic war, an orderly transition to parliamentary government proved impossible. Hasty improvisation prevented a complete revolutionary break with all the Reich's established institutions: as in the Ruhr, so in Hamburg, businessmen moved swiftly to find a *modus vivendi* with moderate socialist leaders. But despite constitutional compromises at the national and state level, the dire economic situation led to recurrent crises of public order until mid 1919. Under these circumstances, the wartime plans for a controlled 'transitional economy' had to be scrapped in favour of a deficit-financed drive to create jobs at any price.

The problems of peace-making also proved greater than had been anticipated. Motivated partly by economic self interest but also by a desire for political influence at home, Warburg, Melchior, Witthoefft and Cuno went to Versailles, armed with a proposal for moderate reparations predicated on a large-scale loan and the return of Germany's lost assets. When these suggestions went unheeded, however, they responded with dire forecasts: excessive reparations demands would lead either to an excessive fiscal contraction, which would drive Germany towards 'the fate of Russia', or to the collapse of the mark and hence a flood of German exports. At first sight, this was an ingenious argument – sophisticated enough to convince Keynes, who became its most ardent propagandist in the West. In the immediate aftermath of the Versailles treaty, the mark did indeed collapse, German exports did sell at bargain-basement prices, and the 'wave of Bolshevism' did threaten to engulf Germany. Yet by March 1920 both predictions had been confounded. The mark had been stabilised as investors speculated on a German recovery; and instead of a Bolshevik takeover, the Republic had to contend with an attempted conservative *putsch*.

The continuation of inflationary fiscal and monetary policies in 1919 had undoubtedly made sense as a response to the exigencies of demobilisation. But it is misleading to argue that their continuation thereafter was necessary to 'save German democracy'.[175] In fact, a very propitious opportunity to stabilise economic policy in early 1920 was missed as a result of largely avoidable policy errors. Although Erzberger's fiscal reforms tended in the right direction, he underestimated the effect of renewed inflation on his new taxes, and wholly failed to bring expenditure under control. Although the currency might have been reformed in 1920, exaggerated fears of the consequences of stabilisation prompted pressure for continued monetary laxity in the form of a low discount rate and intervention against the mark. Although the balance of payments had begun to move towards equilibrium as a result of capital in-flows, the decision to impose trade controls and a social 'levy' had the perverse effects of hampering exports. Finally, although real wages had adjusted themselves downwards during 1919, government measures to stimulate employment and to intervene in industrial disputes led to renewed wage pressure thereafter. For all these reasons, there was a resumption of inflation in 1921/2. But this was not inevitable. Smaller budget deficits, a formal devaluation and a more liberal trade and wages policy would have reduced the risk of a future hyperinflation without unleashing a second revolution.

They might also have been a more effective means of persuading the Allies to revise the terms of the peace. It is true that the Allied demands of 1921 were excessive and could not be paid out of tax and export receipts alone. But it was quite wrong to think, as did Warburg and others, that a deliberate strategy of currency depreciation would be the best way of demonstrating the impossibility of the London

---

[175] Feldman, *Great Disorder*, pp. 854f.

schedule. On the contrary, the German strategy of revision by economic means probably lengthened the life of reparations. It had been easy enough in 1919 to create an initial export advantage for German industry by running deficits and dumping paper marks on the foreign exchanges; but this was not a process which could be constantly repeated. The fall in British and American prices after 1920 and the rapid adjustment of German prices and wages thereafter meant that, far from running a trade surplus, Germany ran a trade deficit of unprecedented size in 1921/2. The strategy of revision-through-depreciation which underlay 'fulfilment' thus wholly backfired, as it relieved rather than increased the pressure on the British and American economies. Here again an earlier attempt at stabilisation might well have been in German interests. Even if the Allied demands could not have been reconciled with balanced budgets, a less deliberately inflationary policy would have exerted more effective pressure on the Allied economies by reducing German imports.

In 1920, Hamburg businessmen had tended to withdraw from politics, alarmed by the political polarisation unleashed by the Kapp *putsch*. By 1922, however, the mood had changed. Frustrated by the sympathy for labour shown by the state and fearful of the consequences of an increasingly imminent liquidity crisis, Cuno and others increasingly favoured a change of domestic regime. At the same time, frustration with the diplomacy of fulfilment prompted an increasingly confrontational stance abroad, which came to a head when Keynes exhorted an enthusiastic audience of businessmen at the Hamburg Overseas Week to call Poincaré's bluff. It seems likely that it was this misconceived advice which finally persuaded Cuno to accept the Chancellorship; though his insistence on a cabinet of business experts, independent of parties and the unions, clearly also reflected the desire for domestic confrontation.

There was great confidence in late 1922 in the idea of a government of *die Wirtschaft*. Yet in practice Cuno's regime proved disastrous. By 1923, there had grown up a fundamental conflict between the interests of the state in combating French occupation of the Ruhr, and the interests of private firms in remaining solvent. As a result, all Cuno's expedients to finance 'passive resistance' were thwarted by his own colleagues, who resisted higher taxation, undermined support for the mark, refused to buy dollar-denominated Treasury bills and opposed his attempt to tighten up exchange controls, with the result that the mark's value all but evaporated. Moreover, Cuno's hopes of French isolation and an American change of heart turned out to be premature. Neither Kent, nor Keynes, nor Dulles was able to persuade the German government that, as in 1918/19, they had no bargaining position from which to bargain. The result of this débâcle was to bring Germany to a state of political disintegration not seen since the time of Napoleon, leaving states, communes and firms struggling to manufacture their own money in the face of radical political challenges from both left and right.

The years 1919–23 witnessed, in this sense, a political crisis every bit as big as the deflationary crisis ten years later – arguably bigger, in the sense that the Reich's very integrity seemed in jeopardy. Yet in 1923/4 it proved possible, with the use of Presidential power, Enabling Laws and emergency decrees, to achieve an economic 'regime change' without destroying Weimar's essential institutions of parliamentarism, federalism and corporatism. Ten years later, by contrast, the economic regime was only changed in the context of a complete restructuring of the political system which replaced these institutions with 'leader principle', the unitary state and a command economy. This has led many historians to the simplistic conclusion that deflationary policies did more political damage to the Republic than inflationary policies. The flaw with this argument is that it was precisely the legacy of the inflation which ensured that the stabilisation of 1924 proved so illusory and the Slump of 1928–32 so severe.

To some extent, of course, it is possible to blame late Weimar's problems on constitutional and party-political defects.[176] There is also a case to be made that the labour and business organisations on which the corporatist 'system' depended failed to provide the necessary underpinning of economic stability; though there are conflicting views as to which side was more to blame.[177] However, these problems were merely symptoms of the underlying political–economic weaknesses inherited from the period before 1924. For, despite the appearance of stabilisation, the fiscal reforms of Luther in reality provided only a temporary respite from the traditional problem of public sector profligacy. The monetary reforms of Schacht did not create a central bank capable of resolving the fundamental conflict between the appetites of the domestic economy and the need for external balance. Ultimately,

---

[176] See in general M. Stürmer, *Koalition und Opposition in der Weimarer Republik, 1924–1928* (Düsseldorf, 1967); idem, 'Der unvollendete Parteienstaat. Zur Vorgeschichte des Präsidialregimes am Ende der Weimarer Republik', in idem (ed.), *Belagerte Civitas*, pp. 310–17; G. Schulz, *Zwischen Demokratie und Diktatur. Verfassungspolitik und Reichsreform in der Weimarer Republik*, 2 vols. (Berlin/New York, 1987); M. Broszat, *Die Machtergreifung. Der Aufstieg der NSDAP und die Zerstörung der Weimarer Republik* (Munich, 1984).

[177] Compare James, *German Slump*, passim with B. Weisbrod, *Schwerindustrie in der Weimarer Republik. Interessenpolitik zwischen Stabilisierung und Krise* (Wuppertal, 1978); Abraham, *Collapse of the Weimar Republic*. Cf. D. Geary, 'Employers, Workers and the Collapse of the Weimar Republic', in Kershaw (ed.), *Weimar*, pp. 92–119.

the entire edifice rested on the flows of foreign capital which followed the Dawes Plan, which was not, in reality, a durable solution of the reparations problem.

The fiscal problems of the period after 1924 were in many respects a continuation of those of the previous five years. The years after 1924 confirmed the Reich's predominance in financial matters, with both the *Länder* and communes remaining dependent on the Reich for revenue, and the Reich's share of total spending rising from 37 per cent to 42 per cent.[178] But the problem of maintaining central control over expenditure – temporarily solved by Luther's emergency decrees – soon returned with the return to normal parliamentary and federal procedures. As a result, spending tended to creep upwards after 1924, at all levels of government. Part of this increase took the form of infrastructural investment by local authorities. But there was also a tendency for public sector pay to increase, as did the costs of debt service – partly as a result of the belated revaluation of government bonds. In particular, there was a general increase in social welfare expenditure: according to one estimate, it increased from 57 per cent of total spending in 1925 to 68 per cent in 1932, compared with just 37 per cent before the war.[179] The problem was that this growth far outstripped the growth of the economy as a whole: total public spending rose from around 25 per cent of NNP in 1925 to a peak of 37 per cent in 1931 and 1932.[180] It also outstripped the growth of revenue.[181] Between 1925 and 1932, the public sector deficit fluctuated at between 1.6 per cent and 3.2 per cent of NNP.[182] As a result, the Reich debt rose from just 2.7 bn. reichsmarks in 1924 to 11.3 bn. reichsmarks six years later; by which time total public debt exceeded 40 per cent of NNP.[183] Local authority borrowing also rose. True, compared with the pre-war period, to say nothing of the inflation years, this was a relatively modest level of public sector borrowing. But it *was* excessive, given the extreme weakness of the market for public bonds, reflected

---

[178] See figure 0.3. See the figures in Witt, 'Auswirkungen', p. 87; Andic and Veverka, 'Government Expenditure', pp. 243–5; Hoffmann, *Wachstum*, p. 791; James, *German Slump*, pp. 39ff., 50f., 375–7; Balderston, *Economic Crisis*, p. 226.

[179] James, *German Slump*, pp. 48f.; Petzina, *Deutsche Wirtschaft*, p. 91. See in general Balderston, *Economic Crisis*, pp. 214–44.

[180] See figure 0.4. Cf. Witt, 'Auswirkungen', p. 87; Hoffmann *et al.*, *Wachstum*, pp. 255f.; Balderston, *Economic Crisis*, p. 226. On the role of local government, K. Hansmeyer (ed.), *Kommunale Finanzpolitik in der Weimarer Republik* (Stuttgart/Berlin/Cologne/Mainz, 1973).

[181] James, *German Slump*, pp. 43f., 130ff., 194; Balderston, *Economic Crisis*, pp. 185f., 245–50.

[182] Calculated from Balderston, *Economic Crisis*, p. 226 and Hoffmann *et al.*, *Wachstum*, pp. 255f.

[183] See figure 1.4. Figures from James, *German Slump*, pp. 375–7; Hoffmann *et al.*, *Wachstum*, pp. 789ff.

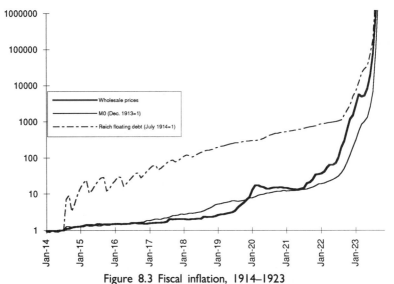

Figure 8.3 Fiscal inflation, 1914–1923
Sources: Bry, Wages, pp. 440–5; Zahlen zur Geldentwertung, p. 5; Holtfrerich,
Inflation, pp. 52ff., 67f.

in the very high yields of the later 1920s. The memory of the inflation
meant that investors had to be enticed back to government paper by
low prices and high interest rates.[184]

In the inflation years unwanted government bonds had, of course,
been readily discounted by the Reichsbank. However, this was no
longer possible as a result of the 1924 reforms of the Reichsbank law.
This left only foreign lenders once again to step into the breach. At
a rough estimate, the net capital inflow into Germany between 1924
and 1930 totalled 17.4 bn. reichsmarks – over 4.5 per cent of NNP
in 1924, 1925, 1927 and 1928 – of which a significant part represented
long – and short-term borrowing by local authorities.[185] Clearly, this
repeat of the great speculation of 1919–22 had certain important advantages, leading some observers to draw overoptimistic conclusions about
Germany's prospects.[186] The resulting economic stimulus in turn meant
that the somewhat reduced burden of reparations was relatively easier

[184] Balderston, *Economic Crisis*, pp. 250–65.
[185] See table 2. Cf. W. McNeil, *American Money and the Weimar Republic* (New York,
1986); James, *German Slump*, p. 95.
[186] J.W. Angell, *The Recovery of Germany* (New Haven, 1929); J.H. Williams, 'Reparation and the Flow of Capital', *American Economic Review*, 20 (Supplement) (1930),
pp. 75–9; J.W. Angell, 'The Reparations Settlement and the International Flow of
Capital', *ibid.*, pp. 80–8; W.A. Brown, 'German Reparations and the International
Flow of Capital', *ibid.*, pp. 88–92.

to shoulder: the total amount paid between 1924 and 1933 did not
exceed 11.1 bn. reichsmarks – at most around 2 per cent of annual
NNP.[187] However, interest payments on such loans accounted for some
5 bn. gold marks between 1924 and 1932, adding to the burden on
the balance of payments.[188] In the absence of a greater reduction in
domestic consumption, the German economy showed no sign of achieving the kind of increase in exports which would be necessary in the
long run to pay reparations and service the debt.[189] Just as one astute
American observer had noted in 1924, the Dawes report had been
'two-faced':

> Germany must have a loan of $200 m. to furnish a gold reserve for her
> currency; but the proceeds of the loan can perfectly well serve that purpose
> and at the same time be spent in Germany to pay reparations in kind. The
> Allies can ultimately obtain 2.5 bn. gold marks a year from Germany, without
> German tax-payers having to pay more than 1.25 bn. gold marks a year.
> Germany's budget must be balanced; but it won't do any harm if it isn't
> balanced right away [. . .].[190]

Or, as Benjamin Strong had foreseen: 'It could all be defeated were
the price readjustments, including wages, to work badly, that is adverse
to her export position.'[191] Except in the depressed year of 1926, there
was a trade deficit every year between 1924 and 1929, reaching as
much as 3.5 per cent of NNP in 1924, 1925 and 1927.[192]

Capital inflows could of course be seen as the problem itself.[193] In
Schacht's eyes, certainly, they threatened to revive inflation and undermine German competitiveness. Bound by a fixed exchange rate and a
strict minimum ratio between its reserves and its note issue, and

---

[187] See table 2. Cf. James, *German Slump*, pp. 21–3.
[188] Cf. A. Klug, 'The Theory and Practice of Reparations and American Lending to
Germany, 1925–1929', *Working Papers in International Economics* (Princeton, 1990).
[189] See J.M. Keynes, 'The German Transfer Problem'; B.G. Ohlin, 'The Reparation
Problem: A Discussion. I: The Transfer Difficulties, Real and Imagined'; J.M.
Keynes, 'The Transfer Problem: A Discussion. II: A Rejoinder'; B.G. Ohlin, 'Mr
Keynes's Views on the Transfer Problem. II: A Rejoinder from Professor Ohlin';
J.M. Keynes, 'Views on the Transfer Problem', *Economic Journal*, 39 (1929), pp.
1–7, 172–82, 400–8. See also F. Machlup, 'The Transfer Problem: Theme and Four
Variations' and 'Foreign Debts, Reparations and the Transfer Problem', in *idem*,
International Payments, Debts and Gold (New York, 1964) pp. 374ff.
[190] Thomas W. Lamont Papers, 176–8 (analysis of Dawes Plan) 18.4.24. See also the
criticisms by J.P. Morgan & Co.; *ibid.*, 176–9, Morgan & Co. to E.C. Grenfell,
19.4.24. Cf. Keynes, *Collected Writings*, XVIII, p. 235.
[191] Federal Reserve Bank of New York, Benjamin Strong Papers, 1000.5, Strong to
P.J. 23/28.4.24.
[192] See table 2.
[193] This was one of the central points at issue between Keynes and Ohlin in their
celebrated debate: cf. Keynes, *Collected Writings*, XI, pp. 451–80; Skidelsky, *Economist as Saviour*, pp. 309ff.

lacking a proper system of open-market operations, the Reichsbank could not easily prevent an increase in its gold and gold-equivalent reserves (from 467 m. reichsmarks at the end of 1924 to 2,838 m. three years later) – as well as in the foreign deposits throughout the banking system – from engendering a corresponding monetary expansion.[194] Between 1924 and 1927, currency in circulation grew at an average annual rate of 13.7 per cent; while broad money (M3) grew at 18 per cent per annum until as late as 1930, allowing a return to gentle inflation at an average rate of around 3 per cent on average.[195] Schacht struggled to limit foreign borrowing by local authorities, but simply drove them from long-term bond issues to short-term borrowing.[196] The difficulty of managing monetary policy under such circumstances was already evident in 1926/7, when reductions in the discount rate designed to stimulate the domestic investment led to capital outflows, which only resumed when interest rates once again rose.[197] But high interest rates tended to worsen the domestic position. By 1928, the dilemma was becoming inescapable: interest rates should have been reduced to boost falling investment, but had to be kept up to avoid capital outflows. Figure 8.4 shows the result: the discount rate rose from 5 per cent in 1927 to 7.5 per cent in mid 1929 as the growth rate of Mo fell from around 10 per cent to zero. This meant a virtually unabated rise in real interest rates and, inevitably, an intensification of the recession.[198]

Moreover, the balance of payments exerted a further restrictive pressure on fiscal policy. Falling revenues and rising expenditures (notably on unemployment benefits) are inevitable – and indeed desirable as 'stabilisers' – in a recession. But the German government was not in a position to run deficits as large as the 1.4 bn. reichsmarks run up by the Reich in 1928: firstly, because it could only finance such deficits abroad; and, secondly, because it continued to owe a huge sum to foreign creditors in the form of reparations. Hilferding's failure to raise a domestic loan, his resort to second-class foreign lenders, and the return of repar-

---

[194] Figures from James, *Reichsbank*, pp. 364–8. Cf. Borchardt, 'A Decade of Debate', pp. 105–9.

[195] See figure 0.5. Cf. G. Hardach, *Weltmarktorientierung und relative Stagnation: Währungspolitik in Deutschland, 1924–1931* (Berlin, 1976).

[196] James, 'Stabilisierung', pp. 73ff.; *idem*, 'Did the Reichsbank Draw the Right Conclusions from the Great Inflation', in Feldman and Müller–Luckner (eds.), *Nachwirkungen*, pp. 211–30. Cf. A. Weber, *Hat Schacht Recht? Die Abhängigkeit der deutschen Wirtschaft vom Ausland* (Munich/Leipzig, 1928).

[197] Sommariva and Tullio, *Macroeconomic History*, pp. 161–6; Balderston, *Economic Crisis*, pp. 150ff.

[198] Taking the difference between nominal interest rates and inflation as a proxy, in the absence of measurable expectations of inflation.

ations to the international agenda at the instigation of the Reparations Agent S. Parker Gilbert in September 1928 underlined both points.[199] The outcome of the Young Committee's deliberations closed the circle; not so much because it came up with yet another 'final' total (121 bn. reichsmarks) and yet another protracted schedule of payments, but because it maintained (indeed in real terms increased) the annual payment of over 2 bn. gold marks while offering a loan of just 1.26 bn. reichsmarks, two-thirds of which the Reich was obliged to hand over directly to the creditors.[200] This news, and the domestic political furore it precipitated, only served to stimulate further capital outflows.[201]

All of these factors made some kind of fiscal and monetary crisis more or less inevitable. Yet the *degree* of deflation was not predetermined. The Müller government had failed to agree on a minor tax increase (unemployment insurance contributions);[202] but its successor, under Heinrich Brüning, embarked on a far more radical policy of expenditure cuts and tax hikes. The reason for this was twofold. Firstly, Brüning seems to have believed that deflationary policies would allow him to implement constitutional changes which would limit the power of the trade unions and the Reichstag.[203] But of equal importance was a foreign policy calculation which, in attempting to achieve reparations revision by instrumentalising domestic economic crisis, was almost exactly the mirror image of the policies adopted by successive governments in 1919 and 1921/2. The difference was that where the earlier government had believed that currency depreciation would force the Allies to change their stance, Brüning, Curtius and Foreign Office diplomats like Weizsäcker, believed that a strict deflationary policy would force the Allies to end

---

[199] Balderston, *Economic Crisis*, pp. 266–87.

[200] Krüger, *Außenpolitik*, pp. 541ff.; Kindleberger, *World in Depression*, p. 304.

[201] Balderston, *Economic Crisis*, pp. 156–73.

[202] Cf. I. Maurer, *Reichsfinanzen und Grosse Koalition: Zur Geschichte des Reichskabinetts Müller, 1928–30* (Bern, 1973).

[203] H. Mommsen, 'Staat und Bürokratie in der Ära Brüning', in G. Jasper (ed.), *Tradition und Reform in der deutschen Politik* (Frankfurt am Main, 1976), pp. 81ff.; *idem*, 'Heinrich Brünings Politik als Reichskanzler: Das Scheitern eines politischen Alleinganges', in K. Holl (ed.), *Wirtschaftskrise und liberale Demokratie. Das Ende der Weimarer Republik und die gegenwärtige Situation* (Göttingen, 1978), pp. 16ff.; W. Jochmann, 'Brünings Deflationspolitik und der Untergang der Weimarer Republik', in Stegmann et al. (eds.), *Industrielle Gesellschaft*, pp. 97–112; W. Conze, 'Die Reichsverfassungsreform als Ziel der Politik Brünings', in Stürmer (ed.), *Belagerte Civitas*, pp. 340–8; P.-C. Witt, 'Finanzpolitik als Verfassungs- und Gesellschaftspolitik. Überlegungen zur Finanzpolitik des Deutschen Reichs in den Jahren 1930 bis 1932', in *G&G*, (1982), pp. 386–414; *idem*, 'Die Auswirkungen der Inflation auf die Finanzpolitik des Deutschen Reiches, 1924–1935', in Feldman and Müller–Luckner (eds.), *Nachwirkungen*, pp. 43ff.; G. Schulz, 'Inflationstrauma, Finanzpolitik und Krisenbekämpfung in den Jahren der Wirtschaftskrise, 1930–3', in *ibid.*, pp. 261–96.

reparations.[204] In his memoirs, Brüning put the point succinctly: Germany was to 'make use of the world crisis [. . .] to put pressure on all the other powers. [. . .] We were able [he recalled] to turn our [economic] sickness into our weapon.'[205] At the time, Hans Posse (of the Economics Ministry) was more precise. The objectives of German policy should be:

1. To work more defensively for the maintenance of as large a trade surplus as possible, to facilitate the debt payments and to control unemployment; [. . . and] 2. To develop an offensive activity to avoid the threat of encirclement as a result of the formation of European blocs.[206]

This meant a series of trade initiatives such as the German–Austrian Customs Union proposal and proposals for new trade treaties with other Danubian states,[207] accompanied by a sharp reduction in German export prices aimed at 'severely damag[ing] the trade of, in particular, the creditor countries'.[208] At the same time, creditor fears of default were to be increased by the 'danger of a National Socialist or a Bolshevik coup' – exactly as German representatives at Versailles had issued calculated warnings about the dangers of Bolshevism.[209] The culmination of the strategy was the proclamation accompanying the Emergency Decree of 5 June 1931, which declared, in language strongly reminiscent of the declarations of 1919 and 1921: 'The continuation of such reparations burdens is not only unbearable for the German economy but must also lead to the ruin of the economy of the whole world.'[210] The policy continued even after 20 June, when the Americans proposed a one-year moratorium on all reparations and war debts. With capital pouring out of Germany as the Austrian banking crisis spread to Berlin, the government rejected French proposals for a 2 bn. reichsmarks loan, and continued to insist on nothing less than 'the whole hog' throughout the Standstill negotiations and the protracted run-up to the Lausanne conference in June–July 1932.[211]

The attempt to use depreciation to achieve revision between 1919 and 1923 had not only failed; it had precipitated a domestic economic

---

[204] Krüger, *Außenpolitik*, pp. 523–35, 553ff.; G. Schulz, 'Reparationen und Krisenprobleme nach dem Wahlsieg der NSDAP 1930. Betrachtungen zur Regierung Brüning' *VSWG*, 67 (1980), pp. 200–22. Cf. J. Baron von Kruedener, 'Could Brüning's Policy of Deflation have been Successful?', in *idem* (ed.), *Economic Crisis*, p. 81.

[205] H. Brüning, *Memoiren 1918–1934* (Stuttgart, 1970), pp. 193, 221, 309, 367.

[206] Krüger, *Außenpolitik*, pp. 522, 536–9.

[207] *Ibid.* pp. 530–5.

[208] *Ibid.*, p. 544.

[209] *Ibid.* Cf. Brüning's comment that the result of the September 1920 Reichstag elections might help 'weaken the united front of our creditors': p. 539f.

[210] E. W. Bennett, *Germany and the Diplomacy of the Financial Crisis 1931* (Cambridge Mass., 1962), pp. 116, 128.

[211] Krüger, *Außenpolitik*, pp. 534–6; Holtfrerich, 'Discussion', p. 159.

disaster. The attempt to achieve the same end by deflation a decade later came closer to success, but with still more deleterious domestic consequences. It was not, it must be stressed, a policy of 'pure' fiscal and monetary orthodoxy. Although taxes were increased and civil service salaries cut, subsidies to agriculture and continuing deficits at the state and local level meant that public sector borrowing was not wholly eliminated. Total public spending was cut by nearly 30 per cent in nominal terms between 1929 and 1932; but the total public deficit remained close to 3 per cent.[212] Similarly, monetary policy ceased to adhere to the rules of the 1924 Reichsbank law in the face of the banking crisis. As a result of capital outflows, the Reichsbank's reserve fell by over 50 per cent in 1931; but this was not translated into a corresponding monetary contraction. The Reichsbank increased its discounting of commercial bills; tacitly breached its 40 per cent reserve:currency ratio, which fell as low as 24 per cent; and dropped its discount rate from its brief peak of 15 per cent to just 4 per cent by the end of 1932.[213] Nevertheless, this scarcely mitigated the deflationary pressure. The continuing high level of public spending reflected the soaring costs of unemployment relief; spending on infrastructural investment, which would have been more economically beneficial, was meanwhile being slashed.[214] Despite a brief increase in M0 in the second half of 1931, broad money continued to contract and prices continued to fall as the Reichsbank continued to restrict credit in other ways. Between January 1929 and January 1933, the annual rate of decrease of wholesale prices averaged 11 per cent (see figure 8.4). In international terms, the aim of an export surplus was certainly achieved in the three years after 1929, albeit as a result of a 65 per cent fall in imports as against a 57 per cent fall in exports. But the effect of these policies on output was devastating. Real NNP fell by 4.6 per cent in 1930, 10.9 per cent in 1931 and 4.9 per cent in 1932; while industrial output fell by 12.4 per cent, 19.7 per cent and 14.4 per cent respectively.[215] An especially important reason for the depth of the trough was the sharp reduction in local authority capital spending caused by the fiscal squeeze.[216] Unemployment, as we have seen, soared to heights not seen since 1923, and then exceeded them, reaching a peak of above 45 per cent of union members in 1932.[217]

---

[212] Cf. Balderston, *Economic Crisis*, pp. 287–317.
[213] James, *Reichsbank*, pp. 173–211; *idem*, 'Did the Reichsbank Draw the Right Conclusions?'.
[214] Balderston, *Economic Crisis*, pp. 332ff.
[215] See figure 2.3 and 2.4.
[216] Balderston, *Economic Crisis*, pp. 332–62.
[217] See figure 2.10.

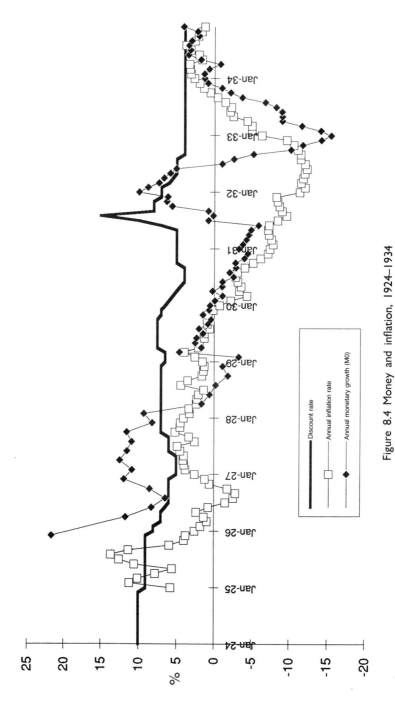

Figure 8.4 Money and inflation, 1924–1934

Sources: Bry, *Wages*, pp. 422–9, 440–5; James, *Reichsbank*, pp. 364–8; Bundesbank, *Währung*, p. 417; Balderston, *Economic Crisis*, p. 148.

As with the period 1920–2, it is reasonable to ask whether an alternative policy might have had less disastrous economic consequences in 1930–2.[218] A number of possible alternatives have been suggested by historians, on the basis of contemporary debate. The Germans could have accepted loans from abroad, regardless of the conditions attached to them;[219] they could have floated the reichsmark;[220] they could have financed job creation by increasing government borrowing (or cutting spending on agricultural subsidies),[221] or *via* the banking system, i.e., by additional money-creation.[222] But there are two arguments which can be advanced against these 'alternatives'. Firstly, even the most radical contemporary schemes would have done too little too late to have significantly improved the economic situation. Secondly, international and domestic constraints made their adoption impossible.[223] Of these, probably the most important was the belief that any attempt at deficit finance or devaluation would lead to a rapid return to hyperinflation.[224] In theory, it would have been possible for a government before 1933 to suspend reparations payments, float the mark, increase public spending and print money; after all, that is more or less what had happened ten

---

[218] C. Holtfrerich, *Alternativen zu Brünings Wirtschaftspolitik in der Weltwirtschaftskrise* (Wiesbaden, 1982); *idem*, 'Was the Policy of Deflation in Germany Unavoidable?', in Kruedener, *Economic Crisis*, pp. 63ff.; *idem*, 'Economic Policy', in Kershaw (ed.), *Weimar*, pp. 65–74; U. Büttner, 'Politische Alternativen zum Brüningschen Deflationskurs; Ein Beitrag zur Diskussion über "ökonomische Zwangslagen" in der Endphase von Weimar', in *VfZ*, 37 (1982), pp. 209–51.

[219] Holtfrerich, 'Discussion', in Kershaw (ed.), *Weimar*, p. 159.

[220] C.S. Maier, 'Die Nicht-Determiniertheit ökonomischer Modelle. Überlegungen zu Knut Borchardts These von der "kranken Wirtschaft" der Weimarer Republik', *G&G*, 11 (1985), pp. 275ff.; Sommariva and Tullio, *Macroeconomic History*, p. 176. Cf. J. Schiemann, *Die deutsche Währung in der Weltwirtschaftskrise, 1929–33. Währungspolitik und Abwertungskontroverse unter den Bedingungen der Reparationen* (Bern, 1980).

[221] J.J. Lee, 'Policy and Performance in the German Economy, 1925–1933: A Comment on the Borchardt Thesis', in M. Laffan (ed.), *The Burden of German History, 1919–1945* (London, 1988), pp. 131–50.

[222] Holtfrerich, 'Was the Policy of Deflation Unavoidable?', in Kruedener (ed.), *Economic Crisis*; B. Weisbrod, 'Industrial Crisis Strategy in the Great Depression', in *ibid.*, p. 61.

[223] K. Borchardt, 'Noch einmal: Alternatives zur Brünings Wirtschaftspolitik', *HZ*, 237 (1983), pp. 67ff.; *idem*, 'Could and Should Germany have Followed Great Britain in Leaving the Gold Standard?', *Journal of European Economic History*, 13 (1984), pp. 471–97; H. James, 'Gab es eine Alternative zur Wirtschaftspolitik Brünings?' *VSWG*, 70 (1983), pp. 523ff.; Kruedener, 'Introduction', in *idem* (ed.), *Economic Crisis*, pp. xi–xxi; Borchardt, 'A Decade of Debate', pp. 99–120; Eichengreen, *Golden Fetters*, pp. 241–6.

[224] Borchardt, 'Inflationsgefahren in der Weltwirtschaftskrise? Zu den Speilräumen der Brüningschen Wirtschaftspolitik, 1930–1932', pp. 21–42; *idem*, 'Das Gewicht der Inflationsangst in den wirtschaftspolitischen Entscheidungsprozessen während der Weltwirtschaftskrise', in Feldman and Müller–Luckner (eds.), *Nachwirkungen*, pp. 233–60. Cf. Balderston, *Economic Crisis*, pp. 315–31; Feldman, *Great Disorder*, p. 853.

years previously, in 1922/3.[225] But the result had been hyperinflation. This fear meant that the slightest hint of an 'alternative' policy tended to accelerate the flight of foreign capital, hence tightening the monetary and fiscal vice. In this way, the earlier crisis decisively limited room for manoeuvre in the later crisis.

Of course, as events after January 1933 were to show, a government capable of overcoming these constraints – in particular, by controlling outflows of capital and avoiding excessive credit creation – could implement a stimulatory policy without precipitating hyperinflation. The problem was that no government before 1933 had the legitimacy to do these things. Politically, it might be said, the deflationary crisis was the mirror image of the inflationary crisis ten years before. The failure of Stresemann's Great Coalition, Ebert's backing for Marx, his use of Enabling Laws to issue emergency decrees, the failure of Seeckt to impose a military dictatorship, the final resort to the polls in 1924: these events, it might be argued, were the farce before the tragedy – the failure of Müller's Great Coalition, Hindenburg's appointment of Brüning, his use of Article 48 to issue emergency decrees, the failure of Papen and Schleicher to impose some kind of dictatorship, the final resort to the polls in 1932. Moreover, both crises were intensified by the same process: politicians seeking to move away from parliamentary government and to achieve foreign policy successes by engineering economic catastrophes. Ultimately, Brüning came closer to getting rid of reparations than Wirth or Cuno: his calculations about the pressure Germany could exert through an economic crisis were closer to the mark than those of the earlier period. But that eventual success abroad had perversely negative consequences at home. Whereas the failure of revisionism in 1922/3 obliged Cuno's successors to cobble Weimar back together again, its success ten years later enabled Brüning's successors to dismantle it. This had less to do with Brüning's increasing reliance on Hindenburg's presidential power to issue decrees, or with the increasing concentration of power in Hindenburg's hands, or, for that matter, with the role played behind the scenes by the economic and military elites. There had been similar developments under Ebert in 1923/4. It had more to do with the results of the elections in September 1930, which saw the National Socialist vote rise by a factor of eight to 6.4 m.; and, in July 1932, which saw the Nazis emerge as the largest Reichstag party with 37.4 per cent of the vote. In view of these results, it is only remarkable that Hitler did not come to power sooner. Paradoxically, it was partly the undemocratic role of Hindenburg which prevented him from doing so.[226]

---

[225] The argument advanced by Borchardt and James that the reformed Reichsbank law ruled this out is not wholly convincing: such legal constraints are easily swept aside in an emergency.

[226] For a different interpretation, see Broszat, *Machtergreifung*.

As voters realised, economic alternatives had become impossible without a political alternative. But why did none of the other, more conservative, authoritarian alternatives prevail? Certainly, there was no shortage of talk in conservative circles about the need for dictatorship to bring about reform of the Reich. Political theorists like Carl Schmitt, politicians like Hans Luther, civil servants like Johannes Popitz, bankers like Hjalmar Schacht, industrialists like Paul Reusch – all were able to discern what was amiss with Weimar, and how a more authoritarian system might resolve its problems.[227] Hamburg businessmen too, notably Warburg, Cuno and Witthoefft, thought along these lines – indeed, had done since the early 1920s, when they had frequently discussed the need to purge the Weimar system of its polycratic and corporatist defects. After the inflation, Warburg was at one with Schacht in his criticism of public sector profligacy and foreign borrowing;[228] while Witthoefft joined Luther's League of Renewal in 1928.[229] Warburg also joined the chorus of business criticism directed against Brüning's deflationary policies in the later part of 1931.[230] But, as the attempts of Papen and Schleicher demonstrated, without an electoral mandate, such ideas could not be implemented on a large enough scale to be effective.[231] And as Brüning later observed, 'the conservative *Bürgertum* with whom one could have formed a strong conservative block in normal times [had been] completely ruined financially and socially by the inflation. It [had] become proletarian in its ideology.'[232] This explains why ultimately, and often reluctantly, businessmen, like the other conservative groupings in Weimar, saw no alternative but to accept Hitler's leadership. As Turner and Neebe have shown, business was far from eager to see Hitler in power, rightly fearing that he intended to increase the power of the state over the economy, and to pursue policies inimical to many business interests.[233] But, as in Hamburg, so at the national level, flexibility was the traditional response of business to a political crisis. When his appointment as Chancellor of a coalition cabinet of the Right was announced in January 1933, few voices were raised in protest. They

---

[227] See, e.g., James, *German Slump*, pp. 47, 76f.
[228] Warburg, *Aufzeichnungen*, pp. 127–33
[229] James, *German Slump*, pp. 76–80.
[230] Büttner, *Staats- und Wirtschaftskrise*, p. 251.
[231] D. Petzina, 'Hauptprobleme der deutschen Wirtschaftspolitik 1932/33', in *VfZ*, 15 (1967), pp. 18ff.; H. Marcon, *Arbeitsbeschaffung der Regierungen Papen und Schleicher* (Frankfurt, 1974); M. Wolffsohn, *Industrie und Handwerk in Konflikt mit staatlicher Wirtschaftspolitik? Studien zur Politik der Arbeitsbeschaffung in Deutschland, 1930–34* (Berlin, 1977).
[232] Feldman, *Great Disorder*, p. 4.
[233] In addition to Turner, *German Big Business*, see also R. Neebe, *Grossindustrie, Staat und NSDAP, 1930–33: Paul Silverberg und der Reichsverband der Deutschen Industrie in der Krise der Weimarer Republik* (Göttingen, 1981).

had no credible alternative; just as they had lacked an alternative to Social Democracy in 1918/19. Hitler had; and only a few businessmen appreciated how radical and how dangerous that alternative was.

In July 1931, following the negotiation of the Standstill agreements on Germany's foreign debts, Carl Melchior had written:

What we have just experienced is the destruction of the ground rules of the capitalist system. Yet the system depends on the strict observance of those very rules. This is the first time that I have had to refuse to fulfil an obligation to which I had freely committed my name simply because the state required me to refuse. The capitalist system in Germany will not survive such a deviation from its rules. For the deviations will constantly increase, and the system will accordingly dissolve.[234]

His old friend Keynes continued to hope that the capitalist system could be saved. In January 1932, he revisited his old haunts in Hamburg to deliver a lecture in which he recommended that Germany follow Britain off the gold standard. But even he had to acknowledge 'the reasons which are at present influencing your authorities away from this decision – the fears, so natural in Germany, of another great inflation'.[235] There was the rub. The truth was that the process Melchior described – the dissolution of the capitalist system in Germany – had begun more than a decade before. In 1923, his partner Max Warburg had written:

I believe in the old capitalistic and individualistic conduct of economic life. [. . .] [H]owever, [. . .] *we shall never be able to successfully combat Bolshevism* [. . .] *if we ourselves sanction individual official robberies committed by states.*[236]

He was, of course, referring to the German property confiscated as reparations after the war. However, the point could have equally been made about the 'official robbery' committed during the inflation, as a result of German fiscal and monetary policy. It was this, more than anything else, which began the dissolution of the German capitalist system. In this sense, the Slump merely concluded what had been begun by the inflation.

[234] Rosenbaum and Sherman, *M.M. Warburg & Co.*, p. 150.
[235] Keynes, *Collected Writings*, XXI, pp. 39–48; Skidelsky, *Economist as Saviour*, p. 435. Ironically, Keynes advised against a unilateral suspension of reparations payments, asking: 'Now that this policy [of fulfilment] has been pursued so steadfastly and for so many years, would it not be a pity not to harvest its fruits now that they are ripening?' On his lack of interest in the contemporary debate on counter-cyclical fiscal policy see G. Garvy, 'Keynes and the Economic Activists of pre-Hitler Germany', *Journal of Political Economy*, 83 (1975), pp. 397ff.
[236] WA, Politische Corrrespondenz, 1923, Warburg to Takahashi, 22.3.23. My emphasis.

Epilogue: Hitler's inflation

The fear of inflation prevented the adoption of radical counter-cyclical policies before 1933. However, it did not prevent voters from turning to Hitler; despite the fact that, on numerous occasions in 1931 and 1932, he was accused of advocating inflationary policies. For example, Brüning used the fear of inflation as a stick with which to beat Hitler during the Presidential elections; while labour leaders like Aufhäuser and Stegerwald alleged that Hitler was attracting big business support by offering a 'second inflation'.[1] This was partly because Hitler had long since established his credentials as an opponent of inflation. As early as 1922, he had decried 'this weak republic [which] throws its pieces of paper about wildly in order to enable its party functionaries [. . .] to feed at the trough'; and NSDAP election propaganda repeatedly cited the inflation as evidence of the Weimar Republic's economic incompetence.[2] Contrary to the predictions of Hitler's opponents, the Nazis continued to stress their commitment to price stability once they had come to power. 'Future monetary policy,' declared Schacht in a radio broadcast immediately after his appointment in March 1933, 'will adhere with unchanging steadfastness to the task of maintaining the value of the mark'; a view explicitly endorsed by Hitler in the Reichstag five days later.[3] Throughout the 1930s and into the war, opposition to 'monetary experiments' was a recurrent theme of Nazi rhetoric: as Hitler put it in 1939, the Reichsbank's task was 'to secure the absolute stability of wages and prices'; the reichsmark was to be 'the most stable [currency] in the world'. 'We embody,' declared Rudolf Brinkmann, the Reichsbank Vice-President in January 1939, 'the iron commitment not to defraud the German people through inflation.'[4] What is more, price indices indicate that this commitment

---

[1] Feldman, 'Einführung', in idem and Müller–Luckner (eds.), Nachwirkungen, p. vii; Borchardt, 'Gewicht der Inflationsangst', ibid., pp. 246–50. Cf. A. Barkai, Nazi Economics, Ideology. Theory and Policy (Oxford/New York/Munich, 1990), pp. 56, 62, 166, 183.
[2] Feldman, Great Disorder, pp. 574f.; Krause, Hamburg wird braun, p. 189.
[3] Marsh, Bundesbank, pp. 109–18.
[4] Ibid., pp. 28–56, 122f.

was honoured. Between 1933 and 1939, the cost-of-living index rose
by just 7 per cent, while annual wholesale price inflation averaged just
1.2 per cent, rising to 2 per cent during the war.[5] It was defeat and
the policy of the occupying powers which unleashed the second German
hyperinflation, which ended with the complete collapse of the currency
in 1946/7.[6]

The fact that inflation remained so low in Nazi Germany requires
some explanation, for, viewed purely in terms of fiscal and monetary
policy, it ought to have been higher. Between 1933 and 1939, total
public spending rose by around 100 per cent; between 1939 and 1943,
by a further 140 per cent.[7] Under the enabling legislation passed in
1933, only a part of that increase had to be financed by taxation
(around 56 per cent between 1933 and 1937, and 33–48 per cent
during the war) so that between 1933 and 1937, total public debt
(excluding around 12 bn. reichsmarks of 'Mefo-bills') rose by 24 per
cent, and by a factor of around ten in the following seven years.[8] The
total fiscal burden by the end of the war was immense: spending was
equivalent to around 73 per cent of GNP, debt to around 250 per
cent of GNP – figures broadly comparable to those in 1917/18. And,
as in the First World War, a high proportion of borrowing by the
end of the war – some 57 per cent – was short term.[9] Monetary
indicators tell a similar, inflationary story. A series of five laws having
lifted the restrictions on government borrowing from the Reichsbank
(ultimately ending its statutory independence),[10] the way was opened
for a second state-led monetary expansion. Between December 1932
and 1938, the volume of currency in circulation rose by 90 per cent,
and in the subsequent six years by a factor of seven.[11] When Wilhelmine
and Weimar governments had pursued such policies, the result had
been inflation, with only very ephemeral benefits in terms of increased
output. Yet, under Hitler, inflation remained low and output growth
was sustained: between 1932 and 1938, GNP grew in real terms at an

---

[5] See figure 0.2.
[6] K.-H. Hansmeyer and R. Caesar, 'Kriegswirtschaft und Inflation, 1936–1948', in
Bundesbank (ed.), *Währung und Wirtschaft*, pp. 418–20. Cf. D. Botting, *In the Ruins
of the Reich* (London, 1986), pp. 286–314.
[7] See figure 0.3; calculated from figures in Andic and Veverka, 'Government Expenditure', pp. 243f.; Milward, *War, Economy and Society*, p. 76.
[8] See figure 1.4; calculated from figures in James, *German Slump*, pp. 375ff.; Hansmeyer
and Caesar, 'Kriegswirtschaft und Inflation', pp. 390ff.; Milward, *War, Economy and
Society*, p. 108.
[9] Hansmeyer and Caesar, 'Kriegswirtschaft und Inflation', p. 405.
[10] *Ibid.*, pp. 372ff. As after 1914, both long-term and short-term government borrowing
had money-creating potential, since long-term bonds could be lombardised at the
Reichsbank and counted as part of its reserve.
[11] *Ibid.*, pp. 413, 417.

annual average rate of 9.8 per cent, and industrial output by as much as 13 per cent per annum; between 1939 and 1943, GNP rose by a further 16 per cent.[12] How was this possible?

The answer is that in a number of fundamental ways Hitler altered the Reich's political economy, effectively overcoming the three constraints which had been responsible for the problems of the past: the power of corporate organisations, the weakness of fiscal and monetary controls, and the external limitations imposed by the balance of payments. Of course, the Slump had begun his work for him, weakening the position of the economic organisations, the states and communes, and moving the economy in the direction of managed trade and exchange controls. But it was Hitler whose vision of a 'synchronised' state – totalitarian in aspiration, if not in practice – completed the process, and stifled resistance to it.

In the case of corporate power, the autonomy of the large concerns and economic associations was steadily reduced, particularly after the promulgation of the Four Year Plan and Hitler's explicit challenge to the competence of the private sector.[13] By the mid 1930s, the money market, the capital market and even the price-setting mechanism were increasingly regulated by the state.[14] Although they continued formally to be privately owned and managed concerns, firms found their freedom of action increasingly curtailed, as they were steadily subordinated to one customer – the state.[15] Even more radically, the state ended the autonomy of organised labour, abolishing the free trade unions and bringing the process of collective bargaining under direct state control through the 'trustees of labour'.[16] The result was that business and labour were unable to compete with the state (and with one another),

[12] Calculated from figures in R.J. Overy, *The Nazi Economic Recovery, 1928–1938* (London, 1982), p. 29; Petzina *et al.* (eds.) *Sozialgeschichtliches Arbeitsbuch*, III, p. 61; Milward, *War, Economy and Society*, p. 76.

[13] U. Wengst, 'Der Reichsverband der deutschen Industrie in den ersten Monaten des Dritten Reiches: Ein Beitrag zum Verhältnis von Grossindustrie und Nationalsozialismus', in *VfZ*, 38 (1980), pp. 94–110; R.J. Overy, 'Heavy industry and the state in Nazi Germany: the Reichswerke crisis', *European History Quarterly* (1985), pp. 313ff.; Noakes and Pridham (eds.), *Nazism*, II, pp. 301–15. Cf. T.W. Mason, 'The Primacy of Politics: Politics and Economics in National Socialist Germany', in S. Woolf (ed.), *The Nature of Fascism* (London, 1968), pp. 165–95.

[14] S. Lurie, *Private Investment in a Controlled Economy: Germany 1933–1939* (London, 1947).

[15] For some contrasting case studies: P. Hayes, *Industry and Ideology. IG Farben in the Nazi Era* (Cambridge, 1987); J.R. Gillingham, *Industry and Politics in the Third Reich. Ruhr Coal, Hitler and Europe* (London, 1985); B.P. Bellon, *Mercedes in Peace and War. German Automobile Workers 1903–1945* (New York, 1990).

[16] See esp. T.W. Mason, *Arbeiterklasse und Volksgemeinschaft. Dokumente und Materialien zur deutschen Arbeiterpolitik, 1936–1939* (Oplanden, 1975); and more recently R. Hachtmann, *Industriearbeit im 'Dritten Reich'. Untersuchungen zu den Lohn- und Arbeitsbedingungen in Deutschland, 1933–1945* (Göttingen, 1989).

in the way that they had in the years of distributional conflict before 1933. True, the restrictions imposed were far from intolerable: undistributed profits rose as a proportion of national income from 0.5 per cent in 1933 to 4.9 per cent in 1939;[17] while workers reaped the benefits of full employment and, according to some figures, higher real wages.[18] But the increase in the state's share of investment and of total capital market issues signified a decisive shift in the economic balance of power from *Wirtschaft* to Reich;[19] just as the fall in wages and consumption as a percentage of national income revealed the limits of working-class prosperity.[20] Above all, the success with which the Nazis were able to control prices – developing and extending the role of the Price Commissioner devised by Brüning in 1931 – symbolised the change.[21] 'I'll see to it that prices remain stable,' declared Hitler. 'That's what my stormtroopers are for.'[22] 'Price raising,' it was decreed in November 1940, was 'economic high treason'. In the words of the Reichsbank Vice-President Kurt Lange in June 1943: 'In an authoritarian state there can be no inflation.'[23]

In this, Hitler effectively learnt the lessons of the First World War, closing many of the gaps which had caused economic controls to fail after 1914. However, this would not have sufficed to control inflation had not the Nazis also transformed the Reich's fiscal system. In many ways, Hitler achieved his early objective: the creation of a 'strong central state power for the Reich'.[24] The enormous increase in armaments and infrastructure expenditure which underlay the Nazi economic recovery was partly financed by swingeing cuts in social expenditures and (some) tax increases: the kind of measures which had proved so difficult to implement in the 1920s. Thus while the percentage of GNP spent on defence rose from 1.2–3.3 per cent in 1933 to 15.2–18.1 per cent in 1938, total public spending as a share of National

---

[17] Noakes and Pridham (eds.), *Nazism*, II, p. 368; Barkai, *Nazi Economics*, p. 257. Cf. M. Sweezy, 'German Corporate Profits, 1926–1938', in *Quarterly Journal of Economics*, 54 (1940).

[18] Noakes and Pridham (eds.), *Nazism*, II, p. 368; Overy, *Economic Recovery*, p. 34; Bry, *Wages*, pp. 329ff.

[19] Forty-six per cent of all investment between 1933 and 1938 was undertaken by the public sector: Overy, *Economic Recovery*, p. 36.

[20] *Ibid.*, p. 34. Wages fell from 64 per cent to 57 per cent of national income; private consumption from 83 per cent to 59 per cent.

[21] Details in Hansmeyer and Caesar, 'Kriegswirtschaft und Inflation', pp. 405–13; James, *German Slump*, pp. 355, 378.

[22] Feldman, *Great Disorder*, p. 855; James, *German Slump*, p. 353.

[23] Hansmeyer and Caesar, 'Kriegswirtschaft und Inflation', p. 413; Marsh, *Bundesbank*, p. 138.

[24] See Noakes and Pridham (eds.), *Nazism*, I, p. 16 (point 25 of the German Workers' Party programme of 1920).

Product did not rise much above 35 per cent.[25] Similarly, the large increases in Reich spending and borrowing were partly compensated for by sharp cuts in state and local authority financing. While Reich expenditure rose by a factor of more than three between 1932 and 1938, communal spending fell by 8 per cent and state spending by 21 per cent.[26] There was a similar reduction in state and communal borrowing. Of course, trends in these directions predated Hitler's accession to power, with the increasing use of decrees to bypass the Reichstag under Brüning, and Papen's coup against Prussia in 1932. But once again it was Hitler who pressed the process forward to its conclusion. True too, Hitler's achievement as a *'Reichsreformer'* should not be exaggerated. In many ways, as Martin Broszat, Hans Mommsen and others have argued, the 'Hitler State' developed its own multiplicity of rival institutions and interests, giving rise to a chaotic system of 'polycracy'.[27] But from an economic point of view, there was a fundamental difference between Nazi polycracy and the 'hyper-pluralism' which characterised the Weimar years: however much administrative chaos there was under Hitler, there was only a very limited sub-division of fiscal power.

The third process which Hitler accelerated was the trend towards autarky: ending the balance of payments constraint by imposing increasingly rigid controls on trade and capital movements. Again, this shift antedated Hitler's appointment as Chancellor. Tariffs had been restored in the mid 1920s; there had already been a move in the direction of bilateral trade; and exchange controls had been imposed in the wake of the banking crisis. As Economics Minister after August 1934, Schacht developed these instruments in his 'New Plan';[28] but he remained at root orthodox about the unsustainability of a large balance of payments deficit. When the pace of rearmament threatened to precipitate a balance of payments crisis, he objected, warning of a new inflation, only to be overruled by Hitler, and effectively subordinated to Göring.[29]

---

[25] Cf. the various figures in Barkai, *Nazi Economics*, pp. 26off.; Andic and Veverka, *Government Expenditure*, pp. 262f.; Milward, *War, Economy and Society*, pp. 25–50; Hansmeyer and Caesar, 'Kriegswirtschaft und Inflation', p. 390; James, *German Slump*, p. 380. The classic early studies are H. Stuebel, 'Die Finanzierung der Aufrüstung im Dritten Reich', in *Europa-Archiv*, 6 (1951), pp. 4128–36; B.H. Klein, *Germany's Economic Preparations for War* (Cambridge, Mass., 1959); and B.A. Carroll, *Design for Total War. Arms and Economics in the Third Reich* (The Hague, 1968).

[26] Calculated from Andic and Veverka, 'Government Expenditure', pp. 244f. Cf. James, *German Slump*, pp. 107f., 371f.

[27] See esp. M. Broszat, *The Hitler State. The Foundation and Development of the Internal Structure of the Third Reich* (London/New York, 1981).

[28] Hansmeyer and Caesar, 'Kriegswirtschaft und Inflation', p. 408; James, *German Slump*, p. 387; Noakes and Pridham (eds.), *Nazism*, II, pp. 266–76.

[29] *Ibid.*, pp. 277–300; W. Carr, *Arms, Autarky and Aggression. A Study in German Foreign Policy, 1933–1939* (London, 1972), pp. 45–65. Cf. H.E. Volkmann, 'Außenhandel und

Schacht was not alone in worrying about inflation. As early as 1936, the Prussian Finance Ministry noted that 'inflation is already with us', a view echoed two years later by the Reichsbank ('a certain, barely recognisable, inflation of the reichsmark has now appeared') and repeated in the famous memorandum to Hitler of January 1939 which accused the government of 'an inflationistic expenditure policy'.[30] Even Schacht's more servile successor Walther Funk could not deny that by 1942, the currency was 'endangered [. . .] on the monetary side, from the permanent increase in purchasing power'.[31] Göring might brazenly cite Frederick the Great as another 'strong inflationist [. . .] in his financial policy',[32] but even he worried in November 1938 that falling consumer goods production and rising public borrowing could signify 'the start of the inflation – and that [would be] the beginning of the end'.[33] In fact – precisely because policy makers did not lose sight of the inflationary danger – Nazi economic policy could probably have been sustainable for some considerable time, in the absence of war: in essentials it did not much differ from the policies adopted in East European socialist states after 1945.[34] Production and employment could have been maintained by high levels of government expenditure, and the inflationary effects of the subsequent monetary overhang suppressed. The price would, as in Eastern Europe, have been a deterioration in labour productivity and capital efficiency, but this would have taken decades to undermine the regime.[35] For, as the case of Hamburg shows, the regime was far from solely reliant on economic prosperity for its legitimacy.[36] It is true that some business spokesmen, including

Aufrüstung in Deutschland, 1933 bis 1939', in F. Forstmeier and H.E. Volkmann (eds.), *Wirtschaft und Rüstung am Vorabend des Zweiten Weltkrieges* (Düsseldorf, 1975), pp. 81ff.; A. Ritschl, 'Die deutsche Zahlungsbilanz 1936–1941 und das Problem des Devisenmangels vor Kriegsbeginn', *VfZ*, 39 (1991), pp. 103–23; D. Petzina, *Autarkiepolitik im Dritten Reich. Die nationalsozialistische Vierjahresplan* (Stuttgart, 1968).

[30] Hansmeyer and Caesar, 'Kriegswirtschaft und Inflation', pp. 382f., 409.

[31] Marsh, *Bundesbank*, pp. 122–8.

[32] Noakes and Pridham (eds.), *Nazism*, II, pp. 287f.

[33] Mason, *Arbeiterklasse und Volksgemeinschaft*, pp. 914, 927, 930.

[34] Temin's recent parallel with the Soviet Union in the 1930s, by contrast, seems less satisfactory: see P. Temin, 'Soviet and Nazi Economic Planning in the 1930s', in *EcHR*, 44 (1991), pp. 573–93.

[35] For a different view T.W. Mason, 'Innere Krise und Angriffskrieg, 1938/9', in Forstmeier and Volkmann (eds.), *Wirtschaft und Rüstung*, pp. 158ff. Cf. R.J. Overy, 'Germany, Domestic Crisis and War in 1939', *P&P*, 116 (1987), pp. 138–68; D. Kaiser, T.W. Mason and R.J. Overy, 'Debate: Germany, "Domestic Crisis" and War in 1939', in *P&P*, 12 (1989), pp. 200–40.

[36] Bruhns *et al.* (eds.), *'Hier war doch alles nicht so schlimm'. Wie die Nazis in Hamburg den Alltag eroberten*; W. Skrentny, '"Hier war alles vernünftiger als anderswo". Hamburg und die Aufarbeitung der NS-Zeit', in G.A.L. Fraktion in der Hamburger Bürgerschaft (ed.), *'Es ist Zeit für die ganze Wahrheit' (K. von Dohnanyi). Aufarbeitung*

Bürgermeister Krogmann and Karl Gottfried Gok of Blohm & Voß, expressed reservations about, respectively, Nazi trade control and 'socialist tendencies in the sense of the implementation of a state subsistence economy (*Bedarfsdeckungswirtschaft*)'.[37] There was also disappointment that Nazi foreign policy did not develop in the direction of a neo-Wilhelmine colonial policy.[38] But on the whole the business community studiously aligned itself with the 'new spirit' of the times.[39] Some trade union leaders also sought accommodation with the new regime, even after the forcible occupation of Trade Union House by the SA;[40] but their efforts were in vain. Although there were occasional alarms about the mood of the Hamburg working-class (notably in 1935, when the Economics Ministry clashed with the Hamburg Trustee of Labour over proposed wage cuts), these hardly constituted evidence of working-class opposition to the regime.[41] Everyday life in Nazi Hamburg may not have been idyllic, but when Hitler and Goebbels visited the city, they found ample evidence of their own popularity;[42] and if the local Nazi leaders – Gauleiter (later Statthalter) Kaufmann and Standartenführer (later Reichskommissar) Richter – were less popular, this hardly mattered. Not only had their formal power in the city been confirmed in the summer of 1933 by the dissolution of the Bürgerschaft and its replacement by a corporatist *Staatsrat*, leaving Bürgermeister Krogmann in an essentially ceremonial role,[43] equally

der NS-Zeit in Hamburg; Die nicht veröffentlichte Senatsbroschure (Hamburg, 1985), pp. 17–47.

[37] Noakes and Pridham (eds.), *Nazism*, II, p. 276; W. Jochmann, 'Gesellschaftliche Gleichschaltung in Hamburg 1933: Freiheit des Individuums oder Sicherheit und Schutz der Gemeinschaft', in *idem* and Büttner (eds.), *Zwischen Demokratie und Diktatur*, p. 105.

[38] M. Lüth, 'Hamburg und die Kolonialpolitik im Dritten Reich', *ZVHG*, 59 (1973), pp. 55–88. Cf. E. Helfferich, *1932–1946. Tatsachen. Ein Beitrag zur Wahrheitsfindung* (Jever, 1968).

[39] Jochmann, 'Gesellschaftliche Gleichschaltung', pp. 106ff.

[40] *Ibid.*, pp. 100f. Cf. K. Ditt, *Sozialdemokraten im Widerstand. Hamburg in der Anfangsphase des Dritten Reiches* (Hamburg, 1984); B. Wulff, 'The Third Reich and the Unemployed. National Socialist Work-Creation Schemes in Hamburg, 1933–4', in Evans and Geary (eds.), *The German Unemployed*, pp. 281–302.

[41] I. Kershaw, *The Nazi Dictatorship. Problems and Perspectives of Interpretation* (London/ New York/Melbourne/Auckland, 1989), p. 77; T.W. Mason, *Sozialpolitik im Dritten Reich* (Opladen, 1977), pp. 158f.; *idem*, 'Arbeiteropposition im nationalsozialistischen Deutschland', in D. Peukert and J. Reulecke (eds.), *Alltag im Nationalsozialismus. Vom Ende der Weimarer Republik bis zum Zweiten Weltkrieg* (Wuppertal, 1981), pp. 293–314.

[42] See, e.g., J. Goebbels, *Die Tagebücher von Joseph Goebbels* (Munich, 1987), Teil I, Bd. II, pp. 434f., 585. Cf. M. Bruhns, C. Preuschaft and W. Skrentny, *Als Hamburg 'erwachte' – Alltag im Nationalsozialismus* (Hamburg, 1983).

[43] Johe, 'Institutionelle Gleichschaltung', in Büttner and Jochmann (eds.), *Zwischen Demokratie und Diktatur*, pp. 82ff. Cf. H. Timpke (ed.), *Dokumente zur Gleichschaltung des Landes Hamburg 1933* (Frankfurt am Main, 1964). For a contemporary attempt

important, the 'synchronisation' of the press and the purges of the police, the civil service, the judiciary and the teaching profession eliminated any possible internal opposition.[44] Moreover, the recruitment of new functionaries to staff the expanding state and party bureaucracy created a foundation of self-interested loyalty. So many people sought jobs of this sort in the period after January 1933 that the initials NSDAP were said to stand for '*Na, Suchst Du Auch ein Pöstchen?*' ('So you're after a job too, eh?').[45] For some observers, this was disillusioning. As Luise Solmitz noted in her diary: 'Unfortunately, [. . .] I see Hitler exchanging *Bonzen* for *Bonzen*, party book for party book.'[46] But criticism more overt than this would soon risk denunciation, arrest, internment – latterly, even death.[47]

Of course, economic recovery and political 'synchronisation' were not ends in themselves for Hitler, but means to other ends. The first of these was war to establish German hegemony in Europe. Historians have long debated how far the war which broke out in 1939 was the war Hitler intended to fight. Certainly, what Hitler intended in 1939 (as with Czechoslovakia the year before) was a short war against a weaker Eastern neighbour, with the West diplomatically neutralised; but his rearmament programme implied a later confrontation with the Western powers, perhaps around 1943.[48] At any event, had the conquest of territory and the establishment of German hegemony in continental Europe been Hitler's sole objective, it is not unimaginable that he might have succeeded. Whatever the inefficiencies of the Nazi economic and administrative system, the Third Reich was still a significantly stronger state than its Wilhelmine predecessor – witness the ease of military victory between 1939 and 1941, and the level of economic mobilisation after January 1942. Moreover, Nazi occupation policy brought real net returns, equivalent to 38.4 per cent of all revenue at

---

to rationalise these changes, see H. Reincke, W. Hävernick and G. Schlotter (eds.), *Hamburg Einst und Jetzt* (Hamburg, 1933), pp. 98–100; and a retrospective attempt to do so, C.V. Krogmann, *Es ging um Deutschlands Zukunft, 1932–1939* (Leonie am Starnberger See, 1977).

[44] O.J. Hale, *The Captive Press in the Third Reich* (Princeton, 1964), pp. 210f.
[45] Jochmann, 'Gesellschaftliche Gleichschaltung', p. 109.
[46] Noakes and Pridham (eds.), *Nazism*, I, p. 134.
[47] Cf. G. Meyer, *Nacht über Hamburg. Berichte und Dokumente, 1933–1945* (Frankfurt am Main, 1971); H. Fangmann, U. Reifner and N. Steinborn, *Parteisoldaten. Die Hamburger Polizei im 'Dritten Reich'* (Hamburg, 1987); Museum für Hamburgische Geschichte (ed.), *'Kola-Fu'. Konzentrationslager und Gestapogefängnis Hamburg-Fühlsbüttel, 1933–1945* (Hamburg, 1983); L. Eiber, *Konzentrationslager Neuengamme, 1938–1945* (Hamburg, 1982).
[48] R.J. Overy, 'Hitler's War and the German Economy: A Reinterpretation', in *EcHR*, 35 (1982), pp. 272–91; *idem*, 'Mobilisation for Total War in Germany, 1939–41', *EcHR*, 103 (1988), pp. 613–39.

the peak of 1943;[49] to say nothing of the 7.5 million foreign workers drafted into the war effort.[50] Of course, there were strains on the home front, as the case of Hamburg illustrates: unrest on the waterfront, a mutiny by Russian POWs, demoralisation after the devastating bombing raids of August 1943, and teenage Americanophilia ('Swing Youth') which the regime viewed with exaggerated anxiety.[51] But the combination of propaganda and terror prevented the kind of internal division which had undermined the military effort in 1917 and 1918.[52] Even as late as 1944, amid the ruins left by the RAF, the architect Konstanty Gutschow was drawing up plans for the rebuilding of Hamburg with skyscrapers for the Party offices and a huge new bridge across the Elbe: 'The Elbe forum of the new Hamburg' was to be 'the midpoint of the Reich in the north and also the world harbour for the Reich', displaying the 'beauty of the truly grand, "the monumental"' on the model of 'Paris [and] Versailles'.[53]

Even Hitler's ultimate objective – the racial 'purification' of Central and Eastern Europe – was far from unpopular. It has frequently been claimed that traditionally cosmopolitan Hamburg was unusually critical of Nazi racial policy.[54] This is misleading. There was no doubting the importance of anti-Semitism to National Socialism: as we have seen, the Nazis had frequently attacked prominent Jews like Max Warburg in their propaganda in the 1920s; and made physical attacks on Jewish property in the key election years of 1930 and 1932. During the torchlit procession of February 1933, as one spectator heard, ' "Death to the Jews" was also sometimes called out and they sang of the blood of the Jews which would squirt from their knives.'[55] Such violence was not immediately unleashed, it is true, though there were some

---

[49] Milward, *War, Economy and Society*, pp. 135–65; cf. *idem*, *The German Economy at War* (London, 1965). Since nearly half of such income came from France, it might be said that Germany recouped a substantial proportion of the reparations it had paid to France in the 1920s. Indeed, the transfer of around 37 per cent of French national income to Germany in 1943 was a far higher burden than Weimar Germany had paid France in any year.

[50] E.L. Homze, *Foreign Labour in Nazi Germany* (Princeton, 1967).

[51] *Ibid.*, p. 295; Milward, *German Economy*, p. 41; Kershaw, '*Hitler Myth*', pp. 201–4; D. Peukert, *Inside Nazi Germany. Conformity, Opposition and Racism in Everyday Life* (London, 1989), pp. 78f., 166f., 199ff.; R. Grunberger, *A Social History of the Third Reich* (London, 1971), p. 360.

[52] See Goebbels's record of a visit to Hamburg in 1940: Goebbels, *Tagebücher*, Teil I, IV, p. 436.

[53] J.M. Diefendorf, 'Konstanty Gutschow and the Reconstruction of Hamburg', *CEH*, 18 (1985), pp. 143–69.

[54] See for example, Peukert, *Inside Nazi Germany*, p. 59, citing a Social Democrat report on the reaction to the *Reichskristallnacht*. But it was the unruly quality to which people were objecting; not the anti-Semitism *per se*.

[55] Noakes and Pridham (eds.), *Nazism*, I, p. 130.

attacks on Jewish businesses before the boycott of April 1933.[56] But the policy of excluding Jews from public, civic and economic life began at once. Within days of Krogmann's appointment as Bürgermeister, Max Warburg and Leo Lippmann lost their positions on the Finance Deputation, and Warburg had to resign from his post with the Reichsbank.[57] Thirty-one Jewish lawyers and judges lost their jobs.[58] At first, Jewish businessmen were simply removed from the supervisory boards of other firms (as in the case of Warburg and the Hapag), but the policy of 'Aryanisation' of Jewish firms was stepped up in December 1935, with a trial of department store directors for alleged 'Rassenschande'; though it was not until June 1938 that Warburg was persuaded to entrust his bank to two non-Jewish associates, Rudolf Brinckmann and Paul Wirtz.[59] For his part, Warburg was torn between the desire to help his fellow Jews emigrate and a personal reluctance to leave Germany. He used his personal contacts with Schacht and his position on the *Reichsvertretung der deutschen Juden* to facilitate the severely restricted transfer of Jews' assets to Palestine and elsewhere;[60] but he and his surviving brother Fritz were only persuaded to leave Hamburg for good after the '*Reichskristallnacht*' in 1938.[61] In all of this, tangible assistance from Gentiles was rare: as when Baron Berenberg-Goßler secured the release of Fritz Warburg after the latter's arrest by the Gestapo in December 1938.[62] For the most part, Hamburg was a '*Mustergau*' with regard to the implementation of Nazi racial and social policy.[63] Gypsies and beggars were deported from the city, and Communist 'breeding grounds' demolished.[64] Around 900 Polish

[56] Jochmann, 'Gesellschaftliche Gleichschaltung', p. 95.
[57] Warburg, *Aufzeichnungen*, pp. 146ff.; Rosenbaum and Sherman, *M.M. Warburg & Co.*, pp. 157f.
[58] Johe, 'Institutionelle Gleichschaltung', p. 75.
[59] A. Barkai, *From Boycott to Annihilation. The Economic Struggle of German Jews, 1933–1943* (Hanover/London, 1989), p. 74; Rosenbaum and Sherman, *M.M. Warburg & Co.*, pp. 165–8; Chernow, *Warburgs*, pp. 472f. See A.J. Sherman, 'A Jewish Bank during the Schacht Era: M.M. Warburg & Co., 1933–1938', in A. Paucker (ed.), *Die Juden in nationalsozialistischen Deutschland, 1933–1943* (Tübingen, 1986), pp. 167–72.
[60] Chernow, *Warburgs*, pp. 401–5; Warburg, *Aufzeichnungen*, pp. 153f.; Rosenbaum and Sherman, *M.M. Warburg & Co.*, p. 161; Attali, *Siegmund Warburg*, pp. 1ff., 111, 116.
[61] E. Warburg, foreword to Warburg, *Aufzeichnungen*, p. v; Rosenbaum and Sherman, *M.M. Warburg & Co.*, p. 160; Attali, *Siegmund Warburg*, pp. 98, 117, 119, 130; Barkai, *Boycott to Annihilation*, pp. 53, 76f., 103f.; Warburg–Spinelli, *Erinnerungen*, pp. 150ff.
[62] *Ibid.*
[63] A. Ebbinghaus, H. Kaupen-Haas and K.-H. Roth, *Heilen und Vernichten im Mustergau Hamburg. Bevölkerungs- und Gesundheitspolitik im Dritten Reich* (Hamburg, 1984).
[64] M. Burleigh and W. Wippermann, *The Racial State. Germany 1933–1945* (Cambridge, 1991), pp. 122, 170–4; K.-H. Roth, 'Städtesanierung und "ausmerzende" Soziologie. Der Fall Andreas Walther und die "Notarbeit der Deutschen Wissenschaften" 1934–

POWs were executed during the war for having sexual relations with Hamburg women.[65] Deportations of Jews from Hamburg to Lodz, Minsk and Riga proceeded routinely from 1941.[66] Most strikingly of all, as Christopher Browning has described, a Reserve Police Battalion from the Hamburg police – around 500 quite 'ordinary men' of working- and lower-middle-class backgrounds – played their part in implementing the 'Final Solution' in occupied Poland. Between July 1942 and November 1943 they shot around 38,000 Jews and deported a further 45,000 to the death camps.[67]

There was, of course, a contradiction between Hitler's military aims and his racial policy. The latter reduced the efficiency of the war effort in numerous ways: removing important economic skills and manpower from the German and Polish economies; alienating the non-Russian populations of the occupied Soviet Union; wasting resources on the annihilation of helpless civilians. Yet it is not quite satisfactory to conclude that Hitler's 'solution' to the German problem failed because of its own internal contradictions. Volatile and inefficient though the regime was, it is too complacent to regard its failure as inevitable: it came too close to military victory over the Soviet Union, and only the most complete military defeat and occupation could destroy it. Ultimately, it was the superiority of the American economy as an engine of production and of the Soviet system as an engine of war mobilisation which proved decisive; and even after this devastating show of superiority, it was still felt necessary to 'denazify' and 'reeducate' the Reich's population – and indeed to occupy and, finally, partition Germany.

The second German hyperinflation of 1944–7 provides the end of this story. The question which remains (but can only be touched upon) is why the West German economy emerged from this second post-war crisis so much more successfully than from the first. Superficially, the problems were similar, if not greater. It took three years rather than five to reform the currency, but in that time the degree of economic dislocation was greater than it had been for most of the post-1918 period: production was lower, and hyperinflation set in much more rapidly. The view that a combination of Marshall Aid, currency reform and deregulation brought about an economic 'miracle' after

1935 in Hamburg', in C. Klingemann (ed.), *Rassenmythos und Sozialwissenschaften in Deutschland* (Opladen, 1987), pp. 370ff.

[65] R. Gellately, *The Gestapo and German Society. Enforcing Racial Policy, 1933–1945* (Oxford, 1990), pp. 235f.

[66] M. Gilbert, *The Holocaust. A Jewish Tragedy* (London, 1986), pp. 213ff., 229, 243.

[67] C.R. Browning, *Ordinary Men. Reserve Police Battalion 101 and the Final Solution in Poland* (New York, 1993). Browning clearly demonstrates that these men were not acting under duress: they were given the option not to participate, which only around 10 per cent took.

1948 is too simplistic: Marshall Aid in itself was relatively limited (as
compared, for example, with the large influx of private American
capital in 1920/2),[68] and in a number of respects the currency reform
and asset-revaluation legislation were little different to those of 1924.[69]
On the other hand, a purely structural interpretation of post-war
recovery – whether it emphasises the strong post-war capital base or
copious labour supply – understates the importance of certain fundamental technical differences in stabilisation policy.[70] Firstly, public
sector finances were turned from surplus to deficit at a crucial point
in 1948/9, allowing the public sector to stimulate saving rather than
inflation.[71] Secondly, the Bank deutscher Länder was equipped with
a far wider range of powers than its predecessor: it could not only
employ the discount rate, but could also conduct open market operations and impose minimum reserve requirements. These devices
ensured that credit expansion was brought under control in 1948/9.[72]
Thirdly, a quite different policy was adopted on the balance of payments: faced with persistent trade deficits, the authorities maintained
exchange controls, but devalued the currency formally in September

[68] H.C. Wallich, *Mainsprings of German Revival* (New Haven, 1955); M.J. Hogan, *The
Marshall Plan. America, Britain and the Reconstruction of Western Europe, 1947–1952*
(New York, 1987); M. Knapp, 'Reconstruction and West-Integration: The impact of
the Marshall Plan on Germany', *Zeitschrift für die gesamte Staatswissenschaft*, 137
(1981), pp. 415 ff.; G. Hardach, 'The Marshall Plan in Germany', in *Journal of
European Economic History*, 16 (1987), pp. 433 ff. Cf. S. Hoffmann and C. S. Maier
(eds.), *The Marshall Plan. A Retrospective* (Boulder, Co./London, 1984); H.-J.
Schröder (ed.), *Marshallplan und Westdeutsche Wiederaufstieg. Positiones – Kontroversen*
(Stuttgart, 1990): C. S. Maier and G. Bischof (eds.), *The Marshall Plan and Germany*
(Oxford/Providence, 1991).

[69] M. Möller, 'Die westdeutsche Währungsreform von 1948', in Deutsche Bundesbank
(ed.), *Währung und Wirtschaft*, pp. 433–83; E. Wandel, *Die Entstehung der Bank
deutscher Länder und die Währungsreform von 1948* (Frankfurt am Main, 1980); A.
Ritschl, 'Die Währungsreform von 1948 und der Wiederaufstieg der westdeutschen
Industrie. Zu den Thesen von Mathias Manz und Werner Abelshauser über die
Produktionswirkungen der Währungsreform', *VfZ*, 33 (1985), pp. 136 ff.; C.
Buchheim, 'Die Währungsreform 1948 in Westdeutschland', in *VfZ*, 36 (1988), pp.
189 ff.

[70] W. Abelshauser, *Wirtschaft in Westdeutschland 1945–1948. Rekonstruktion und Wachstumsbedingungen in der amerikanischen und britischen Zone* (Stuttgart, 1975); *idem*,'Probleme des Wiederaufbaus der westdeutschen Wirtschaft, 1945–1953' in H.A. Winkler
(ed.), *Politische Weichenstellungen in Nachkriegsdeutschland, 1945–1953* (Göttingen,
1979), pp. 208 ff.; *idem*, 'Wiederaufbau vor dem Marshall-Plan. Westeuropas Wachstumschancen und Wirtschaftsordnungspolitik in der zweiten Hälfte der vierziger
Jahre', *VfZ*, 29 (1981), pp. 545 ff.; *idem*, 'West German economic recovery 1945–
1951: A Reassessment', *Three Banks Review*, 135 (1982), pp. 34ff.; C. Kindleberger,
Europe's post-war growth: The Role of the Labour Supply (Cambridge, Mass., 1967).
Cf. B. Klemm and G.J. Trittel, 'Vor dem 'Wirtschaftswunders': Durchbruch zum
Wachstum oder Lähmungskrise? Eine Auseinandersetzung mit W. Abelshausers Inte-
pretation der Wirtschaftsentwicklung, 1945–1948', *VfZ*, 35 (1987), pp. 517 ff.

[71] Balderston, 'Links from Inflation to Depression', p. 177.

[72] Möller, 'Währungreform', pp. 452–9, 466–8.

1949.[73] Finally, because the authorities implementing these policies were not entirely democratically accountable, they were able to continue with them more easily than had Weimar governments, even when they resulted in higher unemployment.[74] In these ways, stabilisation policies were superior to those of the early Weimar years. Indeed, they provide a model for what ought to have been done in 1920.

To some extent, of course, these successes were due to the influence of the American and British occupying forces;[75] not just because of their influence on points of detail (notably the American influence on the new central bank's powers), but also because American and British occupation and the escalation of the Cold War created a stable, not to say rigid, international framework within which the new Federal Republic could establish itself. With characteristic optimism, the exiled Max Warburg had begun to anticipate some of these developments long before Germany's defeat was assured. In October 1940, he wrote a memorandum to Thomas Lamont – whom he had first met at Versailles more than twenty years before – outlining his vision for an American-dominated League of Nations with far more extensive powers than the inter-war League. Warburg acknowledged the need for a 'combination of private enterprise and systematically planned economy'. But what is most striking is his stress on the need for international monetary stability, for 'without [. . .] sound currency conditions [. . .] the new world order cannot be established'.[76] The two discussed these ideas again in April 1942, by which time they had agreed on a 'post-war formula' which was to prove exceedingly prescient:

(1) Feed starving Europe including Germany; (2) Disarm Germany and then police her for years perhaps; (3) Let the USA open up world trade on a free basis so far as can be; (4) Lend gold to the European nations to stabilise their currencies and enable them to trade internationally – incidentally to become good customers of [the] USA.[77]

Here was the lesson Warburg drew from his own experience: post-war Germany could only be stabilised on the basis of currency stability.

Why had he not seen this more clearly in the early 1920s? Why did it take two hyperinflations to teach Germans – even bankers like

---

[73] *Ibid.*, p. 468.

[74] *Ibid.*, p. 473.

[75] See, e.g., I. Turner, 'Great Britain and the Post-war German Currency Reform', in *HJ*, 30, 3 (1987), pp. 685–708; M. Hughes, 'Lastenausgleich unter Sozialismusvergedacht. Amerikanische Besorgnisse, 1945–1949' *VfZ*, 39 (1991), pp. 37–54. Cf. J.H. Bacher, *Priming the German Economy, American Occupation Policies 1945–1948* (Durham, North Carolina, 1971); D. Petzina and W. Euchner (eds.), *Wirtschaftspolitik im britischen Besatzungsgebiet, 1945–1949* (Düsseldorf, 1984).

[76] Baker Library, Harvard, Lamont Papers, 136–12, Warburg Memorandum, 2.10.40.

[77] *Ibid.*, Warburg, Memorandum of a Conversation with Thomas W. Lamont, 3.4.42.

Max Warburg – the benefits of fiscal and monetary stability? This book has attempted to show that, in purely economic terms, the first German hyperinflation was not inevitable. But the kind of men who ought to have argued for (to put it simply) the policies of 1948/9 in 1920/1 were seduced by other possibilities. They saw continued inflation as a way of boosting Germany's recovery, of dampening the threat of revolution and, above all, of undermining the Versailles peace. Yet in every respect, their calculations turned out to be wrong, for the inflation weakened the economy, undermined the political system and failed to bring about a significant revision of the treaty. Then again, even the most prescient economic liberal would probably have struggled to stabilise the fiscal and monetary system permanently in 1920. The structure of the relevant institutions required a far more radical reform than could have been achieved at that time. Indeed, even Hitler could only suppress, rather than eradicate, the inflationary tendencies of the German Reich. For that reason, the historian must hesitate before blaming particular individuals or groups for Weimar's economic instability. The era of inflation which began in the Wilhelmine boom of the 1890s and continued, with only one major interruption, until 1947, had its roots in the nature of the Reich itself – a state whose basic fiscal and monetary structures could never quite fulfil the grand aspirations of its leaders and people. Blood, iron, gold, coal and rye – these elements symbolised the Reich's undoubted strengths. But its fundamental weakness was a matter of paper.

Appendix

Table 1. Weimar finance

1 NNP	2 Reich revenue	3 Reich expend- iture	4 Repar- ations	5 Repar- ations as % of Reich expend- iture	6 Reich deficit	7 Reich deficit as % of NNP	8 Total expendi- tures	9 Total public spending as % NNP
1919 34200	2496	8643			−6054	−17.7	14600	42.7
1920 37700	3171	7098	1236	17.4	−6092	−16.2	16000	42.4
1921 40400	6237	10395	3369	32.4	−4939	−12.2	14800	36.6
1922 42100	4032	6240	2226	35.7	−3953	−9.4	10100	24.0
1923 37900	1785	6543	801	12.2	−8431	−22.2	17900	47.2
1924 44500	4869	4894	281	5.7	−25	−0.1	13600	30.6
1925 67346	4958	5321	1080	20.3	−363	−0.5	16731	24.8
1926 65472	5633	6561	1310	20.0	−928	−1.4	20520	31.3
1927 80466	6697	7154	1779	24.9	−457	−0.6	22513	28.0
1928 83964	6992	8375	2178	26.0	−1383	−1.6	25271	30.1
1929 79491	7215	8042	1965	24.4	−827	−1.0	25685	32.3
1930 71862	7098	8163	1879	23.0	−1065	−1.5	25526	35.5
1931 58484	6059	6548	651	8.6	−489	−0.8	21779	37.2
1932 50782	5448	5819	183	3.1	−371	−0.7	18817	37.0

Notes
Cols. 1, 2, 3, 4, 6 and 8 are in millions of gold marks (1919–23) or reichmarks (1924–32).
Sources
Col. 1: Witt, 'Finanzpolitik', pp. 425f.; Hoffman *et al.*, *Wachstum*, pp. 255f.
Col. 2: Webb, *Hyperinflation*, p. 33, Balderston, *Economic Crisis*, p. 226.
Col. 3: Bresciani, *Inflation*, pp. 437f.; Webb, *Hyperinflation*, p. 37; Balderston, *Economic Crisis*, p. 226.
Col. 4: Holtfrerich, *Inflation*, p. 147; Webb, *Hyperinflation*, pp. 37, 108; Schuker, '"American Reparations"', pp. 378f.; Balderston, *Economic Crisis*, p. 239.
Col. 5: Col. 4 as percentage of Col. 3.
Col. 6: Col. 2 minus Col. 3
Col. 7: Col. 6 as percentage of Col. 1.
Col. 8: Witt, 'Finanzpolitik', pp. 425f.; Balderston, *Economic Crisis*, p. 217.
Col. 9: Col. 8 as percentage of Col. 1.

Table 2. The balance of payments, 1919–1932

	1 NNP	2 Trade balance	3 Trade balance as % NNP	4 Service balance	5 Net interest payments	6 Reparations	7 Reparations as % NNP	8 Net gold balance	9 Net capital movement	10 Net capital movement as % NNP
1919	34200	−4131	−12.0	160	0	−435	−1.3	300	4106	12.0
1920	37700	3	0.0	160	0	−1236	−3.3	300	773	2.1
1921	40400	−692	−1.7	160	0	−3369	−8.3	300	3601	8.9
1922	42100	−2230	−5.3	160	0	−2226	−5.3	300	3996	9.5
1923	37900	−5	0.0	160	0	−801	−2.1	300	346	0.9
1919–19	192300	−7055	−3.7	800	0	−8067	−4.2	1500	12822	6.7
1924	50220	−1816	−3.6	274	159	−281	−0.6	−1255	2919	5.8
1925	67346	−2444	−3.6	462	−6	−1057	−1.6	−90	3135	4.7
1926	65472	793	1.2	532	−173	−1191	−1.8	−568	607	0.9
1927	80466	−2960	−3.7	645	−345	−1584	−2.0	452	3792	4.7
1928	83964	−1311	−1.6	672	−563	−1990	−2.4	−931	4123	4.9
1929	79491	−44	−0.1	712	−800	−2337	−2.9	165	2304	2.9
1930	71862	1558	2.2	538	−1000	−1706	−2.4	120	490	0.7
1931	58484	2778	4.8	450	−1200	−988	−1.7	1653	−2693	−4.6
1932	50782	1052	2.1	265	−900	−160	−0.3	256	−513	−1.0
1924–32	608087	−2394	−0.4	4276	−4987	−11013	−1.8	−198	14164	2.3

Notes

Cols. 1, 2, 4, 5, 6, 8 and 9 are in millions of gold marks (1919–23) or reichmarks (1924–32).

Trade figures are estimates based on incomplete monthly data in the *Monatliche Nachweise*.

Figures for reparations are for total treaty expenses, including occupation costs and payments in kind. This may exaggerage slightly the burden on the balance of payments. Figures for capital movements are estimates.

Sources

Col. 1: Witt 'Finanzpolitik', pp. 424f. Hoffman *et al.*, *Wachstum*, p. 826.

Cols 2, 4, 5, 6, 8 and 9: *Monatliche Nachweise*; Bresciani, *Inflation*, pp. 85, 234; Graham, *Hyperinflation*, p. 265; Laursen & Pedersen, *Hyperinflation*, pp. 69, 101; Holtfrerich, *Inflation*, p. 212; Schuker, '"American Reparations"', pp. 378f.; Hoffmann *et al.*, *Wachstum*, pp. 817ff.; Webb, *Hyperinflation*, pp. 33, 37, 108.

Bibliography

UNPUBLISHED SOURCES

GERMAN FEDERAL REPUBLIC

Bundesarchiv Potsdam; formerly Zentrales Staatsarchiv, Potsdam, Abteilung Sozialismus und Historische Abteilung I

01.01 Reichstag
06.01 Präsidialkanzlei/Büro des Reichspräsidenten
07.01 Alte Reichskanzlei
15.01 Reichsministerium des Innern
15.06 Zentraleinkaufsgesellschaft
15.07 Reichskommissar für die Überwachung der öffentlichen Ordnung
21.01 Reichsfinanzministerium
21.03 Restverwaltung für Reichsaufgaben
25.01 Deutsche Reichsbank: volkswirtschaftliche und statistische Abteilung
31.01 Reichswirtschaftsministerium
32.01 Reichsministerium für wirtschaftliche Demobilmachung
33.01 Reichsministerium für Wiederaufbau
39.01 Reichsarbeitsministerium
70.2e.1 Zentralarbeitsgemeinschaft

Bundesarchiv Koblenz

R2 Reichsfinanzministerium
R28 Reichsbank
R38 Reichsministerium für Wiederaufbau
R43 I Reichskanzlei
R45 II DVP
R45 III DDP
Wilhelm Solf Papers
Friedrich von Loebell Papers
Erich Koch-Weser Papers
Moritz Bonn Papers

Politisches Archiv des Auswärtigen Amts, Bonn

Büro des Reichsministers
Sonderreferat Wirtschaft
  Finanzwesen 16: Währung-Valuta; Devisenpolitik
  Finanzwesen 16A: Stabilisierung der Mark
  Finanzwesen 20: Bankwesen
Abteilung Inland (R32)
Innere Verhältnisse Hamburgs (R3008–R3010)

Staatsarchiv Hamburg

Senat
Bürgerschaft
Arbeiter- und Soldatenrat
Senatskommission für die Reichs- und Auswärtigen Angelegenheiten
Hanseatische Gesandtschaft, Berlin
Demobilmachungskommissar
Deputation für Handel, Schiffahrt und Gewerbe
Kriegsversorgungsamt
Staatliche Pressestelle
Firm and Family Archives
  Arnold Otto Meyer (Franz Witthoefft Papers)
  Familie Sthamer
  Blohm & Voß AG
  Familie Lippmann
  Familie Lamp'l

Prussian State Archive (Stiftung Preussischer Kulturbesitz), Berlin-Dahlem

Rep. 77 Ministerium des Innern
Rep. 842 Justizministerium
Rep. 90 Staatsministerium
Rep. 90j Kriegsakten
Rep. 109 Staatsbank
Rep. 151 Finanzministerium

M.M. Warburg & Co., Hamburg

Max Warburg Papers

Hapag-Lloyd AG, Hamburg

Hapag Firmenakten
Wilhelm Cuno Papers

Haniel Archiv, Franz Haniel & Cie. GmbH, Duisberg (formerly
Historisches Archiv der Gutehoffnungshütte, Oberhausen)

Deutsche Werft Akten
Paul Reusch Papers

Commerzbibliothek, Hamburg

Handelskammer Plenarsitzungen

Hamburg Weltwirtschaftsarchiv

Firmenarchiv (annual reports and press cuttings collection)

UNITED STATES

National Archives, Washington, DC

RG 39 General Records of the Bureau of Accounts, Treasury
RG 59 General Records of the Department of State

Federal Reserve Bank of New York, New York

Benjamin Strong Papers
German Government, Credit and Finance
Reichsbank
Paul M. Warburg Papers

John Fitzgerald Kennedy Library, Boston, Massachusetts

James P. Warburg Papers

Seeley G. Mudd Manuscript Library, Princeton, New Jersey

John Foster Dulles Papers
Fred I. Kent Papers

Sterling Library, Yale University, New Haven, Connecticut

Paul M. Warburg Papers

Baker Library, Harvard Graduate School of Business Administration, Cambridge, Massachusetts

Thomas W. Lamont Papers

UNITED KINGDOM

Public Record Office, Kew

FO 371 Foreign Office

Foreign Office Library, Cornwall House

German Foreign Ministry duplicate series
  Büro des Reichsministers
  NL Stresemann

OFFICIAL PUBLICATIONS AND DOCUMENT COLLECTIONS

Aus Hamburgs Verwaltung und Wirtschaft (Hamburg, 1927)
Akten der Reichskanzlei. Weimarer Republik, Das Kabinett Scheidemann, ed. H. Schulze (Boppard am Rhein, 1971)
Akten der Reichskanzlei. Weimarer Republik, Das Kabinett Bauer, ed. A. Golecki (Boppard am Rhein, 1980)
Akten der Reichskanzlei. Weimarer Republik, Das Kabinett Müller I, ed. M. Vogt (Boppard am Rhein, 1971)
Akten der Reichskanzlei. Weimarer Republik, Das Kabinett Fehrenbach, ed. P. Wulf (Boppard am Rhein, 1972)
Akten der Reichskanzlei. Weimarer Republik, Die Kabinette Wirth I und II., 2 vols., ed. I. Schulze-Bidlingsmaier (Boppard am Rhein, 1973)
Akten der Reichskanzlei. Weimarer Republik, Das Kabinett Cuno, ed. K.-H. Harbeck (Boppard am Rhein, 1968)
Akten der Reichskanzlei. Weimarer Republik, Die Kabinette Stresemann I und II, 2 vols., eds. K.-D. Erdmann and M. Vogt (Boppard am Rhein, 1978)
Akten zur deutschen auswärtigen Politik 1918–1945. Aus dem Archiv des Auswätigen Amtes, ed. H. Rothfels *et al.*, Series A: 1918–1925, vols. I and II (Göttingen, 1982, 1984)
Hamburger Statistische Monatsberichte
Monatliche Nachweise über den auswärtigen Handel Deutschlands
Quellen zur Geschichte des Parlamentarismus und der politischen Parteien: 1. Reihe, Bd. 6, *Die Regierung der Volksbeauftragten 1918/19*, eds. Susanne Miller with Heinrich Potthoff (Düsseldorf, 1969)

Statistik des Deutschen Reiches
Statistik des Hamburgischen Staates
Statistisches Handbuch für den hamburgischen Staat
Statistisches Jahrbuch für das Deutsche Reich
Statistisches Jahrbuch für die Freie und Hansestadt Hamburg
Statistische Mitteilungen über den hamburgischen Staat
Stenographische Berichte über die Sitzungen der Bürgerschaft zu Hamburg
Vierteljahreshefte zur Statistik des Deutschen Reiches
Wirtschaft und Statistik

NEWSPAPERS AND PERIODICALS

Bank-Archiv
Deutsche Allgemeine Zeitung
Deutsche Bergwerks Zeitung
Frankfurter Zeitung
Germania
Hamburger Echo
Hamburger Fremdenblatt
Hamburger Nachrichten
Hamburger Übersee-Jahrbuch
Hamburgische Correspondent
Mitteilungen der Handelskammer zu Hamburg
Vossische Zeitung
Wirtschaftsdienst

SECONDARY WORKS CITED

Abel, A., R. Dornbüsch, J. Huizinga and A. Marcus, 'Money Demand during Hyperinflation', *Journal of Monetary Economics*, 5 (1979), pp. 97–104

Abelshauser, W., *Wirtschaft in Westdeutschland 1945–1948. Rekonstruktion und Wachstumsbedingungen in der amerikanischen und britischen Zone* (Stuttgart, 1975)

'Probleme des Wiederaufbaus der westdeutschen Wirtschaft, 1945–1953', in H.A. Winkler (ed.), *Politische Weichenstellungen in Nachkriegsdeutschland, 1945–1953* (Göttingen, 1979), pp. 208–53

'Wiederaufbau vor dem Marshall-Plan. Westeuropas Wachstumschancen und Wirtschaftsordnungspolitik in der zweiten Hälfte der vierziger Jahre', *VfZ*, 29 (1981), pp. 545–78

'West German economic recovery 1945–1951: A Reassessment', *Three Banks Review*, 135 (1982), pp. 34–53

'Inflation und Stabilisierung. Zum Problem ihrer makroökonomischen Auswirkungen auf die Rekonstruktion der deutschen Wirtschaft nach dem Ersten Weltkrieg', in Büsch and Feldman (eds.), *Historische Prozesse*, pp. 161–74

'Verelendung der Handarbeiter? Zur sozialen Lage der deutschen Arbeiter in der großen Inflation der frühen zwanziger Jahre', in H. Mommsen and W. Schulze (eds.), *Vom Elend der Handarbeit* (Stuttgart, 1982), pp. 445–76

'Freiheitlicher Korporatismus im Kaiserreich und in der Weimarer Republik', in *idem* (ed.), *Die Weimarer Republik als Wohlfahrtsstaat. Zum Verhältnis von Wirtschafts- und Sozialpolitik in der Industriegesellschaft*, VSWG, Beiheft 81 (1987), pp. 147–70

Abelshauser, W. and D. Petzina, 'Krise und Rekonstruktion. Zur Interpretation der gesamtwirtschaftlichen Entwicklung Deutschlands im 20. Jahrhundert', in W.H. Schröder and R. Spree (eds.), *Historische Konjunkturforschung* (Stuttgart, 1981), pp. 75–114

D'Abernon, Lord, *An Ambassador of Peace. Pages from the Diary of Viscount D'Abernon, Berlin, 1920–1926*, 3 vols. (London, 1929–30)

Abraham, D., *The Collapse of the Weimar Republic. Political Economy and Crisis* (Princeton, 1981)

Achterberg, E., *Kleine Hamburger Bankengeschichte* (Hamburg, 1964)

Adler, C., *Felix M. Warburg, A Biographical Sketch* (New York, 1938)

Ahrens, G., 'Die Überwindung der hamburgischen Wirtschaftskrise von 1857 im Spannungsfeld von Privatinitiative und Staatsintervention', *ZVHG*, 64 (1978), pp. 1–29

Ahrens, G. and R. Hauschild-Thiessen, *Die Reeder: Laiesz/Ballin* [Hamburgische Lebensbilder 2] (Hamburg, 1989)

Albertin, L., *Liberalismus und Demokratie am Anfang der Weimarer Republik: Eine vergleichende Analyse der DDP und der DVP* (Düsseldorf, 1972)

Albrecht, G., *Vom Sparen in Hamburg. Hundert Jahre Neue Sparcasse von 1864* (Hamburg, 1964)

Aldcroft, D.H., *The Inter-War Economy. Britain 1919–1939* (London, 1970)

The Twenties. From Versailles to Wall Street, 1919–1929 (Harmondsworth, 1987)

Allen, W.S., 'Farewell to Class Analysis in the Rise of Nazism: a Comment', in *CEH*, 17 (1984), pp. 54–62

Allen, W.S. (ed.), *The Infancy of Nazism: the Memoirs of ex-Gauleiter Alfred Krebs, 1923–1933* (New York, 1976)

Andic, S. and J. Veverka, 'The Growth of Government Expenditure in Germany Since the Unification', *Finanzarchiv*, 23 (1964), pp. 169–278

Angell, J.W., *The Recovery of Germany* (New Haven, 1929)

'The Reparations Settlement and the International Flow of Capital', *American Economic Review*, 20 (Supplement) (1930), pp. 80–8

Applegate, C., 'Localism and the German Bourgeoisie: the "Heimat" Movement in the Rhenish Palatinate before 1914', in Blackbourn and Evans (eds.), *German Bourgeoisie*, pp. 224–54

Arnold, V., *Rätebewegung in der Novemberrevolution. Die Räte als Organisationsformen des Kampfes und der Selbstbestimmung* (Hanover, 1978)

Artaud, D., 'La question des dettes interalliées et la reconstruction de l'Europe', *Revue Historique*, 261 (1979), pp. 362–82

Asendorf, M., F. Kopitzsch, W. Steffani and W. Termin (eds.), *Geschichte der hamburger Bürgerschaft. 125 Jahre gewählter Parlament* (Berlin, 1984)

Attali, J., *A Man of Influence. Sir Siegmund Warburg, 1902–1982* (London, 1986)

Axe, E.W. and H.M. Flinn, 'An Index of General Business Conditions for Germany, 1898–1914', in *Review of Economic Statistics*, 7 (1925), pp. 263–87

Baasch, E., *Die Handelskammer zu Hamburg 1665–1915*, 3 vols. (Hamburg, 1915)

Geschichte Hamburgs, 1814–1918, 2 vols. (Hamburg, 1925)

'Zur Geschichte der Handelskrise von 1857', *ZVHG*, 30 (1929), pp. 81–105

Geschichte des Hamburgischen Zeitungswesens (Hamburg, 1930)

Backer, J.H., *Priming the German Economy, American Occupation Policies 1945–1948* (Durham, North Carolina, 1971)

Bade, K., 'Arbeitsmarkt, Bevölkerung und Wanderungen in der Weimarer Republik', in M. Stürmer (ed.), *Die Weimarer Republik. Belagerte Civitas* (Königstein, 1985), pp. 160–87

'Massenwanderung und Arbeitsmarkt im deutschen Nordosten vom 1880 bis zum Ersten Weltkrieg. Überseeische auswanderung, interne Abwanderung und kontinentale Zuwanderung', *AfS*, 20 (1980), pp. 265–323

von Baden, Prinz Max, *Erinnerungen und Dokumente* (Stuttgart/Berlin/Leipzig, 1927)

Bähr, J., *Staatliche Schlichtung in der Weimarer Republik. Tarifpolitik, Korporatismus und industrieller Konflikt zwischen Inflation und Deflation, 1919–1932* (Berlin, 1989)

Bairoch, P., 'Europe's GNP: 1800–1975', *Journal of European Economic History*, 5 (1976), pp. 273–340

Balderston, T., 'Links between Inflation and Depression: German Capital and Labour Markets 1924–1931', in Feldman and Müller-Luckner (eds.), *Nachwirkungen*, pp. 157–184

'The Origins of Economic Stability in Germany, 1924–1930: Market Forces versus Economic Theory', *VSWG*, 69 (1982), pp. 488–514

'War Finance and Inflation in Britain and Germany', *EcHR*, 42 (1989), pp. 222–44

The German Economic Crisis, 1923–1932 (Berlin, 1993)

Bane, S.L. and R.H. Lutz, *The Blockade of Germany after the Armistice 1918–1919* (Stanford, 1942)

Barclay, D.E., 'A Prussian Socialism? Wichard von Moellendorff and the Dilemma of Economic Planning in Germany 1914–1918', *CEH*, 11 (1978), pp. 50–82

'The Insider as Outsider: Rudolf Wissell's Critique of Social Democratic Economic Policies 1919 to 1920', in Feldman *et al.* (eds.), *Anpassung*, pp. 451–71

'Rudolf Wissell, *Planwirtschaft*, and the Free Trade Unions 1919 to 1923. Some Tentative Observations', in Büsch and Feldman (eds.), *Historische Prozesse*, pp. 295–308

Bariéty, J., 'Les réparations allemandes après la première guerre mondiale. Objet ou prétexte à une politique rhénane de la France', *Bulletin de la Société d'Histoire Moderne* (1973), pp. 20–33

Les relations franco-allemandes après la première guerre mondiale. 10. novembre 1918–10. janvier 1925: de l'execution à la négociation (Paris, 1977)

Barkai, A., *From Boycott to Annihilation. The Economic Struggle of German Jews, 1933–1943* (Hanover/London, 1989)

Nazi Economics. Ideology, Theory and Policy (Oxford/New York/Munich, 1990)

Barth, P., *Otto Dix und die Düsseldorfer Künstlerszene, 1920–1925* (Düsseldorf, 1983)

Baumann, F.-S., *Um den Staat: Ein Beitrag zur Geschichte der Revolution in Hamburg* (Hamburg, 1924)

Becker, O., 'Bismarcks Kampf um die Eingliederung der Hansestädte in die Zolleinheit', in A. v. Brandt and W. Koppe (eds.), *Städtwesen und Bürgertum als geschichtliche Kräfte* (Lübeck, 1953)

Beitel, W. and J. Woettzold, *Deutsch-sowjetische Wirtschaftsbeziehungen in der Zeit der Weimarer Republik. Eine Bilanz in Hinblick auf gegenwärtige Probleme* (Baden-Baden, 1979)

Bellon, B.P., *Mercedes in Peace and War. German Automobile Workers 1903–1945* (New York, 1990)

Bennett, E.W., *Germany and the Diplomacy of the Financial Crisis, 1931* (Cambridge, Mass., 1962)

Berghahn, V.R., *Der Tirpitz Plan* (Düsseldorf, 1970)

Germany and the Approach of War in 1914 (London, 1973)

'Der Bericht der Preußischen Oberrechnungskammer. Wehlers *Kaisserreich* und seine Kritiker', *G&G*, 2 (1976), pp. 125–36

Modern Germany. Society, Economy and Politics in the Twentieth Century (Cambridge, 1987)

Bergmann, C., *Der Weg der Reparationen. Von Versailles über den Dawesplan zum Ziel* (Frankfurt am Main, 1926)

Berlin, J. (ed.), *Das andere Hamburg. Freiheitliche und demokratische Bestrebungen in der Hansestadt seit dem Spätmittelalter* (Hamburg, 1981)

Berlin, J., W.D. Hund *et al.*, *Arbeiterregierung in Hamburg. Die Verhandlungen zwischen ADGB, KPD und SPD nach den Bürgerschaftswahlen 1927* (Hamburg, 1983)

Berthold, R., 'Die Entwicklung der deutschen Agrarproduktion und der Ernährungswirtschaft zwischen 1907 und 1925', *Jahrbuch für Wirtschaftsgeschichte*, 4 (1974), pp. 83–111

Bertrand, C.L., *Revolutionary Situations in Europe 1917–1922. Germany, Italy and Austria-Hungary* (Montreal, 1977)

Bessel, R., *Germany after the First World War* (Oxford, 1993)

Bessel, R. and E. J. Feuchtwanger (eds.), *Social Change and Political Development in Weimar Germany* (Totowa, NJ, 1981)

Beusch, P., *Währungszerfall und Währungsstabilisierung* (Berlin, 1928)

Bieber, H.-J., 'Der Hamburger Hafenarbeiterstreik 1896/1897', in Herzig *et al.* (eds.), *Arbeiter in Hamburg*, pp. 229–45

'Der Streik der Hamburger Hafenarbeiter 1896/1897 und die Haltung des Senats', *ZVHG*, 64 (1978), pp. 91–148

Blackbourn, D., 'The *Mittelstand* in German Society and Politics 1871–1914', *Social History*, 4 (1977), pp. 409–33

'Between Resignation and Volatility: the Petite Bourgeoisie in Nineteenth Century Germany', in G. Crossick and H.-G. Haupt (eds.), *Shopkeepers and Master Artisans in Nineteenth Century Europe* (London, 1984), pp. 35–61

'The *Mittelstand* in German Society and Politics, 1871–1914', *Social History*, 4 (1977), pp. 409–33

'The Politics of Demagogy', *P&P*, 113 (1986), pp. 152–84

Blackbourn, D. and G. Eley, *The Peculiarities of German History. Bourgeois Society and Politics in Nineteenth Century Germany* (Oxford, 1984)

Blackbourn, D. and R.J. Evans (eds.), *The German Bourgeoisie* (London, 1991)

Blaich, F., *Die Wirtschaftskrise 1925/26 und die Reichsregierung* (Kallmünz, 1977)

Der schwarze Freitag. Inflation und Wirtschaftskrise (Munich, 1985)

Blatt, I., 'Die Stellung bürgerlicher Hamburger Zeitungen zur Einführung des Sozialistengesezes', in *ZVHG*, 73 (1987), pp. 61–96

Böhm, E., *Überseehandel und Flottenbau. Hanseatische Kaufmannschaft und deutsche Seerüstung, 1879–1902* (Hamburg 1972)

'Wirtschaft und Politik in Hamburg zur Zeit der Reichsgründung', *ZVHG*, 64 (1978), pp. 31–54

Anwalt der Handels– und Gewerbefreiheit: Staat und Wirtschaft (Beiträge zur Geschichte der Handelskammer Hamburg, vol. 2) (Hamburg, 1981)

Böhme, H., 'Wirtschaftskrise, Merchant Bankers and Verfassungsreform. Zur Bedeutung der Weltwirtschaftskrise von 1857 in Hamburg', *ZVHG*, 54 (1968), pp. 77–128

Frankfurt und Hamburg. Des Deutschen Reiches Silber- und Goldloch und die allerenglischste Stadt des Kontinents (Frankfurt, 1968)

Bohner, T., *Die Woermanns. Vom Werden deutscher Größe* (Berlin, 1935)

Bolland, J., *Die hamburgische Bürgerschaft in alter und neuer Zeit* (Hamburg, 1959)

'Die Gründung der "Hamburgsichen Universität"', in *Universität Hamburg, 1919–1969* (Hamburg, 1969), pp. 21–123

Bonn, M.J., *Die Stabilisierung der Mark* (Berlin, 1922)

Borchardt, K., 'Wachstum und Wechsellagen, 1914–1970', in H. Aubin and W. Zorn (eds.), *Handbuch der deutschen Wirtschafts- und Sozialgeschichte* (Stuttgart, 1976), vol. 2, pp. 696–703

'Währung und Wirtschaft', in Deutsche Bundesbank (ed.), *Währung und Wirtschaft in Deutschland*, pp. 1–53

'Zwangslagen und Handlungsspielräume in der großen Weltwirtschaftskrise der frühen dreißiger Jahre: Zur Revision der überlieferten Geschichtsbildes', *Jahrbuch der Bayerische Akademie der Wissenschaften*, (1979), pp. 87–132

'Noch einmal: Alternativen zur Brünings Wirtschaftspolitik', *HZ*, 237 (1983), pp. 67–83

'Could and Should Germany have Followed Great Britain in Leaving the Gold Standard?', *Journal of European Economic History*, 13 (1984), pp. 471–97

'Inflationsgefahren in der Weltwirtschaftskrise? Zu den Spielräumen der Brüningschen Wirtschaftspolitik, 1930–1932', in W. Engels *et al.* (eds.), *International Capital Movements, Debt and Monetary System Essays in Honour of Wilfried Guth* (Mainz, 1984), pp. 21–42

'Das Gewicht der Inflationsangst in den wirtschaftspolitischen Entscheidungsprozessen während der Weltwirtschaftskrise', in Feldman and Müller-Luckner (eds.), *Nachwirkungen*, pp. 233–60.

'A Decade of Debate about Bruning's Economic Policy', in Kruedener (ed.), *Economic Crisis*, pp. 137–47

'Germany's Experience of Inflation', in *idem, Perspectives on Modern German Economic History and Policy* (Cambridge, 1991), pp. 132–142

Born, K.E., *Die deutsche Bankenkrise 1931* (Munich, 1967)

International Banking in the 19th and 20th Centuries (Leamington Spa, 1983)

Boross, E.A., 'The Role of the State Issuing Bank in the Course of Inflation in Hungary between 1918 and 1924', in Feldman *et al.* (eds.), *Erfahrung*, pp. 188–227

Brackmann, K., *50 Jahre deutsche Afrika-Schiffahrt. Die Geschichte der Woermann-Linie und der Deutschen Ost-Afrika-Linie* (Berlin, 1935)

Brady, R., *The Rationalisation Movement in German Industry* (Berkeley, 1933)

Bramsted, E.K., *Aristocracy and the Middle Classes in Germany* (Chicago, 1964)

Brandt, J., *Hamburgs Finanzen von 1914 bis 1924* (Hamburg, 1924)

Braun, H.-J., *The German Economy in the Twentieth Century. The German Reich and the Federal Republic* (London/New York, 1990)

Bravo, G.F., ' "In the name of our mutual friend." The Keynes-Cuno Affair', *JCH*, 24 (1989), pp. 147–68

Brecht, A., *The Political Education of Arnold Brecht. An Autobiography 1884–1970* (Princeton, 1970)

Brenner, O., 'Die Patriotische Gesellschaft in Hamburg im Wandel von Staat und Gesellschaft', in *idem, Neue Wege der Verfassungs– und Sozialgeschichte* (Göttingen, 1968), pp. 335–44

Bresciani-Turroni, C., *The Economics of Inflation. A Study of Currency Depreciation in Post-War Germany* (London, 1937)

Breuilly, J., 'Kontinuität in der hamburgischen Arbeiterbewegung von 1844 bis 1863?', in Herzig *et al.* (eds.), *Arbeiter in Hamburg*, pp. 139–52

Breuilly, J. and W. Sachsel, *Joachim Friedrich Martens und die deutsche Arbeiterbewegung* (Göttingen, 1984).

Breuilly J. *et al*, 'Zustände und Prozesse – Ein Projekt zur Sozialgeschichte Hamburgs im 19. Jahrhundert', in Verein Hamburg-Jahrbuch, *Hamburger Zustände. Jahrbuch zur Geschichte der Region Hamburg*, I (1988) pp. 1–12

Broszat, M., *The Hitler State. The Foundation and Development of the Internal Structure of the Third Reich* (London/New York, 1981)

Die Machtergreifung. Der Aufstieg der NSDAP und die Zerstörung der Weimarer Republik (Munich, 1984)

Brown, W.A., 'German Reparations and the International Flow of Capital', *American Economic Review*, 20 (Supplement) (1930), pp. 88–92

Browning, C.R., *Ordinary Men. Reserve Police Battalion 101 and the Final Solution in Poland* (New York, 1993)

Bruhns, M., C. Preuschaft and W. Skrentny, *Als Hamburg 'erwachte' – Alltag im Nationalsozialismus* (Hamburg, 1983)

Bruhns, M., et al. (eds.), *'Hier war doch alles nicht so schlimm'. Wie die Nazis in Hamburg den Alltag eroberten* (Hamburg, 1984)

Brüning, H., *Memoiren 1918–1934* (Stuttgart, 1970)

Bry, G., *Wages in Germany 1871–1945* (Princeton, 1960)

Buchheim, C., 'Die Währungsreform 1948 in Westdeutschland', in *VfZ*, 36 (1988), pp. 189–231

Bucholz, A., *Moltke, Schlieffen and Prussian War Planning* (New York/Oxford, 1991)

Bunselmeyer, R., *The Cost of the War, 1914–1918. British Economic War Aims and the Origins of Reparations* (Hamden, Conn., 1975)

Burchardt, L., *Friedenswirtschaft und Kreigsvorsorge. Deutschlands wirtschaftliche Rüstungsbestrebungen vor 1914* (Boppard am Rhein, 1968)

Burg, H., *Inflation und Klassenkampf. Ursachen, Widersprüche und Konsequenzen der Inflation in Imperialismus* (Berlin, 1977)

Burk, K., *Britain, America and the Sinews of War, 1914–1918* (Boston and London, 1985)

Burleigh, M. and W. Wippermann, *The Racial State. Germany 1933–1945* (Cambridge, 1991)

Burnett, P.M., *Reparation at the Paris Peace Conference* (New York, 1940)

Büsch, O. and G.D. Feldman (eds.), *Historische Prozesse der Deutschen Inflation 1914 bis 1924. Ein Tagungsbericht [Einzelveröffentlichungen der historischen Kommission zu Berlin*, Bd. 21] (Berlin, 1978)

Büttner, U., 'Vereinigte Liberalen und Deutsche Demokraten in Hamburg, 1906–1930', *ZVHG*, 63 (1977), pp. 1–34

'Die Finanzpolitik des Hamburger Senats in der Weltwirtschaftskrise, 1929–32', *ZVHG* (1978), pp. 181–226

Hamburg in der Staats- und Wirtschaftskrise, 1928–1931 (Hamburg, 1982)

'Politische Alternativen zum Brüningschen Deflationskurs; Ein Beitrag zur Diskussion über "ökonomische Zwangslagen" in der Endphase von Weimar', *VfZ*, 37 (1982), pp. 209–51

'Die Politik der Hamburger SPD in der Endphase der Weimarer Republik', in Herzig *et al.* (eds.), *Arbeiter in Hamburg*, pp. 457–69

'Die politische Haltung der Hamburger Freien Gewerkschaften in der Weltwirtschaftskrise, 1928–31', in Herzig *et al.* (eds.), *Arbeiter in Hamburg*, pp. 517–28

'Das Ende der Weimarer Republik und der Aufstieg des Nationalsozialismus in Hamburg', in U. Büttner and W. Jochmann (eds.), *Hamburg auf dem Wege ins Dritte Reich. Entwicklungsjahre 1931–3* (Hamburg, 1983), pp. 7–37

'Rettung der Republik oder Systemzerstörung', in U. Büttner and W.

Jochmann (eds.), *Zwischen Demokratie und Diktatur. Nationalsozialistische Machtaneignung in Hamburg. Tendenzen und Reaktionen in Europa* (Hamburg, 1984), pp. 41–65

Politische Gerechtigkeit und sozialer Geist. Hamburg zur Zeit der Weimarer Republik (Hamburg, 1985)

Buxell, G., *100 Jahre Dynamit Nobel* (Troisdorf, 1965)

Cagan, P., 'The Monetary Dynamics of Hyperinflation', in M. Friedman (ed.), *Studies in the Quantity Theory of Money* (Chicago, 1956), pp. 25–117

Canetti, E., *The Torch in my Ear* (London, 1990)

Carr, E.H., *The Bolshevik Revolution, 1917–1923*, 3 vols. (Harmondworth, 1983)

Carr, W., *Arms, Autarky and Aggression. A Study in German Foreign Policy, 1933–1939* (London, 1972)

Carroll, B.A., *Design for Total War. Arms and Economics in the Third Reich* (The Hague, 1968)

Carsten, F., *Revolution in Central Europe 1918–19* (London, 1972)

Caspar, H., 'Die Politik der RGO. Dargestellt am Beispiel der Arbeitslosenpolitik in Hamburg', in *Deutsche Arbeiterbewegung vor dem Faschismus* (Berlin, 1981), pp. 50–79

Cassis, Y., 'Wirtschaftselite und Bürgertum. England, Frankreich und Deutschland um 1900', in Kocka (ed.), *Bürgertum im 19. Jahrhundert*, II, pp. 9–34

Cassis, Y. (ed.), *Finance and Financiers in European History, 1880–1960* (Cambridge, 1993)

Cattaruzza, M., 'Das "Hamburgische Modelle" der Beziehung zwischen Arbeit und Kapital. Organisationsprozesse und Konfliktverhalten auf den Werften 1890–1914', in Herzig *et al.* (eds.), *Arbeiter in Hamburg*, pp. 247–60

Arbeiter und Unternehmer auf den Werften des Kaiserreichs (Wiesbaden, 1988)

Cecil, L., *Albert Ballin. Business and Politics in Imperial Germany* (Princeton, 1967)

Chernow, R., *The Warburgs. The Twentieth Century Odyssey of a Remarkable Jewish Family* (London, 1993)

Chickering, R., *Imperial Germany and a World Without War* (Princeton, 1975)

Childers, T., 'Interest and Ideology: Anti-System Politics in the Era of Stabilisation, 1924–28', in Feldman and Müller-Luckner (eds.), *Nachwirkungen*, pp. 1–20

The Nazi Voter. The Social Foundations of the Fascism in Germany (Chapel Hill, North Carolina/London, 1983)

Claviez, W., *50 Jahre Deutsche Werft, 1918–1968* (Hamburg, 1968)

Cocks G. and K.H. Jarausch (eds.), *German Professions 1800–1950* (Oxford, 1990)

Coetzee, M.S., *The German Army League. Popular Nationalism in Wilhelmine Germany* (Oxford, 1991)

Comfort, R.A., *Revolutionary Hamburg. Labor Politics in the Early Weimar Republic* (Stanford, 1966)

Conze, W., 'Die Reichsverfassungsreform als Ziel der Politik Brünings', in Stürmer (ed.), *Belagerte Civitas*, pp. 340–8

Conzelmann, O., *Der andere Dix* (Stuttgart, 1983)

Coppius, A., *Hamburgs Bedeutung auf dem Gebiete der deutschen Kolonialpolitik* (Berlin, 1905)

Costigliola, F., *Awkward Dominion. American Political, Economic and Cultural Relations with Europe, 1919–1923* (Ithaca, 1984)

Craig, G.A., *Germany, 1866–1945* (Oxford, 1981)

The Germans (Harmondsworth, 1984)

Czada, P., *Die Berliner Elektro-industrie in der Weimarer Zeit. Eine regionalstatistische-wirtschaftshistorische Untersuchung* (Berlin, 1969)

'Große Inflation und Wirtschaftswachstum', in Mommsen *et al.* (eds.), *Industrielles System*, I, pp. 386–94

Dähnhardt, H., *Die Bahrenfelder. Geschichte der Zeitfreiwilligenkorps Groß-Hamburg in den Jahren 1919/20* (Hamburg, 1925)

Dahrendorf, R., *Society and Democracy in Germany* (New York, 1967)

Dann, O. (ed.), *Das Vereinswesen und bürgerliche Gesellschaft in Deutschland* (Munich, 1984)

Danner, L., *Ordnungspolizei Hamburg. Betrachtungen zu ihrer Geschichte 1918–1933* (Hamburg, 1958)

Dasey, R., 'Women's Work and the Family: Women Garment Workers in Berlin and Hamburg before the First World War', in R.J. Evans and W.R. Lee (eds.), *The German Family* (London, 1981), pp. 221–56

Daur, G., *Von Predigern und Bürgern. Eine Hamburgische Kirchengeschichte von der Reformation bis zur Gegenwart* (Hamburg, 1970)

de Bordes, W., *The Austrian Crown: Its Depreciation and Stabilisation* (London, 1924)

Desai, A., *Real Wages in Germany 1871–1913* (Oxford, 1968).

Deumer, R., *Das Hamburger Hypotheken-Kreditwesen* (Hamburg, 1917)

Deutelmoser, M. and B. Ebert, ' "Leichte Mädchen", hohe Herren und energische Frauen', in Berlin (ed.), *Das andere Hamburg*, pp. 140–61

Deutsche Bundesbank (ed.), *Währung und Wirtschaft in Deutschland 1876–1975* (Frankfurt am Main, 1976)

Diamond, S.A., 'Ein Amerikaner in Berlin. Aus den Papieren des Botschafters Alanson B. Houghton 1922–1925', *VfZ*, 27 (1979), pp. 431–70

Diefendorf, J.M., 'Konstanty Gutschow and the Reconstruction of Hamburg', *CEH*, 18 (1985), pp. 143–69

Ditt, K., *Sozialdemokraten im Widerstand. Hamburg in der Anfangsphase des Dritten Reiches* (Hamburg, 1984)

Dockrill, M.L. and J.D. Gould, *Peace without Promise. Britain and the Peace Conference, 1919–1923* (London, 1981)

Domurad, F., 'The Politics of Corporatism: Hamburg Handicraft in the Late Weimar Republic', in Bessel and Feuchtwanger (eds.), *Social Change*, pp. 174–206

Doß, K., *Das deutsche Auswärtige Amt im Übergang vom Kaiserreich zur Weimarer Republik. Die Schülersche Reform* (Düsseldorf, 1977)

Dowie, J.A., '1919–20 is in Need of Attention', *EcHR*, 28, 3 (1975), pp. 429–50

Dukes, J.R. and J. Remak (eds.), *Another Germany: A Reconsideration of the Imperial Era* (Boulder/London, 1988)

Dülffer, J. and K. Holl (eds.), *Bereit zum Krieg. Kriegsmentalität im wilhelminischen Deutschland 1890–1914* (Göttingen, 1986)

Ebbinghaus, A., H. Kaupen-Haas and K.-H. Roth, *Heilen und Vernichten im Mustergau Hamburg. Bevölkerungs- und Gesundheitspolitik im Dritten Reich* (Hamburg, 1984)

Ebeling, H., *Schwarze Chronik einer Weltstadt. Hamburger Kriminalgeschichte 1919–1945* (Hamburg, 1980)

Eckardt, H.W., *Priviligien und Parlament. Auseinandersetzungen um das allgemeine und gleiche Wahlrecht in Hamburg* (Hamburg, 1980)

Ehlert, H.G., *Die wirtschaftlichen Zentralbehörde des Deutschen Reiches, 1914–1919. Das Problem der Gemeinwirtschaft in Krieg und Frieden* (Wiesbaden, 1982)

Eiber, L., *Konzentrationslager Neuengamme, 1938–1945* (Hamburg, 1982)

Eichengreen, B., *Golden Fetters. The Gold Standard and the Great Depression, 1919–1939* (New York/Oxford, 1992)

Eidison, J.R., 'German Club Life as a Local Cultural System', *Comparative Studies in Society and History*, 32 (1990), pp. 357–82.

Eksteins, M., *Rites of Spring. The Great War and the Modern Age* (London, 1989)

Elben, W., *Das Problem der Kontinuität in der deutschen Revolution. Die Politik der Staatssekretäre und der militärischen Führung vom November 1918 bis Februar 1919* (Düsseldorf, 1965)

Eley, G., '*Sammlungspolitik*, Social Imperialism and the German Navy Law of 1898', *Militärgeschichtliche Mitteilungen*, 15 (1974), pp. 29–63

'Capitalism and the Wilhelmine State: Industrial Growth and Political Backwardness, 1890–1918', in *HJ*, 21 (1978), pp. 737–50

Reshaping the German Right. Radical Nationalism and Political Change After Bismarck (New Haven/London, 1980)

Ellis, H.S., *German Monetary Theory, 1865–1933* (Cambridge, Mass., 1934)

Elster, K., *Von der Mark zur Reichsmark. Die Geschichte der deutschen Währung in den Jahren 1914 bis 1924* (Jena, 1928)

Engelhardt, U., '*Bildungsbürgertum*'. *Begriffs- und Dogmengeschichte eines Etiketts* (Stuttgart, 1986)

Die Entwicklung der Gesellschaft 'Harmonie' von 1789 (Hamburg, 1979)

Erdmann, K.D., 'Zur Beurteilung Bethmann Hollwegs', *Geschichte in Wissenschaft und Unterricht*, 15 (1964), pp. 525–40

'War Guilt 1914 Reconsidered. A Balance of New Research', in H.W. Koch (ed.), *The Origins of the First World War* (London, 1984), pp. 334–70

Erger, J., *Der Kapp-Lüttwitz Putsch. Ein Beitrag zur deutschen Innenpolitik 1919/20* (Düsseldorf, 1967)

Ersel, W., *Aktionseinheit stürzt Cuno: Zur Geschichte des Massenkampfes gegen die Cuno Regierung 1923 in Mitteldeutschland* (Berlin, 1963)

Eucken, W., *Kritische Betrachtungen zur deutschen Geldproblem* (Jena, 1923)

Eulenberg, F., 'Die sozialen Wirkungen der Währungsverhältnisse', in *Jahrbücher für Nationalökonomie und Statistik*, 122, 6 (1924), pp. 748–94

Evans, R.J., 'Prostitution, State and Society in Imperial Germany', *P&P*, 70 (1976), pp. 106–29

The Feminist Movement in Germany, 1894–1933 (London, 1976)

'"Red Wednesday" in Hamburg. Social Democrats, Police and Lumpenproletariat in the Suffrage Disturbances of January 17, 1906', *Social History*, 4 (1979), pp. 1–31

'Die Cholera und die Sozialdemokratie: Arbeiterbewegung, Bürgertum und Staat in Hamburg während der Krise von 1892', in Herzig *et al.* (eds.), *Arbeiter in Hamburg*, pp. 203–14

Death in Hamburg. Society and Politics in the Cholera Years 1830–1910 (Oxford, 1987)

Kneipengespräche im Kaiserreich, Stimmungsberichte der Hamburger Politischen Polizei 1892–1914 (Hamburg, 1989)

'Family and Class in the Hamburg Grand Bourgeoisie, 1815–1914', in Blackbourn and Evans (eds.), *German Bourgeoisie*, pp. 115–139

Eyck, E., *A History of the Weimar Republic*, 2 vols. (Oxford, 1962)

Fahning, H., *Bankplatz Hamburg* (Hamburg, 1956)

Falter, J.W., *Hitlers Wähler* (Munich, 1991)

Falter, J.W., T. Lindberger and S. Schumann, *Wahlen und Abstimmungen in der Weimarer Republik: Materialien zum Wahlverhalten, 1919–1933* (Munich, 1986)

Fangmann, H., U. Reifner and N. Steinborn, *Parteisoldaten. Die Hamburger Polizei im 'Dritten Reich'* (Hamburg, 1987)

Farrer, D., *The Warburgs. The Story of a Family* (New York, 1975)

Faulenbach, B., '"Deutscher Sonderweg". Zur Geschichte und Problematik einer zentralen Kategorie des deutschen geschichtlichen Bewußtseins', *Aus Politik und Zeitgeschichte*, 33 (1981), pp. 3–21

Feldman, G.D., *Army, Industry and Labor in Germany, 1914–1918* (Princeton, 1966)

'German Big Business between War and Revolution: The Origins of the Stinnes-Legien Agreement', in G.A. Ritter (ed.), *Entstehung und Wandel der modernen Gesellschaft. Festschrift für Hans Rosenberg zum 65. Geburtstag* (Berlin, 1970), pp. 312–41

'The Origins of the Stinnes-Legien Agreement: A Documentation', *Internationale wissenschaftliche Korrespondenz zur Geschichte der Deutschen Arbeiterbewegung*, 19/20 (1972), pp. 45–102

'Wirtschafts- und sozialpolitische Probleme der deutschen Demobilmachung 1918/19', in Mommsen *et al.* (eds.), *Industrielles System*, II, pp. 618–36

'Die Freien Gewerkschaften und die Zentralarbeitsgemeinschaft 1918–1924', in H.O. Vetter (ed.), *Vom Sozialistengesetz zur Mitbestimmung* (Cologne, 1975), pp. 229–52

'Der deutsche Organisierte Kapitalismus während der Kriegs- und Inflationsjahre, 1914–1923', in Winkler (ed.), *Organisierter Kapitalismus*, pp. 150–171

Iron and Steel in the German Inflation, 1916–1923 (Princeton, 1977)

'The Political Economy of Germany's Relative Stabilisation during the 1920/

21 Depression', in Feldman *et al.* (eds.), *Zwischenbilanz*, pp. 180–206

'The Fate of the Social Insurance System in the German Inflation, 1914 to 1923', in Feldman *et al.* (eds.), *Anpassung*, pp. 433–47

'Weimar from Inflation to Depression: Experiment or Gamble', in *idem* and Müller-Luckner (eds.), *Nachwirkungen*, pp. 385–402

'The Historian and the German Inflation', in Schmukler and Marcus (eds.), *Inflation through the Ages*, pp. 386–99

'Banks and Banking in Germany after the First World War; Strategies of Defence', in Cassis (ed.), *Finance and Financiers*, pp. 243–62

The Great Disorder. Politics, Economics and Society in the German Inflation (New York/Oxford, 1993)

Feldman, G.D. and H. Homburg, *Industrie und Inflation. Studien und Dokumente zur Politik der deutschen Unternehmer, 1916–1923* (Hamburg, 1977)

Feldman, G.D., C.-L. Holtfrerich, G.A. Ritter and P.-C. Witt (eds.), *Die deutsche Inflation. Eine Zwischenbilanz [Beiträge zu Inflation und Wiederaufbau in Deutschland und Europa 1914–1924*, Bd. 1] (Berlin/New York, 1982)

Die Erfahrung der Inflation, [Beiträge zu Inflation und Wiederaufbau in Deutschland und Europa 1914–1924, Bd. 2] (Berlin/New York, 1984)

Die Anpassung an die Inflation [Beiträge zu Inflation und Wiederaufbau in Deutschland und Europa 1914–1924, Bd. 8], (Berlin/New York, 1986)

Die Konsequenzen der Inflation [Einzelveröffentlichungen der Historischen Kommission zu Berlin, Bd. 67. *Beiträge zu Inflation und Wiederaufbau in Deutschland und Europa 1914–1924]* (Berlin, 1989)

Feldman, G.D. and E. Müller-Luckner (eds.), *Die Nachwirkungen der Inflation auf die deutsche Geschichte, 1924–1933* (Munich, 1985)

Feldman, G.D. and I. Steinisch. 'Die Weimarer Republik zwischen Sozial- und Wirtschafts-staat: Die Entscheidung gegen den Achtstundentag', *AfZ*, 18 (1978), pp. 353–75

Felix, D., 'Reparation Reconsidered with a Vengeance', *CEH*, 4, 2 (1971), pp. 171–9

Ferguson, A., *When Money Dies. The Nightmare of the Weimar Collapse* (London, 1975)

Ferguson, N., 'Food and the First World War', *Twentieth Century British History*, 2, 2 (1991), pp. 188–95

'Germany and the Origins of the First World War: New Perspectives', *HJ* 35, 3 (1992), pp. 725–52

'Public Finance and National Security: the Domestic Origins of the First World War Revisited', *P&P* 142 (1994) pp. 141–68

Fink, C., *The Genoa Conference: European Diplomacy, 1921–1922* (Chapel Hill, 1984)

Fischer, F., *Griff nach der Weltmacht. Die Kriegszielpolitik des kaiserlichen Deutschlands, 1914–1918* (Düsseldorf, 1961)

War of Illusions. German Policies from 1911 to 1914 (London/New York, 1975)

Fischer, W., 'Die Weimarer Republik unter den weltwirtschaftlichen Bedingungen der Zwischenkriegszeit', in Mommsen *et al.* (eds.), *Industrielles System*, I, pp. 26–50

'Die deutsche Wirtschaft im Ersten Weltkrieg', in N. Walter (ed.), *Deutschland. Porträt einer Nation*, vol. III: *Wirtschaft* (Gütersloh, 1985)

Flavell, M.K., *George Grosz. A Biography* (New Haven, 1988)

Flemming, J., '"Wege zum sozialen Frieden"? Anfänge staatlicher Arbeitsmarktpolitik in Hamburg', in Herzig *et al.* (eds.), *Arbeiter in Hamburg*, pp. 283–98.

Flemming, J., C.-D. Krohn and P.-C. Witt, 'Sozialverhalten und politische Reaktionen von Gruppen und Institutionen im Inflationsprozeß. Anmerkungen zum Forschungsstand', in Büsch and Feldman (eds.), *Historische Prozesse*, pp. 239–63

Flügel, H., *Die deutschen Welthäfen Hamburg und Bremen* (Jena 1914)

Förster, S., *Der doppelte Militarismus. Die deutsche Heeresrüstungspolitik zwischen Status-quo-Sicherung und Aggression 1890–1913* (Stuttgart, 1985)

Försterling, M., 'Die Hamburgische Bank von 1923 Aktiengesellschaft', in *Hamburger Wirtschaftschronik*, 3 (1965), pp. 1–124

Freimark, P., 'Juden in Hamburg', in *idem* (ed.), *Juden in Preußen – Juden in Hamburg* (Hamburg, 1983), pp. 59–80

Die Hamburger Juden in der Emanzipationsphase, 1780–1870 (Hamburg, 1989)

Frenkel, J.A., 'The Forward Exchange Rate, Expectations and the Demand for Money: the German Hyperinflation', *American Economic Review*, 67 (1977), pp. 653–670

'Further Evidence on Expectations and the Demand for Money during the German Hyperinflation', *Journal of Monetary Economics*, 5 (1979), pp. 81–96

Freudenthal, H., *Vereine in Hamburg, Ein Beitrag zur Geschichte und Volkskunde der Geselligkeit* (Hamburg, 1968)

Frevert, U., 'Bourgeois Honour: Middle-Class Duellists in Germany from the Late Eighteenth to the Early Twentieth Century', in Evans and Blackbourn (eds.), *German Bourgeoisie*, pp. 255–92

von Freyberg, T., *Industrielle Rationalisierung in der Weimarer Republik. Untersucht am Beispielen aus dem Maschinenbau- und der Elektroindustrie* (Frankfurt am Main, 1989)

Freytag, A., *Geschichte des Hamburger Rennclubs und seiner Rennen, 1927–1951* (Hamburg, 1952)

Freytag, C.T., *Die Entwicklung des Hamburger Warenhandels 1871–1900* (Berlin, 1906)

Friedman, M. and A.J. Schwartz, *A Monetary History of the United States, 1867–1960* (Princeton, 1963)

Fritzsche, K., *Politische Romantik und Gegenrevolution. Fluchtwege in der Krise der bürgerlichen Gesellschaft. Das Beispiel des 'Tat' Kreises* (Frankfurt, 1976)

Fulbrook, M., *Germany 1918–1990. The Divided Nation* (London, 1991)

Gall, L., *Bismarck. The White Revolutionary*, 2 vols. (London, 1986)

Gantzel-Kress, G., 'Zur Geschichte des Instituts für Auswärtige Politik. Von der Gründung bis zur nationalsozialistischen Machtübernahme', in K.J. Gantzel (ed.), *Kolonialrechtswissenschaft, Kriegsursachenforschung, Internationale Angelegenheiten* (Baden-Baden, 1983), pp. 23–88

Garvy, G., 'Keynes and the Economic Activists of pre-Hitler Germany', *Journal of Political Economy*, 83 (1975), pp. 391–405

Geary, D., 'Employers, Workers and the Collapse of the Weimar Republic', in Kershaw (ed.), *Weimar*, pp. 92–119

Geiger, T., *Die sozial Schichtung des deutschen Volkes* (Stuttgart, 1932)

Geiss, I., *July 1914. The Outbreak of the First World War: Selected Documents* (London, 1967)

Gelder, L., 'Die Überseeklub 1922–1972', in *Kommerz und Kultur im Amsinck-Haus am Neuen Jungfernstieg* (Hamburg, 1972), pp. 5–58

Gellately, R., *The Politics of Economic Despair: Shopkeepers and German Politics 1890–1914* (London/Beverly Hills, 1974)
The Gestapo and German Society. Enforcing Racial Policy, 1933–1945 (Oxford, 1990)

Gerloff, W., *Die Finanz- und Zollpolitik des Deutschen Reiches 1867–1913* (Jena, 1913)

Gerschenkron, A., *Bread and Democracy in Germany* (Ithaca, 1989)

Gilbert, M., *The Holocaust. A Jewish Tragedy* (London, 1986)

Gillingham, J.R., *Industry and Politics in the Third Reich. Ruhr Coal, Hitler and Europe* (London, 1985)

Gladen, A., 'Der Ruhrbergbau in der Inflationszeit', in Büsch and Feldman (eds.), *Historische Prozesse*, pp. 188–96

Goebbels, J., *Die Tagebücher von Joseph Goebbels: Samtliche Fragmente*, Teil 1, ed. E. Fröhlich, 4 vols. (Munich, 1987)

Goetz, A., *Schiffbau und Schiffahrt. Ein Kapitel von Gestern und Morgen [Mitteilungen des Archivs für Schiffbau und Schiffahrt]* (Hamburg, 1916)

Goldscheid, R., *Staatssozialismus oder Staatskapitalismus* (Jena, 1917)

Gombrich, E.H., *Aby Warburg. An Intellectual Biography* (Oxford, 1970)

Gorlas, J. and D. Peukert (eds.), *Ruhrkampf 1920* (Essen, 1987)

Gossweiler, K., *Großbanken, Industriemonopol, Staat* (Berlin, 1971)

Götz, H.T., *Die Detaillistenkammer Hamburg, 1904–29* (Hamburg, 1929)

Graham, F.D., *Exchange, Prices and Production in Hyperinflation Germany 1920–1923* (Princeton, 1930)

Grebing, H., *Der 'deutsche Sonderweg' in Europa 1806–1945. Eine Kritik* (Stuttgart, 1986)

Greschat, M., 'Krieg und Kriegsbereitschaft im deutschen Protestantismus', in Dülffer and Holl (eds.), *Bereit zum Krieg*, pp. 33–55

Groebel, O., *Deutsche Rohstoffwirtschaft im Weltkrieg* (Stuttgart, 1930)

Groh, D., '"Je eher, desto besser!" Innenpolitische Faktoren für die Präventivkriegsbereitschaft des Deutschen Reiches 1913–14', *Politische Vierteljahresschrift* (1972), pp. 501–21

Grosseinkaufs-Gesellschaft Deutscher Konsumgenossenschaft, *60 Jahre Grosseinkaufs-Gesellschaft Deutscher Konsumgenossenschaft mit beschränkter Haftung Hamburg* (Hamburg, 1954).

Grosz, G., *Abrechnung Folgt!* (Berlin, 1923)

Grunberger, R., *A Social History of the Third Reich* (London, 1971)

Grüttner, M., 'Soziale Hygiene und soziale Kontrolle. Die Sanierung der Hamburger Gängeviertel, 1892–1936', in Herzig *et al.* (eds.), *Arbeiter in Hamburg*, pp. 359–72

'Mobilität und Konfliktverhalten. Der Hamburger Hafenarbeiterstreik 1896/ 7', in K. Tenfelde and H. Volkmann (eds.), *Streik* (Munich, 1984), pp. 143–61

'Unterklassenkriminalität in Hamburg. Güterberaubungen in Hamburger Hafen, 1888–1923', in H. Reif (ed.), *Volk und Obrigkeit* (Frankfurt am Main, 1984), pp. 153–84

Arbeitswelt an der Wasserkante (Göttingen, 1984)

Günther, A., *Die Folgen des Krieges für Einkommen und Lebenshaltung der mittleren Volksschichten Deutschlands* (Stuttgart/Berlin/Leipzig, 1932)

Guttmann, T., *Die Hamburg-Amerika Linie* (Berlin, 1947)

Guttmann, W. and P. Meehan, *The Great Inflation: Germany, 1919–1923* (London, 1975)

Habedank, H., *Zur Geschichte des Hamburger Aufstandes 1923* (Berlin, 1958)

Um Mitbestimmung und Nationalisierung während der Novemberrevolution und im Frühjahr 1919 (Berlin, 1967)

Die Reichsbank in der Weimarer Republik. Zur Rolle der Zentralbank in der Politik des deutschen Imperialismus, 1919–1933 (Berlin, 1981)

Hachtmann, R., *Industriearbeit im 'Dritten Reich'. Untersuchungen zu den Lohn- und Arbeitsbedingungen in Deutschland, 1933–1945* (Göttingen, 1989)

Hahn, A., *Geld und Kredit* (Tübingen, 1924)

Hale, O.J., *The Captive Press in the Third Reich* (Princeton, 1964)

Haller, H., 'Die Rolle der Staatsfinanzen für den Inflationsprozeß', in Deutsche Bundesbank (ed.), *Währung und Wirtschaft*, pp. 137–41

Hallgarten, G.F.W., *Hitler, Reichswehr und Industrie. Zur Geschichte der Jahre 1918–1923* (Frankfurt am Main., 1955)

Hamel, I., *Völkischer Verband und nationale Gewerkschaft. Der Deutschnationale- Handlungsgehilfen Verband 1893–1933* (Frankfurt, 1967)

Hamilton, R.F., *Who Voted for Hitler?* (Princeton, 1982)

Handelskammer Hamburg, *Dokumente zur Geschichte der Handelskammer Hamburg* (Hamburg, 1965)

Repräsentanten der Hamburger Wirtschaft, 1850–1950 (Hamburg, 1984)

Hans, G., *Die Entwicklung der Firma P. Beiersdorf & Co.* (Hamburg, 1915)

Hansmeyer, K.-H. (ed.), *Kommunale Finanzpolitik in der Weimarer Republik* (Stuttgart/Berlin/Cologne/Mainz, 1973)

Hansmeyer, K.-H. and R. Caesar, 'Kriegswirtschaft und Inflation, 1936–1948', in Deutsche Bundesbank (ed.), *Währung und Wirtschaft*, pp. 367–429

Hardach, G., *Weltmarktorientierung und relative Stagnation: Wärungspolitik in Deutschland, 1924–1931* (Berlin, 1976)

The First World War 1914–1918 (Harmondsworth, 1987)

'The Marshall Plan in Germany', in *Journal of European Economic History*, 16 (1987), pp. 433–85

Hardach, K., 'Zur zeitgenössischen Debatte der Nationalökonomen über die Ursachen der deutschen Nachkriegsinflation', in Mommsen *et al.* (eds.), *Industrielles System*, I, pp. 368–75

Harms, O., *Deutsch-Australische Dampfschiffahrtsgesellschaft, Hamburg* (Hamburg, 1933)

Harrod, R.F., *The Life of John Maynard Keynes* (London, 1951)

Hass, H., *Sitte und Kultur in Nachkriegsdeutschland* (Hamburg, 1932)

Hasselmann, E., *Geschichte der deutschen Konsumgenossenschaften* (Frankfurt am Main, 1971)

Haupt, H.-G., *Die radikale Mitte. Lebensweise und Politik von Handwerkern und Kleinhändlern in Deutschland seit 1848* (Munich, 1985)

Haupts, L., *Deutsche Friedenspolitik. Eine Alternative zur Machtpolitik des Ersten Weltkrieges* (Düsseldorf, 1976)

'Zur deutschen und britischen Friedenspolitik in der Krise der Pariser Friedenskonferenz', *HZ*, 217 (1973), pp. 54–98

Hauschild-Thiessen, R., *Bürgerstolz und Kaisertreu. Hamburg und das deutsche Reich von 1871* (Hamburg, 1979)

150 Jahre Grundeigentümer Verein in Hamburg von 1832 e.V. Ein Beitrag zur Geschichte der Freien und Hansestadt Hamburg (Hamburg, 1982)

Hayes, P., *Industry and Ideology. IG Farben in the Nazi Era* (Cambridge, 1987)

Heimer, K., *Geschichte der Hamburg-Amerika Linie*, 2 vols. (Hamburg, 1927)

Heinemann, U., *Die verdrängte Niederlage. Politische Öffentlichkeit und Kriegsschuldfrage in der Weimarer Republik* (Göttingen, 1983)

Helfferich, E., *Zur Geschichte der Firmen Behn, Meyer & Co. und Arnold Otto Meyer*, 2 vols. (Hamburg, 1967)

1932–1946. Tatsachen. Ein Beitrag zur Wahrheitsfindung (Jever, 1968)

Heller, E., *Thomas Mann, The Ironic German* (Cambridge, 1981)

Henderson, W.O., *The Rise of German Industrial Power, 1834–1914* (London, 1975)

Henning, F.-W., *Das industrialisierte Deutschland 1914 bis 1972* (Paderborn, 1974)

Hentschel, V., *Wirtschaft und Wirtschaftspolitik im wilhelminischen Deutschland. Organisierter Kapitalismus und Interventionsstaat?* (Stuttgart, 1978)

'Zahlen und Anmerkungen zum deutschen Außenhandel zwischen dem Ersten Weltkrieg und der Weltwirtschaftskrise', *Zeitschrift für Unternehmensgeschichte*, 31 (1986), pp. 95–116

Hertz-Eichenrode, D., *Wirtschaftskrise und Arbeitsbeschaffung. Konjunkturpolitik 1925/26 und die Grundlagen der Krisenpolitik Brünings* (Frankfurt am Main/New York, 1982)

Herzig, A., 'Organisationsreform und Bewußtseinsprozesse Hamburger Handwerker und Arbeiter in der Zeit 1790–1848', in Herzig *et al.* (eds.), *Arbeiter in Hamburg*, pp. 95–108

Herzig, A. (ed.), *Das alte Hamburg (1500–1848/49). Vergleiche, Beziehungen* (Hamburg, 1989)

Herzig, A., D. Langewiesche and A. Sywottek (eds.), *Arbeiter in Hamburg. Unterschichten, Arbeiter und Arbeiterbewegung seit dem ausgehenden 18. Jahrhundert* (Hamburg, 1982)

Heß, J.C., *'Das ganze Deutschland soll es sein.' Demokratischer Nationalismus in der Weimarer Republik am Beispiel des Deutschen Demokratischen Partei* (Stuttgart, 1978)

Hesse, F., *Die deutsche Wirtschaftslage von 1914 bis 1923. Krieg, Geldblähe und Wechsellagen* (Jena, 1938)

Hesse, H., 'Die Entwicklung der regionalen Einkommensdifferenzen im Wachstumsprozeß der deutschen Wirtschaft vor 1913', in W. Fischer (ed.), *Beiträge zu Wirtschaftswachstum und Wirtschaftsstruktur im 16. und 19. Jahrhundert* (Berlin, 1971), pp. 261–79

Heyn, W., *Das schaffende Hamburg. Hamburg als Versicherungsstadt* (Hamburg, 1939)

Hieke, E., *Zur Geschichte des deutschen Handelshaus Wm. O'Swald & Co.* (Hamburg, 1939)

Rob. M. Sloman Jr. (Hamburg, 1968)

H.C. Stülcken Sohn (Hamburg, 1955)

Hieke, E. and A. Dreyer, *Zur Geschichte des deutschen Handels mit Westafrika. Das hamburgische Handelshaus G.L. Gaiser (1859–1939)* (Hamburg, 1941)

Hillgruber, A., *Germany and the Two World Wars* (Cambridge, Mass., 1981)

'Unter dem Schatten von Versailles – die außenpolitische Belastung der Weimarer Republik: Realität und Perzeption bei den Deutschen', in K.D. Erdmann and H. Schulze (eds.), *Weimar. Selbstpreisgabe einer Demokratie. Eine Bilanz heute* (Düsseldorf, 1980), pp. 177–192

'Revisionismus – Kontinuität und Wandel der Außenpolitik der Weimarer Republik', *HZ*, 237 (1983), pp. 587–621

Hillmann, G. (ed.), *Die Rätebewegung* (Reinbeck bei Hamburg, 1967)

Hintze, O., *Die Niederländische und Hamburgische Familie Amsinck*, 3 vols. (Hamburg, 1932)

Hipp, H., 'Wohnungen für Arbeiter', in Herzig et al. (eds.), *Arbeiter in Hamburg*, pp. 471–81

Wohnstadt Hamburg. Mietshäuser der zwanziger Jahre zwischen Inflation und Weltwirtschaftskrise (Hamburg, 1982)

Hirsch, F. and P. Oppenheimer, 'The Trial of Managed Money', in C. Cipolla, *The Fontana Economic History of Europe*, vol. V (London, 1976), pp. 603–97

Hoffmann, S. and C. Maier (eds.), *The Marshall Plan. A Retrospective* (Boulder, Co./London, 1984)

Hoffmann, W.G., F. Grumbach and H. Hesse, *Das Wachstum der deutschen Wirtschaft seit der Mitte des 19. Jahrhunderts* (Berlin, 1965)

Hogan, M.J., *The Marshall Plan. America, Britain and the Reconstruction of Western Europe, 1947–1952* (New York, 1987)

Hohorst, G., J. Kocka and G.A. Ritter (eds.), *Sozialgeschichtliches Arbeitsbuch*, Bd. II, 'Germany and the International Economy: The Role of the German Inflation in Overcoming the 1920/1 United States 2nd World Depression', in J.J. Lee (ed.), pp. 265–85.

Materialien zur Statistik des Kaiserreichs 1870–1914 (Munich, 1978)

Holborn, H., *A History of Modern Germany*, vol. III, 1840–1945 (London, 1969)

Holtfrerich, C.-L., 'Internationale Verteilungsfolgen der deutschen Inflation', *Kyklos*, 30 (1977), pp. 271–292

'Amerikanischer Kapitalexport und Wiederaufbau der deutschen Wirtschaft 1919–1923 im Vergleich zu 1924–9', *VSWG*, 64 (1977), pp. 497–529

'Die deutsche Inflation 1918 bis 1923 in internationaler Perspektive. Entscheidungsrahmen und Verteilungsfolgen', in Büsch and Feldman (eds.), *Historische Prozesse*, pp. 321–8

'Reichsbankpolitik 1918–1923 zwischen Zahlungsbilanz- und Quantitätstheorie', *Zeitschrift für Wirtschafts- und Sozialwissenschaft*, 13 (1977), pp. 193–214

'Erwartungen des In- und Auslandes und die Geldnachfrage während der Inflation in Deutschland 1920–1923', *Bankhistorisches Archiv*, 6 (1980), pp. 3–19

'Germany and the International Economy: The Role of the German Inflation in Overcoming the 1920/1 United States and World Depression', in J.J. (ed.), pp. 265–85.

Alternativen zu Brünings Wirtschaftspolitik in der Weltwirtschaftskrise (Wiesbaden, 1982)

'Zu höhe Löhne in der Weimarer Republik? Bemerkungen zur Borchardt-These', *G&G*, 10 (1984), pp. 122–41

'Auswirkungen der Inflation auf die Struktur des deutschen Kreditgewerbes', in Feldman and Müller-Luckner (eds.), *Nachwirkungen*, pp. 187–208

'Deutscher Außenhandel und Goldzölle 1919 bis 1923', in Feldman *et al.* (eds.), *Anpassung*, pp. 472–84

'Economic Policy Options and the End of the Weimar Republic', in Kershaw (ed.), *Weimar*, pp. 58–91

'Was the Policy of Deflation Unavoidable?', in Kruedener (ed.), *Economic Crisis*, pp. 63–80

The German Inflation, 1914–1923 (Berlin/New York, 1986)

Homburg, H., 'Die Neuordnung des Marktes nach der Inflation. Probleme und Widerstände am Beispiel der Zusammenschlussprojekte von AEG und Siemens, 1924–1933, oder "Wer hat den längeren Atem?"', in Feldman and Müller-Luckner (eds.), *Nachwirkungen*, pp. 117–54

Homze, E.L., *Foreign Labour in Nazi Germany* (Princeton, 1967)

Hovi, O., 'England und der Gedanke einer Hanserepublik im Herbst 1918', *Publikationen des Instituts für allgemeine Geschichte, Universität Turko, Finland*, 3 (1971), pp. 39–48

Huber, E.R., *Deutsche Verfassungsgeschichte seit 1789*. Bd. IV: *Struktur und Krisen des Kaiserreichs* (Stuttgart, 1969)

Hughes, M.L., 'Economic Interest, Social Attitudes and Creditor Ideology: Popular Responses to Inflation', in Feldman *et al.* (eds.), *Zwischenbilanz*, pp. 395–408

Paying for the German Inflation (Chapel Hill, 1988)

'Lastenausgleich unter Sozialismusverdacht. Amerikanische Besorgnisse, 1945–1949', *VfZ*, 39 (1991), pp. 37–54

Huldermann, B., *Albert Ballin* (London/New York/Toronto/Melbourne, 1922)

Hund, W.D., 'Der 1. Mai 1890', in Berlin (ed.), *Das andere Hamburg*, pp. 119–39

Der Aufstand der KPD 1923 (Opladen, 1983)

Hürten, H., *Der Kapp-Putsch als Wende. Über Rahmenbedingungen der Weimarer Republik seit den Frühjahr 1920* (Opladen, 1989)

Husuung, H.-G., 'Arbeiterschaft und Arbeiterbewegung im Ersten Weltkrieg: Neue Forschungen über Deutschland und England', *HZ*, Sonderheft 15 (1986), pp. 611–64

Huth, W., *Der deutsche Schiffbau und seine Zukunft* (Nieder-Ramstadt bei Darmstadt, 1921)

Jaacks, G., *Festzüge in Hamburg 1696–1913. Bürgerliche Selbtsdarstellung und Geschichtsbewußtsein* (Hamburg, 1972)

'Hermann, Barbarossa, Germania und Hammonia. Nationalsymbole in Hamburger Festzügen des Kaiserreichs', in *Beiträge zur deutschen Volks- und Altertumskunde*, 18 (1979), pp. 57–66

Jacobs, A. and H. Richter, 'Die Grosshandelspreise in Deutschland von 1792 bis 1934', *Sonderhefte des Instituts für Konjunkturforschung*, 37 (1935)

Jacobs, R.L., 'Hyperinflation and the Supply of Money', *Journal of Money, Credit and Banking*, 9 (1977), pp. 287–303

Jacobson, J., 'Strategies of French Foreign Policy after World War I', *JMH* (1983), pp. 78–95

'Is There a New International History of the 1920s?', *AHR*, 88 (1983), pp. 617–45

Jaeckh, E., *Der Goldene Pflug* (Stuttgart, 1955)

Jaeger, R. and C. Steckner, *Zinnober. Kunstszene Hamburg, 1919–33* (Hamburg, 1983)

Jaide, W., *Generationen eines Jahrhunderts. Wechsel der Jugendgeneration im Jahrhundertrend. Zur Sozialgeschichte der Jugend in Deutschland, 1871–1985* (Opladen, 1988)

James, H., 'Gab es eine Alternative zur Wirtschaftspolitik Brünings?', *VSWG*, 70 (1983), pp. 523–41

'The Causes of the German Banking Crisis of 1931', *EcHR*, 37 (1984), pp. 68–87

The Reichsbank and Public Finance in Germany 1924–1933: A Study of the Politics of Economics during the Great Depression (Frankfurt, 1985)

The German Slump. Politics and Economics 1924–1936 (Oxford, 1986)

'Did the Reichsbank draw the Right Conclusions from the Great Inflation?', in Feldman and Müller-Luckner (eds.), *Nachwirkungen*, pp. 211–31

'Die Währungsstabilisierung 1923/4 in internationaler Perspektive', in Abelshauser (ed.), *Weimarer Republik als Wohlfahrtsstaat*, pp. 63–79

'Economic Reasons for the Collapse of Weimar', in Kershaw (ed.), *Weimar*, pp. 30–57

'Banks and Bankers in the German Interwar Depression', in Cassis (ed.), *Finance and Financiers*, pp. 263–82

Jantzen, G., *Hamburgs Ausfuhrhandel im XX. Jahrhundert. Ein Beitrag zur Geschichte eines deutschen Kaufmannstandes und des Verein Hamburger Exporteure, 1903–1953* (Hamburg, 1953)

Hamburgs Ausfuhrhandel im 20. Jahrhundert (Hamburg, 1953)

'Adolf Woermann. Ein politischer Kaufmann in den Wandlungen und Spannungen der imperialistischen Epoche des Reiches', in O. Brunner and D. Gerhard (eds.), *Europa und Übersee. Festschrift für Egmont Zechlin* (Hamburg, 1961), pp. 171–91

Jarausch, K.H., 'The Illusion of Limited War. Chancellor Bethmann Hollweg's Calculated Risk, July 1914', *CEH*, 2 (1969), pp. 48–76

The Unfree Professions. German Lawyers, Teachers and Engineers, 1900–1950 (Oxford, 1990)

Jeck, A., *Wachstum und Verteilung des Volkseinkommens. Untersuchungen und Materialien zur Entwicklung des Volkseinkommensverteilung in Deutschland 1870–1913* (Tübingen, 1970)

Jensen, J., *Presse und politische Polizei. Hamburgs Zeitungen unter den Sozialistengesetz 1878–1890* (Hanover, 1966)

Jessen, A., *Finanzen, Defizit und Notenpresse, 1914–1922* (Berlin, 1923)

Jochmann, W., 'Brünings Deflationspolitik und der Untergang der Weimarer Republik', in Stegmann *et al.* (eds.), *Industrielle Gesellschaft*, pp. 97–112

'Die Ausbreitung des Antisemitismus', in W.E. Mosse (ed.), *Deutsches Judentum in Krieg und Revolution 1916–1923* (Tübingen, 1971), pp. 409–510

'Gesellschaftliche Gleichschaltung in Hamburg 1933: Freiheit des Individuums oder Sicherheit und Schutz der Gemeinschaft', in *idem* and U. Büttner (eds.), *Zwischen Demokratie und Diktatur. Nationalsozialistische Machtaneignung in Hamburg – Tendenzen und Reaktionen in Europa* (Hamburg, 1984), pp. 91–114

Jochmann, W. (ed.), *Im Kampf um die Macht: Hitlers Rede vor dem Hamburger Nationalklub von 1919* (Frankfurt am Main, 1960)

Nationalsozialismus und Revolution. Ursprung und Geschichte der NSDAP in Hamburg 1922–1933. Dokumente (Frankfurt am Main, 1963)

Jochmann, W. and H.-D. Loose (eds.), *Hamburg. Geschichte der Stadt Hamburg und ihre Bewohner*, 2 vols. (Hamburg, 1982)

Johe, W., 'Institutionelle Gleichschaltung in Hamburg 1933: Revolutionäre Umgestaltung oder Widerherstellung traditioneller Ordnungen?', in Jochmann and Büttner (eds.), *Zwischen Demokratie und Diktatur*, pp. 66–90

John, M., *Politics and the Law in Late Nineteenth Century Germany* (Oxford, 1989)

Joll, J., *The Origins of the First World War* (London, 1984)

Jones, C.A., *International Business in the Nineteenth Century. The Rise and Fall of the Cosmopolitan Bourgeoisie* (Brighton, 1987)

Jones, L.E., ' "The Dying Middle": Weimar Germany and the Fragmentation of Bourgeois Politics', *CEH*, 5 (1972), pp. 23–54

'Inflation, Revaluation and the Crisis of Middle Class Politics: A Study of the Dissolution of the German Party System, 1923–1928', *CEH*, 12 (1979), pp. 143–68

'Die Rückwirkungen der Inflation auf die Entwicklung des deutschen Parteiensystems in der Weimarer Republik', in Büsch and Feldman (eds.), *Historische Prozesse*, pp. 288–94

'In the Shadow of Stabilisation: German Liberalism and the Legitimacy Crisis of the Weimar Party System', in Feldman and Müller-Luckner (eds.), *Nachwirkungen*, pp. 21–41

German Liberalism and the Dissolution of the Weimar Party System, 1918–1933 (Chapel Hill, 1988)

Just, M., 'Hamburg als Transithafen für osteuropäische Auswanderer', in Museum für Hanseatische Geschichte (ed.), *'Nach Amerika!'* (Hamburg, 1970), pp. 49–54

Kaelble, H., *Industrialisation and Social Inequality in Nineteenth Century Europe* (Leamington Spa, 1986)

Kaiser, D.E., 'Germany and the Origins of the First World War', *JMH*, 55 (1983), pp. 442–74

Kaiser, D.E., T.W. Mason and R.J. Overy, 'Debate: Germany, "Domestic Crisis" and War in 1939', in *P&P* 12 (1989), pp. 200–40

Karen, O., *Die Hamburger Sparkasse von 1827 in den Jahren 1892 bis 1925* (Hamburg, 1927)

Katzenellbaum, S.S., *Russian Currency and Banking, 1914–1924* (London, 1925)

Kehr, E., 'The Genesis of the Prussian Reserve Officer', in *idem, Economic Interest, Militarism and Foreign Policy in German History* (Berkeley, 1977)

Schlachtflottenbau und Parteipolitik 1894–1901 (Berlin, 1930)

'Soziale und finanzielle Grundlagen der Tirpitzschen Flottenpropaganda', in H.-U. Wehler (ed.), *Der Primat der Innenpolitik* (Berlin, 1970), pp. 134–9

'Englandhaß und Weltpolitik', in H.-U. Wehler (ed.), *Der Primat der Innenpolitik.* (Berlin, 1970), pp. 149–175

Kelter, E., *Hamburg und sein Johanneum im Wandel der Jahrhunderte 1529–1929. Ein Beitrag zur Geschichte unserer Vaterstadt* (Hamburg, 1928)

Kennedy, P.M., *The Rise and Fall of the Great Powers. Economic Change and Military Conflict from 1500 to 2000* (London, 1988)

Kent, B., *The Spoils of War. The Politics, Economics and Diplomacy of Reparations 1918–1932* (Oxford, 1989)

Kernbauer, H., and F. Weber, 'Die Wiener Grossbanken in der Zeit der Kriegs- und Nachkriegsinflation', in Feldman *et al.* (eds.), *Erfahrung*, pp. 142–87

Kershaw, I., *The 'Hitler Myth'. Image and Reality in the Third Reich* (Oxford, 1987)

The Nazi Dictatorship. Problems and Perspectives of Interpretation (London/New York/Melbourne/Auckland, 1989)

Kershaw, I. (ed.), *Weimar: Why did German Democracy Fail?* (London, 1990)

Kessler, Harry Graf, *Tagebücher. 1918 bis 1937* (Frankfurt am Main, 1982)

Keynes, J.M., *The Economic Consequences of the Peace* (London, 1919)

A Revision of the Treaty (London, 1922)

A Tract on Monetary Reform (London, 1923)

'Dr. Melchior, A Defeated Enemy', in *Two Memoirs* (London, 1949)

The Collected Writings of John Maynard Keynes, vol. X, ed. A. Robinson and D.E. Moggridge (Cambridge, 1972)

The Collected Writings of John Maynard Keynes, vol. XVI, ed. E. Johnson (Cambridge, 1977)

The Collected Writings of John Maynard Keynes, vol. XVII, ed. E. Johnson (Cambridge, 1977)

Khan, M., 'The Variability of Expectations in Hyperinflations', *Journal of Political Economy*, 85 (1977), pp. 817–27

Kindleberger, C.P., *Europe's Post-War Growth: The Role of the Labour Supply* (Cambridge, Mass., 1967)

The World in Depression, 1929–1939 (London, 1973)

'A Structural View of the German Inflation', in Feldman *et al.* (eds.), *Erfahrung*, pp. 10–33

A Financial History of Western Europe (London, 1984)

Kipnase, E., *Die Hamburger Hochbahn AG in verkehrspolitischer und sozialpolitischer Beziehung* (Berlin, 1925)

Klein, B.H., *Germany's Economic Preparations for War* (Cambridge, Mass., 1959)

Klein, G., *400 Jahre Hamburger Börse. Eine geschichtliche Darstellung* (Hamburg, 1958)

Kleine-Natrop, F., *Devisenpolitik in Deutschland vor dem Kriege und in der Kriegs- und Nachkriegszeit* (Berlin, 1922)

Klemenz, D., *Die Religionsunterricht in Hamburg von der Kirchenordnung von 1529 bis zum staatlichen Unterrichtsgesetz von 1870* (Hamburg, 1970)

Klemm, B. and G.J. Trittel, 'Vor dem "Wirtschaftswunder": Durchbruch zum Wachstum oder Lähmungskrise? Eine Auseinandersetzung mit W. Abelshausers Intepretation der Wirtschaftsentwicklung, 1945–1948', *VfZ*, 35 (1987), pp. 571–624

Klessmann, E., *Geschichte der Stadt Hamburg* (Hamburg, 1981)

Kludas, A., *Die Geschichte der deutscher Passagier-Schiffahrt, Bd. I: 1850–1914* (Hamburg, 1986)

Kludas, A., D. Maass and S. Sabisch, *Hafen Hamburg* (Hamburg, 1988)

Klug, A., 'The Theory and Practice of Reparations and American Lending to Germany, 1925–1929', *Working Papers in International Economics* (Princeton, 1990)

Kluge, U., *Soldatenräte und Revolution. Studien zur Militärpolitik in Deutschland 1918/19* (Göttingen, 1975)

Die deutsche Revolution 1918/19 (Frankfurt am Main, 1985)

Knapp, M., 'Reconstruction and West-Integration: The Impact of the Marshall Plan on Germany', *Zeitschrift für die gesamte Staatswissenschaft*, 137 (1981), pp. 415–33

Knauss, R., *Die deutsche, englische und französische Kriegsfinanzierung* (Berlin/Leipzig, 1923)

Kocka, J., 'Industrielles Management: Konzeption und Modelle in Deutschland vor 1914', *VSWG*, 56, 3 (1969), pp. 332–72

Unternehmensverwaltung und Angestelltenschaft am Beispiel Siemens, 1847–1914 (Stuttgart, 1969)

Klassengesellschaft im Krieg. Deutsche Sozialgeschichte 1914–1918 (Göttingen, 1973)

'The First World War and the *Mittelstand*. German Artisans and White Collar Workers', *JCH*, 8 (1973), pp. 101–23

Unternehmer in der deutschen Industrialisierung (Göttingen, 1975)

'Familie, Unternehmer und Kapitalismus', *Zeitschrift für Unternehmensgeschichte*, 24. Jg. (1979), pp. 99–135

'Capitalism and Bureaucracy in German Industrialisation before 1914', *EcHR*, 34 (1981), pp. 453–68

'Organisierter Kapitalismus oder Staatsmonopolistischer Kapitalismus? Begriffliche Vorbemerkungen', in Winkler (ed.), *Organisierter Kapitalismus*, pp. 19–35.

'White Collar Employees and Industrial Society in Imperial Germany', in G. Iggers (ed.), *The Social History of Politics* (Leamington Spa, 1985), pp. 113–36

'German History before Hitler. The Debate about the German "Sonderweg"', *JCH*, 23 (1988), pp. 3–16

Kocka, J. (ed.), *Bürgertum im 19. Jahrhundert. Deutschland im europäischen Vergleich*, 3 vols. (Munich, 1988)

Bürger und Bürgerlichkeit im 19. Jahrhundert (Göttingen, 1987)

Bildungsbürgertum im 19. Jahrhundert, Bd. I: *Bildungsbürgertum und Professionalisierung in internationalen Vergleich* (Stuttgart, 1985); Bd. IV: *Politischer Einfluß und gesellschaftliche Formation* (Stuttgart, 1989)

Kolb, E., *Die Arbeiterräte in der deutschen Innenpolitik 1918–19* (Düsseldorf, 1962)

'Rätewirklichkeit und Räteideologie in der deutschen Revolution von 1918–19', in *idem* (ed.), *Vom Kaiserreich zur Weimarer Republik* (Cologne, 1972), pp. 165–84

'Internationale Rahmenbedingungen einer demokratischen Neuordnung in Deutschland 1918/19', in L. Albertin and W. Link (eds.), *Politische Parteien auf dem Weg zur parlamentarischen Demokratie in Deutschland* (Düsseldorf, 1981), pp. 147–76

The Weimar Republic (London, 1988)

Kopitzsch, F., 'Die Hamburgische Gesellschaft zur Beförderung der Künste und nützlichen Gewerbe (Patriotische Gesellschaft von 1765) im Zeitalter der Aufklärung', in R. Vierhaus (ed.), *Deutsche patriotische und gemeinnützige Gesellschaften* (Munich, 1980), pp. 71–118

'Hamburg zwischen Hauptrezess und Franzosenzeit', in W. Rausch (ed.), *Die Städte Mitteleuropas im 17. und 18. Jahrhundert* (Linz, 1981), pp. 181–210

Grundzüge einer Sozialgeschichte der Aufklärung in Hamburg und Altona, 2 vols. (Hamburg, 1982)

'Aufklärung, freie Assoziation und Reform: Das Vereinswesen in Hamburg im 18. und frühen 19. Jahrhundert', in Herzig (ed.), *Das alte Hamburg*, pp. 209–34

Krause, T., 'Revolution in Altona. Die "Novemberrevolution" – Entstehung eines bürgerlichen Traumas', in A. Sywottek (ed.), *Das andere Altona. Beiträge zur Alltagsgeschichte* (Hamburg, 1984)

'Von der Sekte zur Massenpartei. Die Hamburger NSDAP von 1922 bis 1933', in M. Bruhns et al. (eds.), *'Hier war doch alles nicht so schlimm', Wie die Nazis in Hamburg den Alltag eroberten* (Hamburg, 1984), pp. 18–49

Hamburg wird braun. Der Aufstieg der NSDAP von 1921 bis 1933 (Hamburg, 1987)

Kresse, W., *Aus der Vergangenheit des Reiherstiegwerft in Hamburg* (Hamburg, 1927)

Kroboth, R., *Die Finanzpolitik des Deutschen Reiches während der Reichskanzler-schaft Bethmann Hollwegs und die Geld- und Kapitalmarktverhältnisse (1909–1913/14)* (Frankfurt am Main, 1986)

Krogmann, C.V., *Es ging um Deutschlands Zukunft, 1932–1939* (Leonie am Starnberger See, 1977)

Krohn, C.-D., *Stabilisierung und ökonomische Interessen. Die Finanzpolitik des Deutschen Reichs, 1923–1927* (Düsseldorf, 1974)

Die große Inflation in Deutschland, 1918–1923 (Cologne, 1977)

'Helfferich contra Hilferding. Konservative Geldpolitik und die sozialen Folgen der deutschen Inflation, 1918–1923', *VSWG*, 62 (1975), pp. 62–92

Wirtschaftstheorien als politische Interessen. Die akademische Nationalökonomie in Deutschland, 1918–1933 (Frankfurt am Main, 1981)

'Geldtheorien in Deutschland während der Inflation, 1914–1924', in Feldman *et al.* (eds.) *Anpassung*, pp. 3–45

Krohn, H., *Die Juden in Hamburg. Die politische, soziale, kulturelle und politische Entwicklung einer judischen Großstadtgemeinde nach der Emanzipation, 1848–1918* (Hamburg, 1974)

Krohne, R., 'Der Zusammenbruch und der Wiederaufbau der deutschen Seeschiffahrt', in B. Harms (ed.), *Strukturwandlungen der Volkswirtschaft*, Bd. II (Berlin, 1928), pp. 218–49

von Kruedener, J. Baron, 'Die Überförderung der Weimarer Republik als Sozialstaat', *G&G*, 11 (1985), pp. 358–76

'Could Brüning's Policy of Deflation have been Successful?' in *idem* (ed.), *Economic Crisis and Political Collapse. The Weimar Republic, 1924–1933* (New York/Oxford/Munich, 1990), pp. 81–98

Krüger, P., *Deutschland und die Reparationen 1918/19. Die Genesis des Reparationsproblems in Deutschland zwischen Waffenstillstand und Versailler Friedensschluß* (Stuttgart, 1973)

'Die Reparationen und das Scheitern einer Verständigungspolitik auf der Pariser Friedenskonferenz im Jahre 1919', *HZ*, 221 (1975), pp. 326–75

'Die Rolle der Banken und der Industrie in den deutschen reparationspolitischen Entscheidungen nach dem Ersten Weltkrieg', in Mommsen *et al.* (eds.), *Industrielles System*, II, pp. 568–82

'Das Reparationsproblem der Weimarer Republik in fragwürdiger Sicht', *VfZ*, 29 (1981), pp. 21–74

Die Außenpolitik der Republik von Weimar (Darmstadt, 1985)

'Die Auswirkungen der Inflation auf die deutsche Außenpolitik', in Feldman and Müller-Luckner (eds.) *Nachwirkungen*, pp. 297–313

Kuczynski, J., *Die Geschichte der Lage der Arbeiter unter dem Kapitalismus*, Bd. V: *Darstellung der Lage der Arbeiter in Deutschland von 1917/18 bis 1932/33* (Berlin, 1966)

Kunz, A., 'Verteilungskampf oder Interessenkonsensus? Einkommensentwicklung und Sozialverhalten von Arbeitnehmergruppen in der Inflationszeit 1914 bis 1924', in Feldman *et al.* (eds.), *Zwischenbilanz*, pp. 347–84

'Inflation als Verteilungskampf. Eine Bilanz der neueren Forschung', in Abelshauser (ed.), *Weimarer Republik als Wohlfahrtsstaat*, pp. 171–84

'Stand versus Klasse. Beamtenschaft und Gewerkschaften im Konflikt um den Personalabbau 1923/4', *G&G*, 8 (1982), pp. 55–86

'Variants of Social Protest in the German Inflation: The Mobilisation of Civil Servants in City and Countryside, 1920–1924', in Feldman *et al.* (eds.), *Anpassung*, pp. 323–56

Kutz-Bauer, H., *Arbeiterschaft, Arbeiterbewegung und bürgerlicher Staat in der Zeit der Grossen Depression, 1873–1890* (Bonn, 1988)

Lamp'l, W., *Die Revolution in Hamburg/Das groß-hamburgische Revolutionsrecht* (Hamburg, 1921)

Landau, Z. and J. Tomaszweski, 'Poland Between Inflation and Stabilisation 1924–1927', in Feldman *et al.* (eds.), *Erfahrung*, pp. 270–94

Landsburgh, A., *Die Politik der Reichsbank und die Reichschatzanweisungen nach dem Kriege* (Munich, 1924)

Langewiesche, D., '1848/49: Die Revolution in Hamburg – eine vergleichende Skizze', in Herzig (ed.), *Das alte Hamburg*, pp. 177–90

'Wanderungsbewegungen in der Hochindustrialisierungsperiode. Regionale interstadtische und innerstädtische Mobilität in Deutschland 1880–1914', *VSWG*, 64 (1977), pp. 1–40

Langewiesche, D. and K. Schönhover (eds.), *Arbeiter in Deutschland* (Paderborn, 1981)

Laubach, E., *Die Politik der Kabinette Wirth 1921/22* (Lübeck/Hamburg, 1968)

Laufenberg, H., *Hamburg und sein Proletariat im achtzehnten Jahrhundert: Eine wirtschaftshistorische Vorstudie zur Geschichte der modernen Arbeiterbewegung im niederelbischen Städtegebiet* (Hamburg, 1910)

Die Hamburger Revolution (Hamburg, 1919)

Geschichte der Arbeiterbewegung in Hamburg Altona und Umgegend, 2 vols. (Hamburg 1911, 1931).

Laursen, K. and J. Pedersen, *The German Inflation, 1918–1923* (Amsterdam, 1964)

Lawrence, J., M. Dean and J.-L. Robert, 'The outbreak of war and the urban economy. Paris, Berlin and London in 1914', *EcHR* xlv, 3 (1992)

League of Nations, *Memorandum on Production and Trade 1923–1926* (Geneva, 1928)

Leckebusch, G., *Die Beziehung der deutschen Seeschiffswerften zur Eisenindustrie an der Ruhr in der Zeit 1850–1930* (Cologne, 1963)

Lee, J.J., 'Administrators and Agriculture: Aspects of German Agricultural Policy in the First World War', in J.M. Winter (ed.), *War and Economic Development* (Cambridge, 1975), pp. 229–38

'Policy and Performance in the German Economy, 1925–1933: A Comment on the Borchardt Thesis', in M. Laffan (ed.), *The Burden of German History, 1919–1945* (London, 1988), pp. 131–50

Legien, C., *Der Streik der Hafenarbeiter und Seeleute in Hamburg Altona* (Hamburg, 1897)

von Lehe, E. and R. Wiemar, 'Industrie und Gewerbe in Hamburg', in *Heimatchronik der Freien und Hansestadt Hamburg* (Cologne, 1967)

Lehnert, D., 'Rätealltag und Regionalismus in der deutschen Revolution 1918/
    19', in H.-G. Haupt *et al.* (eds.), *Jahrbuch der Arbeiterbewegung. Geschichte
    und Theorie. 1982: Selbstverwaltung und Arbeiterbewegung* (Frankfurt am
    Main, 1982), pp. 73–109
Lessat, A., 'Vom "Corps der Nachtwache" zur modernen Schutzpolizei. Aus
    der 150jährigen Geschichte der Polizeibehörde', in *Hundertfünfzig Jahre
    Hamburger Polizei 1814–1964* (Hamburg, 1964)
Levy, H., *Die Weltmarkt 1913 und heute* (Leipzig/Berlin, 1926)
Levy, R.S., *The Downfall of the anti-Semitic Parties in Imperial Germany* (New
    Haven, 1975)
Linckmeyer, C., *Das katholische Hamburg in Vergangenheit und Gegenwart*
    (Hamburg, 1931)
Lindberg, L.N. and C.S. Maier (eds.), *The Politics of Inflation and Economic
    Stagnation* (Washington, 1985)
Lindemann, M., *Patriots and Paupers. Hamburg 1712–1830* (New York/Oxford,
    1990)
    'Unterschichten und Sozialpolitik in Hamburg, 1799–1814', in Herzig *et al.*
    (eds.), *Arbeiter in Hamburg*, pp. 61–70
Lindenlaub, D., 'Machinebauunternehmen in der Inflation 1919 bis 1923:
    Unternehmenshistorische Überlegungen zu einigen Inflationstheorien', in
    Feldman *et al.* (eds.), *Zwischenbilanz*, pp. 49–106
    *Machinebauunternehmen in der Inflation 1919 bis 1923: Unternehmenshistorische
    Untersuchungen zu einigen Inflationstheorien* (Berlin/New York, 1985)
Link, W., *Die amerikanische Stabilisierungspolitik in Deutschland 1921–1932*
    (Düsseldorf, 1970)
Lippmann, L., *Mein Leben und meine amtliche Tätigkeit. Erinnerungen und ein
    Beitrag zur Finanzgeschichte Hamburgs* (Hamburg, 1964)
Lohalm, U., *Völkischer Radikalismus. Die Geschichte des Deutschvölkischen
    Schutz- und Trutzbundes, 1919–1923* (Hamburg, 1970)
Loose, H.D., 'Abwehr und Resonanz des Kapp-Putsches in Hamburg',
    ZVHG, 56 (1970), pp. 65–96
    'Hansestaat oder Republik Niedersachsen? Territoriale Neuordnungspläne
    für Nordwestdeutschland in der Revolution 1918/19', *ZVHG* (1980), pp.
    95–116
Lorenz, I., *Die Juden in Hamburg zur Zeit der Weimarer Republik*, 2 vols.
    (Hamburg, 1987)
    ' "Ahasver geht nach Eppendorf": Zur Stadtteilkonzentration der Ham-
    burger Juden im 19. und 20. Jahrhundert', *Informationen zur modernen
    Stadtgeschichte* (1987), pp. 23–9
Lotz, W., *Die deutsche Staatsfinanzwirtschaft im Kriege* (Stuttgart, 1927)
Lucas, E., *Märzrevolution im Ruhrgebiet*, 2 vols. (Frankfurt am Main, 1970,
    1973)
Luckau, A., *The German Peace Delegation at the Paris Peace Conference* (New
    York, 1941)
Lund, K., *Das Papiernotgeld von Schleswig-Holstein und Hamburg, 1914–23*
    (Berlin, 1971)
Lurie, S., *Private Investment in a Controlled Economy: Germany 1933–1939*
    (London, 1947)

Lüth, E., *Hamburg und sein Handwerk, 1873–1973* (Hamburg, 1973)

Lüth, E. and H.-D. Loose (eds.), *Bürgermeister Carl Petersen 1868–1933* (Hamburg, 1971)

Lüth, M., 'Hamburg und die Kolonialpolitik im Dritten Reich', *ZVHG*, 59 (1973), pp. 55–88

Lyth, P.J., *Inflation and the Merchant Economy, The Hamburg* Mittelstand, *1914–1924* (New York/Oxford/Munich, 1990)

Maack, E., *Reeder, Schiffe und ein Verband. Zentralverein Deutscher Rheder* (Hamburg, 1957)

Machlup, F., 'The Transfer Problem: Theme and Four Variations' and 'Foreign Debts, Reparations and the Transfer Problem', in *idem, International Payments, Debts and Gold* (New York, 1964), pp. 374ff.

Mai, G., 'Arbeitsmarktregulierung oder Sozialpolitik? Die personelle Demobilmachung in Deutschland 1918 bis 1920/24', in Feldman *et al.* (eds.), *Anpassung*, pp. 202–36

Kriegswirtschaft und Arbeiterbewegung in Württemberg 1914–1918 (Stuttgart, 1983)

Mai, G. (ed.), *Arbeiterschaft in Deutschland 1914–1918. Studien zu Arbeitskampf und Arbeitsmarkt im Ersten Weltkrieg* (Düsseldorf, 1985)

Maier, C.S., *Recasting Bourgeois Europe. Stabilisation in France, Germany and Italy in the Decade after World War I* (Princeton, 1975)

'Coal and Economic Power in the Weimar Republic: the Effects of the Coal Crisis of 1920', in Mommsen *et al.* (eds.), *Industrielles System*, II, pp. 530–42

'The Politics of Inflation in the Twentieth Century', in F. Hirsch and J.H. Goldthorpe (eds.), *The Political Economy of Inflation* (Harvard, 1978), pp. 37–92

'The Truth about the Treaties', *JMH*, 51 (1979), pp. 56–67

'Die deutsche Inflation als Verteilungskonflikt: soziale Ursachen und Auswirkungen im internationalen Vergleich', in Büsch and Feldman (eds.), *Historische Prozesse*, pp. 329–42

'Inflation and Stabilisation in the Wake of Two World Wars: Comparative Strategies and Sacrifices', in Feldman *et al.* (eds.), *Erfahrung*, pp. 106–29

'Die Nicht-Determiniertheit ökonomischer Modelle. Überlegungen zu Knut Borchardts These von der "kranken Wirtschaft" der Weimarer Republik', *G&G*, 11 (1985), pp. 275–94

'The Two Post-war Eras and the Conditions for Stability in Twentieth Century Western Europe', in *idem, In Search of Stability. Explorations in Historical Political Economy* (Cambridge, 1987), pp. 153–84

Maier, C.S. and G. Bischof (eds.), *The Marshall Plan and Germany* (Oxford/ Providence, 1991)

Mandel, D., *The Petrograd Workers and the Soviet Seizure of Power* (London, 1984)

Mann, G., *The History of Germany since 1789* (London, 1987)

Marcon, H., *Arbeitsbeschaffung der Regierungen Papen und Schleicher* (Frankfurt, 1974)

Marks, S., *The Illusion of Peace: International Relations in Europe 1918–33* (New York, 1976)

'Reparations Reconsidered: A Reminder', *CEH*, 2, 4 (1969), pp. 356–65

'The Myths of Reparations', *CEH*, 11 (1978), pp. 231–55

Marschalck, P., *Deutsche Überseewanderung im 19. Jahrhundert. Ein Beitrag zur soziologischen Theorie der Bevölkerung* (Stuttgart, 1973)

Bevölkerungsgeschichte Deutschlands im 19. und 20. Jahrhundert (Frankfurt, 1984)

Marsh, D., *The Bundesbank. The Bank that Rules Europe* (London, 1992)

Martin, R., *Jahrbuch der Millionäre in den Hansestädten* (Berlin, 1912)

Marwedel, G., *Geschichte der Juden in Hamburg, Altona und Wandsbek* (Hamburg, 1982)

März, E., *Austrian Banking and Financial Policy: Creditanstalt at a Turning Point, 1913–1923* (London, 1984)

Mason, T.W., 'The Primacy of Politics: Politics and Economics in National Socialist Germany', in S. Woolf (ed.), *The Nature of Fascism* (London, 1968), pp. 165–95

Arbeiterklasse und Volksgemeinschaft. Dokumente und Materialien zur deutschen Arbeiterpolitik, 1936–1939 (Oplanden, 1975)

Sozialpolitik im Dritten Reich (Opladen, 1977)

'Arbeiteropposition im nationalsozialistischen Deutschland', in D. Peukert and J. Reulecke (eds.), *Alltag im Nationalsozialismus. Vom Ende der Weimarer Republik bis zum Zweiten Weltkrieg* (Wuppertal, 1981), pp. 293–314

Massing, P.W., *Rehearsal for Destruction* (New York, 1949)

Mathies, O., *Hamburgs Reederei, 1814–1914* (Hamburg, 1924)

Maurer, I., *Reichsfinanzen und Grosse Koalition: Zur Geschichte des Reichskabinetts Müller, 1928–30* (Bern, 1973)

May, R., *Kosten der Lebenshaltung in Hamburg seit 1890 [Schriften des Vereins für Sozialpolitik, Bd. 145, 4. Teil, 1]* (Munich/Leipzig, 1915)

Mayer, A.J., *Politics and Diplomacy of Peacemaking. Containment and Counterrevolution at Versailles 1918/19* (New York, 1967)

'Domestic Causes of the First World War', in L. Krieger and F. Stern (eds.), *The Responsibility of Power* (London/Melbourne, 1968), pp. 286–300

McDougall, W.A., *France's Rhineland Diplomacy 1914–1924. The Last Bid for a Balance of Power in Europe* (Princeton, 1978)

'Political Economy versus National Sovereignty', *JMH*, 51 (1979), pp. 4–23

McElligott, A., 'Street Politics in Hamburg', *History Workshop Journal* (1983), pp. 83–90

'Mobilising the Unemployed: the KPD and the Unemployed Workers' Movement in Hamburg-Altona during the Weimar Republic', in R.J. Evans and D. Geary (eds.), *The German Unemployed* (London/Sydney, 1987), pp. 228–60

McKibbin, R., 'Class and Conventional Wisdom. The Conservative Party and the "Public" in Inter-war Britain', in *idem, The Ideologies of Class: Social Relations in Britain, 1880–1950* (Oxford, 1990), pp. 259–48

McNeil, W., *American Money and the Weimar Republic* (New York, 1986)

Mehnke, B., *Armut und Elend in Hamburg, Eine Untersuchung über das öffentliche Armenwesen in der ersten Hälfte des 19. Jahrhunderts* (Hamburg, 1982)

Meinecke, F., *Die deutsche Erhebung von 1914* (Stuttgart, 1914)

Die deutsche Katastrophe (Wiesbaden, 1965)

Menges, F., *Reichsreform und Finanzpolitik. Die Aushöhlung der Eigenstaatlichkeit Bayerns auf finanzpolitischem Wege in der Zeit der Weimarer Republik* (Berlin, 1971)

Merkin, G., 'Towards a Theory of the German Inflation: Some Preliminary Observations', in Feldman *et al.* (eds.), *Zwischenbilanz*, pp. 25–48

Meyer, G., *Nacht über Hamburg. Berichte und Dokumente, 1933–1945* (Frankfurt am Main, 1971)

Meyer, H., *Hamburg als Güterumschlagsplatz vor und nach dem Kriege* (Hamburg, 1930)

Milberg, H., *Schulpolitik in der pluralistischen Gesellschaft. Die politischen und sozialen Aspekte der Schulreform in Hamburg, 1890–1935* (Hamburg, 1970)

Miller, S., *Burgfrieden und Klassenkampf. Die deutsche Sozialdemokratie im Ersten Weltkrieg* (Düsseldorf, 1974)

Die Bürde der Macht. Die deutsche Sozialdemokratie 1918–1920 (Düsseldorf, 1978)

Milward, A.S., *The German Economy at War* (London, 1965)

The Economic effects of Two World Wars in Britain (London/Basingstoke, 1984)

War, Economy and Society, 1939–1945 (Harmondsworth, 1977)

von Moellendorff, W., *Deutsche Gemeinwirtschaft* (Berlin, 1916)

Moeller, R.G., 'Winners as Losers in the German Inflation: Peasant Protest Over the Controlled Economy', in Feldman *et al.* (eds.), *Zwischenbilanz*, pp. 263–75

'The Kaiserreich Recast? Continuity and Change in Modern German Historiography', *Journal of Social History*, 17 (1984), pp. 655–83

Moggridge, D.E., *British Monetary Policy 1924–1931. The Norman Conquest of $4.86* (Cambridge, 1972)

Maynard Keynes. An Economist's Biography (London, 1992)

Mohler, A., *Die konservative Revolution in Deutschland 1918–1932. Grundriß ihrer Weltanschauung* (Stuttgart, 1950)

Möller, M., 'Die westdeutsche Währungsreform von 1948', in Deutsche Bundesbank (ed.), *Währung und Wirtschaft*, pp. 433–83

Mommsen, H., 'Staat und Bürokratie in der Ära Brüning', in G. Jasper (ed.), *Tradition und Reform in der deutschen Politik* (Frankfurt am Main, 1976), pp. 81–137

'Heinrich Brünings Politik als Reichskanzler: Das Scheitern eines politischen Alleinganges', in K. Holl (ed.), *Wirtschaftskrise und liberale Demokratie. Das Ende der Weimarer Republik und die gegenwärtige Situation* (Göttingen, 1978), pp. 16–45

'Die Auflösung des Bürgertums seit dem späten 19. Jahrhundert', in Kocka (ed.), *Bürger und Bürgerlichkeit*, pp. 288–315

Mommsen, H., D. Petzina, B. Weisbrod (eds.), *Industrielles System und Politische Entwicklung in der Weimarer Republik*, 2 vols. (Düsseldorf, 1977)

Mommsen, W.J., 'Domestic Factors in German Foreign Policy before 1914', *CEH*, 6, 1 (1973), pp. 3–43

'Die deutsche Revolution 1918–1920. Politische Revolution und soziale Protestbewegung', *G&G*, 4 (1978), pp. 362–91

'The Topos of Inevitable War in Germany in the Decade before 1914', in
V.R. Berghahn and M. Kitchen (eds.), *Germany in the Age of Total War*
(Totowa, NJ, 1981), pp. 23–45

Max Weber and German Politics 1890–1920 (Chicago/London, 1984)

Möring, M., *Das Lebenswerk Carl Wilhelm Ohlmanns* (Hamburg, 1953)

*1757–1957. 200 Jahre Johannes Schuback & Söhne. Familie und Firma in
Hamburg* (Hamburg, 1957)

100 Jahre Zipperling, Kessler & Co. (Hamburg, 1958)

75 Jahre Carsten Rheder (Hamburg, 1979)

Johann Berenberg, Goßler & Co. (Hamburg, 1962)

175 Jahre Conrad Hinrich Donner (Hamburg, 1973)

Mosbacher, W., 'Reichsbank und Bank von England im Goldstandard vor
1914', *Bankhistorisches Archiv*, 1 (1975)

Mosse, W.E. (ed.), *Juden im wilhelminischen Deutschland 1890–1914* (Tübingen,
1976)

Jews in the German Economy. The German-Jewish Economic Elite, 1820–1935
(Oxford, 1987)

The German-Jewish Economic Elite 1820–1935. A Socio-Cultural Profile
(Oxford 1989)

Mottek, H., W. Becker and A. Schröter, *Wirtschaftsgeschichte Deutschlands.
Ein Grundriß.* Bd. III. *Von der Zeit der Bismarckschen Reichsgründung 1871
bis zur Niederlage des faschistischen deutschen Imperialismus 1945* (Berlin,
1974)

Moulton, H.G. and C.E. McGuire, *Germany's Capacity to Pay. A Study of
the Reparation Problem* (New York, 1923)

Museum für Hamburgische Geschichte (ed.), *'Kola-Fu'. Konzentrationslager
und Gestapogefängnis Hamburg-Fühlsbüttel, 1933–1945* (Hamburg, 1983)

Nahrstedt, W., *Die Entstehung der Freizeit. Dargestellt am Beispiel Hamburgs.
Ein Beitrag zur Strukturgeschichte und zur strukturgeschichtlichen Grundlegung
der Freizeitpädagogik* (Göttingen, 1972)

Neebe, R., *Grossindustrie, Staat und NSDAP, 1930–33: Paul Silverberg und
der Reichsverband der Deutschen Industrie in der Krise der Weimarer Republik*
(Göttingen, 1981)

Nelson, H.I., *Land and Power. British and Allied Policy on Germany's Frontiers
1916–1919*, (London/Toronto, 1963)

Netzband, K.B. and H.P. Widmaier, *Währungs- und Finanzpolitik der Ära
Luther 1923–1925* (Tübingen, 1964)

Neuhaus, R., 'Zum Arbeitskampferfolg der Gewerkschaften vor dem Ersten
Weltkrieg. Streik und Aussperrung auf den Werften 1910', *Internationale
wissenschaftliche Korrespondenz zur Geschichte der deutschen Arbeiterbewegung*, 20 (1984), pp. 498–508

Neumann, P., *Hamburg unter der Regierung des Arbeiter- und Soldatenrats.
Tätigkeitsbericht erstattet im Auftrage der Executive des Arbeiterrats Groß
Hamburgs* (Hamburg, 1919)

Nicholls, A.J., *Weimar and the Rise of Hitler* (London, 1979)

Niehuss, M., *Arbeiterschaft in Krieg und Inflation. Soziale Lage und Schichtung der Arbeiter in Augsburg und Linz, 1910–1925* (Berlin/New York, 1984)

Nipperdey, T., 'Wehlers *Kaiserreich*. Eine kritische Auseinandersetzung', *G&G*, 1 (1975), pp. 539–60

'Verein als soziale Struktur in Deutschland im späten 18. und frühen 19. Jahrhundert', in *idem, Gesellschaft, Kultur, Theorie* (Göttingen, 1976), pp. 174–205

Noakes, J. and G. Pridham (eds.), *Nazism, 1919–1945*, 3 vols. (Exeter, 1983, 1984, 1988)

Nocken, U., 'Corporatism and Pluralism in Modern German History', in Stegmann *et al.* (eds.), *Industrielle Gesellschaft*, pp. 37–56

Nolan, M., *Social Democracy and Society. Working Class Radicalism in Düsseldorf 1800–1920* (Cambridge, 1981)

Nörnberg, H.-J. and D. Schubert, *Massenwohnungsbau in Hamburg. Materialien zur Entstehung und Veränderung Hamburger Arbeiterwohnungen und -siedlungen 1800–1967* (Berlin, 1975)

Novy, K., *Strategien der Sozialisierung: Die Diskussion der Wirtschaftsreform in der Weimarer Republik* (Frankfurt, 1978)

Nurske, R., *The Course and Control of Inflation. A Review of Monetary Experience after World War I* (Geneva, 1946)

Nussbaum, M., 'Unternehmenskonzentration und Investitionsstrategie nach dem Ersten Weltkrieg', *Jahrbuch für Wirtschaftsgeschichte* (1974), pp. 51–75

Obst, A., *Geschichte der Hamburger Bürgervereine* (Hamburg, 1911)

Oeckel, H., *Die revolutionäre Volkswehr 1918/19* (Berlin, 1968)

von Oertzen, P., *Betriebsräte in der Novemberrevolution* (Düsseldorf, 1963)

Offer, A., *The First World War: An Agrarian Interpretation* (Oxford, 1989)

Offermann, G., *Die Geschichte der Neuen Sparcasse von 1864* (Hamburg, 1959)

Offermann, T., 'Arbeiterbewegung, Bürgertum und Staat in Hamburg, 1850–1862/3' in Herzig *et al.* (eds.), *Arbeiter in Hamburg*, pp. 121–37

Oncken, E., *Panzersprung nach Agadir. Die deutsche Politik während der zweiten Marokkokrise 1911* (Düsseldorf, 1981)

Oppens, E., *Der Mandrill. Hamburgs Zwanziger Jahre* (Hamburg, 1969)

Orde, A., *British Policy and European Reconstruction after the First World War* (Cambridge, 1990)

Orsagh, T.J., 'The Probable Geographical Distribution of German Income 1882–1962', *Zeitschrift für die gesamte Staatswissenschaft*, 124 (1968)

Osmond, J., 'Peasant Farming in South and West Germany during War and Inflation 1914 to 1924: Stability and Stagnation', in Feldman *et al.* (eds.), *Zwischenbilanz*, pp. 189–307

Ostasiatischer Verein Hamburg-Bremen zum 60-jährigen Bestehen 1900–60 (Hamburg, 1960)

Ostruba, G., 'Inflation in Oesterreich während und nach dem Ersten bzw. Zweiten Weltkrieg. Ein Vergleich', in Büsch and Feldman (eds.), *Historische Prozesse*, pp. 418–31

Overy, R.J., *The Nazi Economic Recovery, 1928–1938* (London, 1982)

'Hitler's War and the German Economy: A Reinterpretation', in *EcHR*, 35 (1982), pp. 272–91

'Heavy Industry and the State in Nazi Germany: the Reichswerke Crisis', *European History Quarterly* (1985), pp. 313–40

'Germany, Domestic Crisis and War in 1939', *P&P*, 116 (1987), pp. 138–68

'Mobilisation for Total War in Germany, 1939–41', in *EcHR*, 103 (1988), pp. 613–39

Paquet, A., *Die Alte Sparcasse* (Hamburg, 1927)

Parrini, C., *Heir to Empire. United States Economic Diplomacy 1916–1923* (Pittsburgh, 1969)

Die Patriotische Gesellschaft zu Hamburg 1765–1965. Festschrift der Hamburgische–Gesellschaft zur Beförderung der Künste und nützlichen Gewerbe (Hamburg, 1966)

Perrey, H.-J., *Der Russlandausschuß der deutschen Wirtschaft. Die deutsche-sowjetischen Wirtschaftsbeziehungen der Zwischenkriegszeit* (Munich, 1985)

Peterson, L., 'A Social Analysis of KPD Supporters. The Hamburg Insurrectionaries of October 1923', *International Review of Social History*, 28, 2 (1983), pp. 200–39

Petersen, S., ' "Hest ock dahl legt?" August 1791: Generalstreik in Hamburg', in Berlin (ed.), *Das andere Hamburg*, pp. 36–47

Petzina, D., 'Hauptprobleme der deutschen Wirtschaftspolitik 1932/33', *VfZ*, 15 (1967), pp. 18–55

Autarkiepolitik im Dritten Reich. Die nationalsozialistische Vierjahresplan (Stuttgart, 1968)

Die deutsche Wirtschaft in der Zwischenkriegszeit (Wiesbaden, 1977)

'Arbeitslosigkeit in der Weimarer Republik', in Abelshauser (ed.), *Weimarer Republik als wohlfahrtsstaat*, pp. 239–59.

Petzina, D. and W. Euchner (eds.), *Wirtschaftspolitik im britischen Besatzungsgebiet, 1945–1949* (Düsseldorf, 1984)

'Was there a Crisis before the Crisis?' in Kruedener (ed.), *Economic Crisis*, pp. 9–12

Petzina, D., Abelshauser, W. and Foust, A. (eds.), *Sozialgeschichtliches Arbeitsbuch*, Bd. III, *Materialien sur Statistik des Deutschen Reiches 1914–1945* (Munich, 1978)

Petzold, J., *Konservative Theoretiker des deutschen Faschismus. Jungkonservative Ideologen in der Weimarer Republik als geistige Wegbereiter der faschistischen Diktatur* (Berlin, 1982)

Peukert, D., 'The Lost Generation: Youth Unemployment at the End of the Weimar Republic', in R.J. Evans and D. Geary (eds.), *The German Unemployed* (London/Sydney, 1987), pp. 172–93

Inside Nazi Germany. Conformity, Opposition and Racism in Everyday Life (London, 1989)

The Weimar Republic, The Crisis of Classical Modernity (London, 1991)

Pfleiderer, O., 'Die Reichsbank in der Zeit der großen Inflation, die Stabilisierung der Mark und die Aufwertung von Kapitalforderungen', in Deutsche Bundesbank (ed.), *Währung und Wirtschaft*, pp. 157–201

'Das Prinzip "Mark=Mark" in der deutschen Inflation, 1914–1924', in Büsch and Feldman (eds.), *Historische Prozesse*, pp. 69–82

Plagemann, V. (ed.), *Industriekultur in Hamburg. Des Deutschen Reiches Tor zur Welt* (Munich, 1984)

Pogge von Strandmann, H. 'Großindustrie und Rapallopolitik. Deutsch-sowjetische Handelsbeziehungen in der Weimarer Republik', *HZ*, 222 (1976), pp. 265–341

'Rapallo – Strategy in Preventive Diplomacy: New Sources and New Interpretations', in V. Berghahn and M. Kitchen (eds.), *Germany in the Age of Total War. Essays in Honour of Francis Carsten* (London/Totowa, NJ, 1981), pp. 123–46

'Germany and the Coming of War', in *idem* and R.J.W. Evans (eds.), *The Coming of the First World War* (Oxford, 1988), pp. 87–124

Pogge von Strandmann, H. (ed.), *Walther Rathenau. Industrialist, Banker, Intellectual, and Politician. Notes and Diaries 1907–1922* (Oxford, 1985)

Pohl, H. and W. Treue (eds.), *The Concentration Process in the Entrepreneurial Economy since the late Nineteenth Century* (Stuttgart, 1988)

Pohl, M., 'Die Situation der Banken in der Inflationszeit', in Büsch and Feldman (eds.), *Historische Prozesse*, pp. 83–95

Hamburger Bankengeschichte (Mainz, 1986)

Pohlmann, H., *Richard C. Krogmann 1859–1932. Leben und Leistung eines hamburgischen Kaufmanns und Reeders* (Hamburg, 1986)

Postel, R., *Grundriß zur deutschen Verwaltungsgeschichte, 1815–1945*. Bd. 17: Hansestädte und Oldenburg (Marburg/Lahn, 1978)

Potthoff, H., *Gewerkschaften und Politik zwischen Revolution und Inflation* (Düsseldorf, 1979)

Prager, H.G., *Blohm & Voß* (Herford, 1977)

F. Laeisz (Herford, 1980)

Priester, H., *Der Wiederaufbau der deutschen Handelsschiffahrt. Ein Beitrag zur Wirtschaftsgeschichte der Gegenwart* (Berlin, 1926)

Prion, W., *Zwei Vorträge über Scheingewinne* (Jena, 1922)

Prior, K., *100 Jahre Norddeutsche Affinerie* (Hamburg, 1966)

Projektgruppe Arbeiterkultur Hamburg, *Vorwärts und nicht vergessen. Arbeiterkultur in Hamburg um 1930. Materialien zur Geschichte der Weimarer Republik* (Berlin, 1982)

Pulzer, P.G.J., *The Rise of Political anti-Semitism in Germany and Austria* (London, 1988)

Rauh, M., *Föderalismus und Parlamentarismus im wilhelminischen Reich* (Düsseldorf, 1972)

Reichsarchiv, *Der Weltkrieg 1914–1918.* First series, *Die militärischen Operationen zu Lande* (Berlin, 1925)

Reincke, H., W. Haevernick and G. Schlotter (eds.), *Hamburg Einst und Jetzt* (Hamburg, 1933)

Reissner, L., *Hamburg at the Barricades and other Writings on Weimar Germany* (London, 1977)

von Renauld, J., *Die finanzielle Mobilmachung der deutschen Wehrkraft* (Leipzig, 1901)

Reulecke, J., 'Veränderungen des Arbeitskräftepotentials im Deutschen Reich 1900–1933', in Mommsen *et al.* (eds.), *Industrielles System*, I, pp. 84–95

'Phasen und Auswirkungen der Inflation 1914–1923 am Beispiel der Barmer Wirtschaft', in Büsch and Feldman (eds.), *Historische Prozesse*, pp. 175–87 *Geschichte der Urbanisierung in Deutschland* (Frankfurt, 1985).

Reymann, H. and K. Johannsen, *Hamburg als Industrieplatz* (Hamburg, 1930)

Rieger, J., M. Mendel and W. Postelt, *Die Hamburger Konsumgenossenschaft 'Produktion'* (Hamburg, 1949)

Riesser, J., *Finanzielle Kriegsbereitschaft und Kriegsführung* (Jena, 1913)

Ringer, F.K. *The German Inflation of 1923* (New York, 1969)

Ritschl, A., 'Die Währungsreform von 1948 und der Wiederaufstieg der westdeutschen Industrie. Zu den Thesen von Mathias Manz und Werner Abelshauser über die Produktionswirkungen der Währungsreform', *VfZ*, 33 (1985), pp. 136–65

'Zu hohe Löhne in der Weimarer Republik? Eine Auseinandersetzung mit Holtfrerichs Berechnungen zur Lohnposition der Arbeiterschaft, 1925–1932', *G&G*, 16 (1990), pp. 375–402

'Die deutsche Zahlungsbilanz 1936–1941 und das Problem des Devisenmangels vor Kriegsbeginn', *VfZ*, 39 (1991), pp. 103–23

Roerkohl, A., 'Die Lebensmittelversorgung während des Ersten Weltkrieges im Spannungsfeld kommunaler und staatlicher Maßnahmen', in H.-J. Teuteberg (ed.), *Durchbruch zum modernen Massenkonsum. Lebensmittelmärkte und Lebensmittelqualität im Städtewachstum des Industriezeitalters* (Münster, 1987), pp. 309–70

Roesler, K., *Die Finanzpolitik des Deutschen Reiches im Ersten Weltkrieg* (Berlin, 1967)

Rogers, J.H., *The Process of Inflation in France, 1917–1927* (New York, 1929)

Rohrmann, E., *Max von Schinckel* (Hamburg, 1971)

Roth, K.-H., 'Städtesanierung und "ausmerzende" Soziologie. Der Fall Andreas Walther und die "Notarbeit der Deutschen Wissenschaften" 1934–1935 in Hamburg', in C. Klingemann (ed.), *Rassenmythos und Sozialwissenschaften in Deutschland* (Opladen, 1987), pp. 370–93.

Rosenbaum, E., 'Albert Ballin. A Note on the Style of his Economic and Political Activities', *Leo Baeck Institute Yearbook*, 3 (1958), pp. 257–99

Rosenbaum, E. and A.J. Sherman, *M.M. Warburg & Co. 1798–1938. Merchant Bankers of Hamburg* (London, 1979)

Rosenbaum, H., *Formen der Familie. Untersuchungen zum Zusmannenhang von Familienverhältnissen, Sozialstruktur und sozialem Wandel in der deutschen Gesellschaft des 19. Jahrhunderts* (Frankfurt, 1982)

Rosenberg, A., *Imperial Germany and the Birth of the German Republic* (Boston, 1964)

Rosenberg, H., *Große Depression und Bismarckzeit* (Berlin, 1967)

'The Political and Social Consequences of the Great Depression of 1873–1896 in Central Europe', in J.J. Sheehan (ed.), *Imperial Germany* (New York, 1970), pp. 39–60

Roth, A., *Aus der Kampfzeit des Deutschvölkischen Schutz- und Trutzbundes – Eine Erinnerungsschrift vom ehem. Hauptgeschäftsführer Alfred Roth* (Hamburg, 1939)

Rupieper, H.J., *The Cuno Government and Reparations, 1922–1923. Politics and Economics* (The Hague/London/Boston, 1976)

' "Industrie und Reparationen"; Einige Aspekte des Reparationsproblems, 1922–1924', in Mommsen et al. (eds.), *Industrielles System*, II, pp. 582–92

Rürup, R., E. Kolb and G.D. Feldman, 'Die Massenbewegung der Arbeiterschaft in Deutschland am Ende des Ersten Weltkrieges, 1917–1920', *Politische Vierteljahresschrift*, 13 (1972), pp. 84–105

'Demokratische Revolution und "dritter Weg". Die deutsche Revolution 1918/19 in der neueren wissenschaftlichen Diskussion', *G&G*, 9 (1983), pp. 278–301

Ryder, A.J., *The German Revolution of 1918. A Study of German Socialism in War and Revolt* (Cambridge, 1967)

Salemi, M.K., 'Adaptive Expectations, Rational Expectations and Money Demand in Hyperinflation Germany', *Journal of Monetary Economics*, 5 (1979), pp. 593–604

Salemi, M.K. and T.J. Sargent, 'The Demand for Money during Hyperinflation under Rational Expectations: II', *International Economic Review*, 20 (1979), pp. 741–58

Samhaber, E. and O.A. Friedrich, *100 Jahre Weltwirtschaft im Spiegel eines Unternehmens (Phoenix Gummiwerke AG)* (Hamburg, 1956)

Sargent, T.J., 'The Ends of Four Big Inflations', in R.E. Hall (ed.), *Inflation: Causes and Effects* (Chicago, 1982), pp. 41–97

Sargent, T.J. and N. Wallace, 'Rational Expectations and the Dynamics of Hyperinflations', *International Economic Review*, 14 (1973), pp. 328–50

'Rational Expectations and the Theory of Economic Policy', *Journal of Monetary Economics*, 2 (1976), pp. 169–83

Saul, K., *Staat, Industrie und Arbeiterbewegung. Zur Innen- und Sozialpolitik des wilhelminischen Deutschlands 1903–1914* (Düsseldorf, 1974)

' "Verteidigung der bürgerlichen Ordnung" oder Ausgleich der Interessen? Arbeitgeberpolitik in Hamburg-Altona 1896 bis 1914', in Herzig et al. (eds.), *Arbeiter in Hamburg*, pp. 261–82

'Machtsicherung und Gegenoffensive. Zur Entstehung des Arbeitgeberverbandes Hamburg-Altona, 1888–1890', *ZVHG*, 72 (1986), pp. 105–38

Sauvy, A., *Histoire économique de la France entre les deux guerres* (Paris, 1965)

Schacht, H., *The Stabilisation of the Mark* (London, 1927)

Schiemann, J., *Die deutsche Währung in der Weltwirtschaftskrise, 1929–33. Währungspolitik und Abwertungskontroverse unter den Bedingungen der Reparationen* (Bern, 1980)

Schildt, A., 'Hanseatische Vernunft kontra Extremismus? Zum antifaschistischen Kampf der Hamburger Sozialdemokratie, 1929–1933', in Berlin (ed.), *Das andere Hamburg*, pp. 263–82

von Schinckel, M., *Lebenserinnerungen* (Hamburg, 1929)

Schleger, K., 'Mistress and Servant in Nineteenth Century Hamburg', *History Workshop Journal*, 15 (1983), pp. 60–77

Schmack, K., *J.C. Godeffroy & Sohn. Kaufleute zu Hamburg* (Hamburg, 1938)

Schmidt, E.-H., *Heimatheer und Revolution 1918* (Stuttgart, 1981)

Schmidt, G., 'Contradictory Postures and Conflicting Objectives: the July Crisis', in G. Schöllgen (ed.), *Escape into War? The Foreign Policy of Imperial Germany* (Oxford/New York/Munich, 1990), pp. 135–160

Schmidt, W., *Die Revolution von 1848–9 in Hamburg* (Hamburg, 1983)

Schmukler, N. and E. Marcus (eds.), *Inflation through the Ages. Economic, Social, Psychological and Historical Aspects* (New York, 1983)

Schneider, M., 'Deutsche Gesellschaft in Krieg und Währungskrise 1914–1924: Ein Jahrzehnt Forschungen zur Inflation', *AfS*, 16 (1986), pp. 301–19

Scholz, R., 'Lohn und Beschäftigung als Indikatoren für die soziale Lage der Arbeiterschaft in der Inflation', in Feldman *et al.* (eds.) *Anpassung* pp. 278–322

Schönhoff, H.G., *Hamburg im Bundesrat. Die Mitwirkung Hamburgs an der Bildung des Reichswillens 1867–1890* (Hamburg, 1967)

Schönhoven, K., *Expansion und Konzentration. Studien zur Entwicklung der freien Gewerkschaften im wilhelminischen Deutschland, 1890–1914* (Stuttgart, 1980)

Schorske, C.E., *German Social Democracy, 1905–1917* (Cambridge, Mass., 1955)

Fin-de-siècle Vienna. Politics and Culture (Cambridge, 1981)

Schötz, H.O., *Die Kampf um die Mark 1923/24. Die deutsche Währungsstabilisierung unter dem Einfluß der nationalen Interessen Frankreichs, Großbritanniens und der USA* [*Beiträge zur Inflation und Wideraufbau in Deutschland und Europa, 1914–1924*, Bd. 9] (Berlin/New York, 1987)

Schramm, P.E., *Hamburg, Deutschland und die Welt. Leistung und Grenzen hanseatischen Bürgertums in der Zeit zwischen Napoleon I und Bismarck. Ein Kapital deutscher Geschichte* (Munich, 1943)

Deutschland und Übersee. Der deutsche Handel mit den anderen Kontinenten insbes. Afrika, von Karl V. bis zum Bismarck: Geschichte der Rivalität im Wirtschaftsleben (Brunswick/Berlin/Hamburg/Kiel, 1950)

Neun Generationen. 300 Jahre deutscher 'Kulturgeschichte' im Lichte der Schicksale einer Hamburger Bürgerfamilie, 2 vols. (Göttingen, 1963, 1965)

Hamburg – Ein Sonderfall in der Geschichte Deutschlands. Vorträge und Aufsätze (Hamburg, 1964)

Schremmer, D.E., 'Taxation and Public Finance: Britain, France and Germany', in P. Mathias and S. Pollard (eds.), *The Cambridge Economic History of Europe*, vol. VIII. The Industrial Economies: the Development of Economic and Social Policies (Cambridge, 1989), pp. 315–494

Schröder, C.A., *Aus Hamburgs Blütezeit* (Hamburg, 1921)

Schroeder, H.-J., 'Die politische Bedeutung der deutschen Handelspolitik nach dem Ersten Weltkrieg', in Feldman *et al.* (eds.), *Zwischenbilanz*, pp. 235–51

Schroeder, H.-J. (ed.), *Marshallplan und Westdeutsche Wiederaufstieg. Positiones – Kontroversen*, (Stuttgart, 1990)

Schröter, A., *Krieg-Staat-Monopole 1914–1918* (Berlin, 1965)

Schubach, R., *Die Entwicklung der öffentlichen Elektrizitätsversorgung in Hamburg* (Hamburg, 1982)

Schüddekopf, O.-E., *Linke Leute von Rechts. Nationalbolschewismus in Deutschland 1918–1933* (Frankfurt, 1972)

Schuker, S.A., *The End of French Predominance in Europe. The Financial Crisis of 1924 and the Adoption of the Dawes Plan* (Chapel Hill, 1976)

'Finance and Foreign Policy in the Era of the German Inflation: British, French and German Strategies for Economic Reconstruction after the First World War', in Büsch and Feldman (eds.), *Historische Prozesse*, pp. 343–61

'American "Reparations" to Germany, 1919–1933', in Feldman and Müller-Luckner (eds.), *Nachwirkungen*, pp. 335–83

Schult, J., *Geschichte der Hamburger Arbeiter, 1890–1919* (Hamburg, 1967)

Schultze, E. *Not und Verschwendung. Untersuchungen über das deutsche Wirtschaftsschichsal* (Leipzig, 1923)

Schulz, G., 'Reparationen und Krisenprobleme nach dem Wahlsieg der NSDAP 1930. Betrachtungen zur Regierung Brüning', *VSWG*, 67 (1980), pp. 200–22

'Inflationstrauma, Finanzpolitik und Krisenbekämpfung in den Jahren der Wirtschaftskrise, 1930–33', in Feldman and Müller-Luckner (eds.), *Nachwirkungen*, pp. 261–96

Zwischen Demokratie und Diktatur. Verfassungspolitik und Reichsreform in der Weimarer Republik, 2 vols. (Berlin/New York, 1987)

Schulz, P.-R. (ed.), *Wilhelm-Gymnasium Hamburg 1881–1981. Eine Dokumentation über 100 Jahre Wilhelm-Gymnasium* (Hamburg, 1981)

Schulze, H., *Weimar: Deutschland 1917–1933* (Berlin, 1982)

Schumacher, M., *Mittelstandsfront und Republik. Die Wirtschaftspartei – Reichspartei des deutschen Mittelstandes, 1919–1932* (Düsseldorf, 1972)

Schumpeter, J., *Business Cycles* (New York/London, 1939)

Schwabe, K., *Deutsche Revolution und Wilson-Frieden. Die amerikanische und deutsche Friedensstrategie zwischen Idologie und Machtpolitik, 1918/19* (Düsseldorf, 1971)

'Versailles – nach sechzig Jahren', *Neue Politische Literatur*, 24 (1979), pp. 446–75

(ed.), *Die Ruhrkrise, 1923* (Paderborn, 1985)

Schwartz, O., *Die finanzielle Stellung der europäischen Großmächte, zugleich im Hinblick auf ihre finanzielle Kriegsbereitschaft* (Stuttgart, 1913)

Schwarz, M., *MdR. Biographisches Handbuch des Reichstags* (Hanover, 1965)

Schwenck, E., *25 Jahre Verein Hamburger Exporteure* (Hamburg 1928)

Seeger, M., *Die Politik der Reichsbank von 1876–1914 im Lichte der Spielregeln der Goldwährung* (Berlin, 1968)

Sheehan, J.J., 'Liberalism and the City in Nineteenth Century Germany', *P& P*, 51 (1971), pp. 116–37

Sieder, R., *Sozialgeschichte der Familie* (Frankfurt am Main, 1987)

Siegrist, H. (ed.), *Bürgerliche Berufe* (Göttingen, 1988)

Sieveking, H., 'Die Hamburger Bank, 1619–1875', in *Festschrift der Hamburgsichen Universität ihrem Ehrenrektor Herrn Bürgermeister Werner von Melle zum 80. Geburtstag am 18.October 1933 dargebracht* (Hamburg, 1933), pp. 21–110

Sieveking, W., 'Die Patriotische Gesellschaft in den letzten 50 Jahren', in *Die Patriotische Gesellschaft zu Hamburg 1765–1965. Festschrift der Hamburg-*

ischen Gesellschaft zur Beförderung der Künste und nützlichen Gewerbe (Hamburg, 1965)

Silverman, D.P., *Reconstructing Europe after the Great War* (Cambridge, Mass., 1982)

Skidelsky, R., *John Maynard Keynes*, vol. I: *Hopes Betrayed, 1883–1920* (London, 1983); vol II: *The Economist as Saviour, 1920–1937* (London, 1992)

Skrentny, W., ' "Hier war alles vernünftiger als anderswo". Hamburg und die Aufarbeitung der NS-Zeit', in G.A.L. Fraktion in der Hamburger Bürgerschaft (ed.), *'Es is Zeit für die ganze Wahrheit' (K. von Dohnanyi). Aufarbeitung der NS-Zeit in Hamburg; Die nicht veröffentlichte Senatsbroschure* (Hamburg, 1985), pp. 17–47

Smith, S.A., *Red Petrograd. Revolution in the Factories 1917–1918* (Cambridge, 1983)

Sommariva, A. and G. Tullio, *German Macroeconomic History, 1880–1979. A Study of the Effects of Economic Policy on Inflation, Currency Depreciation and Growth* (London, 1987)

Sorkin, D., *The Transformation of German Jewry, 1780–1840* (Oxford, 1987)

Southern, D.B., 'The Revaluation Question in the Weimar Republic', *JMH*, 51 (1979), pp. 1029–53

'The Impact of Inflation: Inflation, the Courts and Revaluation', in Bessel and Feuchtwanger (eds.), *Social Change and Political Development*, pp. 56–76

Soutou, G., 'Die deutschen Reparationen und das Seydoux-Projekt 1920/21', *VfZ*, 23 (1975), pp. 237–70

'Der Einfluß der Schwerindustrie auf die Gestaltung der Frankreichpolitik Deutschlands', in Mommsen *et al.* (eds.), *Industrielles System*, II, pp. 543–51

von Specht, A., *Politische und wirtschaftliche Hintergründe der deutschen Inflation, 1918–1923* (Frankfurt am Main, 1982).

Spree, R., *Wachstumstrends und Konjunkturzyklen in der deutschen Wirtschaft von 1820–1913* (Göttingen, 1978)

Stegmann, D., *Die Erben Bismarcks. Parteien und Verbände in der Spätphase des wilhelminischen Deutschlands. Sammlungspolitik, 1897–1918* (Cologne, 1970)

Stegmann, D., B.-J. Wendt and P.-C. Witt (eds.), *Industrielle Gesellschaft und politisches System. Beiträge zur politischen Sozialgeschichte. Festschrift für Fritz Fischer zum 70. Geburtstag* (Bonn, 1978)

Stehling, J., 'Der Hamburger Arbeiter- und Soldatenrat in der Revolution 1918/19', in Herzig *et al.*, (eds.) *Arbeiter in Hamburg*, pp. 419–28

Stein, H.-K., 'Interessenkonflikte zwischen Großkaufleuten, Handelskammer und Senat in der Frage des Zollanschlusses Hamburgs an das Reich 1866–1881', *ZVHG*, 64 (1978), pp. 55–89

Steinberg, J., 'Diplomatie als Wille und Vorstellung. Die Berliner Mission Lord Haldanes im Februar 1912', in H. Schottelius and W. Deist, *Marine und Marinepolitik 1871–1914* (Düsseldorf, 1972), pp. 263–82

Steinborn, N., 'Militärs auf Abruf – zur Rolle und Entwicklung der Hamburger Polizei', in Verein Hamburg-Jahrbuch (ed.), *Hamburger Zustände. Jahrbuch zur Geschichte der Region Hamburg*, I (1988), pp. 13–18

Steiner, Z.S., *Britain and the Origins of the First World War* (London, 1983)

Stenzel, G., 'Die Industrie', in Deutsche Auslands-Gemeinschaft (ed.), *Hamburg in seiner politischen, wirtschaftlichen und kulturellen Bedeutung* (Hamburg, 1921)

Stern, F., *Gold and Iron. Bismarck, Bleichröder and the Building of the German Empire* (London, 1977)

Stevenson, D., *French War Aims against Germany 1914–1919* (Oxford, 1982)

Stolper, G., K. Häuser and K. Borchardt, *The German Economy, 1870 to the Present* (London, 1967)

Stolten, O., H. Stubbe, E. Krause and M. Leuteritz, *Der Kampf der Sozialdemokratie um das Rathaus in Hamburg* (Hamburg, 1927)

Stolz, G., 'Die Schutzpolizei in Altona und Wandsbek, 1869–1937', *ZVHG*, 63 (1977), pp. 35–68

Stone, N., *The Eastern Front 1914–1917* (London, 1975)

Strobusch, E., *Deutscher Seeschiffbau im 19. und 20. Jahrhundert* (Bremerhaven, 1975)

Stubmann, P., *Gegenwart und Zukunft der Seeschiffahrt* (Berlin, 1916)
  Mein Feld is die Welt, Albert Ballin – sein Leben (Hamburg, 1920)

Stuebel, H., 'Die Finanzierung der Aufrüstung im Dritten Reich', *Europa-Archiv* 6 (1951), pp. 4128–36

Stürmer, M., *Koalition und Opposition in der Weimarer Republik, 1924–1928* (Düsseldorf, 1967)
  'Der unvollendete Parteienstaat. Zur Vorgeschichte des Präsidialregimes am Ende der Weimarer Republik', in idem (ed.), *Die Weimarer Republik Belagerte Civitas*, (Königstein, 1985), pp. 310–17

Süle, T., *Preußische Bürokratietradition. Zur Entwicklung von Verwaltung und Beamtenschaft in Deutschland 1871–1918* (Göttingen, 1988)

Suny, R.G., 'Toward a Social History of the October Revolution', *AHR*, 88 (1983), pp. 31–52

Suval, S., *The Anschluß Question in the Weimar Era* (Baltimore, 1974)

Svennilson, I., *Growth and Stagnation in the European Economy* (Geneva, 1954)

Sweezy, M., 'German Corporate Profits, 1926–1938', *Quarterly Journal of Economics*, 54 (1940)

Tanzler, F., *Die deutschen Arbeitgeberverbände, 1904–1929* (Berlin, 1929).

Tawney, R.H., 'The Abolition of Economic Controls, 1918–1921', *EcHR* (1943), pp. 1–30

Taylor, A.J.P., *The Course of German History* (London, 1961)

Temin, P., 'The Beginning of the Depression in Germany', *EcHR*, 24 (1971), pp. 240–8
  'Soviet and Nazi Economic Planning in the 1930s', *EcHR*, 44 (1991), pp. 573–93

Tenfelde, K., 'Der Durchbruch der Freien Gewerkschaften Deutschlands zur Massenbewegung im letzten Viertel des 19. Jahrhunderts', in G.A. Ritter (ed.), *Arbeiterbewegung, Parteien und Parlamentarismus* (Göttingen, 1976), pp. 55–101

Terhalle, F., 'Geschichte des deutschen Finanzwirtschaft vom Beginn des 19. Jahrhunderts bis zum Schluss des zweiten Weltkrieges', in W. Gerloff and F. Neumark, *Handbuch der Finanzwissenschaft* (Tübingen, 1952). pp. 274–89

Teuteberg, H.-J., 'Die Entstehung des modernen Hamburger Hafens (1886–1896)', *Tradition*, 17 (1972), pp. 257–91

Thimme, A., *Flucht in den Mythos. Die Deutschnationale Volkspartei und die Niederlage von 1918* (Göttingen, 1969)

Tilly, R., 'Unternehmermoral und -verhalten im 19. Jahrhundert. Indizien deutscher Bürgerlichkeit', in Kocka (ed.), *Bürgertum im 19. Jahrhundert*, II, pp. 35–64

Timpke, H. (ed.), *Dokumente zur Gleichschaltung des Landes Hamburg 1933* (Frankfurt am Main, 1964)

von Tirpitz, A., *Deutsche Ohnmachtspolitik im Weltkriege* (Hamburg/Berlin, 1926)

Toury, J., *Soziale und politische Geschichte der Juden in Deutschland 1847–1871. Zwischen Revolution, Reaktion und Emanzipation* (Düsseldorf, 1977)

Trachtenberg, M., 'Reparation at the Paris Peace Conference', *JMH*, 51 (1979), pp. 24–55
Reparation in World Politics: France and European Economic Diplomacy 1916–1923 (New York, 1980)

Tramer, H., 'Die Hamburger Kaiserjuden', *Bulletin des Leo Baeck Instituts*, 3 (1960), pp. 177–89

Treue, W., 'Innovation, Know-How, Rationalisation in the German Shipbuilding Industry 1860–1930', in H. Pohl (ed.), *Innovation, Know-How, Rationalisation and Investment in the German and Japanese Economies* (Wiesbaden, 1982), pp. 103–23

Tschirbs, R., 'Der Ruhrbergbau zwischen Priviligierung und Statusverlust: Lohnpolitik von der Inflation bis zur Rationalisierung (1919–1927)', in Feldman *et al.* (eds.), *Zwischenbilanz*, pp. 308–45

Turner, H.A., *Stresemann and the Politics of the Weimar Republic* (Princeton, 1963)
German Big Business and the Rise of Hitler (Oxford, 1985)

Turner, I., 'Great Britain and the Post-war German Currency Reform', *HJ*, 30, 3 (1987), pp. 685–708

Ullrich, V., *Kriegsalltag. Hamburg im ersten Weltkrieg* (Cologne, 1982)
'Massenbewegung in der Hamburger Arbeiterschaft im Ersten Weltkrieg', in Herzig *et al.* (eds.), *Arbeiter in Hamburg*, pp. 407–18
'Der Januarstreik 1918 in Hamburg, Kiel und Bremen. Eine vergleichende Studie zur Geschichte der Streikbewegung im Ersten Weltkrieg', *ZVHG*, 71 (1985), pp. 45–74

Urban, A., *Staat und Prostitution in Hamburg, 1807–1922* (Hamburg, 1927)

Usborne, C., *The Politics of the Body in Weimar Germany. Reproductive Rights and Duties* (London, 1991)

Vagts, A., 'M.M. Warburg & Co. Ein Bankhaus in der deutschen Weltpolitik, 1905–1933', *VSWG*, 45 (1958), pp. 289–398

Varain, H.J., *Freie Gewerkschaften, Sozialdemokratie und Staat. Die Politik der Generalkommission unter der Führung Carl Legiens, 1890–1920* (Düsseldorf, 1956)

Vereinsbank (ed.), *Hundertjahre Vereinsbank in Hamburg* (Hamburg, 1956)

Verg, E., *Unter der blauen Flagge. 150 Jahre H.M. Gehrekens* (Hamburg, 1980)

Vincent, C.P., *The Politics of Hunger. The Allied Blockade of Germany 1915–1919* (Athens, Ohio, 1985)

Vogt, M., 'Seeckt und die Vorbereitungen zur Stabilisierung der Mark', in Büsch and Feldman (eds.), *Historische Prozesse*, pp. 309–20

'Ansätze für eine rheinische Währung im Spätsommer und Herbst 1923', in Büsch and Feldman (eds.), *Historische Prozesse*, pp. 432–42

'Rudolf Hilferding als Finanzminister im ersten Kabinett Stresemann', in Büsch and Feldman (eds.), *Historische Prozesse*, pp. 127–60

Vogtmeier, M., *Die Familien Mann und Buddenbrook im Lichte der Mehreregenerationen-Familientherapie. Untersuchungen zu Thomas Manns 'Buddenbrooks. Verfall einer Familie'* (Frankfurt, 1987)

Volkmann, H.E., 'Außenhandel und Aufrüstung in Deutschland, 1933 bis 1939', in F. Forstmeier and H.E. Volkmann (eds.), *Wirtschaft und Rüstung am Vorabend des Zweiten Weltkrieges* (Düsseldorf, 1975), pp. 81–131

Volkov, S., *The Rise of Popular Anti-Modernism in Germany. The Urban Master Artisans, 1873–1896* (Princeton, 1978)

'Jüdische Assimilation und jüdische Eigenart im Deutschen Kaiserreich. Ein Versuch', *G&G*, 9 (1983), pp. 331–48

'Die Verbürgerlichung der Juden in Deutschland. Eigenart und Paradigma', in Kocka (ed.), *Bürgertum im 19. Jahrhundert*, II, pp. 343–71

Vondung, K., 'Deutsche Apokalypse 1914', in *idem*, *Das wilhelminischen Bildungsbürgertum* (Göttingen, 1976), pp. 153–71

Voß, A., 'Der Hamburger Aufstand im Oktober 1923', in *idem*, U. Büttner and H. Weber, *Vom Hamburger Aufstand zur politischen Isolierung. Kommunistische Politik in Hamburg und im Dritten Reich* (Hamburg, 1983), pp. 9–54

Wagenführ, R., 'Die Industriewirtschaft. Entwicklungstendenzen der deutschen und internationalen Industrieproduktion, 1860–1932', *Vierteljahreshefte zur Konjunkturforschung*, Sonderheft 31 (1933)

Walker, F.M. and A. Slaven (eds.), *European Ship-Building. 100 Years of Change* (London, 1983), p. 78

Walker, M., *Germany and the Emigration, 1816–1885* (Cambridge, Mass., 1964)

Wallich, H.C., *Mainsprings of German Revival* (New Haven, 1955)

Wandel, E., *Die Entstehung der Bank deutscher Länder und die Währungsreform von 1948* (Frankfurt am Main, 1980)

Warburg, M., *Aus meinen Aufzeichnungen* (Hamburg, 1952)

Warburg-Spinelli, I., *Erinnerungen 1910–1989. 'Die Dringlichkeit des Mitleids und die Einsamkeit, nein zu sagen'* (Hamburg, 1990)

Washausen, H., *Hamburg und die Kolonialpolitik des Deutschen Reiches 1880–1890* (Hamburg, 1968)

Webb, S.B., 'Money Demand and Expectations in the German Hyperinflation:
     A Survey of the Models', in Schmukler and Marcus (eds.), *Inflation
     through the Ages*, pp. 435–49
     'The Supply of Money and Reichsbank Financing of Corporate Debt in
     Germany 1919–1923', *JEcH*, 44 (1984), pp. 499–507
     'Government Debt and Inflationary Expectations as Determinants of the
     Money Supply in Germany, 1919 to 1923', *Journal of Money, Credit and
     Banking* (1985), pp. 479–92
     'Fiscal News and Inflationary Expectations in Germany after World War I',
     JEcH, 46, 3 (1986), pp. 769–94
     Hyperinflation and Stabilisation in Weimar Germany (New York/Oxford, 1989)
Weber, A., *Hat Schacht Recht? Die Abhängigkeit der deutschen Wirtschaft vom
     Ausland* (Munich/Leipzig, 1928)
Wehler, H.-U., *The German Empire 1971–1918* (Leamington Spa, 1985)
Weinberg, G.L., 'The Defeat of Germany in 1918 and the European Balance
     of Power', *CEH* (1969), pp. 248–60
Weisbrod, B., *Schwerindustrie in der Weimarer Republik. Interessenpolitik
     zwischen Stabilisierung und Krise* (Wuppertal, 1978)
     'Economic Power and Political Stability Reconsidered: Heavy Industry in
     the Weimar Republic', *Social History*, 4 (1979), pp. 241–63
     'Industrial Crisis Strategy in the Great Depression', in Kruedener (ed.),
     Economic Crisis, pp. 45–62
Wendemuth, L. and W. Böttcher, *Der Hafen von Hamburg* (Hamburg,
     1927)
Wengst, U., 'Der Reichsverband der deutschen Industrie in den ersten Mon-
     aten des Dritten Reiches: Ein Beitrag zum Verhältnis von Grossindustrie
     und Nationalsozialismus', *VfZ*, 38 (1980), pp. 94–110
Wertheimer, J., *Unwelcome Strangers. East European Jews in Imperial Germany*
     (Oxford/New York, 1987)
Weuster, A., *Theorie der Konsumgenossenschaftsentwicklung. Die deutschen Kon-
     sumgenossenschaften bis zum Ende der Weimarer Zeit* (Berlin, 1980)
Whaley, J., *Religious Toleration and Social Change in Hamburg, 1529–1819*
     (Cambridge, 1985)
Wiedenfeld, K., *Die Organisation der Kriegsrohstoffbewirtschaftung 1914–1918
     im Dienste des deutschen Monopolkapitals* (Berlin, 1955)
Wiegand, F.-M., *Die Notabeln. Untersuchungen zur Geschichte des Wahlrechts
     und der gewählten Bürgerschaft in Hamburg 1859–1919* [Beiträge zur Gesch-
     ichte Hamburgs, Bd. 30] (Hamburg, 1987)
Willett, J., *The New Sobriety, 1917–1933: Art and Politics in the Weimar Period*
     (London, 1978)
     The Theatre of the Weimar Republic (New York/London, 1988)
Williams, J.H., 'German Foreign Trade and the Reparations Payments', *Quar-
     terly Journal of Economics*, 36 (1922)
     'Reparation and the Flow of Capital', *American Economic Review*, 20
     (Supplement) (1930), pp. 75–9
Winkler H.-A., (ed.), *Organisierter Kapitalismus* (Göttingen, 1974)

Von der Revolution zur Stabilisierung. Arbeiter und Arbeiterbewegung in der Weimarer Republik, 1918–1924 (Berlin/Bonn, 1984)

'Die Revolution von 1918/19 und das Problem der Kontinuität in der deutschen Geschichte', *HZ*, 250 (1990), pp. 303–19

Winter, J.M. (ed.), *War and Economic Development. Essays in Memory of David Joslin* (Cambridge, 1975)

The Great War and the British People (Cambridge, 1985)

Wischermann, C., *Wohnen in Hamburg vor dem Ersten Weltkrieg* (Münster, 1983)

Wiskemann, E., *Hamburg und die Welthandelspolitik von den Anfängen bis zur Gegenwart* (Hamburg, 1929)

Witt, F.-W., *Die Hamburger Sozialdemokratie in der Weimarer Republik. Unter besonderer Berücksichtigung der Jahre 1929/30–33* (Hanover, 1971)

Witt, P.-C., *Die Finanzpolitik des Deutschen Reiches, 1903–1913* (Lübeck, 1970)

'Innenpolitik und Imperialismus in der Vorgeschichte des Ersten Weltkrieges' in K. Holl and G. List (eds.), *Liberalismus und imperialistischer Staat* (Göttingen, 1975), pp. 24ff.

'Reichsfinanzminister und Reichsfinanzverwaltung. Zum Problem des Verhältnisses von politischer Führung und bürokratischer Herrschaft in den Anfangsjahren der Weimarer Republik (1918/19–1924)', *VfZ*, 23 (1975), pp. 1–61

'Finanzpolitik und sozialer Wandel in Krieg und Inflation 1918–1924', in Mommsen *et al.* (eds.), *Industrielles System* I, pp. 395–425

'Reichsfinanzen und Rüstungspolitik', in H. Schottelius and W. Deist (eds.), *Marine und Marinepolitik im kaiserlichen Deutschland, 1871–1914* (Düsseldorf, 1981), pp. 146–177

'Finanzpolitik als Verfassungs- und Gesellschaftspolitik. Überlegungen zur Finanzpolitik des Deutschen Reichs in den Jahren 1930 bis 1932', *G&G* (1982), pp. 386–414

'Staatliche Wirtschaftspolitik in Deutschland 1918–1923: Entwicklung und Zerstörung einer modernen wirtschaftspolitischen Strategie', in Feldman *et al.* (eds.), *Zwischenbilanz*, pp. 151–79

'Die Auswirkungen der Inflation auf die Finanzpolitik des Deutschen Reiches, 1924–1935', in Feldman and Müller-Luckner (eds.), *Nachwirkungen*, pp. 43–93

'Anpassung an die Inflation. Das Investitionsverhalten der deutschen Staatsbahnen/Reichsbahn in den Jahren 1914 bis 1923/24', in Feldman *et al.* (eds.), *Anpassung*, pp. 392–432

'Tax Policies, Tax Assessment and Inflation: Towards a Sociology of Public Finances in the German Inflation, 1914 to 1923', in *idem*, *Wealth and Taxation in Central Europe. The History and Sociology of Public Finance* (Leamington Spa/Hamburg/New York, 1987), pp. 137–60

Witthöft, H.J., *Hapag. Hamburg-Amerika Linie* (Herford, 1973)

Wolffsohn, M., *Industrie und Handwerk in Konflikt mit staatlicher Wirtschaftspolitik? Studien zur Politik der Arbeitsbeschaffung in Deutschland, 1930–34* (Berlin, 1977)

Wüest, W.E., *Der Vertrag von Versailles im Licht und Schatten der Kritik: Die Kontroverse um seine wirtschaftlichen Auswirkungen* (Zurich, 1962)

Wulff, B., 'The Third Reich and the Unemployed. National Socialist Work-Creation Schemes in Hamburg, 1933–4', in Evans and Geary (eds.), *The German Unemployed*, pp. 281–302

Wurm, C.A., 'Frankreich, die Reparationen und die interallierten Schulden in den 20er Jahren', in Feldman and Müller–Luckner (eds.) *Nachwirkungen*, pp. 315–33

Zechlin, E., *Die deutsche Politik und die Juden im Ersten Weltkrieg* (Göttingen, 1969)

Krieg und Kriegsrisiko: Zur deutschen Politik im Ersten Weltkrieg (Düsseldorf, 1979)

Zilch, R., *Die Reichsbank und die finanzielle Kriegsvorbereitungen von 1907 bis 1914* (Berlin, 1987)

Zimmermann, L., *Deutsche Außenpolitik in der Ära der Weimarer Republik* (Göttingen, 1958)

Zimmermann, M., *Hamburgischer Patriotismus und deutscher Nationalismus. Die Emanzipation der Juden in Hamburg* (Hamburg, 1979)

Zimmermann, W., A. Günther and R. Meerwarth, *Die Einwirkung des Krieges auf Bevölkerungsbewegung, Einkommen und Lebenshaltung in Deutschland* (Stuttgart/Berlin/Leipzig, 1932)

Zunkel, F., *Industrie und Staatssozialismus. Der Kampf um die Wirtschaftsordnung in Deutschland 1914–1918* (Düsseldorf, 1974)

Unpublished dissertations

Ahrens, W., 'Die sozialistische Genossenschaftswesen in Hamburg 1890–1914. Ein Beitrag zur Sozialgeschichte der Arbeiterbewegung' (Diss. Hamburg, 1970)

Anschütz, H., 'Die Nationalsozialistische Deutsche Arbeiterpartei in Hamburg. Ihre Anfänge bis zur Reichstagswahl vom 14. September 1930' (Diss. Hamburg, 1955)

Behrens, R., 'Die Deutschnationalen in Hamburg' (Diss. Hamburg, 1973)

Cord, A., 'Die soziale Schichtung der Hamburger Bürgerschaft von 1859 bis zum Jahre 1921. Ein Beitrag zur parlamentarischen Geschichte des Kaiserreichs' (Diss. Hamburg, 1961)

Honhart, W., 'The Incomplete Revolution. The Social Democrats' Failure to Transform the German Economy 1918–20' (Ph.D. thesis Duke University, 1972)

Kersten, D., 'Die Kriegsziele der Hamburger Kaufmannschaft im Ersten Weltkrieg 1914–1918' (Diss. Hamburg, 1962)

Koch-Baumgarten, S., 'Zum Problem der Theorie und Politik der "Offensive": Die Märzaktion der KPD 1921 unter besonderer Berücksichtigung Hamburgs und Rheinland-Westfalens' (Diss. Freie Universität Berlin, 1983)

Kohlhaus, H.-H., 'Die Hapag, Cuno und das deutsche Reich, 1920–1933' (Diss. Hamburg, 1952)

Krämer, G., 'Die deutsche Außenhandelskontrolle in der Nachkriegszeit' (Diss. Frankfurt, 1928)

Lyth, P.J., 'The Experience of Urban *Mittelstand* in the German Inflation of 1914 to 1923: the Case of Hamburg' (Ph.D. thesis East Anglia, 1984)

Mueller, C.M., 'Die Auseinandersetzung über Hamburgs Zollanschluß an das Deutsche Reich 1833–1888. Hamburgs Entwicklung von einer Freihafenstadt zu einer Stadt mit Freihafen' (Diss. Freiburg, Switz., 1988)

Rettig, R., 'Die Gewerkschaftsarbeit der KPD von 1918 bis 1925' (Diss. Hamburg, 1954)

Riquarts, K.-G., 'Der Anti-Semitismus als politische Partei in Schleswig-Holstein und Hamburg 1871–1914' (Diss. Kiel, 1975)

Roggendorf, K., 'Die Entwicklung und Bedeutung der H.A.L. unter Berücksichtigung der Vor- und Nachkriegszeit' (Diss. Erlangen, 1922).

Rood, V.P., 'The Hamburg Merchant Marine 1866–1914' (Ph.D thesis University of Wisconsin, 1985)

Schieck, H., 'Der Kampf um die deutsche Wirtschaftspolitik nach dem Novembersturz 1918' (Diss. Heidelberg, 1958)

Tummescheit, H., 'Die Entwicklung der Hamburger Merchant Bankers unter besonderer Berücksichtigung der heute noch bestehenden Firmen' (Diss., Hamburg, 1962)

Ullrich, V., 'Die Hamburger Arbeiterbewegung vom Vorabend des Ersten Weltkrieges bis zur Revolution 1918/19' (Diss. Hamburg, 1976)

Vincent, C.P., 'The Post-World War I Blockade of Germany: An Aspect of the Tragedy of a Nation' (Ph.D. thesis University of Colorado, 1980)

Werling, K., 'Der Preis- und Einkommensmechanismus der Goldwährung. Untersuchung am Beispiel Englands und Deutschlands zwischen 1880 und 1914' (Diss. Hamburg, 1962)

Index